THOUGHT AND EXPERIENCE IN PROSE

SECOND EDITION

Thought
and
Experience
in Prose

EDITED BY

CRAIG R. THOMPSON, *1911~*

PROFESSOR OF ENGLISH, LAWRENCE COLLEGE

AND

JOHN HICKS, *1909~*

PROFESSOR OF ENGLISH, STETSON UNIVERSITY

SECOND EDITION

NEW YORK

OXFORD UNIVERSITY PRESS

1956

© 1951, 1956 BY OXFORD UNIVERSITY PRESS, INC.

SECOND EDITION 1956

LIBRARY OF CONGRESS CATALOGUE CARD NUMBER: 56–5766

PRINTED IN THE UNITED STATES OF AMERICA

Preface

TO SECOND EDITION

In preparing this revision of *Thought and Experience in Prose*, we have taken pains to preserve the book's original purpose and scope, and we have sought to improve it, wherever possible, in accordance with suggestions of teachers who have used the earlier version in their classes and have generously communicated the results of their experience to us. From British and American authors of the past three centuries, with one exception, we have chosen various writings for study and discussion by undergraduate students. We believe that a student who will attend to the selections carefully, analyzing and interpreting them, will become a more perceptive reader and a more discriminating thinker.

This collection has enough variety, we trust, to accommodate itself to the needs of many types of courses. Some of the pieces are short, some long; some are fairly simple, others are not. We have not tried to make either an 'easy' or a 'hard' book, but rather one with sufficient range and diversity of content and style to enable students of different capacities and different interests to use it with profit. This aim accounts also for the number of the selections.

'The light of human minds is perspicuous words,' wrote Hobbes in *Leviathan* (but he warned, too, that 'as men abound in copiousness of language, so they become more wise or more mad than ordinary'). Words, whether by themselves or in the societies called sentences and paragraphs, are constantly shifting in meaning, suggestion, and association. 'A word is not a crystal, transparent and unchanged, it is the skin of a living thought and may vary greatly in color and content according to the circumstances and the time in which it is used.' [1] So Justice Oliver Wendell Holmes observed; and eighteen centuries earlier Plutarch had said much the same thing: 'the use of language is like the currency of coinage in trade: the

[1 Towne v. Eisner, 245 U.S. 418.]

v

coinage which is familiar and well known takes on a different value at different times.' [2] To get at the full meaning of words and sentences, therefore, one must be able and willing to examine them critically, be ready to read between the lines, to respond to subtle suggestions of the context, to sense the tone of a passage, to catch the 'feel' of phrases. It is the mark of maturity in a reader that he not only can read in this fashion, but does so habitually.

The pleasures of prose normally depend on reading that is disciplined and deliberate. Such reading takes practice. If language is complex (as it is), if it has countless subtleties, nuances, evocative powers (as it has), we must respect its difficulties. We must exert ourselves to overcome them. We must not overemphasize them—though overemphasis in this direction hardly seems a clear and present danger in most American education. We do need to be concerned lest students leave our classes with the same inadequacies they brought. We need to try to show each student what good reading involves, and what it does for him. When he has mastered the meanings and syntactical relations of words, and their nice organization into larger forms, his reward will be the satisfaction that understanding brings, at times the excitement of intellectual and intuitional discovery.

In this revision we have omitted some selections used in the earlier edition, and have added certain new ones. Among the examples of biography, fiction, essay, historical narrative, exposition, letters, and argument, most teachers will find some old favorites, but there are also a good many pieces unfamiliar in anthologies. Of these, some deal with political, ethical, and other philosophical or near-philosophical topics; others with diverse, and often lighter, subjects; but all are well written and provocative, and therefore instructive. About half the selections were written in the twentieth century; the rest, with the exception of one from the seventeenth, are almost equally divided between the eighteenth and nineteenth centuries. We have avoided contemporary journalistic pieces. The student has journalism aplenty to read, of both good and bad kinds. Most of it, being ephemeral, is not demanding enough to serve the ends we have in view in this book. Moreover a reader, it seems to us, needs to test himself against writings of other epochs, writings by men with other pre-suppositions than those of his contemporaries. We concur with the judgment of Mr. I. A. Richards that while we must not puzzle our pupils beyond their capacities to solve the puzzles, still we must puzzle them: 'we must give them studies

[2 *Moralia*, 406B (Babbitt's translation).]

which invite them to think. We must *not* give them lessons so well accommodated to their existing modes of thought that no problems of interpretation arise for them. If we do, we are betraying them; we are not preparing them for a world in which everything that really matters will endlessly offer them every sort of chance to misunderstand.' [3]

The professorial guide who uses this book will use it to fit his own methods and his own students. The selections may be read in any order a teacher likes. We have no desire to come between him and his pupils nor do we attempt to impose on this collection any hard and fast arrangement. We do wish, however, to emphasize the numerous connections between the different selections. Every intelligent expression of human thought and experience may be regarded as part of a dense web of relationship. Each selection in this volume is a center from which radiate lines of relationship, direct or indirect, with other pieces.

Explanatory notes and study questions are added for those who want them. Some students may safely ignore the questions; others should find them helpful. For the most part these questions concern meanings, ideas and relations between ideas, and diction. They should enable some readers to see more clearly the main points of the texts, to make more sense of words and structure. The footnotes are admittedly a calculated risk, since in a book of this character notes may easily explain too little or too much. If some of the notes seem elementary or otiose at first we believe nevertheless that they will prove useful to many readers. All footnotes enclosed within square brackets are supplied by the editors; all others are the authors'.

Most of our texts are taken from the first edition or an authoritative reprint of the first edition; some are from later editions ascertained to be reliable. References in the notes to Shakespeare's works use the numbering of the Oxford edition by W. J. Craig. We are happy to thank authors and publishers who have permitted us to reprint materials covered by copyright. In making this revision we are indebted to Isabella McMaster Thompson for special editorial assistance, and to those college and university teachers who have kindly communicated to us the results of their experience with the earlier edition.

'If you wish to have a faculty for reading, read; if for writing, write.' [4]

[3 *A Certain Sort of Interest in Language* (Chap Book published for the College English Association, No. 1, 1941), p. 7.]
[4 Epictetus, *Discourses*, II, xviii (Matheson's translation).]

Provided it be practiced in a critical spirit, this ancient counsel of Epictetus may serve as governing principle to those whose study is language. We remind our colleagues that the philosopher also has a chapter addressed 'to those who undertake the profession of teacher with a light heart.' The high calling of the teacher demands, he says, 'mature years, and a certain way of life, and the guidance of God.' Only indirectly, perhaps, is the instructor in English a teacher of ethics, as was Epictetus. Yet if, by training students to become genuinely discerning and reflective readers, he can help them to become intellectually responsible citizens, he surely performs an ethical as well as intellectual service.

Craig R. Thompson
John Hicks

September 1955

Contents

THOUGHT AND EXPERIENCE IN PROSE

Noah Webster

THE FUTURE OF ENGLISH IN AMERICA

⟨ After graduation in 1778 from Yale (where his studies had been interrupted by service in the Revolutionary army), Webster tried his hand at schoolmastering and the law; later he became a journalist, political pamphleteer, and itinerant lecturer. But his true vocation, almost from college days, was the study, recording, reforming, and teaching of American usage of the English language. In 1783-5 appeared his *Grammatical Institute of the English Language*, consisting of a spelling book, grammar, and reader. Successive editions of his speller, of which many million copies were sold, helped to standardize American spelling, and to some degree American pronunciation, of English. His early ambitions to effect drastic reforms in spelling, however, were gradually modified as he grew older. His first dictionary was published in 1806; *A Grammar of English* in 1807. The 1806 book was a modest affair, but after twenty years' work he issued a greatly enlarged dictionary in 1828, with the title *An American Dictionary of the English Language*. Its scope, and the excellence of its definitions, made the name of Webster synonymous with *dictionary*.

The shrewdness, sincerity, independence, and patriotism of Webster's conception of American English are well exemplified in his *Dissertations on the English Language*, 1789. While acknowledging that English is 'the inheritance which the Americans have received from their British parents,' he insisted that 'as an independent nation, our honor requires us to have a system of our own, in language as well as government.' He was not correct in all his predictions concerning the manifest destiny of English in America, but, more than any other man, he made Americans conscious of their language and studious of its standards.

A REGULAR study of language has, in all civilized countries, formed a part of a liberal education. The Greeks, Romans, Italians and French successfully improved their native tongues, taught them in Acad-

FROM *Dissertations on the English Language*, 1789.

emies at home, and rendered them entertaining and useful to the foreign student.

The English tongue, tho later in its progress towards perfection, has attained to a considerable degree of purity, strength and elegance, and been employed, by an active and scientific nation, to record almost all the events and discoveries of ancient and modern times.

This language is the inheritance which the Americans have received from their British parents. To cultivate and adorn it, is a task reserved for men who shall understand the connection between language and logic, and form an adequate idea of the influence which a uniformity of speech may have on national attachments.

It will be readily admitted that the pleasures of reading and conversing, the advantage of accuracy in business, the necessity of clearness and precision in communicating ideas, require us to be able to speak and write our own tongue with ease and correctness. But there are more important reasons, why the language of this country should be reduced to such fixed principles, as may give its pronunciation and construction all the certainty and uniformity which any living tongue is capable of receiving.

The United States were settled by emigrants from different parts of Europe. But their descendants mostly speak the same tongue; and the intercourse among the learned of the different States, which the revolution has begun, and an America Court will perpetuate, must gradually destroy the differences of dialect which our ancestors brought from their native countries. This approximation of dialects will be certain; but without the operation of other causes than an intercourse at Court, it will be slow and partial. The body of the people, governed by habit, will still retain their respective peculiarities of speaking; and for want of schools and proper books, fall into many inaccuracies, which, incorporating with the language of the state where they live, may imperceptibly corrupt the national language. Nothing but the establishment of schools and some uniformity in the use of books, can annihilate differences in speaking and preserve the purity of the American tongue. A sameness of pronunciation is of considerable consequence in a political view; for provincial accents are disagreeable to strangers and sometimes have an unhappy effect upon the social affections. All men have local attachments, which lead them to believe their own practice to be the least exceptionable. Pride and prejudice incline men to treat the practice of their neighbors with some degree of contempt. Thus small differences in pronunciation at first excite ridicule— a habit of laughing at the singularities of strangers is followed by disrespect

—and without respect friendship is a name, and social intercourse a mere ceremony.

These remarks hold equally true, with respect to individuals, to small societies and to large communities. Small causes, such as a nick-name, or a vulgar tone in speaking, have actually created a dissocial spirit between the inhabitants of the different states, which is often discoverable in private business and public deliberations. Our political harmony is therefore concerned in a uniformity of language.

As an independent nation, our honor requires us to have a system of our own, in language as well as government. Great Britain, whose children we are, and whose language we speak, should no longer be *our* standard; for the taste of her writers is already corrupted, and her language on the decline. But if it were not so, she is at too great a distance to be our model, and to instruct us in the principles of our own tongue.

It must be considered further, that the English is the common root or stock from which our national language will be derived. All others will gradually waste away—and within a century and a half, North America will be peopled with a hundred millions of men, *all speaking the same language*. Place this idea in comparison with the present and possible future bounds of the language in Europe—consider the Eastern Continent as inhabited by nations, whose knowledge and intercourse are embarrassed by differences of language; then anticipate the period when the people of one quarter of the world, will be able to associate and converse together like children of the same family.* Compare this prospect, which is not visionary, with the state of the English language in Europe, almost confined to an Island and to a few millions of people; then let reason and reputation decide, how far America should be dependent on a transatlantic nation, for her standard and improvements in language.

Let me add, that whatever predilection the Americans may have for their native European tongues, and particularly the British descendants for the English, yet several circumstances render a future separation of the American tongue from the English, necessary and unavoidable. The vicinity of the European nations, with the uninterrupted communication in peace, and the changes of dominion in war, are gradually assimilating their respective languages. The English with others is suffering continual

* Even supposing that a number of republics, kingdoms or empires, should within a century arise and divide this vast territory; still the subjects of all will speak the same language, and the consequence of this uniformity will be an intimacy of social intercourse hitherto unknown, and a boundless diffusion of knowledge.

alterations. America, placed at a distance from those nations, will feel, in a much less degree, the influence of the assimilating causes; at the same time, numerous local causes, such as a new country, new associations of people, new combinations of ideas in arts and science, and some inter- course with tribes wholly unknown in Europe, will introduce new words into the American tongue. These causes will produce, in a course of time, a language in North America, as different from the future language of Eng- land, as the modern Dutch, Danish and Swedish are from the German, or from one another: Like remote branches of a tree springing from the same stock; or rays of light, shot from the same center, and diverging from each other, in proportion to their distance from the point of separation.

Whether the inhabitants of America can be brought to a perfect uni- formity in the pronunciation of words, it is not easy to predict; but it is certain that no attempt of the kind has been made, and an experiment, begun and pursued on the right principles, is the only way to decide the question. Schools in Great Britain have gone far towards demolishing local dialects—commerce has also had its influence—and in America these causes, operating more generally, must have a proportional effect.

In many parts of America, people at present attempt to copy the English phrases and pronunciation—an attempt that is favored by their habits, their prepossessions and the intercourse between the two countries. This attempt has, within the period of a few years, produced a multitude of changes in these particulars, especially among the leading classes of people. These changes make a difference between the language of the higher and com- mon ranks; and indeed between the *same* ranks in *different* states; as the rage for copying the English, does not prevail equally in every part of North America.

But besides the reasons already assigned to prove this imitation absurd, there is a difficulty attending it, which will defeat the end proposed by its advocates; which is, that the English themselves have no standard of pronunciation, nor can they ever have one on the plan they propose. The Authors, who have attempted to give us a standard, make the practice of the court and stage in London the sole criterion of propriety in speaking. An attempt to establish a standard on this foundation is both *unjust* and *idle*. It is unjust, because it is abridging the nation of its rights: The *general practice* of a nation is the rule of propriety, and this practice should at least be consulted in so important a matter, as that of making laws for speaking. While all men are upon a footing and no singularities are accounted vulgar or ridiculous, every man enjoys perfect liberty. But when a particular set of men, in exalted stations, undertake to say, 'we are the standards of propriety and elegance, and if all men do not conform to our practice, they shall be accounted vulgar and ignorant,' they take a very great liberty with the rules of the language and the rights of civility.

But an attempt to fix a standard on the practice of any particular class of people is highly absurd: As a friend of mine once observed, it is like fixing a light house on a floating island. It is an attempt to *fix* that which is in itself *variable*; at least it must be variable so long as it is supposed that a local practice has no standard but a *local practice*; that is, no standard but *itself*. While this doctrine is believed, it will be impossible for a nation to follow as fast as the standard changes—for if the gentlemen at court constitute a standard, they are above it themselves, and their practice must shift with their passions and their whims.

But this is not all. If the practice of a few men in the capital is to be the standard, a knowledge of this must be communicated to the whole nation. Who shall do this? An able compiler perhaps attempts to give this practice in a dictionary; but it is probable that the pronunciation, even at court, or on the stage, is not uniform. The compiler therefore must follow his particular friends and patrons; in which case he is sure to be opposed and the authority of his standard called in question; or he must give two pronunciations as the standard, which leaves the student in the same uncertainty as it found him. Both these events have actually taken place in England, with respect to the most approved standards; and of course no one is universally followed.

Besides, if language must vary, like fashions, at the caprice of a court, we must have our standard dictionaries republished, with the fashionable pronunciation, at least once in five years; otherwise a gentleman in the country will become intolerably vulgar, by not being in a situation to adopt the fashion of the day. The *new* editions of them will supersede the *old*, and we shall have our pronunciation to re-learn, with the polite alterations, which are generally corruptions.

Such are the consequences of attempting to make a *local* practice the *standard* of language in a *nation*. The attempt must keep the language in perpetual fluctuation, and the learner in uncertainty.

If a standard therefore cannot be fixed on local and variable custom, on what shall it be fixed? If the most eminent speakers are not to direct

our practice, where shall we look for a guide? The answer is extremely easy;
the *rules of the language itself,* and the *general practice of the nation,* constitute propriety in speaking. If we examine the structure of any language,
we shall find a certain principle of analogy running through the whole. We
shall find in English that similar combinations of letters have usually the
same pronunciation; and that words, having the same terminating syllable,
generally have the accent at the same distance from that termination.
These principles of analogy were not the result of design—they must have
been the effect of accident, or that tendency which all men feel towards
uniformity.* But the principles, when established, are productive of great
convenience, and become an authority superior to the arbitrary decisions
of any man or class of men. There is one exception only to this remark:
When a deviation from analogy has become the universal practice of a
nation, it then takes place of all rules and becomes the standard of
propriety.

The two points therefore, which I conceive to be the basis of a standard
in speaking, are these; *universal undisputed practice,* and the *principle of
analogy. Universal practice* is generally, perhaps always, a rule of propriety;
and in disputed points, where people differ in opinion and practice,
analogy should always decide the controversy.

These are authorities to which all men will submit—they are superior to
the opinions and caprices of the great, and to the negligence and ignorance
of the multitude. The authority of individuals is always liable to be called
in question—but the unanimous consent of a nation, and a fixed principle
interwoven with the very construction of a language, coeval and coexten-
sive with it, are like the common laws of a land, or the immutable rules of
morality, the propriety of which every man, however refractory, is forced
to acknowledge, and to which most men will readily submit. Fashion is

---

* This disposition is taken notice of by Dr. Blair,[1] Lect. 8. Where he observes, 'that
tho the formation of abstract or general conceptions is supposed to be a difficult
operation of the mind, yet such conceptions must have entered into the first formation
of languages'—'this invention of abstract terms requires no great exertion of metaphysical capacity'—'Men are *naturally* inclined to call all those objects which resemble
each other by one common name—We may daily observe this practised by children,
in their first attempts towards acquiring language.'

I cannot, with this great critic, call the process by which *similar* objects acquire the
same name, an act of *abstraction,* or the name an *abstract term.* Logical distinctions
may lead us astray. There is in the mind an *instinctive disposition,* or *principle of association,* which will account for all common names and the analogies in language.

[1 Hugh Blair (1718–1800), Scottish divine and critic. His *Lectures on Rhetoric and
Belles Lettres* (1783) was long used as a textbook.]

usually the child of caprice and the being of a day; principles of propriety are founded in the very nature of things, and remain unmoved and unchanged, amidst all the fluctuations of human affairs and the revolutions of time. . . .

Altho stile, or the choice of words and manner of arranging them, may be necessarily liable to change, yet it does not follow that pronunciation and orthography cannot be rendered in a great measure permanent. An orthography, in which there would be a perfect correspondence between the spelling and pronunciation, would go very far towards effecting this desireable object. The Greek language suffered little or no change in these particulars, for about a thousand years; and the Roman was in a great degree fixed for several centuries.

Rapid changes of language proceed from violent causes; but these causes cannot be supposed to exist in North America. It is contrary to all rational calculation, that the United States will ever be conquered by any one nation, speaking a different language from that of the country. Removed from the danger of corruption by conquest, our language can change only with the slow operation of the causes before-mentioned and the progress of arts and sciences, unless the folly of imitating our parent country should continue to govern us, and lead us into endless innovation. This folly however will lose its influence gradually, as our particular habits of respect for that country shall wear away, and our *amor patriae* [2] acquire strength and inspire us with a suitable respect for our own national character.

We have therefore the fairest opportunity of establishing a national language, and of giving it uniformity and perspicuity, in North America, that ever presented itself to mankind. Now is the time to begin the plan. The minds of the Americans are roused by the events of a revolution; the necessity of organizing the political body and of forming constitutions of government that shall secure freedom and property, has called all the faculties of the mind into exertion; and the danger of losing the benefits of independence, has disposed every man to embrace any scheme that shall tend, in its future operation, to reconcile the people of America to each other, and weaken the prejudices which oppose a cordial union. . . .

On examining the language, and comparing the practice of speaking among the yeomanry of this country, with the stile of Shakespear and Addison, I am constrained to declare that the people of America, in particular the English descendants, speak the most *pure English* now known

[2 Love of country.]

in the world. There is hardly a foreign idiom in their language; by which I mean, a *phrase* that has not been used by the best English writers from the time of Chaucer. They retain a few obsolete *words*, which have been dropt by writers, probably from mere affectation, as those which are substituted are neither more melodious nor expressive. In many instances they retain correct phrases, instead of which the pretended refiners of the language have introduced those which are highly improper and absurd.

Let Englishmen take notice that when I speak of the American yeomanry, the latter are not to be compared to the illiterate peasantry of their own country. The yeomanry of this country consist of substantial independent freeholders, masters of their own persons and lords of their own soil. These men have considerable education. They not only learn to read, write and keep accounts; but a vast proportion of them read newspapers every week, and besides the Bible, which is found in all families, they read the best English sermons and treatises upon religion, ethics, geography and history; such as the works of Watts, Addison, Atterbury, Salmon, &c. In the eastern states, there are public schools sufficient to instruct every man's children, and most of the children are actually benefited by these institutions. The people of distant counties in England can hardly understand one another, so various are their dialects; but in the extent of twelve hundred miles in America, there are very few, I question whether a hundred words, except such as are used in employments wholly local, which are not universally intelligible.

But unless the rage for imitating foreign changes can be restrained, this agreeable and advantageous uniformity will be gradually destroyed. The standard writers abroad give us local practice, the momentary whims of the great, or their own arbitrary rules to direct our pronunciation; and we, the apes of fashion, submit to imitate any thing we hear and see. Sheridan [3] has introduced or given sanction to more arbitrary and corrupt changes of pronunciation, within a few years, than had before taken place in a century; and in Perry's Dictionary,[4] not to mention the errors in what he most arrogantly calls his '*Only sure Guide* to the English Tongue,' there are whole pages in which there are scarcely two or three words marked for a

[3 Thomas Sheridan (1719–88), author of *Lectures on Elocution* (1763) and compiler of a *General Dictionary of the English Language* (1780).]

[4 William Perry's *Only Sure Guide to the English Tongue*, a pronouncing speller and grammar, appeared in 1776.]

just pronunciation. There is no Dictionary yet published in Great Britain, in which so many of the analogies of the language and the just rules of pronunciation are preserved, as in the common practice of the well informed Americans, who have never consulted any foreign standard: Nor is there any grammatical treatise, except Dr. Priestley's,[5] which has explained the real idioms of the language, as they are found in Addison's works, and which remain to this day in the American practice of speaking.

The result of the whole is, that we should adhere to our own practice and general customs, unless it can be made very obvious that such practice is wrong, and that a change will produce some considerable advantage. . . .

[5 Joseph Priestley (1733–1804), scientist and writer on political and religious subjects. In 1761 he published a notable book on *The Rudiments of English Grammar*.]

C. E. Montague

THE BLESSING OF ADAM

¶ This essay is reprinted from A *Writer's Notes on His Trade*, a pleasant and instructive little book with much to say on critical reading as well as the techniques of writing. What is said is the product of shrewd sense and much experience. C. E. Montague (1867–1928) practiced his 'trade' as writer for many years on the staff of *The Manchester Guardian*, one of the most respected newspapers in the English-speaking world. He was also author of half a dozen volumes of fiction and criticism: A *Hind Let Loose* (1910), *Dramatic Values* (1911), *Disenchantment* (1922), *Fiery Particles* (1923), *The Right Place* (1924), *Rough Justice* (1926), *Right Off the Map* (1927), and *Action* (1928).

1

A MAN with some darling craft of his own must scratch his head in wonder when he hears some of the things that are daily said about work. One day he finds labour put down as a curse that came on Adam at the Fall—as if Adam had never done a day's digging before his eviction. Another day we are bidden to hope that if the invention of tricks to save labour can only go on as fast as it is going now, we may yet have no need to work more than two hours a day, or possibly one. Even sages so fully accredited as Mr. Bertrand Russell[1] propose that we should knock off presently for all but four hours a day. He would turn us out for the rest of our time, to get what good we could out of a set of fine abstract nouns— science and art, friendship and love, the contemplation of natural beauty and of the immensity of the universe. Husks, mere husks, unless you peg

[¹ English philosopher and writer. See p. 517.]

FROM A *Writer's Notes on His Trade*, 1930. Reprinted by permission of Chatto & Windus Ltd.

away at them so hard that this, too, becomes work, and so gives you back the delicious fatigues you have lost.

As if we could not see for ourselves that one of the saddest men on earth is he who has made his pile in some business early in life and who only looks in at the office for one or two hours a day to bully the clerks and then return to his Old Masters and roses, the wife of his bosom and the spectacle of the firmament. As if we had never seen children or artists or scientific researchers! A normal child has no spite against work until you have drilled one into him by some form of dis-education. You put him out in a sunny garden to play: he has about him everything that Mr. Bertrand Russell rates highest—sand for engineering science, a paint-box for art, dolls for his affections, a foreground of agreeable landscape and the whole dome of the heavens to contemplate. No good; in half an hour he is plaguing you to let him do some 'real work'; he wants to sweep up dead leaves or to help with the mowing. He will not tire of doing it, either, except in the bodily way, and then he will come again, thirsting for toil, the next morning. So powerful is this innate craving for labour that it may take all the massed resources of a great public school and of a famous and ancient university to make a boy believe that real work is a thing to flee from, like want or disease, and that doing it and 'having a good time' are states naturally and immutably opposed to one another.

Or look at the man of science, the mighty hunter of knowledge, some time when his nose is well down on a hot scent. Offer him a release from all but two hours' work in the day. He will hoot at you. Why, when he goes to bed of a night he probably thinks greedily, 'Only just the few hours that I'm asleep—and those don't really count—and then time for dressing and breakfast, and then I can get at it again. Hurrah!'

2

Consider, above all, the artist. Some years ago the leagued artists of Italy, bitten by the spirit of the age, proclaimed a one-day strike—to 'draw attention,' as the phrase is, to the scurvy mutilation of a portrait by a noble lord who had sat for it and then did not like it. Whether this bolt from blue Southern skies blasted the impious peer is not certain, but every feeling heart knew that it must, at any rate, have inflicted a pretty smart pang on its projectors. For strikes are deeply different things when the work you lay down is a job that suffers from some relative poverty in charm, such as totting up endless small sums at a desk or feeding coal in at the door of a furnace, and when it is one that keeps you full of a pleasant presentiment that before long you will set the Thames or the Tiber on fire with the enormous sparks that are constantly being given off by your genius. Any sound moralist will tell you that your sense of the dignity of labour, and of the moral beauty of sweeping a room as by divine law, ought to make stoking or dusting a task as amusing as that of turning out masterpieces in marble or paint. Yet those of us who do neither of these good things have a rooted notion that it must be some of the best fun in the world to paint as Reynolds [2] did it, and quite poor fun, in a comparative sense, to dust out railway carriages. The cleaner can, as a rule, control for a long time his passion for the act of cleaning for cleaning's sake. But an inspired painter would pretend in vain that he did not mind downing brushes at all, and that football and a little racing were quite good enough to pass the time for him. We pretty well know that, to this grade of labour, work is what alcohol is to the dipsomaniac.

It shows once more the ineradicable goodness of human nature that, knowing this, we pay the artist any wages at all. Tactically we others have him in a cleft stick. A miner who will labour gratis in his vocation is, as Dugald Dalgetty [3] said of the refusal of coined money, a sight seldom seen in a Christian land. But if the world firmly refused to give the artist a farthing for his wares, the passionate creature would still go on painting. He could not give up, and, however rich he might be to the end of the stoppage, the misery of a long strike might be the death of him.

3

If it came to a grand economic dispute, no doubt the artist might try to dissemble this congenital disinclination for striking, in hopes of loosening this fine hold that we of the general public would have upon him. And sometimes the thought is apt to arise—must not a certain amount of this prudent dissimulation be practised by others? Or can it really be that a skilful plumber, or Mr. Bertrand Russell himself, would sincerely like to work at plumbing or at advanced mathematics and political philosophy for only two hours a day? At every congress of organized workmen there seems to run through almost every speech an implication that bodily work is nothing but an evil to be borne only for the sake of the pay that it brings, and that the few poor devils who do no work but try to while away their

[2 English painter (1723-92), famous for his portraits.]
[3 Character in Scott's *Legend of Montrose* (1819).]

shabby days with expensive attempts at self-amusement have got hold of an undue share of happiness, to the exclusion of everybody who is busy. Is it possible that none of the speakers has ever known the kind of pervasive benediction that seems to descend on body and mind after the first hour or two of a day's digging, house-decorating or reaping? Or that delicious satisfaction in every tissue of yourself when you have completed the new hen-house, and stump off at the end of the day to sleep in Elysium, stiff, slow and full of a contentment and serenity passing all understanding?

Of course they have, all of them. There is no kind of work which is not loved passionately by some of those who do it—loved sometimes to the point of selfishness, so that a man will sooner let wife and children go short of food and teaching than give up the work of his choice for some other work on which the family could live better. And yet this kind of true love seems, in our time, to have no more than others of the knack of running smoothly. Like Viola,[4] a good trade unionist will never tell his love. Something keeps the barrister earning his hundred pounds a day from letting out that even if every client were able to bilk him, and did it, still he would stick to his gladiatorial work for the joy and thrill of it, as so many shepherds who piped in Thessaly would manifestly have remained in the business, even if rural labour in those parts had become wholly unremunerative. On all sides the happy toiler's lips are apparently sealed by the real or supposed necessity of taking thought for the possibly evil effect of descants of joy and praise upon the mind of some human paymaster who comes into the affair.

Besides, there is the mischief that so much of our work has been bedevilled by unavoidable changes of circumstance. Childish as it is to think of going back, on any large scale, to archaic hand-work and petty production of all sorts, still the sentimentalists of hand-spinning, hand-weaving and hand-sewing have got hold of one truth—that there is more joy in a person who has slowly and clumsily made a whole piece of cloth single-handed than in ten persons who have made a thousand pieces of cloth between them in the same time, by the aid of several cunning machines which they only half understand. To make the whole of a boat or wheelbarrow or vase with your own hands is to live again through a heart-warming triumph of early mankind's; you become a more or less conscious creator, a chuckling dominator of intractable elements and resistant forces. Little of the glee may be left if your part in making the vase be only to sift or wet the clay for somebody else to throw on the wheel. But it cannot

[4 In Shakespeare's *Twelfth Night*.]

be helped. We can no more go back, at this point in the life of our world, to be like the solitary master-potter of Omar Khayyám [5] wetting his clay for himself in the market-place, than middle-aged men can return to the use of their first teeth or the vocabulary of the nursery. The caravan has to go on; to loiter at any distance behind is to court extinction sooner than it need come. Machinery and mass-production are our fate, and if they have taken the natural delightfulness of work out of a great deal of it, that was when the real Fall came and not when Jehovah told Adam that there was a great deal of perspiration before him.

4

If a Fall it has been, then all the more reason to treasure those species of work which have not been deported from Eden. They may at least keep alive in the minds of the fallen some idea of what life was like in the garden. Even Genesis does not explicitly say, though it allows us to see, what the prime joy of it was—that Adam and Eve were creators as well as creatures—God's fellow-workmen as well as pieces of his handiwork. And that joy of theirs goes on to this day wherever a painter, a writer, or any sort of artist is plying his trade at the top of his form.

In current talk about such activities, and even in the theorising of learned men, it is commonly taken for granted that before a Shakespeare or a Leonardo begins to write or paint a 'Last Supper' or a *Hamlet* he has already before his mind the whole thing which we now see—indeed a good deal more than we are now able to see of the unfortunate 'Last Supper.' The actual painting or writing is taken to be a mere transcribing of this pre-existent vision into paint or words. In one of the smallest and wisest of books about art, Professor Alexander's *Art and the Material*,[6] this grand mistake is put right. Few artists of any sort can and will tell how they do their fine things. But Mr. Alexander has divined it.

That pre-existent vision does not pre-exist at all. It only comes into existence while the technical and physical work of painting or writing goes on. To what may end by being a masterpiece an artist may come at first with a mind empty and stone-cold. It may be that 'Another commonplace model to paint!' was all that Raphael thought as he began the Sistine Madonna. Suppose it so. Well, he gets his tackle out and starts. In a little while the mere feel of the brush in his hand begins to excite him; the cold

[5 See Fitzgerald's translation of *The Rubáiyát of Omar Khayyám*, stanzas 37, 82ff.]
[6 A lecture (1925) by the philosopher Samuel Alexander (1859–1938).]

engine of his mind is warmed a little; it inclines to move; there kindles in him a faint spark of curiosity about the being who is before him; the quickened mind enlivens the hand, and the brush moves more featly; eagerness is growing in all the employed faculties of the man; images, thoughts, memories, sympathies crowd in upon him till he wonders at himself, with a kind of alarm mixed in his delight—will he ever be able to keep himself up to this pitch, he is now so much above par, so strangely endowed, for while it may last, with spiritual insight and also with an unwonted dexterity of hand?

With an ease and confidence that amaze him he sees, infers, conjectures new things behind the fleshen mask of the familiar model's face. A wonderful creature, this sitter! Wonderful creature, a nursing mother! A marvel, all motherhood, all humanity. 'What a piece of work is a man!' [7] So it goes on, and if he can hold long enough the pitch of this exaltation, this mutual stimulation of spiritual and technical power, a masterpiece may come of it, a Sistine Madonna, a Hamlet, or a Gioconda,[8] a thing absolutely new and surpassing, where nothing like it had been before—just what Adam was when first made. For we are to remember that before that exultantly supernormal interaction of imaginative and technical energies began in the man, there was, of all that came afterwards, nothing existent even as a vision in the man's mind—merely the commonplace Hamlet of some old melodrama, or some average middle-class lady or well-built laundress walking about like others in Florence. As Mr. Alexander says, 'The portrait proceeds, not from imaginative anticipation of the portrait that is to be executed, but from a lively and intelligent excitement, using the skilled brush-hand as its instructive organ.'

Art is only work utterly unspoilt, and drudgery is only art gone utterly wrong. But there was no necessary curse on Adam in this matter of work. He went out of Eden with Rome and Athens, Venice and Constantinople to build, and with all the rest of the world to turn, if he chose, into gardens where people could knit in the sun, and workshops where they could whistle over the making of delectable implements, weapons and playthings. That was all blessing, as far as it went, whatever mess the poor fellow may have since made of his chance.

[7 *Hamlet*, II, ii, 323ff.]
[8 Leonardo da Vinci's famous portrait of Mona Lisa.]

Jacques Barzun

HOW TO WRITE AND BE READ

⟦ Mr. Barzun's *Teacher in America*, published in 1944 and re-printed four times in the following year, is a refreshing, sensible, and readable book on teaching. Even a teacher can enjoy it. Mr. Barzun (1907—) has practiced and observed teachers and teaching mainly at Columbia University, which he attended and where he is now Professor of History. He is the author of many articles and books, including *The French Race* (1932), *Race* (1937), *Of Human Freedom* (1939), *Darwin, Marx, Wagner* (1941), *Romanticism and the Modern Ego* (1943), *Berlioz and the Romantic Century* (1950), and *God's Country and Mine* (1954).

> Here and there a touch of good grammar for picturesque-ness.—*Mark Twain.*

WRITING comes before reading, in logic and also in the public mind. No one cares whether you read fast or slow, well or ill, but as soon as you put pen to paper, somebody may be puzzled, angry, bored, or ecstatic; and if the occasion permits, your reader is almost sure to exclaim about the schools not doing their duty. This is the oldest literary tradition, of which here is a modern instance:—

WHAT KIND OF TEACHING IN THE PRIMARY SCHOOLS?
BY 'DISGUSTED'

Recently a letter came into my office from a boy who described himself as a first-year high school student. He wanted *infirmation* about *Africia*, because for his project in the social studies class he had *chozen Africia*. If we could not help him, *were* could he write? In closing, he was ours *sinceerly*. His handwriting was comparable to that of my 6-year-old nephew.

Too bad, but I am not alarmed. This student of 'Africia' may or may not learn to spell: it is not nearly so important as his diction and his sentence structure, which the plaintiff withheld, though they would have better enabled us to judge what the schools were really doing. What I fear about this boy is that when grown-up and provided with a secretary who can spell, he will write something like this:—

DEAR SIR:—

As you know, security prices have been advancing rapidly in the recent past *in belated recognition of the favorable fundamentals that exist.* [Italics mine]

What is decadent about this I shall shortly explain. Meantime, the fact should be faced squarely that good writing is and has always been extremely rare. I do not mean fine writing, but the simple, clear kind that everyone always demands—from others. The truth is that Simple English is no one's mother tongue. It has to be worked for. As an historian, I have plowed through state papers, memoirs, diaries, and letters, and I know that the ability to write has only a remote connection with either intelligence, or greatness, or schooling. Lincoln had no schooling yet became one of the great prose writers of the world. Cromwell went to Cambridge and was hardly ever able to frame an intelligible sentence. Another man of thought and action, Admiral Lord Howe, generally refrained from writing out his plan of battle, so as to save his captains from inevitable misunderstanding. Yet Howe managed to win the famous First of June [1] by tactics that revolutionized the art, and led directly to Nelson's Trafalgar plan—itself a rather muddled piece of prose. Let us then start with no illusion of an imaginary golden age of writing.

Which leaves the problem of doing the best with what nature gives us. And here I have some convictions born of long struggle, with myself and with others. First, I pass by all considerations of penmanship and elementary spelling to remark only that I think it a mistake to start children writing on typewriters, and worse yet to let them grow up unable to do anything but print capitals.

Above the beginner's level, the important fact is that writing cannot be taught exclusively in a course called English Composition. Writing can only be taught by the united efforts of the entire teaching staff. This holds good of any school, college, or university. Joint effort is needed, not merely to 'enforce the rules'; it is needed to insure accuracy in every subject. How can an answer in physics or a translation from the French or an historical

[[1] In a naval battle fought 1 June 1794 he won a great victory over the French. At Trafalgar in 1805 Nelson destroyed the French fleet.]

statement be called correct if the phrasing is loose or the key word wrong? Students argue that the reader of the paper knows perfectly well what is meant. Probably so, but a written exercise is designed to be read; it is not supposed to be a challenge to clairvoyance. My Italian-born tailor periodically sends me a postcard which runs: 'Your clothes is ready and should come down for a fitting.' I understand him, but the art I honor him for is cutting cloth, not precision of utterance. Now a student in college must be inspired to achieve in all subjects the utmost accuracy of perception combined with the utmost artistry of expression. The two merge and develop the sense of good workmanship, of preference for quality and truth, which is the chief mark of the genuinely educated man.

This is obviously a collective task, in which every department and every faculty has a common stake. But it is not enough to give notice that these are the faculty's sentiments. Even supposing that all teachers were willing and able to exert vigilance over written work, there would still be many practical problems of detail. And first, what motive for writing well can the student be made to feel? There is only one valid motive: the desire to be read. You will say that most students have no urge either to write or to be read. True, but (*a*) they know that they have to write and (*b*) most of them want to be well thought of. They should accordingly be made to see that reading the ordinary student paper can be a nuisance and a bore to the teacher, and that the proper aim of writing should be to make it a pleasure. This is another way of saying that most school writing is bad because student and teacher play at writing and reading instead of taking it seriously. The teacher expects second-rate hokum and the student supplies it. Let the teacher assert his rights just as the students do: in many college classes the men protest—quite rightly—when they are asked to read a dull or ill-organized book. Similarly, the instructor may warn the students that when they turn in filler and padding, jargon and lingo, stuff and nonsense, he will mark them down, not only in his grade book, but in his violated soul.

Naturally, this conscious brutality must go with a helping hand; in fact a revision of all usual practices is in order. The embargo on hokum will already work a healthy elimination of bad prose. Then the long Term Paper must be discarded and replaced with the short essay, not more than five typewritten pages in length. Students always ask how long a final paper should be and they are absolutely right in believing that most instructors are impressed by mere bulk. But when one knows how difficult it is to articulate even three measly thoughts around a single point, it is folly to ask eighteen-year-olds to produce thirty- or forty-page monographs that shall be readable. What they produce is an uncarded mattress of quotations, paraphrase, 'however's,' and 'Thus we see's.' Size being aimed at, there is no time for rewriting or reordering the material culled from half a dozen books, and the main effort goes into the irrelevant virtues of neat typing, plentiful footnotes, and the mannerisms of scholarship.

The short paper—and I speak from a large pile accumulated over twelve years—aims and arrives at different ends. It answers the reader's eternal question: Just what are you trying to tell me? It is in that spirit that student writing must be read, corrected, and if need be rewritten. When first presented, it must already be a second or third draft. The only reason I can think of for the somewhat higher average of good writing in France is that the *brouillon* is a national institution. The *brouillon* (literally: scrambled mess) is the first draft, and even the concierge [2] writing to the police about anarchists on the third floor begins with a *brouillon*, later found by his heirs.

Of course it is no use telling an American boy or girl that the essay must be written, laid aside, and rewritten at least once before handing in: the innocents do not know what to do after their first painful delivery. So the simplest thing is to ask early in the term for a good five-page essay, which turns out to be pretty bad. This is fully annotated by the reader and turned back before the next one is called for. But the corrections on it are not merely the conventional *sp., ref., punc.,* and *awk.* which the writers have seen in their margins from the seventh grade on. The comments are intensely and painfully personal, being the responses that an alert reader would feel if he were encountering the essay in print. The result is that even the best students feel abashed, if not actually resentful. To which one can only say that they should resent the neglect in which all their previous teachers have left them.

This neglect has not damaged their grammar so much as their vocabulary. Since the last thing any writer learns is the uses of words, it is no wonder if untutored youths of ability write like the stockbroker whom I quoted about 'favorable fundamentals that exist'—spineless, vague, and incoherent prose. Indeed, the exact parallel comes this moment under my hand, taken from a very able student's report on Newman's *University Sketches:* 'A University that rests on a firm financial foundation has the greater ability to unleash the minds of its students.' Despite the difference in names, the stockbroker is that boy's putative father. Their failure comes

[2 Doorman.]

from a like inattention to meaning—their own and that of the words they use.

This means that words and tone are the main things to be taught. Spelling, grammar, and punctuation do not precede but follow in the order of importance. They follow also quite naturally in the order of facility. Accordingly, the teacher-critic must slowly and carefully explain to the student what each word conveys in its particular context. I find that in the essay just cited I have written such comments as: 'I can't follow—This repeats in disguise—"avocational fruit" suggests alligator pears: why?— We now have about eight "problems" on hand: Begin!—What! more issues and problems?—Commercial lingo—Who is "we"?—Why "cradle": the metaphor is lost—Who says this?—"Patina" is not "clothing"—Don't scold and then trail off in this way—This is your point at last.' In addition, images are changed, synonyms proposed, and bad sentences recast, sometimes in alternative ways, in order to show precisely how the original misleads and how clarity is to be reached.

Tone grows naturally out of diction, but the choice of words betrays feelings of which the young writer is usually unaware. 'Are you pleading, denouncing, coaxing, or laughing? Do you back up this exaggeration? Why suddenly talk down, or turn pedant? If you want to change the mood inside the piece, you must modulate, otherwise your reader will stumble and you will lose him.' The student who learns to quiz himself in this fashion over his first draft is learning not only something about English, about writing, and about thinking, but about the human heart as well.

At the risk of tediousness I repeat that what has to be done is to dramatize the relation between writer and reader. The blunt comments are just a device to break the spell of routine, and though they administer an unpleasant shock at first, they are also flattering. 'Somebody cares about what I want to say.' The teacher is no longer a paid detective hunting stray commas.

To point these lessons up in minute detail to a student of average powers is of course time-consuming—but what else is the teacher there for? Time spent on reading and writing, in any subject, is never a waste, and the reward almost always comes, often astonishingly great. The excitement aroused by the discovery that words live is like finding that you can balance on skates. A new world of motion and of feeling is opened out to the student, a source of some anguish balanced by lifelong delight. George Gissing[3] writes somewhere that he saw an excursion steamer advertised as

[3 English essayist and novelist (1857–1903).]

being 'Replete with Ladies' Lavatories' and he comments on how many people could pass by the sign without a smile. My own favorite recollection is of a guarantee pasted on a modest shop window: 'Hats fitted to the head exclusively'—fun in every ad and at the company's expense.

The pleasure to be taken in words is as innocent and satisfying as the moral effect is clear: unless words are used deftly to set the imagination on its travels, language, literature, conversation, and friendship are full of snares. Much of our modern anxiety about the tyranny of words and of our desire for foolproof Basic [4] comes from the uneasy suspicion that we have lost the art of diction and with it the control over our own minds. This is more serious than it seems, for there is no doubt that the world outside the school largely checks what present instruction attempts, as we shall see. But having spoken of the imagination, let me first meet a likely objection to the advice here proposed. I can fancy some reader for whom school compositions were torture shaking a skeptical head and saying: 'Most young children have very little to say and school assignments blot out even that little.' I agree and the second great practical problem is, What to ask boys and girls to write about?

The don'ts are easy. Don't ask them for 'A vacation experience,' or 'My most embarrassing moment,' or 'I am the Mississippi River.' Such topics will only elicit the driest kind of hokum, though to be fair I must say that they are an improvement on the older practice of expecting infant moralizing and 'What the flag means to me.' Although as a child I enjoyed writing—history chiefly—I can remember the blankness of mind that overtook me when we had to do a *dissertation morale*. I still have a school text with some of those themes checked as having been done—for example: '*The Faithful Dog*.—A poor man has resolved to drown his dog. Thrown into the river, the dog tries to scramble up the bank, but his master lunges out to kill him with a stick. In so doing, he slips and falls. The dog saves him. Remorse of the owner.'

I regret to say that French school life is stuffed with such thorns as these, but I am not sure that the opposite 'progressive' extreme of turning children into researchers on their own is desirable either. The eleven-year-old son of a friend of mine once told me that he was writing a 'project' on Papyrus. Why papyrus? Well, the class had been 'doing' Egypt and each child was assigned one aspect of Egyptian civilization. Where was the

[4 A kind of English developed mainly to help foreigners learn something of the language. It has a vocabulary of about 850 'basic' words. Some books, including the Bible and Plato's *Republic*, have been entirely translated into Basic.]

information to come from? From encyclopedias, museums, friends, and paper manufacturers—hence such letters to strangers as the one about 'Africia' quoted earlier. As I see it, two things are wrong with this scheme. One is that it gives a false freedom; the other is that it hardly trains in the art of composing. Did this boy care at all about Egypt, let alone about the technicalities of papyrology? A child should select a topic that truly engages his interest. To eliminate pretense he must be helped to do this by means of questions and suggestions. At any age, it is very reassuring to be told that you don't really want to write about the Tariff. After two or three casts a real subject emerges, satisfactory to both parties.

Next should come into play the single good feature of the French dissertation, namely its furnishing a plan or program. Depending on the child's age a briefer or longer table of contents should be set out for each theme, either in logically organized form, or pell-mell for the student himself to disentangle. After all, what is wanted is prose, not a riot of fancy. In my experience, even examination questions are answered better when they consist of five or six sentences outlining a topic for discussion. This means further that brevity should never be accounted a fault in itself. After thirty, we can all spin tall tales, mostly secondhand,* but students, even of college age, have had very little conscious experience of life or books and it is no wonder their minds are bone dry. One should moreover keep in view the possibility that in some of them brevity may come from genius. American schoolmarms who relate the anecdote of Lincoln's 'failure' with the Gettysburg Address are just as likely to say at one glance, 'Jane, this is too short.' How do they know? Perhaps they unwittingly agree with the Gettysburg crowd that Everett's speech,[5] being longer, was better.

Some secondary schools, particularly the private ones, require the writing of verse as well as of prose. If the students are really shown how to go about versifying and are not expected to be 'poetic,' there is no harm in it. Verse writing is excellent practice for the prose writer and the striving for correct

* No course, therefore, should ever be called Creative Writing. Let us have at least a collective modesty and leave to charlatans the advertising of 'How to Write Powerful Plays.'

[5 Edward Everett made a long speech on the same occasion (the dedication of the National Cemetery at Gettysburg) on which Lincoln delivered his famous address. Lincoln's was so brief that it disappointed some people and some newspapers. But it should be remembered that many persons had traveled long distances to Gettysburg in order to hear the President; and that although long orations were the fashion then, Lincoln spoke only for a minute or two. It is easy to conjecture that he was finished before some members of his audience had settled down to listening to him; naturally they were disappointed.]

rhythm and rhyme gives the student of literature a feeling for words that may not otherwise be obtained. What can be done in this way before college by a gifted teacher has been shown by the experience of my friend, the poet Dudley Fitts, formerly at Choate and now at Andover. In collegiate circles, it is now well known that a freshman prepared under him is a literate, sometimes a polished writer, who can be safely allowed to skip into advanced work. No doubt Fitts has had his failures like all of us, but it is the successes we are looking for and that count in leavening the mass.

I am not so foolish as to think that carrying out my few suggestions would get rid of illiterate A.B.'s. I am too conscious of my initial point about 'Education,' which is that the school does not work in a vacuum but rather in a vortex of destructive forces. As regards writing, we in the twentieth century must offset not only the constant influence of careless speech and the indifference of parents, but the tremendous output of jargon issuing from the new mechanical means at man's disposal. Worst of all, circumstances have conspired to put the most corrupting force at the very heart of the school system. It is not newspapers, radio scripts, and movies that spoil our tongue so much as textbooks, official documents, commencement speeches, and learned works.*

The rise, at the turn of the century, of what James called 'the softer pedagogy' is responsible for a debasement of language beyond all bounds of forgiveness. The desire to be kind, to sound new, to foster useful attitudes, to appear 'scientific,' and chiefly also the need to produce rapidly, account for this hitherto unheard-of deliquescence. In the victims, the softness goes to the very roots of the mind and turns it into mush. And among the 'new' educators thus afflicted, the Progressive vanguard has naturally outstripped the rest. I shall not multiply examples from catalogues, reports, and speeches, though over the years I have gathered a blush-making collection. I want only to identify the evil because it spreads like the plague.

It consists mainly of what our forefathers called 'cant phrases,' strung together without continuity, like wash on a line. At a faculty meeting, a teacher asks the Director of Admissions why there seem to be more music students applying than before. The Director replies, 'Well, I should say that the forces undergirding the process are societal.' Or a committee chair-

* See Mr. Maury Maverick's excellent denunciation of what he calls Gobbledygook in the *New York Times* for May 21, 1944. The rebuttals attempting to show that roundabout expressions spare shocks to the sick are hardly to the point. The healthy ought to be able to stand directness and even mention of 'death and taxes.' 'Loss of life' and 'fiscal levies' cost just as much in the end.

man wants to know what we do next. 'I think,' says the secretary, 'that we should go on to institute actual implementation.'

Teachers steeped in this medium are bound to ooze it out themselves, particularly if weekly and daily they receive official instructions like these: 'Specify the kinds of change or permanence the student seems to crave, reject, or fear; the reasons given for liking-disliking, giving up-persistence; complaining-boasting. . . It cannot be too strongly emphasized that the observations of characteristics associated with age and background are not being made in the general area of adolescent behavior but under specific and limited conditions—those set by the aims, emphases, and assumptions of one particular faculty.* Moreover, the observations of what appear to be the interests of freshmen conceal a possible ambiguity. The term "interests" may refer to fairly superficial interests in the sense of surprise, pleasure, enjoyment, which are comparatively temporary; or "interests" may involve an awakening curiosity which leads to consistent inquiry along the lines of some project.' The reader must imagine not merely a paragraph taken at random, but pages and pages of similar woolly abstractions, mimeographed at the rate of nine and one-half pounds per person per semester. If the words 'specific' and 'objective' were blotted out of the English language, Progressive Education would have to shut up . . . shop.

As for students in teachers' colleges, the long climb up the ladder of learning comes to mean the mastering of this ghoulish *Desperanto*, so that with the attainment of the M.A. degree, we get the following utterance:—

In the proposed study I wish to describe and evaluate representative programs in these fields as a means of documenting what seems to me a trend of increasing concern with the role of higher education in the improvement of interpersonal and intergroup relations and of calling attention in this way to outstanding contributions in practice.

Some readers might think this quotation very learned and highbrow indeed. But in fact it says nothing definite. It only embodies the disinclination to think. This is a general truth, and nothing is more symptomatic of the whole jargon than the fantastic use and abuse it makes of the phrase 'in terms of.' The fact is worth a moment's attention. 'In terms of' used to refer to things that had terms, like algebra. 'Put the problem in terms of *a* and *b*.' This makes sense. But in educational circles today 'in terms of' means any connection between any two things. 'We should grade students

---

* I regret to say that 'faculty' here means 'faculty member'—a usage so far confined to the progressive schools.

in terms of their effort'—that is, *for* or *according to* their effort. The *New York Public Library Bulletin* prints: 'The first few months of employment would be easier . . . and more efficient in terms of service . . .'—that is, would yield more efficient service. But no one seems to care how or when or why his own two ideas are related. The gap in thought is plugged with 'in terms of.' I have been asked, 'Will you have dinner with me, not tonight or tomorrow, but *in terms of* next week?' A modern Caesar would write: 'All Gaul is to be considered in terms of three parts.' *

From this Educator's patois, easily the worst English now spoken, we ought to pass to the idiom of textbooks, since they are written either by educators or by teachers. Happily, there is a standard set by other books— trade books—and it is not true that all textbooks are as badly written as those on education. On the contrary, it is very encouraging that the leading ones in every field are usually well planned *and* well written. The success of Morison and Commager's *Growth of the American Republic* [6] is only the most recent case in point. Students, nevertheless, are asked to read many ill-written books. There is no excuse for this, though it is by no means the only source of error. We must remember that students do not read only books; they read what every man reads, and this would do no harm—it does no harm—when the mind is trained to resilience by the kind of writing practice I have advocated.

Unfortunately, with the vast increase in public schooling since 1870, an entirely new notion of what is good English has come to prevail. Awakened by free schooling, the people have shown worthy intentions. They want to be right and even elegant, and so become at once suspicious of plainness and pedantic. They purchase all sorts of handbooks that make a fetish of spelling, of avoiding split infinitives, of saying 'it is I' (with the common result of 'between you and I')—in short, dwell on trivialities or vulgarisms which do not affect style or thought in the slightest. But with this intolerance towards crude and plain error goes a remarkable insensitivity to inflated nonsense. Most bad journalism is only highbrow verbosity, yet the popular mind continues to believe that the pedantry which it likes is simple and the simplicity which it finds hard is complex. Here is the opening of a serial thriller in a Boston paper:—

Strange things happen in Chinatown. But even that exotic and perverse district seldom presented drama as fantastic as the secret that hid among the silk

* The objectionable phrase is now to be found in newspapers, business reports, and private correspondence. It is a menace *in terms of* the whole nation.

[6 A chapter of this work is reprinted on pp. 300–321.]

and jade and porcelain splendors of the famous House of the Mandarin on Mulberry Lane.

There is a certain art in this, and I take note of 'porcelain splendors' as the *mot juste* for bathtubs on exhibit. But the passage as a whole contains nothing but arty and highfalutin words, joined by the good will of the reader rather than the mind of the writer. Still, every newspaper reader feels he understands it. Take now a well-known sentence composed of common words, all but two of them single syllables: 'If there are more trees in the world than there are leaves on any one tree, then there must be at least two trees with the same number of leaves.' Read this aloud and almost any listener will respond with 'Huh? Say that again.' For this sentence records a thought, and the Chinatown 'drama' did not.

The close logic in the truly 'simple' sentence makes the contrast sharper, but it would be just as sharp between a feeling clearly put and a feeble attempt to thrill. Thus there is a superstition that the novels of Henry James are written in a 'difficult style.' Yet if you examine them, you will find that the words and sentences—in *The Ambassadors*, for example— are in themselves quite usual. But the feelings they convey are unusual and subtle, and require attention. At the same time they also compel it, which is all that an artist takes pains for in writing.

Conversely, the only thing that can be asked of a writer is that he should know his own meaning and present it as forcibly as he can. The rule has not changed since Byron affirmed that 'easy writing makes damned hard reading.' Hence there is great value, as I think, in having college graduates recognize good prose when they see it, know that a tolerable paragraph must have gone through six or seven versions, and be ready to follow athletically on the trail of articulate thoughts, rather than look for the soapy incline to muddled meaning.

One does not have to go very far for the enjoyment of precise, sinewy writing. The same newspaper that furnishes tripe for the morning meal also brings such rarer tidbits as these: 'They [the robot bombs] are of much the same shape and size as a small fighter plane, with stubby wings. They come over with tails aglow from the propelling rocket force, like little meteors moving at a nightmare pace by dark, and by day like little black planes with tails afire.' This is perfection; and here is poetry: 'Mr. McCaffrey, himself the father of two children, *and therefore schooled in apprehension,* ran across the street . . . shouting a warning.'

When the daily reporter, harried by falling bombs or hustled by a city editor, can write like this, it is depressing to return to agencies closer to the school and find verbal laziness encouraged and imbecility taken for granted. One publisher of reference works sends out a circular stressing the fact that his books give the pronunciation of 'all difficult—"hard-to-say"—words.' Is this where we are after fifty years of quasi-universal literacy? Is the word 'difficult' so difficult that it has to be translated in its own sentence? The question is one for readers, and it is to the subject of reading that I now turn.

Henry David Thoreau
READING

⟨ On Thoreau and *Walden* see p. 383 and pp. 405–14.

Wᴵᴛʜ a little more deliberation in the choice of their pursuits, all men would perhaps become essentially students and observers, for certainly their nature and destiny are interesting to all alike. In accumulating property for ourselves or our posterity, in founding a family or a state, or acquiring fame even, we are mortal; but in dealing with truth we are immortal, and need fear no change nor accident. The oldest Egyptian or Hindoo philosopher raised a corner of the veil from the statue of the divinity; and still the trembling robe remains raised, and I gaze upon as fresh a glory as he did, since it was I in him that was then so bold, and it is he in me that now reviews the vision. No dust has settled on that robe; no time has elapsed since that divinity was revealed. That time which we really improve, or which is improvable, is neither past, present, nor future.

My residence was more favorable, not only to thought, but to serious reading, than a university; and though I was beyond the range of the ordinary circulating library, I had more than ever come within the influence of those books which circulate round the world, whose sentences were first written on bark, and are now merely copied from time to time on to linen paper. Says the poet Mîr Camar Uddîn Mast, 'Being seated to run through the region of the spiritual world; I have had this advantage in books. To be intoxicated by a single glass of wine; I have experienced this pleasure when I have drunk the liquor of the esoteric doctrines.' I kept Homer's Iliad on my table through the summer, though I looked at his page only now and then. Incessant labor with my hands, at first, for I had my house to finish [1] and my beans to hoe at the same time, made more study impos-

[1 See 'Where I Lived, and What I Lived For' (pp. 383–88).]
Fʀᴏᴍ *Walden*, 1854.

sible. Yet I sustained myself by the prospect of such reading in future. I read one or two shallow books of travel in the intervals of my work, till that employment made me ashamed of myself, and I asked where it was then that I lived.

The student may read Homer or Æschylus in the Greek without danger of dissipation or luxuriousness, for it implies that he in some measure emulate their heroes, and consecrate morning hours [2] to their pages. The heroic books, even if printed in the character of our mother tongue, will always be in a language dead to degenerate times; and we must laboriously seek the meaning of each word and line, conjecturing a larger sense than common use permits out of what wisdom and valor and generosity we have. The modern cheap and fertile press, with all its translations, has done little to bring us nearer to the heroic writers of antiquity. They seem as solitary, and the letter in which they are printed as rare and curious, as ever. It is worth the expense of youthful days and costly hours, if you learn only some words of an ancient language, which are raised out of the trivialness of the street, to be perpetual suggestions and provocations. It is not in vain that the farmer remembers and repeats the few Latin words which he has heard. Men sometimes speak as if the study of the classics would at length make way for more modern and practical studies; [3] but the adventurous student will always study classics, in whatever language they may be written and however ancient they may be. For what are the classics but the noblest recorded thoughts of man? They are the only oracles which are not decayed, and there are such answers to the most modern inquiry in them as Delphi and Dodona [4] never gave. We might as well omit to study Nature because she is old. To read well, that is, to read true books in a true spirit, is a noble exercise, and one that will task the reader more than any exercise which the customs of the day esteem. It requires a training such as the athletes underwent, the steady intention almost of the whole life to this object. Books must be read as deliberately and reservedly as they were written.[5] It is not enough even to be able to speak the language of that nation by which they are written, for there is a memorable interval between the spoken and the written language, the language heard and the language read. The one is

[2 On the sacredness of morning see 'Where I Lived, and What I Lived For' (pp. 388–90).]

[3 On the study of classics see selections by Arnold (pp. 120–37) and A. N. Whitehead (pp. 138–51).]

[4 Two celebrated shrines where the oracles of Apollo and Zeus were delivered.]

[5 Compare 'Anonymity: An Enquiry,' by E. M. Forster (pp. 44–53), and E. B. White's essay on Thoreau (pp. 405–14).]

commonly transitory, a sound, a tongue, a dialect merely, almost brutish, and we learn it unconsciously, like the brutes, of our mothers. The other is the maturity and experience of that; if that is our mother tongue, this is our father tongue, a reserved and select expression, too significant to be heard by the ear, which we must be born again in order to speak. The crowds of men who merely *spoke* the Greek and Latin tongues in the middle ages were not entitled by the accident of birth to *read* the works of genius writ-ten in those languages; for these were not written in that Greek or Latin which they knew, but in the select language of literature. They had not learned the nobler dialects of Greece and Rome, but the very materials on which they were written were waste paper to them, and they prized instead a cheap contemporary literature. But when the several nations of Europe had acquired distinct though rude written languages of their own, sufficient for the purposes of their rising literatures, then first learning revived, and scholars were enabled to discern from that remoteness the treasures of antiquity. What the Roman and Grecian multitude could not *hear*, after the lapse of ages a few scholars *read*, and a few scholars only are still read-ing it.

However much we may admire the orator's occasional bursts of elo-quence, the noblest written words are commonly as far behind or above the fleeting spoken language as the firmament with its stars is behind the clouds. *There* are the stars, and they who can may read them. The astrono-mers forever comment on and observe them. They are not exhalations like our daily colloquies and vaporous breath. What is called eloquence in the forum is commonly found to be rhetoric in the study. The orator yields to the inspiration of a transient occasion, and speaks to the mob before him, to those who can *hear* him; but the writer, whose more equable life is his occasion, and who would be distracted by the event and the crowd which inspire the orator, speaks to the intellect and heart of mankind, to all in any age who can *understand* him.

No wonder that Alexander carried the Iliad with him on his expeditions in a precious casket. A written word is the choicest of relics. It is something at once more intimate with us and more universal than any other work of art. It is the work of art nearest to life itself. It may be translated into every language, and not only be read but actually breathed from all human lips; —not be represented on canvas or in marble only, but be carved out of the breath of life itself. The symbol of an ancient man's thought becomes a modern man's speech. Two thousand summers have imparted to the monu-ments of Grecian literature, as to her marbles, only a maturer golden and

autumnal tint, for they have carried their own serene and celestial atmosphere into all lands to protect them against the corrosion of time. Books
are the treasured wealth of the world and the fit inheritance of generations
and nations. Books, the oldest and the best, stand naturally and rightfully
on the shelves of every cottage. They have no cause of their own to plead,
but while they enlighten and sustain the reader his common sense will not
refuse them. Their authors are a natural and irresistible aristocracy in every
society, and, more than kings or emperors, exert an influence on mankind.
When the illiterate and perhaps scornful trader has earned by enterprise
and industry his coveted leisure and independence, and is admitted to the
circles of wealth and fashion, he turns inevitably at last to those still higher
but yet inaccessible circles of intellect and genius, and is sensible only of
the imperfection of his culture and the vanity and insufficiency of all his
riches, and further proves his good sense by the pains which he takes to
secure for his children that intellectual culture whose want he so keenly
feels; and thus it is that he becomes the founder of a family.

Those who have not learned to read the ancient classics in the language
in which they were written must have a very imperfect knowledge of the
history of the human race; for it is remarkable that no transcript of them
has ever been made into any modern tongue, unless our civilization itself
may be regarded as such a transcript. Homer has never yet been printed in
English, nor Æschylus, nor Virgil even,—works as refined, as solidly done,
and as beautiful almost as the morning itself; for later writers, say what we
will of their genius, have rarely, if ever, equalled the elaborate beauty and
finish and the lifelong and heroic literary labors of the ancients. They only
talk of forgetting them who never knew them. It will be soon enough to
forget them when we have the learning and the genius which will enable
us to attend to and appreciate them. That age will be rich indeed when
those relics which we call Classics, and the still older and more than classic
but even less known Scriptures of the nations, shall have still further accumulated, when the Vaticans shall be filled with Vedas and Zendavestas [6]
and Bibles, with Homers and Dantes and Shakspeares, and all the centuries
to come shall have successively deposited their trophies in the forum of the
world. By such a pile we may hope to scale heaven at last.

The works of the great poets have never yet been read by mankind, for
only great poets can read them. They have only been read as the multitude
read the stars, at most astrologically, not astronomically. Most men have

[6 Sacred scriptures of the ancient Hindus and Parsees. Like Emerson, Thoreau was
deeply impressed by Oriental poetry and philosophy.]

learned to read to serve a paltry convenience, as they have learned to cipher in order to keep accounts and not be cheated in trade; but of reading as a noble intellectual exercise they know little or nothing; yet this only is reading, in a high sense, not that which lulls us as a luxury and suffers the nobler faculties to sleep the while, but what we have to stand on tiptoe to read and devote our most alert and wakeful hours to.

I think that having learned our letters we should read the best that is in literature, and not be forever repeating our a b abs, and words of one syllable, in the fourth or fifth classes, sitting on the lowest and foremost form all our lives. Most men are satisfied if they read or hear read, and perchance have been convicted by the wisdom of one good book, the Bible, and for the rest of their lives vegetate and dissipate their faculties in what is called easy reading. There is a work in several volumes in our Circulating Library [7] entitled Little Reading, which I thought referred to a town of that name which I had not been to. There are those who, like cormorants and ostriches, can digest all sorts of this, even after the fullest dinner of meats and vegetables, for they suffer nothing to be wasted. If others are the machines to provide this provender, they are the machines to read it. They read the nine thousandth tale about Zebulon and Sephronia, and how they loved as none had ever loved before, and neither did the course of their true love run smooth,—at any rate, how it did run and stumble, and get up again and go on! how some poor unfortunate got up on to a steeple, who had better never have gone up as far as the belfry; and then, having needlessly got him up there, the happy novelist rings the bell for all the world to come together and hear, O dear! how he did get down again! For my part, I think that they had better metamorphose all such aspiring heroes of universal noveldom into man weathercocks, as they used to put heroes among the constellations, and let them swing round there till they are rusty, and not come down at all to bother honest men with their pranks. The next time the novelist rings the bell I will not stir though the meeting-house burn down. 'The Skip of the Tip-Toe-Hop, a Romance of the Middle Ages, by the celebrated author of "Tittle-Tol-Tan," to appear in monthly parts; a great rush; don't all come together.' All this they read with saucer eyes, and erect and primitive curiosity, and with unwearied gizzard, whose corrugations even yet need no sharpening, just as some little four-year-old bencher his two-cent gilt-covered edition of Cinderella,—without any improvement, that I can see, in the pronunciation, or accent, or emphasis, or any more skill in extracting or inserting the moral. The result is dulness of sight, a

[7 In Concord.]

stagnation of the vital circulations, and a general deliquium and sloughing off of all the intellectual faculties. This sort of gingerbread is baked daily and more sedulously than pure wheat or rye-and-Indian in almost every oven, and finds a surer market.

The best books are not read even by those who are called good readers. What does our Concord culture amount to? There is in this town, with a very few exceptions, no taste for the best or for very good books even in English literature, whose words all can read and spell. Even the college-bred and so called liberally educated men here and elsewhere have really little or no acquaintance with the English classics; and as for the recorded wisdom of mankind, the ancient classics and Bibles, which are accessible to all who will know of them, there are the feeblest efforts any where made to become acquainted with them. I know a woodchopper, of middle age, who takes a French paper, not for news as he says, for he is above that, but to 'keep himself in practice,' he being a Canadian by birth; and when I ask him what he considers the best thing he can do in this world, he says, beside this, to keep up and add to his English. This is about as much as the college bred generally do or aspire to do, and they take an English paper for the purpose. One who has just come from reading perhaps one of the best English books will find how many with whom he can converse about it? Or suppose he comes from reading a Greek or Latin classic in the original, whose praises are familiar even to the so called illiterate; he will find nobody at all to speak to, but must keep silence about it. Indeed, there is hardly the professor in our colleges, who, if he has mastered the difficulties of the language, has proportionally mastered the difficulties of the wit and poetry of a Greek poet, and has any sympathy to impart to the alert and heroic reader; and as for the sacred Scriptures, or Bibles of mankind, who in this town can tell me even their titles? Most men do not know that any nation but the Hebrews have had a scripture. A man, any man, will go considerably out of his way to pick up a silver dollar; but here are golden words, which the wisest men of antiquity have uttered, and whose worth the wise of every succeeding age have assured us of;—and yet we learn to read only as far as Easy Reading, the primers and class-books, and when we leave school, the 'Little Reading,' and story books, which are for boys and beginners; and our reading, our conversation and thinking, are all on a very low level, worthy only of pygmies and manikins.

I aspire to be acquainted with wiser men than this our Concord soil has produced, whose names are hardly known here. Or shall I hear the name of Plato and never read his book? As if Plato were my townsman and I never saw him,—my next neighbor and I never heard him speak or attended to the wisdom of his words. But how actually is it? His Dialogues, which contain what was immortal in him, lie on the next shelf, and yet I never read them. We are under-bred and low-lived and illiterate; and in this respect I confess I do not make any very broad distinction between the illiterateness of my townsman who cannot read at all, and the illiterateness of him who has learned to read only what is for children and feeble intellects. We should be as good as the worthies of antiquity, but partly by first knowing how good they were. We are a race of tit-men, and soar but little higher in our intellectual flights than the columns of the daily paper.

It is not all books that are as dull as their readers. There are probably words addressed to our condition exactly, which, if we could really hear and understand, would be more salutary than the morning or the spring to our lives, and possibly put a new aspect on the face of things for us. How many a man has dated a new era in his life from the reading of a book. The book exists for us perchance which will explain our miracles and reveal new ones. The at present unutterable things we may find somewhere uttered. These same questions that disturb and puzzle and confound us have in their turn occurred to all the wise men; not one has been omitted; and each has answered them, according to his ability, by his words and his life. Moreover, with wisdom we shall learn liberality. The solitary hired man on a farm in the outskirts of Concord, who has had his second birth and peculiar religious experience, and is driven as he believes into silent gravity and exclusiveness by his faith, may think it is not true; but Zoroaster,[8] thousands of years ago, travelled the same road and had the same experience; but he, being wise, knew it to be universal, and treated his neighbors accordingly, and is even said to have invented and established worship among men. Let him humbly commune with Zoroaster then, and through the liberalizing influence of all the worthies, with Jesus Christ himself, and let 'our church'[9] go by the board.

We boast that we belong to the nineteenth century and are making the most rapid strides of any nation. But consider how little this village does for its own culture. I do not wish to flatter my townsmen, nor to be flattered by them, for that will not advance either of us. We need to be provoked,—goaded like oxen, as we are, into a trot. We have a comparatively decent system of common schools, schools for infants only; but excepting

[8 Founder of the ancient Persian religion.]
[9 Thoreau never attended church.]

the half-starved Lyceum [10] in the winter, and latterly the puny beginning of a library suggested by the state, no school for ourselves. We spend more on almost any article of bodily aliment or ailment than on our mental aliment. It is time that we had uncommon schools, that we did not leave off our education when we begin to be men and women. It is time that villages were universities, and their elder inhabitants the fellows of universities, with leisure—if they are indeed so well off—to pursue liberal studies the rest of their lives. Shall the world be confined to one Paris or one Oxford forever? Cannot students be boarded here and get a liberal education under the skies of Concord? Can we not hire some Abelard [11] to lecture to us? Alas! what with foddering the cattle and tending the store, we are kept from school too long, and our education is sadly neglected. In this country, the village should in some respects take the place of the nobleman of Europe. It should be the patron of the fine arts. It is rich enough. It wants only the magnanimity and refinement. It can spend money enough on such things as farmers and traders value, but it is thought Utopian to propose spending money for things which more intelligent men know to be of far more worth. This town has spent seventeen thousand dollars on a townhouse, thank fortune or politics, but probably it will not spend so much on living wit, the true meat to put into that shell, in a hundred years. The one hundred and twenty-five dollars annually subscribed for a Lyceum in the winter is better spent than any other equal sum raised in the town. If we live in the nineteenth century, why should we not enjoy the advantages which the nineteenth century offers? Why should our life be in any respect provincial? If we will read newspapers, why not skip the gossip of Boston and take the best newspaper in the world at once?—not be sucking the pap of 'neutral family' papers, or browsing 'Olive-Branches' here in New England. Let the reports of all the learned societies come to us, and we will see if they know any thing. Why should we leave it to Harper & Brothers and Redding & Co. to select our reading? As the nobleman of cultivated taste surrounds himself with whatever conduces to his culture,—genius—learning—wit—books—paintings—statuary—music—philosophical instruments, and the like; so let the village do,—not stop short at a pedagogue, a parson, a sexton, a parish library, and three selectmen, because our pilgrim forefathers got through a cold winter once on a bleak rock with these. To act collectively is according to the spirit of our institutions; and I am confident

[10 Thoreau lectured occasionally at the Concord Lyceum.]
[11 French philosopher and theologian (1079–1142).]

that, as our circumstances are more flourishing, our means are greater than the nobleman's. New England can hire all the wise men in the world to come and teach her, and board them round the while, and not be provincial at all. That is the *uncommon* school we want. Instead of noblemen, let us have noble villages of men. If it is necessary, omit one bridge over the river, go round a little there, and throw one arch at least over the darker gulf of ignorance which surrounds us.

E. M. Forster

ART FOR ART'S SAKE

⟨ E. M. Forster's high standing among modern English novelists owes most to *A Passage to India* (1924). His earlier novels, *Where Angels Fear to Tread* (1905), *The Longest Journey* (1907), *A Room with a View* (1908), and *Howards End* (1910), though never matching the popularity of *A Passage to India,* have been reprinted in the past decade, and discovered or rediscovered by many readers. His short stories were collected in *The Celestial Omnibus* (1923) and *The Eternal Moment* (1928). Most of Mr. Forster's publications since 1924 are critical or topical essays: *Aspects of the Novel* (1927), *Abinger Harvest* (1936), and *Two Cheers for Democracy* (1951), a volume of studies of political, ethical, and aesthetic subjects. His latest book, *The Hill of Devi* (1953), is another examination of Indian character.

'Art for Art's Sake' is an address delivered before the American Academy of Arts and Letters in 1949. 'I have found by experience,' writes Mr. Forster, 'that the arts act as an antidote against our present troubles and also as a support to our common humanity, and I am glad to emphasise this at a time when they are being belittled and starved.'

I BELIEVE IN art for art's sake. It is an unfashionable belief, and some of my statements must be of the nature of an apology. Fifty years ago I should have faced you with more confidence. A writer or a speaker who chose 'Art for Art's Sake' for his theme fifty years ago could be sure of being in the swim, and could feel so confident of success that he sometimes dressed himself in esthetic costumes suitable to the occasion—in an embroidered dressing-gown, perhaps, or a blue velvet suit with a Lord Fauntleroy collar; or a toga, or a kimono, and carried a poppy or a lily or a long peacock's feather in his mediaeval hand. Times have changed. Not thus can I present either myself or my theme today. My aim rather is to ask you quietly to reconsider for a few minutes a phrase which has been much misused and much abused, but which has, I believe, great importance for us—has, indeed, eternal importance.

Now we can easily dismiss those peacock's feathers and other affectations—they are but trifles—but I want also to dismiss a more dangerous heresy, namely the silly idea that only art matters, an idea which has somehow got mixed up with the idea of art for art's sake, and has helped to discredit it. Many things, besides art, matter. It is merely one of the things that matter, and high though the claims are that I make for it, I want to keep them in proportion. No one can spend his or her life entirely in the creation or the appreciation of masterpieces. Man lives, and ought to live, in a complex world, full of conflicting claims, and if we simplified them down into the esthetic he would be sterilised. Art for art's sake does not mean that only art matters, and I would also like to rule out such phrases as 'The Life of Art,' 'Living for Art,' and 'Art's High Mission.' They confuse and mislead.

What does the phrase mean? Instead of generalising, let us take a specific instance—Shakespeare's *Macbeth*, for example, and pronounce the words, '*Macbeth* for *Macbeth's* sake.' What does that mean? Well, the play has several aspects—it is educational, it teaches us something about legendary Scotland, something about Jacobean England, and a good deal about human nature and its perils. We can study its origins, and study and enjoy its dramatic technique and the music of its diction. All that is true. But *Macbeth* is furthermore a world of its own, created by Shakespeare and existing in virtue of its own poetry. It is in this aspect *Macbeth* for *Macbeth's* sake, and that is what I intend by the phrase 'art for art's sake.' A work of art—whatever else it may be—is a self-contained entity, with a life of its own imposed on it by its creator. It has internal order. It may have external form. That is how we recognise it.

Take for another example that picture of Seurat's [1] which I saw two years ago in Chicago—'*La Grande Jatte*.' Here again there is much to study and to enjoy: the pointillism, the charming face of the seated girl, the nineteenth-century Parisian Sunday sunlight, the sense of motion in immobility. But here again there is something more; '*La Grande Jatte*' forms a world of its own, created by Seurat and existing by virtue of its own poetry: '*La*

[[1] French painter (1859–91).]

Grande Jatte' pour 'La Grande Jatte': l'art pour l'art. Like *Macbeth* it has internal order and internal life.

It is to the conception of order that I would now turn. This is important to my argument, and I want to make a digression, and glance at order in daily life, before I come to order in art.

In the world of daily life, the world which we perforce inhabit, there is much talk about order, particularly from statesmen and politicians. They tend, however, to confuse order with orders, just as they confuse creation with regulations. Order, I suggest, is something evolved from within, not something imposed from without; it is an internal stability, a vital harmony, and in the social and political category it has never existed except for the convenience of historians. Viewed realistically, the past is really a series of *disorders*, succeeding one another by discoverable laws, no doubt, and certainly marked by an increasing growth of human interference, but disorders all the same. So that, speaking as a writer, what I hope for today is a disorder which will be more favourable to artists than is the present one, and which will provide them with fuller inspirations and better material conditions. It will not last—nothing lasts—but there have been some advantageous disorders in the past—for instance, in ancient Athens, in Renaissance Italy, eighteenth-century France, periods in China and Persia —and we may do something to accelerate the next one. But let us not again fix our hearts where true joys are not to be found. We were promised a new order after the first world war through the League of Nations. It did not come, nor have I faith in present promises, by whomsoever endorsed. The implacable offensive of Science forbids. We cannot reach social and political stability for the reason that we continue to make scientific discoveries and to apply them, and thus to destroy the arrangements which were based on more elementary discoveries. If Science would discover rather than apply—if, in other words, men were more interested in knowledge than in power—mankind would be in a far safer position, the stability statesmen talk about would be a possibility, there could be a new order based on vital harmony, and the earthly millennium might approach. But Science shows no signs of doing this: she gave us the internal combustion engine, and before we had digested and assimilated it with terrible pains into our social system, she harnessed the atom, and destroyed any new order that seemed to be evolving. How can man get into harmony with his surroundings when he is constantly altering them? The future of our race is, in this direction, more unpleasant than we care to admit, and it has sometimes seemed to me that its best chance lies through apathy, uninventiveness, and inertia. Universal exhaustion might promote that Change of Heart which is at present so briskly recommended from a thousand pulpits. Universal exhaustion would certainly be a new experience. The human race has never undergone it, and is still too perky to admit that it may be coming and might result in a sprouting of new growth through the decay.

I must not pursue these speculations any further—they lead me too far from my terms of reference and maybe from yours. But I do want to emphasise that order in daily life and in history, order in the social and political category, is unattainable under our present psychology.

Where is it attainable? Not in the astronomical category, where it was for many years enthroned. The heavens and the earth have become terribly alike since Einstein. No longer can we find a reassuring contrast to chaos in the night sky and look up with George Meredith [2] to the stars, the army of unalterable law, or listen for the music of the spheres. Order is not there. In the entire universe there seem to be only two possibilities for it. The first of them—which again lies outside my terms of reference—is the divine order, the mystic harmony, which according to all religions is available for those who can contemplate it. We must admit its possibility, on the evidence of the adepts, and we must believe them when they say that it is attained, if attainable, by prayer. 'O thou who changest not, abide with me,' said one of its poets.[3] '*Ordina questo amor, o tu che m'ami*,' said another: 'Set love in order, thou who lovest me.' The existence of a divine order, though it cannot be tested, has never been disproved.

The second possibility for order lies in the esthetic category, which is my subject here: the order which an artist can create in his own work, and to that we must now return. A work of art, we are all agreed, is a unique product. But why? It is unique not because it is clever or noble or beautiful or enlightened or original or sincere or idealistic or useful or educational— it may embody any of those qualities—but because it is the only material object in the universe which may possess internal harmony. All the others have been pressed into shape from outside, and when their mould is removed they collapse. The work of art stands up by itself, and nothing else does. It achieves something which has often been promised by society, but always delusively. Ancient Athens made a mess—but the *Antigone* [4] stands

[2 See his sonnet, 'Lucifer in Starlight.']
[3 H. F. Lyte, in his familiar hymn, 'Abide with Me' (1847).]
[4 Tragedy by Sophocles (*c.* 441 B.C.).]

up. Renaissance Rome made a mess—but the ceiling of the Sistine got painted. James I made a mess—but there was *Macbeth*. Louis XIV—but there was *Phèdre*.[5] Art for art's sake? I should just think so, and more so than ever at the present time. It is the one orderly product which our muddling race has produced. It is the cry of a thousand sentinels, the echo from a thousand labyrinths; it is the lighthouse which cannot be hidden: *c'est le meilleur témoignage que nous puissions donner de notre dignité.*[6] *Antigone* for *Antigone's* sake, *Macbeth* for *Macbeth's*, 'La Grande Jatte' *pour* 'La Grande Jatte.'

If this line of argument is correct, it follows that the artist will tend to be an outsider in the society to which he has been born, and that the nineteenth-century conception of him as a Bohemian was not inaccurate. The conception erred in three particulars: it postulated an economic system where art could be a full-time job, it introduced the fallacy that only art matters, and it overstressed idiosyncrasy and waywardness—the peacock-feather aspect—rather than order. But it is a truer conception than the one which prevails in official circles on my side of the Atlantic—I don't know about yours: the conception which treats the artist as if he were a particularly bright government advertiser and encourages him to be friendly and matey with his fellow citizens, and not to give himself airs.

Estimable is mateyness, and the man who achieves it gives many a pleasant little drink to himself and to others. But it has no traceable connection with the creative impulse, and probably acts as an inhibition on it. The artist who is seduced by mateyness may stop himself from doing the one thing which he, and he alone, can do—the making of something out of words or sounds or paint or clay or marble or steel or film which has internal harmony and presents order to a permanently disarranged planet. This seems worth doing, even at the risk of being called uppish by journalists. I have in mind an article which was published some years ago in the London *Times*, an article called 'The Eclipse of the Highbrow,' in which the 'Average Man' was exalted, and all contemporary literature was censured if it did not toe the line, the precise position of the line being naturally known to the writer of the article. Sir Kenneth Clark, who was at that time director of our National Gallery, commented on this pernicious doctrine in a letter which cannot be too often quoted. 'The poet and the artist,' wrote Clark, 'are important precisely because they are not average men; because in sensibility, intelligence, and power of invention they far

[5] Tragedy by Racine (1677).]
[6] 'It is the best evidence we could offer of our dignity.']

exceed the average.' These memorable words, and particularly the words 'power of invention,' are the Bohemian's passport. Furnished with it, he slinks about society, saluted now by a brickbat and now by a penny, and accepting either of them with equanimity. He does not consider too anxiously what his relations with society may be, for he is aware of something more important than that—namely the invitation to invent, to create order, and he believes he will be better placed for doing this if he attempts detachment. So round and round he slouches, with his hat pulled over his eyes, and maybe with a louse in his beard, and—if he really wants one—with a peacock's feather in his hand.

If our present society should disintegrate—and who dare prophesy that it won't?—this old-fashioned and démodé figure will become clearer: the Bohemian, the outsider, the parasite, the rat—one of those figures which have at present no function either in a warring or a peaceful world. It may not be dignified to be a rat, but many of the ships are sinking, which is not dignified either—the officials did not build them properly. Myself, I would sooner be a swimming rat than a sinking ship—at all events I can look around me for a little longer—and I remember how one of us, a rat with particularly bright eyes called Shelley, squeaked out, 'Poets are the unacknowledged legislators of the world,' before he vanished into the waters of the Mediterranean.

What laws did Shelley propose to pass? None. The legislation of the artist is never formulated at the time, though it is sometimes discerned by future generations. He legislates through creating. And he creates through his sensitiveness and his power to impose form. Without form the sensitiveness vanishes. And form is as important today, when the human race is trying to ride the whirlwind, as it ever was in those less agitating days of the past, when the earth seemed solid and the stars fixed, and the discoveries of science were made slowly, slowly. Form is not tradition. It alters from generation to generation. Artists always seek a new technique, and will continue to do so as long as their work excites them. But form of some kind is imperative. It is the surface crust of the internal harmony, it is the outward evidence of order.

My remarks about society may have seemed too pessimistic, but I believe that society can only represent a fragment of the human spirit, and that another fragment can only get expressed through art. And I wanted to take this opportunity, this vantage ground, to assert not only the existence of art, but its pertinacity. Looking back into the past, it seems to me that that is all there has ever been: vantage grounds for discussion and creation, little vantage grounds in the changing chaos, where bubbles have been blown and webs spun, and the desire to create order has found temporary gratification, and the sentinels have managed to utter their challenges, and the huntsmen, though lost individually, have heard each other's calls through the impenetrable wood, and the lighthouses have never ceased sweeping the thankless seas. In this pertinacity there seems to me, as I grow older, something more and more profound, something which does in fact concern people who do not care about art at all.

In conclusion, let me summarise the various categories that have laid claim to the possession of Order.

(1) The social and political category. Claim disallowed on the evidence of history and of our own experience. If man altered psychologically, order here might be attainable; not otherwise.

(2) The astronomical category. Claim allowed up to the present century, but now disallowed on the evidence of the physicists.

(3) The religious category. Claim allowed on the evidence of the mystics.

(4) The esthetic category. Claim allowed on the evidence of various works of art, and on the evidence of our own creative impulses, however weak these may be, or however imperfectly they may function. Works of art, in my opinion, are the only objects in the material universe to possess internal order, and that is why, though I don't believe that only art matters, I do believe in Art for Art's Sake.

E. M. Forster
ANONYMITY: AN ENQUIRY

⟨ On E. M. Forster see p. 37.

D o you like to know who a book's by?

The question is more profound than may appear. A poem for example: do we gain more or less pleasure from it when we know the name of the poet? The *Ballad of Sir Patrick Spens*, for example. No one knows who wrote *Sir Patrick Spens*. It comes to us out of the northern void like a breath of ice. Set beside it another ballad whose author is known—*The Rime of the Ancient Mariner*. That, too, contains a tragic voyage and the breath of ice, but it is signed Samuel Taylor Coleridge, and we know a certain amount about this Coleridge. Coleridge signed other poems and knew other poets; he ran away from Cambridge; he enlisted as a Dragoon under the name of Trooper Comberback, but fell so constantly from his horse that it had to be withdrawn from beneath him permanently; he was employed instead upon matters relating to sanitation; he married Southey's sister, and gave lectures; he became stout, pious and dishonest, took opium and died. With such information in our heads, we speak of the *Ancient Mariner* as 'a poem by Coleridge,' but of *Sir Patrick Spens* as 'a poem.' What difference, if any, does this difference between them make upon our minds? And in the case of novels and plays—does ignorance or knowledge of their authorship signify? And newspaper articles—do they impress more when they are signed or unsigned? Thus—rather vaguely—let us begin our quest.

Books are composed of words, and words have two functions to perform: they give information or they create an atmosphere. Often they do both, for the two functions are not incompatible, but our enquiry shall keep them distinct. Let us turn for our next example to Public Notices. There is a word that is sometimes hung up at the edge of a tramline: the word

'Stop.' Written on a metal label by the side of the line, it means that a tram should stop here presently. It is an example of pure information. It creates no atmosphere—at least, not in my mind. I stand close to the label and wait and wait for the tram. If the tram comes, the information is correct; if it doesn't come, the information is incorrect; but in either case it remains information, and the notice is an excellent instance of one of the uses of words.

Compare it with another public notice which is sometimes exhibited in the darker cities of England: 'Beware of pickpockets, male and female.' Here, again, there is information. A pickpocket may come along presently, just like a tram, and we take our measures accordingly. But there is something else besides. Atmosphere is created. Who can see those words without a slight sinking feeling at the heart? All the people around look so honest and nice, but they are not, some of them are pickpockets, male or female. They hustle old gentlemen, the old gentleman glances down, his watch is gone. They steal up behind an old lady and cut out the back breadth of her beautiful sealskin jacket with sharp and noiseless pairs of scissors. Observe that happy little child running to buy sweets. Why does he suddenly burst into tears? A pickpocket, male or female, has jerked his halfpenny out of his hand. All this, and perhaps much more, occurs to us when we read the notice in question. We suspect our fellows of dishonesty, we observe them suspecting us. We have been reminded of several disquieting truths, of the general insecurity of life, human frailty, the violence of the poor, and the fatuous trustfulness of the rich, who always expect to be popular without having done anything to deserve it. It is a sort of *memento mori*,[1] set up in the midst of Vanity Fair. By taking the form of a warning it has made us afraid, although nothing is gained by fear; all we need to do is to protect our precious purses, and fear will not help us to do this. Besides conveying information it has created an atmosphere, and to that extent is literature. 'Beware of pickpockets, male and female,' is not good literature, and it is unconscious. But the words are performing two functions, whereas the word 'Stop' only performed one, and this is an important difference, and the first step in our journey.

Next step. Let us now collect together all the printed matter of the world into a single heap; poetry books, exercise books, plays, newspapers, advertisements, street notices, everything. Let us arrange the contents of the heap into a line, with the works that convey pure information at one end, and the works that create pure atmosphere at the other end, and the

[1 'Remember you must die'; reminder of death, e.g. a skull.]

works that do both in their intermediate positions, the whole line being graded so that we pass from one attitude to another. We shall find that at the end of the pure information stands the tramway notice 'Stop,' and that at the extreme other end is lyric poetry. Lyric poetry is absolutely no use. It is the exact antithesis of a street notice, for it conveys no information of any kind. What's the use of 'A slumber did my spirit seal' or 'Whether on Ida's snowy brow' or 'So we'll go no more a roving' or 'Far in a western brookland'? [2] They do not tell us where the tram will stop or even whether it exists. And, passing from lyric poetry to ballad, we are still deprived of information. It is true that the *Ancient Mariner* describes an antarctic expedition, but in such a muddled way that it is no real help to the explorer, the accounts of the polar currents and winds being hopelessly inaccurate. It is true that the *Ballad of Sir Patrick Spens* refers to the bringing home of the Maid of Norway in the year 1285, but the reference is so vague and confused that the historians turn from it in despair. Lyric poetry is absolutely no use, and poetry generally is almost no use.

But when, proceeding down the line, we leave poetry behind and arrive at the drama, and particularly at those plays that purport to contain normal human beings, we find a change. Uselessness still predominates, but we begin to get information as well. *Julius Caesar* contains some reliable information about Rome. And when we pass from the drama to the novel, the change is still more marked. Information abounds. What a lot we learn from *Tom Jones* [3] about the west countryside! And from *Northanger Abbey* about the same countryside fifty years later! In psychology too the novelist teaches us much. How carefully has Henry James [4] explored certain selected recesses of the human mind! What an analysis of a country rectory in *The Way of All Flesh!* [5] The instincts of Emily Brontë [6] —they illuminate passion. And Proust—how amazingly does Proust [7] describe not only French Society, not only the working of his characters, but the personal equipment of the reader, so that one keeps stopping with a gasp to say 'Oh! how did he find that out about me? I didn't even know it myself until he informed me, but it is so!' The novel, whatever else it may

[2 Opening lines of poems by Wordsworth, Blake, Byron, and A. E. Housman.]

[3 By Henry Fielding (1749). *Northanger Abbey* is one of Jane Austen's novels, 1818.]

[4 American novelist, who lived abroad most of his life. Cf. p. 463, n. 3.]

[5 Novel by Samuel Butler (1903). See selection from it on pp. 455-62.]

[6 English novelist (1818-48), famous for *Wuthering Heights*.]

[7 French novelist (1871-1922); his great work is the series called *À la recherche du temps perdu*.]

be, is partly a notice-board. And that is why many men who do not care for poetry or even for the drama enjoy novels and are well qualified to criticise them.

Beyond the novel we come to works whose avowed aim is information, works of learning, history, sociology, philosophy, psychology, science, etc. Uselessness is now subsidiary, though it still may persist as it does in the *Decline and Fall* or the *Stones of Venice*.[8] And next come those works that give, or profess to give, us information about contemporary events: the newspapers. (Newspapers are so important and so peculiar that I shall return to them later, but mention them here in their place in the procession of printed matter.) And then come advertisements, time tables, the price list inside a taxi, and public notices: the notice warning us against pickpockets, which incidentally produced an atmosphere, though its aim was information, and the pure information contained in the announcement 'Stop.' It is a long journey from lyric poetry to a placard beside a tramline, but it is a journey in which there are no breaks. Words are all of one family, and do not become different because some are printed in a book and others on a metal disc. It is their functions that differentiate them. They have two functions, and the combination of those functions is infinite. If there is on earth a house with many mansions, it is the house of words.

Looking at this line of printed matter, let us again ask ourselves: Do I want to know who wrote that? Ought it to be signed or not? The question is becoming more interesting. Clearly, in so far as words convey information, they ought to be signed. Information is supposed to be true. That is its only reason for existing, and the man who gives it ought to sign his name, so that he may be called to account if he has told a lie. When I have waited for several hours beneath the notice 'Stop,' I have the right to suggest that it be taken down, and I cannot do this unless I know who put it up. Make your statement, sign your name. That's common sense. But as we approach the other function of words—the creation of atmosphere—the question of signature surely loses its importance. It does not matter who wrote 'A slumber did my spirit seal' because the poem itself does not matter. Ascribe it to Ella Wheeler Wilcox [9] and the trams will run as usual. It does not matter much who wrote *Julius Caesar* and *Tom Jones*. They contain descriptions of ancient Rome and eighteenth-century England, and to that extent we wish them signed, for we can judge from the author's name whether the description is likely to be

[8 Best known works of Edward Gibbon (1737–94) and John Ruskin (1819–1900).]
[9 Popular American writer (1885–1919) of bad verse.]

reliable; but beyond that, the guarantee of Shakespeare or Fielding might just as well be Charles Garvice's.[10] So we come to the conclusion, firstly, that what is information ought to be signed; and, secondly, that what is not information need not be signed.

The question can now be carried a step further.

What is this element in words that is not information? I have called it 'atmosphere,' but it requires stricter definition than that. It resides not in any particular word, but in the order in which words are arranged—that is to say, in style. It is the power that words have to raise our emotions or quicken our blood. It is also something else, and to define that other thing would be to explain the secret of the universe. This 'something else' in words is undefinable. It is their power to create not only atmosphere, but a world, which, while it lasts, seems more real and solid than this daily existence of pickpockets and trams. Before we begin to read the *Ancient Mariner* we know that the Polar Seas are not inhabited by spirits, and that if a man shoots an albatross he is not a criminal but a sportsman, and that if he stuffs the albatross afterwards he becomes a naturalist also. All this is common knowledge. But when we are reading the *Ancient Mariner*, or remembering it intensely, common knowledge disappears and uncommon knowledge takes its place. We have entered a universe that only answers to its own laws, supports itself, internally coheres, and has a new standard of truth. Information is true if it is accurate. A poem is true if it hangs together. Information points to something else. A poem points to nothing but itself. Information is relative. A poem is absolute. The world created by words exists neither in space nor time though it has semblances of both, it is eternal and indestructible, and yet its action is no stronger than a flower: it is adamant, yet it is also what one of its practitioners thought it to be, namely, the shadow of a shadow.[11] We can best define it by negations. It is not this world, its laws are not the laws of science or logic, its conclusions not those of common sense. And it causes us to suspend our ordinary judgments.

Now comes the crucial point. While we are reading the *Ancient Mariner* we forget our astronomy and geography and daily ethics. Do we not also forget the author? Does not Samuel Taylor Coleridge, lecturer, opium eater, and dragoon, disappear with the rest of the world of information? We remember him before we begin the poem and after we finish it, but during the poem nothing exists but the poem. Consequently while we

[10 English journalist and novelist (1833–1920).]
[11 A commonplace; perhaps first used by Aeschylus, *Agamemmon*, line 839.]

read the *Ancient Mariner* a change takes place in it. It becomes anonymous, like the *Ballad of Sir Patrick Spens*. And here is the point I would
support: that all literature tends towards a condition of anonymity, and
that, so far as words are creative, a signature merely distracts us from their
true significance. I do not say literature 'ought' not to be signed, because
literature is alive, and consequently 'ought' is the wrong word to use. It
wants not to be signed. That puts my point. It is always tugging in that
direction and saying in effect: 'I, not my author, exist really.' So do the
trees, flowers and human beings say 'I really exist, not God,' and continue
to say so despite the admonitions to the contrary addressed to them by
clergymen and scientists. To forget its Creator is one of the functions of a
Creation. To remember him is to forget the days of one's youth. Literature
does not want to remember. It is alive—not in a vague complementary
sense—but alive tenaciously, and it is always covering up the tracks that
connect it with the laboratory.

It may here be objected that literature expresses personality, that it is the
result of the author's individual outlook, that we are right in asking for his
name. It is his property—he ought to have the credit.

An important objection; also a modern one, for in the past neither
writers nor readers attached the high importance to personality that they
do today. It did not trouble Homer or the various people who were Homer.
It did not trouble the writers in the Greek Anthology who would write
and re-write the same poem in almost identical language, their notion being
that the poem, not the poet, is the important thing, and that by continuous rehandling the perfect expression natural to the poem may be attained.
It did not trouble the mediaeval balladists, who, like the Cathedral
builders, left their works unsigned. It troubled neither the composers nor
the translators of the Bible. The Book of Genesis today contains at least
three different elements—Jahvist, Elohist and Priestly—which were combined into a single account by a committee who lived under King Josiah at
Jerusalem and translated into English by another committee who lived
under King James I at London. And yet the Book of Genesis is literature.
These earlier writers and readers knew that the words a man writes express him, but they did not make a cult of expression as we do today.
Surely they were right, and modern critics go too far in their insistence on
personality.

They go too far because they do not reflect what personality is. Just as
words have two functions—information and creation—so each human mind
has two personalities, one on the surface, one deeper down. The upper

personality has a name. It is called S. T. Coleridge, or William Shakespeare, or Mrs. Humphry Ward.[12] It is conscious and alert, it does things like dining out, answering letters, etc., and it differs vividly and amusingly from other personalities. The lower personality is a very queer affair. In many ways it is a perfect fool, but without it there is no literature, because unless a man dips a bucket down into it occasionally he cannot produce first-class work. There is something general about it. Although it is inside S. T. Coleridge, it cannot be labelled with his name. It has something in common with all other deeper personalities, and the mystic will assert that the common quality is God, and that here, in the obscure recesses of our being, we near the gates of the Divine. It is in any case the force that makes for anonymity. As it came from the depths, so it soars to the heights, out of local questionings; as it is general to all men, so the works it inspires have something general about them, namely beauty. The poet wrote the poem, no doubt, but he forgot himself while he wrote it, and we forget him while we read. What is so wonderful about great literature is that it transforms the man who reads it towards the condition of the man who wrote, and brings to birth in us also the creative impulse. Lost in the beauty where he was lost, we find more than we ever threw away, we reach what seems to be our spiritual home, and remember that it was not the speaker who was in the beginning but the Word.

If we glance at one or two writers who are not first class this point will be illustrated. Charles Lamb and R. L. Stevenson will serve.[13] Here are two gifted, sensitive, fanciful, tolerant, humorous fellows, but they always write with their surface-personalities and never let down buckets into their underworld. Lamb did not try: bbbbuckets, he would have said, are bbeyond me, and he is the pleasanter writer in consequence. Stevenson was always trying oh ever so hard, but the bucket either stuck or else came up again full of the R.L.S. who let it down, full of the mannerisms, the self-consciousness, the sentimentality, the quaintness which he was hoping to avoid. He and Lamb append their names in full to every sentence they write. They pursue us page after page, always to the exclusion of higher joy. They are letter writers, not creative artists, and it is no coincidence that each of them did write charming letters. A letter comes off the surface: it deals with the events of the day or with plans: it is naturally signed. Literature tries to be unsigned. And the proof is that, whereas we are always exclaiming 'How like Lamb!' or 'How typical of Stevenson!' we

[12] English novelist (1851–1920).]
[13] See selections from Lamb and Stevenson on pp. 376–82, 397–404.]

never say 'How like Shakespeare!' or 'How typical of Dante!' We are conscious only of the world they have created, and we are in a sense co-partners in it. Coleridge, in his smaller domain, makes us co-partners too. We forget for ten minutes his name and our own, and I contend that this temporary forgetfulness, this momentary and mutual anonymity, is sure evidence of good stuff. The demand that literature should express personality is far too insistent in these days, and I look back with longing to the earlier modes of criticism where a poem was not an expression but a discovery, and was sometimes supposed to have been shown to the poet by God.

The personality of a writer does become important after we have read his book and begin to study it. When the glamour of creation ceases, when the leaves of the divine tree are silent, when the co-partnership is over, then a book changes its nature, and we can ask ourselves questions about it such as 'What is the author's name?' 'Where did he live?' 'Was he married?' and 'Which was his favourite flower?' Then we are no longer reading the book, we are studying it and making it subserve our desire for information. 'Study' has a very solemn sound. 'I am studying Dante' sounds much more than 'I am reading Dante.' It is really much less. Study is only a serious form of gossip. It teaches us everything about the book except the central thing, and between that and us it raises a circular barrier which only the wings of the spirit can cross. The study of science, history, etc., is necessary and proper, for they are subjects that belong to the domain of information, but a creative subject like literature—to study that is excessively dangerous, and should never be attempted by the immature. Modern education promotes the unmitigated study of literature and concentrates our attention on the relation between a writer's life—his surface life—and his work. That is one reason why it is such a curse. There are no questions to be asked about literature while we read it because 'la paix succède à la pensée,' [14] in the words of Paul Claudel. An examination paper could not be set on the *Ancient Mariner* as it speaks to the heart of the reader, and it was to speak to the heart that it was written, and otherwise it would not have been written. Questions only occur when we cease to realise what it was about and become inquisitive and methodical.

A word in conclusion on the newspapers—for they raise an interesting contributory issue. We have already defined a newspaper as something which conveys, or is supposed to convey, information about passing events. It is true, not to itself like a poem, but to the facts it purports to relate—

[14 'Thought gives way to tranquility.']

like the tram notice. When the morning paper arrives it lies upon the
breakfast table simply steaming with truth in regard to something else.
Truth, truth, and nothing but the truth. Unsated by the banquet, we sally
forth in the afternoon to buy an evening paper, which is published at
midday as the name implies, and feast anew. At the end of the week we
buy a weekly, or a Sunday paper, which as the name implies has been
written on the Saturday, and at the end of the month we buy a monthly.
Thus do we keep in touch with the world of events as practical men should.

And who is keeping us in touch? Who gives us this information upon
which our judgments depend, and which must ultimately influence our
characters? Curious to relate, we seldom know. Newspapers are for the
most part anonymous. Statements are made and no signature appended.
Suppose we read in a paper that the Emperor of Guatemala is dead. Our
first feeling is one of mild consternation; out of snobbery we regret what
has happened, although the Emperor didn't play much part in our lives,
and if ladies we say to one another 'I feel so sorry for the poor Empress.'
But presently we learn that the Emperor cannot have died, because Guatemala is a Republic, and the Empress cannot be a widow, because she does
not exist. If the statement is signed, and we know the name of the goose
who made it, we shall discount anything he tells us in the future. If—which
is more probable—it is unsigned or signed 'Our Special Correspondent'—
we remain defenceless against future misstatements. The Guatemala lad
may be turned on to write about the Fall of the Franc and mislead us over
that.

It seems paradoxical that an article should impress us more if it is unsigned than if it is signed. But it does, owing to the weakness of our
psychology. Anonymous statements have, as we have seen, a universal air
about them. Absolute truth, the collected wisdom of the universe, seems to
be speaking, not the feeble voice of a man. The modern newspaper has
taken advantage of this. It is a pernicious caricature of literature. It has
usurped that divine tendency towards anonymity. It has claimed for information what only belongs to creation. And it will claim it as long as we
allow it to claim it, and to exploit the defects of our psychology. 'The
High Mission of the Press.' Poor Press! as if it were in a position to have a
mission! It is we who have a mission to it. To cure a man through the
newspapers or through propaganda of any sort is impossible: you merely
alter the symptoms of his disease. We shall only be cured by purging our
minds of confusion. The papers trick us not so much by their lies as by
their exploitation of our weakness. They are always confusing the two

functions of words and insinuating that 'The Emperor of Guatemala is dead' and 'A slumber did my spirit seal' belong to the same category. They are always usurping the privileges that only uselessness may claim, and they will do this as long as we allow them to do it.

This ends our enquiry. The question 'Ought things to be signed?' seemed, if not an easy question, at all events an isolated one, but we could not answer it without considering what words are, and disentangling the two functions they perform. We decided pretty easily that information ought to be signed: common sense leads to this conclusion, and newspapers which are largely unsigned have gained by that device their undesirable influence over civilisation. Creation—that we found a more difficult matter. 'Literature wants not to be signed,' I suggested. Creation comes from the depths—the mystic will say from God. The signature, the name, belongs to the surface-personality, and pertains to the world of information, it is a ticket, not the spirit of life. While the author wrote he forgot his name; while we read him we forget both his name and our own. When we have finished reading we begin to ask questions, and to study the book and the author, we drag them into the realm of information. Now we learn a thousand things, but we have lost the pearl of great price, and in the chatter of question and answer, in the torrents of gossip and examination papers we forget the purpose for which creation was performed. I am not asking for reverence. Reverence is fatal to literature. My plea is for something more vital: imagination. Imagination is as the immortal God which should assume flesh for the redemption of mortal passion (Shelley). Imagination is our only guide into the world created by words. Whether those words are signed or unsigned becomes, as soon as the imagination redeems us, a matter of no importance, because we have approximated to the state in which they were written, and there are no names down there, no personality as we understand personality, no marrying or giving in marriage. What there is down there—ah, that is another enquiry, and may the clergymen and the scientists pursue it more successfully in the future than they have in the past.

WRITER AND READER

❰ To hear what a successful writer has to say about his art is always instructive and often enjoyable. Mr. Maugham's *The Summing Up* is as agreeable a book as his best plays and novels. Naturally it is of most interest to readers acquainted with those plays and novels, but even a person who had not read *Of Human Bondage, Cakes and Ale, The Moon and Sixpence, Rain, The Circle,* or *Our Betters* would find *The Summing Up* a provocative account of a writer's development, of his artistic principles, and of his philosophical reflections. It 'is not an autobiography nor is it a book of recollections,' Mr. Maugham says. It is a summing up, written to 'give a coherent picture of my feelings and opinions.'

Since this book appeared (1938), Mr. Maugham has published *A Writer's Notebook* (1949), a different sort of book, and a less considerable one, but not to be missed by anyone who likes *The Summing Up.*

I

I HAVE NEVER had much patience with the writers who claim from the reader an effort to understand their meaning. You have only to go to the great philosophers to see that it is possible to express with lucidity the most subtle reflections. You may find it difficult to understand the thought of Hume,[1] and if you have no philosophical training its implications will doubtless escape you; but no one with any education at all can fail to understand exactly what the meaning of each sentence is. Few people have written English with more grace than Berkeley.[2] There are two sorts of obscurity that you find in writers. One is due to negligence and the

[1 Scottish philosopher and historian (1711–76). See pp. 370–75.]
[2 Irish divine and philosopher (1685–1753).]

other to wilfulness. People often write obscurely because they have never taken the trouble to learn to write clearly. This sort of obscurity you find too often in modern philosophers, in men of science, and even in literary critics. Here it is indeed strange. You would have thought that men who passed their lives in the study of the great masters of literature would be sufficiently sensitive to the beauty of language to write if not beautifully at least with perspicuity. Yet you will find in their works sentence after sentence that you must read twice to discover the sense. Often you can only guess at it, for the writers have evidently not said what they intended.

Another cause of obscurity is that the writer is himself not quite sure of his meaning. He has a vague impression of what he wants to say, but has not, either from lack of mental power or from laziness, exactly formulated it in his mind and it is natural enough that he should not find a precise expression for a confused idea. This is due largely to the fact that many writers think, not before, but as they write. The pen originates the thought. The disadvantage of this, and indeed it is a danger against which the author must be always on his guard, is that there is a sort of magic in the written word. The idea acquires substance by taking on a visible nature, and then stands in the way of its own clarification. But this sort of obscurity merges very easily into the wilful. Some writers who do not think clearly are inclined to suppose that their thoughts have a significance greater than at first sight appears. It is flattering to believe that they are too profound to be expressed so clearly that all who run may read, and very naturally it does not occur to such writers that the fault is with their own minds which have not the faculty of precise reflection. Here again the magic of the written word obtains. It is very easy to persuade oneself that a phrase that one does not quite understand may mean a great deal more than one realizes. From this there is only a little way to go to fall into the habit of setting down one's impressions in all their original vagueness. Fools can always be found to discover a hidden sense in them. There is another form of wilful obscurity that masquerades as aristocratic exclusiveness. The author wraps his meaning in mystery so that the vulgar shall not participate in it. His soul is a secret garden into which the elect may penetrate only after overcoming a number of perilous obstacles. But this kind of obscurity is not only pretentious; it is shortsighted. For time plays it an odd trick. If the sense is meagre time reduces it to a meaningless verbiage that no one thinks of reading. This is the fate that has befallen the lucubrations of those French writers who were seduced by the example of Guillaume Apollinaire. But occasionally it throws a sharp cold light on what had seemed profound and thus discloses the fact that these contortions of language disguised very commonplace notions. There are few of Mallarmé's [3] poems now that are not clear; one cannot fail to notice that his thought singularly lacked originality. Some of his phrases were beautiful; the materials of his verse were the poetic platitudes of his day.

II

Simplicity is not such an obvious merit as lucidity. I have aimed at it because I have no gift for richness. Within limits I admire richness in others, though I find it difficult to digest in quantity. I can read one page of Ruskin with delight, but twenty only with weariness. The rolling period, the stately epithet, the noun rich in poetic associations, the subordinate clauses that give the sentence weight and magnificence, the grandeur like that of wave following wave in the open sea; there is no doubt that in all this there is something inspiring. Words thus strung together fall on the ear like music. The appeal is sensuous rather than intellectual, and the beauty of the sound leads you easily to conclude that you need not bother about the meaning. But words are tyrannical things, they exist for their meanings, and if you will not pay attention to these, you cannot pay attention at all. Your mind wanders. This kind of writing demands a subject that will suit it. It is surely out of place to write in the grand style of inconsiderable things. No one wrote in this manner with greater success than Sir Thomas Browne, but even he did not always escape this pitfall. In the last chapter of *Hydriotaphia* the matter, which is the destiny of man, wonderfully fits the baroque splendour of the language, and here the Norwich doctor produced a piece of prose that has never been surpassed in our literature; but when he describes the finding of his urns in the same splendid manner the effect (at least to my taste) is less happy. When a modern writer is grandiloquent to tell you whether or no a little trollop shall hop into bed with a commonplace young man you are right to be disgusted.

But if richness needs gifts with which everyone is not endowed, simplicity by no means comes by nature. To achieve it needs rigid discipline. So far as I know ours is the only language in which it has been found necessary to give a name to the piece of prose which is described as the purple patch; it would not have been necessary to do so unless it were characteristic. English prose is elaborate rather than simple. It was not always so. Nothing could be more racy, straightforward and alive than the prose of Shakespeare; but it must be remembered that this was dialogue written to

[3 Apollinaire (1880–1918) and Mallarmé (1842–98) were influential French poets.]

be spoken. We do not know how he would have written if like Corneille he had composed prefaces to his plays. It may be that they would have been as euphuistic as the letters of Queen Elizabeth. But earlier prose, the prose of Sir Thomas More, for instance, is neither ponderous, flowery nor oratorical. It smacks of the English soil. To my mind King James's Bible has been a very harmful influence on English prose. I am not so stupid as to deny its great beauty. It is majestical. But the Bible is an oriental book. Its alien imagery has nothing to do with us. Those hyperboles, those luscious metaphors, are foreign to our genius. I cannot but think that not the least of the misfortunes that the Secession from Rome brought upon the spiritual life of our country is that this work for so long a period became the daily, and with many the only, reading of our people. Those rhythms, that powerful vocabulary, that grandiloquence, became part and parcel of the national sensibility. The plain, honest English speech was overwhelmed with ornament. Blunt Englishmen twisted their tongues to speak like Hebrew prophets. There was evidently something in the English temper to which this was congenial, perhaps a native lack of precision in thought, perhaps a naïve delight in fine words for their own sake, an innate eccentricity and love of embroidery, I do not know; but the fact remains that ever since, English prose has had to struggle against the tendency to luxuriance. When from time to time the spirit of the language has reasserted itself, as it did with Dryden and the writers of Queen Anne, it was only to be submerged once more by the pomposities of Gibbon and Dr. Johnson. When English prose recovered simplicity with Hazlitt, the Shelley of the letters and Charles Lamb at his best, it lost it again with De Quincey, Carlyle, Meredith and Walter Pater. It is obvious that the grand style is more striking than the plain. Indeed many people think that a style that does not attract notice is not style. They will admire Walter Pater's, but will read an essay by Matthew Arnold without giving a moment's attention to the elegance, distinction and sobriety with which he set down what he had to say.

The dictum that the style is the man is well known. It is one of those aphorisms that say too much to mean a great deal. Where is the man in Goethe, in his birdlike lyrics or in his clumsy prose? And Hazlitt? But I suppose that if a man has a confused mind he will write in a confused way, if his temper is capricious his prose will be fantastical, and if he has a quick, darting intelligence that is reminded by the matter in hand of a hundred things he will, unless he has great self-control, load his pages with metaphor and simile. There is a great difference between the magniloquence of the Jacobean writers, who were intoxicated with the new wealth that had lately been brought into the language, and the turgidity of Gibbon and Dr. Johnson, who were the victims of bad theories. I can read every word that Dr. Johnson wrote with delight, for he had good sense, charm and wit. No one could have written better if he had not wilfully set himself to write in the grand style. He knew good English when he saw it. No critic has praised Dryden's prose more aptly. He said of him that he appeared to have no art other than that of expressing with clearness what he thought with vigour. And one of his Lives [4] he finished with the words: 'Whoever wishes to attain an English style, familiar but not coarse, and elegant but not ostentatious, must give his days and nights to the volumes of Addison.' But when he himself sat down to write it was with a very different aim. He mistook the orotund for the dignified. He had not the good breeding to see that simplicity and naturalness are the truest marks of distinction.

For to write good prose is an affair of good manners. It is, unlike verse, a civil art. Poetry is baroque. Baroque is tragic, massive and mystical. It is elemental. It demands depth and insight. I cannot but feel that the prose writers of the baroque period, the authors of King James's Bible, Sir Thomas Browne, Glanville,[5] were poets who had lost their way. Prose is a rococo art. It needs taste rather than power, decorum rather than inspiration and vigour rather than grandeur. Form for the poet is the bit and the bridle without which (unless you are an acrobat) you cannot ride your horse; but for the writer of prose it is the chassis without which your car does not exist. It is not an accident that the best prose was written when rococo with its elegance and moderation, at its birth attained its greatest excellence. For rococo was evolved when baroque had become declamatory and the world, tired of the stupendous, asked for restraint. It was the natural expression of persons who valued a civilized life. Humour, tolerance and horse sense made the great tragic issues that had preoccupied the first half of the seventeenth century seem excessive. The world was a more comfortable place to live in and perhaps for the first time in centuries the cultivated classes could sit back and enjoy their leisure. It has been said that good prose should resemble the conversation of a well-bred man. Conversation is only possible when men's minds are free from pressing anxieties.

[4 'Addison,' in *Lives of the English Poets*.]
[5 Seventeenth-century divine. His *Vanity of Dogmatizing* (1661) is remembered because it contains the story from which Matthew Arnold made his poem 'The Scholar Gipsy.']

Their lives must be reasonably secure and they must have no grave concern about their souls. They must attach importance to the refinements of civilization. They must value courtesy, they must pay attention to their persons (and have we not also been told that good prose should be like the clothes of a well-dressed man, appropriate but unobtrusive?), they must fear to bore, they must be neither flippant nor solemn, but always apt; and they must look upon 'enthusiasm' with a critical glance. This is a soil very suitable for prose. It is not to be wondered at that it gave a fitting opportunity for the appearance of the best writer of prose that our modern world has seen, Voltaire. The writers of English, perhaps owing to the poetic nature of the language, have seldom reached the excellence that seems to have come so naturally to him. It is in so far as they have approached the ease, sobriety and precision of the great French masters that they are admirable.

III

I have read that Anatole France tried to use only the constructions and the vocabulary of the writers of the seventeenth century whom he so greatly admired. I do not know if it is true. If so, it may explain why there is some lack of vitality in his beautiful and simple French. But simplicity is false when you do not say a thing that you should say because you cannot say it in a certain way. One should write in the manner of one's period. The language is alive and constantly changing; to try to write like the authors of a distant past can only give rise to artificiality. I should not hesitate to use the common phrases of the day, knowing that their vogue was ephemeral, or slang, though aware that in ten years it might be incomprehensible, if they gave vividness and actuality. If the style has a classical form it can support the discreet use of a phraseology that has only a local and temporary aptness. I would sooner a writer were vulgar than mincing; for life is vulgar, and it is life he seeks.

I think that we English authors have much to learn from our fellow authors in America. For American writing has escaped the tyranny of King James's Bible and American writers have been less affected by the old masters whose mode of writing is part of our culture. They have formed their style, unconsciously perhaps, more directly from the living speech that surrounds them; and at its best it has a directness, a vitality and a drive that give our more urbane manner an air of languor. It has been an advantage to American writers, many of whom at one time or another have been reporters, that their journalism has been written in a more trenchant, nervous, graphic English than ours. For we read the newspaper now as our ancestors read the Bible. Not without profit either; for the newspaper, especially when it is of the popular sort, offers us a part of experience that we writers cannot afford to miss. It is raw material straight from the knacker's yard,[6] and we are stupid if we turn up our noses because it smells of blood and sweat. We cannot, however willingly we would, escape the influence of this workaday prose. But the journalism of a period has very much the same style; it might all have been written by the same hand; it is impersonal. It is well to counteract its effect by reading of another kind. One can do this only by keeping constantly in touch with the writing of an age not too remote from one's own. So can one have a standard by which to test one's own style and an ideal which in one's modern way one can aim at. For my part the two writers I have found most useful to study for this purpose are Hazlitt and Cardinal Newman. I would try to imitate neither. Hazlitt can be unduly rhetorical; and sometimes his decoration is as fussy as Victorian Gothic. Newman can be a trifle flowery. But at their best both are admirable. Time has little touched their style; it is almost contemporary. Hazlitt is vivid, bracing and energetic; he has strength and liveliness. You feel the man in his phrases, not the mean, querulous, disagreeable man that he appeared to the world that knew him, but the man within of his own ideal vision. (And the man within us is as true in reality as the man, pitiful and halting, of our outward seeming.) Newman had an exquisite grace, music, playful sometimes and sometimes grave, a woodland beauty of phrase, dignity and mellowness. Both wrote with extreme lucidity. Neither is quite as simple as the purest taste demands. Here I think Matthew Arnold excels them. Both had a wonderful balance of phrase and both knew how to write sentences pleasing to the eye. Both had an ear of extreme sensitiveness.

If anyone could combine their merits in the manner of writing of the present day he would write as well as it is possible for anyone to write.

IV

Young persons, who are anxious to write, sometimes pay me the compliment of asking me to tell them of certain books necessary for them to read. I do. They seldom read them, for they seem to have little curiosity. They do not care what their predecessors have done. They think they know everything that it is necessary to know of the art of fiction when they have read two or three novels by Mrs. Woolf, one by E. M. Forster, several by

[6 Slaughterhouse for useless horses.]

D. H. Lawrence and, oddly enough, the *Forsyte Saga*. It is true that contemporary literature has a vividness of appeal that classical literature can never have and it is well for a young writer to know what his contemporaries are writing about and how. But there are fashions in literature and it is not easy to tell what intrinsic value there is in a style of writing that happens to be the vogue at the moment. An acquaintance with the great works of the past serves as a very good standard of comparison. I have sometimes wondered whether it is due to their ignorance that many young writers, notwithstanding their facility and cleverness, their skilful technique, so frequently fizzle out. They write two or three books that are not only brilliant, but mature, and then they are done for. But that is not what enriches the literature of a country. For that you must have writers who can produce not just two or three books, but a great body of work. Of course it will be uneven, because so many fortunate circumstances must go together to produce a masterpiece; but a masterpiece is more likely to come as the culminating point of a laborious career than as the lucky fluke of untaught genius. The writer can only be fertile if he renews himself and he can only renew himself if his soul is constantly enriched by fresh experience. There is no more fruitful source of this than the enchanting exploration of the great literatures of the past.

For the production of a work of art is not the result of a miracle. It requires preparation. The soil, be it ever so rich, must be fed. By taking thought, by deliberate effort, the artist must enlarge, deepen and diversify his personality. Then the soil must lie fallow. Like the bride of Christ, the artist waits for the illumination that shall bring forth a new spiritual life. He goes about his ordinary avocations with patience; the subconscious does its mysterious business; and then, suddenly springing, you might think from nowhere, the idea is produced. But like the corn [7] that was sown on stony ground it may easily wither away; it must be tended with anxious care. All the power of the artist's mind must be set to work on it, all his technical skill, all his experience, and whatever he has in him of character and individuality, so that with infinite pains he may present it with the completeness that is fitting to it.

But I am not impatient with the young when, only at their request, I insist, I advise them to read Shakespeare and Swift, and they tell me that they read *Gulliver's Travels* in their nursery and *Henry IV* at school; and if they find *Vanity Fair* unendurable and *Anna Karenina* footling it is their own affair. No reading is worth while unless you enjoy it. There is at

[7 Matthew, xiii, 3–23.]

least this to be said for them that they do not suffer from the self-conceit of knowledge. They are not withdrawn by a wide culture from sympathy with the common run of men who are after all their material. They are nearer to their fellows and the art they practise is not a mystery, but a craft on the same footing as any other. They write novels and plays as unaffectedly as other men build motorcars. This is much to the good. For the artist, the writer especially, in the solitariness of his own mind constructs a world that is different from other men's; the idiosyncrasy that makes him a writer separates him from them and the paradox emerges that though his aim is to describe them truthfully his gift prevents him from knowing them as they really are. It is as though he wanted urgently to see a certain thing and by the act of looking at it drew before it a veil that obscured it. The writer stands outside the very action he is engaged in. He is the comedian who never quite loses himself in the part, for he is at the same time spectator and actor. It is all very well to say that poetry is emotion remembered in tranquillity; but a poet's emotion is specific, a poet's rather than a man's, and it is never quite disinterested. That is why women with their instinctive common sense have so often found the love of poets unsatisfying. It may be that the writers of the present day, who seem to be so much nearer to their raw material, ordinary men among ordinary men, rather than artists in an alien crowd, may break down the barrier that their peculiar gift cannot but raise and so come nearer to the plain truth than has ever been done before. But then you have to make up your mind about the relations between truth and art.

Joseph Conrad

Preface to THE NIGGER OF THE 'NARCISSUS'

⟦ Few great artists have meditated more seriously or more wisely upon their art than Conrad did. He knew which novelists had most to teach him. But he knew, too, what he wanted to do as a writer, and his doctrine of art was his own; it came out of his own character and his own experience. 'My task which I am trying to achieve is, by the power of the written word, to make you hear, to make you feel—it is, before all, to make you *see*. That—and no more, and it is everything. If I succeed, you shall find there according to your deserts: encouragement, consolation, fear, charm—all you demand and, perhaps, also that glimpse of truth for which you have forgotten to ask.'

The best affirmation of Conrad's artistic creed was written near the beginning of his career. It appeared at the end of *The Nigger of the 'Narcissus,'* which was published serially in 1897 (his first novel, *Almayer's Folly*, came out in 1895). This postscript was later published as a preface to editions of *The Nigger*.

See Conrad's 'Il Conde' (pp. 467–80).

A WORK that aspires, however humbly, to the condition of art should carry its justification in every line. And art itself may be defined as a single-minded attempt to render the highest kind of justice to the visible universe, by bringing to ligl.t the truth, manifold and one, underlying its every aspect. It is an attempt to find in its forms, in its colours, in its light, in its shadows, in the aspects of matter and in the facts of life, what of each is fundamental, what is enduring and essential—their one illuminating and convincing quality—the very truth of their existence. The artist, then, like the thinker or the scientist, seeks the truth and makes his appeal. Impressed by the aspect of the world the thinker plunges into ideas, the scientist into facts—whence, presently, emerging they make their

Reprinted by permission of J. M. Dent & Sons, Ltd.

appeal to those qualities of our being that fit us best for the hazardous enterprise of living. They speak authoritatively to our common-sense, to our intelligence, to our desire of peace or to our desire of unrest; not seldom to our prejudices, sometimes to our fears, often to our egoism—but always to our credulity. And their words are heard with reverence, for their concern is with weighty matters; with the cultivation of our minds and the proper care of our bodies: with the attainment of our ambitions: with the perfection of the means and the glorification of our precious aims.

It is otherwise with the artist.

Confronted by the same enigmatical spectacle the artist descends within himself, and in that lonely region of stress and strife, if he be deserving and fortunate, he finds the terms of his appeal. His appeal is made to our less obvious capacities: to that part of our nature which, because of the warlike conditions of existence, is necessarily kept out of sight within the more resisting and hard qualities—like the vulnerable body within a steel armour. His appeal is less loud, more profound, less distinct, more stirring—and sooner forgotten. Yet its effect endures forever. The changing wisdom of successive generations discards ideas, questions facts, demolishes theories. But the artist appeals to that part of our being which is not dependent on wisdom; to that in us which is a gift and not an acquisition—and, therefore, more permanently enduring. He speaks to our capacity for delight and wonder, to the sense of mystery surrounding our lives: to our sense of pity, and beauty, and pain: to the latent feeling of fellowship with all creation—and to the subtle but invincible, conviction of solidarity that knits together the loneliness of innumerable hearts to the solidarity in dreams, in joy, in sorrow, in aspirations, in illusions, in hope, in fear, which binds men to each other, which binds together all humanity—the dead to the living and the living to the unborn.

It is only some such train of thought, or rather of feeling, that can in a measure explain the aim of the attempt, made in the tale which follows, to present an unrestful episode in the obscure lives of a few individuals out of all the disregarded multitude of the bewildered, the simple and the voiceless. For, if there is any part of truth in the belief confessed above, it becomes evident that there is not a place of splendour or a dark corner of the earth that does not deserve, if only a passing glance of wonder and pity. The motive, then, may be held to justify the matter of the work; but this preface, which is simply an avowal of endeavour, cannot end here—for the avowal is not yet complete.

Fiction—if it at all aspires to be art—appeals to temperament. And in truth it must be, like painting, like music, like all art, the appeal of one temperament to all the other innumerable temperaments whose subtle and resistless power endows passing events with their true meaning, and creates the moral, the emotional atmosphere of the place and time. Such an appeal to be effective must be an impression conveyed through the senses; and, in fact, it cannot be made in any other way, because temperament, whether individual or collective, is not amenable to persuasion. All art, therefore, appeals primarily to the senses, and the artistic aim when expressing itself in written words must also make its appeal through the senses, if its high desire is to reach the secret spring of responsive emotions. It must strenuously aspire to the plasticity of sculpture, to the colour of painting, and to the magic suggestiveness of music—which is the art of arts. And it is only through complete, unswerving devotion to the perfect blending of form and substance; it is only through an unremitting never-discouraged care for the shape and ring of sentences that an approach can be made to plasticity, to colour; and the light of magic suggestiveness may be brought to play for an evanescent instant over the commonplace surface of words: of the old, old words, worn thin, defaced by ages of careless usage.

The sincere endeavour to accomplish that creative task, to go as far on that road as his strength will carry him, to go undeterred by faltering, weariness or reproach, is the only valid justification for the worker in prose. And if his conscience is clear, his answer to those who, in the fulness of a wisdom which looks for immediate profit, demand specifically to be edified, consoled, amused; who demand to be promptly improved, or encouraged, or frightened, or shocked, or charmed, must run thus:—My task which I am trying to achieve is, by the power of the written word, to make you hear, to make you feel—it is, before all, to make you *see*. That—and no more, and it is everything. If I succeed, you shall find there according to your deserts: encouragement, consolation, fear, charm—all you demand and, perhaps, also that glimpse of truth for which you have forgotten to ask.

To snatch in a moment of courage, from the remorseless rush of time, a passing phase of life, is only the beginning of the task. The task approached in tenderness and faith is to hold up unquestioningly, without choice and without fear, the rescued fragment before all eyes and in the light of a sincere mood. It is to show its vibration, its colour, its form; and through its movement, its form, and its colour, reveal the substance of its truth—disclose its inspiring secret: the stress and passion within the core of each convincing moment. In a single-minded attempt of that kind, if one be deserving and fortunate, one may perchance attain to such clearness of sincerity that at last the presented vision of regret or pity, of terror or mirth, shall awaken in the hearts of the beholders that feeling of unavoidable solidarity; of the solidarity in mysterious origin, in toil, in joy, in hope, in uncertain fate, which binds men to each other and all mankind to the visible world.

It is evident that he who, rightly or wrongly, holds by the convictions expressed above cannot be faithful to any one of the temporary formulas of his craft. The enduring part of them—the truth which each only imperfectly veils—should abide with him as the most precious of his possessions, but they all: Realism, Romanticism, Naturalism, even the unofficial sentimentalism (which like the poor,[1] is exceedingly difficult to get rid of,) all these gods must, after a short period of fellowship, abandon him—even on the very threshold of the temple—to the stammerings of his conscience and to the outspoken consciousness of the difficulties of his work. In that uneasy solitude the supreme cry of Art for Art, itself, loses the exciting ring of its apparent immorality. It sounds far off. It has ceased to be a cry, and is heard only as a whisper, often incomprehensible, but at times and faintly encouraging.

Sometimes, stretched at ease in the shade of a roadside tree, we watch the motions of a labourer in a distant field, and after a time, begin to wonder languidly as to what the fellow may be at. We watch the movements of his body, the waving of his arms, we see him bend down, stand up, hesitate, begin again. It may add to the charm of an idle hour to be told the purpose of his exertions. If we know he is trying to lift a stone, to dig a ditch, to uproot a stump, we look with a more real interest at his efforts; we are disposed to condone the jar of his agitation upon the restfulness of the landscape; and even, if in a brotherly frame of mind, we may bring ourselves to forgive his failure. We understood his object, and, after all, the fellow has tried, and perhaps he had not the strength—and perhaps he had not the knowledge. We forgive, go on our way—and forget.

And so it is with the workman of art. Art is long and life is short,[2] and success is very far off. And thus, doubtful of strength to travel so far, we talk a little about the aim—the aim of art, which, like life itself, is inspiring, difficult—obscured by mists. It is not in the clear logic of a triumphant conclusion; it is not in the unveiling of one of those heartless secrets which are called the Laws of Nature. It is not less great, but only more difficult.

To arrest, for the space of a breath, the hands busy about the work of

[1] John, xii, 8.]
[2] This maxim is attributed to Hippocrates, fifth century B.C.]

the earth, and compel men entranced by the sight of distant goals to glance for a moment at the surrounding vision of form and colour, of sunshine and shadows; to make them pause for a look, for a sigh, for a smile—such is the aim, difficult and evanescent, and reserved only for a very few to achieve. But sometimes, by the deserving and the fortunate, even that task is accomplished. And when it is accomplished—behold!—all the truth of life is there: a moment of vision, a sigh, a smile—and the return to an eternal rest.

Robert E. Sherwood

HOW F. D. R.'S SPEECHES WERE WRITTEN

❲ In the notes to his play *Abe Lincoln in Illinois,* Mr. Sherwood, reminding us that after Lincoln's election in 1860 Stephen A. Douglas assisted in the composition of the First Inaugural Address, observes that 'There was ghost-writing in high places even then.' For nearly five years during the administration of President Franklin D. Roosevelt, Mr. Sherwood was playing the part of a useful ghost himself. Ghost-writing in high places is going to vex future historians, who will have to guess who wrote a statesman's works, but historians of the Roosevelt era will get invaluable assistance from Mr. Sherwood's record of F. D. R.'s speeches and how they were written. It seems clear that the main ideas and many of the memorable phrases of those speeches were the President's own; the task of working them into coherent discourse was performed by the 'ghosts.'

These pages are from Mr. Sherwood's *Roosevelt and Hopkins* (1948), probably the most important of the numerous revelations so far published of the inner history of the Roosevelt administration.

As I HAVE SAID, Hopkins did not originate policy and then convince Roosevelt it was right. He had too much intelligence as well as respect for his Chief to attempt the role of mastermind. He made it his job to provide a sounding board for discussions of the best means of attaining the goals that the President set for himself. Roosevelt liked to think out loud, but his greatest difficulty was finding a listener who was both understanding and entirely trustworthy. That was Hopkins—and this was the process that Rosenman [1] and I watched over and over again in the prepa-

[1 Judge Samuel I. Rosenman of New York, one of the President's most trusted unofficial aides.]

FROM *Roosevelt and Hopkins.* Copyright 1948 by Robert E. Sherwood. Reprinted by permission of Harper & Brothers.

ration of the speeches and messages in which Roosevelt made known his policies to the nation and to the world. The work that was put in on these speeches was prodigious, for Roosevelt with his acute sense of history knew that all of those words would constitute the bulk of the estate that he would leave to posterity and that his ultimate measurement would depend on the reconciliation of what he said with what he did. Therefore, utmost importance was attached to his public utterances and utmost care exercised in their preparation. In the previous chapter I have mentioned the Cleveland speech [2] which took a night and a day to prepare, but such speed in preparation was unusual, even for a campaign speech, which was necessarily a creature of the moment. The important speeches sometimes required a week or more of hard labor, with a considerable amount of planning before the intensive work started. I don't know what was the record number of distinct drafts of a single speech but it must have been well over twelve, and in the final draft there might not be one sentence that had survived from the first draft. There were of course numerous routine speeches of a ceremonial nature which were not considered of major significance—but, in wartime, even in these Roosevelt was aware that he had a world audience and that everything he said might be material for the propaganda which flooded the air waves. If such a speech were opening a Bond Drive, a first draft would be prepared in the Treasury Department; if it were launching a new campaign for funds for the Red Cross, the Community Chest, National Brotherhood Week, etc., the organization concerned would send in suggestions as to what it wanted the President to say. This submitted material was almost always so rhetorical, so studiously literary, that it did not sound at all like Roosevelt's normal style and it had to be subjected to the process of simplification or even oversimplification that he demanded. He was happiest when he could express himself in the homeliest, even tritest phrases, such as 'common or garden,' 'clear as crystal,' 'rule of thumb,' 'neither here nor there,' 'armchair strategists,' or 'simple as ABC.'

When he wanted to give a speech for some important purpose, whether it was connected with a special occasion or not, he would discuss it first at length with Hopkins, Rosenman and me, telling us what particular points he wanted to make, what sort of audience he wished primarily to reach and what the maximum word limit was to be (he generally put it far too low). He would dictate pages and pages, approaching his main topic, sometimes hitting it squarely on the nose with terrific impact, sometimes rambling so

[2 During the 1940 Presidential campaign.]

far away from it that he couldn't get back, in which case he would say, 'Well—something along those lines—you boys can fix it up.' I think he greatly enjoyed these sessions, when he felt free to say anything he pleased, uttering all kinds of personal insults, with the knowledge that none of it need appear in the final version. When he stopped dictating, because another appointment was due or it was time to go to bed, we would go to the Cabinet Room in the West Wing and start reading through all the assembled material. The President kept a special 'Speech Folder' into which he put newspaper clippings that he had marked, indicating either his approval of some sentiment expressed or indignation that such falsehood should get into print (he could not always remember what the marking signified). There were also all sorts of letters from all sorts of people, known and unknown, containing suggestions as to what he should say, and there were random bits of his own dictation, thoughts that had suddenly occurred to him during preceding days and weeks which might be useful sometime. All of this material was sifted, and added to the newly dictated material with the aid of scissors and paste and a few connecting clauses, until something resembling a coherent speech was put together and fair copies of it made. It was generally two or three times too long. When the President was free to see us again, we handed him this draft and he looked immediately at the last page to see its number, whereupon he announced that at least ninety-two per cent of it must be cut. He then started to read through it, pausing frequently to dictate 'Insert A,' 'Insert G,' etc. Each time he decided to dictate something he said, 'Grace—take a law,' a line he gladly borrowed from the Kaufman-Hart-Rodgers musical show, 'I'd Rather Be Right,' in which George M. Cohan played the part of Franklin D. Roosevelt. The President himself had never seen this show but he enjoyed what he heard about it.

When he had finished dictating inserts, the speech was far longer than it had been and farther from any coherent form. We then returned to the Cabinet Room and started a second draft. This process went on day and night. Sometimes, while the work was in progress, events would intervene —for instance: on a Sunday evening in July, 1943, we were at Shangri-la [3] finishing up a speech devoted primarily to home-front problems—price stabilization, rationing, manpower, etc.—when news came of the fall of Benito Mussolini, and the speech had to be started all over again; this, however, was a pleasure for all.

Most of Roosevelt's work on speeches was done during the evening. We

[3 The President's country lodge in Maryland.]

would gather for the standard cocktail ceremony in the Oval Study at 7:15. The President sat behind his desk, the tray before him. He mixed the ingredients with the deliberation of an alchemist but with what appeared to be a certain lack of precision since he carried on a steady conversation while doing it. His bourbon old-fashioneds were excellent, but I did not care for his Martinis, in which he used two kinds of vermouth (when he had them) and sometimes a dash of absinthe. Hopkins occasionally talked him into making Scotch whisky sours, although he didn't really like them. The usual canapés of cream cheese or fish paste on small circles of toast were served, also popcorn. Roosevelt was an extremely mild drinker—he did not have wine with meals except at large, formal dinners, and I don't recall ever having seen him drink brandy or other liqueurs or a highball; but he certainly loved the cocktail period and the stream of small talk that went with it.

Dinner was generally served in the study about 7:45. It ill becomes a guest to say so, but the White House cuisine did not enjoy a very high reputation. The food was plentiful and, when simple, good—but the chef had a tendency to run amuck on fancy salads. There was one favorite in particular which resembled the productions one finds in the flossier type of tea shoppe: it was a mountain of mayonnaise, slices of canned pineapple, carved radishes, etc. It was served frequently and each time the President merely looked at it and shook his head and murmured sadly, 'No, thank you.' Once when this happened, Sam Rosenman laughed and said, 'Mr. President, you've been in this House for eight years, and for all I know you'll be here eight years more—but they'll never give up trying to persuade you to find out what that salad really tastes like.' Roosevelt was always grateful for delicacies, particularly game, which friends sent in to enliven his diet. I never heard him complain about food or anything else in the way of service, but he did complain bitterly about the security supervision of every article of food sent to him. Once he said, 'I happen to be very fond of roasted peanuts. But if somebody wanted to send me a bag of peanuts, the Secret Service would have to X-ray it and the Department of Agriculture would have to open every shell and test every kernel for poison or high explosives. So, to save trouble, they would just throw the bag away and never tell me about it.' Deeply moved by this, Rosenman and I went to the corner of Pennsylvania Avenue and 15th Street and bought a large bag of peanuts and sneaked it in to the President. He put it under his coat and ate the whole contents.

After dinner he sat on the couch to the left of the fireplace, his feet up on the stool specially built for him, and started reading the latest speech draft. Grace Tully sat next to him, taking more dictation until Dorothy Brady or Toinette Bachelder came in to relieve her. Sometimes Roosevelt read the speech out loud, to see how it sounded, for every word was judged not by its appearance in print but by its effectiveness over the radio. About 10 o'clock, a tray with drinks was brought in. The President sometimes had a glass of beer but more often a horse's neck (ginger ale and lemon peel). He was by now yawning and losing interest in the speech and he usually went to bed before eleven. During these evening sessions, the telephone almost never rang. Now and then a dispatch might be brought in, which Roosevelt would read and pass on to Hopkins without a word or a change of expression, but otherwise one would have thought this house the most peaceful, remote retreat in a war-wracked world.

After leaving the Study, we would spend most of the night in the Cabinet Room producing another draft which would go to the President with his breakfast in the morning. Sometimes we would send a call for help to Archibald MacLeish, Librarian of Congress, who would come in late at night to help bring a diffuse speech into focus. More than once, before the White House windows were blacked out after Pearl Harbor, Mrs. Roosevelt saw the lights burning in the Cabinet Room at 3:00 A.M. and telephoned down to tell us we were working too hard and should go to bed. Of course, the fact was that she herself was sitting up working at that hour.

We had to get up early in the morning to be ready for summons in case the President wanted to work on the speech before his first appointment. We generally had breakfast on trays in Hopkins' room and it was rarely a cheerful gathering. The draft that had been completed a few hours previously looked awful in the morning light and the judgment on it that we most often expressed was, 'I only hope that the reputation of Franklin Delano Roosevelt does not depend on this terrible speech.'

After the session in the President's bedroom, Rosenman and I went over to the Cabinet Room to await the summons. The signal bells announced the President's approach to his office and we stood by the French windows leading out to the colonnade and watched him go by in his armless, cushionless, uncomfortable wheelchair, pushed by his Negro valet, Chief Petty Officer Arthur Prettyman. Accompanying him was the detail of Secret Service men, some of them carrying the large, overflowing wire baskets of papers on which he had been working the night before and the dispatches that had come in that morning. When Fala came abreast of the wheelchair as it rolled along, Roosevelt would reach down and scratch his neck. This progress to the day's work by a crippled man was a sight to stir the most torpid imagination; for here was a clear glimpse of the Roosevelt that the people believed him to be—the chin up, the cigarette holder tilted at what was always described as 'a jaunty angle' and the air of irrepressible confidence that whatever problems the day might bring, he would find a way to handle them. The fact that this confidence was not always justified made it none the less authentic and reassuring.

When I saw the President go by on these mornings, I felt that nobody who worked for him had a right to feel tired. That was not an unusual feeling: it went all through the wartime Administration in Washington, extending to all sorts of people, some of whom disagreed with him politically and most of whom never laid eyes on him. It was, I think, Henry Pringle [4] who, when working in a government agency shortly after Pearl Harbor, suggested as a wall slogan for bureaucrats' offices: EXHAUSTION IS NOT ENOUGH!

The speeches had to be checked and counterchecked with various departments and agencies, most of all with the Army and Navy; many speeches that were sent over to the War Department came back with corrections and suggestions penciled in the handwriting of General Marshall. The work of the so-called 'ghost writers' consisted largely of the painstaking, arduous verification of facts and figures. We felt, 'The New York Times can make mistakes—the World Almanac can make mistakes—but the President of the United States must not make mistakes.' This constant thought imposed a harrowing responsibility. After 1940, the White House had its resident statistician—Isador Lubin, the Commissioner of Labor Statistics, who was constantly available and incalculably valuable to Roosevelt and to Hopkins in checking every decimal point.

Although the speeches were usually seen in advance by the War and Navy Departments and sometimes (though not always) by the State Department, they were kept otherwise under close wraps of secrecy. There were always various eminent officials who wanted to know what the President was going to say. They were particularly anxious to make sure that he was going to include the several pages of material that they had submitted on their own particular departments. They knew they could get nowhere with Hopkins in their quest of inside information; so they concentrated on Rosenman, who would fob them off with the misstatement that, 'The President is weighing that in his mind right now.' We used to derive enjoyment from the thought of various important personages around

[4 Journalist and biographer.]

Washington listening to the Presidential broadcasts and then, as the strains of 'The Star Spangled Banner' broke out at the finish, cursing, 'He didn't use a *word* of that stuff that I sent him.' It was even more enjoyable to picture the amazed expression of some anonymous citizen in Council Bluffs who had written a letter to the President and then heard something from that letter incorporated in a Fireside Chat.

On the final two days of preparation of a speech Roosevelt would really buckle down to serious work and then what had seemed a formless, aimless mess of words would begin to assume tautness and sharpness. He studied every implication for its effect on various groups in the nation and on allies and enemies and neutrals. He paid a great deal of attention to the punctuation, not for its correctness but for its aid or hindrance to him in reading the speech aloud. Grace Tully liked to insert a great many commas, and the President loved to strike them out. He once said to her, 'Grace! How many times do I have to tell you not to waste the taxpayers' commas?' He liked dashes, which were visual aids, and hated semicolons and parentheses. I don't think he ever used the sonorous phrase, 'And I quote—.' If he had to have quotation marks, he did not refer to them, knowing they would appear in the printed version.

In the final draft of a speech, every word was counted and Roosevelt finally decided the precise number that he would be able to crowd into thirty minutes. His sense of timing was phenomenal. His normal rate was 100 words a minute, but he would say, 'There are some paragraphs in this speech that I can take quickly so I can handle a total of 3,150 words'— and that did not mean 3,162. At other times, he would feel that he had to be deliberate in his delivery and the words would have to be cut to 2,800. This cutting was the most difficult work of all because, by the time we had come to the ninth or tenth draft, we felt sure the speech had been boiled down to the ultimate monosyllable. Roosevelt's estimates were rarely off more than a split second on his broadcasts. Speeches before audiences were difficult to estimate, of course, because crowd responses are unpredictable, but he was generally accurate even on these. In the Teamsters' speech,[5] the roars of laughter and applause were so frequent and prolonged that the speech ran some fifteen minutes overtime, but that did not upset Roosevelt at all despite the fact that, since it was a campaign speech, the Democratic National Committee had to pay the heavy excess charges.

When a speech was finally closed up, about six o'clock in the evening,

[5 A speech delivered during the 1944 campaign at a dinner of the International Brotherhood of Teamsters in Washington.]

the President was wheeled over to Dr. McIntire's office for the sinus treatments that were a regular part of his day. Then he went upstairs for cocktails and dinner, after which he chatted or worked on his correspondence or his stamp albums, without seeming to give much attention to the final reading copy of his speech which was typed on special limp paper, to avoid rustling noises as he turned the pages, and bound in a black leather looseleaf folder. But when he started to broadcast he seemed to know it by heart. When he looked down at his manuscript, he was usually not looking at the words he was then speaking but at the next paragraph to determine where he would put his pauses and which of his large assortment of inflections he would employ. As one who has had considerable experience in the theater, I marveled at the unfailing precision with which he made his points, his grace in reconciling the sublime with the ridiculous, as though he had been rehearsing these lines for weeks and delivering them before audiences for months. Those who worked with him on speeches were all too well aware that he was no slave to his prepared text. He could and did ad-lib at will, and that was something which always amused him greatly. During the days of preparation, Hopkins, Rosenman and I would sometimes unite in opposition to some line, usually of a jocose nature, which the President wanted to include. It was our duty to make every effort to avoid being yes men and so we kept at him until we had persuaded him that the line should be cut out; but, if he really liked it well enough, he would keep it in mind and then ad-lib it, and later would be full of apologies to us for his 'unfortunate slip of the tongue.' He was almost always immensely good humored about the arguments we offered him—he liked to appear persecuted and complain that 'They won't let me say anything of my own in my own speech.' There were times, however, when he was worn out and angered by something else and then he would be cantankerous with us because we were the only convenient targets; we learned that on such occasions it was best to shut up and to revive our arguments later after he had had some rest and felt more amiable. Referring again to my experience in the theater, I can testify that he was normally the most untemperamental genius I have ever encountered. That is one of the reasons why he was able to sleep so well at night.

During the campaign of 1940, Carl Sandburg came to call at the White House and had a long talk with the President who said to him, 'Why don't you go down to Missy LeHand's office and dictate some of the things you've just been saying to me?' Sandburg did so and said, among other things:

The Gettysburg speech of Abraham Lincoln or the farewell address of Robert E. Lee to his Army, would be, in our American street talk, 'just a lot of words,' unless we look behind the words, unless we see words throwing long shadows—and out of the shadows arises the mystery of man consecrated to mystic causes. . .

If we go back across American history we find that as a nation among the other nations of the world this country has never kept silence as to what it stands for. For a hundred and fifty years and more we have told the world that the American Republic stands for a certain way of life. No matter what happened to the map of Europe, no matter what changes of government and systems went on there, no matter what old thrones and dynasties crashed to make way for something else, no matter what new philosophies and orbits of influence were proclaimed, America never kept silence.

Despite his strenuous avoidance of solemnity, and the frivolousness and irrelevance of his small talk when he was off the record, Roosevelt knew that he was the voice of America to the rest of the world. In the darkest days before and after Pearl Harbor he expressed the hopes of civilized humanity. Churchill's was the gallant voice of the unconquerable warrior, but Roosevelt's was the voice of liberation, the reassurance of the dignity of man. His buoyancy, his courage, his confidence renewed hope in those who feared that they had forever lost it. Roosevelt seemed to take his speeches lightly, but no one knew better than he that, once he had the microphone before him, he was speaking for the eternal record—his words were, as Sandburg said, 'throwing long shadows.'

In a foreword to an anthology of Roosevelt speeches, Harry Hopkins wrote:

Roosevelt made many great speeches. But some were not so good. He occasionally did not try, because he was frankly bored. A President of the United States has to speak many times on subjects which do not interest him. He would prefer to read a book or go to bed.

This was particularly true of the last two years of Roosevelt's life, when he made just as few speeches as possible and rarely appeared to take a great deal of interest in those that he did make. The time of challenge when words were the only weapons had at last passed and great and terrible events were speaking for themselves. He seemed to relax to save himself for the time when events would cease and words would again become the instruments of international politics.

THE STORY OF JOSEPH

❡ It is safe to assert that more new English translations of the Bible were published in the first half of the twentieth century than in the preceding three hundred years. In some respects the gap between the King James Bible of 1611 and its complete revision in 1885 was fortunate, for if the sixteenth- and early seventeenth-century versions were by modern standards of scholarship defective, they were nevertheless felicitous in style. Tyndale and Coverdale had an instinctive feeling for language as well as a passion to 'search the scriptures'; perhaps the two things are not unrelated. These men and the makers of the Geneva version of 1560 and Rheims-Douai of 1582–1609, and above all the committee that gave us the so-called Authorized or King James Bible of 1611 made the Bible popular literature in English.

From the present standpoint all these translations had very serious faults. Textual criticism and textual and archaeological discoveries in the past century have so vastly advanced our knowledge of the Bible that new translations or drastic revisions become imperative. However splendid the phrases and rhythms of Tudor or Jacobean versions, accuracy and an idiom more intelligible to the plain reader of the present time are yet greater matters if the Bible is to be read and valued as it needs to be.

Of the completely fresh translations of the whole Bible into English in the twentieth century, probably the most successful are those by Dr. James Moffatt, a Scot; by Monsignor Ronald Knox, an Englishman; and by five American and Canadian scholars (Professors J. M. Powis Smith, Edgar J. Goodspeed, Theophile J. Meek, Alexander R. Gordon, and Leroy Waterman), who called theirs the 'American' translation. Concerning their rendering of the Old Testament (1927), Dr. Smith writes: 'It tries to be American in the sense that the writings of Lincoln, Roosevelt, and Wilson are American. This does not imply any limitation of our mother-tongue, but if anything an enrichment of it. Least of all does it mean that the translation is for Americans only; it aims at being easily understood wherever English is spoken. In general we have been loyal to the Hebrew in its use of symbolic and figurative language; occasionally where such figures would not be clear to the reader, we have translated the figure into more familiar terms.'

The Authorized or King James Version of the Bible was the work of a committee—one of the very few products of committee labor to have literary distinction. It was suggested in 1604 by a Puritan divine, Dr. Reynolds, and sponsored by the King. Two subcommittees, as we should call them, worked at the project in London, two in Oxford, and two in Cambridge. Still another subcommittee, chosen from these six, revised their draft. The book was published in 1611.

The King James Version was based directly on the earlier translations of William Tyndale (1525ff.) and Miles Coverdale (1535), and on the revision of Coverdale's translation, the 'Great Bible' (1539). The Geneva Bible of 1560, which was the favorite version with the Puritans, and the Roman Catholic translation, the Rheims-Douai of 1582–1609, were also consulted by the makers of the Authorized Version. But the Tyndale and Coverdale translations were by far their most important aids.

I

JOSEPH, being seventeen years old, was feeding the flock with his brethren; and the lad was with the sons of Bilhah, and with the sons of Zilpah, his father's wives: and Joseph brought unto his father their evil report.

Now Israel[1] loved Joseph more than all his children, because he was the son of his old age: and he made him a coat of many colours. And when his brethren saw that their father loved him more than all his brethren, they hated him, and could not speak peaceably unto him.

And Joseph dreamed a dream, and he told it his brethren: and they hated him yet the more. And he said unto them,

'Hear, I pray you, this dream which I have dreamed: for, behold, we were binding sheaves in the field, and, lo, my sheaf arose, and also stood upright; and, behold, your sheaves stood round about, and made obeisance to my sheaf.'

[1 Jacob.]
FROM the Authorized Version of 1611.

II

AT THE age of seventeen Joseph used to accompany his brothers in looking after the flocks, being a mere lad alongside the sons of Bilhah and Zilpah, his father's wives; and Joseph brought a bad report of them to their father.

Now Israel loved Joseph more than any of his other sons, because he was the son of his old age; so he made a long cloak for him. When his brothers saw that their father loved him more than any of his brothers, they hated him, and could not say a good word about him.

Joseph had a dream which he told to his brothers, so that they hated him all the more. He said to them,

'Listen to this dream that I have had. While we were binding sheaves in the field, my sheaf rose up and remained standing, while your sheaves gathered round it, and made obeisance to my sheaf!'

FROM *The Complete Bible, An American Translation*, 1931. Reprinted by permission of the University of Chicago Press.

And his brethren said to him,

'Shalt thou indeed reign over us? or shalt thou indeed have dominion over us?'

And they hated him yet the more for his dreams, and for his words.

And he dreamed yet another dream, and told it his brethren, and said,

'Behold, I have dreamed a dream more; and, behold, the sun and the moon and the eleven stars made obeisance to me.'

And he told it to his father, and to his brethren: and his father rebuked him, and said unto him,

'What is this dream that thou hast dreamed? Shall I and thy mother and thy brethren indeed come to bow down ourselves to thee to the earth?'

And his brethren envied him; but his father observed the saying.

And his brethren went to feed their father's flock in Shechem. And Israel said unto Joseph,

'Do not thy brethren feed the flock in Shechem? come, and I will send thee unto them.'

And he said to him, 'Here am I.'

And he said to him,

'Go, I pray thee, see whether it be well with thy brethren, and well with the flocks; and bring me word again.'

So he sent him out of the vale of Hebron, and he came to Shechem. And a certain man found him, and, behold, he was wandering in the field: and the man asked him, saying,

'What seekest thou?'

And he said,

'I seek my brethren: tell me, I pray thee, where they feed their flocks.'

His brothers said to him,

'Are you indeed to be king over us; would you actually rule us?'

So they hated him all the more for his dreams and for his words.

Then he had another dream which he recounted to his brothers.

'I have just had another dream,' he said, 'and the sun, moon, and eleven stars made obeisance to me!'

When he recounted it to his father and his brothers, his father reproved him, saying to him,

'What is this dream that you have had? Am I actually to come with your mother and your brothers, and make obeisance to the earth to you?'

But while his brothers became jealous of him, his father kept the matter in mind.

After his brothers had gone off to pasture their father's flocks at Shechem, Israel said to Joseph,

'Are not your brothers pasturing the flocks at Shechem? Come, let me send you to them.'

'I am ready,' he replied.

So he said to him,

'Go and see how your brothers are, and the flocks; and bring me back word.'

So he despatched him from the valley of Hebron; and he arrived at Shechem. But a man found him wandering about the country; so the man asked him,

'What are you looking for?'

'I am looking for my brothers,' he said; 'do tell me where they are pasturing the flocks.'

And the man said,

'They are departed hence; for I heard them say, "Let us go to Dothan."'

And Joseph went after his brethren, and found them in Dothan. And when they saw him afar off, even before he came near unto them, they conspired against him to slay him.

And they said one to another, 'Behold, this dreamer cometh. Come now therefore, and let us slay him, and cast him into some pit, and we will say, "Some evil beast hath devoured him": and we shall see what will become of his dreams.'

And Reuben heard it, and he delivered him out of their hands; and said, 'Let us not kill him.'

And Reuben said unto them, 'Shed no blood, but cast him into this pit that is in the wilderness, and lay no hand upon him'; that he might rid him out of their hands, to deliver him to his father again.

And it came to pass, when Joseph was come unto his brethren, that they stripped Joseph out of his coat, his coat of many colours that was on him; and they took him, and cast him into a pit: and the pit was empty, there was no water in it.

And they sat down to eat bread: and they lifted up their eyes and looked, and, behold, a company of Ishmaelites came from Gilead with their camels bearing spicery and balm and myrrh, going to carry it down to Egypt. And Judah said unto his brethren,

'What profit is it if we slay our

The man said,

'They have moved from here; for I heard them say, "Let us go to Dothan."'

So Joseph followed his brothers, and found them at Dothan. But they saw him in the distance, and before he could reach them, they plotted against him to kill him.

'There comes the dreamer yonder!' they said to one another. 'Come now, let us kill him, and throw him into one of the pits. We can say that a wild beast devoured him. Then we shall see what his dreams will come to.'

But when Reuben heard this, he tried to save him from their hands; so he said,

'Let us not take his life.'

'Do not shed any blood,' Reuben said to them; 'throw him into the pit here in the wilderness, but do not lay hands on him' (his idea being to save him from their hands, and restore him to his father).

As soon as Joseph reached his brothers, they stripped him of his cloak (the long cloak that he was wearing), and seizing him, they threw him into the pit. The pit, however, was empty, with no water in it.

Then they sat down to eat a meal; but raising their eyes, they saw a caravan of Ishmaelites coming from Gilead, with their camels carrying gum, balm, and laudanum, which they were engaged in taking down to Egypt. Thereupon Judah said to his brothers,

'What is the good of killing our

brother, and conceal his blood? Come
and let us sell him to the Ishmaelites,
and let not our hand be upon him;
for he is our brother and our flesh.'

And his brethren were content.
Then there passed by Midianites mer-
chantmen; and they drew and lifted
up Joseph out of the pit, and sold Joseph to the Ishmaelites for twenty
pieces of silver: and they brought Joseph into Egypt.

And Reuben returned unto the pit;
and, behold, Joseph was not in the pit;
and he rent his clothes. And he returned unto his brethren, and said,
'The child is not; and I, whither shall
I go?'

And they took Joseph's coat, and
killed a kid of the goats, and dipped
the coat in the blood; and they sent
the coat of many colours, and they
brought it to their father; and said,
'This have we found: know now
whether it be thy son's coat or no.'

And he knew it, and said,
'It is my son's coat; an evil beast
hath devoured him; Joseph is without
doubt rent in pieces.'

And Jacob rent his clothes, and put
sackcloth upon his loins, and mourned
for his son many days. And all his sons
and all his daughters rose up to comfort him; but he refused to be comforted; and he said,
'For I will go down into the grave
unto my son mourning.'

Thus his father wept for him.

And Joseph was brought down to
Egypt; and Potiphar, an officer of
Pharaoh, captain of the guard, an
Egyptian, bought him of the hands of

brother and covering up his blood?
Come, let us sell him to the Ishmaelites, and not lay hands on him; for
after all he is our brother, our own
flesh.'

His brothers agreed. Some Midian-
ite traders passed by, so pulling Joseph up, they lifted him out of the pit.
They sold Joseph to the Ishmaelites
for twenty shekels of silver; and they
took him to Egypt.

So when Reuben went back to the
pit, there was no Joseph in the pit.
Then he tore his clothes, and returning to his brothers, said,
'The boy is gone! And I, how can I
go home?'

Then they took Joseph's cloak, and
killing a goat, they dipped the cloak in
the blood. So they soiled the long
cloak, and then they brought it to
their father, saying,
'We found this; see whether it is
your son's cloak or not.'

Examining it, he said,
'It is my son's cloak! Some wild
beast has devoured him; Joseph must
be torn to pieces.'

Then Jacob tore his clothes, and
girded himself with sackcloth, and
mourned for his son for a long time.
His sons and daughters all tried to
console him, but he would not be
consoled.

'No,' he said, 'I will go down mourning to Sheol to my son.'

Thus did his father weep for him.

When Joseph was taken down to
Egypt, Potiphar, an Egyptian, an officer of Pharaoh, his head steward,
bought him from the Ishmaelites who

the Ishmaelites, which had brought him down thither. And the Lord was with Joseph, and he was a prosperous man; and he was in the house of his master the Egyptian. And his master saw that the Lord was with him, and that the Lord made all that he did to prosper in his hand. And Joseph found grace in his sight, and he served him: and he made him overseer over his house, and all that he had he put into his hand. And it came to pass from the time that he had made him overseer in his house, and over all that he had, that the Lord blessed the Egyptian's house for Joseph's sake; and the blessing of the Lord was upon all that he had in the house, and in the field. And he left all that he had in Joseph's hand; and he knew not ought he had, save the bread which he did eat.

And Joseph was a goodly person, and well favoured. And it came to pass after these things, that his master's wife cast her eyes upon Joseph: and she said,

'Lie with me.'

But he refused, and said unto his master's wife,

'Behold, my master wotteth not what is with me in the house, and he hath committed all that he hath to my hand! There is none greater in this house than I; neither hath he kept back any thing from me but thee, because thou art his wife: how then can I do this great wickedness, and sin against God?'

And it came to pass, as she spake to Joseph day by day, that he hearkened

had taken him down there. The Lord was with Joseph, so that he became a prosperous man. He lived in the house of his master, the Egyptian; and his master noticed that the Lord was with him and that the Lord made everything prosper with him that he undertook; so Joseph found favor with him, and was made his personal attendant; then he made him superintendent of his household, and put him in charge of all his property. From the time that he made him superintendent of his household and all his property, the Lord blessed the house of the Egyptian for Joseph's sake, the Lord's blessing resting on everything that belonged to him, both indoors and outdoors. So he left everything that he had to Joseph's charge, and having him, gave no concern to anything, except the food that he ate.

Now Joseph was so handsome and good-looking that some time later the wife of his master took a fancy to Joseph, and said,

'Lie with me.'

But he refused, saying to his master's wife,

'Having me, my master is giving no concern to anything in the house, but has committed all his property to my charge; there is no one in this household greater than I; he has kept nothing from me except yourself, and that because you are his wife. How then can I commit this great crime, and sin against God?'

Though she spoke to Joseph day after day, he would not listen to her

not unto her, to lie by her, or to be with her. And it came to pass about this time, that Joseph went into the house to do his business; and there was none of the men of the house there within. And she caught him by his garment, saying,

'Lie with me': and he left his garment in her hand, and fled, and got him out.

And it came to pass, when she saw that he had left his garment in her hand, and was fled forth, that she called unto the men of her house, and spake unto them, saying,

'See, he hath brought in a Hebrew unto us to mock us; he came in unto me to lie with me, and I cried with a loud voice; and it came to pass, when he heard that I lifted up my voice and cried, that he left his garment with me, and fled, and got him out.'

And she laid up his garment by her, until his lord came home.

And she spake unto him according to these words, saying,

'The Hebrew servant, which thou hast brought unto us, came in unto me to mock me; and it came to pass, as I lifted up my voice and cried, that he left his garment with me, and fled out.'

And it came to pass, when his master heard the words of his wife, which she spake unto him, saying, 'After this manner did thy servant to me'; that his wrath was kindled. And Joseph's master took him, and put him into the prison, a place where the king's prisoners were bound: and he was there in the prison.

solicitations to lie with her, or be with her. One day, however, when he went into the house to do his work, none of the household servants being anywhere in the house, she caught hold of his coat, saying,

'Lie with me.'

But he fled, leaving the coat in her hands, and went outdoors. When she saw that he had fled outdoors, leaving his coat in her hands, she called her household servants, and said to them,

'See how he has brought this Hebrew fellow into our house to violate us! He came into my room to lie with me, but I screamed; and as soon as he heard me scream and call, he fled, leaving his coat beside me, and went outdoors.'

So she left the coat beside her until his master came home, and then told him this same story.

'The Hebrew slave whom you brought into our house came into my room to violate me, but as soon as I screamed and called, he fled outdoors, leaving his coat beside me.'

When Joseph's master heard the statements of his wife who said to him, 'This is the way your slave treated me,' his anger blazed, and Joseph's master took him and threw him into the prison where state prisoners were confined. So he lay there in prison.

But the Lord was with Joseph, and showed him mercy, and gave him favour in the sight of the keeper of the prison. And the keeper of the prison committed to Joseph's hand all the prisoners that were in the prison; and whatsoever they did there, he was the doer of it. The keeper of the prison looked not to any thing that was under his hand; because the Lord was with him, and that which he did, the Lord made it to prosper.

And it came to pass after these things that the butler of the king of Egypt and his baker had offended their lord the king of Egypt. And Pharaoh was wroth against two of his officers, against the chief of the butlers, and against the chief of the bakers. And he put them in ward in the house of the captain of the guard, into the prison, the place where Joseph was bound. And the captain of the guard charged Joseph with them, and he served them: and they continued a season in ward. And they dreamed a dream both of them, each man his dream in one night, each man according to the interpretation of his dream, the butler and the baker of the king of Egypt, which were bound in the prison. And Joseph came in unto them in the morning, and looked upon them, and, behold, they were sad. And he asked Pharaoh's officers that were with him in the ward of his lord's house, saying,

'Wherefore look ye so sadly to-day?'

And they said unto him, 'We have dreamed a dream, and there is no interpreter of it.'

And Joseph said unto them,

The Lord, however, was with Joseph and was kind to him, and got him into the good graces of the jailer, so that the jailer put Joseph in charge of all the prisoners who were in the jail, and he looked after everything that was done there. The jailer exercised no oversight over anything in his charge, because the Lord was with him, and the Lord made whatever he undertook prosper.

Some time after these events the butler and the baker of the king of Egypt offended their lord, the king of Egypt, so that Pharaoh became angry with his two officers, the chief butler and the chief baker, and put them in custody in the head steward's house, in the prison where Joseph was confined. The head steward intrusted Joseph with them, and he waited on them. After they had been in custody some time, they both had dreams on the same night, each having a dream of different meaning—the butler and the baker of the king of Egypt who were confined in the prison. When Joseph came to them in the morning, he saw that they were worried, so he asked Pharaoh's officers who were in custody with him in his master's house,

'Why do you look so gloomy to-day?'

'We have had dreams,' they replied, 'and there is no one to interpret them.'

Joseph said to them,

'Do not interpretations belong to God? tell me them, I pray you.'

And the chief butler told his dream to Joseph, and said to him,

'In my dream, behold, a vine was before me; and in the vine were three branches: and it was as though it budded, and her blossoms shot forth; and the clusters thereof brought forth ripe grapes; and Pharaoh's cup was in my hand: and I took the grapes, and pressed them into Pharaoh's cup, and I gave the cup into Pharaoh's hand.'

And Joseph said unto him,

'This is the interpretation of it. The three branches are three days. Yet within three days shall Pharaoh lift up thine head, and restore thee unto thy place: and thou shalt deliver Pharaoh's cup into his hand, after the former manner when thou wast his butler. But think on me when it shall be well with thee, and show kindness, I pray thee, unto me, and make mention of me unto Pharaoh, and bring me out of this house: for indeed I was stolen away out of the land of the Hebrews: and here also have I done nothing that they should put me into the dungeon.'

When the chief baker saw that the interpretation was good, he said unto Joseph,

'I also was in my dream, and, behold, I had three white baskets on my head: and in the uppermost basket there was of all manner of bakemeats for Pharaoh; and the birds did eat them out of the basket upon my head.'

And Joseph answered and said,

'This is the interpretation thereof.

'Does not dream interpretation belong to God? Pray recount them to me.'

So the chief butler recounted his dream to Joseph.

'In my dream,' he said to him, 'there was a vine in front of me, and on the vine were three branches. As soon as it budded, its blossoms shot up, its clusters ripened into grapes. With Pharaoh's cup in my hand, I took the grapes, and squeezing them into Pharaoh's cup, I placed the cup in Pharaoh's hand.'

Joseph said to him,

'This is its interpretation: the three branches represent three days; within three days Pharaoh shall summon you, and restore you to your position, so that you shall place Pharaoh's cup in his hand as you used to do when you were his butler; so, if you will be good enough to keep me in mind when prosperity comes to you, do me the kindness of mentioning me to Pharaoh, and so liberate me from this house; for I was really kidnapped from the land of the Hebrews, and further, I have done nothing here that I should be put into a dungeon.'

When the chief baker found that the interpretation was favorable, he said to Joseph,

'I too had a dream; in mine there were three open-work baskets on my head, and in the top basket was some of every kind of baked food for Pharaoh, but the birds were eating it out of the basket on my head.'

Joseph answered,

'This is its interpretation: the three

The three baskets are three days. Yet within three days shall Pharaoh lift up thy head from off thee, and shall hang thee on a tree; and the birds shall eat thy flesh from off thee.'

And it came to pass the third day, which was Pharaoh's birthday, that he made a feast unto all his servants: and he lifted up the head of the chief butler and of the chief baker among his servants. And he restored the chief butler unto his butlership again; and he gave the cup into Pharaoh's hand. But he hanged the chief baker: as Joseph had interpreted to them. Yet did not the chief butler remember Joseph, but forgot him.

And it came to pass at the end of two full years that Pharaoh dreamed: and, behold, he stood by the river. And, behold, there came up out of the river seven well favoured kine and fatfleshed; and they fed in a meadow. And, behold, seven other kine came up after them out of the river, ill favoured and leanfleshed; and stood by the other kine upon the brink of the river. And the ill favoured and leanfleshed kine did eat up the seven well favoured and fat kine. So Pharaoh awoke. And he slept and dreamed the second time: and, behold, seven ears of corn came up upon one stalk, rank and good. And, behold, seven thin ears and blasted with the east wind sprung up after them. And the seven thin ears devoured the seven rank and full ears. And Pharaoh awoke, and, behold, it was a dream.

And it came to pass in the morning that his spirit was troubled; and he sent and called for all the magicians

baskets represent three days; within three days Pharaoh shall summon you, and hang you on a tree, and the birds shall eat the flesh off you.'

On the third day, which was Pharaoh's birthday, he held a feast for all his officials; and among his officials he summoned the chief butler and the chief baker. The chief butler he restored to his duties, so that he again placed the cup in Pharaoh's hand; but the chief baker he hanged, as Joseph had told them in his interpretation. The chief butler, however, did not keep Joseph in mind, but forgot him.

Two whole years later Pharaoh dreamed that he was standing beside the Nile, when seven beautiful, fat cows came up out of the Nile, and browsed in the sedge. After them seven other cows came up out of the Nile, ugly and thin, and stood beside the other cows on the bank of the Nile. Then the thin, ugly cows ate up the seven beautiful, fat cows, whereupon Pharaoh awoke. When he fell asleep again, he had a second dream: there were seven ears of grain growing on a single stalk, fine and plump, and after them there sprouted seven other ears, thin and blasted by the east wind. Then the thin ears swallowed up the seven fine, full ears, whereupon Pharaoh awoke, only to find it a dream!

Next morning he was so perturbed that he sent for all the magicians and wise men of Egypt. To them Pharaoh

of Egypt, and all the wise men thereof: and Pharaoh told them his dream; but there was none that could interpret them unto Pharaoh. Then spake the chief butler unto Pharaoh, saying,

'I do remember my faults this day. Pharaoh was wroth with his servants, and put me in ward in the captain of the guard's house, both me and the chief baker: and we dreamed a dream in one night, I and he; we dreamed each man according to the interpretation of his dream. And there was there with us a young man, a Hebrew, servant to the captain of the guard; and we told him, and he interpreted to us our dreams; to each man according to his dream he did interpret. And it came to pass, as he interpreted to us, so it was; me he restored unto mine office, and him he hanged.'

Then Pharaoh sent and called Joseph, and they brought him hastily out of the dungeon: and he shaved himself, and changed his raiment, and came in unto Pharaoh. And Pharaoh said unto Joseph,

'I have dreamed a dream, and there is none that can interpret it: and I have heard say of thee that thou canst understand a dream to interpret it.'

And Joseph answered Pharaoh, saying, 'It is not in me: God shall give Pharaoh an answer of peace.'

And Pharaoh said unto Joseph,

'In my dream, behold, I stood upon the bank of the river. And, behold, there came up out of the river seven kine, fatfleshed and well favoured; and they fed in a meadow. And, behold, seven other kine came up after them,

recounted his dreams, but no one could interpret them for Pharaoh. Then the chief butler said to Pharaoh,

'I would today recall my offense, how Pharaoh became angry with his servants, and put them in custody in the house of the head steward, myself and the chief baker. On the same night we had dreams, he and I, each of us having a dream of different meaning. With us there was a Hebrew youth, a slave belonging to the head steward, and when we recounted our dreams to him, he interpreted them for us, giving each the proper interpretation of his dream. And it fell out just as he had indicated in the interpretation; I was restored to my position, while the other was hanged.'

Thereupon Pharaoh sent for Joseph, and he was brought hurriedly from the dungeon. When he had shaved and changed his clothes, he came into Pharaoh's presence.

'I have had a dream,' Pharaoh said to Joseph, 'but there is no one to interpret it. However, I have heard it said of you that you know how to interpret dreams.'

'Apart from God can Pharaoh be given a favorable response?' Joseph answered Pharaoh.

Then Pharaoh said to Joseph,

'I dreamed that I was standing on the bank of the Nile, when seven fat and beautiful cows came up out of the Nile, and browsed in the sedge. After them came up seven other cows, thin and very ugly and lean—I have

poor and very ill favoured and lean-fleshed, such as I never saw in all the land of Egypt for badness. And the lean and the ill favoured kine did eat up the first seven fat kine; and when they had eaten them up, it could not be known that they had eaten them; but they were still ill favoured, as at the beginning. So I awoke. And I saw in my dream, and, behold, seven ears came up in one stalk, full and good. And, behold, seven ears, withered, thin, and blasted with the east wind, sprung up after them. And the thin ears devoured the seven good ears: and I told this unto the magicians; but there was none that could declare it to me.'

And Joseph said unto Pharaoh, 'The dream of Pharaoh is one. God hath showed Pharaoh what he is about to do. The seven good kine are seven years; and the seven good ears are seven years: the dream is one. And the seven thin and ill favoured kine that came up after them are seven years; and the seven empty ears blasted with the east wind shall be seven years of famine. This is the thing which I have spoken unto Pharaoh. What God is about to do he showeth unto Pharaoh. Behold, there come seven years of great plenty throughout all the land of Egypt, and there shall arise after them seven years of famine; and all the plenty shall be forgotten in the land of Egypt; and the famine shall consume the land. And the plenty shall not be known in the land by reason of that famine following; for it shall be very grievous. And for that the dream was doubled unto Pharaoh

never seen such poor cows in all the land of Egypt. Then the lean, ugly cows ate up the first seven fat cows; they passed right into them, but no one would have known that they had done so—they looked just as bad as before. Then I awoke.

'In another dream I saw seven ears of grain growing on a single stalk, full and plump, and after them there sprouted seven other ears, withered, thin, and blasted by the east wind. Then the thin ears swallowed up the seven plump ears. I told this to the magicians, but there was no one to explain it to me.'

Joseph said to Pharaoh, 'Pharaoh's dream is simple; God would reveal to Pharaoh what he is about to do. The seven fat cows represent seven years, and the seven plump ears represent seven years—it is a single dream. The seven lean and ugly cows that came up after them represent seven years, and so do the seven empty ears blasted by the east wind; there are to be seven years of famine. It is as I told Pharaoh, God would show Pharaoh what he is about to do. Seven years of great plenty are coming throughout all the land of Egypt, but following them there will be seven years of famine, so that the plenty will all be forgotten in the land of Egypt; the famine will devastate the land, and the plenty will become quite unknown in the land because of that famine which is to follow; for it will be very severe. The fact that the dream was sent twice to Pharaoh in two

twice; it is because the thing is established by God, and God will shortly bring it to pass. Now therefore let Pharaoh look out a man discreet and wise, and set him over the land of Egypt. Let Pharaoh do this, and let him appoint officers over the land, and take up the fifth part of the land of Egypt in the seven plenteous years. And let them gather all the food of those good years that come, and lay up corn under the hand of Pharaoh, and let them keep food in the cities. And that food shall be for store to the land against the seven years of famine, which shall be in the land of Egypt; that the land perish not through the famine.'

And the thing was good in the eyes of Pharaoh, and in the eyes of all his servants. And Pharaoh said unto his servants,

'Can we find such a one as this is, a man in whom the Spirit of God is?'

And Pharaoh said unto Joseph,

'Forasmuch as God hath showed thee all this, there is none so discreet and wise as thou art. Thou shalt be over my house, and according unto thy word shall all my people be ruled: only in the throne will I be greater than thou.'

And Pharaoh said unto Joseph,

'See, I have set thee over all the land of Egypt.'

And Pharaoh took off his ring from his hand, and put it upon Joseph's hand, and arrayed him in vestures of fine linen, and put a gold chain about his neck; and he made him to ride in the second chariot which he had; and

forms means that the matter is absolutely settled by God, and that God will soon bring it about. Now, then, let Pharaoh find a shrewd and prudent man, and put him in control of the land of Egypt. Let Pharaoh proceed to appoint officials over the land to forearm the land of Egypt during the seven years of plenty; let them collect all the food of these good years that are coming, and under the authority of Pharaoh store up grain for food in the cities, and hold it there. The food shall serve as a reserve for the land against the seven years of famine that are to befall the land of Egypt, so that the land may not perish from the famine.'

The proposal commended itself to Pharaoh and all his courtiers, and Pharaoh said to his courtiers,

'Can we find a man with the spirit of God in him like this one?'

So Pharaoh said to Joseph,

'Since God has made all this known to you, there is no one so shrewd and prudent as you; you shall be in charge of my palace, and all my people shall be obedient to your commands; it is only in the matter of the throne itself that I shall be your superior.'

Thereupon Pharaoh said to Joseph,

'I hereby put you in charge of the whole land of Egypt.'

And taking the signet ring from his finger, Pharaoh put it on Joseph's finger; he dressed him in linen robes, put a gold chain round his neck, and had him ride in the second of his chariots, with people shouting 'Bow

they cried before him, 'Bow the knee': and he made him ruler over all the land of Egypt.

And Pharaoh said unto Joseph,

'I am Pharaoh, and without thee shall no man lift his hand or foot in all the land of Egypt.'

And Pharaoh called Joseph's name Zaphnath-paaneah; and he gave him to wife Asenath the daughter of Poti-pherah priest of On. And Joseph went out over all the land of Egypt.

And Joseph was thirty years old when he stood before Pharaoh king of Egypt.

And Joseph went out from the presence of Pharaoh, and went throughout all the land of Egypt. And in the seven plenteous years the earth brought forth by handfuls. And he gathered up all the food of the seven years, which were in the land of Egypt, and laid up the food in the cities: the food of the field, which was round about every city, laid he up in the same. And Joseph gathered corn as the sand of the sea, very much, until he left numbering; for it was without number.

And unto Joseph were born two sons before the years of famine came, which Asenath the daughter of Poti-pherah priest of On bore unto him. And Joseph called the name of the first born Manasseh. 'For God,' said he, 'hath made me forget all my toil, and all my father's house.' And the name of the second called he Eph-raim: 'For God hath caused me to be fruitful in the land of my affliction.'

And the seven years of plenteous-ness, that was in the land of Egypt,

down!' before him, thus putting him in charge of the whole land of Egypt.

'Although I continue as Pharaoh,' said Pharaoh to Joseph, 'yet without your consent shall no one stir hand or foot in all the land of Egypt.'

Then Pharaoh called Joseph's name Zaphenath-paneah, and married him to Asenath, the daughter of Potiphera, priest of On; and Joseph's fame spread throughout the land of Egypt.

Joseph was thirty years old when he entered the service of Pharaoh, king of Egypt.

After leaving the presence of Pha-raoh, Joseph made a tour through the whole land of Egypt. During the seven years of plenty the land produced abundant crops; so he collected all the food of the seven years when there was plenty in the land of Egypt, and thus stored food in the cities, storing in each city the food from the fields around it. Joseph stored up grain like the sands of the sea, in great quanti-ties, until he ceased to keep account of it; for it was past measuring.

Before the years of famine came, two sons were born to Joseph by Ase-nath, the daughter of Potiphera, priest of On. Joseph called the name of the first-born Manasseh [forgetfulness]; 'For,' said he, 'God has made me for-get all about my hardships and my father's home.' The name of the sec-ond he called Ephraim [fruitfulness]; 'For God has made me fruitful in the land of my misfortune.'

When the seven years of plenty that had prevailed in the land of Egypt were ended. And the seven years of dearth began to come, according as Joseph had said: and the dearth was in all lands; but in all the land of Egypt there was bread.

And when all the land of Egypt was famished, the people cried to Pharaoh for bread: and Pharaoh said unto all the Egyptians,

'Go unto Joseph; what he saith to you, do.'

And the famine was over all the face of the earth. And Joseph opened all the storehouses, and sold unto the Egyptians; and the famine waxed sore in the land of Egypt. And all countries came into Egypt to Joseph for to buy corn; because that the famine was so sore in all lands.

Now when Jacob saw that there was corn in Egypt, Jacob said unto his sons,

'Why do ye look one upon another?' And he said, 'Behold, I have heard that there is corn in Egypt: get you down thither, and buy for us from thence; that we may live, and not die.'

And Joseph's ten brethren went down to buy corn in Egypt. But Benjamin, Joseph's brother, Jacob sent not with his brethren; for he said, 'Lest peradventure mischief befall him.' And the sons of Israel came to buy corn among those that came: for the famine was in the land of Canaan.

And Joseph was the governor over the land, and he it was that sold to all the people of the land: and Joseph's brethren came, and bowed down themselves before him with their faces to the earth. And Joseph saw his brethren, and he knew them, but made

came to an end, the seven years of famine set in, as Joseph had said.

There was famine in all lands, but throughout all the land of Egypt there was food.

When all the land of Egypt became famished, the people cried to Pharaoh for food; so Pharaoh announced to all Egypt,

'Go to Joseph, and do what he tells you.'

The famine spread all over the land, so Joseph threw open all that he had locked up, and sold grain to the Egyptians, since the famine was severe in the land of Egypt. People from all lands came to Joseph in Egypt to buy grain; for the famine was severe all over the earth.

When Jacob learned that there was grain in Egypt, he said to his sons,

'Why do you stare at one another? I have just heard,' he said, 'that there is grain in Egypt; go down there, and buy some for us there, that we may live and not die.'

So ten of Joseph's brothers went down to buy grain in Egypt, since Jacob would not let Joseph's brother Benjamin go with his other brothers; 'Lest,' thought he, 'harm should befall him.' Thus the Israelites came with the rest to buy grain; for the famine was in the land of Canaan.

Now Joseph was the vizier of the land; it was he who sold the grain to all the people of the land. So Joseph's brothers came and prostrated themselves before him, with their faces to the ground. When Joseph saw his brothers, he recognized them, but he himself strange unto them, and spoke roughly unto them; and he said unto them,

'Whence come ye?'

And they said, 'From the land of Canaan to buy food.'

And Joseph knew his brethren, but they knew not him. And Joseph remembered the dreams which he dreamed of them, and said unto them,

'Ye are spies; to see the nakedness of the land ye are come.'

And they said unto him,

'Nay, my lord, but to buy food are thy servants come. We are all one man's sons; we are true men, thy servants are no spies.'

And he said unto them, 'Nay, but to see the nakedness of the land ye are come.'

And they said,

'Thy servants are twelve brethren, the sons of one man in the land of Canaan; and, behold, the youngest is this day with our father, and one is not.'

And Joseph said unto them,

'That is it that I spoke unto you, saying, "Ye are spies." Hereby ye shall be proved: by the life of Pharaoh ye shall not go forth hence, except your youngest brother come hither. Send one of you, and let him fetch your brother, and ye shall be kept in prison, that your words may be proved, whether there be any truth in you: or else by the life of Pharaoh surely ye are spies.'

'And he put them all together into

treated them as if he were a stranger, and spoke harshly to them.

'Where have you come from?' he said to them.

'From the land of Canaan to buy food,' they said.

Joseph recognized his brothers, but they did not recognize him. Remembering the dreams that he had had about them, Joseph said to them,

'You are spies; you have come to find out the condition of the land!'

'No, my lord,' they said to him, 'your servants have come to buy food. We are all sons of one man; we are honest men; your servants are not spies.'

'Not so,' he said to them; 'but you have come to find out the condition of the land.'

But they said,

'Your servants are brothers, twelve in all; we are sons of a certain man in the land of Canaan; the youngest is at present with our father, while the other is no more.'

But Joseph said to them,

'It is as I told you; you are spies. By this you shall be put to the proof: as Pharaoh lives, you shall not leave this place unless your youngest brother comes here. Send one of your number to fetch your brother, while the rest of you remain in custody. Thus shall your statements be put to the proof as to whether you are truthful or not. As Pharaoh lives, you are spies!'

So he bundled them off to prison

ward three days. And Joseph said unto them the third day,

'This do, and live; for I fear God. If ye be true men, let one of your brethren be bound in the house of your prison: go ye, carry corn for the famine of your houses: but bring your youngest brother unto me; so shall your words be verified, and ye shall not die.'

And they did so. And they said one to another,

'We are verily guilty concerning our brother, in that we saw the anguish of his soul, when he besought us, and we would not hear; therefore is this distress come upon us.'

And Reuben answered them, saying,

'Spake I not unto you, saying, "Do not sin against the child"; and ye would not hear? therefore, behold, also his blood is required.'

And they knew not that Joseph understood them; for he spake unto them by an interpreter. And he turned himself about from them, and wept; and returned to them again, and communed with them, and took from them Simeon, and bound him before their eyes. Then Joseph commanded to fill their sacks with corn, and to restore every man's money into his sack, and to give them provision for the way: and thus did he unto them. And they laded their asses with the corn, and departed thence.

And as one of them opened his sack to give his ass provender in the

for three days, but on the third day Joseph said to them,

'Since I am one who fears God, you may save your lives, if you do this: if you are honest men, let one of you brothers remain confined in your prison and then the rest of you, go and take grain home to your starving households; but you must bring me your youngest brother. Thus shall your words be verified, and you shall not die.'

They proceeded to do so, saying to one another,

'Unfortunately, we were to blame about our brother, upon whose distress, when he pleaded with us for mercy, we gazed unmoved; that is why this distress has come to us.'

Then Reuben spoke up and said to them,

'Did I not say to you, "Do not sin against the lad"? But you paid no attention; so now comes a reckoning for his blood!'

They did not know that Joseph heard them; for the intermediary was between them. He turned from them, and wept. On coming back to them, he spoke to them, took Simeon from them, and imprisoned him in their presence. Joseph then ordered their receptacles to be filled with grain, the money of each of them to be replaced in his sack, and provisions to be given them for the journey. This was done for them. Then they loaded their asses with their grain, and departed.

At the camping-place for the night one of them opened his sack to give

inn, he espied his money; for, behold, it was in his sack's mouth.

And he said unto his brethren, 'My money is restored; and, lo, it is even in my sack': and their heart failed them, and they were afraid, saying one to another,

'What is this that God hath done unto us?'

And they came unto Jacob their father unto the land of Canaan, and told him all that befell unto them; saying,

'The man, who is the lord of the land, spake roughly to us, and took us for spies of the country. And we said unto him, "We are true men; we are no spies: we be twelve brethren, sons of our father; one is not, and the youngest is this day with our father in the land of Canaan." And the man, the lord of the country, said unto us, "Hereby shall I know that ye are true men; leave one of your brethren here with me, and take food for the famine of your households, and be gone: and bring your youngest brother unto me: then shall I know that ye are no spies, but that ye are true men: so will I deliver you your brother, and ye shall traffick in the land." '

And it came to pass as they emptied their sacks, that, behold, every man's bundle of money was in his sack: and when both they and their father saw the bundles of money, they were afraid. And Jacob their father said unto them,

'Me have ye bereaved of my children: Joseph is not, and Simeon is

his ass some fodder, and there he saw his money in the mouth of his sack!

'My money has been put back! It is right here inside my sack!' he said to his brothers.

Thereupon their hearts sank, and they turned to one another in fear, saying,

'What is this that God has done to us?'

On reaching their father Jacob in the land of Canaan, they told him all that had befallen them:

'The man, the lord of the land, talked harshly to us, making us out to be spies of the land. But we said to him, "We are honest men; we are not spies. We are brothers on our father's side, twelve in all; one is no more, and the youngest is at present with our father in the land of Canaan." Then the man, the lord of the land, said to us, "By this I shall find out whether you are honest men: leave one of your brothers with me, and taking something for your famishing households, be off; and then bring me your youngest brother. Thus shall I know that you are not spies, but honest men. I will restore your brother to you, and you will be free to trade in the land." '

When they came to empty their sacks, there was the money-packet of each in his sack! On seeing their money-packets, both they and their father were dismayed, and their father Jacob said to them,

'It is I that you bereave. Joseph is no more, Simeon is no more, and now

not, and ye will take Benjamin away:
all these things are against me.'

And Reuben spoke unto his father,
saying,

'Slay my two sons, if I bring him
not to thee: deliver him into my hand,
and I will bring him to thee again.'

And he said,

'My son shall not go down with
you; for his brother is dead, and he is
left alone: if mischief befall him by
the way in the which ye go, then shall
ye bring down my gray hairs with sorrow to the grave.'

And the famine was sore in the
land. And it came to pass, when they
had eaten up the corn which they had
brought out of Egypt, their father said
unto them,

'Go again, buy us a little food.'

And Judah spake unto him, saying,

'The man did solemnly protest unto
us, saying, "Ye shall not see my face,
except your brother be with you." If
thou wilt send our brother with us, we
will go down and buy thee food. But
if thou wilt not send him, we will not
go down: for the man said unto us,
"Ye shall not see my face, except
your brother be with you." '

And Israel said, 'Wherefore dealt
ye so ill with me, as to tell the man
whether ye had yet a brother?'

And they said, 'The man asked us
straitly of our state, and of our kindred, saying, "Is your father yet alive?
have ye another brother?" and we told
him according to the tenor of these
words: could we certainly know that

you would take Benjamin! It is on me
that all this falls.'

Reuben said to his father,

'You may kill my two sons if I do
not bring him home to you! Put him
in my charge, and I will bring him
back to you.'

But he said,

'My son shall not go down with
you; for his brother is dead, and he
alone is left. If harm were to befall
him on the journey that you make,
you would bring my gray hairs down
to Sheol in sorrow.'

The famine continued severe in the
land, so when they had finished eating
all the grain which they had brought
from Egypt, their father said to them,

'Go again, and buy us a little food.'

But Judah said to him,

'The man strictly warned us: "You
cannot have audience with me unless
your brother is with you." If you are
ready to let our brother go with us,
we will go down and buy food for
you; but if you are not ready to let
him go, we cannot go down; for the
man said to us, "You cannot have audience with me unless your brother is
with you." '

'Why did you bring this trouble on
me,' said Israel, 'by telling the man
that you had another brother?'

They said,

'The man persisted in asking about
ourselves and our family—"Is your
father still living? Have you another
brother?" We only gave him the information demanded by these questions of his. How could we possibly

he would say, "Bring your brother down"? '

And Judah said unto Israel his father,

'Send the lad with me, and we will arise and go; that we may live, and not die, both we, and thou, and also our little ones. I will be surety for him; of my hand shalt thou require him: if I bring him not unto thee, and set him before thee, then let me bear the blame for ever: for except we had lingered, surely now we had returned this second time.'

And their father Israel said unto them,

'If it must be so now, do this; take of the best fruits in the land in your vessels, and carry down the man a present, a little balm, and a little honey, spices, and myrrh, nuts, and almonds. And take double money in your hand; and the money that was brought again in the mouth of your sacks, carry it again in your hand; peradventure it was an oversight. Take also your brother, and arise, go again unto the man. And God Almighty give you mercy before the man, that he may send away your other brother, and Benjamin. If I be bereaved of my children, I am bereaved.'

And the men took that present, and they took double money in their hand, and Benjamin; and rose up, and went down to Egypt, and stood before Joseph. And when Joseph saw Benjamin with them, he said to the ruler of his house,

'Bring these men home, and slay, and make ready; for these men shall dine with me at noon.'

know that he would say, "Bring your brother down"?'

'Let the lad go with me,' said Judah to his father Israel; 'but we must go at once, if we would save our lives and not die, both we, you, and our dependents. I will be surety for him; you may hold me responsible for him. If I do not bring him back to you and set him before you, you may blame me for it all my life; in fact if we had not wasted so much time, we could have made a second trip by now.'

Then their father Israel said to them,

'If it must be so, then do this: take some of the country's best in your receptacles, and take it down to the man as a present—a little balm, a little honey, gum, laudanum, pistachio nuts, and almonds. Also take double the money with you, and so take back with you the money that was replaced in the mouths of your sacks—perhaps there was a mistake. Take your brother too, and go, return to the man. May God Almighty grant you such kindness with the man that he will release your other brother for you, as well as Benjamin. As for me, as I am bereaved, I am bereaved.'

So the men took this present, and taking double the money with them, as well as Benjamin, they started off, went down to Egypt, and stood in the presence of Joseph. When Joseph saw Benjamin with them, he said to his house-steward,

'Take the men home, kill an animal, and get it ready; for the men are to dine with me at noon.'

And the man did as Joseph bade; and the man brought the men into Joseph's house. And the men were afraid, because they were brought into Joseph's house; and they said,

'Because of the money that was returned in our sacks at the first time are we brought in; that he may seek occasion against us, and fall upon us, and take us for bondmen, and our asses.'

And they came near to the steward of Joseph's house, and they communed with him at the door of the house, and said,

'O sir, we came indeed down at the first time to buy food; and it came to pass, when we came to the inn, that we opened our sacks, and, behold, every man's money was in the mouth of his sack, our money in full weight: and we have brought it again in our hand. And other money have we brought down in our hands to buy food: we cannot tell who put our money in our sacks.'

And he said, 'Peace be to you, fear not: your God, and the God of your father, hath given you treasure in your sacks: I had your money.'

And he brought Simeon out unto them.

And the man brought the men into Joseph's house, and gave them water, and they washed their feet; and he gave their asses provender. And they made ready the present against Joseph came at noon; for they heard that they should eat bread there. And when Joseph came home, they brought him the present which was in their

The man did as Joseph said, and brought the men to Joseph's house. On being brought to Joseph's house, the men became frightened, saying,

'It is because of the money which reappeared in our sacks the first time that we are being brought in, so that he may devise some pretext against us, and falling upon us, take us into slavery, together with our asses.'

So they went up to Joseph's house-steward, and spoke to him at the doorway of the house.

'If you please, sir,' they said, 'we came down the first time specially to buy food, but when we reached the camping-place for the night, and opened our sacks, there was each man's money in the mouth of his sack —our money in full. Accordingly we have brought it back with us, and we have brought other money down with us to buy food. We do not know who put our money in our sacks.'

'Be at ease,' he said, 'do not be afraid! It must have been your God, the God of your fathers, who put treasure in your sacks for you. I received your money.'

Then he brought Simeon out to them.

After bringing the men into Joseph's house, the man gave them water to wash their feet, and he gave them fodder for their asses. Then they set out the present in anticipation of Joseph's arrival at noon; for they had heard that they were to dine there. When Joseph came home, they brought him the present that they had carried into hand into the house, and bowed themselves to him to the earth. And he asked them of their welfare, and said, 'Is your father well, the old man of whom ye spake? Is he yet alive?'

And they answered, 'Thy servant our father is in good health, he is yet alive.' And they bowed down their heads, and made obeisance.

And he lifted up his eyes, and saw his brother Benjamin, his mother's son, and said,

'Is this your younger brother, of whom ye spake unto me?'

And he said, 'God be gracious unto thee, my son.'

And Joseph made haste; for his bowels did yearn upon his brother: and he sought where to weep; and he entered into his chamber, and wept there. And he washed his face, and went out, and refrained himself and said,

'Set on bread.'

And they set on for him by himself, and for them by themselves, and for the Egyptians, which did eat with him, by themselves: because the Egyptians might not eat bread with the Hebrews; for that is an abomination unto the Egyptians. And they sat before him, the firstborn according to his birthright, and the youngest according to his youth: and the men marvelled one at another. And he took and sent messes unto them from before him: but Benjamin's mess was five times so much as any of theirs. And they drank, and were merry with him.

And he commanded the steward of his house, saying,

the house, and bowed to the ground before him. He asked after their health.

'Is your father well,' he said, 'the old man of whom you spoke? Is he still living?'

'Your servant, our father, is well; he is still living,' they said, bowing in homage to him.

Raising his eyes, he saw his brother Benjamin, the son of his own mother, and said,

'Is this your youngest brother, of whom you told me?'

'May God be gracious to you, my son!' he said.

Thereupon Joseph hastily sought a place to weep; for his heart was deeply stirred at sight of his brother; he retired to his room, and wept there. Then he bathed his face, and came out, and controlling himself, said,

'Serve the meal.'

The meal was served, separately for him, for them, and for the Egyptians that were dining with him; for the Egyptians could not eat with the Hebrews, because that would be abhorrent to the Egyptians. They were seated in his presence in order of age, from the oldest to the youngest, so that the men stared at one another in amazement. Portions were carried from his own table to them, but Benjamin's portion was five times as much as any other's. So they feasted, and drank with him.

He then gave orders to his house-steward,

'Fill the men's sacks with food, as much as they can carry, and put every man's money in his sack's mouth. And put my cup, the silver cup, in the sack's mouth of the youngest, and his corn money.'

And he did according to the word that Joseph had spoken.

As soon as the morning was light, the men were sent away, they and their asses. And when they were gone out of the city, and not yet far off, Joseph said unto his steward,

'Up, follow after the men; and when thou dost overtake them, say unto them, "Wherefore have ye rewarded evil for good? Is not this it in which my lord drinketh, and whereby indeed he divineth? ye have done evil in so doing." '

And he overtook them, and he spake unto them these same words. And they said unto him,

'Wherefore saith my lord these words? God forbid that thy servants should do according to this thing. Behold, the money, which we found in our sacks' mouths, we brought again unto thee out of the land of Canaan: how then should we steal out of thy lord's house silver or gold? With whomsoever of thy servants it be found, both let him die, and we also will be my lord's bondmen.'

And he said, 'Now also let it be according unto your words: he with whom it is found shall be my servant; and ye shall be blameless.'

Then they speedily took down every

'Fill the men's sacks as full as they will hold with food, and put each man's money in the mouth of his sack; in the mouth of the sack belonging to the youngest put my cup, the silver cup, along with his money for the grain.'

He followed the instructions which Joseph gave.

With the dawn of morning the men with their asses were sent on their way. Although they had left the city, they had not gone far, when Joseph said to his house-steward,

'Run at once after the men, and when you overtake them, say to them, "Why have you returned evil for good? Why have you stolen my silver cup? Is not this the one from which my lord drinks, which in fact he uses for divination? It is a wicked thing that you have done." '

So he overtook them, and addressed these words to them; but they said to him,

'Why should my lord speak like this? Your servants would never think of doing such a thing! Why, we even brought you back from the land of Canaan the money that we found in the mouths of our sacks. How then could we steal silver or gold from your master's house? That one of your servants in whose possession it is found shall die, and the rest of us will become slaves to my lord.'

'Although it may indeed be just as you say,' he said, 'yet the one in whose possession it is found shall become my slave, but the rest of you shall be held blameless.'

Then each of them quickly lowered

man his sack to the ground, and opened every man his sack. And he searched, and began at the eldest, and left at the youngest: and the cup was found in Benjamin's sack. Then they rent their clothes, and laded every man his ass, and returned to the city.

And Judah and his brethren came to Joseph's house; for he was yet there: and they fell before him on the ground.

And Joseph said unto them,

'What deed is this that ye have done? wot ye not that such a man as I can certainly divine?'

And Judah said,

'What shall we say unto my lord? what shall we speak? or how shall we clear ourselves? God hath found out the iniquity of thy servants: behold, we are my lord's servants, both we, and he also with whom the cup is found.'

And he said, 'God forbid that I should do so: but the man in whose hand the cup is found, he shall be my servant; and as for you, get you up in peace unto your father.'

Then Judah came near unto him, and said,

'Oh, my lord, let thy servant, I pray thee, speak a word in my lord's ears, and let not thine anger burn against thy servant: for thou art even as Pharaoh. My lord asked his servants, saying, "Have ye a father, or a brother?" And we said unto my lord, "We have a father, an old man, and a child of his old age, a little one; and his brother is dead, and he alone is left of his mother, and his father loveth him." And thou saidst unto thy

his sack to the ground, and opened it, and search being made, beginning with the oldest and ending with the youngest, the cup was found in Benjamin's sack. Thereupon they tore their clothes, and each having reloaded his ass, they returned to the city.

Judah and his brothers arrived at the house of Joseph, while he was still there, so they flung themselves on the ground before him.

'What is this that you have done?' Joseph said to them. 'Did you not know that a man like me would be sure to use divination?'

Judah said,

'What can we say to my lord? What can we urge? How can we prove our innocence? God has discovered the crime of your servants; here we are, the slaves of my lord, both we and he in whose possession the cup has been found.'

'I could not think of doing such a thing,' he said; 'only the man in whose possession the cup has been found shall be my slave; the rest of you are free to go back to your father.'

Then Judah went up to him, and said,

'If you please, my lord, let your servant speak a word in the ear of my lord, and your anger not blaze against your servant; for you are the equal of Pharaoh himself. My lord asked his servants, "Have you a father or a brother?" And we said to my lord, "We have an aged father, and a young brother, the child of his old age; his brother is dead, so that he alone is left of his mother's children, and his father loves him." Then you said to your servants, "Bring him down unto me, that I may set mine eyes upon him." And we said unto my lord, "The lad cannot leave his father: for if he should leave his father, his father would die." And thou saidst unto thy servants, "Except your youngest brother come down with you, ye shall see my face no more."

'And it came to pass when we came up unto thy servant my father, we told him the words of my lord. And our father said, "Go again, and buy us a little food." And we said, "We cannot go down: if our youngest brother be with us, then will we go down: for we may not see the man's face, except our youngest brother be with us." And thy servant my father said unto us, "Ye know that my wife bore me two sons; and the one went out from me, and I said, 'Surely he is torn in pieces'; and I saw him not since: and if ye take this also from me, and mischief befall him, ye shall bring down my gray hairs with sorrow to the grave."

'Now therefore when I come to thy servant my father, and the lad be not with us; seeing that his life is bound up in the lad's life; it shall come to pass, when he seeth that the lad is not with us, that he will die: and thy servants shall bring down the gray hairs of thy servant our father with sorrow to the grave. For thy servant became surety for the lad unto my father, saying, "If I bring him not unto thee, then I shall bear the blame to my father for ever." Now therefore, I pray thee, let thy servant abide in-

servants, "Bring him down to me that I may see him." But we told my lord, "The boy cannot leave his father; his father would die if he were to leave him." Whereupon you said to your servants, "Unless your youngest brother comes down with you, you cannot have audience with me again."

'When we went back to your servant, my father, we reported to him the words of my lord. Then our father said, "Go again and buy a little food for us." But we said, "We cannot go down; if our youngest brother accompanies us, we can go down; for we shall not be allowed to have audience with the man unless our youngest brother is with us." Then your servant, my father, said to us, "You know that my wife bore me only two children; then one of them left me, and I think he must surely have been torn to pieces; for I have never seen him since. If then you take this one from me too, and harm befall him, you will bring down my gray hairs to Sheol in trouble."

'And now, when I rejoin your servant, my father, and the boy not with us, his life is so bound up with the boy's that he will die when he sees that there is no boy, and your servants will bring down the gray hairs of your servant, our father, to Sheol in sorrow; for your servant went surety for the boy to my father, saying, "If I do not bring him back to you, let my father blame me for it all my life." Now then, pray let your servant remain in the boy's place as my lord's slave, but let the boy go back with his brothers;

stead of the lad a bondman to my lord; and let the lad go up with his brethren. For how shall I go up to my father, and the lad be not with me? lest peradventure I see the evil that shall come on my father.'

Then Joseph could not refrain himself before all them that stood by him; and he cried,

'Cause every man to go out from me.'

And there stood no man with him, while Joseph made himself known unto his brethren. And he wept aloud: and the Egyptians and the house of Pharaoh heard. And Joseph said unto his brethren,

'I am Joseph; doth my father yet live?'

And his brethren could not answer him; for they were troubled at his presence. And Joseph said unto his brethren,

'Come near to me, I pray you.'

And they came near. And he said, 'I am Joseph your brother, whom ye sold into Egypt. Now therefore be not grieved, nor angry with yourselves, that ye sold me hither: for God did send me before you to preserve life. For these two years hath the famine been in the land: and yet there are five years, in the which there shall neither be earing nor harvest. And God sent me before you to preserve you a posterity in the earth, and to save your lives by a great deliverance. So now it was not you that sent me hither, but God: and he hath made me a father to Pharaoh, and lord of all his house, and a ruler throughout all the land of Egypt. Haste ye, and

for how can I go back to my father unless the boy is with me, and witness the agony that would come to my father?'

Joseph could no longer control himself before all his attendants, so he cried out,

'Have everyone withdraw from me.'

So there was no one with Joseph when he made himself known to his brothers; but he wept so loudly that the Egyptians heard it, and Pharaoh's household heard it. Joseph said to his brothers,

'I am Joseph. Is my father still living?'

But his brothers could not answer him, because they were so dismayed at being in his presence. So Joseph said to his brothers,

'Come nearer to me.'

When they came nearer, he said, 'I am your brother Joseph whom you sold into Egypt. Now do not be distressed nor angry with yourselves that you sold me here; for it was to save life that God sent me ahead of you; for it is two years now that the famine has prevailed in the land, but there are still five years in which there will be no plowing or reaping. God sent me ahead of you to insure you a remnant in the earth, and to be the means of a remarkable escape for you. So then it was not you, but God who sent me here, and made me a father to Pharaoh, lord of all his house, and ruler over all the land of Egypt. Hurry back to my father and say to him,

go up to my father, and say unto him, "Thus saith thy son Joseph, 'God hath made me lord of all Egypt: come down unto me, tarry not: and thou shalt dwell in the land of Goshen, and thou shalt be near unto me, thou, and thy children, and thy children's children, and thy flocks, and thy herds, and all thou hast: and there will I nourish thee; for yet there are five years of famine; lest thou, and thy household, and all that thou hast, come to poverty.' " And, behold, your eyes see, and the eyes of my brother Benjamin, that it is my mouth that speaketh unto you. And ye shall tell my father of all my glory in Egypt, and of all that ye have seen; and ye shall haste and bring down my father hither.'

And he fell upon his brother Benjamin's neck, and wept; and Benjamin wept upon his neck. Moreover he kissed all his brethren, and wept upon them: and after that his brethren talked with him.

And the fame thereof was heard in Pharaoh's house, saying,

'Joseph's brethren are come': and it pleased Pharaoh well, and his servants. And Pharaoh said unto Joseph,

'Say unto thy brethren, "This do ye; lade your beasts, and go, get you unto the land of Canaan; and take your father and your households and come unto me: and I will give you the good of the land of Egypt, and ye shall eat the fat of the land. Now thou art commanded, this do ye; take your wagons out of the land of Egypt for your little ones, and for your wives, and bring your father, and come. Also

"Thus speaks your son Joseph: 'Since God has made me lord of all Egypt, come down to me without delay. You shall live in the land of Goshen, and be near me, you, your sons, your grandsons, your flocks, your herds, and all that belong to you; and there I will provide for you, lest you, your household, and all that belong to you come to want; for there are still five years of famine to come.' " You can see for yourselves and my brother Benjamin for himself that it is I who speak to you. You must tell my father all about my splendor in Egypt, and all that you have seen; hurry and bring my father here.'

Then he fell on the neck of his brother Benjamin and wept, while Benjamin wept on his neck. He kissed all his brothers, and wept on their shoulders, after which his brothers talked with him.

When the news was received at Pharaoh's palace that Joseph's brothers had arrived, Pharaoh was delighted, as were also his courtiers. Pharaoh said to Joseph,

'Say to your brothers, "Do this: load your animals, go back to the land of Canaan, and taking your father and your households, come to me, and I will give you the best of the land of Egypt, so that you shall eat the fat of the land. Also, carry out this order: take wagons from the land of Egypt for your little ones and your wives; convey your father in them, and come back. Never mind your goods; for the regard not your stuff; for the good of all the land of Egypt is yours." '

And the children of Israel did so: and Joseph gave them wagons, according to the commandment of Pharaoh, and gave them provisions for the way. To all of them he gave each man changes of raiment; but to Benjamin he gave three hundred pieces of silver, and five changes of raiment. And to his father he sent after this manner; ten asses laden with the good things of Egypt, and ten she-asses laden with corn and bread and meat for his father by the way. So he sent his brethren away, and they departed: and he said unto them,

'See that ye fall not out by the way.'

And they went up out of Egypt, and came into the land of Canaan unto Jacob their father, and told him, saying,

'Joseph is yet alive, and he is governor over all the land of Egypt.'

And Jacob's heart fainted, for he believed them not. And they told him all the words of Joseph, which he had said unto them: and when he saw the wagons which Joseph had sent to carry him, the spirit of Jacob their father revived. And Israel said,

'It is enough; Joseph my son is yet alive: I will go and see him before I die.'

And Israel took his journey with all that he had, and came to Beer-sheba, and offered sacrifices unto the God of his father Isaac. And God spake unto Israel in the visions of the night, and said, 'Jacob, Jacob.'

And he said, 'Here am I.'

And he said, 'I am God, the God of

best of the whole land of Egypt will be yours." '

The sons of Israel did so. Joseph gave them wagons in accord with the command of Pharaoh, and he also gave them provisions for the journey. To each of them he gave a festal garment, but to Benjamin he gave three hundred shekels of silver and five festal garments. To his father he sent likewise ten asses loaded with the best products of Egypt, and ten she-asses loaded with grain, bread, and provisions for his father on the journey. Then he sent his brothers away; and as they left, he said to them,

'Do not get too excited on the way.'

So they went up from Egypt, and came to the land of Canaan, to their father Jacob.

'Joseph is still living, and he is ruler over all the land of Egypt,' they told him.

But he was so stunned that he would not believe them. However, when they told him all that Joseph had said to them, and he saw the wagons that Joseph had sent to convey him, their father Jacob recovered.

'Enough!' said Israel; 'my son Joseph is still living; I will go and see him before I die.'

So Israel set out with all that belonged to him. On reaching Beer-sheba, he offered sacrifices to the God of his father Isaac. In a vision by night God spoke to Israel.

'Jacob! Jacob!' he said.

'Here I am,' he said.

'I am El, the God of your father,'

thy father: fear not to go down into Egypt; for I will there make of thee a great nation: I will go down with thee into Egypt; and I will also surely bring thee up again: and Joseph shall put his hand upon thine eyes.'

And Jacob rose up from Beer-sheba: and the sons of Israel carried Jacob their father, and their little ones, and their wives, in the wagons which Pharaoh had sent to carry him. And they took their cattle, and their goods, which they had gotten in the land of Canaan, and came into Egypt, Jacob, and all his seed with him: his sons, and his sons' sons with him, his daughters, and his sons' daughters, and all his seed brought he with him into Egypt.

And he sent Judah before him unto Joseph, to direct his face unto Goshen; and they came into the land of Goshen. And Joseph made ready his chariot, and went up to meet Israel his father, to Goshen, and presented himself unto him; and he fell on his neck, and wept on his neck a good while.

And Israel said unto Joseph, 'Now let me die, since I have seen thy face, because thou art yet alive.'

And Joseph said unto his brethren, and unto his father's house,

'I will go up, and shew Pharaoh, and say unto him, "My brethren, and my father's house, which were in the land of Canaan, are come unto me; and the men are shepherds, for their trade hath been to feed cattle; and they have brought their flocks, and their herds, and all that they have." And it shall come to pass, when Pha-

he said; 'do not be afraid to go down to Egypt; for there I will make you a great nation. I will myself go down to Egypt with you—yes, and I will bring you up again, when Joseph's hand shall close your eyes.'

Then Jacob set out from Beersheba; and the sons of Israel conveyed their father Jacob, with their little ones and their wives, in the wagons which Pharaoh had sent to convey him. Taking their live stock and the property which they had acquired in the land of Canaan, Jacob and all his family migrated to Egypt; his sons and his grandsons accompanied him, as well as his daughters and his grand-daughters; he brought all his family with him into Egypt.

Israel sent Judah ahead of him to Joseph in Goshen, to appear before him. On their arrival in the land of Goshen Joseph hitched the horses to his chariot, and went up to meet his father Israel in Goshen. When he presented himself to him, he fell on his neck, weeping again and again on his neck.

'Now at last I may die,' Israel said to Joseph, 'after having seen from your very self that you are still alive.'

Then Joseph said to his brothers and his father's household,

'I will go and tell Pharaoh, and say to him, "My brothers and my father's household who used to live in the land of Canaan have come to me. Since the men are shepherds, having to do with live stock, they have brought their flocks and herds and everything that they own." Accordingly, when Pharaoh summons you, and says to you,

raoh shall call you, and shall say,
"What is your occupation?" that ye
shall say, "Thy servants' trade hath
been about cattle from our youth even
until now, both we, and also our
fathers": that ye may dwell in the
land of Goshen; for every shepherd is
an abomination unto the Egyptians.'

Then Joseph came and told Pharaoh, and said,

'My father and my brethren, and
their flocks, and their herds, and all
that they have, are come out of the
land of Canaan; and, behold, they are
in the land of Goshen.'

And he took some of his brethren,
even five men, and presented them
unto Pharaoh.

And Pharaoh said unto his brethren, 'What is your occupation?'

And they said unto Pharaoh, 'Thy
servants are shepherds, both we, and
also our fathers.' They said moreover
unto Pharaoh, 'For to sojourn in the
land are we come; for thy servants
have no pasture for their flocks; for
the famine is sore in the land of Canaan: now therefore, we pray thee, let
thy servants dwell in the land of
Goshen.'

And Pharaoh spake unto Joseph,
saying,

'Thy father and thy brethren are
come unto thee: The land of Egypt is
before thee; in the best of the land
make thy father and brethren to dwell;
in the land of Goshen let them dwell:
and if thou knowest any men of activity among them, then make them
rulers over my cattle.'

And Joseph brought in Jacob his

"What is your occupation?" you must
say, "Your servants have been concerned with live stock from our youth
until now, both we and our fathers"
—in order that you may settle in the
land of Goshen; for shepherds are all
abhorrent to the Egyptians.'

So Joseph came and told Pharaoh.

'My father and brothers,' he said,
'together with their flocks and herds
and everything that they own, have
come from the land of Canaan, and
are now in the land of Goshen.'

Taking five of the ablest of his
brothers, he presented them to Pharaoh.

'What is your occupation?' Pharaoh said to his brothers.

'Your servants are shepherds,' they
said to Pharaoh, 'both we and our
fathers. We have come to settle as
immigrants in the land,' they said to
Pharaoh; 'for there is no pasture for
the flocks belonging to your servants,
because the famine is so severe in the
land of Canaan. Pray let your servants
settle, then, in the land of Goshen.'

Then Pharaoh said to Joseph,

'Now that your father and brothers
have joined you, the land of Egypt is
at your disposal; settle your father and
brothers in the best part of the land;
let them settle in the land of Goshen,
and if you know of any competent
men among them, put them in charge
of my own live stock.'

Then Joseph brought his father Ja-

father, and set him before Pharaoh: and Jacob blessed Pharaoh.

And Pharaoh said unto Jacob, 'How old art thou?'

And Jacob said unto Pharaoh, 'The days of the years of my pilgrimage are an hundred and thirty years: few and evil have the days of the years of my life been, and have not attained unto the days of the years of the life of my fathers in the days of their pilgrimage.'

And Jacob blessed Pharaoh, and went out from before Pharaoh.

And Joseph placed his father and his brethren, and gave them a possession in the land of Egypt, in the best of the land, in the land of Rameses, as Pharaoh had commanded. And Joseph nourished his father, and his brethren, and all his father's household, with bread, according to their families.

And there was no bread in all the land; for the famine was very sore, so that the land of Egypt and all the land of Canaan fainted by reason of the famine. And Joseph gathered up all the money that was found in the land of Egypt, and in the land of Canaan, for the corn which they bought: and Joseph brought the money into Pharaoh's house. And when money failed in the land of Egypt, and in the land of Canaan, all the Egyptians came unto Joseph, and said,

'Give us bread: for why should we die in thy presence? for the money faileth.'

cob and presented him to Pharaoh, and Jacob paid his respects to Pharaoh.

'How old are you?' Pharaoh said to Jacob.

'The length of my life as an immigrant has been one hundred and thirty years,' Jacob said to Pharaoh; 'few and hard have been the years of my life; they have not equaled the number of years that my fathers lived in their lifetime as immigrants.'

After paying his respects to Pharaoh, Jacob withdrew from the presence of Pharaoh.

So Joseph settled his father and brothers, giving them property in the land of Egypt in the very best part of the land, in the land of Rameses, as Pharaoh had commanded. Joseph provided his father and brothers and all his father's household with food sufficient for the needs of the dependents.

There was now no food anywhere in the land; for the famine was very severe, so that the lands of Egypt and Canaan were languishing because of the famine. Joseph had gathered up all the money that was to be found in the lands of Egypt and Canaan in payment for the grain which was bought, and had brought the money to Pharaoh's palace. So when the money was exhausted in the lands of Egypt and Canaan, all the Egyptians came to Joseph, saying,

'Give us food; why should we die right under your eyes, just because our money is gone?'

And Joseph said, 'Give your cattle; and I will give you for your cattle, if money fail.'

And they brought their cattle unto Joseph: and Joseph gave them bread in exchange for horses, and for the flocks, and for the cattle of the herds, and for the asses: and he fed them with bread for all their cattle for that year.

When that year was ended, they came unto him the second year, and said unto him,

'We will not hide it from my lord, how that our money is spent; my lord also hath our herds of cattle; there is not ought left in the sight of my lord, but our bodies, and our lands: wherefore shall we die before thine eyes, both we and our land? buy us and our land for bread, and we and our land will be servants unto Pharaoh: and give us seed, that we may live, and not die, that the land be not desolate.'

And Joseph bought all the land of Egypt for Pharaoh; for the Egyptians sold every man his field, because the famine prevailed over them: so the land became Pharaoh's. And as for the people, he removed them to cities from one end of the borders of Egypt even to the other end thereof. Only the land of the priests bought he not; for the priests had a portion assigned them of Pharaoh, and did eat their portion which Pharaoh gave them: wherefore they sold not their lands.

Then Joseph said unto the people, 'Behold, I have bought you this day and your land for Pharaoh: lo, here is

'Give me your live stock,' said Joseph; 'I will give you food in exchange for your live stock, if your money is gone.'

So they brought their live stock to Joseph, and Joseph gave them food in exchange for horses, sheep, cattle, and asses; thus he supported them with food that year in exchange for all their live stock.

When that year was over, they came to him the next year, and said to him,

'We would hide nothing from my lord; but our money is gone, and our live stock has come into the possession of my lord; there is nothing left for my lord except our persons and our lands. Why should we perish before your very eyes, both we and our land? Buy us and our land in exchange for food, and we and our land shall become feudatory to Pharaoh; but give us seed that we may live and not die, and the land not become a waste.'

So Joseph bought all the land of Egypt for Pharaoh; for everyone of the Egyptians sold his field, because the famine was so severe on them. Thus the land became Pharaoh's, and the people themselves he transferred to the towns from one end of Egypt's domain to the other. It was only the priests' land that he did not buy; for the priests had a subvention from Pharaoh, and lived off the subvention which Pharaoh gave them; that was why they did not have to sell their land.

'Observe,' said Joseph to the people, 'that I have today bought you and your land for Pharaoh. Here is seed

seed for you, and ye shall sow the land. And it shall come to pass in the increase, that ye shall give the fifth part unto Pharaoh, and four parts shall be your own, for seed of the field, and for your food, and for them of your household, and for food for your little ones.'

And they said, 'Thou hast saved our lives: let us find grace in the sight of my lord, and we will be Pharaoh's servants.'

And Joseph made it a law over the land of Egypt unto this day, that Pharaoh should have the fifth part; except the land of the priests only, which became not Pharaoh's.

And Israel dwelt in the land of Egypt, in the country of Goshen; and they had possessions therein, and grew, and multiplied exceedingly.

And Jacob lived in the land of Egypt seventeen years: so that the whole age of Jacob was an hundred forty and seven years.

for you to sow the land; a fifth of the crop you shall give to Pharaoh, and four fifths shall go to yourselves as seed for the fields, and as food for yourselves and your households, and as food for your little ones.'

'You have saved our lives,' they said, 'we would thank my lord; and we will becomes slaves to Pharaoh.'

So Joseph made it a statute for the land in Egypt, which continues to this day, that a fifth of the produce should go to Pharaoh, the land of the priests alone being exempt from Pharaoh's claims.

So the Israelites settled in the land of Egypt, in the land of Goshen, where they acquired property, were prolific, and became very numerous.

Jacob lived in the land of Egypt for seventeen years, so that the length of Jacob's life was one hundred and forty-seven years.

John Henry Newman
LIBERAL KNOWLEDGE

❲ In 1852 Newman published *Discourses on the Scope and Nature of University Education, Addressed to the Catholics of Dublin*. These discourses he delivered after he had been appointed Rector of the Irish Catholic University, to which he devoted seven years of his life and for which he had high hopes, although they finally came to nothing. In 1859 he revised the *Discourses* and limited the title to *The Scope and Nature of University Education*. In 1873 he made further changes and added ten essays, dividing the book into 'University Teaching' and 'University Essays,' and gave the volume the title of *The Idea of a University*.

Newman's conception of a university was in some respects startlingly unlike that prevalent today. He thought of it mainly as a place of teaching. It was not, for him, a place of research, least of all scientific research. On the other hand, his idea of liberal knowledge, of intellectual training for its own sake, was one that is as valid today as ever. He held that the main object of liberal education is not morality or religion. Its function is to train the mind. As Woodrow Wilson once said when he was president of Princeton, 'The object of a university is intellect; as a university its only object is intellect.' Newman insists that liberal education, philosophy in short, is an end worth pursuing for itself. Religion and morality are more urgent, but they are the province of other agencies than the university.

I

. . . KNOWLEDGE is one thing, virtue is another; good sense is not conscience, refinement is not humility, nor is largeness and justness of view faith. Philosophy, however enlightened, however profound, gives no command over the passions, no influential motives, no vivifying principles.

FROM *The Idea of a University*, 1852, 1859, 1873.

Liberal Education makes not the Christian, not the Catholic, but the gentleman. It is well to be a gentleman, it is well to have a cultivated intellect, a delicate taste, a candid, equitable, dispassionate mind, a noble and courteous bearing in the conduct of life;—these are the connatural qualities of a large knowledge; they are the objects of a University; I am advocating, I shall illustrate and insist upon them; but still, I repeat, they are no guarantee for sanctity or even for conscientiousness, they may attach to the man of the world, to the profligate, to the heartless,—pleasant, alas, and attractive as he shows when decked out in them. Taken by themselves, they do but seem to be what they are not; they look like virtue at a distance, but they are detected by close observers, and on the long run; and hence it is that they are popularly accused of pretence and hypocrisy, not, I repeat, from their own fault, but because their professors and their admirers persist in taking them for what they are not, and are officious in arrogating for them a praise to which they have no claim. Quarry the granite rock with razors, or moor the vessel with a thread of silk; then may you hope with such keen and delicate instruments as human knowledge and human reason to contend against those giants, the passion and the pride of man.

Surely we are not driven to theories of this kind, in order to vindicate the value and dignity of Liberal Knowledge. Surely the real grounds on which its pretensions rest are not so very subtle or abstruse, so very strange or improbable. Surely it is very intelligible to say, and that is what I say here, that Liberal Education, viewed in itself, is simply the cultivation of the intellect, as such, and its object is nothing more or less than intellectual excellence. Every thing has its own perfection, be it higher or lower in the scale of things; and the perfection of one is not the perfection of another. Things animate, inanimate, visible, invisible, all are good in their kind, and have a *best* of themselves, which is an object of pursuit. Why do you take such pains with your garden or your park? You see to your walks and turf and shrubberies; to your trees and drives; not as if you meant to make an orchard of the one, or corn or pasture land of the other, but because there is a special beauty in all that is goodly in wood, water, plain, and slope, brought all together by art into one shape, and grouped into one whole. Your cities are beautiful, your palaces, your public buildings, your territorial mansions, your churches; and their beauty leads to nothing beyond itself. There is a physical beauty and a moral: there is a beauty of person, there is a beauty of our moral being, which is natural virtue; and in like manner there is a beauty, there is a perfection, of the intellect. There is an ideal perfection in these various subject-matters, towards which individual instances are seen to rise, and which are the standards for all instances whatever. The Greek divinities and demigods, as the statuary has moulded them, with their symmetry of figure, and their high forehead and their regular features, are the perfection of physical beauty. The heroes, of whom history tells, Alexander, or Cæsar, or Scipio, or Saladin, are the representatives of that magnanimity or self-mastery which is the greatness of human nature. Christianity too has its heroes, and in the supernatural order, and we call them Saints. The artist puts before him beauty of feature and form; the poet, beauty of mind; the preacher, the beauty of grace: then intellect too, I repeat, has its beauty, and it has those who aim at it. To open the mind, to correct it, to refine it, to enable it to know, and to digest, master, rule, and use its knowledge, to give it power over its own faculties, application, flexibility, method, critical exactness, sagacity, resource, address, eloquent expression, is an object as intelligible (for here we are inquiring, not what the object of a Liberal Education is worth, nor what use the Church makes of it, but what it is in itself), I say, an object as intelligible as the cultivation of virtue, while, at the same time, it is absolutely distinct from it.

This indeed is but a temporal object, and a transitory possession; but so are other things in themselves which we make much of and pursue. The moralist will tell us that man, in all his functions, is but a flower which blossoms and fades, except so far as a higher principle breathes upon him, and makes him and what he is immortal. Body and mind are carried on into an eternal state of being by the gifts of Divine Munificence; but at first they do but fail in a failing world; and if the powers of intellect decay, the powers of the body have decayed before them, and, as an Hospital or an Almshouse, though its end be ephemeral, may be sanctified to the service of religion, so surely may a University, even were it nothing more than I have as yet described it. We attain to heaven by using this world well, though it is to pass away; we perfect our nature, not by undoing it, but by adding to it what is more than nature, and directing it towards aims higher than its own. . .

II

. . . That training of the intellect, which is best for the individual himself, best enables him to discharge his duties to society. The Philosopher, indeed, and the man of the world differ in their very notion, but the methods, by which they are respectively formed, are pretty much the same.

The Philosopher has the same command of matters of thought, which the true citizen and gentleman has of matters of business and conduct. If then a practical end must be assigned to a University course, I say it is that of training good members of society. Its art is the art of social life, and its end is fitness for the world. It neither confines its views to particular professions on the one hand, nor creates heroes or inspires genius on the other. Works indeed of genius fall under no art; heroic minds come under no rule; a University is not a birthplace of poets or of immortal authors, of founders ot schools, leaders of colonies, or conquerors of nations. It does not promise a generation of Aristotles or Newtons, of Napoleons or Washingtons, of Raphaels or Shakespeares, though such miracles of nature it has before now contained within its precincts. Nor is it content on the other hand with forming the critic or the experimentalist, the economist or the engineer, though such too it includes within its scope. But a University training is the great ordinary means to a great but ordinary end; it aims at raising the intellectual tone of society, at cultivating the public mind, at purifying the national taste, at supplying true principles to popular enthusiasm and fixed aims to popular aspiration, at giving enlargement and sobriety to the ideas of the age, at facilitating the exercise of political power, and refining the intercourse of private life. It is the education which gives a man a clear conscious view of his own opinions and judgments, a truth in developing them, an eloquence in expressing them, and a force in urging them. It teaches him to see things as they are, to go right to the point, to disentangle a skein of thought, to detect what is sophistical, and to discard what is irrelevant. It prepares him to fill any post with credit, and to master any subject with facility. It shows him how to accommodate himself to others, how to throw himself into their state of mind, how to bring before them his own, how to influence them, how to come to an understanding with them, how to bear with them. He is at home in any society, he has common ground with every class; he knows when to speak and when to be silent; he is able to converse, he is able to listen; he can ask a question pertinently, and gain a lesson seasonably, when he has nothing to impart himself; he is ever ready, yet never in the way; he is a pleasant companion, and a comrade you can depend upon; he knows when to be serious and when to trifle, and he has a sure tact which enables him to trifle with gracefulness and to be serious with effect. He has the repose of a mind which lives in itself, while it lives in the world, and which has resources for its happiness at home when it cannot go abroad. He has a gift which serves him in public, and supports him in retirement, without which good fortune is but vulgar, and with which failure and disappointment have a charm. The art which tends to make a man all this, is in the object which it pursues as useful as the art of wealth or the art of health, though it is less susceptible of method, and less tangible, less certain, less complete in its result. . .

III

. . . At this day the 'gentleman' is the creation, not of Christianity, but of civilization. But the reason is obvious. The world is content with setting right the surface of things; the Church aims at regenerating the very depths of the heart. She ever begins with the beginning; and, as regards the multitude of her children, is never able to get beyond the beginning, but is continually employed in laying the foundation. She is engaged with what is essential, as previous and as introductory to the ornamental and the attractive. She is curing men and keeping them clear of mortal sin; she is 'treating of justice and chastity, and the judgment to come:' she is insisting on faith and hope, and devotion, and honesty, and the elements of charity; and has so much to do with precept, that she almost leaves it to inspirations from Heaven to suggest what is of counsel and perfection. She aims at what is necessary rather than at what is desirable. She is for the many as well as for the few. She is putting souls in the way of salvation, that they may then be in a condition, if they shall be called upon, to aspire to the heroic, and to attain the full proportions, as well as the rudiments, of the beautiful.

Such is the method, or the policy (so to call it), of the Church; but Philosophy looks at the matter from a very different point of view: what have Philosophers to do with the terror of judgment or the saving of the soul? Lord Shaftesbury [1] calls the former a sort of 'panic fear.' Of the latter he scoffingly complains that 'the saving of souls is now the heroic passion of exalted spirits.' Of course he is at liberty, on his principles, to pick and choose out of Christianity what he will; he discards the theological, the mysterious, the spiritual; he makes selection of the morally or esthetically beautiful. To him it matters not at all that he begins his teaching where he should end it; it matters not that, instead of planting the tree, he merely crops its flowers for his banquet; he only aims at the present life, his philosophy dies with him; if his flowers do but last to the end of his

---

[1 English philosopher (1671–1713). He held that virtue is a kind of beauty and is therefore governable by taste. Newman criticizes his opinions in the chapter from which this excerpt is taken, 'Liberal Knowledge Viewed in Relation to Religion.']

revel, he has nothing more to seek. When night comes, the withered leaves may be mingled with his own ashes; he and they will have done their work, he and they will be no more. Certainly, it costs little to make men virtuous on conditions such as these; it is like teaching them a language or an accomplishment, to write Latin or to play on an instrument,—the profession of an artist, not the commission of an Apostle.

This embellishment of the exterior is almost the beginning and the end of philosophical morality. This is why it aims at being modest rather than humble; this is how it can be proud at the very time that it is unassuming. To humility indeed it does not even aspire; humility is one of the most difficult of virtues both to attain and to ascertain. It lies close upon the heart itself, and its tests are exceedingly delicate and subtle. Its counterfeits abound; however, we are little concerned with them here, for, I repeat, it is hardly professed even by name in the code of ethics which we are reviewing. As has been often observed, ancient civilization had not the idea, and had no word to express it: or rather, it had the idea, and considered it a defect of mind, not a virtue, so that the word which denoted it conveyed a reproach. As to the modern world, you may gather its ignorance of it by its perversion of the somewhat parallel term 'condescension.' Humility or condescension, viewed as a virtue of conduct, may be said to consist, as in other things, so in our placing ourselves in our thoughts on a level with our inferiors; it is not only a voluntary relinquishment of the privileges of our own station, but an actual participation or assumption of the condition of those to whom we stoop. This is true humility, to feel and to behave as if we were low; not, to cherish a notion of our importance, while we affect a low position. Such was St. Paul's humility,[2] when he called himself 'the least of the saints;' such the humility of those many holy men who have considered themselves the greatest of sinners. It is an abdication, as far as their own thoughts are concerned, of those prerogatives or privileges to which others deem them entitled. Now it is not a little instructive to contrast with this idea, Gentlemen,—with this theological meaning of the word 'condescension,'—its proper English sense; put them in juxta-position, and you will at once see the difference between the world's humility and the humility of the Gospel. As the world uses the word, 'condescension' is a stooping indeed of the person, but a bending forward, unattended with any the slightest effort to leave by a single inch the seat in which it is so firmly established. It is the act of a superior, who protests to himself, while he commits it, that he is superior still, and that he is doing nothing else

[2 See Ephesians, iii, 8.]

but an act of grace towards those on whose level, in theory, he is placing himself. And this is the nearest idea which the philosopher can form of the virtue of self-abasement; to do more than this is to his mind a meanness or an hypocrisy, and at once excites his suspicion and disgust. What the world is, such it has ever been; we know the contempt which the educated pagans had for the martyrs and confessors of the Church; and it is shared by the anti-Catholic bodies of this day.

Such are the ethics of Philosophy, when faithfully represented; but an age like this, not pagan, but professedly Christian, cannot venture to reprobate humility in set terms, or to make a boast of pride. Accordingly, it looks out for some expedient by which it may blind itself to the real state of the case. Humility, with its grave and self-denying attributes, it cannot love; but what is more beautiful, what more winning, than modesty? what virtue, at first sight, simulates humility so well? though what in fact is more radically distinct from it? In truth, great as is its charm, modesty is not the deepest or the most religious of virtues. Rather it is the advanced guard or sentinel of the soul militant, and watches continually over its nascent intercourse with the world about it. It goes the round of the senses; it mounts up into the countenance; it protects the eye and ear; it reigns in the voice and gesture. Its province is the outward deportment, as other virtues have relation to matters theological, others to society, and others to the mind itself. And being more superficial than other virtues, it is more easily disjoined from their company; it admits of being associated with principles or qualities naturally foreign to it, and is often made the cloak of feelings or ends for which it was never given to us. So little is it the necessary index of humility, that it is even compatible with pride. The better for the purpose of Philosophy; humble it cannot be, so forthwith modesty becomes its humility.

Pride, under such training, instead of running to waste in the education of the mind, is turned to account; it gets a new name; it is called self-respect; and ceases to be the disagreeable, uncompanionable quality which it is in itself. Though it be the motive principle of the soul, it seldom comes to view; and when it shows itself, then delicacy and gentleness are its attire, and good sense and sense of honour direct its motions. It is no longer a restless agent, without definite aim; it has a large field of exertion assigned to it, and it subserves those social interests which it would naturally trouble. It is directed into the channel of industry, frugality, honesty, and obedience; and it becomes the very staple of the religion and morality held in honour in a day like our own. It becomes the safeguard of chastity, the guarantee of veracity, in high and low; it is the very household god of society, as at present constituted, inspiring neatness and decency in the servant girl, propriety of carriage and refined manners in her mistress, uprightness, manliness, and generosity in the head of the family. It diffuses a light over town and country; it covers the soil with handsome edifices and smiling gardens; it tills the field, it stocks and embellishes the shop. It is the stimulating principle of providence on the one hand, and of free expenditure on the other; of an honourable ambition, and of elegant enjoyment. It breathes upon the face of the community, and the hollow sepulchre is forthwith beautiful to look upon.

Refined by the civilization which has brought it into activity, this self-respect infuses into the mind an intense horror of exposure, and a keen sensitiveness of notoriety and ridicule. It becomes the enemy of extravagances of any kind; it shrinks from what are called scenes; it has no mercy on the mock-heroic, on pretence or egotism, on verbosity in language, or what is called prosiness in conversation. It detests gross adulation; not that it tends at all to the eradication of the appetite to which the flatterer ministers, but it sees the absurdity of indulging it, it understands the annoyance thereby given to others, and if a tribute must be paid to the wealthy or the powerful, it demands greater subtlety and art in the preparation. Thus vanity is changed into a more dangerous self-conceit, as being checked in its natural eruption. It teaches men to suppress their feelings, and to control their tempers, and to mitigate both the severity and the tone of their judgments. As Lord Shaftesbury would desire, it prefers playful wit and satire in putting down what is objectionable, as a more refined and good-natured, as well as a more effectual method, than the expedient which is natural to uneducated minds. It is from this impatience of the tragic and the bombastic that it is now quietly but energetically opposing itself to the unchristian practice of duelling, which it brands as simply out of taste, and as the remnant of a barbarous age; and certainly it seems likely to effect what Religion has aimed at abolishing in vain.

Hence it is that it is almost a definition of a gentleman to say he is one who never inflicts pain. This description is both refined and, as far as it goes, accurate. He is mainly occupied in merely removing the obstacles which hinder the free and unembarrassed action of those about him; and he concurs with their movements rather than takes the initiative himself. His benefits may be considered as parallel to what are called comforts or conveniences in arrangements of a personal nature: like an easy chair or a good fire, which do their part in dispelling cold and fatigue, though nature

provides both means of rest and animal heat without them. The true gentleman in like manner carefully avoids whatever may cause a jar or a jolt in
the minds of those with whom he is cast;—all clashing of opinion, or col-
lision of feeling, all restraint, or suspicion, or gloom, or resentment; his
great concern being to make every one at their ease and at home. He has
his eyes on all his company; he is tender towards the bashful, gentle
towards the distant, and merciful towards the absurd; he can recollect to
whom he is speaking; he guards against unseasonable allusions, or topics
which may irritate; he is seldom prominent in conversation, and never
wearisome. He makes light of favours while he does them, and seems to be
receiving when he is conferring. He never speaks of himself except when
compelled, never defends himself by a mere retort, he has no ears for slan-
der or gossip, is scrupulous in imputing motives to those who interfere with
him, and interprets every thing for the best. He is never mean or little in
his disputes, never takes unfair advantage, never mistakes personalities or
sharp sayings for arguments, or insinuates evil which he dare not say out.
From a long-sighted prudence, he observes the maxim of the ancient sage,[3]
that we should ever conduct ourselves towards our enemy as if he were one
day to be our friend. He has too much good sense to be affronted at insults,
he is too well employed to remember injuries, and too indolent to bear
malice. He is patient, forbearing, and resigned, on philosophical principles;
he submits to pain, because it is inevitable, to bereavement, because it is
irreparable, and to death, because it is his destiny. If he engages in controversy of any kind, his disciplined intellect preserves him from the blunder-
ing discourtesy of better, perhaps, but less educated minds; who, like blunt
weapons, tear and hack instead of cutting clean, who mistake the point in
argument, waste their strength on trifles, misconceive their adversary, and
leave the question more involved than they find it. He may be right or
wrong in his opinion, but he is too clear-headed to be unjust; he is as simple
as he is forcible, and as brief as he is decisive. Nowhere shall we find greater
candour, consideration, indulgence: he throws himself into the minds of
his opponents, he accounts for their mistakes. He knows the weakness of
human reason as well as its strength, its province and its limits. If he be an
unbeliever, he will be too profound and large-minded to ridicule religion
or to act against it; he is too wise to be a dogmatist or fanatic in his infidel-
ity. He respects piety and devotion; he even supports institutions as venerable, beautiful, or useful, to which he does not assent; he honours the min-

[3 This maxim is attributed to Bias of Pirene, one of the Seven Sages of ancient
Greece.]

isters of religion, and it contents him to decline its mysteries without assail-
ing or denouncing them. He is a friend of religious toleration, and that, not
only because his philosophy has taught him to look on all forms of faith
with an impartial eye, but also from the gentleness and effeminacy of feeling, which is the attendant on civilization.

Matthew Arnold

LITERATURE AND SCIENCE

❰ Arnold's 'Literature and Science' is a powerful defense of the
role of letters in education. T. H. Huxley's 'Science and Culture,'
to which it is in part a reply, was an equally clear and astute argument for the educational value of physical science. To judge merely
by the present ratio of students of Greek to students of physics,
Huxley was at least the better prophet; yet we hear many voices
warning us that the need for the humanities was never greater than
it is now. In considering such questions we need to read the 'best
that has been thought and said' about them. Arnold's essay is a
contribution we should not omit.

'Literature and Science' was originally a lecture delivered at the
University of Cambridge. Arnold revised it for his American lecture
tour of 1883–4 and afterwards published it in *Discourses in America*. The text printed here is this revised one.

P

RACTICAL people [1] talk with a smile of Plato and of his absolute ideas; and it is impossible to deny that Plato's ideas do often seem
unpractical and impracticable, and especially when one views them in connection with the life of a great work-a-day world like the United States.
The necessary staple of the life of such a world Plato regards with disdain;
handicraft and trade and the working professions he regards with disdain;
but what becomes of the life of an industrial modern community if you
take handicraft and trade and the working professions out of it? The base
mechanic arts and handicrafts, says Plato, bring about a natural weakness
in the principle of excellence in a man, so that he cannot govern the ignoble
growths in him, but nurses them, and cannot understand fostering any
other. Those who exercise such arts and trades, as they have their bodies, he

[1 See the selection by Macaulay, pp. 547–55.]
FROM *Discourses in America*, 1885.

says, marred by their vulgar businesses, so they have their souls, too, bowed and broken by them. And if one of these uncomely people has a mind to seek self-culture and philosophy, Plato compares him to a bald little tinker,[2] who has scraped together money, and has got his release from service, and has had a bath, and bought a new coat, and is rigged out like a bridegroom about to marry the daughter of his master who has fallen into poor and helpless estate.

Nor do the working professions fare any better than trade at the hands of Plato. He draws for us an inimitable picture of the working lawyer, and of his life of bondage; he shows how this bondage from his youth up has stunted and warped him, and made him small and crooked of soul, encompassing him with difficulties which he is not man enough to rely on justice and truth as means to encounter, but has recourse, for help out of them, to falsehood and wrong. And so, says Plato, this poor creature is bent and broken, and grows up from boy to man without a particle of soundness in him, although exceedingly smart and clever in his own esteem.

One cannot refuse to admire the artist who draws these pictures. But we say to ourselves that his ideas show the influence of a primitive and obso- lete order of things, when the warrior caste and the priestly caste were alone in honour and the humble work of the world was done by slaves. We have now changed all that; the modern majority consists in work, as Emerson declares; and in work, we may add, principally of such plain and dusty kind as the work of cultivators of the ground, handicraftsmen, men of trade and business, men of the working professions. Above all is this true in a great industrious community such as that of the United States.

Now education, many people go on to say, is still mainly governed by the ideas of men like Plato, who lived when the warrior caste and the priestly or philosophical class were alone in honour, and the really useful part of the community were slaves. It is an education fitted for persons of leisure in such a community. This education passed from Greece and Rome to the feudal communities of Europe, where also the warrior caste and the priestly caste were alone held in honour and where the really useful and working part of the community, though not nominally slaves as in the pagan world, were practically not much better off than slaves, and not more seriously regarded. And how absurd it is, people end by saying, to inflict this education upon an industrious modern community, where very few indeed are persons of leisure, and the mass to be considered has not leisure, but is bound, for its own great good, and for the great good of the world at

[2 See Plato's *Republic*, VI, 495.]

large, to plain labour and to industrial pursuits, and the education in question tends necessarily to make men dissatisfied with these pursuits and unfitted for them!

That is what is said. So far I must defend Plato, as to plead that his view of education and studies is in the general, as it seems to me, sound enough, and fitted for all sorts and conditions of men, whatever their pursuits may be. 'An intelligent man,' says Plato, 'will prize those studies which result in his soul getting soberness, righteousness, and wisdom, and will less value the others.' I cannot consider *that* a bad description of the aim of education, and of the motives which should govern us in the choice of studies, whether we are preparing ourselves for a hereditary seat in the English House of Lords or for the pork trade in Chicago.

Still I admit that Plato's world was not ours, that his scorn of trade and handicraft is fantastic, that he had no conception of a great industrial community such as that of the United States, and that such a community must and will shape its education to suit its own needs. If the usual education handed down to it from the past does not suit it, it will certainly before long drop this and try another. The usual education in the past has been mainly literary. The question is whether the studies which were long supposed to be the best for all of us are practically the best now; whether others are not better. The tyranny of the past, many think, weighs on us injuriously in the predominance given to letters in education. The question is raised whether, to meet the needs of our modern life, the predominance ought not now to pass from letters to science; and naturally the question is nowhere raised with more energy than here in the United States. The design of abasing what is called 'mere literary instruction and education,' and of exalting what is called 'sound, extensive, and practical scientific knowledge,' [3] is, in this intensely modern world of the United States, even more perhaps than in Europe, a very popular design, and makes great and rapid progress.

I am going to ask whether the present movement for ousting letters from their old predominance in education, and for transferring the predominance in education to the natural sciences, whether this brisk and flourishing movement ought to prevail, and whether it is likely that in the end it really will prevail. An objection may be raised which I will anticipate. My own studies have been almost wholly in letters, and my visits to the field of the natural sciences have been very slight and inadequate, although

[3 These quotations are from the instructions of Sir Josiah Mason for the founding of a college in Birmingham (opened 1880), now part of the University of Birmingham.]

those sciences have always strongly moved my curiosity. A man of letters, it will perhaps be said, is not competent to discuss the comparative merits of letters and natural science as means of education. To this objection I reply, first of all, that his incompetence, if he attempts the discussion but is really incompetent for it, will be abundantly visible; nobody will be taken in; he will have plenty of sharp observers and critics to save mankind from that danger. But the line I am going to follow is, as you will soon discover, so extremely simple, that perhaps it may be followed without failure even by one who for a more ambitious line of discussion would be quite incompetent.

Some of you may possibly remember a phrase of mine which has been the object of a good deal of comment; an observation to the effect that in our culture, the aim being *to know ourselves and the world*, we have, as the means to this end, *to know the best which has been thought and said in the world*.[4] A man of science, who is also an excellent writer and the very prince of debaters, Professor Huxley,[5] in a discourse at the opening of Sir Josiah Mason's college at Birmingham, laying hold of this phrase, expanded it by quoting some more words of mine, which are these: 'The civilized world is to be regarded as now being, for intellectual and spiritual purposes, one great confederation, bound to a joint action and working to a common result; and whose members have for their proper outfit a knowledge of Greek, Roman, and Eastern antiquity, and of one another. Special local and temporary advantages being put out of account, that modern nation will in the intellectual and spiritual sphere make most progress, which most thoroughly carries out this programme.'

Now on my phrase, thus enlarged, Professor Huxley remarks that when I speak of the above-mentioned knowledge as enabling us to know ourselves and the world, I assert *literature* to contain the materials which suffice for thus making us know ourselves and the world. But it is not by any means clear, says he, that after having learnt all which ancient and modern literatures have to tell us, we have laid a sufficiently broad and deep foundation for that criticism of life, that knowledge of ourselves and the world, which constitutes culture. On the contrary, Professor Huxley declares that he finds himself 'wholly unable to admit that either nations or individuals will really advance, if their outfit draws nothing from the stores of physical

[4 Arnold's quotations in this paragraph are from his 'The Function of Criticism at the Present Time' (1864).]

[5 Thomas Henry Huxley, biologist, writer, and defender of Darwinism. See his lecture, 'Science and Culture' (1880).]

science. An army without weapons of precision, and with no particular base of operations, might more hopefully enter upon a campaign on the Rhine, than a man, devoid of a knowledge of what physical science has done in the last century, upon a criticism of life.'

This shows how needful it is for those who are to discuss any matter together, to have a common understanding as to the sense of the terms they employ,—how needful, and how difficult. What Professor Huxley says, implies just the reproach which is so often brought against the study of *belles lettres*,[6] as they are called: that the study is an elegant one, but slight and ineffectual; a smattering of Greek and Latin and other ornamental things, of little use for any one whose object is to get at truth, and to be a practical man. So, too, M. Renan [7] talks of the 'superficial humanism' of a school-course which treats us as if we were all going to be poets, writers, preachers, orators, and he opposes this humanism to positive science, or the critical search after truth. And there is always a tendency in those who are remonstrating against the predominance of letters in education, to understand by letters *belles lettres*, and by *belles lettres* a superficial humanism the opposite of science or true knowledge.

But when we talk of knowing Greek and Roman antiquity, for instance, which is the knowledge people have called the humanities,[8] I for my part mean a knowledge which is something more than a superficial humanism, mainly decorative. 'I call all teaching *scientific*,' says Wolf,[9] the critic of Homer, 'which is systematically laid out and followed up to its original sources. For example: a knowledge of classical antiquity is scientific when the remains of classical antiquity are correctly studied in the original languages.' There can be no doubt that Wolf is perfectly right; that all learning is scientific which is systematically laid out and followed up to its original sources, and that a genuine humanism is scientific.

When I speak of knowing Greek and Roman antiquity, therefore, as a help to knowing ourselves and the world, I mean more than a knowledge of so much vocabulary, so much grammar, so many portions of authors in the Greek and Latin languages, I mean knowing the Greeks and Romans, and their life and genius, and what they were and did in the world; what we get from them, and what is its value. That, at least, is the ideal; and

[6 In ordinary usage, literature; but as Arnold remarks in this same paragraph, the term '*belles lettres*,' as sometimes used, implies an elegance or superficiality that he is careful to exclude from 'letters' and 'literature.']

[7 French writer on history and religion (1823–1892).]

[8 Compare the selection by Whitehead (pp. 138–51).]

[9 Eminent German classical scholar (1759–1824).]

when we talk of endeavouring to know Greek and Roman antiquity, as a help to knowing ourselves and the world, we mean endeavouring so to know them as to satisfy this ideal, however much we may still fall short of it.

The same also as to knowing our own and other modern nations, with the like aim of getting to understand ourselves and the world. To know the best that has been thought and said by the modern nations, is to know, says Professor Huxley, 'only what modern *literatures* have to tell us; it is the criticism of life contained in modern literature.' And yet 'the distinctive character of our times,' he urges, 'lies in the vast and constantly increasing part which is played by natural knowledge.' And how, therefore, can a man, devoid of knowledge of what physical science has done in the last century, enter hopefully upon a criticism of modern life?

Let us, I say, be agreed about the meaning of the terms we are using. I talk of knowing the best which has been thought and uttered in the world; Professor Huxley says this means knowing *literature*. Literature is a large word; it may mean everything written with letters or printed in a book. Euclid's *Elements* and Newton's *Principia* are thus literature. All knowledge that reaches us through books is literature. But by literature Professor Huxley means *belles lettres*. He means to make me say, that knowing the best which has been thought and said by the modern nations is knowing their *belles lettres* and no more. And this is no sufficient equipment, he argues, for a criticism of modern life. But as I do not mean, by knowing ancient Rome, knowing merely more or less of Latin *belles lettres*, and taking no account of Rome's military, and political, and legal, and administrative work in the world; and as, by knowing ancient Greece, I understand knowing her as the giver of Greek art, and the guide to a free and right use of reason and to scientific method, and the founder of our mathematics and physics and astronomy and biology,—I understand knowing her as all this, and not merely knowing certain Greek poems, and histories, and treatises, and speeches,—so as to the knowledge of modern nations also. By knowing modern nations, I mean not merely knowing their *belles lettres*, but knowing also what has been done by such men as Copernicus, Galileo, Newton, Darwin. 'Our ancestors learned,' says Professor Huxley, 'that the earth is the centre of the visible universe, and that man is the cynosure of things terrestrial; and more especially was it inculcated that the course of nature had no fixed order, but that it could be, and constantly was, altered.' But for us now, continues Professor Huxley, 'the notions of the beginning and the end of the world entertained by our forefathers are no longer credible. It is very certain that the earth is not the chief body in the material universe, and that the world is not subordinated to man's use. It is even more certain that nature is the expression of a definite order, with which nothing interferes.' 'And yet,' he cries, 'the purely classical education advocated by the representatives of the humanists in our day gives no inkling of all this!'

In due place and time I will just touch upon that vexed question of classical education; but at present the question is as to what is meant by knowing the best which modern nations have thought and said. It is not knowing their *belles lettres* merely which is meant. To know Italian *belles lettres*, is not to know Italy, and to know English *belles lettres* is not to know England. Into knowing Italy and England there comes a great deal more, Galileo and Newton amongst it. The reproach of being a superficial humanism, a tincture of *belles lettres*, may attach rightly enough to some other disciplines; but to the particular discipline recommended when I proposed knowing the best that has been thought and said in the world, it does not apply. In that best I certainly include what in modern times has been thought and said by the great observers and knowers of nature.

There is, therefore, really no question between Professor Huxley and me as to whether knowing the great results of the modern scientific study of nature is not required as a part of our culture, as well as knowing the products of literature and art. But to follow the processes by which those results are reached, ought, say the friends of physical science, to be made the staple of education for the bulk of mankind. And here there does arise a question between those whom Professor Huxley calls with playful sarcasm 'the Levites [10] of culture,' and those whom the poor humanist is sometimes apt to regard as its Nebuchadnezzars.[11]

The great results of the scientific investigation of nature we are agreed upon knowing, but how much of our study are we bound to give to the processes by which those results are reached? The results have their visible bearing on human life. But all the processes, too, all the items of fact, by which those results are reached and established, are interesting. All knowledge is interesting to a wise man, and the knowledge of nature is interesting to all men. It is very interesting to know, that, from the albuminous white of the egg, the chick in the egg gets the materials for its flesh, bones, blood, and feathers; while from the fatty yolk of the egg, it gets the heat and

[10 Members of the tribe of Levi had charge of the Hebrew temple and its sacred vessels.]

[11 Enemies; tyrants over the chosen people. Nebuchadnezzar was a Babylonian king; see the stories about him in the Old Testament.]

energy which enable it at length to break its shell and begin the world. It is less interesting, perhaps, but still it is interesting, to know that when a taper burns, the wax is converted into carbonic acid and water. Moreover, it is quite true that the habit of dealing with facts, which is given by the study of nature, is, as the friends of physical science praise it for being, an excellent discipline. The appeal, in the study of nature, is constantly to observation and experiment; not only is it said that the thing is so, but we can be made to see that it is so. Not only does a man tell us that when a taper burns the wax is converted into carbonic acid and water, as a man may tell us, if he likes, that Charon [12] is punting his ferry-boat on the river Styx, or that Victor Hugo [13] is a sublime poet, or Mr. Gladstone [14] the most admirable of statesmen; but we are made to see that the conversion into carbonic acid and water does actually happen. This reality of natural knowledge it is, which makes the friends of physical science contrast it, as a knowledge of things, with the humanist's knowledge, which is, say they, a knowledge of words. And hence Professor Huxley is moved to lay it down that, 'for the purpose of attaining real culture, an exclusively scientific education is at least as effectual as an exclusively literary education.' And a certain President of the Section for Mechanical Science in the British Association [15] is, in Scripture phrase, 'very bold,' and declares that if a man, in his mental training, 'has substituted literature and history for natural science, he has chosen the less useful alternative.' But whether we go these lengths or not, we must all admit that in natural science the habit gained of dealing with facts is a most valuable discipline, and that every one should have some experience of it.

More than this, however, is demanded by the reformers. It is proposed to make the training in natural science the main part of education, for the great majority of mankind at any rate. And here, I confess, I part company with the friends of physical science, with whom up to this point I have been agreeing. In differing from them, however, I wish to proceed with the utmost caution and diffidence. The smallness of my own acquaintance with the disciplines of natural science is ever before my mind, and I am fearful of doing these disciplines an injustice. The ability and pugnacity of the partisans of natural science make them formidable persons to contradict. The tone of tentative inquiry, which befits a being of dim faculties and

[12 In classical mythology he ferried souls across the Styx.]
[13 The French poet. Arnold disapproved of him and his works.]
[14 Prime Minister, 1868–74, 1880–85, 1886, 1892–4.]
[15 The British Association for the Advancement of Science.]

bounded knowledge, is the tone I would wish to take and not to depart from. At present it seems to me, that those who are for giving to natural knowledge, as they call it, the chief place in the education of the majority of mankind, leave one important thing out of their account: the constitution of human nature. But I put this forward on the strength of some facts not at all recondite, very far from it; facts capable of being stated in the simplest possible fashion, and to which, if I so state them, the man of science will, I am sure, be willing to allow their due weight.

Deny the facts altogether, I think, he hardly can. He can hardly deny, that when we set ourselves to enumerate the powers which go to the building up of human life, and say that they are the power of conduct, the power of intellect and knowledge, the power of beauty, and the power of social life and manners,—he can hardly deny that this scheme, though drawn in rough and plain lines enough, and not pretending to scientific exactness, does yet give a fairly true representation of the matter. Human nature is built up by these powers; we have the need for them all. When we have rightly met and adjusted the claims of them all, we shall then be in a fair way for getting soberness and righteousness, with wisdom. This is evident enough, and the friends of physical science would admit it.

But perhaps they may not have sufficiently observed another thing: namely, that the several powers just mentioned are not isolated, but there is, in the generality of mankind, a perpetual tendency to relate them one to another in divers ways. With one such way of relating them I am particularly concerned now. Following our instinct for intellect and knowledge, we acquire pieces of knowledge; and presently, in the generality of men, there arises the desire to relate these pieces of knowledge to our sense for conduct, to our sense for beauty,—and there is weariness and dissatisfaction if the desire is baulked. Now in this desire lies, I think, the strength of that hold which letters have upon us.

All knowledge is, as I said just now, interesting; and even items of knowledge which from the nature of the case cannot well be related, but must stand isolated in our thoughts, have their interest. Even lists of exceptions have their interest. If we are studying Greek accents it is interesting to know that *pais* and *pas*, and some other monosyllables of the same form of declension, do not take the circumflex upon the last syllable of the genitive plural, but vary, in this respect, from the common rule. If we are studying physiology, it is interesting to know that the pulmonary artery carries dark blood and the pulmonary vein carries bright blood, departing in this respect from the common rule for the division of labour between the veins and the arteries. But every one knows how we seek naturally to combine the pieces of our knowledge together, to bring them under general rules, to relate them to principles; and how unsatisfactory and tiresome it would be to go on forever learning lists of exceptions, or accumulating items of fact which must stand isolated.

Well, that same need of relating our knowledge, which operates here within the sphere of our knowledge itself, we shall find operating, also, outside that sphere. We experience, as we go on learning and knowing,—the vast majority of us experience,—the need of relating what we have learnt and known to the sense which we have in us for conduct, to the sense which we have in us for beauty.

A certain Greek prophetess of Mantineia in Arcadia, Diotima [16] by name, once explained to the philosopher Socrates that love, and impulse, and bent of all kinds, is, in fact, nothing else but the desire in men that good should forever be present to them. This desire for good, Diotima assured Socrates, is our fundamental desire, of which fundamental desire every impulse in us is only some one particular form. And therefore this fundamental desire it is, I suppose,—this desire in men that good should be forever present to them,—which acts in us when we feel the impulse for relating our knowledge to our sense for conduct and to our sense for beauty. At any rate, with men in general the instinct exists. Such is human nature. And the instinct, it will be admitted, is innocent, and human nature is preserved by our following the lead of its innocent instincts. Therefore, in seeking to gratify this instinct in question, we are following the instinct of self-preservation in humanity.

But, no doubt, some kinds of knowledge cannot be made to directly serve the instinct in question, cannot be directly related to the sense for beauty, to the sense for conduct. These are instrument-knowledges; they lead on to other knowledges, which can. A man who passes his life in instrument-knowledges is a specialist. They may be invaluable as instruments to something beyond, for those who have the gift thus to employ them; and they may be disciplines in themselves wherein it is useful for every one to have some schooling. But it is inconceivable that the generality of men should pass all their mental life with Greek accents or with formal logic. My friend Professor Sylvester,[17] who is one of the first mathematicians in the world, holds transcendental doctrines as to the virtue of

[16 See Plato's *Symposium*.]
[17 J. J. Sylvester (1814–97) was a professor at Johns Hopkins, 1877–83, and at Oxford, 1883–97.]

mathematics, but those doctrines are not for common men. In the very Senate House and heart of our English Cambridge I once ventured, though not without an apology for my profaneness, to hazard the opinion that for the majority of mankind a little of mathematics, even, goes a long way. Of course this is quite consistent with their being of immense importance as an instrument to something else; but it is the few who have the aptitude for thus using them, not the bulk of mankind.

The natural sciences do not, however, stand on the same footing with these instrument-knowledges. Experience shows us that the generality of men will find more interest in learning that, when a taper burns, the wax is converted into carbonic acid and water, or in learning the explanation of the phenomenon of dew, or in learning how the circulation of the blood is carried on, than they find in learning that the genitive plural of *pais* and *pas* does not take the circumflex on the termination. And one piece of natural knowledge is added to another, and others are added to that, and at last we come to propositions so interesting as Mr. Darwin's famous proposition [18] that 'our ancestor was a hairy quadruped furnished with a tail and pointed ears, probably arboreal in his habits.' Or we come to propositions of such reach and magnitude as those which Professor Huxley delivers, when he says that the notions of our forefathers about the beginning and the end of the world were all wrong, and that nature is the expression of a definite order with which nothing interferes.

Interesting, indeed, these results of science are, important they are, and we should all of us be acquainted with them. But what I now wish you to mark is, that we are still, when they are propounded to us and we receive them, we are still in the sphere of intellect and knowledge. And for the generality of men there will be found, I say, to arise, when they have duly taken in the proposition that their ancestor was 'a hairy quadruped furnished with a tail and pointed ears, probably arboreal in his habits,' there will be found to arise an invincible desire to relate this proposition to the sense in us for conduct, and to the sense in us for beauty. But this the men of science will not do for us, and will hardly even profess to do. They will give us other pieces of knowledge, other facts, about other animals and their ancestors, or about plants, or about stones, or about stars; and they may finally bring us to those great 'general conceptions of the universe, which are forced upon us all,' says Professor Huxley, 'by the progress of physical science.' But still it will be *knowledge* only which they give us; knowledge not put for us into relation with our sense for conduct, our sense

[18] In *The Descent of Man*, part III, ch. xxi.]

for beauty, and touched with emotion by being so put; not thus put for us, and therefore, to the majority of mankind, after a certain while, unsatisfy- ing, wearying.

Not to the born naturalist, I admit. But what do we mean by a born naturalist? We mean a man in whom the zeal for observing nature is so uncommonly strong and eminent, that it marks him off from the bulk of mankind. Such a man will pass his life happily in collecting natural knowl- edge and reasoning upon it, and will ask for nothing, or hardly anything, more. I have heard it said that the sagacious and admirable naturalist whom we lost not very long ago, Mr. Darwin,[19] once owned to a friend that for his part he did not experience the necessity for two things which most men find so necessary to them,—religion and poetry; science and the domestic affections, he thought, were enough. To a born naturalist, I can well under- stand that this should seem so. So absorbing is his occupation with nature, so strong his love for his occupation, that he goes on acquiring natural knowledge and reasoning upon it, and has little time or inclination for thinking about getting it related to the desire in man for conduct, the desire in man for beauty. He relates it to them for himself as he goes along, so far as he feels the need; and he draws from the domestic affections all the additional solace necessary. But then Darwins are extremely rare. Another great and admirable master of natural knowledge, Faraday,[20] was a Sandemanian. That is to say, he related his knowledge to his instinct for conduct and to his instinct for beauty, by the aid of that respectable Scot- ·tish sectary, Robert Sandeman.[21] And so strong, in general, is the demand of religion and poetry to have their share in a man, to associate themselves with his knowing, and to relieve and rejoice it, that, probably, for one man amongst us with the disposition to do as Darwin did in this respect, there are at least fifty with the disposition to do as Faraday.

Education lays hold upon us, in fact, by satisfying this demand. Profes- sor Huxley holds up to scorn mediæval education, with its neglect of the knowledge of nature, its poverty even of literary studies, its formal logic devoted to 'showing how and why that which the Church said was true must be true.' But the great mediæval Universities were not brought into

[19 It is true that he had lost his taste for literature, but he affirmed that 'if I had to live my life again, I would have made a rule to read some poetry and listen to some music at least once every week' (*Life and Letters of Charles Darwin*, ed. Francis Darwin, 1889, 1, 81).]

[20 English physicist and chemist (1791–1867) who made revolutionary discoveries concerning electricity.]

[21 Leader of a small sect of independent Presbyterians in the eighteenth century.]

being, we may be sure, by the zeal for giving a jejune and contemptible education. Kings have been their nursing fathers, and queens have been their nursing mothers, but not for this. The mediæval Universities came into being, because the supposed knowledge, delivered by Scripture and the Church, so deeply engaged men's hearts, by so simply, easily, and power-fully relating itself to their desire for conduct, their desire for beauty. All other knowledge was dominated by this supposed knowledge and was sub-ordinated to it, because of the surpassing strength of the hold which it gained upon the affections of men, by allying itself profoundly with their sense for conduct, their sense for beauty.

But now, says Professor Huxley, conceptions of the universe fatal to the notions held by our forefathers have been forced upon us by physical sci-ence. Grant to him that they are thus fatal, that the new conceptions must and will soon become current everywhere, and that every one will finally perceive them to be fatal to the beliefs of our forefathers. The need of humane letters, as they are truly called, because they serve the paramount desire in men that good should be forever present to them,—the need of humane letters, to establish a relation between the new conceptions, and our instinct for beauty, our instinct for conduct, is only the more visible. The Middle Age could do without humane letters, as it could do without the study of nature, because its supposed knowledge was made to engage its emotions so powerfully. Grant that the supposed knowledge disappears, its power of being made to engage the emotions will of course disappear along with it,—but the emotions themselves, and their claim to be engaged and satisfied, will remain. Now if we find by experience that humane letters have an undeniable power of engaging the emotions, the importance of humane letters in a man's training becomes not less, but greater, in pro-portion to the success of modern science in extirpating what it calls 'mediæval thinking.'

Have humane letters, then, have poetry and eloquence, the power here attributed to them of engaging the emotions, and do they exercise it? And if they have it and exercise it, *how* do they exercise it, so as to exert an influ-ence upon man's sense for conduct, his sense for beauty? Finally, even if they both can and do exert an influence upon the senses in question, how are they to relate to them the results,—the modern results,—of natural science? All these questions may be asked. First, have poetry and eloquence the power of calling out the emotions? The appeal is to experience. Experi-ence shows that for the vast majority of men, for mankind in general, they have the power. Next, do they exercise it? They do. But then, *how* do they exercise it so as to affect man's sense for conduct, his sense for beauty? And this is perhaps a case for applying the Preacher's words: 'Though a man labour to seek it out, yet he shall not find it; yea, farther, though a wise man think to know it, yet shall he not be able to find it.' * Why should it be one thing, in its effect upon the emotions, to say, 'Patience is a virtue,' and quite another thing, in its effect upon the emotions, to say with Homer,

τλητὸν γὰρ Μοῖραι θυμὸν θέσαν ἀνθρώποισιν—†

'for an enduring heart have the destinies appointed to the children of men'? Why should it be one thing, in its effect upon the emotions, to say with the philosopher Spinoza,[22] *Felicitas in ea consistit quod homo suum esse conservare potest*—'Man's happiness consists in his being able to preserve his own essence,' and quite another thing, in its effect upon the emotions, to say with the Gospel,[23] 'What is a man advantaged, if he gain the whole world, and lose himself, forfeit himself?' How does this difference of effect arise? I cannot tell, and I am not much concerned to know; the important thing is that it does arise, and that we can profit by it. But how, finally, are poetry and eloquence to exercise the power of relating the modern results of natural science to man's instinct for conduct, his instinct for beauty? And here again I answer that I do not know *how* they will exercise it, but that they can and will exercise it I am sure. I do not mean that modern philosophical poets and modern philosophical moralists are to come and relate for us, in express terms, the results of modern scientific research to our instinct for conduct, our instinct for beauty. But I mean that we shall find, as a matter of experience, if we know the best that has been thought and uttered in the world, we shall find that the art and poetry and eloquence of men who lived, perhaps, long ago, who had the most limited natural knowledge, who had the most erroneous conceptions about many important matters, we shall find that this art, and poetry, and eloquence, have in fact not only the power of refreshing and delighting us, they have also the power,—such is the strength and worth, in essentials, of their authors' criticism of life,—they have a fortifying, and elevating, and quickening, and suggestive power, capable of wonderfully helping us to

* *Ecclesiastes*, viii, 17.
† *Iliad*, xxiv, 49.
[22 Famous Dutch philosopher, of Jewish descent (1632–77).]
[23 Matthew, xvi, 26.]

relate the results of modern science to our need for conduct, our need for beauty. Homer's conceptions of the physical universe were, I imagine, grotesque; but really, under the shock of hearing from modern science that 'the world is not subordinated to man's use, and that man is not the cynosure of things terrestrial,' I could, for my own part, desire no better comfort than Homer's line which I quoted just now,

τλητὸν γὰρ Μοῖραι θυμὸν θέσαν ἀνθρώποισιν—

'for an enduring heart have the destinies appointed to the children of men'!

And the more that men's minds are cleared, the more that the results of science are frankly accepted, the more that poetry and eloquence come to be received and studied as what in truth they really are,—the criticism of life by gifted men, alive and active with extraordinary power at an unusual number of points;—so much the more will the value of humane letters, and of art also, which is an utterance having a like kind of power with theirs, be felt and acknowledged, and their place in education be secured.

Let us therefore, all of us, avoid indeed as much as possible any invidious comparison between the merits of humane letters, as means of education, and the merits of the natural sciences. But when some President of a Section for Mechanical Science insists on making the comparison, and tells us that 'he who in his training has substituted literature and history for natural science has chosen the less useful alternative,' let us make answer to him that the student of humane letters only, will, at least, know also the great general conceptions brought in by modern physical science; for science, as Professor Huxley says, forces them upon us all. But the student of the natural sciences only, will, by our very hypothesis, know nothing of humane letters; not to mention that in setting himself to be perpetually accumulating natural knowledge, he sets himself to do what only specialists have in general the gift for doing genially. And so he will probably be unsatisfied, or at any rate incomplete, and even more incomplete than the student of humane letters only.

I once mentioned in a school-report, how a young man in one of our English training colleges having to paraphrase the passage in *Macbeth* beginning,

Can'st thou not minister to a mind diseased?

turned this line into, 'Can you not wait upon the lunatic?' And I remarked what a curious state of things it would be, if every pupil of our national schools knew, let us say, that the moon is two thousand one hundred and sixty miles in diameter, and thought at the same time that a good para-phrase for

Can'st thou not minister to a mind diseased?

was, 'Can you not wait upon the lunatic?' If one is driven to choose, I think I would rather have a young person ignorant about the moon's diam-eter, but aware that 'Can you not wait upon the lunatic?' is bad, than a young person whose education had been such as to manage things the other way.

Or to go higher than the pupils of our national schools. I have in my mind's eye a member of our British Parliament who comes to travel here in America, who afterwards relates his travels, and who shows a really masterly knowledge of the geology of this great country and of its mining capabilities, but who ends by gravely suggesting that the United States should borrow a prince from our Royal Family, and should make him their king, and should create a House of Lords of great landed proprietors after the pattern of ours; and then America, he thinks, would have her future happily and perfectly secured. Surely, in this case, the President of the Section for Mechanical Science would himself hardly say that our member of Parliament, by concentrating himself upon geology and mineralogy, and so on, and not attending to literature and history, had 'chosen the more useful alternative.'

If then there is to be separation and option between humane letters on the one hand, and the natural sciences on the other, the great majority of mankind, all who have not exceptional and overpowering aptitudes for the study of nature, would do well, I cannot but think, to choose to be edu-cated in humane letters rather than in the natural sciences. Letters will call out their being at more points, will make them live more.

I said that before I ended I would just touch on the question of classical education, and I will keep my word. Even if literature is to retain a large place in our education, yet Latin and Greek, say the friends of progress, will certainly have to go. Greek is the grand offender in the eyes of these gentlemen. The attackers of the established course of study think that against Greek, at any rate, they have irresistible arguments. Literature may perhaps be needed in education, they say; but why on earth should it be Greek literature? Why not French or German? Nay, 'has not an English-man models in his own literature of every kind of excellence?' [24] As before, it is not on any weak pleadings of my own that I rely for convincing the

[24 An inexact quotation of Huxley's words.]

gainsayers; it is on the constitution of human nature itself, and on the instinct of self-preservation in humanity. The instinct for beauty *is* set in human nature, as surely as the instinct for knowledge is set there, or the instinct for conduct. If the instinct for beauty is served by Greek literature and art as it is served by no other literature and art, we may trust to the instinct of self-preservation in humanity for keeping Greek as part of our culture. We may trust to it for even making the study of Greek more prevalent than it is now. Greek will come, I hope, some day to be studied more rationally than at present; but it will be increasingly studied as men increasingly feel the need in them for beauty, and how powerfully Greek art and Greek literature can serve this need. Women will again study Greek, as Lady Jane Grey [25] did; I believe that in that chain of forts, with which the fair host of the Amazons are now engirdling our English universities, I find that here in America, in colleges like Smith College in Massachusetts, and Vassar College in the State of New York, and in the happy families of the mixed universities out West, they are studying it already.

Defuit una mihi symmetria prisca,—'The antique symmetry was the one thing wanting to me,' said Leonardo da Vinci; and he was an Italian. I will not presume to speak for the Americans, but I am sure that, in the Englishman, the want of this admirable symmetry of the Greeks is a thousand times more great and crying than in any Italian. The results of the want show themselves most glaringly, perhaps, in our architecture, but they show themselves, also, in all our art. *Fit details strictly combined, in view of a large general result nobly conceived;* that is just the beautiful *symmetria prisca* of the Greeks, and it is just where we English fail, where all our art fails. Striking ideas we have, and well executed details we have; but that high symmetry which, with satisfying and delightful effect, combines them, we seldom or never have. The glorious beauty of the Acropolis at Athens did not come from single fine things stuck about on that hill, a statue here, a gateway there;—no, it arose from all things being perfectly combined for a supreme total effect. What must not an Englishman feel about our deficiencies in this respect, as the sense for beauty, whereof this symmetry is an essential element, awakens and strengthens within him! what will not one day be his respect and desire for Greece and its *symmetria prisca,* when the scales drop from his eyes as he walks the London streets, and he sees such a lesson in meanness, as the Strand, for instance, in its true deformity! But here we are coming to our friend Mr. Ruskin's

[25 Great-granddaughter of Henry VII. Executed in 1554 because of her husband's and her father's complicity in rebellion against Mary Tudor.]

province,[26] and I will not intrude upon it, for he is its very sufficient guardian.

And so we at last find, it seems, we find flowing in favour of the humanities the natural and necessary stream of things, which seemed against them when we started. The 'hairy quadruped furnished with a tail and pointed ears, probably arboreal in his habits,' this good fellow carried hidden in his nature, apparently, something destined to develop into a necessity for humane letters. Nay, more; we seem finally to be even led to the further conclusion that our hairy ancestor carried in his nature, also, a necessity for Greek.

And, therefore, to say the truth, I cannot really think that humane letters are in much actual danger of being thrust out from their leading place in education, in spite of the array of authorities against them at this moment. So long as human nature is what it is, their attractions will remain irresistible. As with Greek, so with letters generally: they will some day come, we may hope, to be studied more rationally, but they will not lose their place. What will happen will rather be that there will be crowded into education other matters besides, far too many; there will be, perhaps, a period of unsettlement and confusion and false tendency; but letters will not in the end lose their leading place. If they lose it for a time, they will get it back again. We shall be brought back to them by our wants and aspirations. And a poor humanist may possess his soul in patience, neither strive nor cry, admit the energy and brilliancy of the partisans of physical science, and their present favour with the public, to be far greater than his own, and still have a happy faith that the nature of things works silently on behalf of the studies which he loves, and that, while we shall all have to acquaint ourselves with the great results reached by modern science, and to give ourselves as much training in its disciplines as we can conveniently carry, yet the majority of men will always require humane letters; and so much the more, as they have the more and the greater results of science to relate to the need in man for conduct, and to the need in him for beauty.

[26 Ruskin (1819–1900) often wrote about the ugliness of Victorian life and urged people to take a different attitude toward art from that which he found prevalent among them.]

A. N. Whitehead

TECHNICAL EDUCATION AND ITS RELATION TO SCIENCE AND LITERATURE

[A. N. Whitehead (1861–1947) often wrote as vividly and challengingly in his more popular books as he wrote profoundly in his formal mathematical and philosophical treatises. Adequate judgment of his *Principia Mathematica* (with Bertrand Russell, 1910), *Principles of Natural Knowledge* (1919), *The Concept of Nature* (1920), or *Process and Reality* (1929) must be left to specialists, but even the non-specialist, if he is familiar with the intellectual history of the twentieth century, is aware of the influence and importance of those books. There are other books, addressed to the general educated public, which have been almost as provocative in their spheres as *Principia Mathematica* and *Process and Reality* are in theirs. Of these the best are *Science and the Modern World* (1925), *Religion in the Making* (1926), *The Aims of Education* (1929), and *Adventures of Ideas* (1933).

'Technical Education and Its Relation to Science and Literature,' first published in Whitehead's *The Organisation of Thought* (1917), was reprinted in *The Aims of Education*. Of the latter work he wrote: 'The references to the educational system concern England. The failures and successes of the system in that country are somewhat different from those in America. But such references are merely illustrative: the general principles apply equally to both countries.'

THE subject of this address is Technical Education. I wish to examine its essential nature and also its relation to a liberal education. Such an inquiry may help us to realise the conditions for the successful

FROM *The Aims of Education and Other Essays*, 1929. Copyright by The Macmillan Company and used with their permission.

working of a national system of technical training. It is also a very burning question among mathematical teachers; for mathematics is included in most technological courses.

Now it is unpractical to plunge into such a discussion without framing in our own minds the best ideal towards which we desire to work, however modestly we may frame our hopes as to the result which in the near future is likely to be achieved.

People are shy of ideals; and accordingly we find a formulation of the ideal state of mankind placed by a modern dramatist * in the mouth of a mad priest: 'In my dreams it is a country where the State is the Church and the Church the people: three in one and one in three. It is a commonwealth in which work is play and play is life: three in one and one in three. It is a temple in which the priest is the worshipper and the worshipper the worshipped: three in one and one in three. It is a god-head in which all life is human and all humanity divine: three in one and one in three. It is, in short, the dream of a madman.'

Now the part of this speech to which I would direct attention is embodied in the phrase, 'It is a commonwealth in which work is play and play is life.' This is the ideal of technical education. It sounds very mystical when we confront it with the actual facts, the toiling millions, tired, discontented, mentally indifferent, and then the employers—— I am not undertaking a social analysis, but I shall carry you with me when I admit that the present facts of society are a long way off this ideal. Furthermore, we are agreed that an employer who conducted his workshop on the principle that 'work should be play' would be ruined in a week.

The curse that has been laid on humanity, in fable and in fact, is, that by the sweat of its brow shall it live. But reason and moral intuition have seen in this curse the foundation for advance. The early Benedictine monks rejoiced in their labours because they conceived themselves as thereby made fellow-workers with Christ.

Stripped of its theological trappings, the essential idea remains, that work should be transfused with intellectual and moral vision and thereby turned into a joy, triumphing over its weariness and its pain.[1] Each of us will re-state this abstract formulation in a more concrete shape in accordance with his private outlook. State it how you like, so long as you do not lose the main point in your details. However you phrase it, it remains the sole real hope of toiling humanity; and it is in the hands of technical

* Cf. BERNARD SHAW: *John Bull's Other Island.*
[[1] Cf. 'The Blessing of Adam,' pp. 10–15.]

teachers, and of those who control their spheres of activity, so to mould the nation that daily it may pass to its labours in the spirit of the monks of old.

The immediate need of the nation is a large supply of skilled workmen, of men with inventive genius, and of employers alert in the development of new ideas.

There is one—and only one—way to obtain these admirable results. It is by producing workmen, men of science, and employers who enjoy their work. View the matter practically in the light of our knowledge of average human nature. Is it likely that a tired, bored workman, however skilful his hands, will produce a large output of first-class work? He will limit his production, will scamp his work, and be an adept at evading inspection; he will be slow in adapting himself to new methods; he will be a focus of discontent, full of unpractical revolutionary ideas, controlled by no sympathetic apprehension of the real working of trade conditions. If, in the troubled times which may be before us, you wish appreciably to increase the chance of some savage upheaval, introduce widespread technical education and ignore the Benedictine ideal. Society will then get what it deserves.

Again, inventive genius requires pleasurable mental activity as a condition for its vigorous exercise. 'Necessity is the mother of invention' is a silly proverb. 'Necessity is the mother of futile dodges' is much nearer to the truth. The basis of the growth of modern invention is science, and science is almost wholly the outgrowth of pleasurable intellectual curiosity.

The third class are the employers, who are to be enterprising. Now it is to be observed that it is the successful employers who are the important people to get at, the men with business connections all over the world, men who are already rich. No doubt there will always be a continuous process of rise and fall of businesses. But it is futile to expect flourishing trade, if in the mass the successful houses of business are suffering from atrophy. Now if these men conceive their businesses as merely indifferent means for acquiring other disconnected opportunities of life, they have no spur to alertness. They are already doing very well, the mere momentum of their present business engagements will carry them on for their time. They are not at all likely to bother themselves with the doubtful chances of new methods. Their real soul is in the other side of their life. Desire for money will produce hardfistedness and not enterprise. There is much more hope for humanity from manufacturers who enjoy their work than from those who continue in irksome business with the object of founding hospitals.

Finally, there can be no prospect of industrial peace so long as masters and men in the mass conceive themselves as engaged in a soulless operation of extracting money from the public. Enlarged views of the work performed, and of the communal service thereby rendered, can be the only basis on which to found sympathetic cooperation.

The conclusion to be drawn from this discussion is, that alike for masters and for men a technical or technological education, which is to have any chance of satisfying the practical needs of the nation, must be conceived in a liberal spirit as a real intellectual enlightenment in regard to principles applied and services rendered. In such an education geometry and poetry are as essential as turning laths.

The mythical figure of Plato may stand for modern liberal education as does that of St. Benedict for technical education. We need not entangle ourselves in the qualifications necessary for a balanced representation of the actual thoughts of the actual men. They are used here as symbolic figures typical of antithetical notions. We consider Plato in the light of the type of culture he now inspires.

In its essence a liberal education is an education for thought and for æsthetic appreciation. It proceeds by imparting a knowledge of the masterpieces of thought, of imaginative literature, and of art. The action which it contemplates is command. It is an aristocratic education implying leisure. This Platonic ideal has rendered imperishable services to European civilisation. It has encouraged art, it has fostered that spirit of disinterested curiosity which is the origin of science, it has maintained the dignity of mind in the face of material force, a dignity which claims freedom of thought. Plato did not, like St. Benedict, bother himself to be a fellow-worker with his slaves; but he must rank among the emancipators of mankind. His type of culture is the peculiar inspiration of the liberal aristocrat, the class from which Europe derives what ordered liberty it now possesses. For centuries, from Pope Nicholas V [2] to the school of the Jesuits, and from the Jesuits to the modern headmasters of English public schools, this educational ideal has had the strenuous support of the clergy.

For certain people it is a very good education. It suits their type of mind and the circumstances amid which their life is passed. But more has been claimed for it than this. All education has been judged adequate or defective according to its approximation to this sole type.

The essence of the type is a large discursive knowledge of the best literature. The ideal product of the type is the man who is acquainted with the best that has been written. [3] He will have acquired the chief languages, he

[2] He was Pope from 1437 to 1455.]
[3] See Arnold, p. 123.]

will have considered the histories of the rise and fall of nations, the poetic expression of human feeling, and have read the great dramas and novels. He will also be well grounded in the chief philosophies, and have attentively read those philosophic authors who are distinguished for lucidity of style.

It is obvious that, except at the close of a long life, he will not have much time for anything else if any approximation is to be made to the fulfilment of this programme. One is reminded of the calculation in a dialogue of Lucian [4] that, before a man could be justified in practising any one of the current ethical systems, he should have spent a hundred and fifty years in examining their credentials.

Such ideals are not for human beings. What is meant by a liberal culture is nothing so ambitious as a full acquaintance with the varied literary expression of civilised mankind from Asia to Europe, and from Europe to America. A small selection only is required; but then, as we are told, it is a selection of the very best. I have my doubts of a selection which includes Xenophon and omits Confucius, but then I have read through neither in the original. The ambitious programme of a liberal education really shrinks to a study of some fragments of literature included in a couple of important languages.

But the expression of the human spirit is not confined to literature. There are the other arts, and there are the sciences. Also education must pass beyond the passive reception of the ideas of others. Powers of initiative must be strengthened. Unfortunately initiative does not mean just one acquirement—there is initiative in thought, initiative in action, and the imaginative initiative of art; and these three categories require many subdivisions.

The field of acquirement is large, and the individual so fleeting and so fragmentary: classical scholars, scientists, headmasters are alike ignoramuses.

There is a curious illusion that a more complete culture was possible when there was less to know. Surely the only gain was, that it was more possible to remain unconscious of ignorance. It cannot have been a gain to Plato to have read neither Shakespeare, nor Newton, nor Darwin. The achievements of a liberal education have in recent times not been worsened. The change is that its pretensions have been found out.

My point is, that no course of study can claim any position of ideal completeness. Nor are the omitted factors of subordinate importance. The insistence in the Platonic culture on disinterested intellectual appreciation is a psychological error. Action and our implication in the transition of

[4 Greek writer (second century), famous for his satires and dialogues.]

events amid the inevitable bond of cause to effect are fundamental. An education which strives to divorce intellectual or æsthetic life from these fundamental facts carries with it the decadence of civilisation. Essentially culture should be for action, and its effect should be to divest labour from the association of aimless toil. Art exists that we may know the deliverances of our senses as good. It heightens the sense-world.[5]

Disinterested scientific curiosity is a passion for an ordered intellectual vision of the connection of events. But the goal of such curiosity is the marriage of action to thought. This essential intervention of action even in abstract science is often overlooked. No man of science wants merely to know. He acquires knowledge to appease his passion for discovery. He does not discover in order to know, he knows in order to discover. The pleasure which art and science can give to toil is the enjoyment which arises from successfully directed intention. Also it is the same pleasure which is yielded to the scientist and to the artist.

The antithesis between a technical and a liberal education is fallacious. There can be no adequate technical education which is not liberal, and no liberal education which is not technical: that is, no education which does not impart both technique and intellectual vision. In simpler language, education should turn out the pupil with something he knows well and something he can do well. This intimate union of practice and theory aids both. The intellect does not work best in a vacuum. The stimulation of creative impulse requires, especially in the case of a child, the quick transition to practice. Geometry and mechanics, followed by workshop practice, gain that reality without which mathematics is verbiage.

There are three main methods which are required in a national system of education, namely, the literary curriculum, the scientific curriculum, the technical curriculum. But each of these curricula should include the other two. What I mean is, that every form of education should give the pupil a technique, a science, an assortment of general ideas, and æsthetic appreciation, and that each of these sides of his training should be illuminated by the others. Lack of time, even for the most favoured pupil, makes it impossible to develop fully each curriculum. Always there must be a dominant emphasis. The most direct æsthetic training naturally falls in the technical curriculum in those cases when the training is that requisite for some art or artistic craft. But it is of high importance in both a literary and a scientific education.

The educational method of the literary curriculum is the study of language, that is, the study of our most habitual method of conveying to

[5 Cf. Forster, pp. 37–43, and Conrad, pp. 63–7.]

others our states of mind. The technique which should be acquired is the technique of verbal expression, the science is the study of the structure of language and the analysis of the relations of language to the states of mind conveyed. Furthermore, the subtle relations of language to feeling, and the high development of the sense organs to which written and spoken words appeal, lead to keen æsthetic appreciations being aroused by the successful employment of language. Finally, the wisdom of the world is preserved in the masterpieces of linguistic composition.

This curriculum has the merit of homogeneity. All its various parts are co-ordinated and play into each other's hands. We can hardly be surprised that such a curriculum, when once broadly established, should have claimed the position of the sole perfect type of education. Its defect is unduly to emphasise the importance of language. Indeed the varied importance of verbal expression is so overwhelming that its sober estimation is difficult. Recent generations have been witnessing the retreat of literature, and of literary forms of expression, from their position of unique importance in intellectual life. In order truly to become a servant and a minister of nature something more is required than literary aptitudes.

A scientific education is primarily a training in the art of observing natural phenomena, and in the knowledge and deduction of laws concerning the sequence of such phenomena. But here, as in the case of a liberal education, we are met by the limitations imposed by shortness of time. There are many types of natural phenomena, and to each type there corresponds a science with its peculiar modes of observation, and its peculiar types of thought employed in the deduction of laws. A study of science in general is impossible in education, all that can be achieved is the study of two or three allied sciences. Hence the charge of narrow specialism urged against any education which is primarily scientific. It is obvious that the charge is apt to be well-founded; and it is worth considering how, within the limits of a scientific education and to the advantage of such an education, the danger can be avoided.

Such a discussion requires the consideration of technical education. A technical education is in the main a training in the art of utilising knowledge for the manufacture of material products. Such a training emphasises manual skill, and the co-ordinated action of hand and eye, and judgment in the control of the process of construction. But judgment necessitates knowledge of those natural processes of which the manufacture is the utilisation. Thus somewhere in technical training an education in scientific knowledge is required. If you minimize the scientific side, you will confine it to the scientific experts; if you maximize it, you will impart it in some measure to the men, and—what is of no less importance—to the directors and managers of the businesses.

Technical education is not necessarily allied exclusively to science on its mental side. It may be an education for an artist or for apprentices to an artistic craft. In that case æsthetic appreciation will have to be cultivated in connection with it.

An evil side of the Platonic culture has been its total neglect of technical education as an ingredient in the complete development of ideal human beings. This neglect has arisen from two disastrous antitheses, namely, that between mind and body, and that between thought and action. I will here interject, solely to avoid criticism, that I am well aware that the Greeks highly valued physical beauty and physical activity. They had, however, that perverted sense of values which is the nemesis of slave-owning.

I lay it down as an educational axiom that in teaching you will come to grief as soon as you forget that your pupils have bodies. This is exactly the mistake of the post-renaissance Platonic curriculum. But nature can be kept at bay by no pitchfork;[6] so in English education, being expelled from the classroom, she returned with a cap and bells in the form of all-conquering athleticism.

The connections between intellectual activity and the body, though diffused in every bodily feeling, are focussed in the eyes, the ears, the voice, and the hands. There is a co-ordination of senses and thought, and also a reciprocal influence between brain activity and material creative activity. In this reaction the hands are peculiarly important. It is a moot point whether the human hand created the human brain, or the brain created the hand. Certainly the connection is intimate and reciprocal. Such deep-seated relations are not widely atrophied by a few hundred years of disuse in exceptional families.

The disuse of hand-craft is a contributory cause to the brain-lethargy of aristocracies, which is only mitigated by sport where the concurrent brain-activity is reduced to a minimum and the hand-craft lacks subtlety. The necessity for constant writing and vocal exposition is some slight stimulus to the thought-power of the professional classes. Great readers, who exclude other activities, are not distinguished by subtlety of brain. They tend to be timid conventional thinkers. No doubt this is partly due to their excessive knowledge outrunning their powers of thought; but it is partly due to the lack of brain-stimulus from the productive activities of hand or voice.

In estimating the importance of technical education we must rise above

[6 Horace, *Ep.*, I, x, 24.]

the exclusive association of learning with book-learning. First-hand knowledge is the ultimate basis of intellectual life. To a large extent book-learning conveys second-hand information, and as such can never rise to the importance of immediate practice. Our goal is to see the immediate events of our lives as instances of our general ideas. What the learned world tends to offer is one second-hand scrap of information illustrating ideas derived from another second-hand scrap of information. The second-handedness of the learned world is the secret of its mediocrity. It is tame because it has never been scared by facts. The main importance of Francis Bacon's influence does not lie in any peculiar theory of inductive reasoning which he happened to express, but in the revolt against second-hand information of which he was a leader.

The peculiar merit of a scientific education should be, that it bases thought upon first-hand observation; and the corresponding merit of a technical education is, that it follows our deep natural instinct to translate thought into manual skill, and manual activity into thought.

The thought which science evokes is logical thought. Now logic is of two kinds: the logic of discovery and the logic of the discovered.

The logic of discovery consists in the weighing of probabilities, in discarding details deemed to be irrelevant, in divining the general rules according to which events occur, and in testing hypotheses by devising suitable experiments. This is inductive logic.

The logic of the discovered is the deduction of the special events which, under certain circumstances, would happen in obedience to the assumed laws of nature. Thus when the laws are discovered or assumed, their utilisation entirely depends on deductive logic. Without deductive logic science would be entirely useless. It is merely a barren game to ascend from the particular to the general, unless afterwards we can reverse the process and descend from the general to the particular, ascending and descending like the angels on Jacob's ladder.[7] When Newton had divined the law of gravitation he at once proceeded to calculate the earth's attractions on an apple at its surface and on the moon. We may note in passing that inductive logic would be impossible without deductive logic. Thus Newton's calculations were an essential step in his inductive verification of the great law.

Now mathematics is nothing else than the more complicated parts of the art of deductive reasoning, especially where it concerns number, quantity, and space.

In the teaching of science, the art of thought should be taught: namely,

[7 Genesis, xxviii, 12.]

the art of forming clear conceptions applying to first-hand experience, the art of divining the general truths which apply, the art of testing divinations, and the art of utilising general truths by reasoning to more particular cases of some peculiar importance. Furthermore, a power of scientific exposition is necessary, so that the relevant issues from a confused mass of ideas can be stated clearly, with due emphasis on important points.

By the time a science, or a small group of sciences, has been taught thus amply, with due regard to the general art of thought, we have gone a long way towards correcting the specialism of science. The worst of a scientific education based, as necessarily must be the case, on one or two particular branches of science, is that the teachers under the influence of the examination system are apt merely to stuff their pupils with the narrow results of these special sciences. It is essential that the generality of the method be continually brought to light and contrasted with the speciality of the particular application. A man who only knows his own science, as a routine peculiar to that science, does not even know that. He has no fertility of thought, no power of quickly seizing the bearing of alien ideas. He will discover nothing, and be stupid in practical applications.

This exhibition of the general in the particular is extremely difficult to effect, especially in the case of younger pupils. The art of education is never easy. To surmount its difficulties, especially those of elementary education, is a task worthy of the highest genius. It is the training of human souls.

Mathematics, well taught, should be the most powerful instrument in gradually implanting this generality of idea. The essence of mathematics is perpetually to be discarding more special ideas in favour of more general ideas, and special methods in favour of general methods. We express the conditions of a special problem in the form of an equation, but that equation will serve for a hundred other problems, scattered through diverse sciences. The general reasoning is always the powerful reasoning, because deductive cogency is the property of abstract form.

Here, again, we must be careful. We shall ruin mathematical education if we use it merely to impress general truths. The general ideas are the means of connecting particular results. After all, it is the concrete special cases which are important. Thus in the handling of mathematics in your results you cannot be too concrete, and in your methods you cannot be too general. The essential course of reasoning is to generalise what is particular, and then to particularise what is general. Without generality there is no reasoning, without concreteness there is no importance.

Concreteness is the strength of technical education. I would remind you that truths which lack the highest generality are not necessarily concrete facts. For example, $x + y = y + x$ is an algebraic truth more general than $2 + 2 = 4$. But 'two and two make four' is itself a highly general proposition lacking any element of concreteness. To obtain a concrete proposition immediate intuition of a truth concerning particular objects is requisite; for example, 'these two apples and those apples together make four apples' is a concrete proposition, if you have direct perception or immediate memory of the apples.

In order to obtain the full realisation of truths as applying, and not as empty formulæ, there is no alternative to technical education. Mere passive observation is not sufficient. In creation only is there vivid insight into the properties of the object thereby produced. If you want to understand anything, make it yourself, is a sound rule. Your faculties will be alive, your thoughts gain vividness by an immediate translation into acts. Your ideas gain that reality which comes from seeing the limits of their application.

In elementary education this doctrine has long been put into practice. Young children are taught to familiarise themselves with shapes and colours by simple manual operations of cutting out and of sorting. But good though this is, it is not quite what I mean. That is practical experience before you think, experience antecedent to thought in order to create ideas, a very excellent discipline. But technical education should be much more than that: it is creative experience while you think, experience which realises your thought, experience which teaches you to co-ordinate act and thought, experience leading you to associate thought with foresight and foresight with achievement. Technical education gives theory, and a shrewd insight as to where theory fails.

A technical education is not to be conceived as a maimed alternative to the perfect Platonic culture: namely, as a defective training unfortunately made necessary by cramped conditions of life. No human being can attain to anything but fragmentary knowledge and a fragmentary training of his capacities. There are, however, three main roads along which we can proceed with good hope of advancing towards the best balance of intellect and character: these are the way of literary culture, the way of scientific culture, the way of technical culture. No one of these methods can be exclusively followed without grave loss of intellectual activity and of character. But a mere mechanical mixture of the three curricula will produce bad results in the shape of scraps of information never interconnected or utilised. We have already noted as one of the strong points of the traditional literary culture that all its parts are co-ordinated. The problem of education is to retain the dominant emphasis, whether literary, scientific, or technical, and without loss of co-ordination to infuse into each way of education something of the other two. . . .

In considering the intellectual side of the curriculum we must be guided by the principle of the co-ordination of studies. In general, the intellectual studies most immediately related to manual training will be some branches of science. More than one branch will, in fact, be concerned; and even if that be not the case, it is impossible to narrow down scientific study to a single thin line of thought. It is possible, however, provided that we do not press the classification too far, roughly to classify technical pursuits according to the dominant science involved. We thus find a sixfold division, namely, (1) Geometrical techniques, (2) Mechanical techniques, (3) Physical techniques, (4) Chemical techniques, (5) Biological techniques, (6) Techniques of commerce and of social servcie.

By this division, it is meant that apart from auxiliary sciences some particular science requires emphasis in the training for most occupations. We can, for example, reckon carpentry, ironmongery, and many artistic crafts among geometrical techniques. Similarly agriculture is a biological technique. Probably cookery, if it includes food catering, would fall midway between biological, physical, and chemical sciences, though of this I am not sure.

The sciences associated with commerce and social service would be partly algebra, including arithmetic and statistics, and partly geography and history. But this section is somewhat heterogeneous in its scientific affinities. Anyhow the exact way in which technical pursuits are classified in relation to science is a detail. The essential point is, that with some thought it is possible to find scientific courses which illuminate most occupations. Furthermore, the problem is well understood, and has been brilliantly solved in many of the schools of technology and junior technical schools throughout the country.

In passing from science to literature, in our review of the intellectual elements of technical education, we note that many studies hover between the two: for example, history and geography. They are both of them very essential in education, provided that they are the right history and the right geography. Also books giving descriptive accounts of general results, and trains of thought in various sciences fall in the same category. Such books should be partly historical and partly expository of the main ideas which have finally arisen. Their value in education depends on their quality as mental stimulants. They must not be inflated with gas on the wonders of science, and must be informed with a broad outlook.

It is unfortunate that the literary element in education has rarely been considered apart from grammatical study. The historical reason is, that when the modern Platonic curriculum was being formed Latin and Greek were the sole keys which rendered great literature accessible. But there is no necessary connection between literature and grammar. The great age of Greek literature was already past before the arrival of the grammarians of Alexandria. Of all types of men to-day existing, classical scholars are the most remote from the Greeks of the Periclean times.

Mere literary knowledge is of slight importance. The only thing that matters is, how it is known. The facts related are nothing. Literature only exists to express and develop that imaginative world which is our life, the kingdom which is within us. It follows that the literary side of a technical education should consist in an effort to make the pupils enjoy literature. It does not matter what they know, but the enjoyment is vital. The great English Universities, under whose direct authority school-children are examined in plays of Shakespeare, to the certain destruction of their enjoyment, should be prosecuted for soul murder.

Now there are two kinds of intellectual enjoyment: the enjoyment of creation, and the enjoyment of relaxation. They are not necessarily separated. A change of occupation may give the full tide of happiness which comes from the concurrence of both forms of pleasure. The appreciation of literature is really creation. The written word, its music, and its associations, are only the stimuli. The vision which they evoke is our own doing. No one, no genius other than our own, can make our own life live. But except for those engaged in literary occupations, literature is also a relaxation. It gives exercise to that other side which any occupation must suppress during the working hours. Art also has the same function in life as has literature.

To obtain the pleasure of relaxation requires no help. The pleasure is merely to cease doing. Some such pure relaxation is a necessary condition of health. Its dangers are notorious, and to the greater part of the necessary relaxation nature has affixed, not enjoyment, but the oblivion of sleep. Creative enjoyment is the outcome of successful effort and requires help for its initiation. Such enjoyment is necessary for high-speed work and for original achievement.

To speed up production with unrefreshed workmen is a disastrous economic policy. Temporary success will be at the expense of the nation, which, for long years of their lives, will have to support worn-out artisans— unemployables. Equally disastrous is the alternation of spasms of effort with periods of pure relaxation. Such periods are the seed-times of degeneration, unless rigorously curtailed. The normal recreation should be change of activity, satisfying the cravings of instincts. Games afford such activity. Their disconnection emphasises the relaxation, but their excess leaves us empty.

It is here that literature and art should play an essential part in a healthily organised nation. Their services to economic production would be only second to those of sleep or of food. I am not now talking of the training of an artist, but of the use of art as a condition of healthy life. It is analogous to sunshine in the physical world.

When we have once rid our minds of the idea that knowledge is to be exacted, there is no especial difficulty or expense involved in helping the growth of artistic enjoyment. All school-children could be sent at regular intervals to neighbouring theatres where suitable plays could be subsidised. Similarly for concerts and cinema films. Pictures are more doubtful in their popular attraction; but interesting representations of scenes or ideas which the children have read about would probably appeal. The pupils themselves should be encouraged in artistic efforts. Above all the art of reading aloud should be cultivated. The Roger de Coverley essays of Addison are perfect examples of readable prose.

Art and literature have not merely an indirect effect on the main energies of life. Directly, they give vision. The world spreads wide beyond the deliverances of material sense, with subtleties of reaction and with pulses of emotion. Vision is the necessary antecedent to control and to direction. In the contest of races which in its final issues will be decided in the workshops and not on the battlefield, the victory will belong to those who are masters of stores of trained nervous energy, working under conditions favourable to growth. One such essential condition is Art.

If there had been time, there are other things which I should like to have said: for example, to advocate the inclusion of one foreign language in all education. From direct observation I know this to be possible for artisan children. But enough has been put before you to make plain the principles with which we should undertake national education.

In conclusion, I recur to the thought of the Benedictines, who saved for mankind the vanishing civilisation of the ancient world by linking together knowledge, labour and moral energy. Our danger is to conceive practical affairs as the kingdom of evil, in which success is only possible by the extrusion of ideal aims. I believe that such a conception is a fallacy directly negatived by practical experience. In education this error takes the form of a mean view of technical training. Our forefathers in the dark ages saved themselves by embodying high ideals in great organisations. It is our task, without servile imitation, boldly to exercise our creative energies.

C. H. Haskins
THE EARLIEST UNIVERSITIES

⟨ C. H. Haskins (1870–1937) was an eminent American historian, noted for his studies of mediaeval civilization. A graduate of Johns Hopkins University, he taught there, at the University of Wisconsin, and for many years (1902–31) at Harvard, where he was also Dean of the Graduate School of Arts and Sciences from 1908 to 1924. He was the author of *The Normans in European History* (1915), *Norman Institutions* (1918), *The Rise of Universities* (1923), *Studies in the History of Mediaeval Science* (1924), *The Renaissance of the Twelfth Century* (1927), and *Studies in Mediaeval Culture* (1929). *The Rise of Universities*, originally a course of lectures delivered at Brown University, has chapters on the earliest universities, the mediaeval professor, and the mediaeval student. We reprint nearly all of the first and a few pages of the second chapters.

U NIVERSITIES, LIKE cathedrals and parliaments, are a product of the Middle Ages. The Greeks and the Romans, strange as it may seem, had no universities in the sense in which the word has been used for the past seven or eight centuries. They had higher education, but the terms are not synonymous. Much of their instruction in law, rhetoric, and philosophy it would be hard to surpass, but it was not organized into the form of permanent institutions of learning. A great teacher like Socrates gave no diplomas; if a modern student sat at his feet for three months, he would demand a certificate, something tangible and external to show for it—an excellent theme, by the way, for a Socratic dialogue. Only in the twelfth and thirteenth centuries do there emerge in the world those features of organized education with which we are most familiar, all that machinery of instruction represented by faculties and colleges and courses

FROM *The Rise of Universities*, 1923, published by Henry Holt & Co.

of study, examinations and commencements and academic degrees. In all these matters we are the heirs and successors, not of Athens and Alexandria, but of Paris and Bologna. . . .

The occasion for the rise of universities was a great revival of learning, not that revival of the fourteenth and fifteenth centuries to which the term is usually applied, but an earlier revival, less known though in its way quite as significant, which historians now call the renaissance of the twelfth century. So long as knowledge was limited to the seven liberal arts of the early Middle Ages, there could be no universities, for there was nothing to teach beyond the bare elements of grammar, rhetoric, logic, and the still barer notions of arithmetic, astronomy, geometry, and music, which did duty for an academic curriculum. Between 1100 and 1200, however, there came a great influx of new knowledge into western Europe, partly through Italy and Sicily, but chiefly through the Arab scholars of Spain—the works of Aristotle, Euclid, Ptolemy,[1] and the Greek physicians, the new arithmetic, and those texts of the Roman law which had lain hidden through the Dark Ages. In addition to the elementary propositions of triangle and circle, Europe now had those books of plane and solid geometry which have done duty in schools and colleges ever since; instead of the painful operations with Roman numerals—how painful one can readily see by trying a simple problem of multiplication or division with these characters—it was now possible to work readily with Arabic figures; in the place of Boethius[2] the 'Master of them that know'[3] became the teacher of Europe in logic, metaphysics, and ethics. In law and medicine men now possessed the fulness of ancient learning. This new knowledge burst the bonds of the cathedral and monastery schools and created the learned professions; it drew over mountains and across the narrow seas eager youths who, like Chaucer's Oxford clerk of a later day, 'would gladly learn and gladly teach,'[4] to form in Paris and Bologna those academic gilds which have given us our first and our best definition of a university, a society of masters and scholars.

To this general statement concerning the twelfth century there is one partial exception, the medical university of Salerno. Here, a day's journey to the south of Naples, in territory at first Lombard and later Norman, but still in close contact with the Greek East, a school of medicine had existed as early as the middle of the eleventh century, and for perhaps two hundred years thereafter it was the most renowned medical centre in

[1 The geographer and astronomer (2nd cent. A.D.).]
[2 Roman statesman and philosopher (c. 475-525).]
[3 Aristotle; see p. 165.]
[4 See the *Canterbury Tales*, Prologue, 308.]

Europe. In this 'city of Hippocrates' the medical writings of the ancient Greeks were expounded and even developed on the side of anatomy and surgery, while its teachings were condensed into pithy maxims of hygiene which have not yet lost their vogue—'after dinner walk a mile,' etc. Of the academic organization of Salerno we know nothing before 1231, and when in this year the standardizing hand of Frederick II regulated its degrees Salerno had already been distanced by newer universities farther north. Important in the history of medicine, it had no influence on the growth of university institutions.

If the University of Salerno is older in time, that of Bologna has a much larger place in the development of higher education. And while Salerno was known only as a school of medicine, Bologna was a many-sided institution, though most noteworthy as the centre of the revival of the Roman law. Contrary to a common impression, the Roman law did not disappear from the West in the early Middle Ages, but its influence was greatly diminished as a result of the Germanic invasions. Side by side with the Germanic codes, Roman law survived as the customary law of the Roman population, known no longer through the great law books of Justinian but in elementary manuals and form-books which grew thinner and more jejune as time went on. The *Digest*, the most important part of the *Corpus Juris Civilis*, disappears from view between 603 and 1076; only two manuscripts survived; in Maitland's [5] phrase, it 'barely escaped with its life.' Legal study persisted, if at all, merely as an apprenticeship in the drafting of documents, a form of applied rhetoric. Then, late in the eleventh century, and closely connected with the revival of trade and town life, came a revival of law, foreshadowing the renaissance of the century which followed. This revival can be traced at more than one point in Italy, perhaps not first at Bologna, but here it soon found its centre for the geographical reasons which, then as now, made this city the meeting-point of the chief routes of communication in northern Italy. Some time before 1100 we hear of a professor named Pepo, 'the bright and shining light of Bologna'; by 1119 we meet with the phrase *Bononia docta*.[6] At Bologna, as at Paris, a great teacher stands at the beginning of university development. The teacher who gave Bologna its reputation was one Irnerius, perhaps the most famous of the many great professors of law in the Middle Ages. Just what he wrote and what he taught are still subjects of dispute among scholars, but he seems to have fixed the method of 'glossing' the law texts upon the basis of a comprehensive use of the whole *Corpus Juris*, as con-

[5 English legal historian (1850–1906).]
[6 'Bologna the learned.']

trasted with the meagre epitomes of the preceding centuries, fully and finally separating the Roman law from rhetoric and establishing it firmly as a subject of professional study. Then, about 1140, Gratian, a monk of San Felice, composed the *Decretum* which became the standard text in canon law, thus marked off from theology as a distinct subject of higher study; and the preëminence of Bologna as a law school was fully assured.

A student class had now appeared, expressing itself in correspondence and in poetry, and by 1158 it was sufficiently important in Italy to receive a formal grant of rights and privileges from Emperor Frederick Barbarossa, though no particular town or university is mentioned. By this time Bologna had become the resort of some hundreds of students, not only from Italy but from beyond the Alps. Far from home and undefended, they united for mutual protection and assistance, and this organization of foreign, or Transmontane, students was the beginning of the university. In this union they seem to have followed the example of the gilds already common in Italian cities. Indeed, the word university means originally such a group or corporation in general, and only in time did it come to be limited to gilds of masters and students, *universitas societas magistrorum discipulorumque.* Historically, the word university has no connection with the universe or the universality of learning; it denotes only the totality of a group, whether of barbers, carpenters, or students did not matter. The students of Bologna organized such a university first as a means of protection against the townspeople, for the price of rooms and necessaries rose rapidly with the crowd of new tenants and consumers, and the individual student was helpless against such profiteering. United, the students could bring the town to terms by the threat of departure as a body, secession, for the university, having no buildings, was free to move, and there are many historic examples of such migrations. Better rent one's rooms for less than not rent them at all, and so the student organizations secured the power to fix the prices of lodgings and books through their representatives.

Victorious over the townsmen, the students turned on 'their other enemies, the professors.' Here the threat was a collective boycott, and as the masters lived at first wholly from the fees of their pupils, this threat was equally effective. The professor was put under bond to live up to a minute set of regulations which guaranteed his students the worth of the money paid by each. We read in the earliest statutes (1317) that a professor might not be absent without leave, even a single day, and if he desired to leave town he had to make a deposit to ensure his return. If he failed to secure an audience of five for a regular lecture, he was fined as if absent—a poor lecture indeed which could not secure five hearers! He must begin with the bell and quit within one minute after the next bell. He was not allowed to skip a chapter in his commentary, or postpone a difficulty to the end of the hour, and he was obliged to cover ground systematically, so much in each specific term of the year. No one might spend the whole year on introduction and bibliography! Coercion of this sort presupposes an effective organization of the student body, and we hear of two and even four universities of students, each composed of 'nations' and presided over by a rector. Emphatically Bologna was a student university, and Italian students are still quite apt to demand a voice in university affairs. When I first visited the University of Palermo I found it just recovering from a riot in which the students had broken the front windows in a demand for more frequent, and thus less comprehensive, examinations. At Padua's seventh centenary last May the students practically took over the town, with a programme of processions and ceremonies quite their own and an amount of noise and tumult which almost broke up the most solemn occasions and did break the windows of the greatest hall in the city.

Excluded from the 'universities' of students, the professors also formed a gild or 'college,' requiring for admission thereto certain qualifications which were ascertained by examination, so that no student could enter save by the gild's consent. And, inasmuch as ability to teach a subject is a good test of knowing it, the student came to seek the professor's license as a certificate of attainment, regardless of his future career. This certificate, the license to teach (*licentia docendi*), thus became the earliest form of academic degree. Our higher degrees still preserve this tradition in the words master (*magister*) and doctor, originally synonymous, while the French even have a *licence*. A Master of Arts was one qualified to teach the liberal arts; a Doctor of Laws, a certified teacher of law. And the ambitious student sought the degree and gave an inaugural lecture, even when he expressly disclaimed all intention of continuing in the teaching profession. Already we recognize at Bologna the standard academic degrees as well as the university organization and well-known officials like the rector.

Other subjects of study appeared in course of time, arts, medicine, and theology, but Bologna was preëminently a school of civil law, and as such it became the model of university organization for Italy, Spain, and southern France, countries where the study of law has always had political and social as well as merely academic significance. Some of these universities became Bologna's competitors, like Montpellier and Orleans as well as the Italian schools nearer home. Frederick II founded the University of Naples in 1224 so that the students of his Sicilian kingdom could go to a Ghibelline school at home instead of the Guelfic centre in the North.[7] Rival Padua was founded two years earlier as a secession from Bologna, and only last year, on the occasion of Padua's seven-hundredth anniversary, I saw the ancient feud healed by the kiss of peace bestowed on Bologna's rector amid the encores of ten thousand spectators. Padua, however, scarcely equalled Bologna in our period, even though at a later age Portia[8] sent thither for legal authority, and though the university still shines with the glory of Galileo.

In northern Europe the origin of universities must be sought at Paris, in the cathedral school of Notre-Dame. By the beginning of the twelfth century in France and the Low Countries learning was no longer confined to monasteries but had its most active centres in the schools attached to cathedrals, of which the most famous were those of Liège, Rheims, Laon, Paris, Orleans, and Chartres. The most notable of these schools of the liberal arts was probably Chartres, distinguished by a canonist like St. Ives and by famous teachers of classics and philosophy like Bernard and Thierry. As early as 991 a monk of Rheims, Richer, describes the hardships of his journey to Chartres in order to study the *Aphorisms* of Hippocrates of Cos; while from the twelfth century John of Salisbury, the leading northern humanist of the age, has left us an account of the masters which we shall later have occasion to cite. Nowhere else today can we drop back more easily into a cathedral city of the twelfth century, the peaceful town still dominated by its church and sharing, now as then,

> the minster's vast repose.
> Silent and gray as forest-leaguered cliff
> Left inland by the ocean's slow retreat,
> . . . . patiently remote
> From the great tides of life it breasted once,
> Hearing the noise of men as in a dream.

By the time the cathedral stood complete, with its 'dedicated shapes of saints and kings,' it had ceased to be an intellectual centre of the first importance, overshadowed by Paris fifty-odd miles away, so that Chartres never became a university.

The advantages of Paris were partly geographical, partly political as the

[7 Guelfs and Ghibellines, rival political parties in mediaeval Italy. Guelfs were, in the main, supporters of the popes; Ghibellines, of the emperors.]
[8 In Shakespeare's *Merchant of Venice*.]

capital of the new French monarchy, but something must be set down to
the influence of a great teacher in the person of Abelard. This brilliant
young radical, with his persistent questioning and his scant respect for
titled authority, drew students in large numbers wherever he taught,
whether at Paris or in the wilderness. At Paris he was connected with the
church of Mont-Sainte-Geneviève longer than with the cathedral school,
but resort to Paris became a habit in his time, and in this way he had a
significant influence on the rise of the university. In an institutional sense
the university was a direct outgrowth of the school of Notre-Dame, whose
chancellor alone had authority to license teaching in the diocese and thus
kept his control over the granting of university degrees, which here as at
Bologna were originally teachers' certificates. The early schools were within
the cathedral precincts on the Ile de la Cité, that tangled quarter about
Notre-Dame pictured by Victor Hugo which has long since been de-
molished. A little later we find masters and scholars living on the Little
Bridge (Petit-Pont) which connected the island with the Left Bank of the
Seine—this bridge gave its name to a whole school of philosophers, the
Parvipontani—but by the thirteenth century they have overrun the Left
Bank, thenceforth the Latin Quarter of Paris.

At what date Paris ceased to be a cathedral school and became a university, no one can say, though it was certainly before the end of the
twelfth century. Universities, however, like to have precise dates to cele-
brate, and the University of Paris has chosen 1200, the year of its first
royal charter. In that year, after certain students had been killed in a town
and gown altercation, King Philip Augustus issued a formal privilege which
punished his prévôt and recognized the exemption of the students and
their servants from lay jurisdiction, thus creating that special position of
students before the courts which has not yet wholly disappeared from the
world's practice, though generally from its law. More specific was the first
papal privilege, the bull *Parens scientiarum* of 1231, issued after a two
years' cessation of lectures growing out of a riot in which a band of students, having found 'wine that was good and sweet to drink,' beat up the
tavern keeper and his friends till they in turn suffered from the prévôt and
his men, a dissension in which the thirteenth century clearly saw the hand
of the devil. Confirming the existing exemptions, the Pope goes on to
regulate the discretion of the chancellor in conferring the license, at the
same time that he recognizes the right of the masters and students 'to make
constitutions and ordinances regulating the manner and time of lectures
and disputations, the costume to be worn,' attendance at masters' funerals,
the lectures of bachelors, necessarily more limited than those of fully fledged

masters, the price of lodgings, and the coercion of members. Students must not carry arms, and only those who frequent the schools regularly are to enjoy the exemptions of students, the interpretation in practice being attendance at not less than two lectures a week.

While the word university does not appear in these documents, it is taken for granted. A university in the sense of an organized body of masters existed already in the twelfth century; by 1231 it had developed into a corporation, for Paris, in contrast to Bologna, was a university of masters. There were now four faculties, each under a dean: arts, canon law (civil law was forbidden at Paris after 1219), medicine, and theology. The masters of arts, much more numerous than the others, were grouped into four 'nations': the French, including the Latin peoples; the Norman; the Picard, including also the Low Countries; and the English, comprising England, Germany, and the North and East of Europe. These four nations chose the head of the university, the rector, as he is still generally styled on the Continent, whose term, however, was short, being later only three months. If we may judge from such minutes as have survived, much of the time of the nations was devoted to consuming the fees collected from new members and new officers, or, as it was called, drinking up the surplus—at the Two Swords near the Petit-Pont, at the sign of Our Lady in the Rue S.-Jacques, at the Swan, the Falcon, the Arms of France, and scores of similar places. A learned monograph on the taverns of mediaeval Paris has been written from the records of the English nation alone. The artificial constitution of the nations seems to have encouraged rather than diminished the feuds and rivalries between the various regions represented at Paris, of which Jacques de Vitry has left a classic description.*

They wrangled and disputed not merely about the various sects or about some discussions; but the differences between the countries also caused dissensions, hatreds, and virulent animosities among them, and they impudently uttered all kinds of affronts and insults against one another. They affirmed that the English were drunkards and had tails; the sons of France proud, effeminate, and carefully adorned like women. They said that the Germans were furious and obscene at their feasts; the Normans, vain and boastful; the Poitevins, traitors and always adventurers. The Burgundians they considered vulgar and stupid. The Bretons were reputed to be fickle and changeable, and were often reproached for the death of Arthur. The Lombards were called avaricious, vicious, and cowardly; the Romans, seditious, turbulent, and slanderous; the Sicilians, tyrannical and cruel; the inhabitants of Brabant, men of

* As translated by Munro, *The Mediaeval Student*, p. 19.

blood, incendiaries, brigands, and ravishers; the Flemish, fickle, prodigal, gluttonous, yielding as butter, and slothful. After such insults, from words they often came to blows.'

Another university institution which goes back to twelfth-century Paris is the college. Originally merely an endowed hospice or hall of residence, the college early became an established unit of academic life at many universities. 'The object of the earliest college-founders was simply to secure board and lodging for poor scholars who could not pay for it themselves'; but in course of time the colleges became normal centres of life and teaching, absorbing into themselves much of the activity of the university. The colleges had buildings and endowments, if the university had not. There was a college at Paris as early as 1180; there were sixty-eight by 1500, and the system survived until the Revolution, to leave behind it only fragments of buildings or local names like the Sorbonne of today, sole memento of that Collège de la Sorbonne founded for theologians by a confessor of St. Louis in the thirteenth century. Many other continental universities had their colleges, one of which, the ancient College of Spain at Bologna, still survives for the delectation of the few Spanish youths who reach its quiet courtyard. But of course the ultimate home of the college was Oxford and Cambridge, where it came to be the most characteristic feature of university life, arrogating to itself practically all teaching as well as direction of social life, until the university became merely an examining and degree-conferring body. Here the older colleges like Balliol, Merton, and Peterhouse date from the thirteenth century.

Paris was preëminent in the Middle Ages as a school of theology, and, as theology was the supreme subject of mediaeval study, 'Madame la haute science' it was called, this means that it was preëminent as a university. 'The Italians have the Papacy, the Germans have the Empire, and the French have Learning,' ran the old saying; and the chosen abode of learning was Paris. Quite naturally Paris became the source and the model for northern universities. Oxford branched off from this parent stem late in the twelfth century, likewise with no definite date of foundation; Cambridge began somewhat later. The German universities, none of them older than the fourteenth century, were confessed imitations of Paris. Thus the Elector Palatine, Ruprecht, in founding the University of Heidelberg in 1386—for these later universities were founded at specific dates—provides that it 'shall be ruled, disposed, and regulated according to the modes and matters accustomed to be observed in the University of Paris, and that as a handmaid of Paris—a worthy one let us hope—it shall imitate the steps of Paris in every way possible, so that there shall be four faculties,' four nations and a rector, exemptions for students and their servants, and even caps and gowns for the several faculties 'as has been observed at Paris.' *

By the end of the Middle Ages at least eighty universities had been founded in different parts of Europe.† Some of these were short-lived, many were of only local importance, others like Salerno flourished only to die, but some like Paris and Montpellier, Bologna and Padua, Oxford and Cambridge, Vienna and Prague and Leipzig, Coimbra and Salamanca, Cracow and Louvain, have an unbroken history of many centuries of distinction. And the great European universities of more recent foundation, like Berlin, Strasbourg, Edinburgh, Manchester, and London, follow in their organization the ancient models. In America the earliest institutions of higher learning reproduced the type of the contemporary English college at a time when the university in England was eclipsed by its constituent colleges; but in the creation of universities in the later nineteenth century, America turned to the universities of the Continent and thus entered once more into the ancient inheritance. Even in the colonial period a sense of the general university tradition survived, for the charter of Rhode Island College [9] in 1764 grants 'the same privileges, dignities, and immunities enjoyed by the American colleges, and European universities.'

What then is our inheritance from the oldest of universities? In the first place it is not buildings or a type of architecture, for the early universities had no buildings of their own, but on occasion used private halls and neighboring churches. After all, as late as 1775 the First Baptist Church in Providence was built 'for the publick worship of Almighty God, and also for holding Commencement in'! Indeed one who seeks to reconstruct the life of ancient universities will find little aid in their existing remains. Salerno retains no monuments of its university, though its rare old cathedral, where Hildebrand lies buried, must have seen the passing of many generations of would-be physicians. In the halls and coats of arms of 'many-domed Padua proud' we behold the Renaissance, not the Middle Ages. Even Bologna, *Bononia docta*, with its leaning towers and cool arcades, has no remains of university architecture earlier than the fourteenth century, from which date the oldest monuments of its professors of law gathered now into the municipal museum. Montpellier and Orleans preserve

* Translated in E. F. Henderson, *Select Historical Documents of the Middle Ages*, pp. 262–266.
† Table in Rashdall, *Universities*, I, p. xxviii; map at beginning of Vol. II and in Shepherd, *Historical Atlas* (New York, 1911), p. 100.
[9 Now Brown University, where this lecture was delivered.]

nothing from this period. Paris, too often careless of its storied past, can show today only the ancient church of Saint-Julien-le-Pauvre, where university meetings were often held, unless we count, as we should, the great cathedral in the Cité whence the university originally sprang. The oldest Cambridge college, Peterhouse, has only a fragment of its earliest buildings; the finest Cambridge monument, King's College chapel, is of the late fifteenth century. More than all others Oxford gives the deepest impression of continuity with an ancient past, Matthew Arnold's Oxford, 'so venerable, so lovely . . . steeped in sentiment as she lies, spreading her gardens to the moonlight, and whispering from her towers the last enchantments of the Middle Age'; yet so far as the actual college buildings are concerned they have much more of sentiment than of the Middle Ages. Only at Merton, which fixed the college type at Oxford, do any of the present structures carry us back of 1300, and nowhere is there much of the fourteenth century. Those venerable glories of Oxford, the Bodleian library, the tower of Magdalen, and the hall of Christ Church, belong to a much later age, the period of the Tudors, and thus by ordinary reckoning to modern times. When we say how very mediaeval, we often mean how very Tudor!

Neither does the continuity lie in academic form and ceremony, in spite of occasional survivals, like the conferring of degrees by the ring or the kiss of peace, or the timing of examinations by the hour glass as I have seen it at Portuguese Coimbra. Academic costume has in it some element of tradition where it is a daily dress as at Oxford, Cambridge, and Coimbra, but in America the tradition was broken by our ancestors, and the formal cap and gown current in the United States today are a product of modern Albany rather than of mediaeval Paris and Bologna. Even in their ancient homes the costumes have changed. 'It is probable,' says Rashdall, 'that no gown now worn in Oxford has much resemblance to its mediaeval ancestor.' A student of mediaeval Padua would not recognize the variegated procession which wound through its streets last summer; Robert de Sorbon would rub his eyes at the non-mediaeval styles of the gorgeous gowns which were massed on the stage of the great hall of the Sorbonne when President Wilson received his honorary degree in 1918.

It is, then, in institutions that the university tradition is most direct. First, the very name university, as an association of masters and scholars leading the common life of learning. Characteristic of the Middle Ages as such a corporation is, the individualistic modern world has found nothing to take its place. Next, the notion of a curriculum of study, definitely laid down as regards time and subjects, tested by an examination and leading to a degree, as well as many of the degrees themselves—bachelor, as a stage toward the mastership, master, doctor, in arts, law, medicine, and theology. Then the faculties, four or more, with their deans, and the higher officers such as chancellors and rectors, not to mention the college, wherever the residential college still survives. The essentials of university organization are clear and unmistakable, and they have been handed down in unbroken continuity. They have lasted more than seven hundred years—what form of government has lasted so long? Very likely all this is not final—nothing is in this world of flux—but it is singularly tough and persistent, suited to use and also to abuse, like Bryce's [10] university with a faculty 'consisting of Mrs. Johnson and myself,' or the 'eleven leading universities' of a certain state of the Middle West! Universities are at times criticised for their aloofness or their devotion to vocationalism, for being too easy or too severe, and drastic efforts have been made to reform them by abolishing entrance requirements or eliminating all that does not lead directly to bread and butter; but no substitute has been found for the university in its main business, the training of scholars and the maintenance of the tradition of learning and investigation. The glory of the mediaeval university, says Rashdall, was 'the consecration of Learning,' and the glory and the vision have not yet perished from the earth. 'The mediaeval university,' it has been said, 'was the school of the modern spirit.' . . .

The basis of education in the early Middle Ages consisted, as we have seen, of the so-called seven liberal arts. Three of these, grammar, rhetoric, and logic, were grouped as the trivium; the remaining four, arithmetic, geometry, astronomy, and music, made up the quadrivium. The first group was the more rudimentary, but the second was rudimentary enough. The number was fixed and the content standardized during the decadence of ancient learning, and the whole conception reached the Middle Ages chiefly in the book of a certain Martianus Capella, written in the early fifth century. These later ages of classical antiquity, in condensing and desiccating knowledge for their own more limited intelligence, were also unconsciously preparing for later times those small and convenient packages which alone could be carried as a *viaticum* through the stormy times of the Dark Ages. It was almost wholly as formulated in a few standard texts that the learning of the ancient world was transmitted to mediaeval times, and the authority of these manuals was so great that a list of those in use in any period affords an accurate index of the extent of its knowledge and the nature of its instruction. It was a bookish age, with great

[10] James Bryce, British scholar and diplomat. The reference is to a passage in his *The American Commonwealth* (1888).]

reverence for standard authorities, and its instruction followed closely the written word.

In the monastic and cathedral schools of the earlier period the text-books were few and simple, chiefly the Latin grammars of Donatus and Priscian with some elementary reading-books, the logical manuals of Boethius, as well as his arithmetic and music, a manual of rhetoric, the most elementary propositions of geometry, and an outline of practical astronomy such as that of the Venerable Bede.[11] Of Greek, of course, there was none. This slender curriculum in arts was much enlarged by the renaissance of the twelfth century, which added to the store of western knowledge the astronomy of Ptolemy, the complete works of Euclid, and the Aristotelian logic, while at the same time under the head of grammar great stimulus was given to the study and reading of the Latin classics. This classical revival, which is noteworthy and comparatively little known, centred in such cathedral schools as Chartres and Orleans, where the spirit of a real humanism showed itself in an enthusiastic study of ancient authors and in the production of Latin verse of a really remarkable quality. Certain writings of one of these poets, Bishop Hildebert of Le Mans, were even mistaken for 'real antiques' by later humanists. Nevertheless, though brilliant, this classical movement was short-lived, crushed in its early youth by the triumph of logic and the more practical studies of law and rhetoric. In the later twelfth century John of Salisbury inveighs against the logicians of his day, with their superficial knowledge of literature; in the university curriculum of the thirteenth century, literary studies have quite disappeared. Toward 1250, when a French poet, Henri d'Andeli, wrote his *Battle of the Seven Arts*, the classics are already the ancients, fighting a losing battle against the moderns:

> Logic has the students,
> Whereas Grammar is reduced in numbers.
>
>   .   .   .   .
>
> Civil Law rode gorgeously
> And Canon Law rode haughtily
> Ahead of all the other arts.

If the absence of the ancient classics and of vernacular literature is a striking feature of the university curriculum in arts, an equally striking fact is the amount of emphasis placed on logic or dialectic. The earliest university statutes, those of Paris in 1215, require the whole of Aristotle's logical works, and throughout the Middle Ages these remain the backbone of the

[11 British monk (673–735), famous as historian and scholar.]

arts course, so that Chaucer can speak of the study of logic as synonymous with attendance at a university—

> That un-to logik hadde longe y-go.

In a sense this is perfectly just, for logic was not only a major subject of study itself, it pervaded every other subject as a method and gave tone and character to the mediaeval mind. Syllogism, disputation, the orderly marshalling of arguments for and against specific theses, these became the intellectual habit of the age in law and medicine as well as in philosophy and theology. The logic, of course, was Aristotle's, and the other works of the philosopher soon followed, so that in the Paris course of 1254 we find also the *Ethics*, the *Metaphysics*, and the various treatises on natural science which had at first been forbidden to students. To Dante Aristotle had become 'the Master of them that know,' by virtue of the universality of his method no less than of his all-embracing learning. 'The father of book knowledge and the grandfather of the commentator,' no other writer appealed so strongly as Aristotle to the mediaeval reverence for the text-book and the mediaeval habit of formal thought. Doctrines like the eternity of matter which seemed dangerous to faith were explained away, and great and authoritative systems of theology were built up by the methods of the pagan philosopher. And all idea of literary form disappeared when everything depended on argument alone.

If the study of the classics became confined to examples and excerpts designed to illustrate the rules of grammar, rhetoric had a somewhat different fate by reason of its practical applications. The intellectual life of the Middle Ages was not characterized by spontaneous or widely diffused power of literary expression. Few were able to write, still fewer could compose a letter, and the professional scribes and notaries on whom devolved the greater part of the labor of mediaeval correspondence fastened upon the letter-writing of the period the stereotyped formalism of a conventional rhetoric. Regular instruction in the composition of letters and official acts was given in the schools and chanceries, and numerous professors, called *dictatores*, went about from place to place teaching this valuable art— 'often and exceeding necessary for the clergy, for monks suitable, and for laymen honorable,' as one rhetorician tells us. By the thirteenth century such masters had found a place in certain universities, especially in Italy and Southern France, and they advertised their wares in a way that has been compared to the claims of a modern business course—short and practical, with no time wasted on outgrown classical authors but everything fresh and snappy and up-to-date, ready to be applied the same day if need be! Thus one professor at Bologna derides the study of Cicero, whom he cannot recall having read, and promises to train his students in writing every sort of letter and official document which was demanded of the notaries and secretaries of his day. Since . . . such teachers specialized in the composition of student letters, chiefly skilful appeals to the parental purse, their practical utility was at once apparent. 'Let us,' says one writer, 'take as our theme today that a poor and diligent student at Paris is to write his mother for necessary expenses.' Would not every listener be sure that here at least he had found 'the real thing'? The professor of rhetoric might also be called in to draft a university prospectus, like the circular issued in 1229 by the masters of the new University of Toulouse setting forth its superiority to Paris—theologians teaching in the pulpits and preaching at the street corners, lawyers magnifying Justinian and physicians Galen, professors of grammar and logic, and musicians with their organs, lectures on the books of natural philosophy then forbidden at Paris, low prices, a friendly populace, the way now prepared by the extirpation of the thorns of heresy, a land flowing with milk and honey, Bacchus reigning in the vineyards and Ceres in the fields under the mild climate desired by the philosophers of old, with plenary indulgence for all masters and students. Who could resist such an appeal from the South?

With grammar and rhetoric reduced to a subordinate position and the studies of the quadrivium receiving but scant attention, the arts course was mainly a course in logic and philosophy, plus so much of the natural sciences as could be apprehended by the scholastic study of the 'natural books' of Aristotle. Laboratories there were none until long after the Middle Ages were past, and of history and the social sciences nothing was heard in universities until still later. Hard, close drill on a few well-thumbed books was the rule. The course in arts led normally to the master's degree in six years, with the baccalaureate somewhere on the way. Graduation in arts was the common preparation for professional study, being regularly required for theology and usual for intending lawyers and physicians. A sound tradition, to which the American world has given too little attention!

Gilbert Highet
THE AMERICAN STUDENT AS I SEE HIM

❪ Gilbert Highet (1906—), a native of Scotland and a graduate of Glasgow and Oxford, has been Professor of Greek and Latin at Columbia University since 1938, except for wartime service with the British Army. He has written *The Classical Tradition* (1949), a stimulating survey of the Greek and Latin influences on Western literature; *Juvenal The Satirist* (1954); and several volumes of essays. Earlier he had translated Werner Jaeger's *Paideia* (1939–44).

It might not be unfair to remark that the present essay was based on the experiences of a few years in one metropolitan university; and Mr. Highet writes that he would not say the same things if he were treating this theme today. For all that, it remains an excellent statement of how the American student of a generation ago impressed a European scholar.

For some further impressions, see Mr. Highet's *The Art of Teaching* (1950).

T HE AMERICAN SCHOLAR I have long known and long respected. The American student I met first as an ambitious but depressed graduate working in the hard Scottish medical schools; then as an exotic graft [1] on Oxford's gnarled trunk (like Vergil's tree, 'admiring strange new leaves and fruit unlike her own' [2]); and finally in several of the great universities of his own country. I like studying him, and he, by now inured to the fads of his preceptors, supports with surprising affability the endless process of being studied.

As far as I can judge, he is unlike any other student in the whole world. For one thing, he often works three or four hours a day at some job which

[1 Rhodes scholars, apparently.]
[2 *Georgics*, II, 82.]

FROM *The American Scholar*, Autumn, 1941. Copyright 1941 by *The American Scholar*. Reprinted by permission of *The American Scholar* and of the author.

is at least extra-curricular, if not extra-mural.³ My friends at St. Andrews and Glasgow were often poor—much poorer than the freshmen whom I see cheerfully filing clippings or toting luncheon trays—but in term-time they never worked at anything outside their studies. The vast mythology of Scottish education is full of stories about the crofter's son who lived all term in half a room on a barrel of oatmeal and a barrel of herrings brought from home, and then walked a hundred miles back to Inverquharity with the gold medal. And that ideal still persists. Occasionally British and French undergraduates do a little tutoring, and a dozen or two are book-shifters in the libraries or demonstrators in the labs; but they don't *work*. James Joyce's miserable Stephen Dedalus ⁴ in Dublin, drinking watery tea and eating fried bread while he fingered his parents' pawn tickets, would have been far better for a decent meal earned by honest work.

But it is not, or seldom, done. The feeling is that it would interfere with real work and equally real play: that it would keep the undergraduate from having his full share in the life of the university. And there is some truth in this. To spend three or four hours a day on something wholly unacademic nearly always narrows the student's interest in his academic work. He is apt to feel that it too can be done in the same way: two lectures, four hours at his job, four hours' study, and then stop. This therefore is one of the reasons why so few undergraduates in the universities here aspire to honors, compete for prizes, carry their interest in their courses further than the term paper. In France and Britain, on the other hand, it is common for lecturers to get notes from their undergraduate hearers questioning some statement, seeking a reference, asking for extended treatment of some difficulty. A not very intelligent pupil of my own at Oxford handed me a verse translation of six idylls of Theocritus, which he had made in his spare time during the two winter terms; in Jules Romains' *Les Hommes de Bonne Volonté* a student at the École Normale Supérieure translates and annotates the choric odes of Sophocles, just for fun; and, at all the British universities, essay and poem competitions are nearly always burdensome to mark, there are so many competitors. But they would not have the energy, or even the interest, to do all that, if they had to manage a laundry agency for four hours a day.

The American student himself feels this; for when he becomes a graduate student, a radical change comes over him—a change far greater than the corresponding change in other countries. He will doggedly set himself

[³ Compare Hutton, 'The Cult of the Average,' p. 180.]
[⁴ In *A Portrait of the Artist as a Young Man*.]

to read and classify every Elizabethan sonnet, or memorize every decision arising out of the Snite Act; he will plunge into labyrinthine bibliographies, from whose depths he can be heard faintly crying, as if he battled with unseen monsters, and from which he emerges through the gate of ivory, pale but uplifted, like Aeneas [5] from the world of the dead; and when you and I make jokes to him, he will copy them and write 'laughter' in the margin. It is scarcely too much to say that he then feels himself for the first time to be a whole-time student; and the only thing to be regretted about this metamorphosis is that it often keeps him from being a whole-time member of the university, that he is so often debarred by it from games and societies and other junior academic activities. He feels, not without a certain justice, that he is paying for the comparative diffuseness of his undergraduate days. There is another way of putting this. No European country thinks that education is, or ought to be, wholly democratic. Not even the United States does, in the last resort—for, in awarding fellowships and scholarships, its universities base their distribution not on *need* but on *achievement*. The principle of competition, thus tacitly acknowledged, is carried much further in Europe. In France * the A. B. examination is a national contest, whose winners are rewarded not only with the civic tributes which the French know so well how to dispense, but with prizes, money, trips to Cambodia and certainty of a favorable start in their careers. The bad side of this is obvious—suicides are not at all uncommon among disappointed or overworked candidates, and a man's whole life can be darkened by a sense of his own inescapable inferiority, publicly and competitively demonstrated. But it makes the students read, and read hard. All scholarships in Britain (except a very few assigned to localities or family names) are awarded on the basis of a long and difficult competitive examination. And there are very many more scholarships there than there are in this country: scholarships are endowed and awarded by cities, counties, prep schools, 'public' schools, colleges, universities, alumni societies, guilds and national associations. Besides those, there are hundreds upon hundreds of rich scholarships dependent on the wills of long-dead benefactors. I went through one university on money left by a thread manufacturer who died about 1850, and through another on the rentals of farms bequeathed for the purpose by a Court official of King James the First. It would not be too

[5 *Aeneid*, vi, 893–8.]

* This refers of course to France before it was invaded by the Germans, and before its government determined to assist its conqueror in attaining his own ideal, *die Vernichtung Frankreichs*, 'the destruction of France.'

much to say that the rich man who, in the United States, gives $50,000
for cancer research, gives £10,000 in Britain to support 'a student who
desires to enter the medical profession, said student to be selected by an
examination on the fundamentals of . . .' The University of Oxford is
thought to be full of the leisure class. Yet in 1937 60 per cent of its students were wholly or partially supported by scholarships; and all those
scholarships had to be won by keen and difficult competition. From a certain Scots university there is one, and only one, scholarship which will take
you to Oxford; and it is competed for by every student who wants it: pre-
lawyers, chemists, historians, economists, mathematicians, philologists,
they all sit there glowering at one another in the same examination room,
and furiously laboring at the twelve three-hour papers on which their future
depends. It is a painful ordeal; but it makes you study! Not only in France
but in Britain too, enormous emphasis is laid on the exact position of a
student in his class. Those who simply collect their grades and their clubs
and leave are little regarded, must, practically speaking, have jobs waiting
for them; find the higher careers closed. Those who try for honors find
themselves arranged into a natural hierarchy, which, *ceteris paribus*,[6] represents their comparative chances of getting a good position when they
graduate.

The American student, if I know him, would not care for this system.
He would, I think, feel that it too highly rewarded the 'grind' and under-
valued the character-building and social qualities of college life; he would
conclude it was unfair to boys who happened to attend schools which gave
them less careful preparation for academic competition; ultimately he
would think that, by subjecting him to a constant implied pressure, it deprived him of a good deal of his liberty. And yet, it seems to me that it
would do him good, and improve the service of schools and universities to
individuals and to the state.

Take only one broad consideration. The development of government all
over the world, in the democracies as well as in the despotisms, is towards
a more numerous, more elaborate, and more highly trained bureaucracy.
For good or bad, every national government now interests itself in the lives
of its citizens far more closely than at any time since the Byzantine empire.
Therefore it is necessary, year by year, for it to command a great supply of
diverse and well-trained officials, mostly specialists of one kind or another.
In the despotisms these officials are produced by the Party machine,
selected and trained by a system which is at least methodically similar to

[6 Other things being equal.]

education. In the democracies they are at present produced and trained by no system, except in a few fields like jurisprudence and public health. In Great Britain the diplomatic service, the higher branches of the civil service, and certain other administrative departments are recruited by rigorous competitive examinations for which, in practice, candidates prepare throughout the universities and even during their last years at school. That system is thought to work well, although it is limited in extent. But many educators feel that the bureaucracies, both local and national, ought to be wholly staffed by men and women trained *on purpose*, and that in the democracies the schools and universities ought to be the organizations which produce and train them. Many a large store will not engage salesmen and saleswomen unless they are college graduates with noticeably good records; it is ludicrous that states and colleges should be less careful about choosing their executives. If we are to have a mandarinate, let us be as sensible as the Chinese in selecting our mandarins. If we want intelligent officials let us train them and discipline them and sift them by competitive examination and reward them with good, appropriate jobs, instead of letting our universities annually pour out a huge undifferentiated mass of graduates, from which only luck or exceptional perseverance will direct the right man to the right place in the social machine.

However, at present that is not done; and the American student, except in a few eccentric universities, estimates his achievement by time spent, which is quantitative, rather than by competitive achievement, which is qualitative. And yet he is at heart emulous. If it is presented civilly and winningly to him, he will welcome authority. He would welcome it still more if it were organized: if he felt that in school and at college its consistent purpose was to make him fit for a career which depended not entirely on his own whim, but on a long series of tests of his abilities and a constructive estimate of his character and capacity.

Another unique attribute characterizes the American student: his huge numbers. Can four real universities exist in one city? Can it be possible that in one state fifty or sixty thousand youths and maidens are capable of the activity required to absorb a university education? Are the inhabitants of California (whose very name derives from a romance describing the Earthly Paradise) so talented that they can every year produce a myriad of university graduates? And what educators could be at once so inspiring and so industrious as to teach, effectively, this enormous horde? Or, finally, can the vast multitudes of adolescents in the United States all be so much more talented than their coevals in Canada, in France, in Sweden?

The paradox, of course, conceals a dichotomy. To put it bluntly and generally, the American student who is not preparing for a profession does not often go to the university in pursuit of higher education. He goes to complete the education which his school left incomplete. He has been badly schooled. It is not his fault, and not wholly the fault of the school. But it is a pity. It sometimes strikes me with a sense of pathos to read the grave works on education, ranging all the way from Mortimer Adler's *How to Read a Book* to the bulletins of the Carnegie Institute for Educational Research, which treat the American school system in total detachment from all others, as if it could learn nothing from Europe, and teach Europe nothing—still less other continents. Mr. Adler, in his efforts to teach his patients how to read books, makes one or two cursory references to the situation in Europe, and throughout the rest of his prescription treats the American student as a chimera bombinating in the void. But of course he finds it difficult to read Locke or Dante when he gets to college. He has seldom been compelled to read anything difficult in school. And a comparison, however invidious, would demonstrate that. I went to a perfectly ordinary school in Scotland, P.S. 93 as it were. In my last three years (ages 15–18) we were forced to read and understand *Hamlet, Macbeth, Henry IV*, Chaucer's *Prologue* and *Knight's Tale, Polyeucte, Le Cid, Le Misanthrope, Eugénie Grandet, Seven Against Thebes, The Persians, Iliad* xvi and xviii, *Aeneid* ii, iv, and vi, Livy ix and several other books. And we read them. (Dickens and Scott and Thackeray and so on, we had read long before.) We had to, under that stringent discipline. We could write a character of Macduff or Célimène, we could reproduce the various explanations and emendations of the 'dram of eale' in *Hamlet*, we could compare the shields of Achilles and Aeneas, we could write little essays on Balzac's idea of realism. They were not very good; but they proved that we had read the books. And we were not alone. In Edinburgh they were doing the same. Bristol Grammar School was doing even more. Sheffield and Manchester and London and Newcastle were doing at least as much. French schools are still more arduous, although they concentrate more closely on the classics of their own tongue; and so, in a more limited way, were Scandinavian and Dutch schools, and even German schools before the despotism.

Now why does the average American student need to learn how to read a book? Why does he approach *Hamlet* or *Crime and Punishment* with a mixture of awe and bravado, and usually look up from it with such puzzled delight and half-understood emotion? Manifestly because he has been ill taught at school. And, so far, that is nobody's fault: certainly not his; but there are two main reasons for the fact.

For one thing, the system of mass-education has nowhere else been applied to a population so huge and so various. Only a nation so gallant and so confident as the United States would have dreamt of administering approximately the same education to the children of long-settled western Europeans, recent central European immigrants, and many millions of emancipated Negroes, of whom Bigger Thomas [7] with his revolt and his tragedy may well be partially symbolic. Whenever I ask my pupils about their schooling they invariably say, if they went to public school, that they were held back by the size of the classes or by lazy and recalcitrant classmates. One of the best students I have ever had praised the history master at his public school most highly, but added that he was forced to devote himself almost wholly to the upper one third of his class. In one of his more frankly autobiographical essays Mr. James Thurber describes a tough school in Columbus, Ohio, as it was a generation ago; and even if we allow for humorous exaggeration there is still the ring of truth in the sentence about his enormous Negro protector, Floyd: 'I was one of the ten or fifteen male pupils in Sullivant School who always, or almost always, knew their lessons, and I believe Floyd admired the mental prowess of a youngster who knew how many continents there were and whether or not the sun was inhabited.' And the problem is complicated by the almost inevitable rigidity of the school system. It is true that many high schools have recently endeavored to work out special courses of study for pupils who are more intelligent than the average; but such readjustments are not yet common, are nearly everywhere tentative, and often meet with opposition. It is a task of almost inconceivable difficulty to raise the educational standards of an entire population; for at least two thirds of the boys and girls now leaving American schools are much more highly educated than their parents were. This difficulty does not exist in western European countries, and it fills me with admiration to see the courage and tenacity with which it is being faced here. But, in education more than in other things, each generation stands on the shoulders of its predecessor, and in another decade or so a great part of this difficulty will have been removed.

The other reason is the comparatively lax discipline of schools in the United States. High school pupils spend appreciably less time in school here than they do in Britain, and much less than they do in France. In school they spend less time on actual study, because of the surprising

[7 Principal character in Richard Wright's novel, *Native Son*.]

amount of attention paid to extra-curricular activities. They spend far less time on preparation at home. And there is much less *drive* behind their learning than there is in western European schools. In the last two years at an ordinary British city school, corresponding to a good high school here, the ordinary pupil averages at least five and a half hours of actual classroom work in school and three hours' preparation at home, with a minimum of six hours' preparation at week ends. The working hours of two good provincial lycées in France, where friends of mine taught during the early '30s, are literally almost double those of an American high school.* Any extracurricular occupation, like producing the school magazine, or football practice, or rehearsing in the school orchestra, takes place outside working hours. And there is a constant disciplinary pressure to keep the pupils at work, to keep them actively attentive, to pull up the laggards and push on the leaders. Attendances are rigidly kept: an incident such as that reported in the New York papers in 1940, when a squad of policemen and truant officers 'combed' the cinemas on two different mornings and rounded up nearly two thousand school children A.W.O.L., is frankly inconceivable. If anything like it occurred in Europe it would be instantly followed by the discharge or demotion of dozens of school teachers. It may not be unfair to suggest that some of the laxity observable in American schools is due to the much higher proportion of women acting as teachers. Adolescent boys cannot be properly disciplined by women, and adolescent girls only with much difficulty. But there are other reasons, which are too well known or too controversial to be discussed here. The fact remains. The American high school student has a far better time, but he does far less work than his European counterpart.

Accordingly the American student, when he reaches college, is not so well prepared as the average European freshman. He has not read so much, and he does not know how to read and write so well. He does not buy nearly so many books for his own enjoyment, if indeed he buys any at all. One distinction seems to me particularly significant. English and French undergraduates are apt to publish little magazines in which they practise fine writing: the first sonnet, the first political manifesto, chapters from the first autobiographical novel and so on. The American student hardly ever produces an imitation literary review. Instead, he produces an imitation of a daily newspaper, or occasionally an imitation of a comic weekly. Almost every distinguished contemporary French and British writer wrote

---

* The same system at an earlier date is admirably described by the Abbé Ernest Dimnet in his autobiography, *My Old World* (Simon and Schuster, New York: 1935). Arduous as it was, he has nothing but praise for it.

his first publishable work when he was an undergraduate; almost no distinguished American writer wrote anything at college which in any way prefigured his later work.

If I have not misunderstood the fairly widespread movement towards establishing 'junior colleges' and the frequently emphasized distinction between the first biennium of college work and the second, they are based on this same fact: that some fairly intensive work is required to make up the deficiencies of the schools. Viewed in this light, the multitudinousness of the American student becomes (although still a little bewildering) intelligible and sympathetic.

The third quality which forces itself on the observer of the American student is his freedom. He will, without great heart-searching, move from one university to another—a thing almost never done in France or Britain, and in Germany chiefly by very earnest undergraduates in search of a particular kind of specialized teaching or even of a particular professor. He will give up college altogether with a facility which still amazes me, although the dean's office usually knows exactly what proportion of the student body can be expected to drop out annually. He will in college drop subjects on which he spent four years in school; and he will take eccentric subjects or anomalous combinations of subjects with complete nonchalance. He is infinitely less cut to pattern (even allowing for his numbers) than the European student. In an English university it is often possible to tell what particular college an undergraduate attends, and even what school he came from, after five minutes' general conversation; but seldom in the United States.

This has its good side and its bad. It makes the American student far more self-reliant—one of my chief difficulties in Oxford was handling the timid, sheltered, hampered boy who might prove to be brilliant and might almost equally well be defeated and crushed; such difficulties hardly ever present themselves here. But, on the other hand, it makes him rather irresponsible, and even restless and discontented. Far too much is left to his own choice, at a time when he is scarcely capable of making a choice. Thanks to the kindly laxity initiated by President Eliot,[8] he is free to take astronomy 17, comparative religion 1, government 33, Spanish drama in translation 21 and hygiene 2A (hygiene 2A is compulsory). A semester of that would, at best, produce a healthy cross between Sir Isaac Newton and the Duke of Plaza-Toro. It is no wonder that the mixture sometimes fails to act, and discourages him that gives and him that takes. The opposite extreme is seen in the English 'public' schools, where a schoolboy good at

[8 Of Harvard, 1869–1909. He championed the elective curriculum.]

history will be tutored from the age of fifteen till the age of eighteen to win a history scholarship at a good college specializing in history, will spend three or four years reading history for a first class in the final examinations, and then take history at his examination for entrance to the home civil service. (Usually, he will spend most of his time on the same period of history—e.g. medieval history, with special emphasis on the 12th century.) * Both extremes are dangerous. The British extreme is often as narrowing as the other is bewildering: it needs, as an offset, the manifold external interests which only a great university and experienced tutors can give. But it has one merit in itself: it sets a premium on unremitting hard work and the long view. The other extreme broadens the student's mind; but it often broadens it without deepening it.

Thus it is that the American student in his last two years at school does not often know what he is going to be, and still less often knows what he will learn in his university; and in the first two years at the university (if he is not firmly steered by his parents into a profession) seldom knows how he will spend his junior and senior years, and how they will dovetail into his future. From one point of view, this shows a genuine, disinterested love of learning, a magnificent belief in the virtues of the university; but from another it means waste of good effort, waste of priceless time, waste of irreplaceable enthusiasm. The task of the university is to cast such a light on a man's youth as will illuminate him through his life, and yet to keep the light unblurred by the shadows of the temporary and the inessential. This task is always supremely difficult, but its difficulty is here enhanced by the inadequateness of the liaison between schools and universities and the lack of emphasis on the essentials of education. The schools have more than enough to do. They cannot tackle this job. It is for the American universities to look, like the wise man, before and after: to induce the student to surrender most of his freedom of choice for a more stable set of patterns in education. Wherever such compulsory patterns have been introduced he needs little persuasion to accept them; at Columbia he looks back on the arduous humanities course with feelings of pleasure and gratitude, not unmingled with surprise. He is a good fellow, the American student: he is energetic and ambitious; but he lacks direction, as the young do everywhere. 'For,' says Thomas Burton, 'as he that plays for nothing will not heed his game; no more will voluntary employment so thoroughly affect a student, except he be very intent of himself.' And, in these bad days, few of us are very intent of ourselves.

* An interesting document showing one boy's revolt against this system is Christopher Isherwood's autobiography, *Lions and Shadows*, Hogarth Press, London: 1938.

Graham Hutton
THE CULT OF THE AVERAGE

❴ The scope and purpose of Graham Hutton's excellent book, *Midwest at Noon*, from which 'The Cult of the Average' is taken, are best described in his own words: 'In the middle of the journey of my life and by the accident of war, I came to live in the Middle West. It was the region of America which I had always liked best, where I felt and was made to feel most at home, and where I spent the most absorbing, interesting, and happy years of a not uneventful life. The longer I lived there, the more I became convinced that the Midwest and its people were largely unknown, widely misinterpreted, and greatly misunderstood. I also came to believe that the Midwest today was not what it had been and what American folklore makes it out to be.' He felt this so strongly, he adds, that he had to write a book.

Unlike some of his predecessors among foreign observers of the Midwest, Mr. Hutton knows thoroughly the region he writes about. He went everywhere in it, talked to everybody, and enjoyed himself. 'There has not been one unpleasant experience in my journeyings. . . I have never lost a dime or anything else—not even my British accent!'

T O THE GREAT majority of midwesterners, however and wherever they live, the education of their children is most important. It arouses much private and public discussion in political circles, in the home, and in many voluntary associations. It is the charter for the equality of children, for which so many immigrants came to the region. The teaching of 'the young idea' [1] is not a social institution which 'just growed' with Midwest society and is viewed as part of the order of Nature. It is one of those recent

[1 'To teach the young idea how to shoot' (Thomson, *The Seasons*).]

FROM *Midwest at Noon*, 1946. Reprinted by permission of the University of Chicago Press.

man-made institutions which, like much else in the region, is periodically taken out, examined, transformed, and set to work anew. Political changes or voluntary movements see to that, even if the transformations are not as complete as the majority would like them to be.

It is recent; very recent. Public education on any ordered scale in the region is scarcely more than a hundred years old. It was called forth from a busy people mainly by the great efforts of women, New Englanders, ministers, and a few leading citizens. It has had to change vastly and frequently to fit new peoples with new ideas as they populated the region. It has had to assimilate their children and equip them with Americanism. It achieved the widest regional literacy in America before 1914. It has had to keep pace with big changes as the various new forms of transport and the quicker communication of ideas transformed a region of insulated agricultural settlers into one of the greatest industrial regions of the world, if not the greatest. And as they are all still changing, still in the process of 'becoming,' so is Midwest public education. It is as complex and as varied as the life of the people.

As in many countries a long time ago, and in most today, the main problem of Midwest education was that of teaching the 'three R's' to the children of farmers. It was at this stage that many men and women with a little learning, much zeal for the young, and natural teaching ability started rudimentary classes in an attic, a store, a 'church,' or in their own cabins. Lincoln learned eagerly, arduously, and therefore well from such teachers.* But this rudimentary education was unorganized. It was education for the necessarily ignored and ignorant children of a rural, segregated, and hardworking people. When railroads were built and roads were made, waves of immigrants and settlers came both to towns and to country, and then educational institutions multiplied exceedingly. The individual teachers remained, but in little red schoolhouses built for them. These schoolhouses are fresh in the memory of many midwesterners today, and they are still a majority of the schools out in the countryside. They are the monument of the vanishing Old Midwest. But they are still important. The United States Office of Education in 1938 stated that more than half the public-school buildings in America consisted of one room and that most individual teachers were teaching the children through eight grades of study. The problem

---

* See Kunigunde Duncan and D. F. Nichols, *Mentor Graham, the Man Who Taught Lincoln* (Chicago: University of Chicago Press, 1944). This book gives a valuable and fascinating account of the beginnings of education in Indiana and Illinois. See also Lloyd Lewis, *John S. Wright, Prophet of the Prairies* (Chicago: Prairie Farmer Publishing Co., 1941).

reflected by these figures is mainly that of the South, Southwest, and Great Plains regions; but in the Old Midwest today it is apparent as soon as you enter purely agricultural counties and townships.

The majority of midwesterners today view problems of the public education of young people up to the age of eighteen under four main headings. These headings correspond to the four main purposes which education of all kinds must serve. First in order of importance, education must assimilate different children from widely differing economic or family backgrounds to 'the American way.' Whether the school is private or public, in city or town or country, the first aim is to make good American citizens out of widely differing young people. This means that it must iron out disparities, establish an American average to which pupils must conform, and necessarily must also to a substantial degree standardize them. All education does that, everywhere; but in the Midwest there are clear reasons why it must do it to a greater extent. A Swiss, Swedish, Dutch, French, or British child comes to school in those European countries from a family which is already long and closely assimilated to a national or folk pattern of life and thought. That is not so in most of America; and in the Midwest it is less so than in the East and South. Education is therefore from the outset not just, nor even first, a matter of mere learning; not a matter of 'leading forth from' the pupil the capacities he or she may possess. It is more a matter of 'putting in' standards of good Americanism and of general knowledge. But as that is by no means *all* it is in the Midwest, in education we also find extremes, contrasts, paradoxes, problems, and difficulties not found in other regions and lands, or not found to the same extent.

Secondly, education must mold or establish the individual's character and temperament. It must make the pupil self-dependent at the same time as it makes him a 'good mixer,' a member of the community, and a playing member of the all-American team. It must make him adaptable in a country and region of great differences, extremes, and rapid change. It must also make him resourceful in a region of marked individualism, initiative, and enterprise. Clearly, the task facing the teacher is exacting. He, or more frequently she, must reconcile the accent on individual character with the accent on the average, the pattern, and the community.

Thirdly, education must provide a general, average standard of learning as the young person's start in life—he and she are entitled to it on the basis of equality. The adult citizen, which the pupil will become, will find adaptation, understanding of society, and mixing with his fellows much easier if all of them, when young, share in the same broad pattern and elements of learning. This third aim of education is the most distinctively midwestern. It comes down, in clear and unbroken descent from the earliest days of primitive education in the Old Midwest, tinged with strong feelings of equality and democracy.

Fourthly, and only as far as is compatible with the attainment of these other three aims, education must be selective. It must provide courses in anything for which pupils show a desire or an aptitude. In other words, it must sieve out the pupils who will best profit from a college education, it must spot the able individuals who stand out from the average, and it must give them as much individual tuition or as great an opportunity to become more outstanding as it can afford—but always giving priority to the first three aims.

The midwesterner always distrusted intellectually outstanding people, geniuses of the mind (though not of 'practical affairs'), nonconformists in general, and the abnormal. To this extent he showed, and still shows, a remarkable similarity to the Englishman who dislikes things that 'are not done.' But, unlike most Englishmen, he believed and still believes that all young people, until their majority, have an equal right to a university education and the ability equally to profit from it, even if he knows the results are bound to be unequal. Accordingly, almost as early and as fast as private colleges were founded in the Midwest—mainly by easterners—midwesterners themselves set up state universities. Later, the leading citizens in big cities founded and endowed city colleges which added to the number available to young people. The standards of many of these had to be pitched low, to suit anyone who came to them.

Any student can 'work his or her way' through college, if the student wants to. A greater proportion of public high-school students than in any other land, or than in most other regions of America, want a 'college education' badly enough to work their way through. Those whose parents are able and willing to pay for them, send them 'through college.' It is the sacrifice by modest Midwest parents which is made with the least questioning. The extent of that sacrifice is largely unseen, especially by the children; but it is ungrudgingly made in hundreds of thousands of little homes. Thanks to rich benefactors, alumni, or state funds, the universities charge proportionately lower fees than the universities of Europe; but for parents who send their children through college, it is costly. To keep a young person there until he or she is twenty or twenty-one is bound to be so. And that, again, is why so many young people 'work their way through.'

Yet, to a smaller but still to a large extent, college education is viewed by the majority of midwesterners in much the same way as education in the public schools. The aims are much the same and certainly rank in the same order. The standards are very 'practical' in the midwesterner's understanding of that word. The student is there to gain accomplishments that will make of him a worthy citizen. He is there to learn social arts and graces, the common life of sports and games, and the vocabulary of adult life. He is there to acquire knowledge, to take it in. He is there to acquire a training which will prove both practical and profitable in getting his living; to acquire 'basic skills.' And a minority are there to nourish genius, secure as much individual tuition as they can, enter the tantalizing portals of the life of the mind, and make their own individual contributions to it. Learning is still the 'basic skills' or 'book-larnin' ' that mark the public grade and high schools, as it marked the old midwesterners' idea of education in general.

In school and college alike there is what seems to a European a strange reverence for books and the printed word. It may not be entirely fanciful to ascribe this to the wide extent of illiteracy in the region until one long lifetime ago; and to the reverence for 'the Word' and the few men who could read and expound it in those days. Yet it is found all through American educational life. Certainly the heavy dependence of the first Midwest colleges upon religion and churches made their presidents and faculties rather dogmatic. It confined teachers within restraints from which they only began to break free in the 1890's and 1900's. Not all of them are free now. And if they are free from religious restraint, they certainly are not free from political and ideological restraints. But, to whatever it is due, 'book-larnin' ' seems to bulk inordinately large in Midwest universities—with notable exceptions.

The notable exceptions are famous throughout the world of learning: to name but a few, the University of Chicago, Northwestern University in Evanston, the University of Michigan at Ann Arbor, the University of Wisconsin at Madison, the State University of Iowa at Iowa City, and the University of Minnesota at Minneapolis. The region is equally rich in smaller private or denominational colleges of sound tradition, great learning, and much influence in the humanities: Grinnell * and Cornell in Iowa, Lawrence in Wisconsin, Knox in Illinois, Carleton in Minnesota, Oberlin in Ohio, and many others.

But within varying limits it seems to the stranger that the Midwest, and to a smaller extent the American, high school's and college's emphasis is

* It was to the Reverend J. B. Grinnell that Horace Greeley in 1853 said, 'Go West, young man, go West and grow up with the country.'

heavily upon *indoctrination* rather than on *education* in the strict Latin meaning of those words; on putting in rather than on bringing out; upon instilling the ideas of others rather than on criticizing them or getting the student to form ideas of his own; upon examinations of the student's absorptive capacity rather than of his originality or exposition; upon assimilation rather than on an independent, critical power to reason and to discriminate. These may seem like hard sayings, and this is not a treatise on education. But these observations are those of the leading educators of America who began and still lead a revolt, much of which borrowed its force and its leading exponents from great and exceptional Midwest colleges and schools. What Harper of the University of Chicago disliked and tried, with success, to change, Hutchins of the same university tries, in different ways, to change today. And there are many such men in the private or state universities of the region now dedicated to the task of reducing emphasis on mass-produced learning, on papers and textbooks and examinations, on grading and 'points' and classification systems which treat young minds like sides of beef, counts of yarn, or qualities of tobacco.

In many high schools and colleges the student is graded by credits and marks not on his originality but on knowledge of facts, lectures, and books. Even the examination papers are questionnaires or quizzes by which the student's rank or grade is established. And the teachers are so overworked, giving lectures and grading or marking innumerable papers, that there is little time for individual tuition or seminars. All this results in a standardized pattern of college or high-school education—open to all, the same for all, but hard on teacher and student alike. It is highly significant that the leading universities of the region are famous for their *postgraduate* departments and professors and that only among these can the outstanding graduate, the young man or woman who departs from the average or mass, find the necessary individual tuition, cherishing, and nourishment.

In the main, the best of European high-school and college education aims to *make* the student critical, both of his teacher and of what is being taught. It aims to discover and then develop the original and independent qualities or capacities of the young mind. The only outstanding exceptions were in the universities of the old Germany, in which the professors delivered their lectures, devoted themselves to postgraduate work and research, were a great force in public life, enjoyed high social status, and gave individual tuition to a favored few. American universities were vastly influenced by those of Germany between 1840 and 1900. Much of that influence, despite the revolt against it which began at the close of last century, still remains—particularly in the Midwest.

Clearly, here are the sources of some of those characteristics which we have already noted of the bulk of adult midwesterners: respect for and devotion to the average, a lack of discrimination, a passion for facts, and less ability to manipulate them. Here, once more, is another instance of a Midwest paradox of extremes: emphasis on individualism but also on a standardized average, the greatest tolerance in the world but equally great emphasis on conformity. What is taught as fact from an approved textbook to large classes of different young midwesterners in high schools, with the aim of making them one and indivisible, often ends either by crystallizing prejudices or by creating terrible problems for those university professors who later on try to develop an original, independent, and critical faculty in those same young minds. What the public schools do, many of the best universities, both state and private, have to try to undo. It was the *esprit de corps* which Emerson [2] found and liked in England a century ago. But American educators visiting England since 1918, and especially today, find more striking, and commend more, the individual originality of young Britishers in high schools and universities. And the visitors are not by any means all easterners.

From the outset, midwesterners firmly believed that all human knowledge could be reduced to the level of popular understanding. The forerunner of the 'digest' of today, and of the textbooks that tell all about everything, was the Midwest man's and woman's 'Companion to Knowledge' of the 1830's to 1860's. It was a thoroughly laudable aim that all knowledge should be 'understanded of the people'; and in a society of settlers and small towns largely inhabited by a homogeneous population, it was almost feasible. It did not, however, become feasible when the population changed and became bewilderingly diverse. The average of Americanism to which the children of alien immigrants had to conform naturally suggested an average level of understanding, an average of potted knowledge which should be each child's birthright. But the average had to be lower in terms of knowledge, wider in terms of social accomplishments, behavior, and 'basic skills.' And, as each child was democratically equal, it followed that the pace of the class should be set within the average pupil's range of ability —often, indeed, within that of the slightly backward pupils, to be on the safe side. The great differences among the children's families and the new-

[² See his *English Traits*.]

ness of the Midwest naturally resulted in the deliberate 'patterning' of young Americans. The pledge to the flag filled the gap made by the absence of any formal religious instruction or prayers. The teaching of patriotism and what it means to be an American was bound up with the teaching of history from textbooks approved, and even commissioned on well-defined lines, by politicians. The results are not always good for a sound conception of history or of other peoples, or for independent and critical judgment. But they are doubtless good for Americanism. The Midwest has proved that.

The children of alien immigrants, and the immigrants' votes, have altered the content of education to a large extent. It is surprising to a European today to find that most pupils in Midwest high schools and many at college can read, but cannot understand, the great speeches of Calhoun, Webster, Clay, and Douglas. It is doubtful if Midwest schools and colleges today can teach their masterly style and logic; and many midwesterners themselves deplore the passing of the clear simplicity of Lincoln's English, as shown not in his great orations but in his letter to General Hooker.[3] The generation of midwesterners which passed from the scene in the 1920's certainly could comprehend the language of its fathers' day and age. To the pupils in high schools and to many students in college since 1920, that language and the fine logic and reason in those speeches are alien, archaic, and well-nigh incomprehensible. The American, the Americanism, and the American language of today are all very different from those of 1860. They are changing fast; and this is reflected in education.

Whatever schools and colleges may lack in developing an independent critical faculty or originality in their young people, they offset by developing practical and technical skills. The great inventors, industrialists, and businessmen of the region have richly endowed technical institutions, separately or as parts of a university, which are the envy of scientists all over the world. It is in branches of technique that the Midwest boy or girl most easily and naturally achieves self-expression: for in these fields of practical knowledge or skill, formulas or a technical vocabulary are manipulated instead of 'abstract ideas.' The midwesterners' emphasis on the practical, their insistent query, 'Will it work?' and their readiness to try anything once have more than justified themselves in the fields of natural science, medicine, transport, psychology, agriculture, meteorology, and commerce.

[3 Presumably Lincoln's letter of 26 January 1863, appointing General Hooker to the command of the Army of the Potomac.]

It is natural that this emphasis should spill over into social studies. It leads not only many businessmen but also many principals, presidents, and professors to believe that departments dedicated to what are misleadingly termed 'the social sciences' can be, or should be, as practical, precise, and prophetical as those concerned with the natural sciences. It is natural, too, that they cannot be so practical. But it is also imperative that they should be encouraged in every way to undertake fearless and impartial research. Yet there are still great difficulties for historians, political scientists, economists, and sociologists.

These studies of human society are greatly influenced by currents of contemporary political thought. Principals, presidents, and professors have to tread with extreme delicacy along these dangerous paths, for they have the care of students whose parents have strong political convictions, much distrust of what is called 'pure speculation,' and a consuming hatred for what is termed 'advanced thought' or described as 'radicalism.' The situation of these teachers in public high schools, and especially in state universities, is not particularly enviable. It accounts for the colorlessness of much that is taught in the social studies. Neutrality must be preserved. In these subjects teaching goes on under limitations and restraints imposed by intolerance or the fear of it. It is just another of the contrasts in the region. The contrast is heightened by the extreme brilliance of achievements in the more 'practical' fields of study and research. But it has a bearing on the tendency of many great or promising thinkers and teachers to quit the region and its colleges. The brilliance and originality seem fated, in the main, to be nourished and developed in 'practical' studies and skills. The young sense this as quickly as the teachers, and the ship sails forward with a heavy list to one side. The master and his crew do all they can to redress the balance. But it is on the side of the humanities,[4] arts, and social studies that the vessel lacks equipoise.

In all the leading high schools and universities of the region this struggle is going on with characteristic nobility of purpose and vigor. But it would be wrong to say that it is nearly settled, that it is easy, or that the issue is beyond question. And that, too, is not the problem of educators in the Midwest alone. What one can say is that if the outcome is successful there, it will more affect the Midwest way of life, and be more fruitful there, than it will anywhere else in America; and that all Americans will then be astonished at the richness of promise and performance. For the latent talent is boundless.

[4 See Whitehead, pp. 138–51.]

If you turn away from the current disputes between educators in all
countries to look at young people themselves, you are greatly encouraged
and comforted. Whatever Midwest education's problems may be, whatever
it may lack, its results in making good American citizens are great and
undeniable. It is natural that midwesterners should want it to be better
than it is. But they need not make the best the enemy of the good. The
good is all around them.

Midwest boys and girls, young men and women, are more like those of
democratic Sweden and Switzerland than any others in Europe. The East
of America may still place more of a premium on sheer intellectual and
cultural abilities, it may still be the mirror of fashion and mold of form [5]
in these fields, but it is in the Midwest schools that you can best study the
educational system as it turns out sturdy, convivial, generous, and human
young Americans. Not a little of the gallantry and intrepidity of the very
young Midwest boys in the second World War is due to their schools and
teachers; and a surprisingly large number of those who returned recognized
it and went back to the school to tell the teachers so.

For this, the nonintellectual side of the school curriculum and of school
life in general is responsible. Whether in a one-room schoolhouse or in the
most up-to-date and beautifully appointed schools in the world—and both
are numerous in the region—the accent is as much on the young pupils as
potential members of the community as it is on what they can be made to
absorb, what mental capacities they possess, or what intellectual faculties
they can develop. Who dare say, today, in our vexed age, that this is wrong?
Humanity has suffered more from frustrated intellectuals than from low-
brows or hearties. The latter are social; the former antisocial.

The pupils are encouraged to run their own social life in their own way
and by their own elected nominees. Not all schools, least of all those in the
countryside, can afford teachers and facilities to make this social side of
school life resemble what it is in the best schools of the region. But in many
schools in well-to-do suburban communities, big cities, large towns, and
smaller towns, the high-school pupils of both sexes are now social types
with a life and lingo of their own. In many high schools I know, I found
that the seniors had balloted for the following choices among their number and in each sex: best-looking, most popular, most original, best personality, best dancer, biggest flirt, most bashful, best leader, best athlete, best

[5 See *Hamlet*, III, i, 162.]

dressed, funniest laugh, most industrious, most sophisticated, most naïve, blushing beauty, most conceited, biggest show-off, best mannered, most photogenic, most business-like, best natured, teacher's pet, most sportsman-like, biggest eater, wittiest, biggest bluffer, laziest, peppiest, and most likely to succeed. The names were all published in the newspaper edited, managed, and run by the pupils themselves. The average age of seniors in these schools would be a little under seventeen and a half; but among juniors, sophomores, and freshmen a corresponding independence, sense of humor, community spirit, and readiness to give and take as members of the community were as well marked. The emphasis of the young everywhere is on good comradeship; but these lists show a remarkably heavy emphasis on the social achievements and a remarkably light one on anything else. They are typical in that.

Coeducation is responsible for much of this. If it interferes with purely intellectual learning, and if it leads to more sex problems for the young in the cities than out in the country, it results in an enormous net gain. In school hours the constant comradeship between the sexes, the differences of ability, and the scholastic competition between them are all to the good. This is most noticeable out in the country, where the smaller numbers of pupils of both sexes, in groups, form a little nation of their own. They have easy access to sports and open-air games, winter and summer. They work and play together virtually year in, year out. In the towns and cities this comradeship in active relaxation is rarer.

The young people have acute problems of their own. They are generally adept at solving them. But there is now a rift between both teachers and parents, on the one hand, and children on the other, which may grow wider. Already it is causing much concern, and in the Midwest it is particularly obvious. For decades, indeed for generations, children in the Midwest have been taught in school, and often in the home, that their region is the most go-ahead in America and, therefore, in the world; that the past is dead; that the future alone is important, for it is made into today.

While all this is natural enough in the Midwest, it is also natural that it should have the widespread effect of making young people identify their parents with a remote past, as if those parents had been pioneers who cleared the ground for their homes from the forest primeval and shot Indians off it. It has made Midwest youth more impatient of advice and of counsel drawn from both teachers' and parents' experience (they are of almost the same generation) than most of the youth of America—and that, by European standards, is saying a lot. It has probably helped to make them the extraordinarily self-reliant, capable, and resourceful young people they are. But now the social problems of America, nowhere more extreme than in the Midwest, are forcing teachers and parents alike to look around them, to examine their own institutions, the foundations of their beliefs and ideas, and even to look backward to the past.

The young people sense the prevailing confusion of beliefs, the extremes and opposites, the divisions and frictions, but are as impatient as ever of 'old-fashioned ideas.' Teachers and parents are in a quandary, for they are divided among themselves on great social, political, or economic issues. What are they to tell the young? The parents can make their own decisions what version or what gloss they put upon these issues at home when they talk with the young people or before them. But the teachers and the schools are 'on the spot.' If a teacher ventures anything like an opinion on any of these issues, or says anything that could be taken as an opinion, he or she may lose a job. The control of education by the immediate locality and its opinion is far stronger in the Midwest than it is almost anywhere else. It is far stronger than the influence of local opinion on law and the enforcement of it. This results not in giving 'the young idea' a lead toward clarity but in ignoring or soft-pedaling many vital and interesting questions of the day.

It is noteworthy that the young people debate these questions in clubs and discussion groups which they run for themselves; but to get help and guidance from impartial adults is both rare and difficult. Many American parents and teachers were worried in the second World War about boys of nineteen fighting for their country and others, merely because Uncle Sam told them to. American correspondents abroad testified that many young men had only the vaguest ideas of America's foreign policy, her relationships with other countries including those of South America, and of economics, labor relations, or political institutions in general. This is not isolationism, nor is it due to it. It can be found in the armies of all belligerents in varying degrees. It reflects educational problems. It is the outcome of a public education which makes boys mature early and treats them as men in almost all respects, but agrees in the main not to teach them anything on controversial issues—or to teach it in such a neutral way that no judgment or conclusion can be reached. It forms one of the most vexing of postwar problems. It is one on which the veterans who choose to take their college education after the war will have a profound influence. That influence is already apparent.

Many of the parents' problems do not, however, arise from the teaching curriculum. They arise from the emphasis on social life at school. In no schools is this social life more organized, or better provision for it made, than in many Midwest educational institutions. But it produces problems. The life is that of a mature and adult group with freedoms, codes of behavior, personal relationships, rules of conformity, fashions, and a vocabulary of its own. Parents want their children to mature young, and both parents and teachers do all they can to insure it. The greatest proof of that is the extent of liberty allowed to the young. But that liberty, like all liberty, cannot easily or safely be cut into neat slices and kept in iceboxes, to be brought out at schooltime or for well-defined occasions.

Liberty is the most pervasive of all atmospheres. In many if not most cities and towns of the region the social liberty and self-government of young people at school, which are means to maturity, often become means to revolt; and revolt does not break out at school or college. It breaks out in the home. Social life, when baulked, deteriorates into the rule of gangs among boys and girls. Some of the worst of the juvenile gangs were composed of girls in their teens. More frequently, and less harmfully, it becomes the domination of the group by exclusive cliques, which makes problems for many children and their parents. In the small rural towns the heavy wine of personal and group liberty makes young people even more restless, for parental, conventional, and religious restraints are far greater there. The standardization of all-American relaxations and diversions by the movies, radio, magazines, and comic strips affects the young in towns and country alike. Their chafings against parental control become more acute and frequent. And naturally this all-pervading atmosphere affects the schoolwork of many pupils.

Nevertheless, the pattern of good Americanism which the schools set before their pupils is sound. Like many Midwest characteristics, it is flexible and adaptable. It can take a lot of beating. Like their parents, the young people carry a heavy cargo of common sense. They can see an adult's viewpoint because they are more mature. They are the freest, most natural, most poised young people in all countries of the Western world; and that is true from kindergarten or nursery school through college. No young people anywhere are more attractive. Nowhere else can a grown-up get as much enjoyment from being among the younger generation. That is an enormous tribute to parents, teachers, and young people alike. Alongside this the costs, the exceptions, and the problems seem minor and manageable: which is true of so much in the Midwest.

George Santayana
CLASSIC LIBERTY

❦ George Santayana was born in Spain (1863) but grew up in the United States. He was educated at Harvard, where he taught philosophy as the colleague of Josiah Royce and William James from 1889 until 1912. He resigned in 1912, after (we are told) receiving a legacy, which freed him from teaching; as Dr. Johnson observed, 'a man who has enough without teaching, will probably not teach.' He lived in Europe from 1912 until his death in 1952.

His *Life of Reason* (1905), *Scepticism and Animal Faith* (1923), *The Realm of Essence* (1928), *The Realm of Matter* (1930), *The Realm of Truth* (1937) are familiar to students of philosophy. Better known to most readers are his *Character and Opinion in the United States* (1920), *Soliloquies in England* (1922), *Obiter Scripta* (1935), and his novel, *The Last Puritan* (1935). In his last decade he published three volumes of reminiscences.

Soliloquies in England and *The Last Puritan* are products of those periods in his life when he was 'attracted into an unfeigned participation in social pleasures and in political hopes.' He believes that they are therefore 'the most approachable of my writings for the general reader; but even here, though some interest may be aroused, I doubt that the unconverted or unconvertible will find much ultimate satisfaction.' Most of the *Soliloquies* were written during the war years of 1914–18.

W HEN ancient peoples defended what they called their liberty, the word stood for a plain and urgent interest of theirs: that their cities should not be destroyed, their territory pillaged, and they themselves sold into slavery. For the Greeks in particular liberty meant even more than this. Perhaps the deepest assumption of classic philosophy is that nature

FROM *Soliloquies in England*, 1922, published by Charles Scribner's Sons.

and the gods on the one hand and man on the other, both have a fixed character; that there is consequently a necessary piety, a true philosophy, a standard happiness, a normal art. The Greeks believed, not without reason, that they had grasped these permanent principles better than other peoples. They had largely dispelled superstition, experimented in government, and turned life into a rational art. Therefore when they defended their liberty what they defended was not merely freedom to live. It was freedom to live well, to live as other nations did not, in the public experimental study of the world and of human nature. This liberty to discover and pursue a natural happiness, this liberty to grow wise and to live in friendship with the gods and with one another, was the liberty vindicated at Thermopylae [1] by martyrdom and at Salamis [2] by victory.

As Greek cities stood for liberty in the world, so philosophers stood for liberty in the Greek cities. In both cases it was the same kind of liberty, not freedom to wander at hazard or to let things slip, but on the contrary freedom to legislate more precisely, at least for oneself, and to discover and codify the means to true happiness. Many of these pioneers in wisdom were audacious radicals and recoiled from no paradox. Some condemned what was most Greek: mythology, athletics, even multiplicity and physical motion. In the heart of those thriving, loquacious, festive little ant-hills, they preached impassibility and abstraction, the unanswerable scepticism of silence. Others practised a musical and priestly refinement of life, filled with metaphysical mysteries, and formed secret societies, not without a tendency to political domination. The cynics railed at the conventions, making themselves as comfortable as possible in the rôle of beggars and mocking parasites. The conservatives themselves were radical, so intelligent were they, and Plato wrote the charter [3] of the most extreme militarism and communism, for the sake of preserving the free state. It was the swan-song of liberty, a prescription to a diseased old man to become young again and try a second life of superhuman virtue. The old man preferred simply to die.

Many laughed then, as we may be tempted to do, at all those absolute physicians of the soul, each with his panacea. Yet beneath their quarrels the wranglers had a common faith. They all believed there was a single solid natural wisdom to be found, that reason could find it, and that man-

[1 The Greeks under Leonidas of Sparta made a heroic defense against the Persians at the narrow pass of Thermopylae, in eastern Greece, in 480 B.C., but were defeated through treachery.]

[2 An island off the southwestern coast of Attica, where in 480 B.C. the Greeks won a great victory over the Persian fleet.]

[3 His *Republic*.]

kind, sobered by reason, could put it in practice. Mankind has continued to run wild and like barbarians to place freedom in their very wildness, till we can hardly conceive the classic assumption of Greek philosophers and cities, that true liberty is bound up with an institution, a corporate scientific discipline, necessary to set free the perfect man, or the god, within us.

Upon the dissolution of paganism the Christian church adopted the classic conception of liberty. Of course, the field in which the higher politics had to operate was now conceived differently, and there was a new experience of the sort of happiness appropriate and possible to man; but the assumption remained unchallenged that Providence, as well as the human soul, had a fixed discoverable scope, and that the business of education, law, and religion was to bring them to operate in harmony. The aim of life, salvation, was involved in the nature of the soul itself, and the means of salvation had been ascertained by a positive science which the church was possessed of, partly revealed and partly experimental. Salvation was simply what, on a broad view, we should see to be health, and religion was nothing but a sort of universal hygiene.

The church, therefore, little as it tolerated heretical liberty, the liberty of moral and intellectual dispersion, felt that it had come into the world to set men free, and constantly demanded liberty for itself, that it might fulfil this mission. It was divinely commissioned to teach, guide, and console all nations and all ages by the self-same means, and to promote at all costs what it conceived to be human perfection. There should be saints and as many saints as possible. The church never admitted, any more than did any sect of ancient philosophers, that its teaching might represent only an eccentric view of the world, or that its guidance and consolations might be suitable only at one stage of human development. To waver in the pursuit of the orthodox ideal could only betray frivolity and want of self-knowledge. The truth of things and the happiness of each man could not lie elsewhere than where the church, summing up all human experience and all divine revelation, had placed it once for all and for everybody. The liberty of the church to fulfil its mission was accordingly hostile to any liberty of dispersion, to any radical consecutive independence, in the life of individuals or of nations.

When it came to full fruition this orthodox freedom was far from gay; it was called sanctity. The freedom of pagan philosophers too had turned out to be rather a stiff and severe pose; but in the Christian dispensation this austerity of true happiness was less to be wondered at, since life on earth was reputed to be abnormal from the beginning, and infected with hereditary disease. The full beauty and joy of restored liberty could hardly become evident in this life. Nevertheless a certain beauty and joy did radiate visibly from the saints; and while we may well think their renunciations and penances misguided or excessive, it is certain that, like the Spartans and the philosophers, they got something for their pains. Their bodies and souls were transfigured, as none now found upon earth. If we admire without imitating them we shall perhaps have done their philosophy exact justice. Classic liberty was a sort of forced and artificial liberty, a poor perfection reserved for an ascetic aristocracy in whom heroism and refinement were touched with perversity and slowly starved themselves to death.

Since those days we have discovered how much larger the universe is, and we have lost our way in it. Any day it may come over us again that our modern liberty to drift in the dark is the most terrible negation of freedom. Nothing happens to us as we would. We want peace and make war. We need science and obey the will to believe, we love art and flounder among whimsicalities, we believe in general comfort and equality and we strain every nerve to become millionaires. After all, antiquity must have been right in thinking that reasonable self-direction must rest on having a determinate character and knowing what it is, and that only the truth about God and happiness, if we somehow found it, could make us free. But the truth is not to be found by guessing at it, as religious prophets and men of genius have done, and then damning every one who does not agree. Human nature, for all its substantial fixity, is a living thing with many varieties and variations. All diversity of opinion is therefore not founded on ignorance; it may express a legitimate change of habit or interest. The classic and Christian synthesis from which we have broken loose was certainly premature, even if the only issue of our liberal experiments should be to lead us back to some such equilibrium. Let us hope at least that the new morality, when it comes, may be more broadly based than the old on knowledge of the world, not so absolute, not so meticulous, and not chanted so much in the monotone of an abstracted sage.

Thomas Jefferson and John Adams
NATURAL ARISTOCRACY

⟨[Thomas Jefferson (1743–1826; President, 1801–9) and John Adams (1735–1826; President, 1797–1801) had been acquainted since the days of the Continental Congress, to which Jefferson was a delegate from Virginia and Adams from Massachusetts. This acquaintance soon became one of mutual respect and then, more slowly, ripened into friendship. Despite serious estrangements caused by differences in political philosophy and by party conflicts, the friendship grew stronger with the years; for, as Jefferson wrote to Adams in 1812, they had been 'fellow laborers in the same cause, struggling for what is most valuable to man, his right of self-government; laboring always at the same oar, with some wave ever ahead, threatening to overwhelm us, yet passing harmless under our bark we knew not how, we rode through the storm with heart and hand, and made a happy port.' Some years after their retirement from the turmoils of public life, their memories, sympathies, and ideas found expression in letters exchanged between Monticello and Quincy. This correspondence, opened by Adams in 1812, continued until their deaths. The two friends died on the same day, 4 July (appropriately enough) 1826.

Jefferson to Adams
Monticello, October 28, 1813.

. . . I AGREE with you that there is a natural aristocracy among men. The grounds of this are virtue and talents. Formerly, bodily powers gave place among the aristoi.[1] But since the invention of gunpowder has armed the weak as well as the strong with missile death, bodily strength, like beauty, good humor, politeness and other accomplishments, has become but an auxiliary ground for distinction. There is also an artificial aristocracy, founded on wealth and birth, without either virtue or talents; for with these it would belong to the first class. The natural aristocracy I consider as the

[1 Aristocrats.]

most precious gift of nature, for the instruction, the trusts, and government of society. And indeed, it would have been inconsistent in creation to have formed man for the social state, and not to have provided virtue and wisdom enough to manage the concerns of the society. May we not even say, that that form of government is the best, which provides the most effectually for a pure selection of these natural aristoi into the offices of government? The artificial aristocracy is a mischievous ingredient in government, and provision should be made to prevent its ascendency. On the question, what is the best provision, you and I differ; but we differ as rational friends, using the free exercise of our reason, and mutually indulging its errors. You think it best to put the pseudo-aristoi into a separate chamber of legislation, where they may be hindered from doing mischief by their co-ordinate branches, and where, also, they may be a protection to wealth against the agrarian and plundering enterprises of the majority of the people. I think that to give them power in order to prevent them from doing mischief is arming them for it, and increasing instead of remedying the evil. For if the co-ordinate branches can arrest their action, so may they that of the co-ordinates. Mischief may be done negatively as well as positively. Of this, a cabal in the Senate [2] of the United States has furnished many proofs. Nor do I believe them necessary to protect the wealthy; because enough of these will find their way into every branch of the legislature to protect themselves. From fifteen to twenty legislatures of our own, in action for thirty years past, have proved that no fears of an equalization of property are to be apprehended from them. I think the best remedy is exactly that provided by all our constitutions, to leave to the citizens the free election and separation of the aristoi from the pseudo-aristoi, of the wheat from the chaff. In general they will elect the really good and wise. In some instances, wealth may corrupt, and birth blind them; but not in sufficient degree to endanger the society.

It is probable that our difference of opinion may, in some measure, be produced by a difference of character in those among whom we live. From what I have seen of Massachusetts and Connecticut [3] myself, and still more from what I have heard, and the character given of the former by yourself, who know them so much better, there seems to be in those States a traditionary reverence for certain families, which has rendered the offices of the

[2] It is not clear which cabal Jefferson alludes to. Like most Presidents, he and Adams (cf. p. 200) were vexed by Congressional opposition to their policies.]
[3] New England Federalists, especially Connecticut ones, were extremely hostile to Jefferson throughout his Presidency.]

government nearly hereditary in those families. I presume that from an early period of your history, members of those families happening to possess virtue and talents have honestly exercised them for the good of the people, and by their services have endeared their names to them. In coupling Connecticut with you, I mean it politically only, not morally. For having made the Bible the common law of their land, they seem to have modeled their morality on the story of Jacob and Laban.[4] But although this hereditary succession to office with you may, in some degree, be founded in real family merit, yet in a much higher degree it has proceeded from your strict alliance of Church and State.[5] These families are canonised in the eyes of the people on common principles, 'you tickle me, and I will tickle you.' In Virginia we have nothing of this. Our clergy, before the revolution, having been secured against rivalship by fixed salaries, did not give themselves the trouble of acquiring influence over the people. Of wealth, there were great accumulations in particular families, handed down from generation to generation, under the English law of entails.[6] But the only object of ambition for the wealthy was a seat in the King's Council. All their court was paid to the crown and its creatures; and they Philipised [7] in all collisions between the King and the people. Hence they were unpopular; and that unpopularity continues attached to their names. A Randolph, a Carter, or a Burwell must have great personal superiority over a common competitor to be elected by the people even at this day. At the first session of our legislature after the Declaration of Independence, we passed a law abolishing entails. And this was followed by one abolishing the privilege of primogeniture,[8] and dividing the lands of intestates equally among all their children, or other representatives. These laws, drawn by myself, laid the axe to the root of pseudo-aristocracy. And had another

[4 See Genesis, chs. xxix–xxxi.]

[5 In Massachusetts and Connecticut the Congregational Churches possessed special privileges, as the Anglican Church once had in the Southern states. Massachusetts and Connecticut were many years behind the other states in severing official ties between Church and State.]

[6 This law permitted landed estates (and slaves attached to them) to be settled inalienably; the estate could not, ordinarily, be broken up. Jefferson's bill abolishing entails made landed property easily distributable and negotiable, like any other property. Some of the wealthy landowners strongly opposed Jefferson's successful attempt to deprive them of an ancient privilege.]

[7 Supported the aims and policies of a foreign power rather than those of their own country, as some Athenians did in the days of Philip of Macedon.]

[8 The law of primogeniture gave all the inheritance to the eldest son. Jefferson himself was an eldest son.]

which I prepared been adopted by the legislature, our work would have been complete. It was a bill for the more general diffusion of learning.[9] This proposed to divide every county into wards of five or six miles square, like your townships; to establish in each ward a free school for reading, writing and common arithmetic; to provide for the annual selection of the best subjects [10] from these schools, who might receive, at the public expense, a higher degree of education at a district school; and from these district schools to select a certain number of the most promising subjects, to be completed at an University, where all the most useful sciences should be taught. Worth and genius would thus have been sought out from every condition of life, and completely prepared by education for defeating the competition of wealth and birth for public trusts. My proposition had, for a further object, to impart to these wards those portions of self-government for which they are best qualified, by confiding to them the care of their poor, their roads, police, elections, the nomination of jurors, administration of justice in small cases, elementary exercises of militia; in short to have made them little republics, with a warden at the head of each, for all those concerns which, being under their eye, they would better manage than the larger republics of the county or State. A general call of ward meetings by their wardens on the same day through the State would at any time produce the genuine sense of the people on any required point, and would enable the State to act in mass, as your people have so often done, and with so much effect, by their town meetings. The law for religious freedom,[11] which made a part of this system, having put down the aristocracy of the clergy, and restored to the citizen the freedom of the mind, and those of entails and descents nurturing an equality of condition among them, this on education would have raised the mass of the people to the high ground of moral respectability necessary to their own safety, and to orderly government; and would have completed the great object of qualifying them to select the veritable aristoi, for the trusts of government, to the exclusion of the pseudalists; and the same Theognis [12] who has fur-

[9 This bill did not pass, but public education continued to be one of Jefferson's strongest interests. Under his leadership the University of Virginia was established in 1819. He laid out its grounds, designed its buildings, planned its curriculum, and selected its first faculty.]

[10 The best students.]

[11 The law entirely separated Church and State in Virginia, where all taxpayers had been taxed to support the Anglican Church whether members of that Church or not. Jefferson considered his long struggle for this law one of his greatest services to his state.]

[12 Greek poet, sixth century B.C.]

nished the epigraphs of your two letters, assures us that ["Good men, Cyrnus, have never ruined a state']. Although this law has not yet been acted on but in a small and inefficient degree, it is still considered as before the legislature, with other bills of the revised code, not yet taken up, and I have great hope that some patriotic spirit will, at a favorable moment, call it up, and make it the key-stone of the arch of our government.

With respect to aristocracy, we should further consider, that before the establishment of the American States, nothing was known to history but the man of the old world, crowded within limits either small or over-charged, and steeped in the vices which that situation generates. A government adapted to such men would be one thing; but a very different one, that for the man of these States. Here every one may have land to labor for himself, if he chooses; or, preferring the exercise of any other industry, may exact for it such compensation as not only to afford a comfortable subsistence, but wherewith to provide for a cessation from labor in old age. Every one, by his property, or by his satisfactory situation, is interested in the support of law and order. And such men may safely and advantageously reserve to themselves a wholesome control over their public affairs, and a degree of freedom, which, in the hands of the *canaille* [13] of the cities of Europe, would be instantly perverted to the demolition and destruction of everything public and private. The history of the last twenty-five years of France, and of the last forty years in America, nay of its last two hundred years, proves the truth of both parts of this observation.

But even in Europe a change has sensibly taken place in the mind of man.[14] Science has liberated the ideas of those who read and reflect, and the American example has kindled feelings of right in the people. An insurrection has consequently begun, of science, talents, and courage, against rank and birth, which have fallen into contempt. It has failed in its first effort, because the mobs of the cities, the instrument used for its accomplishment, debased by ignorance, poverty, and vice, could not be restrained to rational action. But the world will recover from the panic of this first catastrophe. Science is progressive, and talents and enterprise on the alert. Resort may be had to the people of the country, a more governable power from their principles and subordination; and rank, and birth, and tinsel-aristocracy will finally shrink into insignificance, even there.

[13 Rabble.]

[14 Referring to the French Revolution and its consequences. As our Minister to France from 1785 to 1789, Jefferson witnessed the outbreak of the Revolution. His account of it can be read in his *Autobiography*.]

This, however, we have no right to meddle with. It suffices for us, if the moral and physical condition of our own citizens qualifies them to select the able and good for the direction of their government, with a recurrence of elections at such short periods as will enable them to displace an unfaithful servant, before the mischief he meditates may be irremediable.

I have stated my opinion on a point on which we differ, not with a view to controversy, for we are both too old to change opinions which are the result of a long life of inquiry and reflection; but on the suggestions of a former letter of yours, that we ought not to die before we have explained ourselves to each other. We acted in perfect harmony, through a long and perilous contest for our liberty and independence. A constitution has been acquired, which, though neither of us thinks perfect, yet both consider as competent to render our fellow citizens the happiest and the securest on whom the sun has ever shone. If we do not think exactly alike as to its imperfections, it matters little to our country, which, after devoting to it long lives of disinterested labor, we have delivered over to our successors in life, who will be able to take care of it and of themselves.

From Adams's Reply
Quincy, November 15, 1813.

We are now explicitly agreed upon one important point, viz., that there is a natural aristocracy among men, the grounds of which are virtue and talents. You very justly indulge a little merriment upon this solemn subject of aristocracy. I often laugh at it too, for there is nothing in this world more ridiculous than the management of it by all the nations of the earth; but while we smile, mankind have reason to say to us, as the frogs said to boys, what is sport to you are wounds and death to us. When I consider the weakness, the folly, the pride, the vanity, the selfishness, the artifice, the low craft and mean cunning, the want of principle, the avarice, the unbounded ambition, the unfeeling cruelty of a majority of those (in all nations) who are allowed an aristocratical influence, and, on the other hand, the stupidity with which the more numerous multitude not only become their dupes, but even love to be taken in by their tricks, I feel a stronger disposition to weep at their destiny, than to laugh at their folly. But though we have agreed in one point, in words, it is not yet certain that we are perfectly agreed in sense. Fashion has introduced an indeterminate use of the word talents. Education, wealth, strength, beauty, stature, birth, marriage, graceful attitudes and motions, gait, air, complexion, physiognomy, are talents, as well as genius, science, and learning. Any one of these talents that in fact commands or influences two votes in society gives to the man who possesses it the character of an aristocrat, in my sense of the word. Pick up the first hundred men you meet, and make a republic. Every man will have an equal vote; but when deliberations and discussions are opened, it will be found that twenty-five, by their talents, virtues being equal, will be able to carry fifty votes. Every one of these twenty-five is an aristocrat in my sense of the word, whether he obtains his one vote in addition to his own by his birth, fortune, figure, eloquence, science, learning, craft, cunning, or even his character for good fellowship, and a *bon vivant*. . .

   Your distinction between natural and artificial aristocracy does not appear to me founded. Birth and wealth are conferred upon some men as imperiously by nature as genius, strength, or beauty. The heir to honors, and riches, and power, has often no more merit in procuring these advantages than he has in obtaining a handsome face or an elegant figure. When aristocracies are established by human laws, and honor, wealth, and power are made hereditary by municipal laws and political institutions, then I acknowledge artificial aristocracy to commence; but this never commences till corruption in elections become dominant and uncontrollable. But this artificial aristocracy can never last. The everlasting envies, jealousies, rivalries, and quarrels among them; their cruel rapacity upon the poor ignorant people, their followers, compel them to set up Caesar, a demagogue, to be a monarch, a master; *pour mettre chacun à sa place*.[15] Here you have the origin of all artificial aristocracy, which is the origin of all monarchies. And both artificial aristocracy and monarchy, and civil, military, political, and hierarchical despotism have all grown out of the natural aristocracy of virtues and talents. We, to be sure, are far remote from this. Many hundred years must roll away before we shall be corrupted. Our pure, virtuous, public-spirited, federative republic will last forever, govern the globe, and introduce the perfection of man; his perfectibility being already proved by Price, Priestley, Condorcet, Rousseau, Diderot, and Godwin.[16] Mischief has been done by the Senate of the United States. I have known and felt more of this mischief than Washington, Jefferson, and Madison, all together. But this has been all caused by the constitutional power of the Senate, in executive business, which ought to be immediately, totally, and essentially abolished. Your distinction between the [aristoi] and [pseudo-

[15 'To put everyone in his place.']

[16 Adams was skeptical, and at times scornful, of the pretensions of the writers he names in this ironical passage. Price, Priestley, and Godwin were English radicals and controversialists; Priestley was a correspondent of Jefferson's. Condorcet, Rousseau, and Diderot were important French writers on moral, political, and philosophical topics.]

aristoi] will not help the matter. I would trust one as well as the other with unlimited power. The law wisely refuses an oath as a witness in his own case, to the saint as well as the sinner. . .

You suppose a difference of opinion between you and me on the subject of aristocracy. I can find none. I dislike and detest hereditary honors, offices, emoluments, established by law. So do you. I am for excluding legal, hereditary distinctions from the United States as long as possible. So are you. I only say that mankind have not yet discovered any remedy against irresistible corruption in elections to offices of great power and profit, but making them hereditary.

James Madison
THE FEDERALIST. NO. X

❴ The Convention of May–September 1787 adopted a Constitution
of the United States to replace the Articles of Confederation and
'form a more perfect Union.' But to be in force, the new Constitution had to be ratified by nine of the thirteen states, and ratification
was far from assured. In the months after the Convention Alexander Hamilton, James Madison, and John Jay wrote a series of articles
designed to win public support for the Constitution by explaining
and defending it. These *Federalist* papers became, and have remained, the classic commentary on the Constitutional foundations
of American government.

Of the 85 *Federalist* papers, 79 appeared in New York newspapers. Madison is believed to have written at least 24 of them in
addition to Number x (printed in *The New York Packet*, 23 November 1787), which is his best-known contribution to the series.

The Constitution was ratified in 1788.

To the People of the State of New York:

AMONG the numerous advantages promised by a well-
constructed Union, none deserves to be more accurately developed than
its tendency to break and control the violence of faction. The friend of
popular governments never finds himself so much alarmed for their character and fate, as when he contemplates their propensity to this dangerous
vice. He will not fail, therefore, to set a due value on any plan which, without violating the principles to which he is attached, provides a proper cure
for it. The instability, injustice, and confusion introduced into the public
councils, have, in truth, been the mortal diseases under which popular
governments have everywhere perished; as they continue to be the favorite
and fruitful topics from which the adversaries to liberty derive their most
specious declamations. The valuable improvements made by the American

constitutions[1] on the popular models, both ancient and modern, cannot certainly be too much admired; but it would be an unwarrantable partiality, to contend that they have as effectually obviated the danger on this side, as was wished and expected. Complaints are everywhere heard from our most considerate and virtuous citizens, equally the friends of public and private faith, and of public and personal liberty, that our governments are too unstable, that the public good is disregarded in the conflicts of rival parties, and that measures are too often decided, not according to the rules of justice and the rights of the minor party, but by the superior force of an interested and overbearing majority. However anxiously we may wish that these complaints had no foundation, the evidence of known facts will not permit us to deny that they are in some degree true. It will be found, indeed, on a candid review of our situation, that some of the distresses under which we labor have been erroneously charged on the operation of our governments; but it will be found, at the same time, that other causes will not alone account for many of our heaviest misfortunes; and, particularly, for that prevailing and increasing distrust of public engagements, and alarm for private rights, which are echoed from one end of the continent to the other.[2] These must be chiefly, if not wholly, effects of the unsteadiness and injustice with which a factious spirit has tainted our public administrations.

By a faction, I understand a number of citizens, whether amounting to a majority or minority of the whole, who are united and actuated by some common impulse of passion, or of interest, adverse to the rights of other citizens, or to the permanent and aggregate interests of the community.

There are two methods of curing the mischiefs of faction: the one, by removing its causes; the other, by controlling its effects.

There are again two methods of removing the causes of faction: the one, by destroying the liberty which is essential to its existence; the other, by giving to every citizen the same opinions, the same passions, and the same interests.

It could never be more truly said than of the first remedy, that it was worse than the disease. Liberty is to faction what air is to fire, an aliment without which it instantly expires. But it could not be less folly to abolish liberty, which is essential to political life, because it nourishes faction, than

[1 The Articles of Confederation (which the Constitution adopted in 1787 was to supersede) seem to be meant, but probably Madison also has in mind the constitutions of the various states.]

[2 This may refer to Shays's Rebellion in Massachusetts, in the autumn of 1786, which shocked the country and which was not forgotten by the framers of the Constitution.]

it would be to wish the annihilation of air, which is essential to animal life, because it imparts to fire its destructive agency.

The second expedient is as impracticable as the first would be unwise. As long as the reason of man continues fallible, and he is at liberty to exercise it, different opinions will be formed. As long as the connection subsists between his reason and his self-love, his opinions and his passions will have a reciprocal influence on each other; and the former will be objects to which the latter will attach themselves. The diversity in the faculties of men, from which the rights of property [3] originate, is not less an insuperable obstacle to a uniformity of interests. The protection of these faculties is the first object of government. From the protection of different and unequal faculties of acquiring property, the possession of different degrees and kinds of property immediately results; and from the influence of these on the sentiments and views of the respective proprietors, ensues a division of the society into different interests and parties.

The latent causes of faction are thus sown in the nature of man; and we see them everywhere brought into different degrees of activity, according to the different circumstances of civil society. A zeal for different opinions concerning religion, concerning government, and many other points, as well of speculation as of practice; an attachment to different leaders ambitiously contending for pre-eminence and power; or to persons of other descriptions whose fortunes have been interesting to the human passions, have, in turn, divided mankind into parties, inflamed them with mutual animosity, and rendered them much more disposed to vex and oppress each other than to co-operate for their common good. So strong is this propensity of mankind to fall into mutual animosities, that where no substantial occasion presents itself, the most frivolous and fanciful distinctions have been sufficient to kindle their unfriendly passions and excite their most violent conflicts. But the most common and durable source of factions has been the various and unequal distribution of property. Those who hold and those who are without property have ever formed distinct interests in society. Those who are creditors, and those who are debtors, fall under a like discrimination. A landed interest, a manufacturing interest, a mercantile interest, a moneyed interest, with many lesser interests, grow up of necessity in civilized nations, and divide them into different classes, actuated by different sentiments and views. The regulation of these various and interfering interests forms the principal task of modern legislation, and

[3 Compare Madison's ideas on property with those of Emerson ('Politics'), pp. 210–21, and Jefferson, pp. 194–9.]

involves the spirit of party and faction in the necessary and ordinary operations of the government.

No man is allowed to be a judge in his own cause, because his interest would certainly bias his judgment, and, not improbably, corrupt his integrity. With equal, nay with greater reason, a body of men are unfit to be both judges and parties at the same time; yet what are many of the most important acts of legislation, but so many judicial determinations, not indeed concerning the rights of single persons, but concerning the rights of large bodies of citizens? And what are the different classes of legislators but advocates and parties to the causes which they determine? Is a law proposed concerning private debts? It is a question to which the creditors are parties on one side and the debtors on the other. Justice ought to hold the balance between them. Yet the parties are, and must be, themselves the judges; and the most numerous party, or, in other words, the most powerful faction must be expected to prevail. Shall domestic manufactures be encouraged, and in what degree, by restrictions on foreign manufactures? are questions which would be differently decided by the landed and the manufacturing classes, and probably by neither with a sole regard to justice and the public good. The apportionment of taxes on the various descriptions of property is an act which seems to require the most exact impartiality; yet there is, perhaps, no legislative act in which greater opportunity and temptation are given to a predominant party to trample on the rules of justice. Every shilling with which they overburden the inferior number, is a shilling saved to their own pockets.

It is in vain to say that enlightened statesmen will be able to adjust these clashing interests, and render them all subservient to the public good. Enlightened statesmen will not always be at the helm. Nor, in many cases, can such an adjustment be made at all without taking into view indirect and remote considerations, which will rarely prevail over the immediate interest which one party may find in disregarding the rights of another or the good of the whole.

The inference to which we are brought is, that the *causes* of faction cannot be removed, and that relief is only to be sought in the means of controlling its *effects*.

If a faction consists of less than a majority, relief is supplied by the republican principle, which enables the majority to defeat its sinister views by regular vote. It may clog the administration, it may convulse the society; but it will be unable to execute and mask its violence under the forms of the Constitution. When a majority is included in a faction, the form of popular government, on the other hand, enables it to sacrifice to its ruling passion or interest both the public good and the rights of other citizens. To secure the public good and private rights against the danger of such a faction, and at the same time to preserve the spirit and the form of popular government, is then the great object to which our inquiries are directed. Let me add that it is the great desideratum by which this form of government can be rescued from the opprobrium under which it has so long labored, and be recommended to the esteem and adoption of mankind.

By what means is this object attainable? Evidently by one of two only. Either the existence of the same passion or interest in a majority at the same time must be prevented, or the majority, having such coexistent passion or interest, must be rendered, by their number and local situation, unable to concert and carry into effect schemes of oppression. If the impulse and the opportunity be suffered to coincide, we well know that neither moral nor religious motives can be relied on as an adequate control. They are not found to be such on the injustice and violence of individuals, and lose their efficacy in proportion to the number combined together, that is, in proportion as their efficacy becomes needful.

From this view of the subject it may be concluded that a pure democracy, by which I mean a society consisting of a small number of citizens, who assemble and administer the government in person, can admit of no cure for the mischiefs of faction. A common passion or interest will, in almost every case, be felt by a majority of the whole; a communication and concert result from the form of government itself; and there is nothing to check the inducements to sacrifice the weaker party or an obnoxious individual. Hence it is that such democracies have ever been spectacles of turbulence and contention; have ever been found incompatible with personal security or the rights of property; and have in general been as short in their lives as they have been violent in their deaths. Theoretic politicians, who have patronized this species of government, have erroneously supposed that by reducing mankind to a perfect equality in their political rights, they would, at the same time, be perfectly equalized and assimilated in their possessions, their opinions, and their passions.

A republic, by which I mean a government in which the scheme of representation takes place, opens a different prospect, and promises the cure for which we are seeking. Let us examine the points in which it varies from pure democracy, and we shall comprehend both the nature of the cure and the efficacy which it must derive from the Union.

The two great points of difference between a democracy and a republic

are: first, the delegation of the government, in the latter, to a small number of citizens elected by the rest; secondly, the greater number of citizens,
and greater sphere of country, over which the latter may be extended.

The effect of the first difference is, on the one hand, to refine and enlarge
the public views, by passing them through the medium of a chosen body
of citizens, whose wisdom may best discern the true interest of their country, and whose patriotism and love of justice will be least likely to sacrifice it to temporary or partial considerations. Under such a regulation, it
may well happen that the public voice, pronounced by the representatives
of the people, will be more consonant to the public good than if pronounced by the people themselves, convened for the purpose. On the other
hand, the effect may be inverted. Men of factious tempers, of local prejudices, or of sinister designs, may, by intrigue, by corruption, or by other
means, first obtain the suffrages, and then betray the interests, of the
people. The question resulting is, whether small or extensive republics are
more favorable to the election of proper guardians of the public weal; and
it is clearly decided in favor of the latter by two obvious considerations:

In the first place, it is to be remarked that, however small the republic
may be, the representatives must be raised to a certain number, in order to
guard against the cabals of a few; [4] and that, however large it may be, they
must be limited to a certain number, in order to guard against the confusion of a multitude. Hence, the number of representatives in the two
cases not being in proportion to that of the two constituents, and being
proportionally greater in the small republic, it follows that, if the proportion of fit characters be not less in the large than in the small republic, the
former will present a greater option, and consequently a greater probability
of a fit choice.

In the next place, as each representative will be chosen by a greater number of citizens in the large than in the small republic, it will be more difficult for unworthy candidates to practise with success the vicious arts by
which elections are too often carried; and the suffrages of the people being
more free, will be more likely to centre in men who possess the most
attractive merit and the most diffusive and established characters.

It must be confessed that in this, as in most other cases, there is a mean,
on both sides of which inconveniences will be found to lie. By enlarging
too much the number of electors, you render the representative too little
acquainted with all their local circumstances and lesser interests; as by

[4 On the danger of obstruction by strongly organized minorities see also the Jefferson-
Adams letters, pp. 194–201.]

reducing it too much, you render him unduly attached to these, and too little fit to comprehend and pursue great and national objects. The federal Constitution forms a happy combination in this respect; the great and aggregate interests being referred to the national, the local and particular to the State legislatures.

The other point of difference is, the greater number of citizens and extent of territory which may be brought within the compass of republican than of democratic government; and it is this circumstance principally which renders factious combinations less to be dreaded in the former than in the latter. The smaller the society, the fewer probably will be the distinct parties and interests composing it; the fewer the distinct parties and interests, the more frequently will a majority be found of the same party; and the smaller the number of individuals composing a majority, and the smaller the compass within which they are placed, the more easily will they concert and execute their plans of oppression. Extend the sphere, and you take in a greater variety of parties and interests; you make it less probable that a majority of the whole will have a common motive to invade the rights of other citizens; or if such a common motive exists, it will be more difficult for all who feel it to discover their own strength, and to act in unison with each other. Besides other impediments, it may be remarked that, where there is a consciousness of unjust or dishonorable purposes, communication is always checked by distrust in proportion to the number whose concurrence is necessary.

Hence, it clearly appears, that the same advantage which a republic has over a democracy, in controlling the effects of faction, is enjoyed by a large over a small republic,—is enjoyed by the Union over the States composing it. Does the advantage consist in the substitution of representatives whose enlightened views and virtuous sentiments render them superior to local prejudices and to schemes of injustice? It will not be denied that the representation of the Union will be most likely to possess these requisite endowments. Does it consist in the greater security afforded by a greater variety of parties, against the event of any one party being able to outnumber and oppress the rest? In an equal degree does the increased variety of parties comprised within the Union, increase this security. Does it, in fine, consist in the greater obstacles opposed to the concert and accomplishment of the secret wishes of an unjust and interested majority? Here, again, the extent of the Union gives it the most palpable advantage.

The influence of factious leaders may kindle a flame within their particular States, but will be unable to spread a general conflagration through the other States. A religious sect may degenerate into a political faction in a part of the Confederacy; [5] but the variety of sects dispersed over the entire face of it must secure the national councils against any danger from that source. A rage for paper money, for an abolition of debts, for an equal division of property, or for any other improper or wicked project, will be less apt to pervade the whole body of the Union than a particular member of it; in the same proportion as such a malady is more likely to taint a particular county or district, than an entire State.

In the extent and proper structure of the Union, therefore, we behold a republican remedy for the diseases most incident to republican government. And according to the degree of pleasure and pride we feel in being republicans, ought to be our zeal in cherishing the spirit and supporting the character of Federalists.   PUBLIUS.

[5] 'Confederacy' here and 'Federalists' in the next paragraph do not, of course, have the restricted meanings familiar to students of nineteenth-century American history. 'Confederacy' here means merely the association of states existent when Madison was writing. 'Federalists' is not the name of an organized political party but a term denoting those who wanted the Constitution to be ratified and who supported the kind of federal union advocated by the *Federalist* papers.]

Ralph Waldo Emerson
POLITICS

❡ A good many readers in this generation may find Emerson's 'Politics' quaint if nothing worse. If they approve of his doubts about property, they will nevertheless think that his exaltation of the individual above the State is somewhat remote from the way the world goes now. 'Good men must not obey the laws too well.' 'A party is perpetually corrupted by personality.' 'The less government we have, the better.' 'The appearance of character makes the State unnecessary.' These are not maxims of the modern State, in either its democratic or its totalitarian manifestations. 'If men can be educated, the institutions will share their improvement, and the moral sentiment will write the law of the land,' Emerson insists. His 'Politics' remains an uncompromising affirmation of faith in idealism, in the supreme worth of the individual, and of conviction that in the long run it is individuals who make States good, not States that make individuals good.

'Politics' was first published in the second series of Emerson's *Essays*, 1844.

IN DEALING with the State, we ought to remember that its institutions are not aboriginal, though they existed before we were born: that they are not superior to the citizen: that every one of them was once the act of a single man: every law and usage was a man's expedient to meet a particular case: that they all are imitable, all alterable; we may make as good; we may make better. Society is an illusion to the young citizen. It lies before him in rigid repose, with certain names, men, and institutions, rooted like oak-trees to the centre, round which all arrange themselves the best they can. But the old statesman knows that society is fluid; there are no such roots and centres; but any particle may suddenly become the centre

FROM *Essays*, Second Series, 1844.

of the movement, and compel the system to gyrate round it, as every man of strong will, like Pisistratus,[1] or Cromwell, does for a time, and every man of truth, like Plato, or Paul, does forever. But politics rest on necessary foundations, and cannot be treated with levity. Republics abound in young civilians, who believe that the laws make the city, that grave modifications of the policy and modes of living, and employments of the population, that commerce, education, and religion, may be voted in or out; and that any measure, though it were absurd, may be imposed on a people, if only you can get sufficient voices to make it a law. But the wise know that foolish legislation is a rope of sand, which perishes in the twisting; that the State must follow, and not lead the character and progress of the citizen; the strongest usurper is quickly got rid of; and they only who build on Ideas, build for eternity; and that the form of government which prevails, is the expression of what cultivation exists in the population which permits it. The law is only a memorandum. We are superstitious, and esteem the statute somewhat: so much life as it has in the character of living men, is its force. The statute stands there to say, yesterday we agreed so and so, but how feel ye this article to-day? Our statute is a currency, which we stamp with our own portrait: it soon becomes unrecognizable, and in process of time will return to the mint. Nature is not democratic, nor limited-monarchical, but despotic, and will not be fooled or abated of any jot of her authority, by the pertest of her sons: and as fast as the public mind is opened to more intelligence, the code is seen to be brute and stammering. It speaks not articulately, and must be made to. Meantime the education of the general mind never stops. The reveries of the true and simple are prophetic. What the tender poetic youth dreams, and prays, and paints to-day, but shuns the ridicule of saying aloud, shall presently be the resolutions of public bodies, then shall be carried as grievance and bill of rights through conflict and war, and then shall be triumphant law and establishment for a hundred years, until it gives place, in turn, to new prayers and pictures. The history of the State sketches in coarse outline the progress of thought, and follows at a distance the delicacy of culture and of aspiration.

The theory of politics, which has possessed the mind of men, and which they have expressed the best they could in their laws and in their revolutions, considers persons and property[2] as the two objects for whose protec-

---

[1 Ruler of Athens, 560–527 B.C.]

[2 See Jefferson, pp. 194–9; Madison, *Federalist,* No. x, pp. 202–9; Becker, 'The Reality,' pp. 235–51.]

tion government exists. Of persons, all have equal rights, in virtue of being identical in nature. This interest, of course, with its whole power demands a democracy. Whilst the rights of all as persons are equal, in virtue of their access to reason, their rights in property are very unequal. One man owns his clothes, and another owns a county. This accident, depending, primarily, on the skill and virtue of the parties, of which there is every degree, and, secondarily, on patrimony, falls unequally, and its rights, of course, are unequal. Personal rights, universally the same, demand a government framed on the ratio of the census: property demands a government framed on the ratio of owners and of owning. Laban,[3] who has flocks and herds, wishes them looked after by an officer on the frontiers, lest the Midianites shall drive them off, and pays a tax to that end. Jacob has no flocks or herds, and no fear of the Midianites, and pays no tax to the officer. It seemed fit that Laban and Jacob should have equal rights to elect the officer, who is to defend their persons, but that Laban, and not Jacob, should elect the officer who is to guard the sheep and cattle. And, if question arise whether additional officers or watch-towers should be provided, must not Laban and Isaac, and those who must sell part of their herds to buy protection for the rest, judge better of this, and with more right, than Jacob, who, because he is a youth and a traveller, eats their bread and not his own?

In the earliest society the proprietors made their own wealth, and so long as it comes to the owners in the direct way, no other opinion would arise in any equitable community, than that property should make the law for property, and persons the law for persons.

But property passes through donation or inheritance to those who do not create it. Gift, in one case, makes it as really the new owner's, as labor made it the first owner's: in the other case, of patrimony, the law makes an ownership, which will be valid in each man's view according to the estimate which he sets on the public tranquillity.

It was not, however, found easy to embody the readily admitted principle, that property should make law for property, and persons for persons: since persons and property mixed themselves in every transaction. At last it seemed settled, that the rightful distinction was, that the proprietors should have more elective franchise than non-proprietors, on the Spartan principle of 'calling that which is just, equal; not that which is equal, just.'

That principle [4] no longer looks so self-evident as it appeared in former

[3 See Genesis, xxix–xxxi.]

[4 Property qualifications for voting existed in many states until the 1820's.]

times, partly, because doubts have arisen whether too much weight had not been allowed in the laws, to property, and such a structure given to our usages, as allowed the rich to encroach on the poor, and to keep them poor; but mainly, because there is an instinctive sense, however obscure and yet inarticulate, that the whole constitution of property, on its present tenures, is injurious, and its influence on persons deteriorating and degrading; that truly, the only interest for the consideration of the State, is persons: that property will always follow persons; that the highest end of government is the culture of men: and if men can be educated, the institutions will share their improvement, and the moral sentiment will write the law of the land.

If it be not easy to settle the equity of this question, the peril is less when we take note of our natural defences. We are kept by better guards than the vigilance of such magistrates as we commonly elect. Society always consists, in greatest part, of young and foolish persons. The old, who have seen through the hypocrisy of courts and statesmen, die, and leave no wisdom to their sons. They believe their own newspaper, as their fathers did at their age. With such an ignorant and deceivable majority, States would soon run to ruin, but that there are limitations, beyond which the folly and ambition of governors cannot go. Things have their laws, as well as men; and things refuse to be trifled with. Property will be protected. Corn will not grow, unless it is planted and manured; but the farmer will not plant or hoe it, unless the chances are a hundred to one, that he will cut and harvest it. Under any forms, persons and property must and will have their just sway. They exert their power, as steadily as matter its attraction. Cover up a pound of earth never so cunningly, divide and subdivide it; melt it to liquid, convert it to gas; it will always weigh a pound: it will always attract and resist other matter, by the full virtue of one pound weight;—and the attributes of a person, his wit and his moral energy, will exercise, under any law or extinguishing tyranny, their proper force,—if not overtly, then covertly; if not for the law, then against it; if not wholesomely, then poisonously; with right, or by might.

The boundaries of personal influence it is impossible to fix, as persons are organs of moral or supernatural force. Under the dominion of an idea, which possesses the minds of multitudes, as civil freedom, or the religious sentiment, the powers of persons are no longer subjects of calculation. A nation of men unanimously bent on freedom, or conquest, can easily confound the arithmetic of statists, and achieve extravagant actions, out of all proportion to their means; as, the Greeks, the Saracens, the Swiss, the Americans, and the French have done.

In like manner, to every particle of property belongs its own attraction. A cent is the representative of a certain quantity of corn or other commodity. Its value is in the necessities of the animal man. It is so much warmth, so much bread, so much water, so much land. The law may do what it will with the owner of property, its just power will still attach to the cent. The law may in a mad freak say, that all shall have power except the owners of property: they shall have no vote. Nevertheless, by a higher law, the property will, year after year, write every statute that respects property. The non-proprietor will be the scribe of the proprietor. What the owners wish to do, the whole power of property will do, either through the law, or else in defiance of it. Of course, I speak of all the property, not merely of the great estates. When the rich are outvoted, as frequently happens, it is the joint treasury of the poor which exceeds their accumulations. Every man owns something, if it is only a cow, or a wheelbarrow, or his arms, and so has that property to dispose of.

The same necessity which secures the rights of person and property against the malignity or folly of the magistrate, determines the form and methods of governing, which are proper to each nation, and to its habit of thought, and nowise transferable to other states of society. In this country, we are very vain of our political institutions, which are singular in this, that they sprung, within the memory of living men, from the character and condition of the people, which they still express with sufficient fidelity, —and we ostentatiously prefer them to any other in history. They are not better, but only fitter for us. We may be wise in asserting the advantage in modern times of the democratic form, but to other states of society, in which religion consecrated the monarchical, that and not this was expedient. Democracy is better for us, because the religious sentiment of the present time accords better with it. Born democrats, we are nowise qualified to judge of monarchy, which, to our fathers living in the monarchical idea, was also relatively right. But our institutions, though in coincidence with the spirit of the age, have not any exemption from the practical defects which have discredited other forms. Every actual State is corrupt. Good men must not obey the laws too well. What satire on government can equal the severity of censure conveyed in the word *politic*, which now for ages has signified *cunning*, intimating that the State is a trick?

The same benign necessity and the same practical abuse appear in the parties into which each State divides itself, of opponents and defenders of the administration of the government. Parties are also founded on instincts, and have better guides to their own humble aims than the sagacity of their leaders. They have nothing perverse in their origin, but rudely mark some real and lasting relation. We might as wisely reprove the east wind, or the frost, as a political party, whose members, for the most part, could give no account of their position, but stand for the defence of those interests in which they find themselves. Our quarrel with them begins, when they quit this deep natural ground at the bidding of some leader, and, obeying personal considerations, throw themselves into the maintenance and defence of points, nowise belonging to their system. A party is perpetually corrupted by personality. Whilst we absolve the association from dishonesty, we cannot extend the same charity to their leaders. They reap the rewards of the docility and zeal of the masses which they direct. Ordinarily, our parties are parties of circumstance, and not of principle; as, the planting interest in conflict with the commercial; the party of capitalists, and that of operatives; parties which are identical in their moral character, and which can easily change ground with each other, in the support of many of their measures. Parties of principle, as, religious sects, or the party of free-trade, of universal suffrage, of abolition of slavery, of abolition of capital punishment, degenerate into personalities, or would inspire enthusiasm. The vice of our leading parties in this country (which may be cited as a fair specimen of these societies of opinion) is, that they do not plant themselves on the deep and necessary grounds to which they are respectively entitled, but lash themselves to fury in the carrying of some local and momentary measure, nowise useful to the commonwealth. Of the two great parties,[5] which, at this hour, almost share the nation between them, I should say, that, one has the best cause, and the other contains the best men. The philosopher, the poet, or the religious man, will, of course, wish to cast his vote with the democrat, for free-trade, for wide suffrage, for the abolition of legal cruelties in the penal code, and for facilitating in every manner the access of the young and the poor to the sources of wealth and power. But he can rarely accept the persons whom the so-called popular party propose to him as representatives of these liberalities. They have not at heart the ends which give to the name of democracy what hope and virtue are in it. The spirit of our American radicalism is destructive and aimless: it is not loving; it has no ulterior and divine ends; but is destructive only out of hatred and selfishness. On the other side, the conservative party, composed of the most moderate, able, and cultivated part of the population, is timid, and merely defensive of property. It vindicates no right, it aspires to no real good, it brands no crime, it proposes no generous

[5 The Democratic and the Whig.]

policy, it does not build, nor write, nor cherish the arts, nor foster religion, nor establish schools, nor encourage science, nor emancipate the slave, nor befriend the poor, or the Indian, or the immigrant. From neither party, when in power, has the world any benefit to expect in science, art, or humanity, at all commensurate with the resources of the nation.

I do not for these defects despair of our republic. We are not at the mercy of any waves of chance. In the strife of ferocious parties, human nature always finds itself cherished, as the children of the convicts at Botany Bay [6] are found to have as healthy a moral sentiment as other children. Citizens of feudal states are alarmed at our democratic institutions lapsing into anarchy; and the older and more cautious among ourselves are learning from Europeans to look with some terror at our turbulent freedom. It is said that in our license of construing the Constitution, and in the despotism of public opinion, we have no anchor; and one foreign observer thinks he has found the safeguard in the sanctity of Marriage among us; and another thinks he has found it in our Calvinism. Fisher Ames [7] expressed the popular security more wisely, when he compared a monarchy and a republic, saying, 'that a monarchy is a merchantman, which sails well, but will sometimes strike on a rock, and go to the bottom; whilst a republic is a raft, which would never sink, but then your feet are always in water.' No forms can have any dangerous importance, whilst we are befriended by the laws of things. It makes no difference how many tons weight of atmosphere presses on our heads, so long as the same pressure resists it within the lungs. Augment the mass a thousand fold, it cannot begin to crush us, as long as reaction is equal to action. The fact of two poles, of two forces, centripetal and centrifugal, is universal, and each force by its own activity develops the other. Wild liberty develops iron conscience. Want of liberty, by strengthening law and decorum, stupefies conscience. 'Lynch-law' prevails only where there is greater hardihood and self-subsistency in the leaders. A mob cannot be a permanency: everybody's interest requires that it should not exist, and only justice satisfies all.

We must trust infinitely to the beneficent necessity which shines through all laws. Human nature expresses itself in them as characteristically as in statues, or songs, or railroads, and an abstract of the codes of nations would be a transcript of the common conscience. Governments have their origin in the moral identity of men. Reason for one is seen to be reason for an-

[6] British penal colony off New South Wales.]

[7] Massachusetts Federalist (1758–1808), prominent in the politics of the Washington administration, 1789–97.]

other, and for every other. There is a middle measure which satisfies all parties, be they never so many, or so resolute for their own. Every man finds a sanction for his simplest claims and deeds in decisions of his own mind, which he calls Truth and Holiness. In these decisions all the citizens find a perfect agreement, and only in these; not in what is good to eat, good to wear, good use of time, or what amount of land, or of public aid, each is entitled to claim. This truth and justice men presently endeavor to make application of, to the measuring of land, the apportionment of service, the protection of life and property. Their first endeavors, no doubt, are very awkward. Yet absolute right is the first governor; or, every government is an impure theocracy. The idea, after which each community is aiming to make and mend its law, is, the will of the wise man. The wise man, it cannot find in nature, and it makes awkward but earnest efforts to secure his government by contrivance; as, by causing the entire people to give their voices on every measure; or, by a double choice to get the representation of the whole; or, by a selection of the best citizens; or, to secure the advantages of efficiency and internal peace, by confiding the government to one, who may himself select his agents. All forms of government symbolize an immortal government, common to all dynasties and independent of numbers, perfect where two men exist, perfect where there is only one man.

Every man's nature is a sufficient advertisement to him of the character of his fellows. My right and my wrong, is their right and their wrong. Whilst I do what is fit for me, and abstain from what is unfit, my neighbor and I shall often agree in our means, and work together for a time to one end. But whenever I find my dominion over myself not sufficient for me, and undertake the direction of him also, I overstep the truth, and come into false relations to him. I may have so much more skill or strength than he, that he cannot express adequately his sense of wrong, but it is a lie, and hurts like a lie both him and me. Love and nature cannot maintain the assumption: it must be executed by a practical lie, namely, by force. This undertaking for another, is the blunder which stands in colossal ugliness in the governments of the world. It is the same thing in numbers, as in a pair, only not quite so intelligible. I can see well enough a great difference between my setting myself down to a self-control, and my going to make somebody else act after my views: but when a quarter of the human race assume to tell me what I must do, I may be too much disturbed by the circumstances to see so clearly the absurdity of their command. Therefore, all public ends look vague and quixotic beside private ones. For, any laws but those which men make for themselves, are laughable. If I put myself in the place of my child, and we stand in one thought, and see that things are thus or thus, that perception is law for him and me. We are both there, both act. But if, without carrying him into the thought, I look over into his plot, and, guessing how it is with him, ordain this or that, he will never obey me. This is the history of governments,—one man does something which is to bind another. A man who cannot be acquainted with me, taxes me; looking from afar at me, ordains that a part of my labor shall go to this or that whimsical end, not as I, but as he happens to fancy. Behold the consequence. Of all debts, men are least willing to pay the taxes. What a satire is this on government! Everywhere they think they get their money's worth, except for these.

Hence, the less government we have, the better,—the fewer laws, and the less confided power. The antidote to this abuse of formal Government, is, the influence of private character, the growth of the Individual; the appearance of the principal to supersede the proxy; the appearance of the wise man, of whom the existing government is, it must be owned, but a shabby imitation. That which all things tend to educe, which freedom, cultivation, intercourse, revolutions, go to form and deliver, is character; that is the end of nature, to reach unto this coronation of her king. To educate the wise man, the State exists; and with the appearance of the wise man, the State expires. The appearance of character makes the State unnecessary. The wise man is the State. He needs no army, fort, or navy,— he loves men too well; no bribe, or feast, or palace, to draw friends to him; no vantage ground, no favorable circumstance. He needs no library, for he has not done thinking; no church, for he is a prophet; no statute book, for he has the lawgiver; no money, for he is value; no road, for he is at home where he is; no experience, for the life of the creator shoots through him, and looks from his eyes. He has no personal friends, for he who has the spell to draw the prayer and piety of all men unto him, needs not husband and educate a few, to share with him a select and poetic life. His relation to men is angelic; his memory is myrrh to them; his presence, frankincense and flowers.

We think our civilization near its meridian, but we are yet only at the cock-crowing and the morning star. In our barbarous society the influence of character is in its infancy. As a political power, as the rightful lord who is to tumble all rulers from their chairs, its presence is hardly yet suspected. Malthus and Ricardo [8] quite omit it; the Annual Register is silent; in the

[8] Thomas Malthus (1766–1834) and David Ricardo (1772–1823), celebrated English economists.]

Conversations' Lexicon, it is not set down; the President's Message, the Queen's Speech, have not mentioned it; and yet it is never nothing. Every thought which genius and piety throw into the world, alters the world. The gladiators in the lists of power feel, through all their frocks of force and simulation, the presence of worth. I think the very strife of trade and ambition are confession of this divinity; and successes in those fields are the poor amends, the fig-leaf with which the shamed soul attempts to hide its nakedness. I find the like unwilling homage in all quarters. It is because we know how much is due from us, that we are impatient to show some petty talent as a substitute for worth. We are haunted by a conscience of this right to grandeur of character, and are false to it. But each of us has some talent, can do somewhat useful, or graceful, or formidable, or amusing, or lucrative. That we do, as an apology to others and to ourselves, for not reaching the mark of a good and equal life. But it does not satisfy *us*, whilst we thrust it on the notice of our companions. It may throw dust in their eyes, but does not smooth our own brow, or give us the tranquillity of the strong when we walk abroad. We do penance as we go. Our talent is a sort of expiation, and we are constrained to reflect on our splendid moment, with a certain humiliation, as somewhat too fine, and not as one act of many acts, a fair expression of our permanent energy. Most persons of ability meet in society with a kind of tacit appeal. Each seems to say, 'I am not all here.' Senators and presidents have climbed so high with pain enough, not because they think the place specially agreeable, but as an apology for real worth, and to vindicate their manhood in our eyes. This conspicuous chair is their compensation to themselves for being of a poor, cold, hard nature. They must do what they can. Like one class of forest animals, they have nothing but a prehensile tail: climb they must, or crawl. If a man found himself so rich-natured that he could enter into strict relations with the best persons, and make life serene around him by the dignity and sweetness of his behavior, could he afford to circumvent the favor of the caucus and the press, and covet relations so hollow and pompous, as those of a politician? Surely nobody would be a charlatan, who could afford to be sincere.

The tendencies of the times favor the idea of self-government, and leave the individual, for all code, to the rewards and penalties of his own constitution, which work with more energy than we believe, whilst we depend on artificial restraints. The movement in this direction has been very marked in modern history. Much has been blind and discreditable, but the nature of the revolution is not affected by the vices of the revolters; for this is a purely moral force. It was never adopted by any party in history, neither can be. It separates the individual from all party, and unites him, at the same time, to the race. It promises a recognition of higher rights than those of personal freedom, or the security of property. A man has a right to be employed, to be trusted, to be loved, to be revered. The power of love, as the basis of a State, has never been tried. We must not imagine that all things are lapsing into confusion, if every tender protestant be not compelled to bear his part in certain social conventions: nor doubt that roads can be built, letters carried, and the fruit of labor secured, when the government of force is at an end. Are our methods now so excellent that all competition is hopeless? could not a nation of friends even devise better ways? On the other hand, let not the most conservative and timid fear anything from a premature surrender of the bayonet, and the system of force. For, according to the order of nature, which is quite superior to our will, it stands thus; there will always be a government of force, where men are selfish; and when they are pure enough to abjure the code of force, they will be wise enough to see how these public ends of the post-office, of the highway, of commerce, and the exchange of property, of museums and libraries, of institutions of art and science, can be answered.

We live in a very low state of the world, and pay unwilling tribute to governments founded on force. There is not, among the most religious and instructed men of the most religious and civil nations, a reliance on the moral sentiment, and a sufficient belief in the unity of things to persuade them that society can be maintained without artificial restraints, as well as the solar system; or that the private citizen might be reasonable, and a good neighbor, without the hint of a jail or a confiscation. What is strange too, there never was in any man sufficient faith in the power of rectitude, to inspire him with the broad design of renovating the State on the principle of right and love. All those who have pretended this design, have been partial reformers, and have admitted in some manner the supremacy of the bad State. I do not call to mind a single human being who has steadily denied the authority of the laws, on the simple ground of his own moral nature. Such designs, full of genius and full of fate as they are, are not entertained except avowedly as air-pictures. If the individual who exhibits them, dare to think them practicable, he disgusts scholars and churchmen; and men of talent, and women of superior sentiments, cannot hide their contempt. Not the less does nature continue to fill the heart of youth with suggestions of this enthusiasm, and there are now men,—if indeed I can speak in the plural number,—more exactly, I will say, I have just been conversing with one man, to whom no weight of adverse experience will make it for a moment appear impossible, that thousands of human beings might exercise towards each other the grandest and simplest sentiments, as well as a knot of friends, or a pair of lovers.

John Stuart Mill
ON LIBERTY

❮ With Mill, as with most progressive political thinkers of the eighteenth and nineteenth centuries, the watchword was liberty. Times have changed, and the arguments in *On Liberty* now seem inadequate to many readers; to some they are as out of date as the *laissez-faire* economics and the 'free enterprise' of the era Mill lived in. But they are not dead ideas. For in welfare states, planned societies, and socialism the problem of individual liberty not only remains unanswered but becomes more perplexing than ever. Mill was firmly convinced that 'Apart from the peculiar tenets of individual thinkers, there is also in the world at large an increasing inclination to stretch unduly the powers of society over the individual, both by the force of opinion and even by that of legislation: and as the tendency of all the changes taking place in the world is to strengthen society and diminish the power of the individual, this encroachment is not one of the evils which tend spontaneously to disappear, but, on the contrary, to grow more and more formidable.' The question he posed in 1859, 'how to make the fitting adjustment between individual independence and social control,' we are trying to answer today. To look for precise solutions to the problems of the 1950's in this essay of the 1850's would be unreasonable. But as an argument for the enduring values of individualism and the preciousness of personal liberty it is still an eloquent and persuasive work.

The selection reprinted here is the introductory chapter of Mill's essay.

T̄HE SUBJECT of this Essay is not the so-called Liberty of the Will, so unfortunately opposed to the misnamed doctrine of Philosophical Necessity; but Civil, or Social Liberty: the nature and limits of the power which can be legitimately exercised by society over the individual. A ques-

FROM *On Liberty*, 1859.

tion seldom stated, and hardly ever discussed, in general terms, but which profoundly influences the practical controversies of the age by its latent presence, and is likely soon to make itself recognized as the vital question of the future. It is so far from being new, that, in a certain sense, it has divided mankind, almost from the remotest ages; but in the stage of progress into which the more civilized portions of the species have now entered, it presents itself under new conditions, and requires a different and more fundamental treatment.

The struggle between Liberty and Authority is the most conspicuous feature in the portions of history with which we are earliest familiar, particularly in that of Greece, Rome, and England. But in old times this contest was between subjects, or some classes of subjects, and the government.[1] By liberty, was meant protection against the tyranny of the political rulers. The rulers were conceived (except in some of the popular governments of Greece) as in a necessarily antagonistic position to the people whom they ruled. They consisted of a governing One, or a governing tribe or caste, who derived their authority from inheritance or conquest; who, at all events, did not hold it at the pleasure of the governed, and whose supremacy men did not venture, perhaps did not desire, to contest, whatever precautions might be taken against its oppressive exercise. Their power was regarded as necessary, but also as highly dangerous; as a weapon which they would attempt to use against their subjects, no less than against external enemies. To prevent the weaker members of the community from being preyed upon by innumerable vultures, it was needful that there should be an animal of prey stronger than the rest, commissioned to keep them down. But as the king of the vultures would be no less bent upon preying on the flock than any of the minor harpies, it was indispensable to be in a perpetual attitude of defence against his beak and claws. The aim, therefore, of patriots, was to set limits to the power which the ruler should be suffered to exercise over the community; and this limitation was what they meant by liberty. It was attempted in two ways. First, by obtaining a recognition of certain immunities, called political liberties or rights, which it was to be regarded as a breach of duty in the ruler to infringe, and which, if he did infringe, specific resistance, or general rebellion, was held to be justifiable. A second, and generally a later expedient, was the establishment of constitutional checks; by which the consent of the community, or of a body of some sort supposed to represent its interests, was made a necessary condition to some of the more important acts of the gov-

[1 See Santayana, pp. 190–93, and Becker, pp. 235–40.]

erning power. To the first of these modes of limitation, the ruling power, in most European countries, was compelled, more or less, to submit. It was not so with the second; and to attain this, or when already in some degree possessed, to attain it more completely, became everywhere the principal object of the lovers of liberty. And so long as mankind were content to combat one enemy by another, and to be ruled by a master, on condition of being guaranteed more or less efficaciously against his tyranny, they did not carry their aspirations beyond this point.

A time, however, came, in the progress of human affairs, when men ceased to think it a necessity of nature that their governors should be an independent power, opposed in interest to themselves. It appeared to them much better that the various magistrates of the State should be their tenants or delegates, revocable at their pleasure. In that way alone, it seemed, could they have complete security that the powers of government would never be abused to their disadvantage. By degrees, this new demand for elective and temporary rulers became the prominent object of the exertions of the popular party, wherever any such party existed; and superseded, to a considerable extent, the previous efforts to limit the power of rulers. As the struggle proceeded for making the ruling power emanate from the periodical choice of the ruled, some persons began to think that too much importance had been attached to the limitation of the power itself. *That* (it might seem) was a resource against rulers whose interests were habitually opposed to those of the people. What was now wanted was, that the rulers should be identified with the people; that their interest and will should be the interest and will of the nation. The nation did not need to be protected against its own will. There was no fear of its tyrannizing over itself. Let the rulers be effectually responsible to it, promptly removable by it, and it could afford to trust them with power of which it could itself dictate the use to be made. Their power was but the nation's own power, concentrated, and in a form convenient for exercise. This mode of thought, or rather perhaps of feeling, was common among the last generation of European liberalism, in the Continental section of which, it still apparently predominates. Those who admit any limit to what a government may do, except in the case of such governments as they think ought not to exist, stand out as brilliant exceptions among the political thinkers of the Continent. A similar tone of sentiment might by this time have been prevalent in our own country, if the circumstances which for a time encouraged it had continued unaltered.

But, in political and philosophical theories, as well as in persons, success discloses faults and infirmities which failure might have concealed from observation. The notion, that the people have no need to limit their power over themselves, might seen axiomatic, when popular government was a thing only dreamed about, or read of as having existed at some distant period of the past. Neither was that notion necessarily disturbed by such temporary aberrations as those of the French Revolution, the worst of which were the work of an usurping few, and which, in any case, belonged, not to the permanent working of popular institutions, but to a sudden and convulsive outbreak against monarchical and aristocratic despotism. In time, however, a democratic republic [2] came to occupy a large portion of the earth's surface, and made itself felt as one of the most powerful members of the community of nations; and elective and responsible government became subject to the observations and criticisms which wait upon a great existing fact. It was now perceived that such phrases as 'self-government,' and 'the power of the people over themselves,' do not express the true state of the case. The 'people' who exercise the power, are not always the same people with those over whom it is exercised; and the self-government spoken of, is not the government of each by himself, but of each by all the rest. The will of the people, moreover, practically means, the will of the most numerous or the most active *part* of the people; the majority, or those who succeed in making themselves accepted as the majority: the people, consequently, *may* desire to oppress a part of their number; and precautions are as much needed against this, as against any other abuse of power. The limitation, therefore, of the power of government over individuals, loses none of its importance when the holders of power are regularly accountable to the community, that is, to the strongest party therein. This view of things, recommending itself equally to the intelligence of thinkers and to the inclination of those important classes in European society to whose real or supposed interests democracy is adverse, has had no difficulty in establishing itself; and in political speculations 'the tyranny of the majority' is now generally included among the evils against which society requires to be on its guard.

Like other tyrannies, the tyranny of the majority was at first, and is still vulgarly, held in dread, chiefly as operating through the acts of the public authorities. But reflecting persons perceived that when society is itself the tyrant—society collectively, over the separate individuals who compose it —its means of tyrannizing are not restricted to the acts which it may do by the hands of its political functionaries. Society can and does execute its

[2 The United States.]

own mandates: and if it issues wrong mandates instead of right, or any mandates at all in things with which it ought not to meddle, it practises a social tyranny more formidable than many kinds of political oppression, since, though not usually upheld by such extreme penalties, it leaves fewer means of escape, penetrating much more deeply into the details of life, and enslaving the soul itself. Protection, therefore, against the tyranny of the magistrate is not enough; there needs protection also against the tyranny of the prevailing opinion and feeling; against the tendency of society to impose, by other means than civil penalties, its own ideas and practices as rules of conduct on those who dissent from them; to fetter the development, and, if possible, prevent the formation, of any individuality not in harmony with its ways, and compel all characters to fashion themselves upon the model of its own. There is a limit to the legitimate interference of collective opinion with individual independence; and to find that limit, and maintain it against encroachment, is as indispensable to a good condition of human affairs, as protection against political despotism.

But though this proposition is not likely to be contested in general terms, the practical question, where to place the limit—how to make the fitting adjustment between individual independence and social control— is a subject on which nearly everything remains to be done. All that makes existence valuable to any one, depends on the enforcement of restraints upon the actions of other people. Some rules of conduct, therefore, must be imposed, by law in the first place, and by opinion on many things which are not fit subjects for the operation of law. What these rules should be, is the principal question in human affairs; but if we except a few of the most obvious cases, it is one of those which least progress has been made in resolving. No two ages, and scarcely any two countries, have decided it alike; and the decision of one age or country is a wonder to another. Yet the people of any given age and country no more suspect any difficulty in it, than if it were a subject on which mankind had always been agreed. The rules which obtain among themselves appear to them self-evident and self-justifying. This all but universal illusion is one of the examples of the magical influence of custom, which is not only, as the proverb says, a second nature, but is continually mistaken for the first. The effect of custom, in preventing any misgiving respecting the rules of conduct which mankind impose on one another, is all the more complete because the subject is one on which it is not generally considered necessary that reasons should be given, either by one person to others, or by each to himself. People are accustomed to believe, and have been encouraged in the belief by some who aspire to the character of philosophers, that their feelings, on subjects of this nature, are better than reasons, and render reasons unnecessary. The practical principle which guides them to their opinions on the regulation of human conduct, is the feeling in each person's mind that everybody should be required to act as he, and those with whom he sympathizes, would like them to act. No one, indeed, acknowledges to himself that his standard of judgment is his own liking; but an opinion on a point of conduct, not supported by reasons, can only count as one person's preference; and if the reasons, when given, are a mere appeal to a similar preference felt by other people, it is still only many people's liking instead of one. To an ordinary man, however, his own preference, thus supported, is not only a perfectly satisfactory reason, but the only one he generally has for any of his notions of morality, taste, or propriety, which are not expressly written in his religious creed; and his chief guide in the interpretation even of that. Men's opinions, accordingly, on what is laudable or blameable, are affected by all the multifarious causes which influence their wishes in regard to the conduct of others, and which are as numerous as those which determine their wishes on any other subject. Sometimes their reason —at other times their prejudices or superstitions: often their social affections, not seldom their antisocial ones, their envy or jealousy, their arrogance or contemptuousness: but most commonly, their desires or fears for themselves—their legitimate or illegitimate self-interest. Wherever there is an ascendant class, a large portion of the morality of the country emanates from its class interests, and its feelings of class superiority. The morality between Spartans and Helots, between planters and negroes, between princes and subjects, between nobles and roturiers, between men and women, has been for the most part the creation of these class interests and feelings: and the sentiments thus generated, react in turn upon the moral feelings of the members of the ascendant class, in their relations among themselves. Where, on the other hand, a class, formerly ascendant, has lost its ascendancy, or where its ascendancy is unpopular, the prevailing moral sentiments frequently bear the impress of an impatient dislike of superiority. Another grand determining principle of the rules of conduct, both in act and forbearance, which have been enforced by law or opinion, has been the servility of mankind towards the supposed preferences or aversions of their temporal masters, or of their gods. This servility, though essentially selfish, is not hypocrisy; it gives rise to perfectly genuine sentiments of abhorrence; it made men burn magicians and heretics. Among so many baser influences, the general and obvious interests of society have of course had a share, and a large one, in the direction of the moral sentiments: less, however, as a matter of reason, and on their own account, than as a consequence of the sympathies and antipathies which grew out of them: and sympathies and antipathies which had little or nothing to do with the interests of society, have made themselves felt in the establishment of moralities with quite as great force.

The likings and dislikings of society, or of some powerful portion of it, are thus the main thing which has practically determined the rules laid down for general observance, under the penalties of law or opinion. And in general, those who have been in advance of society in thought and feeling, have left this condition of things unassailed in principle, however they may have come into conflict with it in some of its details. They have occupied themselves rather in inquiring what things society ought to like or dislike, than in questioning whether its likings or dislikings should be a law to individuals. They preferred endeavoring to alter the feelings of mankind on the particular points on which they were themselves heretical, rather than make common cause in defence of freedom, with heretics generally. The only case in which the higher ground has been taken on principle and maintained with consistency, by any but an individual here and there, is that of religious belief: a case instructive in many ways, and not least so as forming a most striking instance of the fallibility of what is called the moral sense: for the *odium theologicum*,[3] in a sincere bigot, is one of the most unequivocal cases of moral feeling. Those who first broke the yoke of what called itself the Universal Church, were in general as little willing to permit difference of religious opinion as that church itself. But when the heat of the conflict was over, without giving a complete victory to any party, and each church or sect was reduced to limit its hopes to retaining possession of the ground it already occupied; minorities, seeing that they had no chance of becoming majorities, were under the necessity of pleading to those whom they could not convert, for permission to differ. It is accordingly on this battle-field, almost solely, that the rights of the individual against society have been asserted on broad grounds of principle, and the claim of society to exercise authority over dissentients openly controverted. The great writers to whom the world owes what religious liberty it possesses, have mostly asserted freedom of conscience as an indefeasible right, and denied absolutely that a human being is accountable to others for his religious belief. Yet so natural to mankind is intolerance in whatever they really care about, that religious freedom has hardly anywhere

[3 Detestation felt by one theologian or sect for another.]

been practically realized, except where religious indifference, which dislikes to have its peace disturbed by theological quarrels, has added its weight to the scale. In the minds of almost all religious persons, even in the most tolerant countries, the duty of toleration is admitted with tacit reserves. One person will bear with dissent in matters of church government, but not of dogma; another can tolerate everybody, short of a Papist or an Unitarian; another, every one who believes in revealed religion; a few extend their charity a little further, but stop at the belief in a God and in a future state. Wherever the sentiment of the majority is still genuine and intense, it is found to have abated little of its claim to be obeyed.

In England, from the peculiar circumstances of our political history, though the yoke of opinion is perhaps heavier, that of law is lighter, than in most other countries of Europe; and there is considerable jealousy of direct interference, by the legislative or the executive power, with private conduct; not so much from any just regard for the independence of the individual, as from the still subsisting habit of looking on the government as representing an opposite interest to the public. The majority have not yet learnt to feel the power of the government their power, or its opinions their opinions. When they do so, individual liberty will probably be as much exposed to invasion from the government, as it already is from public opinion. But, as yet, there is a considerable amount of feeling ready to be called forth against any attempt of the law to control individuals in things in which they have not hitherto been accustomed to be controlled by it; and this with very little discrimination as to whether the matter is, or is not, within the legitimate sphere of legal control; insomuch that the feeling, highly salutary on the whole, is perhaps quite as often misplaced as well grounded in the particular instances of its application. There is, in fact, no recognized principle by which the propriety or impropriety of government interference is customarily tested. People decide according to their personal preferences. Some, whenever they see any good to be done, or evil to be remedied, would willingly instigate the government to undertake the business; while others prefer to bear almost any amount of social evil, rather than add one to the departments of human interests amenable to governmental control. And men range themselves on one or the other side in any particular case, according to this general direction of their sentiments; or according to the degree of interest which they feel in the particular thing which it is proposed that the government should do; or according to the belief they entertain that the government would, or would not, do it in the manner they prefer; but very rarely on account of any opinion to which they consistently adhere, as to what things are fit to be done by a government. And it seems to me that, in consequence of this absence of rule or principle, one side is at present as often wrong as the other; the interference of government is, with about equal frequency, improperly invoked and improperly condemned.

The object of this Essay is to assert one very simple principle, as entitled to govern absolutely the dealings of society with the individual in the way of compulsion and control, whether the means used be physical force in the form of legal penalties, or the moral coercion of public opinion. That principle is, that the sole end for which mankind are warranted, individually or collectively, in interfering with the liberty of action of any of their number, is self-protection. That the only purpose for which power can be rightfully exercised over any member of a civilized community, against his will, is to prevent harm to others. His own good, either physical or moral, is not a sufficient warrant. He cannot rightfully be compelled to do or forbear because it will be better for him to do so, because it will make him happier, because, in the opinions of others, to do so would be wise, or even right. These are good reasons for remonstrating with him, or reasoning with him, or persuading him, or entreating him, but not for compelling him, or visiting him with any evil, in case he do otherwise. To justify that, the conduct from which it is desired to deter him must be calculated to produce evil to some one else. The only part of the conduct of any one, for which he is amenable to society, is that which concerns others. In the part which merely concerns himself, his independence is, of right, absolute. Over himself, over his own body and mind, the individual is sovereign.

It is, perhaps, hardly necessary to say that this doctrine is meant to apply only to human beings in the maturity of their faculties. We are not speaking of children, or of young persons below the age which the law may fix as that of manhood or womanhood. Those who are still in a state to require being taken care of by others, must be protected against their own actions as well as against external injury. For the same reason, we may leave out of consideration those backward states of society in which the race itself may be considered as in its nonage. The early difficulties in the way of spontaneous progress are so great, that there is seldom any choice of means for overcoming them; and a ruler full of the spirit of improvement is warranted in the use of any expedients that will attain an end, perhaps otherwise unattainable. Despotism is a legitimate mode of government in dealing with barbarians, provided the end be their improvement, and the means justified by actually effecting that end. Liberty, as a principle, has no application to any state of things anterior to the time when mankind have become capable of being improved by free and equal discussion. Until then, there is nothing for them but implicit obedience to an Akbar [4] or a Charlemagne,[5] if they are so fortunate as to find one. But as soon as mankind have attained the capacity of being guided to their own improvement by conviction or persuasion (a period long since reached in all nations with whom we need here concern ourselves), compulsion, either in the direct form or in that of pains and penalties for non-compliance, is no longer admissible as a means to their own good, and justifiable only for the security of others.

It is proper to state that I forego any advantage which could be derived to my argument from the idea of abstract right, as a thing independent of utility. I regard utility as the ultimate appeal on all ethical questions; but it must be utility in the largest sense, grounded on the permanent interests of man as a progressive being. Those interests, I contend, authorize the subjection of individual spontaneity to external control, only in respect to those actions of each, which concern the interest of other people. If any one does an act hurtful to others there is a *primâ facie* [6] case for punishing him, by law, or, where legal penalties are not safely applicable, by general disapprobation. There are also many positive acts for the benefit of others, which he may rightfully be compelled to perform; such as, to give evidence in a court of justice; to bear his fair share in the common defence, or in any other joint work necessary to the interest of the society of which he enjoys the protection; and to perform certain acts of individual beneficence, such as saving a fellow creature's life, or interposing to protect the defenceless against ill-usage, things which whenever it is obviously a man's duty to do, he may rightfully be made responsible to society for not doing. A person may cause evil to others not only by his actions but by his inaction, and in either case he is justly accountable to them for the injury. The latter case, it is true, requires a much more cautious exercise of compulsion than the former. To make any one answerable for doing evil to others, is the rule; to make him answerable for not preventing evil, is, comparatively speaking, the exception. Yet there are many cases clear enough and grave enough to justify that exception. In all things which regard the external relations of the individual, he is *de jure* [7] amenable to those whose interests

[4 Emperor of Hindustan (1542–1605).]
[5 Charles the Great (742–814), King of the Franks and Emperor of the West.]
[6 On first appearance, obvious.]
[7 By right.]

are concerned, and if need be, to society as their protector. There are often good reasons for not holding him to the responsibility; but these reasons must arise from the special expediences of the case: either because it is a kind of case in which he is on the whole likely to act better, when left to his own discretion, than when controlled in any way in which society have it in their power to control him; or because the attempt to exercise control would produce other evils, greater than those which it would prevent. When such reasons as these preclude the enforcement of responsibility, the conscience of the agent himself should step into the vacant judgment-seat, and protect those interests of others which have no external protection; judging himself all the more rigidly, because the case does not admit of his being made accountable to the judgment of his fellow-creatures.

But there is a sphere of action in which society, as distinguished from the individual, has, if any, only an indirect interest; comprehending all that portion of a person's life and conduct which affects only himself, or, if it also affects others, only with their free, voluntary, and undeceived consent and participation. When I say only himself, I mean directly, and in the first instance: for whatever affects himself, may affect others *through* himself; and the objection which may be grounded on this contingency, will receive consideration in the sequel. This, then, is the appropriate region of human liberty. It comprises, first, the inward domain of consciousness; demanding liberty of conscience, in the most comprehensive sense; liberty of thought and feeling; absolute freedom of opinion and sentiment on all subjects, practical or speculative, scientific, moral, or theological. The liberty of expressing and publishing opinions may seem to fall under a different principle, since it belongs to that part of the conduct of an individual which concerns other people; but, being almost of as much importance as the liberty of thought itself, and resting in great part on the same reasons, is practically inseparable from it. Secondly, the principle requires liberty of tastes and pursuits; of framing the plan of our life to suit our own character; of doing as we like, subject to such consequences as may follow; without impediment from our fellow-creatures, so long as what we do does not harm them, even though they should think our conduct foolish, perverse, or wrong. Thirdly, from this liberty of each individual, follows the liberty, within the same limits, of combination among individuals; freedom to unite, for any purpose not involving harm to others: the persons combining being supposed to be of full age, and not forced or deceived.

No society in which these liberties are not, on the whole, respected, is free, whatever may be its form of government; and none is completely free in which they do not exist absolute and unqualified. The only freedom which deserves the name, is that of pursuing our own good in our own way, so long as we do not attempt to deprive others of theirs, or impede their efforts to obtain it. Each is the proper guardian of his own health, whether bodily, or mental and spiritual. Mankind are greater gainers by suffering each other to live as seems good to themselves, than by compelling each to live as seems good to the rest.

Though this doctrine is anything but new, and, to some persons, may have the air of a truism, there is no doctrine which stands more directly opposed to the general tendency of existing opinion and practice. Society has expended fully as much effort in the attempt (according to its lights) to compel people to conform to its notions of personal, as of social excellence. The ancient commonwealths thought themselves entitled to practise, and the ancient philosophers countenanced, the regulation of every part of private conduct by public authority, on the ground that the State had a deep interest in the whole bodily and mental discipline of every one of its citizens; a mode of thinking which may have been admissible in small republics surrounded by powerful enemies, in constant peril of being subverted by foreign attack or internal commotion, and to which even a short interval of relaxed energy and self-command might so easily be fatal, that they could not afford to wait for the salutary permanent effects of freedom. In the modern world, the greater size of political communities, and above all, the separation between the spiritual and temporal authority (which placed the direction of men's consciences in other hands than those which controlled their worldly affairs), prevented so great an interference by law in the details of private life; but the engines of moral repression have been wielded more strenuously against divergence from the reigning opinion in self-regarding, than even in social matters; religion, the most powerful of the elements which have entered into the formation of moral feeling, having almost always been governed either by the ambition of a hierarchy, seeking control over every department of human conduct, or by the spirit of Puritanism. And some of those modern reformers who have placed themselves in strongest opposition to the religions of the past, have been noway behind either churches or sects in their assertion of the right of spiritual domination: M. Comte,[8] in particular, whose social system, as unfolded in his *Traité de Politique Positive*, aims at establishing (though by moral more than by legal appliances) a despotism of society over the

[8 French philosopher (1798–1857), founder of the 'positivistic' philosophy. Mill gave him financial help.]

individual, surpassing anything contemplated in the political ideal of the most rigid disciplinarian among the ancient philosophers.

Apart from the peculiar tenets of individual thinkers, there is also in the world at large an increasing inclination to stretch unduly the powers of society over the individual, both by the force of opinion and even by that of legislation: and as the tendency of all the changes taking place in the world is to strengthen society, and diminish the power of the individual, this encroachment is not one of the evils which tend spontaneously to disappear, but, on the contrary, to grow more and more formidable. The disposition of mankind, whether as rulers or as fellow-citizens, to impose their own opinions and inclinations as a rule of conduct on others, is so energetically supported by some of the best and by some of the worst feelings incident to human nature, that it is hardly ever kept under restraint by anything but want of power; and as the power is not declining, but growing, unless a strong barrier of moral conviction can be raised against the mischief, we must expect, in the present circumstances of the world, to see it increase. . .

Carl Becker

THE REALITY

⟦ Carl Becker (1873–1945) taught history at Dartmouth College, at the University of Kansas, and, from 1917 until his death, at Cornell University. His best-known books are *The Declaration of Independence* (1922), *The Heavenly City of the Eighteenth Century Philosophers* (1932), *Everyman His Own Historian* (1935), *Modern Democracy* (1941), and *New Liberties for Old* (1942). *Modern Democracy* consists of lectures delivered at the University of Virginia in 1940. The first lecture, 'The Ideal,' sketched the theory of democratic society. The lecture reprinted here was the second one.

'Research, though laborious, is easy; imagination, though delightful, is difficult.' Becker's books have in them both the labors of research and the play of imagination. Among recent historians he was unusual for the ease and clarity of his style.

> Men mistook the pernicious channels in which selfish propensities had been flowing for the propensities themselves, which were sure to find new channels when the old had been destroyed.—*James Bryce.*[1]

> Those who own the country ought to govern it.—*John Jay.*[2]

I

In the preceding lecture we were concerned with the ideal form of democracy. It is obvious that the reality does not strictly conform to this ideal. There is nothing remarkable in that. The ideal is always better

[1 British scholar and diplomat (1838–1922). His *The American Commonwealth* was the best book of its time, and one of the best of any time, on America.]

[2 Statesman (1745–1829); first Chief Justice of the United States. He wrote some of the *Federalist* papers (see p. 202).]

From *Modern Democracy*, 1941. Reprinted by permission of the Yale University Press.

than the real—otherwise there would be no need for ideals. We have been told, as if it were a surprising thing, that in Russia the Revolution has been betrayed. But it was bound to be betrayed. It is in the nature of revolutions to be betrayed,[3] since life and history have an inveterate habit of betraying the ideal aspirations of men. In this sense the liberal-democratic revolution [4] was likewise bound to be betrayed—men were sure to be neither so rational nor so well-intentioned as the ideology conceived them to be. But while a little betrayal is a normal thing, too much is something that calls for explanation. The liberal-democratic revolution has been so far betrayed, the ideal so imperfectly portrayed in the course of events, that its characteristic features cannot easily be recognized in any democratic society today. In this lecture I shall attempt to disclose some of the essential reasons for the profound discord between democracy as it was ideally projected and democracy as a going concern.

Stated in general terms the essential reason is that the idea of liberty, as formulated in the eighteenth century, although valid enough for that time, has in one fundamental respect ceased to be applicable to the situation in which we find ourselves. In the eighteenth century the most obvious oppressions from which men suffered derived from governmental restraints on the free activity of the individual. Liberty was therefore naturally conceived in terms of the emancipation of the individual from such restraints. In the economic realm this meant the elimination of governmental restraints on the individual in choosing his occupation, in contracting for the acquisition and disposal of property, and the purchase and sale of personal services. But in our time, as a result of the growing complexities of a technological society, the emancipation of the individual from governmental restraint in his economic activities has created new oppressions, so that for the majority of men liberty can be achieved only by an extension of governmental regulation of competitive business enterprise. It is in the economic realm that the traditional idea of liberty is no longer applicable; in the economic realm, accordingly, that the discord between democracy as an ideal and democracy as a going concern is most flagrant, most disillusioning, and most dangerous.

In order to elaborate this statement it will be well, first of all, to note the chief characteristics of the social situation in the eighteenth century—

[3 See Jefferson on the French Revolution, p. 198.]

[4 That realized politically by the American and French revolutions and, so far as the United States was concerned, expressed doctrinally in the Declaration of Independence, the Constitution, and the *Federalist* papers.]

the situation against which the liberal-democratic revolution was directed, and from which the eighteenth-century conception of liberty emerged as an obvious and valid rationalization.

From the twelfth to the seventeenth century the cardinal economic fact in western Europe was the rise of an industrial capitalist class in the towns; the cardinal political fact was the consolidation of royal power over all classes and corporations within definite territorial limits. The chief obstacles encountered by kings in this political process were two: first, the feudal vassals who claimed, and often exercised, virtual independence within their domains; second, the Roman Church, which claimed to be superior to the civil power, was in large part a self-governing institution, and exercised in fact over the king's subjects an authority independent of, and often in conflict with, the authority of the king.

In this three-cornered struggle for power, kings were sometimes supported by the church against the nobles, sometimes by the nobles against the church; but the persistent and effective support against both church and nobility came from the rising industrial class. Merchants and traders always found the turbulence of the nobility bad for business, and were usually willing, however painful it may have been, to supply the king with some of the money he needed to establish orderly government. Thus in the course of centuries, chiefly with the aid of the industrial bourgeois class, kings gradually reduced the nobles to the status of landed proprietors who retained, as the price of submission, the distinctions and prerogatives of a superior social class.

Meantime, the long struggle for the subordination of the church to royal power was virtually completed by the upheaval known as the Protestant Reformation, and it was the growing power and heretical ideas of the industrial classes that made the Reformation successful. Everywhere stronger in the towns than in the country, stronger in industrialized than in nonindustrialized countries, the Protestant Reformation was in effect a revolt of the middle classes against a church which, being controlled by a landed aristocracy, enforced ethical standards and religious practices unsuited to the temper and contrary to the interests of an industrial society. The chief political result of the Reformation was that by breaking the power of Rome it enhanced the power of kings, and by enhancing the power of kings it subordinated the church to the state, and thereby reduced the clergy, like the nobility, to the status of a privileged social class.

Thus in the seventeenth century, as a result of the rise of an industrial capitalist class, the consolidation of royal power, and the survival of nobles and clergy as privileged classes within the state, there emerged in western Europe a social system that was everywhere much the same. The prevailing form of government was absolute monarchy. In theory the power of the king rested upon the doctrine of divine right, supplemented by the Roman Law precept 'What the Prince wills has the force of law.' In practice the power of the king rested upon the support of nobles, clergy, and the rich bourgeois industrialists and financiers, and functioned for the most part to their advantage by exploiting an underlying population of peasants and workers.

It was what we should call a highly regimented system—a system in which the rights and obligations of the individual, always subject to the arbitrary will of the king, were normally determined by the rights and obligations appertaining to the class in which he was born. Generally speaking, there was for the individual neither freedom of occupation, nor of opinion or religion, nor any recognized method by which he might initiate or modify the law and custom by which his thought and conduct were controlled. The character of the liberal-democratic revolution which occurred from the seventeenth to the nineteenth centuries was conditioned by this fact. Dispensing with verbal refinements, all revolutions are made in behalf of liberty—freedom from some sort of real or fancied oppression; and in a social situation in which the individual was so obviously restrained and oppressed by law and custom not of his own making, it was inevitable that liberty should be conceived in terms of the emancipation of the individual from social and political control.

The revolution was initiated and directed, not by those who were most oppressed, but by those who were most aware of oppression and most competent to denounce and resist it—that is to say, not by the brutalized and ignorant peasants and workers, but by the educated and well-to-do middle classes. The bourgeoisie derived their power neither from birth nor office, but from money, that abstract and supple measure of the material value of all things. They acquired the education, cultivated the virtues, and developed the mentality appropriate to the occupations that engaged them. Occupied with practical affairs, with defined and determinable relations, with concrete things and their disposal and calculable cash value, they cultivated the virtues of thrift and prudence, dependability and sound judgment, and developed a pragmatic and skeptical temper, averse to the mystical and other-worldly, little disposed to slavish adherence to tradition, easily adaptable to the new and the experimental.

In every country the liberal-democratic revolution developed, with occasional violent upheavals, in the measure that the bourgeoisie acquired power and became class conscious—became aware, that is to say, of their peculiar class interests and virtues; and of the frustration of their interests and virtues by rococo class distinctions, and by arbitrary royal decrees which hampered business enterprise and deprived them of their property for the benefit of an aristocracy which they regarded as less intelligent, less moral, and less socially useful than themselves. The central, dramatic episode in the rise of liberal-democracy was the French Revolution; and it was in connection with this episode that there appeared in western Europe an exceptionally able group of intellectuals who rationalized the social situation by identifying the middle-class interests and virtues with the rights of all men—the right of all men to equality of status and of opportunity, to freedom of occupation and of economic enterprise, to freedom of opinion and of religion, and to freedom from arbitrary political authority.

II

Fortunately for the bourgeoisie and for the revolution, the interests of the middle classes were, in one respect, identical with the interests of the great majority. The liberal-democratic revolution could not have been won if it had been fought on behalf of bourgeois class interests alone. Of all the liberties demanded, freedom of economic enterprise was the one least stressed by the Philosophers [5] and of least importance for the purposes of revolutionary propaganda. The liberty which could be demanded with most assurance and denied with least grace was liberty of person and of opinion—freedom of religion, freedom of speech and the press, freedom of learning and of teaching, freedom from the insane brutalities practiced in the civil and ecclesiastical administration of justice and in the punish-ment of crimes. In proclaiming the worth and dignity of the individual, in demanding the emancipation of men from the inhumanity of man to man, the bourgeois spokesmen were appealing to interests transcending all class lines. They were appealing to the spirit of Christianity against its practices, and espousing the cause with which all the saints and sages of the world had been identified. In doing so they injected into the liberal-democratic revolution the quality of a religious crusade, and thereby enlisted the widespread support which alone could assure its success.

[5 Name given to a number of eighteenth-century French writers on philosophical and political topics; Diderot, D'Alembert, and Condorcet belong to this group. They were skeptical, anticlerical, and antimonarchical. Through their advocacy of liberty they helped to prepare the way for the French Revolution. See Becker's study, *The Heavenly City of the Eighteenth Century Philosophers*.]

The political and economic interests of the bourgeoisie could not, unfortunately, be thus identified with the interests of all. On the contrary, the interests of the bourgeoisie, both in the political and the economic realm, proved in the long run to be in sharp conflict with the interests of the masses. It was the interest of the bourgeoisie to deny to the masses the political privileges which they demanded for themselves; while the freedom of economic enterprise which enriched bourgeois employers turned out to be, for the proletarian peasants and workers, no more than the old subjection under new forms. As liberal-democracy emerged into the light of day, this conflict of class interests became more obvious and more disastrous; and it is this conflict which in our time has created those profound social discords which so largely nullify the theory and threaten to undermine the stability of democratic institutions.

In the earlier stages of the revolution, when the chief task was to deprive kings and aristocrats of political power and social privilege, this latent conflict between middle- and lower-class interests was not apparent. For the time being, indeed, it did not exist. The tyranny of kings and aristocrats, so effectively denounced by the Philosophers, was real enough, and so long as it existed all the unprivileged, bourgeois and people alike, had a common interest in resisting it. The doctrine that all men had a natural right to govern themselves seemed then but a simple truth, and the bourgeoisie could accept it without bothering too much about its practical application, all the more so since only by accepting it could they enlist the support of the people in destroying absolute monarchy and class privilege. In all the great 'revolutionary days'—the English civil wars in the seventeenth century, the American and the French revolutions at the close of the eighteenth, the South American wars of independence, the revolutions of 1830 and 1848—in all these crucial struggles in which the tyranny of kings and aristocrats was still the central issue, the bourgeoisie and the people are found united in the effort to win political freedom by overthrowing the existing regime. They differed only in the respective parts which they played in the struggle: the function of the bourgeoisie was to take the initiative and supply the ideas; the function of the people was to erect the barricades and supply the necessary force.

It is always easier for diverse groups to unite for the destruction of an existing regime than it is to unite for the construction of a new one. Having united to destroy the tyranny of kings and aristocrats, the bourgeoisie and the people were divided on the question of what political liberty should mean in practice. The doctrine that all men had a natural right to govern themselves was interpreted by the people to mean that all adult male citizens should share in choosing the magistrates and shaping the laws by which the community was governed. By the bourgeoisie it was interpreted to mean, as John Jay put it, that 'those who own the country ought to govern it.' In this respect the first result of the revolution was everywhere essentially a victory for the bourgeoisie. Kings lost their absolute power, aristocrats lost their special privileges, or most of them; but political liberty —the right to choose the magistrates and enact the laws by which the community was governed—was limited to the people of property;[6] the masses, having served their purpose by erecting the barricades, found themselves still excluded from what Guizot[7] called 'the political country.'

Having thus, with the aid of the people, elbowed kings and aristocrats out of the seats of power, the bourgeoisie promptly united with the aristocrats to control the state. They had a common interest in excluding the people from political privilege, but in the competition for votes and power within the political country their interests were opposed. There accordingly emerged, for the promotion of their respective interests, two political parties which, although known by different names in different countries, we may call conservative and liberal. Conservative parties were composed for the most part of the landed aristocracy, the clergy of the established churches, high-placed bureaucrats, and hangers-on of royal courts. In some countries, more royalist than the king, they at first entertained the vain hope of restoring the ancient regime; but in any case they defended the interests of land against capital, the established church against dissenting religions, and old social distinctions and aristocratic prestige against the leveling influence of democratic customs. Liberal parties were composed of the educated and well-to-do middle classes—businessmen, professional people, middle-class intellectuals, perhaps a few liberalized aristocrats. Occupying a middle position, the liberal parties fought on two fronts: equally opposed to absolutism and democracy, they were defenders of liberty against kings and aristocrats, but defenders of their own newly acquired privilege against the people.

In this situation, there emerged a third political party—variously called republican, progressive liberal, radical—which for convenience we may call democratic. The democratic party represented those who were still excluded from the political country—at first more particularly the industrial workers, who were most oppressed and the first to become class conscious. They

[6 See p. 211 and note.]
[7 French statesman and historian (1787–1874).]

were commonly led by middle-class intellectuals, who formulated for them a doctrine and a program. The doctrine was the pure liberal-democratic ideology which middle-class liberals professed in theory but denied in practice—the doctrine that all men had a natural right to govern themselves; and the chief point in the program was accordingly the extension of the suffrage to all adult male citizens, in the confident belief that the workers, once possessed of the right to vote for those who made the laws, could correct by legislation the economic inequalities that oppressed them.

In the course of time, after much fruitless effort and some abortive uprisings, the people were admitted to the political country—in the United States during the period from about 1830 to 1840, in European countries for the most part during the last three decades of the century. To this result both logic and political tactics contributed. In point of logic, it was difficult for middle-class Liberals, who had won political privilege by advocating the right of all men to govern themselves, to refute the argument that the masses as well as the classes should enjoy that right. But it was less the logic of the ideology than of political strategy that determined the outcome. As the fear of kings declined and the revolution was accepted as an accomplished fact, the opposition between upper-class Liberal and Conservative parties declined also. Agreeing upon fundamentals, they were chiefly divided by the competitive struggle for votes; and it seemed obvious that the party which first pleased the masses by giving them the right to vote would stand the best chance of winning their support at the polls. Generally speaking, therefore, at least so far as European countries are concerned, it can hardly be said that the people forced their way into the political country. Quite as often as not they were admitted by Conservative or Liberal party governments, each of which, in the particular instance, hoped to increase its voting strength by enlarging the electorate.

The adoption of universal manhood suffrage was thought at the time to be a signal triumph for democracy. And it did in fact add something to the power of the people, since it compelled upper-class parties to take account of popular opinion in formulating policies and devising measures that would appeal to the mass of the voters. But on the whole, the admission of the people to the political country did very little to increase their power or improve the conditions under which they lived. Political control remained, as before, essentially in the hands of upper-class political parties.

Many reasons may be advanced for the failure of the people to profit by their apparent victory. When they entered the political country they found the upper classes intrenched in all the strategic positions. The forms and procedure of representative institutions were already established; political parties, representing for the most part the upper classes, were well organized; and the technique for selecting candidates and manipulating elections was such that politics was a profession only men of property and social position could enter with much chance of success. In theory the masses were free to present to the electorate the measures that seemed to them desirable for the public good; in fact the means of propaganda were freely available only to the educated and well-to-do. In theory the poor man could vote for candidates of his own choosing; in fact his choice was limited to candidates who represented the dominant upper-class parties. It is true that in the course of time the people organized working-class socialist parties of their own; but while such parties often obtained from conservative or liberal governments measures designed to protect the interests of the poor, effective political control still remained in the hands of those who could easily afford the expensive luxury of self-government.

These are the superficial reasons for the failure of political equality to safeguard the interests of the people. The more fundamental reason is to be found in the economic structure of the society that emerged from the liberal-democratic revolution. Individual liberty in the political realm proved inadequate because individual liberty in the economic realm failed to bring about even that minimum degree of equality of possessions and of opportunity without which political equality is scarcely more than an empty form. This point, since it is fundamental, calls for some elaboration.

III

The principle of individual freedom in the economic realm, although not much stressed in the propaganda of the great crusading days, was always an integral part of the liberal-democratic ideology. For the needed emancipation of industry from the hampering restraints of monopolistic privilege and petty governmental regulation, it was a sound working principle; but applied without qualifications it could only benefit the industrial bourgeoisie at the expense of the underlying population of peasants and workers. As set forth in the *Wealth of Nations*,[8] and in the more rigorous and apparently more scientific works of the English classical economists, the principle was indeed scarcely more than pure rationalization of the business interests of capitalist employers; but this ominous fact was long concealed because the principle was formulated in terms of the word liberty, the magic of which was sufficient at that time to give a general

[8 An extremely influential treatise on economics by Adam Smith, published in 1776.]

sanction even to the brutalities of cutthroat competition and the systematic degradation of women and children. The present misery of the workers could be more easily contemplated and dismissed because it could be regarded as a necessary but temporary phase in the operation of a divinely ordained law of progress. The average humane middle-class man, whether employer or not, could therefore accept the principle of individual freedom in the economic realm, along with the other great freedoms, since it so happily enabled him to reconcile his selfish with his altruistic impulses by assuring him that he could best serve God and his neighbor by doing as he pleased. 'Private advantage a public benefit'—such was the succinct formula by which the prosperous middle classes justified their amiable expectation that when everyone was free all would presently be equal, when all were equal everyone would presently have enough, when all had enough no one would any longer be unjust or inhumane.

The expectation was surely naïve, in no sort of harmony with the relevant facts of social experience. Even under the most favorable circumstances, a society of uprooted and freely competing individuals must have functioned to the advantage of the few who by good fortune, intelligence, or lack of scruple were able to acquire wealth and employ it to advance their interests through the mechanism of politics: the times would always be ripe for a sufficient number of not-too-good men to come to the aid of the party. But this result was greatly accelerated and intensified by those changes in the economic and material conditions of life which, effected without blare of trumpets and scarcely perceived at the time, are now known as the industrial or technological revolution of modern times.

Technological is the better term. Industrial is wholly inadequate to denote one of the two or three major revolutions in the history of the human race. Man is a tool-using animal, and all civilization is conditioned by the sources of natural power known to him and the mechanical appliances he can invent to make such power available for use. The first great epoch of discovery and invention takes us back before the time of recorded history. All the more obvious sources of natural power—gravitation, fire, wind and water, domesticated animals, the fertility of the soil—and the simple hand tools, weapons, utensils, and appliances for making such power available were known to primitive man. From the time of the invention of writing, some five or six thousand years ago, until comparatively recent times few if any new sources of natural power, except crude explosives and magnetic force, were discovered; and during all that long time the mechanical appliances available, although more numerous and greatly perfected, were essentially of the same order as those employed from time immemorial.

But we are now living in the second great epoch of discovery and invention. Since the seventeenth century, the discovery of steam power, gas, electricity, and radiation have made possible those innumerable tools and appliances, those complicated and powerful machines, and those delicate instruments of precision which elicit our wonder and our admiration. The result has been that the new technology, by giving men unprecedented control over material things, has transformed the relatively simple agricultural communities of the eighteenth century into societies far more complex and impersonal than anything the prophets of liberal-democracy could have imagined—mechanized Leviathans which Thomas Jefferson at least would have regarded as unreal and fantastic and altogether unsuited to the principles of liberty and equality as he understood them.

I need not say that the influence of the technological revolution has not been confined to any particular aspect of social life. On the contrary, it has exerted and still exerts a decisive influence in modifying all the habitual patterns of thought and conduct. But I am here concerned with the influence of the technological revolution in accelerating and intensifying that concentration of wealth and power in the hands of a few which the principles of individual freedom in the economic realm would in any case have tended to bring about.

The first and most obvious result of the technological revolution has been to increase the amount of wealth in the form of material things which can be produced in a given time by a given population. For example, in 1913 there was produced in Great Britain seven billion yards of cotton cloth for export alone. In 1750 the total population of Great Britain, working with the mechanical appliances then available, could have produced only a small fraction of that amount. A second result of the technological revolution is that, as machines are perfected and become more automatic, man power plays a relatively less important part in the production of a given amount of wealth in a given time. Fifty years ago, when all type was set by hand, the labor of several men was required to print, fold, and arrange in piles the signatures of a book. Today machines can do it all, and far more rapidly; little man power is required, except that a mechanic, who may pass the time sitting in a chair, must be present in case anything goes wrong with the machine. And finally, a third result of the technological revolution is that, under the system of private property in the means of production and the price system as a method of distributing wealth, the greater part of the wealth produced, since it is produced by the machines, goes to those who own or control the machines, while those who work the machines receive that part only which can be exacted by selling their services in a market where wages are impersonally adjusted to the necessities of the machine process.

I use the phrase 'own *or* control the machines' for the reason that, as a result of modern technology and business organization, those who own private property in the means of production do not necessarily control it. The ownership of property is now a highly intangible and illusive concept. Mass production calls for enormous industrial plants which are commonly managed by corporations and financed by selling corporation stock to the investing public. If I buy ten shares of General Motors I may be said to own that amount of General Motors property, but I have no control of it. The property is controlled by those who own a majority of the stock, and the majority of the stock is commonly owned by a few persons. Ownership, as far as I am concerned, consists in the possession of a slip of paper which gives me a lively hope that those who control the property will periodically send me a check for a certain sum of money: if they fail to do so there is nothing I can do about it. By the intricate device of the holding company, control may be still further concentrated and still further divorced from ownership: several corporations may be controlled by a few persons who have little or no interest in the operating companies except to manipulate and exploit them for financial gain. Thus it happens that while the owner- ship of private property in the means of production may be widely dis- tributed, the effective control of that property is likely to be concentrated in the hands of a few.

If the concept of ownership is intangible and illusive, the concept of property is no less so. The value of General Motors property resides, not in the physical plant and the financial assets alone, but essentially in the business as a going concern. To be a prosperous going concern, the cor- poration must be able to purchase labor and supplies at a cost that will enable it to sell its products throughout the entire community at a profit. For this reason General Motors cannot live or die to itself alone. Its pros- perity, and therefore the value of its property, conditions and is condi- tioned by the prosperity of innumerable individuals and business enter- prises—the enterprises, large and small throughout the community and even throughout the world, which sell its cars and supply it with raw material, fuel, and equipment; the individuals who, as laborers or stockholders, are associated with General Motors and with the many enterprises that are integrated with it.

The value of private property in the means of production is thus not a private matter. It is both cause and effect in the functioning of a highly integrated and delicately adjusted industrial structure that touches the public interest at every point. That the few who control private property in the means of production should be wealthy men is no great matter. What matters is that their control of the means of production gives them an indeterminate and impersonal power over the lives and fortunes of millions of people unknown to them—power which they are sometimes unwilling but far more often quite unable to use for the public good.

In any society there is bound to be a close connection between economic and political power. In any society those who possess economic power, like other people, are disposed to identify their economic interests with the general good, and to promote their interests through the mechanism of politics and propaganda. But in modern industrial societies, based upon democratic political control and the principle of free economic enterprise, the beneficiaries of private property in the means of production are in a peculiarly advantageous position for molding opinion and shaping legislation. Their advantage arises less from the fact that they can and do spend money freely for those purposes, than from the fact that political procedure and the instruments of propaganda are so integrated with the industrial system that legislation and opinion more or less automatically respond to the pressure of the system of free enterprise from which their economic power is derived.

In democratic societies political power is mediated through political parties organized primarily for the purpose of obtaining control of the government by winning elections. To win elections a political party must of course formulate a program of legislation that will appeal to the voters. But elections are not won on the merits of a program alone. The winning of an election is a practical business enterprise, which calls for a capital investment in the form of a campaign fund, and for an intricate organization of employees—a political machine managed by professional politicians whose business it is to deliver the vote. Contributions to the campaign fund may be made from interested or disinterested motives; but the largest contributions will commonly be made by wealthy men or corporations expecting in return that the party will not, at the very least, be altogether indifferent to the kind of legislation they desire.

The professional politician, whose business it is to deliver the vote, is concerned primarily with the vote of those whose loyalty to the party is determined less by the merits of the party program than by the disposition of the party to confer tangible benefits upon them. The function of the highest species of politician is to handle the patronage, to distribute appointive offices to those who can best serve the party. The function of the lowest species of politician—the *déclassé* [9] ward heeler— is to do what respectable statesmen know must be done but are prevented by the mores [10] from doing themselves, namely, to see to it that the poor and dispossessed are provided with a minimum of subsistence, and not too much hampered in their private enterprises, even sometimes if they happen to be on the wrong side of the fence, by the majesty of the law. In delivering the vote, the ward heeler is the henchman of the political boss, the political boss has the necessary contacts with the party leaders who hold elective or appointive offices, and the political leaders have the necessary personal and social contacts with the businessmen who contribute so generously to the campaign fund. In every community, large or small, there is this unavowed, undercover integration of economic and political power; and apart from some unanticipated ethical disturbance in the climate of opinion, legislation, always defended by statesmen in terms of the common good, is always insensibly influenced by the pressure of the predominant industrial interest.

In molding opinion, no less than in shaping legislation, those who possess economic power have a great advantage over the general run of citizens. This is not to say that freedom of speech and the press does not exist in democratic societies. One has only to compare nondemocratic with democratic societies to realize that, in a very real and important sense, it does exist. In democratic societies any man may freely express his opinion without first looking furtively over his shoulder to see if a government spy is in the offing; any man may publish a book or a newspaper without first submitting it to an official censor. This is the fundamentally important privilege; and no cataloguing of incidental violations of civil liberties, serious and deplorable as they are, can obscure the fact that through the press and the radio detailed information about events, and the most diverse opinions, are with little let or hindrance daily and hourly presented to the people.

Nevertheless, the average individual, although free to express his ideas, plays a distinctly minor role in the molding of opinion: his role is not to initiate, but passively to receive information and ideas presented to him

[9 Said of one who has lost social standing.]
[10 Customs.]

by others. The propaganda of social or political opinion, to be effective under modern conditions, must be organized; and its promoters will have an indifferent success unless they resort to mass production and distribution of their wares. The chief instruments of propaganda—the press and broadcasting stations—are not readily available to the average individual for conveying his ideas: they can be effectively used only by the government, political parties and party leaders, prominent organizations, wealthy men and business corporations, associations organized for specific purposes, and the writers of books which publishing houses find it worth while to publish.

Even more important is the fact that the instruments of propaganda are themselves business corporations organized and financed for profit, and as such subject to those influences that condition and are conditioned by the system of free economic enterprise. Newspapers are free to print all the news that's fit to print; but they cannot consistently propagate ideas that will alienate the business interests whose paid advertisements enable them to distribute profits to the stockholders. Broadcasting corporations are free from government censorship, or reasonably so, reasonably free to broadcast what they will; but in the last analysis they will not broadcast that which seriously offends the prevailing mores, or the business enterprises which, in this country at least, sponsor and finance their programs of entertainment. In democratic societies free and impartial discussion, from which the truth is supposed to emerge, is permitted and does occur. But the thinking of the average man is largely shaped by a wealth of factual information and the conflicting opinions which the selective process of competitive business enterprise presents to him for consideration: information, the truth of which he cannot verify; ideas, formulated by persons he does not know, and too often inspired by private economic interests that are never avowed.

Such, in broad outline, are the circumstances that may serve to explain the profound discord between democracy as an ideal and as a reality. In terms of the ideal there should have emerged from the liberal-democratic revolution a relatively simple society of free, equal, and prosperous citizens, fraternally coöperating to effect, by rational discussion and mutual concession, the common good. In fact there emerged an extremely complex society in which highly intricate and impersonal economic forces, stronger than good will or deliberate intention or rational direction, brought about an increasing concentration of wealth and power in the hands of the fortunate few, and thereby nullified, for the majority of the people, many of those essential liberties which provide both the theoretical justification and the necessary conditions for the practical success of democratic institutions.

This discord, long since perceived by the discerning, has in our time become so flagrant that in many countries the ideal has been abandoned as an illusion. In these countries new social philosophies now prevail which maintain that the attempt to apply the principles of individual liberty, not only in the economic but in the political and the intellectual realm, was a fundamental error, and is responsible for the social and international conflicts which now bewilder and distress the world.

To accept this view implies the end of democratic institutions as we know them, and the renunciation of that faith in the worth and dignity of the individual which we have cherished even if we have not always justified it in action. I do not accept this view. I believe that in the long run it will prove mistaken—fatal to any way of life that can rightly be called civilized. But I also believe that if the democratic way of life is to survive we must give to the traditional concept of freedom a more positive content. The traditional concept of individual liberty is essentially negative. The freedom it emphasizes is freedom from constraint, and indeed from a particular kind of constraint, that is to say, governmental constraint. In the economic realm the result of freeing the individual from governmental constraint is that today far too many people are always in danger of losing those positive goods without which freedom from governmental constraint is of no value. What the average man now needs is the opportunity to acquire by his own effort, in an occupation for which he is fitted, the economic security which is essential to decent and independent living. This opportunity has now disappeared for something like a quarter of the working population. In my opinion it can only be restored, if at all, by such governmental regulations of our economy as may be necessary to enable private economic enterprise to function effectively and for the common good.

If then the democratic way of life is to survive we must distinguish the kinds of individual freedom that are essential to it from those that are unessential or disastrous. Broadly speaking, the kinds that are essential are those which the individual enjoys in his intellectual and political activities; the kinds that are unessential are the relatively unrestrained liberties he has hitherto enjoyed in his economic activities. The distinction is comparatively easy to make in theory, but will be extremely difficult to effect in practice. Not the least of the difficulties arises from the fact that in the traditional ideology the freedom of the individual in the political, the intellectual, and the economic realms are so intimately associated that they seem to stand or fall together. The result is that any proposal to regulate by governmental authority the system of free economic enterprise is sure to be opposed on the ground that if the system of free economic enterprise cannot be maintained the other freedoms of democracy, freedom of thought and political freedom, must in the end be abandoned also. Whether this is true can only be determined by the event. Whatever the event may be, the difficult but essential task which confronts all democratic societies today may be formulated as follows: how in practice to curtail the freedom of the individual in economic enterprise sufficiently to effect that equality of opportunity and of possessions without which democracy is an empty form, and at the same time to preserve that measure of individual freedom in intellectual and political life without which it cannot exist.

George Orwell

POLITICS AND THE ENGLISH LANGUAGE

❲ 'George Orwell' (Eric Blair) was born in India in 1903, and educated at Eton. He served in the Indian Imperial Police in Burma, 1922–7 (see his essay, 'Shooting an Elephant'), then lived in Paris and London, writing, and supporting himself by odd jobs. During the Spanish Civil War in the 1930's, he fought in the Loyalist Army and was wounded. He spent the rest of his life in England, dying in 1950.

His earlier books, including *Down and Out in Paris and London* (1933), *The Road to Wigan Pier* (1937), and *Homage to Catalonia* (1938), were duly noticed, but he was not widely read abroad until the appearance of his satire on dictatorships, *Animal Farm* (1945), and *1984* (1949), a powerful vision of the totalitarian society Orwell seemed to expect. Besides these books, he wrote essays that are collected in *Critical Essays* (1946), *Shooting an Elephant* (1950), and *Such, Such Were the Joys* (1953).

Orwell described himself in 1942 as 'definitely "left," but I believe that a writer can remain honest only if he keeps free of party labels.' As a believer in liberty, as one who insisted on facing facts and who demanded honesty of writers and politicians, he argued that there is an essential relation between prose and politics. 'The present political chaos is connected with the decay of language,' he wrote in 1946; 'political speech and writing are largely the defence of the indefensible.' The deliberate ambiguities of bureaucratic language are, he felt, the characteristic devices of men who are enemies of liberty.

Most people who bother with the matter at all would admit that the English language is in a bad way, but it is generally assumed that we cannot by conscious action do anything about it. Our civilization is decadent and our language—so the argument runs—must inevitably share in the general collapse. It follows that any struggle against the abuse of language is a sentimental archaism, like preferring candles to electric light or hansom cabs to aeroplanes. Underneath this lies the half-conscious belief that language is a natural growth and not an instrument which we shape for our own purposes.

Now, it is clear that the decline of a language must ultimately have political and economic causes: it is not due simply to the bad influence of this or that individual writer. But an effect can become a cause, reinforcing the original cause and producing the same effect in an intensified form, and so on indefinitely. A man may take to drink because he feels himself to be a failure, and then fail all the more completely because he drinks. It is rather the same thing that is happening to the English language. It becomes ugly and inaccurate because our thoughts are foolish, but the slovenliness of our language makes it easier for us to have foolish thoughts. The point is that the process is reversible. Modern English, especially written English, is full of bad habits which spread by imitation and which can be avoided if one is willing to take the necessary trouble. If one gets rid of these habits one can think more clearly, and to think clearly is a necessary first step towards political regeneration: so that the fight against bad English is not frivolous and is not the exclusive concern of professional writers. I will come back to this presently, and I hope that by that time the meaning of what I have said here will have become clearer. Meanwhile, here are five specimens of the English language as it is now habitually written.

These five passages have not been picked out because they are especially bad—I could have quoted far worse if I had chosen—but because they illustrate various of the mental vices from which we now suffer. They are a little below the average, but are fairly representative samples. I number them so that I can refer back to them when necessary:

(1) I am not, indeed, sure whether it is not true to say that the Milton who once seemed not unlike a seventeenth-century Shelley had not become, out of an experience ever more bitter in each year, more alien [sic] to the founder of that Jesuit sect which nothing could induce him to tolerate.

Professor Harold Laski
(Essay in Freedom of Expression).

(2) Above all, we cannot play ducks and drakes with a native battery of idioms which prescribes such egregious collocations of vocables as the Basic *put up with* for *tolerate* or *put at a loss* for *bewilder*.

Professor Lancelot Hogben (Interglossa).

(3) On the one side we have the free personality: by definition it is not neurotic, for it has neither conflict nor dream. Its desires, such as they are, are transparent, for they are just what institutional approval keeps in the forefront of consciousness; another institutional pattern would alter their number and intensity; there is little in them that is natural, irreducible, or culturally dangerous. But *on the other side,* the social bond itself is nothing but the mutual reflection of these self-secure integrities. Recall the definition of love. Is not this the very picture of a small academic? Where is there a place in this hall of mirrors for either personality or fraternity?

Essay on psychology in *Politics* (New York).

(4) All the 'best people' from the gentlemen's clubs, and all the frantic fascist captains, united in common hatred of Socialism and bestial horror of the rising tide of the mass revolutionary movement, have turned to acts of provocation, to foul incendiarism, to medieval legends of poisoned wells, to legalize their own destruction of proletarian organizations, and rouse the agitated petty-bourgeoisie to chauvinistic fervor on behalf of the fight against the revolutionary way out of the crisis.

Communist pamphlet.

(5) If a new spirit is to be infused into this old country, there is one thorny and contentious reform which must be tackled, and that is the humanization and galvanization of the B.B.C. Timidity here will bespeak canker and atrophy of the soul. The heart of Britain may be sound and of strong beat, for instance, but the British lion's roar at present is like that of Bottom in Shakespeare's *Midsummer Night's Dream*—as gentle as any sucking dove. A virile new Britain cannot continue indefinitely to be traduced in the eyes, or rather ears, of the world by the effete languors of Langham Place, brazenly masquerading as 'standard English.' When the Voice of Britain is heard at nine o'clock, better far and infinitely less ludicrous to hear aitches honestly dropped than the present priggish, inflated, inhibited, school-ma'amish arch braying of blameless bashful mewing maidens!

Letter in *Tribune*

Each of these passages has faults of its own, but, quite apart from avoidable ugliness, two qualities are common to all of them. The first is staleness of imagery; the other is lack of precision. The writer either has a meaning and cannot express it, or he inadvertently says something else, or he is almost indifferent as to whether his words mean anything or not. This mixture of vagueness and sheer incompetence is the most marked characteristic of modern English prose, and especially of any kind of political writing. As soon as certain topics are raised, the concrete melts into the abstract and no one seems able to think of turns of speech that are not hackneyed: prose consists less and less of *words* chosen for the sake of their meaning, and more and more of *phrases* tacked together like the sections of a prefabricated hen-house. I list below, with notes and examples, various of the tricks by means of which the work of prose-construction is habitually dodged:

Dying metaphors. A newly invented metaphor assists thought by evoking a visual image, while on the other hand a metaphor which is technically 'dead' (e.g. *iron resolution*) has in effect reverted to being an ordinary word and can generally be used without loss of vividness. But in between these two classes there is a huge dump of worn-out metaphors which have lost all evocative power and are merely used because they save people the trouble of inventing phrases for themselves. Examples are: *Ring the changes on, take up the cudgels for, toe the line, ride roughshod over, stand shoulder to shoulder with, play into the hands of, no axe to grind, grist to the mill, fishing in troubled waters, on the order of the day, Achilles' heel, swan song, hotbed.* Many of these are used without knowledge of their meaning (what is a 'rift,' for instance?), and incompatible metaphors are frequently mixed, a sure sign that the writer is not interested in what he is saying. Some metaphors now current have been twisted out of their original meaning without those who use them even being aware of the fact. For example, *toe the line* is sometimes written *tow the line.* Another example is *the hammer and the anvil,* now always used with the implication that the anvil gets the worst of it. In real life it is always the anvil that breaks the hammer, never the other way about: a writer who stopped to think what he was saying would be aware of this, and would avoid perverting the original phrase.

Operators or *verbal false limbs.* These save the trouble of picking out appropriate verbs and nouns, and at the same time pad each sentence with extra syllables which give it an appearance of symmetry. Characteristic phrases are *render inoperative, militate against, make contact with, be subjected to, give rise to, give grounds for, have the effect of, play a leading part (role) in, make itself felt, take effect, exhibit a tendency to, serve the purpose of, etc., etc.* The keynote is the elimination of simple verbs. Instead of being a single word, such as *break, stop, spoil, mend, kill,* a verb becomes a *phrase*, made up of a noun or adjective tacked on to some general-purposes verb such as *prove, serve, form, play, render*. In addition, the passive voice is wherever possible used in preference to the active, and noun constructions are used instead of gerunds (*by examination of* instead of *by examining*). The range of verbs is further cut down by means of the *-ize* and *de-* formations, and the banal statements are given an appearance of profundity by means of the *not un-* formation. Simple conjunctions and prepositions are replaced by such phrases as *with respect to, having regard to, the fact that, by dint of, in view of, in the interests of, on the hypothesis that*; and the ends of sentences are saved from anticlimax by such resounding commonplaces as *greatly to be desired, cannot be left out of account, a development to be expected in the near future, deserving of serious consideration, brought to a satisfactory conclusion*, and so on and so forth.

Pretentious diction. Words like *phenomenon, element, individual* (as noun), *objective, categorical, effective, virtual, basic, primary, promote, constitute, exhibit, exploit, utilize, eliminate, liquidate*, are used to dress up simple statement and give an air of scientific impartiality to biased judgments. Adjectives like *epoch-making, epic, historic, unforgettable, triumphant, age-old, inevitable, inexorable, veritable*, are used to dignify the sordid processes of international politics, while writing that aims at glorifying war usually takes on an archaic color, its characteristic words being: *realm, throne, chariot, mailed fist, trident, sword, shield, buckler, banner, jackboot, clarion*. Foreign words and expressions such as *cul de sac, ancien régime, deus ex machina, mutatis mutandis, status quo, gleichschaltung, weltanschauung*, are used to give an air of culture and elegance. Except for the useful abbreviations *i.e., e.g.*, and *etc.*, there is no real need for any of the hundreds of foreign phrases now current in English. Bad writers, and especially scientific, political and sociological writers, are nearly always haunted by the notion that Latin or Greek words are grander than Saxon ones, and unnecessary words like *expedite, ameliorate, predict, extraneous, deracinated, clandestine, subaqueous* and hundreds of others constantly gain ground from their Anglo-Saxon opposite numbers.[1] The jargon peculiar to Marxist writing (*hyena, hangman, cannibal, petty bourgeois, these gentry,*

---

[1] An interesting illustration of this is the way in which the English flower names which were in use till very recently are being ousted by Greek ones, *snapdragon* becoming *antirrhinum*, *forget-me-not* becoming *myosotis*, etc. It is hard to see any practical reason for this change of fashion: it is probably due to an instinctive turning-away from the more homely word and a vague feeling that the Greek word is scientific.

lacquey, flunkey, mad dog, White Guard, etc.) consists largely of words and phrases translated from Russian, German or French; but the normal way of coining a new word is to use a Latin or Greek root with the appropriate affix and, where necessary, the -ize formation. It is often easier to make up words of this kind (*deregionalize, impermissible, extramarital, non-fragmentary* and so forth) than to think up the English words that will cover one's meaning. The result, in general, is an increase in slovenliness and vagueness.

Meaningless words. In certain kinds of writing, particularly in art criticism and literary criticism, it is normal to come across long passages which are almost completely lacking in meaning.[2] Words like *romantic, plastic, values, human, dead, sentimental, natural, vitality,* as used in art criticism, are strictly meaningless, in the sense that they not only do not point to any discoverable object, but are hardly ever expected to do so by the reader. When one critic writes, 'The outstanding feature of Mr. X's work is its living quality,' while another writes, 'The immediately striking thing about Mr. X's work is its peculiar deadness,' the reader accepts this as a simple difference of opinion. If words like *black* and *white* were involved, instead of the jargon words *dead* and *living,* he would see at once that language was being used in an improper way. Many political words are similarly abused. The word *Fascism* has now no meaning except in so far as it signifies 'something not desirable.' The words *democracy, socialism, freedom, patriotic, realistic, justice,* have each of them several different meanings which cannot be reconciled with one another. In the case of a word like *democracy,* not only is there no agreed definition, but the attempt to make one is resisted from all sides. It is almost universally felt that when we call a country democratic we are praising it: consequently the defenders of every kind of régime claim that it is a democracy, and fear that they might have to stop using the word if it were tied down to any one meaning. Words of this kind are often used in a consciously dishonest way. That is, the person who uses them has his own private definition, but allows his hearer to think he means something quite different. Statements like *Marshal Pétain was a true patriot, The Soviet Press is the freest in the world,*

[2] Example: 'Comfort's catholicity of perception and image, strangely Whitmanesque in range, almost the exact opposite in aesthetic compulsion, continues to evoke that trembling atmospheric accumulative hinting at a cruel, an inexorably serene timelessness. . . . Wrey Gardiner scores by aiming at simple bull's-eyes with precision. Only they are not so simple, and through this contented sadness runs more than the surface bitter-sweet of resignation.' (*Poetry Quarterly.*)

The Catholic Church is opposed to persecution, are almost always made with intent to deceive. Other words used in variable meanings, in most cases more or less dishonestly, are: *class, totalitarian, science, progressive, reactionary, bourgeois, equality.*

Now that I have made this catalogue of swindles and perversions, let me give another example of the kind of writing that they lead to. This time it must of its nature be an imaginary one. I am going to translate a passage of good English into modern English of the worst sort. Here is a well-known verse from *Ecclesiastes*:

'I returned and saw under the sun, that the race is not to the swift, nor the battle to the strong, neither yet bread to the wise, nor yet riches to men of understanding, nor yet favour to men of skill; but time and chance happeneth to them all.'

Here it is in modern English:

'Objective consideration of contemporary phenomena compels the conclusion that success or failure in competitive activities exhibits no tendency to be commensurate with innate capacity, but that a considerable element of the unpredictable must invariably be taken into account.'

This is a parody, but not a very gross one. Exhibit (3), above, for instance, contains several patches of the same kind of English. It will be seen that I have not made a full translation. The beginning and ending of the sentence follow the original meaning fairly closely, but in the middle the concrete illustrations—race, battle, bread—dissolve into the vague phrase 'success or failure in competitive activities.' This had to be so, because no modern writer of the kind I am discussing—no one capable of using phrases like 'objective consideration of contemporary phenomena'—would ever tabulate his thoughts in that precise and detailed way. The whole tendency of modern prose is away from concreteness. Now analyse these two sentences a little more closely. The first contains forty-nine words but only sixty syllables, and all its words are those of everyday life. The second contains thirty-eight words of ninety syllables: eighteen of its words are from Latin roots, and one from Greek. The first sentence contains six vivid images, and only one phrase ('time and chance') that could be called vague. The second contains not a single fresh, arresting phrase, and in spite of its ninety syllables it gives only a shortened version of the meaning contained in the first. Yet without a doubt it is the second kind of sentence that is gaining ground in modern English. I do not want to exaggerate. This kind of writing is not yet universal, and outcrops of simplicity will occur here and there in the worst-written page. Still, if you or I were told to write a few lines on the uncertainty of human fortunes, we should probably come much nearer to my imaginary sentence than to the one from *Ecclesiastes*.

As I have tried to show, modern writing at its worst does not consist in picking out words for the sake of their meaning and inventing images in order to make the meaning clearer. It consists in gumming together long strips of words which have already been set in order by someone else, and making the results presentable by sheer humbug. The attraction of this way of writing is that it is easy. It is easier—even quicker, once you have the habit—to say *In my opinion it is not an unjustifiable assumption that* than to say *I think*. If you use ready-made phrases, you not only don't have to hunt about for words; you also don't have to bother with the rhythms of your sentences, since these phrases are generally so arranged as to be more or less euphonious. When you are composing in a hurry—when you are dictating to a stenographer, for instance, or making a public speech—it is natural to fall into a pretentious, Latinized style. Tags like *a consideration which we should do well to bear in mind* or *a conclusion to which all of us would readily assent* will save many a sentence from coming down with a bump. By using stale metaphors, similes and idioms, you save much mental effort, at the cost of leaving your meaning vague, not only for your reader but for yourself. This is the significance of mixed metaphors. The sole aim of a metaphor is to call up a visual image. When these images clash—as in *The Fascist octopus has sung its swan song, the jackboot is thrown into the melting pot*—it can be taken as certain that the writer is not seeing a mental image of the objects he is naming; in other words he is not really thinking. Look again at the examples I gave at the beginning of this essay. Professor Laski (1) uses five negatives in fifty-three words. One of these is superfluous, making nonsense of the whole passage, and in addition there is the slip *alien* for akin, making further nonsense, and several avoidable pieces of clumsiness which increase the general vagueness. Professor Hogben (2) plays ducks and drakes with a battery which is able to write prescriptions, and, while disapproving of the everyday phrase *put up with*, is unwilling to look *egregious* up in the dictionary and see what it means; (3), if one takes an uncharitable attitude towards it, is simply meaningless: probably one could work out its intended meaning by reading the whole of the article in which it occurs. In (4), the writer knows more or less what he wants to say, but an accumulation of stale phrases chokes him like tea leaves blocking a sink. In (5), words and meaning have almost parted company. People who write in this manner usually have a general emotional meaning—they dislike one thing and want to express solidarity with another—but they are not interested in the detail of what they are saying. A scrupulous writer, in every sentence that he writes, will ask himself at least four questions, thus: What am I trying to say? What words will express it? What image or idiom will make it clearer? Is this image fresh enough to have an effect? And he will probably ask himself two more: Could I put it more shortly? Have I said anything that is avoidably ugly? But you are not obliged to go to all this trouble. You can shirk it by simply throwing your mind open and letting the ready-made phrases come crowding in. They will construct your sentences for you—even think your thoughts for you, to a certain extent—and at need they will perform the important service of partially concealing your meaning even from yourself. It is at this point that the special connection between politics and the debasement of language becomes clear.

In our time it is broadly true that political writing is bad writing. Where it is not true, it will generally be found that the writer is some kind of rebel, expressing his private opinions and not a 'party line.' Orthodoxy, of whatever color, seems to demand a lifeless, imitative style. The political dialects to be found in pamphlets, leading articles, manifestos, White Papers and the speeches of under-secretaries do, of course, vary from party to party, but they are all alike in that one almost never finds in them a fresh, vivid, home-made turn of speech. When one watches some tired hack on the platform mechanically repeating the familiar phrases—*bestial atrocities, iron heel, bloodstained tyranny, free peoples of the world, stand shoulder to shoulder*—one often has a curious feeling that one is not watching a live human being but some kind of dummy: a feeling which suddenly becomes stronger at moments when the light catches the speaker's spectacles and turns them into blank discs which seem to have no eyes behind them. And this is not altogether fanciful. A speaker who uses that kind of phraseology has gone some distance towards turning himself into a machine. The appropriate noises are coming out of his larynx, but his brain is not involved as it would be if he were choosing his words for himself. If the speech he is making is one that he is accustomed to make over and over again, he may be almost unconscious of what he is saying, as one is when one utters the responses in church. And this reduced state of consciousness, if not indispensable, is at any rate favorable to political conformity.

In our time, political speech and writing are largely the defence of the indefensible. Things like the continuance of British rule in India, the Russian purges and deportations, the dropping of the atom bombs on

Japan, can indeed be defended, but only by arguments which are too brutal for most people to face, and which do not square with the professed aims of political parties. Thus political language has to consist largely of euphemism, question-begging and sheer cloudy vagueness. Defenceless villages are bombarded from the air, the inhabitants driven out into the countryside, the cattle machine-gunned, the huts set on fire with incendiary bullets: this is called *pacification*. Millions of peasants are robbed of their farms and sent trudging along the roads with no more than they can carry: this is called *transfer of population* or *rectification of frontiers*. People are imprisoned for years without trial, or shot in the back of the neck or sent to die of scurvy in Arctic lumber camps: this is called *elimination of unreliable elements*. Such phraseology is needed if one wants to name things without calling up mental pictures of them. Consider for instance some comfortable English professor defending Russian totalitarianism. He cannot say outright, 'I believe in killing off your opponents when you can get good results by doing so.' Probably, therefore, he will say something like this:

'While freely conceding that the Soviet régime exhibits certain features which the humanitarian may be inclined to deplore, we must, I think, agree that a certain curtailment of the right to political opposition is an unavoidable concomitant of transitional periods, and that the rigors which the Russian people have been called upon to undergo have been amply justified in the sphere of concrete achievement.'

The inflated style is itself a kind of euphemism. A mass of Latin words falls upon the facts like soft snow, blurring the outlines and covering up all the details. The great enemy of clear language is insincerity. When there is a gap between one's real and one's declared aims, one turns as it were instinctively to long words and exhausted idioms, like a cuttlefish squirting out ink. In our age there is no such thing as 'keeping out of politics.' All issues are political issues, and politics itself is a mass of lies, evasions, folly, hatred and schizophrenia. When the general atmosphere is bad, language must suffer. I should expect to find—this is a guess which I have not sufficient knowledge to verify—that the German, Russian and Italian languages have all deteriorated in the last ten or fifteen years, as a result of dictatorship.

But if thought corrupts language, language can also corrupt thought. A bad usage can spread by tradition and imitation, even among people who should and do know better. The debased language that I have been discussing is in some ways very convenient. Phrases like *a not unjustifiable assumption, leaves much to be desired, would serve no good purpose, a consideration which we should do well to bear in mind,* are a continuous temptation, a packet of aspirins always at one's elbow. Look back through this essay, and for certain you will find that I have again and again committed the very faults I am protesting against. By this morning's post I have received a pamphlet dealing with conditions in Germany. The author tells me that he 'felt impelled' to write it. I open it at random, and here is almost the first sentence that I see: '[The Allies] have an opportunity not only of achieving a radical transformation of Germany's social and political structure in such a way as to avoid a nationalistic reaction in Germany itself, but at the same time of laying the foundations of a co-operative and unified Europe.' You see, he 'feels impelled' to write—feels, presumably, that he has something new to say—and yet his words, like cavalry horses answering the bugle, group themselves automatically into the familiar dreary pattern. This invasion of one's mind by ready-made phrases (*lay the foundations, achieve a radical transformation*) can only be prevented if one is constantly on guard against them, and every such phrase anaesthetizes a portion of one's brain.

I said earlier that the decadence of our language is probably curable. Those who deny this would argue, if they produced an argument at all, that language merely reflects existing social conditions, and that we cannot influence its development by any direct tinkering with words and constructions. So far as the general tone or spirit of a language goes, this may be true, but it is not in detail. Silly words and expressions have often disappeared, not through any evolutionary process but owing to the conscious action of a minority. Two recent examples were *explore every avenue* and *leave no stone unturned,* which were killed by the jeers of a few journalists. There is a long list of flyblown metaphors which could similarly be got rid of if enough people could interest themselves in the job; and it should also be possible to laugh the *not un-* formation out of existence,[3] to reduce the amount of Latin and Greek in the average sentence, to drive out foreign phrases and strayed scientific words, and, in general, to make pretentiousness unfashionable. But all these are minor points. The defence of the English language implies more than this, and perhaps it is best to start by saying what it does *not* imply.

To begin with it has nothing to do with archaism, with the salvaging of obsolete words and turns of speech, or with the setting up of a 'standard

---

[3] One can cure oneself of the *not un-* formation by memorizing this sentence: *A not unblack dog was chasing a not unsmall rabbit across a not ungreen field.*

English' which must never be departed from. On the contrary, it is especially concerned with the scrapping of every word or idiom which has outworn its usefulness. It has nothing to do with correct grammar and syntax,
which are of no importance so long as one makes one's meaning clear, or
with the avoidance of Americanisms, or with having what is called a 'good
prose style.' On the other hand it is not concerned with fake simplicity and
the attempt to make written English colloquial. Nor does it even imply in
every case preferring the Saxon word to the Latin one, though it does imply
using the fewest and shortest words that will cover one's meaning. What is
above all needed is to let the meaning choose the word, and not the other
way about. In prose, the worst thing one can do with words is to surrender
to them. When you think of a concrete object, you think wordlessly, and
then, if you want to describe the thing you have been visualizing you
probably hunt about till you find the exact words that seem to fit it. When
you think of something abstract you are more inclined to use words from
the start, and unless you make a conscious effort to prevent it, the existing
dialect will come rushing in and do the job for you, at the expense of
blurring or even changing your meaning. Probably it is better to put off
using words as long as possible and get one's meaning as clear as one can
through pictures or sensations. Afterwards one can choose—not simply
accept—the phrases that will best cover the meaning, and then switch
round and decide what impression one's words are likely to make on
another person. This last effort of the mind cuts out all stale or mixed
images, all prefabricated phrases, needless repetitions, and humbug and
vagueness generally. But one can often be in doubt about the effect of a
word or a phrase, and one needs rules that one can rely on when instinct
fails. I think the following rules will cover most cases:

(i) Never use a metaphor, simile or other figure of speech which you
are used to seeing in print.

(ii) Never use a long word where a short one will do.

(iii) If it is possible to cut a word out, always cut it out.

(iv) Never use the passive where you can use the active.

(v) Never use a foreign phrase, a scientific word or a jargon word if you
can think of an everyday English equivalent.

(vi) Break any of these rules sooner than say anything outright
barbarous.

These rules sound elementary, and so they are, but they demand a deep
change of attitude in anyone who has grown used to writing in the style

now fashionable. One could keep all of them and still write bad English, but one could not write the kind of stuff that I quoted in those five specimens at the beginning of this article.

I have not here been considering the literary use of language, but merely language as an instrument for expressing and not for concealing or preventing thought. Stuart Chase and others have come near to claiming that all abstract words are meaningless, and have used this as a pretext for advocating a kind of political quietism. Since you don't know what Fascism is, how can you struggle against Fascism? One need not swallow such absurdities as this, but one ought to recognize that the present political chaos is connected with the decay of language, and that one can probably bring about some improvement by starting at the verbal end. If you simplify your English, you are freed from the worst follies of orthodoxy. You cannot speak any of the necessary dialects, and when you make a stupid remark its stupidity will be obvious, even to yourself. Political language—and with variations this is true of all political parties, from Conservatives to Anarchists—is designed to make lies sound truthful and murder respectable, and to give an appearance of solidity to pure wind. One cannot change this all in a moment, but one can at least change one's own habits, and from time to time one can even, if one jeers loudly enough, send some worn-out and useless phrase—some *jackboot, Achilles' heel, hotbed, melting pot, acid test, veritable inferno* or other lump of verbal refuse—into the dustbin where it belongs.

Edmund Burke

REFLECTIONS ON THE REVOLUTION
IN FRANCE

❰ The contrast between Burke as champion of Ireland and the American Colonies, and Burke as the implacable enemy of the French Revolution, is perennially fascinating and instructive to the student of political thought. Whatever the private reasons that may have contributed to the severity of his judgments on the French people in their struggle for better government, Burke condemned the revolutionary movement from the first. It was not the September massacres of 1792 nor the execution of the king, in January 1793, that moved him to opposition—those events merely confirmed his prophecies—but even the efforts of the National Assembly of 1789 to create a constitutional government caused him to dread and denounce a political force that many of his countrymen enthusiastically applauded.

Burke's most extensive examination and indictment of 'French principles' was his *Reflections on the Revolution in France* (1790), a work originating in 'a correspondence between the Author and a very young gentleman at Paris, who did him the honour of desiring his opinion upon the important transactions which then, and have ever since, so much occupied the attention of all men.' Seven thousand copies, we are told, were sold within a week. His *Reflections* at once made Burke the leading voice in British hostility to France; hostility that ended, as Burke foresaw, in war between the two countries.

Despite his blindness to what was good in the French Revolution, Burke had a clear eye to its dangers. The excesses he feared, and the military dictatorship he predicted, did come to pass. This very combination of blindness and foresight helps to give the *Reflections* an enduring interest and relevance.

O N THE forenoon of the 4th of November last, Doctor Richard Price, a non-conforming minister of eminence, preached at the

FROM *Reflections on the Revolution in France*, 1790.

dissenting meeting-house of the Old Jewry, to his club or society, a very extraordinary miscellaneous sermon, in which there are some good moral and religious sentiments, and not ill expressed, mixed up with a sort of porridge of various political opinions and reflections: but the Revolution in France is the grand ingredient in the cauldron. I consider the address transmitted by the Revolution Society to the National Assembly, through Earl Stanhope, as originating in the principles of the sermon, and as a corollary from them. It was moved by the preacher of that discourse. It was passed by those who came reeking from the effect of the sermon, without any censure or qualification, expressed or implied. If, however, any of the gentlemen concerned shall wish to separate the sermon from the resolution, they know how to acknowledge the one, and to disavow the other. They may do it: I cannot.

For my part, I looked on that sermon as the public declaration of a man much connected with literary caballers, and intriguing philosophers; with political theologians, and theological politicians, both at home and abroad. I know they set him up as a sort of oracle; because, with the best intentions in the world, he naturally *philippizes*,[1] and chants his prophetic song in exact unison with their designs.

That sermon is in a strain which I believe has not been heard in this kingdom, in any of the pulpits which are tolerated or encouraged in it, since the year 1648; when a predecessor of Dr. Price, the Reverend Hugh Peters, made the vault of the king's own chapel at St. James's ring with the honour and privilege of the saints, who, with the 'high praises of God in their mouths, and a *two*-edged sword in their hands, were to execute judgment on the heathen, and punishments upon the *people*; to bind their *kings* with chains, and their *nobles* with fetters of iron.' * Few harangues from the pulpit, except in the days of your league in France, or in the days of our solemn league and covenant in England, have ever breathed less of the spirit of moderation than this lecture in the Old Jewry. Supposing, however, that something like moderation were visible in this political sermon, yet politics and the pulpit are terms that have little agreement. No sound ought to be heard in the church but the healing voice of Christian charity. The cause of civil liberty and civil government gains as little as that of religion by this confusion of duties. Those who quit their proper character to assume what does not belong to them are, for the greater part, ignorant both of the character they leave, and of the character they assume. Wholly unacquainted with the world in which they are so fond of meddling, and

[¹ See p. 196, n.7.]
* Ps. cxlix.

inexperienced in all its affairs, on which they pronounce with so much confidence, they have nothing of politics but the passions they excite. Surely the church is a place where one day's truce ought to be allowed to the dissensions and animosities of mankind. . . .

These gentlemen of the Old Jewry, in all their reasonings on the Revolution of 1688, have a revolution which happened in England about forty years before, and the late French Revolution, so much before their eyes, and in their hearts, that they are constantly confounding all the three together. It is necessary that we should separate what they confound. We must recall their erring fancies to the *acts* of the Revolution which we revere, for the discovery of its true *principles*. If the *principles* of the Revolution of 1688 are anywhere to be found, it is in the statute called the *Declaration of Right*. In that most wise, sober, and considerate declaration, drawn up by great lawyers and great statesmen, and not by warm and inexperienced enthusiasts, not one word is said, nor one suggestion made, of a general right 'to choose our own *governors*; to cashier them for misconduct: and to *form* a government for *ourselves*.'

This Declaration of Right (the act of the 1st of William and Mary, sess. 2, ch. 2) is the corner-stone of our constitution, as reinforced, explained, improved, and in its fundamental principles for ever settled. It is called 'An act for declaring the rights and liberties of the subject, and for *settling* the *succession* of the crown.' You will observe, that these rights and this succession are declared in one body, and bound indissolubly together. . . .

The two Houses, in the act of King William, did not thank God that they had found a fair opportunity to assert a right to choose their own governors, much less to make an election the *only lawful* title to the crown. Their having been in a condition to avoid the very appearance of it, as much as possible, was by them considered as a providential escape. They threw a politic, well-wrought veil over every circumstance tending to weaken the rights which in the meliorated order of succession they meant to perpetuate, or which might furnish a precedent for any future departure from what they had then settled for ever. Accordingly, that they might not relax the nerves of their monarchy, and that they might preserve a close conformity to the practice of their ancestors, as it appeared in the declaratory statutes of Queen Mary * and Queen Elizabeth, in the next clause they vest, by recognition, in their majesties *all* the legal prerogatives of the crown, declaring, 'that in them they are most *fully*, rightfully, and *entirely*, invested, incorporated, united, and annexed.' In the clause which follows,

---

* 1st Mary, sess. 3, ch. 1.

for preventing questions, by reason of any pretended titles to the crown, they declare (observing also in this the traditionary language, along with the traditionary policy of the nation, and repeating as from a rubric the language of the preceding acts of Elizabeth and James) that on the preserving 'a *certainty* in the SUCCESSION thereof, the unity, peace, and tranquillity of this nation, doth, under God, wholly depend.'

They knew that a doubtful title of succession would but too much resemble an election; and that an election would be utterly destructive of the 'unity, peace, and tranquillity of this nation,' which they thought to be considerations of some moment. To provide for these objects, and therefore to exclude for ever the Old Jewry doctrine of 'a right to choose our own governors,' they follow with a clause, containing a most solemn pledge, taken from the preceding act of Queen Elizabeth, as solemn a pledge as ever was or can be given in favour of an hereditary succession, and as solemn a renunciation as could be made of the principles by this Society imputed to them. 'The lords spiritual and temporal, and commons, do, in the name of all the people aforesaid, most humbly and faithfully submit *themselves, their heirs, and posterities for ever*; and do faithfully promise, that they will stand to, maintain, and defend their said majesties, and also the *limitation of the crown*, herein specified and contained, to the utmost of their powers,' &c., &c.

So far is it from being true, that we acquired a right by the Revolution to elect our kings, that if we had possessed it before, the English nation did at that time most solemnly renounce and abdicate it, for themselves, and for all their posterity for ever. . . .

Far am I from denying in theory, full as far is my heart from withholding in practice (if I were of power to give or to withhold) the *real* rights of men. In denying their false claims of right, I do not mean to injure those which are real, and are such as their pretended rights would totally destroy. If civil society be made for the advantage of man, all the advantages for which it is made become his right. It is an institution of beneficence; and law itself is only beneficence, acting by a rule. Men have a right to live by that rule; they have a right to justice, as between their fellows, whether their fellows are in politic function or in ordinary occupation. They have a right to the fruits of their industry; and to the means of making their industry fruitful. They have a right to the acquisitions of their parents; to the nourishment and improvement of their offspring; to instruction in life, and to consolation in death. Whatever each man can separately do, without trespassing upon others, he has a right to do for himself; and he has a right to a fair portion of all which society, with all its combinations of skill and force, can do in his favour. In this partnership all men have equal rights; but not to equal things. He that has but five shillings in the partnership has as good a right to it as he that has five hundred pounds has to his larger proportion. But he has not a right to an equal dividend in the product of the joint stock; and as to the share of power, authority, and direction which each individual ought to have in the management of the state, that I must deny to be amongst the direct original rights of man in civil society; for I have in my contemplation the civil social man, and no other. It is a thing to be settled by convention.

If civil society be the offspring of convention, that convention must be its law. That convention must limit and modify all the descriptions of constitution which are formed under it. Every sort of legislative, judicial, or executory power are its creatures. They can have no being in any other state of things; and how can any man claim, under the conventions of civil society, rights which do not so much as suppose its existence?—rights which are absolutely repugnant to it? One of the first motives to civil society, and which becomes one of its fundamental rules, is, *that no man should be judge in his own cause.* By this each person has at once divested himself of the first fundamental right of uncovenanted man, that is, to judge for himself, and to assert his own cause. He abdicates all right to be his own governor. He inclusively, in a great measure, abandons the right of self-defence, the first law of nature. Man cannot enjoy the rights of an uncivil and of a civil state together. That he may obtain justice, he gives up his right of determining what it is in points the most essential to him. That he may secure some liberty, he makes a surrender in trust of the whole of it.

Government is not made in virtue of natural rights, which may and do exist in total independence of it; and exist in much greater clearness, and in a much greater degree of abstract perfection; but their abstract perfection is their practical defect. By having a right to everything, they want everything. Government is a contrivance of human wisdom to provide for human *wants.* Men have a right that these wants should be provided for by this wisdom. Among these wants is to be reckoned the want, out of civil society, of a sufficient restraint upon their passions. Society requires not only that the passions of individuals should be subjected, but that even in the mass and body, as well as in the individuals, the inclinations of men should frequently be thwarted, their will controlled, and their passions brought into subjection. This can only be done *by a power out of themselves;* and not, in the exercise of its function, subject to that will and to those passions which it is its office to bridle and subdue. In this sense the restraints on men, as well as their liberties, are to be reckoned among their rights. But as the liberties and the restrictions vary with times and circum-stances, and admit of infinite modifications, they cannot be settled upon any abstract rule; and nothing is so foolish as to discuss them upon that principle.

The moment you abate anything from the full rights of men, each to govern himself, and suffer any artificial, positive limitation upon those rights, from that moment the whole organization of government becomes a consideration of convenience. This it is which makes the constitution of a state, and the due distribution of its powers, a matter of the most delicate and complicated skill. It requires a deep knowledge of human nature and human necessities, and of the things which facilitate or obstruct the various ends which are to be pursued by the mechanism of civil institutions. The state is to have recruits to its strength, and remedies to its distempers. What is the use of discussing a man's abstract right to food or medicine? The question is upon the method of procuring and administering them. In that deliberation I shall always advise to call in the aid of the farmer and the physician, rather than the professor of metaphysics.

The science of constructing a commonwealth, or renovating it, or re-forming it, is, like every other experimental science, not to be taught *a priori*. Nor is it a short experience that can instruct us in that practical science; because the real effects of moral causes are not always immediate; but that which in the first instance is prejudicial may be excellent in its remoter operation, and its excellence may arise even from the ill effects it produces in the beginning. The reverse also happens; and very plausible schemes, with very pleasing commencements, have often shameful and lamentable conclusions. In states there are often some obscure and almost latent causes, things which appear at first view of little moment, on which a very great part of its prosperity or adversity may most essentially depend. The science of government being therefore so practical in itself, and in-tended for such practical purposes, a matter which requires experience, and even more experience than any person can gain in his whole life, however sagacious and observing he may be, it is with infinite caution that any man ought to venture upon pulling down an edifice which has answered in any tolerable degree for ages the common purposes of society, or on building it up again, without having models and patterns of approved utility before his eyes.

These metaphysic rights entering into common life, like rays of light which pierce into a dense medium, are, by the laws of nature, refracted from their straight line. Indeed, in the gross and complicated mass of human passions and concerns, the primitive rights of men undergo such a variety of refractions and reflections, that it becomes absurd to talk of them as if they continued in the simplicity of their original direction. The nature of man is intricate; the objects of society are of the greatest possible complexity: and therefore no simple disposition or direction of power can be suitable either to man's nature, or to the quality of his affairs. When I hear the simplicity of contrivance aimed at and boasted of in any new political constitutions, I am at no loss to decide that the artificers are grossly ignorant of their trade, or totally negligent of their duty. The simple governments are fundamentally defective, to say no worse of them. If you were to contemplate society in but one point of view, all these simple modes of polity are infinitely captivating. In effect each would answer its single end much more perfectly than the more complex is able to attain all its complex purposes. But it is better that the whole should be imperfectly and anomalously answered, than that, while some parts are provided for with great exactness, others might be totally neglected, or perhaps materially injured, by the over-care of a favourite member.

The pretended rights of these theorists are all extremes: and in proportion as they are metaphysically true, they are morally and politically false. The rights of men are in a sort of *middle*, incapable of definition, but not impossible to be discerned. The rights of men in governments are their advantages; and these are often in balances between differences of good; in compromises sometimes between good and evil, and sometimes between evil and evil. Political reason is a computing principle: adding, subtracting, multiplying, and dividing, morally, and not metaphysically or mathematically, true moral denominations.

By these theorists the right of the people is almost always sophistically confounded with their power. The body of the community, whenever it can come to act, can meet with no effectual resistance; but till power and right are the same, the whole body of them has no right inconsistent with virtue, and the first of all virtues, prudence. Men have no right to what is not reasonable, and to what is not for their benefit. . . .

History will record, that on the morning of the 6th of October, 1789, the King and Queen of France, after a day of confusion, alarm, dismay, and slaughter, lay down, under the pledged security of public faith, to indulge nature in a few hours of respite, and troubled, melancholy repose. From this sleep the queen was first startled by the voice of the sentinel at her door, who cried out to her to save herself by flight—that this was the last proof of fidelity he could give—that they were upon him, and he was dead. Instantly he was cut down. A band of cruel ruffians and assassins, reeking with his blood, rushed into the chamber of the queen, and pierced with a hundred strokes of bayonets and poniards the bed, from whence this persecuted woman had but just time to fly almost naked, and, through ways unknown to the murderers, had escaped to seek refuge at the feet of a king and husband, not secure of his own life for a moment.

This king, to say no more of him, and this queen, and their infant children, (who once would have been the pride and hope of a great and generous people,) were then forced to abandon the sanctuary of the most splendid palace in the world, which they left swimming in blood, polluted by massacre, and strewed with scattered limbs and mutilated carcases. Thence they were conducted into the capital of their kingdom. Two had been selected from the unprovoked, unresisted, promiscuous slaughter which was made of the gentlemen of birth and family who composed the king's body-guard. These two gentlemen, with all the parade of an execution of justice, were cruelly and publicly dragged to the block, and beheaded in the great court of the palace. Their heads were stuck upon spears, and led the procession; whilst the royal captives who followed in the train were slowly moved along, amidst the horrid yells, and shrilling screams, and frantic dances, and infamous contumelies, and all the unutterable abominations of the furies of hell, in the abused shape of the vilest of women. After they had been made to taste, drop by drop, more than the bitterness of death, in the slow torture of a journey of twelve miles, protracted to six hours, they were, under a guard, composed of those very soldiers who had thus conducted them through this famous triumph, lodged in one of the old palaces of Paris, now converted into a Bastile for kings. . . .

It is now sixteen or seventeen years since I saw the Queen of France, then the dauphiness, at Versailles; and surely never lighted on this orb, which she hardly seemed to touch, a more delightful vision. I saw her just above the horizon, decorating and cheering the elevated sphere she just began to move in,—glittering like the morning-star, full of life, and splendour and joy. Oh! what a revolution! and what a heart must I have, to contemplate without emotion that elevation and that fall! Little did I dream when she added titles of veneration to those of enthusiastic, distant, respectful love, that she should ever be obliged to carry the sharp antidote against disgrace concealed in that bosom; little did I dream that I should have lived to see such disasters fallen upon her in a nation of gallant men, in a nation of men of honour, and of cavaliers. I thought ten thousand swords must have leaped from their scabbards to avenge even a look that threatened her with insult. But the age of chivalry is gone. That of sophisters, economists, and calculators has succeeded; and the glory of

Europe is extinguished forever. Never, never more, shall we behold that generous loyalty to rank and sex, that proud submission, that dignified obedience, that subordination of the heart, which kept alive, even in servitude itself, the spirit of an exalted freedom. The unbought grace of life, the cheap defence of nations, the nurse of manly sentiment and heroic enterprise is gone! It is gone, that sensibility of principle, that chastity of honour, which felt a stain like a wound, which inspired courage whilst it mitigated ferocity, which ennobled whatever it touched, and under which vice itself lost half its evil by losing all its grossness.

This mixed system of opinion and sentiment had its origin in the ancient chivalry; and the principle, though varied in its appearance by the varying state of human affairs, subsisted and influenced through a long succession of generations, even to the time we live in. If it should ever be totally extinguished, the loss, I fear, will be great. It is this which has given its character to modern Europe. It is this which has distinguished it under all its forms of government, and distinguished it to its advantage, from the states of Asia, and possibly from those states which flourished in the most brilliant periods of the antique world. It was this, which, without confounding ranks, had produced a noble equality, and handed it down through all the gradations of social life. It was this opinion which mitigated kings into companions, and raised private men to be fellows with kings. Without force or opposition, it subdued the fierceness of pride and power; it obliged sovereigns to submit to the soft collar of social esteem, compelled stern authority to submit to elegance, and gave a dominating vanquisher of laws to be subdued by manners.

But now all is to be changed. All the pleasing illusions, which made power gentle, and obedience liberal, which harmonized the different shades of life, and which, by a bland assimilation, incorporated into politics the sentiments which beautify and soften private society, are to be dissolved by this new conquering empire of light and reason. All the decent drapery of life is to be rudely torn off. All the superadded ideas, furnished from the wardrobe of a moral imagination, which the heart owns, and the understanding ratifies, as necessary to cover the defects of our naked, shivering nature, and to raise it to dignity in our own estimation. are to be exploded as a ridiculous, absurd, and antiquated fashion.

On this scheme of things, a king is but a man, a queen is but a woman; a woman is but an animal; and an animal not of the highest order. All homage paid to the sex in general as such, and without distinct views, is to be regarded as romance and folly. Regicide, and parricide, and sacrilege, are but fictions of superstition, corrupting jurisprudence by destroying its simplicity. The murder of a king, or a queen, or a bishop, or a father, are only common homicide; and if the people are by any chance, or in any way, gainers by it, a sort of homicide much the most pardonable, and into which we ought not to make too severe a scrutiny. . . .

Society is indeed a contract. Subordinate contracts for objects of mere occasional interest may be dissolved at pleasure—but the state ought not to be considered as nothing better than a partnership agreement in a trade of pepper and coffee, calico or tobacco, or some other such low concern, to be taken up for a little temporary interest, and to be dissolved by the fancy of the parties. It is to be looked on with other reverence; because it is not a partnership in things subservient only to the gross animal existence of a temporary and perishable nature. It is a partnership in all science; a partnership in all art; a partnership in every virtue, and in all perfection. As the ends of such a partnership cannot be obtained in many generations, it becomes a partnership not only between those who are living, but between those who are living, those who are dead, and those who are to be born. Each contract of each particular state is but a clause in the great primeval contract of eternal society, linking the lower with the higher natures, connecting the visible and invisible world, according to a fixed compact sanctioned by the inviolable oath which holds all physical and all moral natures, each in their appointed place. This law is not subject to the will of those who by an obligation above them, and infinitely superior, are bound to submit their will to that law. The municipal corporations of that universal kingdom are not morally at liberty at their pleasure, and on their speculations of a contingent improvement, wholly to separate and tear asunder the bands of their subordinate community, and to dissolve it into an unsocial, uncivil, unconnected chaos of elementary principles. It is the first and supreme necessity only, a necessity that is not chosen, but chooses, a necessity paramount to deliberation, that admits no discussion, and demands no evidence, which alone can justify a resort to anarchy. This necessity is no exception to the rule; because this necessity itself is a part too of that moral and physical disposition of things, to which man must be obedient by consent or force: but if that which is only submission to necessity should be made the object of choice, the law is broken, nature is disobeyed, and the rebellious are outlawed, cast forth, and exiled, from this world of reason, and order, and peace, and virtue, and fruitful penitence, into the antagonist world of madness, discord, vice, confusion, and unavailing sorrow.

Thomas Paine

THE RIGHTS OF MAN

❪ Paine (1737–1809), an Englishman who emigrated to America in 1774 (with an introduction from Franklin), supported the cause of the Colonies by his famous pamphlets, *Common Sense* (1776) and *The Crisis* (1776–1783). He served in the Revolutionary army, and afterward held various political posts. In 1787 he went back to England. His *Rights of Man* (1791–2) compelled him to flee to France to avoid prosecution. He was given the title of French citizen and became a member of the Convention in the following year (he voted against the execution of Louis XVI), but got into trouble and barely escaped the guillotine. While in prison he worked on his *Age of Reason* (1793). He returned to America in 1802. His criticism of George Washington in 1796, as well as the notoriety of his *Age of Reason*, which attacked Christianity, cost him most of his popularity in America. He died in New York in 1809.

The *Rights of Man* is an elaborate reply to Burke's *Reflections on the Revolution in France*. It denies Burke's doctrine that one generation can bind succeeding ones to a form of government, expounds the 'natural' and 'civil' rights of mankind, and defends the French Revolution. As an argument for radical republicanism, Paine's book became a classic.

A MONG the incivilities by which nations or individuals provoke and irritate each other, Mr. Burke's pamphlet on the French Revolution is an extraordinary instance. Neither the people of France, nor the National Assembly, were troubling themselves about the affairs of England, or the English Parliament; and that Mr. Burke should commence an unprovoked attack upon them, both in Parliament and in public, is a conduct that cannot be pardoned on the score of manners, nor justified

FROM *The Rights of Man*, 1791-2.

on that of policy. There is scarcely an epithet of abuse to be found in the English language, with which Mr. Burke has not loaded the French nation and the National Assembly. Every thing which rancor, prejudice, ignorance, or knowledge could suggest, are poured forth in the copious fury of near four hundred pages. In the strain and on the plan Mr. Burke was writing, he might have written on to as many thousands. When the tongue or the pen is let loose in a frenzy of passion, it is the man and not the subject that becomes exhausted.

Hitherto Mr. Burke has been mistaken and disappointed in the opinions he had formed of the affairs of France; but such is the ingenuity of his hope, or the malignancy of his despair, that it furnishes him with new pretenses to go on. There was a time when it was impossible to make Mr. Burke believe there would be any revolution in France. His opinion then was, that the French had neither spirit to undertake it, nor fortitude to support it; and now that there is one, he seeks an escape by condemning it.

Not sufficiently content with abusing the National Assembly, a great part of his work is taken up with abusing Dr. Price (one of the best-hearted men that lives), and the two societies in England known by the name of the Revolution Society, and the Society for Constitutional Information.

Dr. Price [1] had preached a sermon on the 4th of November, 1789, being the anniversary of what is called in England the Revolution, which took place in 1688. Mr. Burke, speaking of this sermon, says, 'The political divine proceeds dogmatically to assert that, by the principles of the Revolution, the people of England have acquired three fundamental rights:

'1. To choose our own governors.

'2. To cashier them for misconduct.

'3. To frame a government for ourselves.'

Dr. Price does not say that the right to do these things exists in this or in that person, or in this or in that description of persons, but that it exists in the *whole*; that it is a right resident in the nation. Mr. Burke, on the contrary, denies that such a right exists in the nation, either in whole or in part, or that it exists any where; and, what is still more strange and marvelous, he says, 'that the people of England utterly disclaim such a right, and that they will resist the practical assertion of it with their lives and fortunes.'

That men should take up arms, and spend their lives and fortunes, *not*

[1 See pp. 265-7.]

to maintain their rights, but to maintain they have *not* rights, is an entirely new species of discovery, and suited to the paradoxical genius of Mr. Burke.

The method which Mr. Burke takes to prove that the people of England had no such rights, and that such rights do not now exist in the nation, either in whole or in part, or any where at all, is of the same marvelous and monstrous kind with what he has already said; for his arguments are, that the persons, or the generation of persons, in whom they did exist, are dead, and with them the right is dead also.

To prove this, he quotes a declaration made by Parliament about a hundred years ago, to William and Mary, in these words: 'The Lords Spiritual and Temporal, and Commons, do, in the name of the people aforesaid,' (meaning the people of England then living) 'most humbly and faithfully *submit* themselves, their *heirs* and *posterities*, for EVER.' He also quotes a clause of another act of Parliament made in the same reign, the terms of which, he says, 'bind us,' (meaning the people of that day) 'our *heirs* and our *posterity*, to *them*, their *heirs* and *posterity*, to the end of time.'

Mr. Burke conceives his point sufficiently established by producing these clauses, which he enforces by saying that they exclude the right of the nation for *ever*. And not yet content with making such declarations, repeated over and over again, he further says, 'that if the people of England possessed such a right before the Revolution,' (which he acknowledges to have been the case, not only in England but throughout Europe, at an early period,) 'yet that the *English nation* did, at the time of the Revolution, most solemnly renounce and abdicate it, for themselves, and for *all their posterity, for ever.*'

As Mr. Burke occasionally applies the poison drawn from his horrid principles, not only to the English nation, but to the French Revolution and the National Assembly, and charges that august, illuminated and illuminating body of men with the epithet of *usurpers*, I shall, *sans cérémonie*, place another system of principles in opposition to his.

The English Parliament of 1688 did a certain thing, which, for themselves and their constituents, they had a right to do, and which it appeared right should be done: But, in addition to this right, which they possessed by delegation, *they set up another right by assumption*, that of binding and controlling posterity to the end of time.

The case, therefore, divides itself into two parts; the right which they possessed by delegation, and the right which they set up by assumption. The first is admitted; but with respect to the second, I reply:—

There never did, there never will, and there never can exist a parliament, or any description of men, or any generation of men, in any country, possessed of the right or the power of binding and controlling posterity to the '*end of time*,' or of commanding forever how the world shall be governed, or who shall goven it; and therefore, all such clauses, acts or declarations, by which the makers of them attempt to do what they have neither the right nor the power to do, nor the power to execute, are in themselves null and void.

Every age and generation must be as free to act for itself, *in all cases*, as the ages and generation which preceded it. The vanity and presumption of governing beyond the grave, is the most ridiculous and insolent of all tyrannies.

Man has no property in man; neither has any generation a property in the generations which are to follow. The Parliament or the people of 1688, or of any other period, had no more right to dispose of the people of the present day, or to bind or to control them *in any shape whatever*, than the Parliament or the people of the present day have to dispose of, bind, or control those who are to live a hundred or a thousand years hence.

Every generation is, and must be, competent to all the purposes which its occasions require. It is the living, and not the dead, that are to be accommodated. When man ceases to be, his power and his wants cease with him; and having no longer any participation in the concerns of this world, he has no longer any authority in directing who shall be its governors, or how its government shall be organized, or how administered.

I am not contending for nor against any form of government, nor for nor against any party here or elsewhere. That which a whole nation chooses to do, it has a right to do. Mr. Burke says, No. Where then *does* the right exist? I am contending for the rights of the *living*, and against their being willed away, and controlled and contracted for, by the manuscript assumed authority of the dead; and Mr. Burke is contending for the authority of the dead over the rights and freedom of the living.

There was a time when kings disposed of their crowns by will upon their death-beds, and consigned the people, like beasts of the field, to whatever successor they appointed. This is now so exploded as scarcely to be remembered, and so monstrous as hardly to be believed. But the parliamentary clauses upon which Mr. Burke builds his political church, are of the same nature.

The laws of every country must be analogous to some common principle. In England, no parent or master, nor all the authority of Parliament, omnipotent as it has called itself, can bind or control the personal freedom even of an individual beyond the age of twenty-one years. On what ground of right, then, could the Parliament of 1688, or any other parliament, bind all posterity for ever?

Those who have quitted the world, and those who are not yet arrived in it, are as remote from each other, as the utmost stretch of moral imagination can conceive. What possible obligation, then, can exist between them; what rule or principle can be laid down, that two nonentities, the one out of existence, and the other not in, and who never can meet in this world, that the one should control the other to the end of time?

In England, it is said that money cannot be taken out of the pockets of the people without their consent. But who authorized, or who could authorize the Parliament of 1688 to control and take away the freedom of posterity, and limit and confine their right of acting in certain cases for ever, who were not in existence to give or to withhold their consent?

A greater absurdity cannot present itself to the understanding of man, than what Mr. Burke offers to his readers. He tells them, and he tells the world to come, that a certain body of men, who existed a hundred years ago, made a law; and that there does not now exist in the nation, nor ever will, nor ever can, a power to alter it. Under how many subtilties, or absurdities, has the divine right to govern been imposed on the credulity of mankind! . . .

When a man reflects on the condition which France was in from the nature of her government, he will see other causes for revolt than those which immediately connect themselves with the person or character of Louis XVI. There were, if I may so express it, a thousand despotisms to be reformed in France, which had grown up under the hereditary despotism of the monarchy, and became so rooted as to be in a great measure independent of it. Between the monarchy, the parliament, and the church, there was a *rivalship* of despotism; besides the feudal despotism operating locally, and the ministerial despotism operating everywhere.

But Mr. Burke, by considering the King as the only possible object of a revolt, speaks as if France was a village, in which every thing that passed must be known to its commanding officer, and no oppression could be acted but what he could conveniently control. Mr. Burke might have been in the Bastille his whole life, as well under Louis XVI and neither the one nor the other have known that such a man as Mr. Burke existed. The despotic principles of the government were the same in both reigns, though the dispositions of the men were as remote as tyranny and benevolence.

What Mr. Burke considers as a reproach to the French Revolution (that of bringing it forward under a reign more mild than the preceding ones), is one of its highest honors. The revolutions that have taken place in other European countries, have been excited by personal hatred. The rage was against the man, and he became the victim. But, in the instance of France, we see a revolution generated in the rational contemplation of the rights of man, and distinguishing from the beginning between persons and principles.

But Mr. Burke appears to have no idea of principles, when he is contemplating governments. 'Ten years ago,' says he, 'I could have felicitated France on her having a government, without inquiring what the nature of that government was, or how it was administered.'

Is this the language of a rational man? Is it the language of a heart feeling as it ought to feel for the rights and happiness of the human race? On this ground, Mr. Burke must compliment every government in the world, while the victims who suffer under them, whether sold into slavery, or tortured out of existence, are wholly forgotten.

It is power, and not principles, that Mr. Burke venerates; and under this abominable depravity, he is disqualified to judge between them. Thus much for his opinion as to the occasion of the French Revolution. I now proceed to other considerations.

I know a point in America called Point-no-Point; because as you proceed along the shore, gay and flowery as Mr. Burke's language, it continually recedes and presents itself at a distance before you; but when you have got as far as you can go, there is no point at all. Just thus it is with Mr. Burke's three hundred and fifty-six pages. It is therefore difficult to reply to him. But as the points he wishes to establish may be inferred from what he abuses, it is in his paradoxes that we must look for his arguments.

As to the tragic paintings by which Mr. Burke has outraged his own imagination, and seeks to work upon that of his readers, they are very well calculated for theatrical representation, where facts are manufactured for the sake of show, and accommodated to produce, through the weakness of sympathy, a weeping effect. But Mr. Burke should recollect that he is writing history, and not *plays*; and that his readers will expect truth, and not the spouting rant of high-toned declamation.

When we see a man dramatically lamenting in a publication intended to be believed, that, 'The age of chivalry is gone! that *The glory of Europe is extinguished forever!* that *The unbought grace of life* (if any one knows what it is), *the cheap defense of nations, the nurse of manly sentiment and heroic enterprise, is gone!'* [2] and all this because the Quixotic age of chivalric nonsense is gone, what opinion can we form of his judgment, or what regard can we pay to his facts?

In the rhapsody of his imagination, he has discovered a world of windmills,[3] and his sorrows are, that there are no Quixotes to attack them. But if the age of aristocracy, like that of chivalry, should fall, and they had originally some connection, Mr. Burke, the trumpeter of the order, may continue his parody to the end, and finish with exclaiming, '*Othello's occupation's gone!'* [4]

Notwithstanding Mr. Burke's horrid paintings, when the French Revolution is compared with that of other countries, the astonishment will be, that it is marked with so few sacrifices; but this astonishment will cease when we reflect that *principles* and not *persons*, were the meditated objects of destruction. The mind of the nation was acted upon by a higher stimulus than what the consideration of persons could inspire, and sought a higher conquest than could be produced by the downfall of an enemy.

[2 See pp. 272–3.]
[3 As Don Quixote does in Cervantes' novel.]
[4 *Othello*, III, iii, 358.]

Arnold J. Toynbee

CIVILIZATION ON TRIAL

❡ 'Civilization on Trial' is an essay taken from one of Mr. Toynbee's minor books, but its ideas are good examples, briefly set forth, of some of the themes expounded so elaborately in his *magnum opus*, A *Study of History*. In the English-speaking world Mr. Toynbee is unquestionably one of the most widely read of contemporary writers on history. This eminence is due almost entirely to A *Study of History*, which began to appear in 1933 but did not become well known outside of Great Britain until the shock of the Second World War caused many common readers to reexamine their presuppositions about the nature of history and of civilization. Six volumes of A *Study of History* were published between 1933 and 1939; four more in 1954. Whatever one may think of the philosophical, ethical, and religious theses in this work—and they have been much debated among scholars—it is a treatise whose erudition, originality, and force are undeniable.

After a few years as Fellow and Tutor of Balliol College, Oxford, Mr. Toynbee was Professor of Byzantine and Modern Greek Language, Literature, and History at the University of London, 1919 to 1924, and since 1925 has been Director of Studies at the Royal Institute of International Affairs. From 1915 to 1919 and again from 1939 to 1943 he was engaged in war work.

I

OUR PRESENT Western outlook on history is an extraordinarily contradictory one. While our historical horizon has been expanding vastly in both the space dimension and the time dimension, our historical vision—what we actually do see, in contrast to what we now could see if we chose—has been contracting rapidly to the narrow field of what a horse sees between its blinkers or what a U-boat commander sees through his periscope.

This is certainly extraordinary; yet it is only one of a number of contradictions of this kind that seem to be characteristic of the times in which we are living. There are other examples that probably loom larger in the minds of most of us. For instance, our world has risen to an unprecedented degree of humanitarian feeling. There is now a recognition of the human rights of people of all classes, nations and races; yet at the same time we have sunk to perhaps unheard-of depths of class warfare, nationalism, and racialism. These bad passions find vent in cold-blooded, scientifically planned cruelties; and the two incompatible states of mind and standards of conduct are to be seen to-day, side by side, not merely in the same world, but sometimes in the same country and even in the same soul.

Again, we now have an unprecedented power of production side by side with unprecedented shortages. We have invented machines to work for us, but have less spare labour than ever before for human service—even for such an essential and elementary service as helping mothers to look after their babies. We have persistent alternations of widespread unemployment with famines of man-power. Undoubtedly, the contrast between our expanding historical horizon and our contracting historical vision is something characteristic of our age. Yet, looked at in itself, what an astonishing contradiction it is!

Let us remind ourselves first of the recent expansion of our horizon. In space, our Western field of vision has expanded to take in the whole of mankind over all the habitable and traversable surface of this planet, and the whole stellar universe in which this planet is an infinitesimally small speck of dust. In time, our Western field of vision has expanded to take in all the civilizations that have risen and fallen during these last 6000 years; the previous history of the human race back to its genesis between 600,000 and a million years ago; the history of life on this planet back to perhaps 800 million years ago. What a marvelous widening of our historical horizon! Yet, at the same time, our field of historical vision has been contracting; it has been tending to shrink within the narrow limits in time and space of the particular republic or kingdom of which each of us happens to be a citizen. The oldest surviving Western states—say France or England—have so far had no more than a thousand years of continuous political existence; the largest existing Western state—say Brazil or the United States—embraces only a very small fraction of the total inhabited surface of the Earth.

Before the widening of our horizon began—before our Western seamen circumnavigated the globe, and before our Western cosmogonists and geologists pushed out the bounds of our universe in both time and space—our pre-nationalist mediaeval ancestors had a broader and juster historical vision than we have to-day. For them, history did not mean the history of one's own parochial community; it meant the history of Israel, Greece, and Rome. And even if they were mistaken in believing that the world was created in 4004 B.C., it is at any rate better to look as far back as 4004 B.C. than to look back no farther than the Declaration of Independence or the voyages of the *Mayflower* or Columbus or Hengist and Horsa. ¹ (As a matter of fact, 4004 B.C. happens, though our ancestors did not know this, to be a quite important date: it approximately marks the first appearance of representatives of the species of human society called civilizations.)

Again, for our ancestors, Rome and Jerusalem meant much more than their own home towns. When our Anglo-Saxon ancestors were converted to Roman Christianity at the end of the sixth century of the Christian era, they learned Latin, studied the treasures of sacred and profane literature to which a knowledge of the Latin language gives access, and went on pilgrimages to Rome and Jerusalem—and this in an age when the difficulties and dangers of travelling were such as to make modern war-time travelling seem child's play. Our ancestors seem to have been big-minded, and this is a great intellectual virtue as well as a great moral one, for national histories are unintelligible within their own time limits and space limits.

II

In the time dimension, you cannot understand the history of England if you begin only at the coming of the English to Britain, any better than you can understand the history of the United States if you begin only at the coming of the English to North America. In the space dimension, likewise, you cannot understand the history of a country if you cut its outlines out of the map of the world and rule out of consideration anything that has originated outside that particular country's frontiers.

What are the epoch-making events in the national histories of the United States and the United Kingdom? Working back from the present towards the past, I should say they were the two world wars, the Industrial Revolution, the Reformation, the Western voyages of discovery, the Renaissance, the conversion to Christianity. Now I defy anyone to tell the history

[¹ Hengist and Horsa were leaders of the Jutish invasion of England, *c*. A.D. 449.]

of either the United States or the United Kingdom without making these events the cardinal ones, or to explain these events as local American or local English affairs. To explain these major events in the history of any Western country, the smallest unit that one can take into account is the whole of Western Christendom. By Western Christendom I mean the Roman Catholic and Protestant world—the adherents of the Patriarchate of Rome who have maintained their allegiance to the Papacy, together with the former adherents who have repudiated it.

But the history of Western Christendom, too, is unintelligible within its own time limits and space limits. While Western Christendom is a much better unit than the United States or the United Kingdom or France for a historian to operate with, it too turns out, on inspection, to be inadequate. In the time dimension, it goes back only to the close of the Dark Ages following the collapse of the western part of the Roman Empire; that is, it goes back less than 1300 years, and 1300 years is less than a quarter of the 6000 years during which the species of society represented by Western Christendom has been in existence. Western Christendom is a civilization belonging to the third of the three generations of civilizations that there have been so far.

In the space dimension, the narrowness of the limits of Western Christendom is still more striking. If you look at the physical map of the world as a whole, you will see that the small part of it which is dry land consists of a single continent—Asia—which has a number of peninsulas and off-lying islands. Now, what are the farthest limits to which Western Christendom has managed to expand? You will find them at Alaska and Chile on the west and at Finland and Dalmatia on the east. What lies between those four points is Western Christendom's domain at its widest. And what does that domain amount to? Just the tip of Asia's European peninsula, together with a couple of large islands. (By these two large islands, I mean, of course, North and South America.) Even if you add in the outlying and precarious footholds of the Western world in South Africa, Australia, and New Zealand, its total habitable present area amounts to only a very minor part of the total habitable area of the surface of the planet. And you cannot understand the history of Western Christendom within its own geographical limits.

Western Christendom is a product of Christianity, but Christianity did not arise in the Western world; it arose outside the bounds of Western Christendom, in a district that lies today within the domain of a different civilization: Islam. We Western Christians did once try to capture from the Muslims the cradle of our religion in Palestine. If the Crusades had succeeded, Western Christendom would have slightly broadened its footing on the all-important Asiatic mainland. But the Crusades ended in failure.

Western Christendom is merely one of five civilizations that survive in the world to-day; and these are merely five out of about nineteen that one can identify as having come into existence since the first appearance of representatives of this species of society about 6000 years ago.

III

To take the four other surviving civilizations first: if the firmness of a civilization's foothold on the continent—by which I mean the solid landmass of Asia—may be taken as giving a rough indication of that civilization's relative expectation of life, then the other four surviving civilizations are 'better lives'—in the jargon of the life insurance business—than our own Western Christendom.

Our sister civilization, Orthodox Christendom, straddles the continent from the Baltic to the Pacific and from the Mediterranean to the Arctic Ocean: it occupies the northern half of Asia and the eastern half of Asia's European peninsula. Russia overlooks the back doors of all the other civilizations; from White Russia and North-Eastern Siberia she overlooks the Polish and Alaskan back doors of our own Western world; from the Caucasus and Central Asia she overlooks the back doors of the Islamic and Hindu worlds; from Central and Eastern Siberia she overlooks the back door of the Far Eastern world.

Our half-sister civilization, Islam, also has a firm footing on the continent. The domain of Islam stretches from the heart of the Asiatic continent in North-Western China all the way to the west coast of Asia's African peninsula. At Dakar, the Islamic world commands the continental approaches to the straits that divide Asia's African peninsula from the island of South America. Islam also has a firm footing in Asia's Indian peninsula.

As for the Hindu society and the Far Eastern society, it needs no demonstration to show that the 400 million Hindus and the 400 or 500 million Chinese have a firm foothold on the continent.

But we must not exaggerate the importance of any of these surviving civilizations just because, at this moment, they happen to be survivors. If, instead of thinking in terms of 'expectation of life,' we think in terms of achievement, a rough indication of relative achievement may be found in the giving of birth to individual souls that have conferred lasting blessings on the human race.

Now who are the individuals who are the greatest benefactors of the living generation of mankind? I should say: Confucius and Lao-tse; [2] the Buddha; the Prophets of Israel and Judah; Zoroaster, Jesus, and Muhammad; and Socrates. And not one of these lasting benefactors of mankind happens to be a child of any of the five living civilizations. Confucius and Lao-tse were children of a now extinct Far Eastern civilization of an earlier generation; the Buddha was the child of a now extinct Indian civilization of an earlier generation. Hosea, Zoroaster, Jesus, and Muhammad were children of a now extinct Syrian civilization. Socrates was the child of a now extinct Greek civilization.

Within the last 400 years, all the five surviving civilizations have been brought into contact with each other as a result of the enterprise of two of them: the expansion of Western Christendom from the tip of Asia's European peninsula over the ocean, and the expansion of Orthodox Christendom overland across the whole breadth of the Asiatic continent.

The expansion of Western Christendom displays two special features: being oceanic, it is the only expansion of a civilization to date that has been literally world-wide in the sense of extending over the whole habitable portion of the Earth's surface; and, owing to the 'conquest of space and time' by modern mechanical means, the spread of the network of Western material civilization has brought the different parts of the world into far closer physical contact than ever before. But, even in these points, the expansion of the Western civilization differs in degree only, and not in kind, from the contemporary overland expansion of Russian Orthodox Christendom, and from similar expansions of other civilizations at earlier dates.

There are earlier expansions that have made important contributions towards the present unification of mankind—with its corollary, the unification of our vision of human history. The now extinct Syrian civilization was propagated to the Atlantic coasts of Asia's European and African peninsulas westward by the Phoenicians, to the tip of Asia's Indian peninsula south-eastwards by the Himyarites [3] and Nestorians,[4] and to the Pacific

[2 Founder (sixth century B.C.) of Taoism, one of the main religions (along with Buddhism and Confucianism) of China.]

[3 A group of ancient South Arabian tribes.]

[4 Fifth-century Christians who were deemed heretical because of their views on the nature of Christ. They flourished until the fourteenth century; there are still Nestorian Christians in the East.]

north-eastwards by the Manichaeans [5] and Nestorians. It expanded in two directions overseas and in a third direction overland. Any visitor to Peking will have seen a striking monument of the Syrian civilization's overland cultural conquests. In the trilingual inscriptions of the Manchu Dynasty of China at Peking, the Manchu and Mongol texts are inscribed in the Syriac form of our alphabet, not in Chinese characters.

Other examples of the expansion of now extinct civilizations are the propagation of the Greek civilization overseas westwards to Marseilles by the Greeks themselves, overland northwards to the Rhine and Danube by the Romans, and overland eastwards to the interiors of India and China by the Macedonians; and the expansion of the Sumerian civilization in all directions overland from its cradle in 'Iraq.

IV

As a result of these successive expansions of particular civilizations, the whole habitable world has now been unified into a single great society. The movement through which this process has been finally consummated is the modern expansion of Western Christendom. But we have to bear in mind, first, that this expansion of Western Christendom has merely completed the unification of the world and has not been the agency that has produced more than the last stage of the process; and, second, that, though the unification of the world has been finally achieved within a Western framework, the present Western ascendancy in the world is certain not to last.

In a unified world, the eighteen non-Western civilizations—four of them living, fourteen of them extinct—will assuredly reassert their influence. And as, in the course of generations and centuries, a unified world gradually works its way toward an equilibrium between its diverse component cultures, the Western component will gradually be relegated to the modest place which is all that it can expect to retain in virtue of its intrinsic worth by comparison with those other cultures—surviving and extinct—which the Western society, through its modern expansion, has brought into association with itself and with one another.

History, seen in this perspective, makes, I feel, the following call upon historians of our generation and of the generations that will come after ours. If we are to perform the full service that we have the power to perform for our fellow human beings—the important service of helping them

[5] The Manichaean religion, a mixture of Christianity and Zoroastrianism, was widespread in both East and West in the fourth and fifth centuries of this era.]

to find their bearings in a unified world—we must make the necessary effort of imagination and effort of will to break our way out of the prison walls of the local and short-lived histories of our own countries and our own cultures, and we must accustom ourselves to taking a synoptic view of history as a whole.

Our first task is to perceive, and to present to other people, the history of all the known civilizations, surviving and extinct, as a unity. There are, I believe, two ways in which this can be done.

One way is to study the encounters between civilizations, of which I have mentioned four outstanding examples. These encounters between civilizations are historically illuminating, not only because they bring a number of civilizations into a single focus of vision, but also because, out of encounters between civilizations, the higher religions have been born— the worship, perhaps originally Sumerian, of the Great Mother and her Son who suffers and dies and rises again; Judaism and Zoroastrianism, which sprang from an encounter between the Syrian and Babylonian civilizations; Christianity and Islam, which sprang from an encounter between the Syrian and Greek civilizations; the Mahayana form of Buddhism and Hinduism, which sprang from an encounter between the Indian and Greek civilizations. The future of mankind in this world—if mankind is going to have a future in this world—lies, I believe, with these higher religions that have appeared within the last 4000 years (and all but the first within the last 3000 years), and not with the civilizations whose encounters have provided opportunities for the higher religions to come to birth.

A second way of studying the history of all the known civilizations as a unity is to make a comparative study of their individual histories, looking at them as so many representatives of one particular species of the genus Human Society. If we map out the principal phases in the histories of civilizations—their births, growths, breakdowns, and declines—we can compare their experiences phase by phase; and by this method of study we shall perhaps be able to sort out their common experiences, which are specific, from their unique experiences, which are individual. In this way we may be able to work out a morphology of the species of society called civilizations.

If, by the use of these two methods of study, we can arrive at a unified vision of history, we shall probably find that we need to make very far-going adjustments of the perspective in which the histories of divers civilizations and peoples appear when looked at through our peculiar present-day Western spectacles.

In setting out to adjust our perspective, we shall be wise, I suggest, to proceed simultaneously on two alternative assumptions. One of these alternatives is that the future of mankind may not, after all, be going to be catastrophic and that, even if the Second World War prove not to have been the last, we shall survive the rest of this batch of world wars as we survived the first two bouts, and shall eventually win our way out into calmer waters. The other possibility is that these first two world wars may be merely overtures to some supreme catastrophe that we are going to bring on ourselves.

This second, more unpleasant, alternative has been made a very practical possibility by mankind's unfortunately having discovered how to tap atomic energy before we have succeeded in abolishing the institution of war. Those contradictions and paradoxes in the life of the world in our time, which I took as my starting point, also look like symptoms of serious social and spiritual sickness, and their existence—which is one of the portentous features in the landscape of contemporary history—is another indication that we ought to take the more unpleasant of our alternatives as a serious possibility, and not just as a bad joke.

On either alternative, I suggest that we historians ought to concentrate our own attention—and direct the attention of our listeners and readers—upon the histories of those civilizations and peoples which, in the light of their past performances, seem likely, in a unified world, to come to the front in the long run in one or other of the alternative futures that may be lying in wait for mankind.

v

If the future of mankind in a unified world is going to be on the whole a happy one, then I would prophesy that there is a future in the Old World for the Chinese, and in the island of North America for the *Canadiens*. Whatever the future of mankind in North America, I feel pretty confident that these French-speaking Canadians, at any rate, will be there at the end of the story.

On the assumption that the future of mankind is to be very catastrophic, I should have prophesied, even as lately as a few years ago, that whatever future we might be going to have would lie with the Tibetans and the Eskimos, because each of these peoples occupied, till quite lately, an unusually sheltered position. 'Sheltered' means, of course, sheltered from the dangers arising from human folly and wickedness, not sheltered from the rigors of the physical environment. Mankind has been master of its physical environment, sufficiently for practical purposes, since the middle palaeo-lithic age; since that time, man's only dangers—but these have been deadly dangers—have come from man himself. But the homes of the Tibetans and the Eskimos are sheltered no longer, because we are on the point of managing to fly over the North Pole and over the Himalayas, and both Northern Canada and Tibet would (I think) be likely to be theatres of a future Russo-American war.

If mankind is going to run amok with atom bombs, I personally should look to the Negrito Pygmies of Central Africa to salvage some fraction of the present heritage of mankind. (Their eastern cousins in the Philippines and in the Malay Peninsula would probably perish with the rest of us, as they both live in what have now come to be dangerously exposed positions.)

The African Negritos are said by our anthropologists to have an unex-pectedly pure and lofty conception of the nature of God and of God's re-lation to man. They might be able to give mankind a fresh start; and, though we should then have lost the achievements of the last 6000 to 10,000 years, what are 10,000 years compared to the 600,000 or a million years for which the human race has already been in existence?

The extreme possibility of catastrophe is that we might succeed in ex-terminating the whole human race, African Negritos and all.

On the evidence of the past history of life on this planet, even that is not entirely unlikely. After all, the reign of man on the Earth, if we are right in thinking that man established his present ascendancy in the middle palaeolithic age, is so far only about 100,000 years old, and what is that compared to the 500 million or 800 million years during which life has been in existence on the surface of this planet? In the past, other forms of life have enjoyed reigns which have lasted for almost inconceivably longer periods—and which yet at last have come to an end. There was a reign of the giant armored reptiles which may have lasted about 80 million years; say from about the year 130 million to the year 50 million before the present day. But the reptiles' reign came to an end. Long before that—perhaps 300 million years ago—there was a reign of giant armoured fishes—creatures that had already accomplished the tremendous achievement of growing a movable lower jaw. But the reign of the fishes came to an end.

The winged insects are believed to have come into existence about 250 million years ago. Perhaps the higher winged insects—the social insects that have anticipated mankind in creating an institutional life—are still waiting for their reign on Earth to come. If the ants and bees were one day to acquire even that glimmer of intellectual understanding that man has possessed in his day, and if they were then to make their own shot at seeing history in perspective, they might see the advent of the mammals, and the brief reign of the human mammal, as almost irrelevant episodes, 'full of sound and fury, signifying nothing.' [6]

The challenge to us, in our generation, is to see to it that this interpretation of history shall not become the true one.

[[6] *Macbeth*, v, v, 27–8.]

Benjamin Franklin
REMARKS
CONCERNING THE SAVAGES OF NORTH AMERICA

❪ Franklin's skill in political and social satire is attested by the many short pieces, most of them journalistic, that he wrote in the odd moments of his long and extraordinarily busy life. 'An Edict of the King of Prussia,' 'Rules by Which a Great Empire May Be Reduced to a Small One,' 'A Dialogue Between Britain, France, Spain, Holland, Saxony, and America,' and the one reprinted here are among the most familiar.

He was long interested in Indian affairs, a subject of no small importance to a Pennsylvanian in the eighteenth century, and he had a firsthand knowledge of the Indians themselves. In 1753 he was one of three commissioners appointed by the Governor to go to Carlisle, then a frontier post, to make a treaty with the chiefs of the Six Nations. The account of this episode in his *Autobiography* (not wholly accurate) relates that the Indians behaved well until the treaty was concluded because they were denied rum while official business was attended to. Then they all got drunk on rum furnished by the whites, and caused a great tumult. On the following day they apologized for their conduct. 'This backwoods mission of 1753 was the beginning of Franklin's career in diplomacy' (Carl Van Doren, *Benjamin Franklin*, ch. vii).

Europeans of the eighteenth century idealized the 'noble savage,' whereas there is an American saying that 'The best Indian is a dead Indian.' Franklin knew both good and bad ones, but was consistently sympathetic with Indians and, like William Penn, thought they and the white men could live in mutual peace and justice. It was the whites who all too often broke the treaties and who took advantage of the red men's fatal weakness for alcohol. In 'Remarks Concerning the Savages of North America' (1784 or earlier) Franklin amusingly contrasts the manners of the two races, with a permissible exaggeration and an ironic sobriety that recall *Gulliver's Travels*. The description of the white men going to church to hear 'good things' is worthy of Swift at his best.

REPRINTED FROM *The Writings of Benjamin Franklin*, ed. A. H. Smyth, 1907, by permission of Mr. Howard C. Myers, Jr.

SAVAGES we call them, because their Manners differ from ours, which we think the Perfection of Civility; they think the same of theirs.

Perhaps, if we could examine the Manners of different Nations with Impartiality, we should find no People so rude, as to be without any Rules of Politeness; nor any so polite, as not to have some Remains of Rudeness.

The Indian Men, when young, are Hunters and Warriors; when old, Counsellors; for all their Government is by Counsel of the Sages; there is no Force, there are no Prisons, no Officers to compel Obedience, or inflict Punishment. Hence they generally study Oratory, the best Speaker having the most Influence. The Indian Women till the Ground, dress the Food, nurse and bring up the Children, and preserve and hand down to Posterity the Memory of public Transactions. These Employments of Men and Women are accounted natural and honourable. Having few artificial Wants, they have abundance of Leisure for Improvement by Conversation. Our laborious Manner of Life, compared with theirs, they esteem slavish and base; and the Learning, on which we value ourselves, they regard as frivolous and useless. An Instance of this occurred at the Treaty of Lancaster,[1] in Pennsylvania, *anno* 1744, between the Government of Virginia and the Six Nations. After the principal Business was settled, the Commissioners from Virginia acquainted the Indians by a Speech, that there was at Williamsburg a College,[2] with a Fund for Educating Indian youth; and that, if the Six Nations would send down half a dozen of their young Lads to that College, the Government would take care that they should be well provided for, and instructed in all the Learning of the White People. It is one of the Indian Rules of Politeness not to answer a public Proposition the same day that it is made; they think it would be treating it as a light matter, and that they show it Respect by taking time to consider it, as of a Matter important. They therefore deferr'd their Answer till the Day following; when their Speaker began, by expressing their deep Sense of the kindness of the Virginia Government, in making them that Offer; 'for we know,' says he, 'that you highly esteem the kind of Learning taught in those

[1 In a letter written 4 July 1744, Franklin describes it in slightly different terms as a treaty 'between the governments of Virginia, Maryland, and Pennsylvania on one side, and the United Five Nations of Indians on the other.']
[2 The College of William and Mary.]

Colleges, and that the Maintenance of our young Men, while with you, would be very expensive to you. We are convinc'd, therefore, that you mean to do us Good by your Proposal; and we thank you heartily. But you, who are wise, must know that different Nations have different Conceptions of things; and you will therefore not take it amiss, if our Ideas of this kind of Education happen not to be the same with yours. We have had some Experience of it; Several of our young People were formerly brought up at the Colleges of the Northern Provinces; they were instructed in all your Sciences; but, when they came back to us, they were bad Runners, ignorant of every means of living in the Woods, unable to bear either Cold or Hunger, knew neither how to build a Cabin, take a Deer, or kill an Enemy, spoke our Language imperfectly, were therefore neither fit for Hunters, Warriors, nor Counsellors; they were totally good for nothing. We are however not the less oblig'd by your kind Offer, tho' we decline accepting it; and, to show our grateful Sense of it, if the Gentlemen of Virginia will send us a Dozen of their Sons, we will take great Care of their Education, instruct them in all we know, and make *Men* of them.'

Having frequent Occasions to hold public Councils, they have acquired great Order and Decency in conducting them. The old Men sit in the foremost Ranks, the Warriors in the next, and the Women and Children in the hindmost. The Business of the Women is to take exact Notice of what passes, imprint it in their Memories (for they have no Writing), and communicate it to their Children. They are the Records of the Council, and they preserve Traditions of the Stipulations in Treaties 100 Years back; which, when we compare with our Writings, we always find exact. He that would speak, rises. The rest observe a profound Silence. When he has finish'd and sits down, they leave him 5 or 6 Minutes to recollect, that, if he has omitted any thing he intended to say, or has any thing to add, he may rise again and deliver it. To interrupt another, even in common Conversation, is reckon'd highly indecent. How different this is from the conduct of a polite British House of Commons, where scarce a day passes without some Confusion, that makes the Speaker hoarse in calling *to Order*; and how different from the Mode of Conversation in many polite Companies of Europe, where, if you do not deliver your Sentence with great Rapidity, you are cut off in the middle of it by the Impatient Loquacity of those you converse with, and never suffer'd to finish it!

The Politeness of these Savages in Conversation is indeed carried to Excess, since it does not permit them to contradict or deny the Truth of what is asserted in their Presence. By this means they indeed avoid Disputes; but then it becomes difficult to know their Minds, or what Impression you make upon them. The Missionaries who have attempted to convert them to Christianity, all complain of this as one of the great Difficulties of their Mission. The Indians hear with Patience the Truths of the Gospel explain'd to them, and give their usual Tokens of Assent and Approbation; you would think they were convinc'd. No such matter. It is mere Civility.

A Swedish Minister, having assembled the chiefs of the Susquehanah Indians, made a Sermon to them, acquainting them with the principal historical Facts on which our Religion is founded; such as the Fall of our first Parents by eating an Apple, the coming of Christ to repair the Mischief, his Miracles and Suffering, &c. When he had finished, an Indian Orator stood up to thank him. 'What you have told us,' says he, 'is all very good. It is indeed bad to eat Apples. It is better to make them all into Cyder. We are much oblig'd by your kindness in coming so far, to tell us these Things which you have heard from your Mothers. In return, I will tell you some of those we have heard from ours. In the Beginning, our Fathers had only the Flesh of Animals to subsist on; and if their Hunting was unsuccessful, they were starving. Two of our young Hunters, having kill'd a Deer, made a Fire in the Woods to broil some Part of it. When they were about to satisfy their Hunger, they beheld a beautiful young Woman descend from the Clouds, and seat herself on that Hill, which you see yonder among the blue Mountains. They said to each other, it is a Spirit that has smelt our broiling Venison, and wishes to eat of it; let us offer some to her. They presented her with the Tongue; she was pleas'd with the Taste of it, and said, "Your kindness shall be rewarded; come to this Place after thirteen Moons, and you shall find something that will be of great Benefit in nourishing you and your Children to the latest Generations." They did so, and, to their Surprise, found Plants they had never seen before; but which, from that ancient time, have been constantly cultivated among us, to our great Advantage. Where her right Hand had touched the Ground, they found Maize; where her left hand had touch'd it, they found Kidney-Beans; and where her Backside had sat on it, they found Tobacco.' The good Missionary, disgusted with this idle Tale, said, 'What I delivered to you were sacred Truths; but what you tell me is mere Fable, Fiction, and Falshood.' The Indian, offended, reply'd, 'My brother, it seems your Friends have not done you Justice in your Education; they have not well instructed you in the Rules of common Civility. You saw that we, who understand and practise those Rules, believ'd all your stories; why do you refuse to believe ours?'

When any of them come into our Towns, our People are apt to crowd round them, gaze upon them, and incommode them, where they desire to be private; this they esteem great Rudeness, and the Effect of the Want of Instruction in the Rules of Civility and good Manners. 'We have,' say they, 'as much Curiosity as you, and when you come into our Towns, we wish for Opportunities of looking at you; but for this purpose we hide ourselves behind Bushes, where you are to pass, and never intrude ourselves into your Company.'

Their Manner of entring one another's village has likewise its Rules. It is reckon'd uncivil in travelling Strangers to enter a Village abruptly, without giving Notice of their Approach. Therefore, as soon as they arrive within hearing, they stop and hollow, remaining there till invited to enter. Two old Men usually come out to them, and lead them in. There is in every Village a vacant Dwelling, called *the Strangers' House*. Here they are plac'd, while the old Men go round from Hut to Hut, acquainting the Inhabitants, that Strangers are arriv'd, who are probably hungry and weary; and every one sends them what he can spare of Victuals, and Skins to repose on. When the Strangers are refresh'd, Pipes and Tobacco are brought; and then, but not before, Conversation begins, with Enquiries who they are, whither bound, what News, &c.; and it usually ends with offers of Service, if the Strangers have occasion of Guides, or any Necessaries for continuing their Journey; and nothing is exacted for the Entertainment.

The same Hospitality, esteem'd among them as a principal Virtue, is practis'd by Private Persons; of which Conrad Weiser,[3] our Interpreter, gave me the following Instance. He had been naturaliz'd among the Six Nations, and spoke well the Mohock Language. In going thro' the Indian Country, to carry a Message from our Governor to the Council at Onondaga,[4] he call'd at the Habitation of Canassatego, an old Acquaintance, who embrac'd him, spread Furs for him to sit on, plac'd before him some boil'd Beans and Venison, and mix'd some Rum and Water for his Drink. When he was well refresh'd, and had lit his Pipe, Canassatego began to converse with him; ask'd how he had far'd the many Years since they had seen each other; whence he then came; what occasion'd the Journey, &c. Conrad answered all his Questions; and when the Discourse began to flag, the Indian, to continue it, said, 'Conrad, you have lived long among the

[3 He was the chief interpreter between the Indians and the Pennsylvania government.]

[4 In New York, near the present Syracuse.]

white People, and know something of their Customs; I have been sometimes at Albany, and have observed, that once in Seven Days they shut up
their Shops, and assemble all in the great House; tell me what it is for?
What do they do there?' 'They meet there,' says Conrad, 'to hear and learn
good Things.' 'I do not doubt,' says the Indian, 'that they tell you so; they
have told me the same; but I doubt the Truth of what they say, and I will
tell you my Reasons. I went lately to Albany to sell my Skins and buy
Blankets, Knives, Powder, Rum, &c. You know I us'd generally to deal with
Hans Hanson; but I was a little inclin'd this time to try some other Merchant. However, I call'd first upon Hans, and asked him what he would
give for Beaver. He said he could not give any more than four Shillings a
Pound; "but," says he, "I cannot talk on Business now; this is the Day when
we meet together to learn *Good Things,* and I am going to the Meeting."
So I thought to myself, "Since we cannot do any Business to-day, I may
as well go to the meeting too," and I went with him. There stood up a
Man in Black, and began to talk to the People very angrily. I did not understand what he said; but, perceiving that he look'd much at me and at
Hanson, I imagin'd he was angry at seeing me there; so I went out, sat
down near the House, struck Fire, and lit my Pipe, waiting till the Meeting
should break up. I thought too, that the Man had mention'd something of
Beaver, and I suspected it might be the Subject of their Meeting. So, when
they came out, I accosted my Merchant. "Well, Hans," says I, "I hope you
have agreed to give more than four Shillings a Pound." "No," says he, "I
cannot give so much; I cannot give more than three shillings and sixpence."
I then spoke to several other Dealers, but they all sung the same song,—
Three and sixpence,—Three and sixpence. This made it clear to me, that
my Suspicion was right; and, that whatever they pretended of meeting to
learn *good Things,* the real purpose was to consult how to cheat Indians in
the Price of Beaver. Consider but a little, Conrad, and you must be of my
Opinion. If they met so often to learn *good Things,* they would certainly
have learnt some before this time. But they are still ignorant. You know
our Practice. If a white Man, in travelling thro' our Country, enters one of
our Cabins, we all treat him as I treat you; we dry him if he is wet, we warm
him if he is cold, we give him Meat and Drink, that he may allay his Thirst
and Hunger; and we spread soft Furs for him to rest and sleep on; we
demand nothing in return. But, if I go into a white Man's House at Albany,
and ask for Victuals and Drink, they say, "Where is your Money?" and if
I have none, they say, "Get out, you Indian Dog." You see they have not
yet learned those little *Good Things,* that we need no Meetings to be in-

structed in, because our Mothers taught them to us when we were Children; and therefore it is impossible their Meetings should be, as they say, for any such purpose, or have any such Effect; they are only to contrive *the Cheating of Indians in the Price of Beaver.'*

NOTE.—It is remarkable that in all Ages and Countries Hospitality has been allow'd as the Virtue of those whom the civiliz'd were pleas'd to call Barbarians. The Greeks celebrated the Scythians for it. The Saracens possess'd it eminently, and it is to this day the reigning Virtue of the wild Arabs. St. Paul,[5] too, in the Relation of his Voyage and Shipwreck on the Island of Melita says the Barbarous People shewed us no little kindness; for they kindled a fire, and received us every one, because of the present Rain, and because of the Cold.—F.

[5 See Acts, xxviii, 1–2.]

Samuel Eliot Morison
and *Henry Steele Commager*

THE UNITED STATES IN 1790 *

⟦ *The Growth of the American Republic,* from which these pages
are taken, is without question the most popular, as it is probably
the best, short history of the United States. When first published in
1930 it was a one-volume work but has been expanded in successive
editions until it is now more than twice its original length.

Samuel Eliot Morison (1887—), Professor of American History
in Harvard University, wrote his first history of the United States
while teaching at Oxford (*The Oxford History of the United
States,* 1927). He is author of *The Maritime History of Massachusetts* (1921), *The Puritan Pronaos* (1936), and *Admiral of the
Ocean Sea* (1942), a life of Columbus, which received a Pulitzer
Prize. As historian of the United States Navy in World War II, he
has published nine volumes of the *History of United States Naval
Operations in World War II,* and more are to follow. He is also
the author of an elaborate *Tercentennial History of Harvard University,* which won international honors. In conception and scope it
is unrivaled as a history of a university.

Henry Steele Commager (1902—) is, like Mr. Morison, a prolific and popular writer on American history. His books include
Theodore Parker (1936), *Majority Rule and Minority Rights*
(1943), and *The American Mind* (1950); he has collaborated in
and edited many other publications. He is Professor of History in
Columbia University.

1. GENERALITIES

O<small>NLY</small> twenty-five years since the Stamp Act; only fourteen
years since the Thirteen Colonies declared 'to a candid world' that they
were 'and of right ought to be, free and independent States.' It is already

---

* We have taken the year 1790, rather than 1789, as the central point of this description, because it was the year of the first federal census, which supplies the first statistics,
incomplete to be sure and not very accurate, for the United States.

F<small>ROM</small> *The Growth of the American Republic,* revised and enlarged edition, 1950.
Copyright 1930, 1937, 1942, 1950, by Oxford University Press, Inc. Reprinted by permission of the publishers.

time to take stock, and see what sort of country it was when the Federal Constitution was newly established, and Washington had been President for less than a year.

Much had been said in the debates over the Constitution about the enhanced prestige that it would give to the United States. Official Europe was not impressed. Not that they perceived danger in American republicanism. With Washington's army disbanded, and the navy dismantled, the United States was hardly a feather in the balance of power. Merchants and traders, however, were not so indifferent to the new nation, if it could be called a nation. As a source of raw materials for Europe, the United States was not yet in a class with the West Indies; but for a country of such vast empty spaces, it was an important market. Even with the Mississippi as its western boundary, the United States was equal in area to the British Isles, France, Germany, Spain, and Italy. Less than half this territory had yet come under the effective jurisdiction of the United States or of any state; and the population of four millions, including seven hundred thousand Negro slaves, was dispersed over an expanse of coastal plain and upland slightly more extensive than France. But if the trans-Appalachian country were ever settled, it would surely break off from the Thirteen States. So at least believed the few Europeans who gave the matter a thought.

Whatever the future might promise the United States in wealth and power seemed to be denied by political vagaries. America was attempting simultaneously three political experiments, which the accumulated wisdom of Europe deemed likely to fail: independence, republicanism, and federal union. While the British and the Spanish empires touched the states on three sides, their independence could hardly be maintained without more of that European aid by which it had been won; and an independence so maintained would be only nominal. Republicanism promised instability; and federalism, dissolution. Since the Renaissance, the uniform tendency in Europe had been towards centralized monarchy; federal republics had maintained themselves only in small areas, such as the Netherlands and Switzerland. Most European observers believed that the history of the American Union would be short and stormy.

It was still too early to aver that the Americans had conquered the forest. Volney [1] wrote that during his journey in 1796 through the length and breadth of the United States, he scarcely travelled for more than three miles together on open and cleared land. 'Compared with France, the entire

[[1] French scholar (1757–1820). He spent three years, 1795–8, in the United States and in 1803 published a narrative of his experiences.]

country is one vast wood.' Only in southern New England, and the eastern portion of the Middle States, did the cultivated area exceed the woodland; and the clearings became less frequent as one approached the Appalachians.

The larger part of the American people then lived under isolated conditions, but in a land of such plenty that exertion had no attraction for the unambitious. The ocean and its shores yielded plenty of fish; the tidal rivers teemed with salmon, sturgeon, herring, and shad in due season, and the upland streams with trout; every kind of game was plentiful, from quail and raccoon to wild turkey and deer; and at times the flights of wild pigeon darkened the air. Cattle and swine throve on the woodland herbage and mast; Indian corn ripened quickly in the hot summer nights; even sugar could be obtained from the maple, or honey from wild bees. The American of the interior, glutted with nature's bounty and remote from a market, had no immediate incentive to produce much beyond his own actual needs; yet the knowledge that easier life could be had often pressed him westward to more fertile lands, or to a higher scale of living. Hence the note of personal independence that was, and in the main still is, dominant in American life. 'The means of subsistence being so easy in the country,' wrote an English observer in 1796, 'and their dependence on each other consequently so trifling, that spirit of servility to those above them so prevalent in European manners, is wholly unknown to them; and they pass their lives without any regard to the smiles or the frowns of men in power.'

However independent of those above him the average American might be, he was dependent on those about him for help in harvest, in raising his house-frame, and in illness. In a new country you turn to your neighbors for many offices and functions that, in a riper community, are performed by government or by specialists. Hence the dual nature of the American: individualism and herd instinct, indifference and kindliness. Isolation in American foreign policy is an authentic outcome of community isolation, as are the recent American relief organizations of primitive interdependence.

In 1790 there were only six cities (Philadelphia, New York, Boston, Charleston, Baltimore, and Salem) in the United States with a population of eight thousand or over; and their combined numbers included only three per cent of the total population.* Their aspect was not unlike that of provincial towns in Great Britain, for a native American architectural style had not yet been invented. Brick houses in the Georgian style, often detached and surrounded with gardens and shrubbery; inns with capacious

* The proportion of urban to rural population did not pass ten per cent until after 1840.

yards and stables; shops and stores with overhanging signs; places of worship with graceful spires after Sir Christopher Wren; market houses or city halls of the same style, often placed in the middle of a broad street or square, with arcades to serve as stalls or merchants' exchange; somewhat ramshackle unpainted wooden houses where the poorer people lived, but hardly one without a bit of garden or yard. Wealth was not a conspicuous feature of the United States in 1790. Almost a century had to elapse before a European could find here anything impressive in the way of shops, mansions, architecture, or high living. Nor was there anything to match the poverty of a European city; and even the slave population of the Carolina rice-fields was less wretched than the contemporary Irish peasant.[2]

Except for iron, the vast mineral resources of the country were practically untouched, and iron smelting remained primitive, owing to the abundance of wood, long after the British had made technical improvements. Agriculture was the main occupation of nine-tenths of the people. Except along the Hudson, practically every farmer was a freeholder. Except among the Pennsylvania Germans and the more enlightened country gentry of the South, the methods of agriculture were incredibly wasteful and primitive, with little sign of the improved culture and implements that were then transforming rural England. Wheat bread was largely an upper-class luxury. Indian corn was the principal food crop, with rye a poor second. Brown 'rye and Injun' bread, corn-pone or hoe-cake, and hasty-pudding or hominy, with salt pork or codfish, washed down by rum, cider, or whisky, according to locality, formed the farmer's staple diet from Maine to Georgia. As early as 1780 the Marquis de Chastellux noted the prevalence of hot biscuits, the bountiful breakfasts of the South, and 'the American custom of drinking coffee with meat, vegetables, or other food.' Frontier conditions still prevailed over the larger part of the 'Old West' which had been settled within the last fifty years. The houses were commonly log cabins of one or two rooms and a cock-loft; the fields were full of stumps, and acres of dead trees strangled by girdling were a depressing sight to travellers.

Bad roads were one of the penalties that Americans paid for their dispersed settlement and aversion from taxation. In 1790 the difficulties of communication were so great that a detour of several hundred miles by river and ocean was often preferable to an overland journey of fifty miles. It was almost as difficult to assemble the first Congress of the United States as to convene church councils in the Middle Ages. There was a main post-road from Wiscasset in Maine to Savannah in Georgia, over which passen-

[2 See Swift's A Modest Proposal (pp. 329–37).]

gers and mails were transported by light open stage-wagons, in approximately so many days as the railway now requires hours. It took twenty-nine days for the news of the Declaration of Independence to reach Charleston from Philadelphia. Bridges were few, even over the rivers and streams that were unfordable; the wooden pile structure across the Charles at Boston was considered an immense feat of engineering. Washington managed to visit almost every state in the Union in his own coach without serious mishap; but he had to choose a season when the roads were passable, and to undergo discomforts and even dangers. Most of the roads were merely wide tracks through the forest, full of rocks and stumps and enormous holes. Many that are marked on the early maps were mere bridle-paths or Indian trails, that would admit no wheeled vehicle. Northern farmers reserved their heavy hauling for winter, when snow made even the worst trace practicable for sledges; whilst upland Southerners got their tobacco to tidewater by pivoting a pair of shafts to a hogshead, and rolling it down on the bilge. Inns were to be found at frequent intervals along the main roads; but they commonly fulfilled the function of neighborhood pot-house better than resting-place for the weary wayfarer. The food was cheap and plentiful, but meals could be had only at stated hours—as in the largest American hotels within recent memory. A traveller was fortunate to secure a bed to himself, or to arrive on the first evening after the sheets were changed. Lieutenant Anburey, late of Burgoyne's army, regretted that he could not safely horsewhip the landlord who overcharged him. He might have fought the landlord, however, with bare fists, and been thought a better man for it.

Now that America has become famous for its sanitation, and for hotels with as many thousand baths as bedrooms, it is worth noting that in the eighteenth and early nineteenth centuries America impressed European tourists as an uncommonly dirty country. From persons at that time accustomed to London or Paris, this meant a good deal. Even in the larger towns streets were seldom paved and never cleaned, offal was deposited in the docks, and, without wire screens, houses were defenseless against the swarms of flies and other winged pests that summer brought. As no one had yet heard of disease germs, there were intermittent outbreaks of typhoid and yellow fever in the seaports as far north as New Hampshire; and the frontiersmen were racked every summer by malarial fevers and agues,[3] transmitted by mosquitoes. Flower gardens were rare; and the pioneer, regarding trees as enemies, neither spared them nor planted them for purposes of shade. Country farmhouses in the older-settled region were almost

[3 See Brogan (pp. 322–3).]

invariably of wood, usually unpainted, resembling dingy boxes surrounded by unseemly household litter. Stoutly and honestly built as they were, the colonial houses that have survived long enough to acquire white paint, green blinds, lawns, shrubs, and century-old shade trees, are seen to have both distinction and beauty. In the eighteenth century, however, no one found much to admire in America in the works of man; and few Americans had the taste or leisure to appreciate the rugged grandeur of their mountains and forests, and their majestic rivers, swift rapids, and mighty waterfalls.

The United States of 1790 was not a nation, by any modern standard. Materials of a nation were present, but cohesive force was wanting. An English origin for the bulk of the people made a certain cultural homogeneity; the Maine fisherman could understand the Georgian planter much more readily than a Kentishman could understand a Yorkshireman, or an Alsatian a Breton. Political institutions, though decentralized, were fairly constant in form through the length and breadth of the land. But there was no tradition of union behind the War of Independence, and it was difficult to discover a common interest upon which union could be built. Most citizens of the United States in 1790, if asked their country or nation, would not have answered American, but Carolinian, Virginian, Pennsylvanian, Jerseyman, New Yorker, or New Englander. A political nexus had been found, but unless a national tradition were soon established, the United States would develop a particularism similar to the states of Germany and Italy. Already the problem was becoming complicated by the formation of settlements on the western waters, beyond the Appalachians. In the meantime, it would require the highest statesmanship to keep the thirteen commonwealths together, so widely did they differ in origin, tradition, religion, and economic interests. The Federal Constitution made it possible; but few observers in 1790 thought it probable.

2. NEW ENGLAND

In New England, climate, soil, and religion had produced in a century and a half a strongly individualized type, the Yankee, perhaps the most persistent ingredient of the American mixture.

The Yankee was the American Scot; and New England was an eighteenth-century Scotland without the lairds. A severe climate, a grudging soil that had to be cleared of boulders as well as trees, and a stern puritan faith, dictated the four gospels of education, thrift, ingenuity, and righteousness. By necessity rather than choice, the New Englanders had acquired an aptitude for maritime enterprise and trading. They hailed with joy the new and wider opportunities for seafaring opened by freedom from the Acts of Trade. The seamen of Salem had already ventured to the East Indies with much success when Boston, in 1790, celebrated the return of her ship *Columbia*, laden with tea, silk, and porcelain, from a voyage around the world. On her next voyage the *Columbia* sailed up a great river that Vancouver had passed by, gave it her name, and to its banks her flag.

The five New England States were divided, politically, into townships, about thirty square miles on an average, containing from a hundred to several thousand people. Each was a unit for purposes of local government, conducting its own affairs by town meeting and selectmen, supporting common schools by local taxes, and electing annually to the state legislature a representative, whose votes and doings were keenly scrutinized by his constituents. The nucleus of every township was the meeting-house, part town hall, part place of worship, bordering on the village green. Outlying farms, by 1790, in most places outnumbered those with a village house-plot; and the common fields had been divided in severalty, and enclosed by uncemented stone walls. There was plenty of wood to supply the large open fireplaces. Families were large, but estates were seldom divided below a hundred acres; a Yankee farmer hoped to make a scholar or minister out of one son, to provide for a second with a tract of wilderness, and let the rest earn their living by working for hire, going to sea, or learning a trade. Until 1830 or thereabouts the American merchant marine was manned largely by New England lads who were seeking the wherewithal to purchase land and set up housekeeping.

Puritanism had become less grim than in the seventeenth, less petty than in the nineteenth century. 'Holy days' were still proscribed, and the puritan Sabbath was still observed; but there was plenty of frisking at rural barn-raisings and corn-huskings; and much drinking on public occasions such as ship-launchings, ordinations, college commencements, and Thanksgiving Day—the puritan substitute for Christmas, which in course of time became an additional day of merry-making. On the whole, living was plain in New England; and the ample, generous tone of new countries was little in evidence. Even in the family of President Adams, we are told, the children were urged to a double portion of hasty pudding, in order to spare the meat that was to follow. Idleness was the cardinal sin. If a Yankee had nothing else to do, he whittled barrel-bungs from a pine stick, or carved a model of his latest ship; and he usually had much else to do. New England housewives spun, wove, and tailored their woolen garments, and made cloth for sale. Small fulling mills and paper mills were established at the numerous waterfalls, and distilleries in the seaports turned West India molasses into that grateful if dangerous beverage, New England rum. Wooden ware was made by snow-bound farmers for export to the West Indies, nails were cut and headed from wrought iron rods at fireside forges, and in some parts there was a domestic industry of shoemaking. Connecticut, in particular, had attained a nice balance between farming, seafaring, and handicraft, which made the people of that state renowned for steady habits and mechanical ingenuity. Before the century was out, Eli Whitney of New Haven devised the cotton gin and interchangeable parts for firearms: inventions which, for weal or woe, have deeply affected the human race. New England was ripe for an abrupt transition from handicraft to the factory system; but the success of her seafarers, and the facility of emigration, postponed industrial revolution for another generation. The intellectual flowering was all in the future.

For a good inside view of New England by an outsider, we are indebted to the South American patriot Francisco de Miranda, who travelled through that region in the summer of 1784. An intelligent member of an old Spanish family, brought up in Carácas and familiar with Spain, Miranda found much in New England that was kindly, pleasant, and in good taste. At New Haven he is taken over Yale College by President Stiles, converses with a classically educated miller who had been a cavalry captain in the late war, and views the famous Blue Laws in the town archives. Proceeding to Wethersfield, he attends Sabbath meeting, and admires the manner in which the psalms and responses are sung by the congregation, trained by a music master. At Windsor, the men are ill-dressed and the women ill-favored, but he enjoys a lively literary conversation with John Trumbull, as well as with the innkeeper. This worthy is discovered reading Rollin's *Ancient History*, and discusses with Miranda the comparative merits of the ancients and the moderns, stoutly maintaining Ben Franklin to be a better man than Aristides.[4] Thence to Middletown, and a boat excursion on the river with General Parsons and other good fellows, drinking copiously of punch 'in pure republican style,' which was probably not so different from the present style. Newport he thought justly called the paradise of New England, containing, besides hospitable natives, a large company of ladies and gentlemen from Charleston, S. C., who were already using the place as a summer resort. The leading lights of Providence, on

[4 'The Just'; Athenian statesman and general, fifth century B.C.]

the other hand, were provincial and vulgar, Commodore Esek Hopkins even insisting that there was no such place as the City of Mexico.

Miranda entered Boston armed with letters of introduction to the 'best people,' whose ladies he found vain, luxurious, and too much given to the use of cosmetics. Boston society was so fast, in that year of post-war extravagance, that he predicted bankruptcy within twenty years. Samuel Adams, however, was still faithful to republican simplicity. After carefully inspecting Harvard College, Miranda reports it better suited to turn out Protestant clergymen than intelligent and liberal citizens. He visits the studio of the self-taught painter, Edward Savage, and predicts that with a European education his talent will take him far. (Savage never visited Europe, but his portrait of Washington is the best likeness we have of that great man.) From Boston, Miranda takes the eastward road to Portsmouth, N. H., and is much impressed by the thrift and prosperity of the North Shore of Massachusetts. 'Liberty inspires such intelligence and industry in these towns . . . that the people out of their slender resources maintain their large families, pay heavy taxes, and live with comfort and taste, a thousand times happier than the proprietors of the rich mines and fertile lands of Mexico, Peru, Buenos Aires, Carácas, and the whole Spanish-American continent.'

The New Englanders were very well satisfied with themselves in 1790, and had reason to be; for they had struck root in a region where nature was not lavish, and produced a homogeneous, cohesive, and happy society. Disorderly as colonists when royal governors attempted to thwart their will, the Yankees quickly passed through the cruder phases of democracy. For another generation the leadership of their clergy, well-to-do merchants, and conservative lawyers would not be successfully challenged. Outside New England, where they were familiar as traders and pedlars, the Yankees were regarded much as Scotchmen then were by the English: often envied, sometimes respected, but generally disliked.

3. THE MIDDLE STATES

New York State was heterogeneous in 1790, and was never destined to attain homogeneity. The Dutch 'Knickerbocker' families shared a social ascendancy with the descendants of English and Huguenot merchants. There were many villages where Dutch was still spoken, and Albany was still thoroughly Dutch, ruled by mynheers who lived in substantial brick houses with stepped gables. But the Netherlandish element comprised only one-sixth of the three hundred thousand inhabitants of New York State. For the rest, there were Germans in the Mohawk valley and Ulster county; a few families of Sephardic [5] Jews at New York City; an appreciable element of Scotch and Irishmen, and a strong majority of English, among whom the Yankee element was fast increasing.

New York was only the fifth state in population in 1790; a fourfold increase in thirty years made it first in 1820. It was the settlement of the interior that made the difference. In 1790 the inhabited area of New York followed the Hudson river from New York City to Albany, whence one branch of settlement continued up the Mohawk towards Lake Erie, and a thin line of clearings pushed up by Lake George and Lake Champlain, which Burgoyne had found a wilderness. There were also a few islands of settlement such as Cooperstown, where James Fenimore Cooper was cradled in the midst of the former hunting grounds of the Six Nations. Socially, New York was still the most aristocratic of the states, in spite of the extensive confiscation and subdividing of loyalists' estates; for most of the patroons managed to retain their vast properties. One out of every seven New York families held slaves in 1790, and nine more years elapsed before gradual emancipation began. The qualifications for voting and for office were high. For a generation the story of New York politics was to be, in the main, a struggle for the prestige and profit of office between the great whig families, struggles waged by the means familiar to English politics of the time. These landlords were wont to improve their fortunes through alliances with mercantile families, with lawyer-statesmen like Hamilton and Rufus King, and by speculation in Western land.

New York City owed its prosperity, and its thirty-three thousand inhabitants, to a unique position at the mouth of the Hudson river, the greatest tidal inlet between the St. Lawrence and the Plata. It was the natural gateway to the Iroquois country, which was settled between 1790 and 1820; and in 1825 the Erie Canal, following the lowest watershed between the Atlantic States and the Lakes, made New York City the principal gateway to the West, and the financial center of the Union. The merchants did not need to be so venturesome as those of New England and Baltimore, and they spent more on good living than on churches and schools. They too had a family college—Columbia (late King's); but while Boston was forming learned institutions, and Philadelphia supporting a literary journal and a Philosophical Society, New York was founding the Columbian Order, better known as Tammany Hall. Yet it was in the midst of this wealthy, gay, and somewhat cynical society that Alexander Hamilton reached manhood, and Washington Irving was born.

[5 Spanish and Portuguese.]

New Jersey, a farming state of less than two hundred thousand people, has been compared with a barrel tapped at both ends by New York and Philadelphia. Travellers along the road between these two cities admired the Jersey apple orchards, the well-cultivated farms, and, at the pleasant village of Princeton, the College of New Jersey whose Nassau Hall, 180 feet long and four stories high, was reputed to be the largest building in the Thirteen States. At the falls of the Passaic river, near Newark, an incorporated company had just founded Paterson, the first factory village in America. South of this main road was a region of pine barrens and malarial marshes.

Pennsylvania, the second largest state in the Union, with a population of 435,000, had acquired a certain uniformity in diversity. Her racial heterogeneity, democratic polity, and social structure, ranging from wealthy and sophisticated merchants to the wildest frontiersmen, made Pennsylvania a microcosm of the America to be. Philadelphia, with its evenly spaced and numbered streets crossing at right angles, had been the principal port of immigration for a century previous to 1825; and the boat-shaped Conestoga wagons of the Pennsylvania Dutch needed but slight improvement to become the 'prairie schooner' of westward advance.

Pennsylvania was still in the throes of democratic experiments. Her radical state constitution, with a unicameral legislature and a plural executive, had become notoriously factious and incompetent. In 1790 a new constitution with a bicameral legislature was adopted, but manhood suffrage was retained; and this laid a firm foundation for subsequent democratization of Pennsylvania.

Philadelphia, admirably situated at the junction of the Delaware and Schuylkill rivers, and with a population of forty-five thousand in 1790, was easily the first city in the United States for commerce, architecture, and culture. During the next ten years it was the seat of the Federal Government and of a more brilliant republican court than the city of Washington was to show for a century to come. Owing largely to Quaker influence, Philadelphia was well provided with penal and charitable institutions, amateur scientists and budding literati. It was 'by Delaware's green banks' that Tom Moore in 1804 found Dennie and Ingersoll and Brockden Brown,[6] but for whom

[6 Joseph Dennie (1768–1812), 'the American Addison,' published two volumes of essays. Jared Ingersoll (1782–1862) wrote fiction, history, and poetry; his novel, *Inchiquin* (1810) received some European attention. Brockden Brown (1771–1810), the most important of these three early American writers, is remembered for his novels, *Wieland* (1798), *Arthur Mervyn* (1799), *Ormond* (1799), and *Edgar Huntly* (1799).]

Columbia's days were done,
Rank without ripeness, quickened without sun.

These 'sacred few' were producing pallid imitations of the *Spectator*, dreary tragedies of medieval Europe, novels of mystery and horror. Hugh Brackenridge of Pittsburgh alone expressed the rich color and wilderness flavor of youthful Pennsylvania.

A few miles from Philadelphia one reached the garden spot of eighteenth-century America, a belt of rich limestone soil that crossed the Susquehanna river, and extended into Maryland and the Valley of Virginia. The fortunate inhabitants of this region were reaping huge profits in 1790 by reason of the European crop failures of 1789; and were to prosper still more through the wars that flowed from the French Revolution. 'The whole country is well cultivated,' wrote a Dutch financier who passed through this region in 1794, 'and what forests the farmers keep are stocked with trees of the right kind—chestnut, locust, walnut, maple, white oak. It is a succession of hills, not too high, and the aspect of the country is very beautiful.' Lancaster, with four thousand inhabitants, was the largest inland town in the United States. Here and in the limestone belt, the bulk of the farmers and townspeople were German. They were by far the best husbandmen in America, using a proper rotation, with clover and root crops. Their houses were commonly of stone, and heated by stoves; their fences of stout posts and rails; but what most impressed strangers were the great barns, with huge gable-end doors, through which a loaded wagon could drive onto a wide threshing-floor, flanked by spacious hay-lofts, cattle and sheep pens, and horse stables. The Germans were divided into a number of sects, some of which, like the Amish Mennonites, have retained their quaint costumes and puritanism into the twentieth century. They supported six weekly newspapers in their own language, and were as keen household manufacturers as the Yankees; but Chastellux found them lacking in public spirit, compared with the English-speaking Americans, 'content . . . with being only the spectators of their own wealth,' and with the standards of a German peasant.

Lancaster was the parting point for two streams of westward emigration. One wagon road took a southwesterly direction, crossed the Potomac at Harper's Ferry, and entered the Shenandoah valley of Virginia, between the Blue Ridge and the Unakas. The Pittsburgh wagon road struck out northwesterly, crossed the Susquehanna by ford or ferry at Harrisburg (the future capital of Pennsylvania), and followed the beautiful wooded valley of the Juniata to its headwaters. This region was inhabited mainly by Ulstermen, although in the easternmost section they were rapidly being bought out by the more thrifty and land-hungry Germans. North of it, and west of the upper Susquehanna, Pennsylvania was still a mountainous virgin forest. After a long, painful pull up the rocky, rutty wagon road, to an elevation of some 2,500 feet, you attained the Alleghany front, an escarp-ment from which, by a rolling, densely wooded plateau, you descended westward to where the Alleghany and Monongahela rivers come together to form the Ohio. At this point you reached Pittsburgh, a thriving village in the midst of virgin coal and iron deposits, the most important of three inner gateways to the far West. Already fleets of covered wagons were bringing in settlers destined for Kentucky, and goods to be distributed down the mighty valley of the Ohio and Mississippi.

4. THE SOUTH

Twenty-five miles south of Philadelphia the post-road crossed the Mason and Dixon line,* an internal boundary that bulks large in American his-tory. Originally drawn to divide Pennsylvania from Delaware and Mary-land, in 1790 it was already recognized as the boundary between the farm-ing, or commercial, and the plantation states. From 1804 to 1865 it divided the free and the slave states; and even yet it is the boundary of sentiment between North and South.

Delaware, formerly an autonomous portion of the Penn proprietary, was the least populous state of the Union; and apart from the flour-milling regions about Wilmington, a farming community, steadfastly conservative in politics. Maryland, with 320,000 souls, one-third of them slaves, was the northernmost state where slavery was an essential part of the economic system. The old English Catholic families still retained some of the better plantations on both shores of Chesapeake Bay; the Irish Carrolls of Carroll-ton provided a 'signer,' a United States Senator, and the first Roman Cath-olic bishop in the United States. Maryland produced the best wheat flour in America, and a variety of tobacco chiefly appreciated by the French. The lowland planters were famous for hospitality, and for the various and

* The Mason and Dixon line is the parallel latitude of 39° 43' 26.3" between the southwestern corner of Pennsylvania and the arc of a circle of twelve miles' radius drawn from Newcastle (Delaware) as a center; and along that arc to the Delaware river. It was run in 1763–1767 by two English surveyors named Mason and Dixon, in conse-quence of Lord Hardwicke's decision, in 1750, of a long-standing controversy between the proprietors of Maryland and Pennsylvania. But there have been interstate contro-versies about parts of it even in the present century.

delicious methods devised by their black cooks for preparing the oysters, soft-shell crabs, terrapin, shad, canvasback ducks, and other delicacies afforded by Chesapeake Bay. Annapolis, the pleasant and hospitable state capital, had just been made the seat of St. John's College. Later, the town was to be saved from decay by the United States Naval Academy.

Baltimore, a mere village before the War of Independence, was approaching Boston in population. A deep harbor on Chesapeake Bay, water-driven flour mills, and proximity to wheat-growing regions made it the metropolis for an important section of Pennsylvania, in preference to Philadelphia. Baltimore was already famous for belles, one of whom married Napoleon Bonaparte's brother Jerome, and for swift schooners, the Baltimore clippers that made excellent privateers and successful pirates. The Maryland Piedmont was much like the limestone belt of Pennsylvania: a rich rolling grain country tilled by English and German farmers, with the aid of a few slaves. This region, in combination with Baltimore, neutralized the Tidewater aristocracy, and gradually drew Maryland into the social and economic orbit of the Northern states.

From Baltimore a road that long remained the despair of travellers traversed Maryland to Georgetown, just below the Great Falls of the Potomac. Here, at the head of navigation, the City of Washington was being planned. Crossing the river, one entered the Old Dominion, with a population of 748,000, of which forty per cent were slaves.*

Virginia is today but a fragment of the imperial domain that was granted to the Virginia Company in 1606; and less than half the size of the state in 1790. Kentucky was lopped off as a separate state of the Union in 1792, and West Virginia in 1863. But even without Kentucky, Virginia was the most populous, proud, and wealthy American commonwealth.

The Tidewater or coastal plain of Virginia, east of the fall line which passes through Washington, Richmond, and Petersburg, consists of a series of long narrow peninsulas separated by the navigable estuaries of the Potomac, Rappahannock, York, and James rivers. There were no towns excepting Portsmouth and Norfolk, and scarcely even a village. County seats were merely a court house, church, and tavern at some convenient cross-roads. Tobacco warehouse-receipts, and bills of exchange on your London merchant, who did your shopping in the metropolis, served as currency. 'Even now,' wrote John Randolph in 1813, 'the old folks talk of "going home to England." ' But by 1790 the Tidewater had seen its best days. The state capital had been transferred to Richmond, at the falls of

* Not including the 74,000 in Kentucky (17 per cent slaves).

the James; only William and Mary College kept Williamsburg alive. Norfolk, not yet recovered from the fire of 1776, was a poor-looking seaport of less than thirty-five hundred people. The forest was reconquering exhausted tobacco fields, the wiser planters were laying down their lands to wheat and grass, and the wisest were emigrating to Kentucky. One of the best plantations of the Virginia Tidewater, Davies Randolph's 'Presqu'ile' at Bermuda Hundred on the James, was described by the Duc de la Rochefoucauld-Liancourt, in 1795. It contained 750 acres, of which 400 were wood and marsh, and 350 were cultivated by eight Negroes, two horses, and four oxen. This area was divided into forty-acre fields by the usual Virginia or worm fence, made of split rails, notched near the ends, and intersected in a zigzag pattern in order to dispense with posts. 'No sort of fencing is more expensive or wasteful of timber,' wrote Washington; but those improving farmers who attempted hedges were thwarted by the enterprise of American hogs and cattle. Mr. Randolph used manure on but one of his fields. His system of rotation was corn, oats, wheat, rye, fallow: an improvement over the customary one of corn, wheat, and pasturage, which John Taylor called a scheme of tillage founded in contempt of the earth and terminating in its murder. With a modest average yield of ten to twelve bushels per acre, Presqu'ile brought its owner from $1,800 to $3,500 annually; and he valued the plantation at $20,000. The proportion of labor to acreage was so small that the condition of the land compared 'very indifferently with the most ordinary husbandry of Europe.' Apart from the mansion houses, the appearance of Virginia plantations, with their ill-cultivated fields, straggling fences, and dilapidated Negroes' cabins, was slovenly in the extreme. A traveller going south from Pennsylvania looked in vain for tidy agriculture until he reached the rice plantations of South Carolina.

By 1790 the Virginia Piedmont between the fall line and the Blue Ridge, for the most part a fruitful, rolling country, had become the seat of all that was healthy and vigorous in the plantation system; and Richmond, as the principal outlet of the James river valley, was flourishing. Most of the great Virginia statesmen of the revolutionary and early republican eras were either born in this region or grew to manhood in its wilder margins. The 'First Families of Virginia,' a rural aristocracy of native origin, reproduced the high sense of honor and public spirit of the English aristocracy, as well as the amenities of English country life. They frequently combined planting with the practice of law, but left trade to their inferiors, commerce to the agents of British mercantile firms, and navigation to the Yankees. Prepared by private tutors or at schools kept by Scotch clergymen for Princeton or William and Mary, trained to administration by managing their large estates, and to politics by representing their counties in the Virginia Assembly, the planters stepped naturally and gracefully into the leadership of the nation. It was no accident that Jefferson of Virginia drafted the Declaration of Independence, that Washington of Virginia led the army and became the first President, that Madison of Virginia fathered the Federal Constitution, that Marshall of Virginia became the greatest American jurist, and that he and Taylor of Virginia [7] led the two opposing schools of American political thought.

If the proper object of society be to produce and maintain an aristocracy,[8] Virginia had achieved it. If it be to maintain a high general level of comfort and intelligence, she had not. Below the 'first families,' but continually pushing into their level by marriage, was a class of lesser planters, to which Patrick Henry belonged: a class generous and hospitable, but uneducated, provincial, and rude. Below them was an unstable and uneasy class of yeomen, outnumbering the planters in the Piedmont. Descended largely from indentured servants and deported convicts, these peasants, as the gentry called them, were illiterate, ferocious, and quarrelsome. Self-contained plantations, with slave artisans and mechanics, left small demand for skilled white labor, and made small farms unprofitable. Hence the Virginia yeoman had but the alternative of migrating westward, or of becoming 'poor white trash' despised even by the slaves. It was already doubtful in 1790 that any community could endure half slave and half free; presently it would be doubtful if the nation could thus endure.

In the lowlands the slaves outnumbered the whites; in the Piedmont they comprised about one-third of the total population. They supported the economic system, and contributed much to the quality of Virginia leadership. Jefferson's oft-quoted passage, that 'the whole commerce between master and slave is a perpetual exercise of the most boisterous passions,' can only have applied to new and inexperienced members of the planter class; for the successful management of Negroes required tact, patience, forbearance, an even temper, and a sense of humor. Few denied that slavery was a moral evil and a menace to the country. Almost every educated Virginian hoped to make real the opening words of his Bill of Rights 'that all men are by nature free and independent.' But a state whose population was forty per cent black naturally quailed before such a social

[7 John Taylor of Caroline (1753–1824).]
[8 See Jefferson, pp. 194–9.]

revolution. Jefferson counted on the young abolitionists that Chancellor Wythe was making in William and Mary College. But in a few years' time the cotton gin gave chattel slavery a new lease of life; and, shortly after Jefferson died, a young professor of William and Mary began to preach the doctrine that Negro slavery was justified by history and ordained by God.

As one rode westward across the Virginia Piedmont, with the crest-line of the Blue Ridge looming in the distance, the forest became more dense, the large plantations less numerous, the farms of independent yeomen more frequent, and the cultivation of tobacco gave place to corn and grazing. Between the Blue Ridge and the higher folds of the Appalachians lies the Shenandoah valley peopled as we have seen by Scotch and Germans, and feeling itself a province apart from lowland and Piedmont until 1861. It was here, in Rockingham county, that Abraham Lincoln, grandfather of the President, lived until 1784; and at Staunton in Augusta county, Woodrow Wilson was born in 1856. Still less did the trans-Appalachian part of Virginia, a densely wooded plateau sloping to the upper Ohio, resemble the Virginia of the planters. In 1790 it was a frontier more primitive even than Kentucky. In 1861 it refused to follow the Old Dominion out of the Union, and became the State of West Virginia.

South from Petersburg in Virginia, through a level, sandy country of pine forest, a two days' journey took you to Halifax, one of several petty seaports of North Carolina. This 'tar-heel state' possessed a very different character from her neighbors on either side. Her population was the result of two distinct streams of secondary and fairly recent colonization: Virginia yeomen who settled in the coastal plain; those who followed the Shenandoah valley into the Piedmont and the Great Smoky mountains. Along the Roanoke river there was an overflow of plantations from Virginia; but the greater part of the coastal plain, a hundred miles or more wide, consisted of pine barrens with soil too sandy for wheat or tobacco, and extensive marshes like the Dismal Swamp. The river mouths were landlocked against vessels drawing above ten feet by the barrier beaches that enclosed Pamlico and Albemarle Sounds. This region, therefore, was sparsely settled, and its chief exports were naval stores: tar, turpentine, and pine timber. President Washington, travelling through it in 1791, found it 'the most barren country he ever beheld,' without 'a single house of an elegant appearance.'

The Piedmont of North Carolina was a thriving region of upland farms, supporting a large population of Germans, Ulstermen, English, and Highland Scotch. There was little communication between coast and Piedmont through the pine barrens, and less sympathy. Petersburg, Va., and Charleston, S. C., were nearer or more convenient markets for the upland farmers than the petty ports of their own state. Local particularism was so strong that the legislature abandoned Governor Tryon's 'palace' at Newbern, and became peripatetic. Only by creating a new state capital, at Raleigh on the falls of the Neuse river, could it manage to settle down.

The plantation system never obtained a strong foothold in North Carolina; the state remained a farming democracy, aided by rather than based upon chattel slavery. Among its white population of three hundred thousand in 1790, less than one-third owned slaves; and the proportion was even smaller in 1860.* For such a community a democratic policy was natural and inevitable; but without the leaven of popular education, a land-locked region was not apt to make much progress. Honest mediocrity was typical of North Carolina statesmanship from the eighteenth century to the twentieth, when the industrial revolution brought wealth, material progress, enthusiasm for learning, and accomplishment in the arts.

There was no such dearth of great figures, as we have seen, in South Carolina. The coastal plain of that state has a sub-tropical climate. In Charleston, its only city, the ravages of war were quickly repaired and the gay old life was resumed; in 1790, with a population of sixteen thousand, it was the fourth city in America, and metropolis of the lower South.† The Rev. Jedidiah Morse in his *American Geography* (1789) wrote, 'In no part of America are the social blessings enjoyed more rationally and liberally than in Charleston. Unaffected hospitality, affability, ease in manners and address, and a disposition to make their guests welcome, easy and pleased with themselves, are characteristics of the respectable people of Charleston.' One can well imagine that stiff New England Calvinist succumbing to the graceful attentions of a Charleston family, while he sipped their Madeira wine on a spacious verandah overlooking a tropical garden.

The South Carolina planters went to their country houses in November, when the first frosts removed the danger of fever; and took their families back to Charleston for the gay season from January to March. Early spring, a most anxious period in rice culture, was passed in the plantation man-

---

* With a total population of 400,000 in 1790 (one-quarter slave), North Carolina was the fourth state in the Union, just ahead of New York. But North Carolina's interior had already been settled, and New York's had not. New York reached the million mark in 1810; North Carolina only in 1870; in 1920 North Carolina had three million to New York's twelve and a half; and its largest city fell short of a hundred thousand.

† In 1940 Charleston had only 71,275 inhabitants, but more distinction and flavor than any one of the hundred American cities that exceeded it in size.

sion—shaded by a classic portico, and surrounded by groves of live oaks, hung with Spanish moss. The hot months would be spent at a summer house in the pine hills, or at Newport. Popular education was little attended to, but the College of Charleston was established in 1785, and the more opulent families continued to send their sons to Old England or New England for higher education.

Rice, the economic basis of the lower country, required intensive cultivation, along such parts of the tidal rivers as permitted artificial flooding with fresh water. These regions were so unhealthy for white people that black labor, immune from malaria, was a necessity; and in no part of the United States were slaves so numerous. Out of sixteen hundred heads of families in the rural part of the Charleston district, in 1790, thirteen hundred held slaves to the number of forty-three thousand. South Carolina not only blocked abolition of the African slave trade in the Federal Constitution, but reopened traffic by state law in 1803.

Indigo culture had been abandoned with the loss of the Parliamentary bounty; but the South Carolina planters, in 1790, were experimenting with the long staple sea-island cotton; and the next year Robert Owen spun into yarn the first two bags of it that were sent to England. The short staple upland cotton, which could be grown inland, was so difficult to separate from its seed as to be unmarketable until after the cotton gin was invented in 1793. One effect of this momentous discovery was to extend the plantation system into the Piedmont, the more populous section. In 1790 the upland people had just won their first victory by transferring the state capital up-country, to Columbia; but the Piedmont was still underrepresented in the legislature, and poor men were denied office by high property qualifications. John C. Calhoun, who was destined to weld the South and divide the Union, was a boy of eight in the upper country, in 1790.

Across the Savannah river from South Carolina lay Georgia, which retained few traces of General Oglethorpe's pious experiment. The objects of his benevolence, poor debtors and Scotch highlanders, wedged between hostile Indians on one side and a plantation colony on the other, had led a miserable existence. As soon as the prohibition of rum, slaves, and large holdings was removed, Georgia developed, as had South Carolina, a slave-holding rice coast, a belt of infertile pine barrens, and a rolling, wooded Piedmont of hunters and frontier farmers, who racially belonged to the usual Southern mixed upland stock. These Georgia 'crackers' were vigorous and lawless, hard drinkers and rough fighters. Desperately eager to despoil the Creek Indians of their fertile cornfields across the Oconee river, the up-country Georgians gave constant trouble to the Federal Government.

5. 'AMERICA THE HOPE OF THE WORLD'

Such, in their broader outlines, were the Thirteen States, and the people thereof, seven years after the war. They were singularly fortunate and happy. Of such a people, so circumstanced, the friends of liberty in Europe had high expectations. The French statesman Turgot wrote in his famous letter of 1778 to Dr. Price: [9]

This people is the hope of the human race. It may become the model. It ought to show the world by facts, that men can be free and yet peaceful, and may dispense with the chains in which tyrants and knaves of every colour have presumed to bind them, under pretext of the public good. The Americans should be an example of political, religious, commercial and industrial liberty. The asylum they offer to the oppressed of every nation, the avenue of escape they open, will compel governments to be just and enlightened; and the rest of the world in due time will see through the empty illusions in which policy is conceived. But to obtain these ends for us, America must secure them to herself; and must not become, as so many of your ministerial writers have predicted, a mass of divided powers, contending for territory and trade, cementing the slavery of peoples by their own blood.

Dr. Price printed Turgot's letter in 1785, together with some hundred pages of his own advice to the young republic. Slavery must be abolished. America must adopt a system of education that will 'teach *how* to think, rather than *what* to think, or to lead into the best way of searching for truth, rather than to instruct in truth itself.' The American States should foster an equal distribution of property; and to this end they must renounce foreign trade, as well as foreign alliances.

The Atlantic must be crossed before they can be attacked. . . Thus singularly happy, why should they seek connexions with Europe, and expose themselves to the danger of being involved in its quarrels?—What have they to do with its politics?—Is there anything very important to them which they can draw from thence—except *infection?*—indeed, I tremble when I think of that rage for trade which is likely to prevail among them.

Here is the policy of isolation, laid down in terms that America found too Spartan; and something more than a suggestion of the political system

[9 Clergyman, philosopher, and political controversialist (1723-91). He supported the American and French revolutions. See pp. 265-7 and 276.]

later known as Jeffersonian democracy. But there was one dominant force in United States history that few foresaw in 1785: the expansive force. With such a prize as the West at their back doors, the people of the United States would have been more than human had they been content with a 'state of nature' between the Atlantic and the Appalachians. For a century to come, the subduing of the temperate regions of North America to the purposes of civilized life was to be the main business of the United States. In 1790 the boundaries of the republic included eight hundred thousand, in 1860 three million square miles. In 1790 the population was four million; in 1950 one hundred and forty-nine million. This folk movement, comparable only with the barbaric invasions of Europe, gives the history of the United States a different quality from that of modern Europe; different even from that of Canada and Australia, by reason of the absence of exterior control. The advancing frontier, with growing industrialism, set the rhythm of American society, colored its politics, and rendered more difficult the problem of union. Yet, as Turgot warned us, only union could secure the gain and fulfil the promise of the American Revolution.

Thomas Bland Hollis, another English radical who looked to the rising star in the West, wrote to the President of Harvard College in 1788: 'Our papers mention that there is an intention of having the Olympic games revived in America. All her friends wish it and say she is capable of it: having acted upon Greek principles you should have Greek exercises.' Her friends saw no reason why literature and the arts should not spring into new life in a new world, fostered by liberty. One of them, ten years later, recorded with his disappointment the popular excuse: 'We are but a young people—let us grow.' How often has that excuse been repeated, and how constantly has it been true! Grow they did; but not as Rome, neither as Greece. Their astounding expansion was a continuous adventure in pioneering, a constant renewal of the nation's youth through fresh contact with a receding frontier. The American of today, with all his wealth, pride, and power, is still unmistakably young and inexperienced in the ways of the world that he is now called upon to set right for the second time in one generation.

The frontier has vanished with the wild Indian, and America's youth is waning fast. Some thought, during the great depression, that it had altogether gone, and that a premature old age was settling over American society. They were wrong. It is the story of a youthful people that you are to read; of a people constantly in movement, expanding and upheaving, blithely accepting new forces that were to strain their body politic, seeking to assimilate them to the democratic principle and to recover equilibrium between liberty and order, or security. And, as we write, America, with all the confidence and idealism of youth, is organizing her resources as never before to restore the peace, the productivity and the freedom of the Western World. Possibly that effort will destroy her youthfulness forever. We believe not; that, on the contrary, the faith and energy of the United States are still, in an even deeper sense than in 1778, 'the hope of the human race.'

D. W. Brogan

AMERICAN CLIMATE

⟨ Mr. Brogan's description of what passes for climate in America is a typical chapter from his *The American Character* (1944), a shrewd and entertaining account of the United States by an observer who knows the land and its people better than most Americans do. The author (1900—) is now Professor of Political Science at the University of Cambridge. Besides this and other books on the United States (including *Government of the People*, a study of the American political system, 1933, *U. S. A.*, 1941, and *An Introduction to American Politics*, 1954), he has written *The English People* (1943), *The Development of Modern France, 1870–1939* (1940), and *The Free State* (1945).

IT WAS NOT surprising that the Americans, at the end of their long march from ocean to ocean, should have too hastily assumed that they 'had America licked.' But it was an error, all the same. The continent remained not so much hostile as capricious; the gorgeous West, pouring out wealth with lavish hand, often had more than a hand inside the glove. The settlers in the South and in the Mississippi Valley had had to deal with diseases that, to northern Europeans, were very hard to manage. There was yellow fever, coming in from the West Indies; there was pellagra; there was hookworm; there was malaria. Some of these diseases became manageable as modern medical technology developed; Gorgas and Manson and Pasteur and Ross [1] not only made the Panama Canal a possibility—they

[1 W. C. Gorgas (1854–1920) did much to free Cuba and, later, Panama from yellow fever. He was chief sanitary officer of the Panama Canal Commission. Sir Patrick Manson (1844–1922), 'the father of tropical medicine,' was the first to suggest that malaria is carried by mosquitoes. Louis Pasteur (1822–95) was the founder of modern bacteriology. Sir Ronald Ross (1857–1932) specialized in the study of tropical diseases, notably malaria.]

also made an easier and safer life possible in the continental United States. Pellagra is curable mainly through a rise in economic standards, and—so far as that has come about—pellagra has been cured; although in the poverty-stricken and decaying regions of the South it is still a menace to white and black poor alike—and a disease that makes life disagreeable in Umbria has even less to make it tolerable in the derelict regions of Georgia. Malaria needs fighting by cleanliness, and this, too, involves economic factors, for it is far harder for the poor to be clean than for the rich. Hookworm is highly debilitating, but you are much less likely to get it if you wear shoes— and shoes cost money; there is nothing romantic about being a barefoot boy in the hookworm belt. Improved water supply, improved medical services, even the rudiments of organized sanitation were necessary to turn the depressed and despised 'mudsills' of the South—once denounced for their quite sensible habit of eating 'dirt' (i.e., earth) as a remedy for the deficiencies caused by hookworm—into healthy and energetic citizens. The work of the Rockefeller Foundation and of the state and federal governments did more for this southern problem than cubic miles of southern oratory—although some excellent oratory was devoted to getting the South to accept northern aid. . .

But the South was especially handicapped, climatically, historically, racially, economically. The problem of making the Middle West habitable was much easier; it required wealth and energy and scientific knowledge, which the region acquired in abundance. It also required a high degree of political efficiency, which was not so abundant. The Chicago drainage canal, though a reasonably adequate solution for Chicago, was less attractive to her downstream neighbors. But other breakdowns only prove that human institutions are human; a local collapse of sanitary efficiency is no more to be wondered at in Chicago than in Croydon.

Even the most favored regions had their drawbacks. The first settlers who moved into the Pacific slope were richly rewarded. Oregon, reasonably warm, well wooded, well watered, was more like Devon than like Illinois. And California, to the pioneers coming over the High Sierra or round the Horn, was a new Canaan. Indeed, as the first Americans began to visit the California coast, the great empty land with its scattered Mexican ranches was more like the world of Abraham than like the new machine world that already existed on the other side of the Atlantic. California cried out for more energetic settlers, and a swarm of Moses appeared to seize the land where, in its last spasm of imperial energy, Spain had created the little missions of San Francisco, Santa Barbara, San Luis Rey, San Luis Obispo, San

Diego, and—destined to a highly paradoxical destiny—the village called
after 'Our Lady, Queen of the Angels.' California had many attractions,
but one struck home in the Great Valley: it had no malaria; 'the shakes'
were unknown. But, as the unkind Frenchman said of New Zealand, 'There
are no snakes, but a great many Scotchmen,' and even California had its
drawbacks. It had no weather, only the most perfect climate in the world,
where season followed season in perfect regularity, with hardly an exceptional day. It seemed to be too good to be true. It was. The most regular
feature of San Francisco weather was the summer fog, and in even more
favored Southern California (as a saboteur from Florida put it in *The
New Yorker*), 'there is no rain, but the heavy dew sometimes washes away
the railroad bridges.' All around Los Angeles, the justification for this hit
below the belt can be seen; empty river beds lined with concrete, provided
with admirable bridges, recalling the Manzanares at Madrid. But the old
joke to the effect that the Madrileños [2] ought to sell the bridges and buy
a river is pointless in the California outpost of New Spain, for when the
rains do come, they come down with a speed and exuberance that are
worthy of the Golden State; seven inches in two days makes very necessary indeed the bridges and parapets that control the *arroyos* [3] turned
torrents. Nor are floods the only trouble in California. The State has no
equivalent of those terrible lightning storms of the Middle West, but it
does have earthquakes. Significantly, it is still a little tactless to refer (in
San Francisco) to 'the earthquake of 1906'—you should say 'the Fire,' because that result of the natural catastrophe is less painful to recall. Fire is
a manageable enemy of man and an old one, but when the foundations
of the earth move, the most optimistic Californian is reminded of the un-
tamable nature of the American land.

And at the other side of the continent, the rival paradise of Florida
has had its bad shocks: in sudden frosts that kill the citrus crops; in devastating tornadoes that wreck the Miami waterfront as thoroughly as a
second-class air raid could, or sweep the sea over such bold works of man
as the road across the Atlantic to Key West.

In the other parts of America, the savage possibilities of the climate
are never forgotten. All Ohio remembers the great flood year of 1913,
whose impact on Columbus Mr. Thurber [4] has made familiar to English
readers. From that disaster came an elaborate and expensive system of flood

[2] Citizens of Madrid.]
[3] Rivulets.]
[4] See his 'The Day the Dam Broke' in *My Life and Hard Times*.]

control in Columbus, in Dayton, in all southwestern Ohio. But other river towns in other states have had their own and much more recent disasters. The Wabash does not, alas for the citizens of Indiana, always stay within its banks; and when we get to the Mississippi, we are faced with the greatest engineering problem in the western world. Only the great rivers of China have so bad a record. The floods starting when the ice and snow melt, fifteen hundred miles away from the subtropical delta, present a problem every year. And the news that is flashed down the river has the urgency of an air-raid alert, for ten feet of extra water at Paducah may mean disaster if something is not done *at once* at Vicksburg. So men and boys, white and black, are called out to pile cotton bales and sandbags on the threatened levees; women and children get ready to flee from the rising wall of water being funneled down the river. And somewhere the sides of the funnel give way and tens of thousands are made homeless, hundreds are drowned, and an economic catastrophe that would ruin a minor European state has to be coped with.

Even in the long-settled East, the water is still restive. The Connecticut River, normally as placid as the Thames at Teddington, sometimes goes on the rampage, reminding the inhabitants of cities like Hartford that life and property are still insecure. Great storms drive the sea over the summer cottages of Block Island. And there was an historical appropriateness in the comment Nature provided for the end of the tercentenary celebration at Harvard, for on the last day the great 'storm wind of the equinox' that had been rushing up the coast from Florida struck Cambridge (Massachusetts) with a force unknown to Cambridge (England). It showed that for the sons of the Puritans the God of their Fathers was still an angry God of storm and rain like Him who had smitten the army of Sisera [5] and had later toughened the New Englanders.

Even when there are no catastrophes, there are constant climatic problems. The mere range of temperature is a problem. How do you plan your life in a place like Bismarck, North Dakota, where the July temperatures have ranged between 32° F. and 108°, and the January temperatures between 45° below zero and 60° above? What do you do, even in normally kindly New Orleans, where the January temperatures have ranged between 15° and 82° and the July temperatures between 35° and 102°? In Wyoming at the source of the Colorado River, there is frost in every month of the year; over many states there is never any frost at all for decades at a time. *But* no part of the United States—not Texas, not Florida,

[5 See Judges, iv, v.]

not California—is free from frost that will, when by a freak it does come, kill lemons and oranges and avocados and break the hearts or strain the consciences of local boosters.

It seems likely that not until this century did the Americans really adjust themselves to the climate—as far as it is humanly possible to do do. Those who were of British origin were especially handicapped, coming as they did from an island where no one had been really comfortable in winter between the departure of the Romans and the coming of the more exigent type of American tourist. It is worth noting that one of the most important inventions of that most representative of Americans, Franklin, was an efficient stove (another was the lightning conductor). But to make houses even reasonably airtight was a problem; the log cabin, whether or not it was of Finnish origin, was a solution better than any that English practice would suggest. The continuous series of farm buildings—house, stables, barn, all in line so that the farmer could pass from the kitchen to the horses and on to the cattle without going into the bitter air—was another necessary adjustment; moreover, it provided a fine range of buildings that could be turned into rumpus rooms, garages, etc., when city folk took over the New Hampshire countryside. With primitive central heating, the last lap was entered on. It is possibly no accident, again, that the most modern thermostatic systems of central heating owe their essential equipment to a firm in Minneapolis where the winter cold can kill ten times as often as it can on the milder Atlantic. An Iowa farm, painted in midwinter by Grant Wood, with its red barn and dominating silo is highly functional: devoted to the job of keeping men and stock alive and food and feed usable through the long siege of winter. No American farm-bred boy or girl is likely to think that he or she has America licked.

Nor, indeed, is the town boy, who, as he grows up, will have at least one memory of a great and killing cold spell, even if it does not become so legendary as the great New York freezes of 1837 and 1888. Gardeners will long remember the late winter of 1933–34 which killed so many plants and shrubs on Long Island; and all regions of America, except the South and the Pacific Coast, have their own stories of death by cold, of stalled buggies or sleighs or even cars, of the dangers of bad chains or defective car-heaters, of a winter climate that always bears watching.

And summer demands it even more. For the early settlers were even less acclimated (as Americans put it) to heat than to cold. For one thing, as Professor S. E. Morison has pointed out, they wore far too many and too thick clothes. Even the Andalusians of Columbus' crews wore too many garments for a Caribbean summer. North Europeans did worse. There were economic obstacles, of course; until cotton textiles became cheap and abundant around 1800, linen was expensive and woolens uncomfortable. But there was more in it than that. Long after adequate textiles were abundant and cheap, fashion—not merely style but moral fashion—kept too many clothes on the American man and still more on the American woman. Men might wear 'dusters' like Lincoln, or 'seersuckers' like the prosperous middle class of the eighties. If they were prepared to be conspicuous, they might wear white linen suits like Mark Twain. But they still wore too much and, for dress occasions, they had to wear 'Prince Alberts' (i.e., frock coats), tall hats, broadcloth, and starched collars and shirts. Theodore Roosevelt was regarded as pretty eccentric and reckless of the conventions, yet his typical costume was very formal and very uncomfortable indeed, compared with that of his niece's husband, the President of the United States today. It was still thought worthy of note when William Jennings Bryan took his coat off at Dayton, Tennessee, and defended Genesis in his shirt-sleeves [6]—and that was not quite twenty years ago. And the uniform of the American army that went to France in 1917–18 included a stiff cloth collar that made the British officer's uniform the envy of his semi-strangled comrades in arms.

As for the women, to look at fashion magazines of 1900, to read in *Middletown* of the clothes worn in Indiana in the summer a generation ago, even to recall the fuss made about the length of bathing-suit skirts and other problems of sartorial morals twenty years ago, is to be struck with astonishment as were the Greeks who learned from Herodotus that among the Lydians it was thought shameful even for men to be seen naked. No one, least of all a woman, need be overclothed in an American summer today. Indeed, unless she is clever with the needle or can afford custom-made clothes, any American woman who resolved to wear at least half as much as her mother used to would be baffled in any department store however big. The South Sea Islanders, put into 'Mother Hubbards' by American missionaries and in consequence suffering discomfort, or even death, have been thoroughly avenged.

It is not only the American house that has at last been adapted to the American climate. American food has, too. Although Americans have always, by European standards, been abundantly fed, they have not until recently been well fed. One early difficulty of adjustment was that of diet; the average pioneer wanted the roast beef of old England or its equivalent,

[6 At the famous 'Monkey Trial' in 1925.]

and was not to be put off with such new-fangled dishes as turkeys, tomatoes, corn, etc. He did adjust himself fairly quickly, but only in the sense of adding American items to European, not of balancing his diet or making it suit the climate and the work he had to do.

Of course some classes and some regions have been badly fed for economic reasons. 'Hog and hominy,' the diet of the Confederate army, was bad, but any other diet would have been a novelty to Southern poor whites. Negroes were and often are badly fed from any point of view. But travelers and critical Americans alike long lamented the monotony of American food, the good food ruined in that enemy to the pursuit of happiness, the frying-pan; the saleratus [7] bread which was debited with the American sallow complexion and the melancholy view of life characteristic of many Americans in middle age. Until modern storage methods came in, the severity of both winter and summer made variety in diet difficult. Ice, indeed, was an early American passion; in water, in coffee, in juleps and other alcoholic concoctions. But it was ice cut and stored in a New England winter and shipped to South Carolina—and India—in a highly speculative voyage. For if most of your cargo arrived safe, your fortune was made, while if your ship was becalmed, all you had was extra water ballast of no market value. One of the minor hardships of the Southern gentry in the War between the States was the shortage of ice, no laughing matter in the mint-julep country of tidewater Virginia.

With the coming of artificial ice, the worst was over and ice in summer became almost as necessary as coal in winter. European pioneers made refrigerator cars possible, to the profit of the meat-packers of Chicago and the fruit-growers of California and Florida. But American men still ate too much meat, ate it too often, and did not balance it with sufficient fruit and vegetables. It is only in modern times, very modern times, that the American diet has become varied, light, and suitable for the climate. The electric refrigerator is becoming a necessity; deep freezing promises new culinary resources, and air conditioning promises a new climate—indoors, at any rate. There is no visible prospect of any method of obviating the Turkish-bath sensation that hits the person who goes out from an air-conditioned train or store or movie house on a very hot day. It is still too early to relax. America has always managed to keep her children on their toes; she still manages to do so. But the day is not in sight on which science and business together will be able to guarantee the climate and natural resources of California to the whole Union—or even to California.

[7 Baking soda.]

Jonathan Swift

A MODEST PROPOSAL

FOR PREVENTING THE CHILDREN OF POOR
PEOPLE IN IRELAND FROM BEING A BURDEN
TO THEIR PARENTS OR COUNTRY, AND FOR
MAKING THEM BENEFICIAL TO THE PUBLIC.
1729.

❬ One of the minor ironies of Swift's life was his popularity with the Irish, despite his reluctance to be an Irishman. He had served the Irish Church well as a negotiator for concessions from the English government, but after his pamphleteering for the Tories between 1710 and 1714 he hoped to be rewarded by an ecclesiastical appointment in England. This hope failed (according to tradition, because Queen Anne had been offended by A *Tale of a Tub*, 1704); the best he could get was the deanery of St. Patrick's Cathedral, Dublin. To Dublin he went (1714), but he was a disappointed man. He visited London in 1726 and 1727, but after that never again left Ireland.

The 'saeva indignatio' of his genius, plus political circumstances, made Swift on several occasions the champion of Irish protest against economic exploitation by England. In 1720 he advised the Irish in a pamphlet, *The Universal Use of Irish Manufacture*, to boycott English goods and buy those of Irish manufacture instead. By his *Drapier's Letters* of 1724 he forced the English government to drop a scheme of allowing one William Wood to mint copper coins for Irish use. Swift convinced his readers that the money would be ruinous to Ireland.

Some of his most striking and most somber descriptions of human depravity, those of the Yahoos in the fourth book of *Gulliver's Travels*, must have been suggested, in part, by the miserable condition of the Irish peasantry. But for indignation at man's callous inhumanity to man nothing in literature surpasses A *Modest Proposal*. The masterly and terrible irony of this tract accomplishes what anger alone could never do. It shocks, and it was meant to shock, as few writings have done.

I T IS a melancholy object to those who walk through this great town,[1] or travel in the country, when they see the streets, the roads, and cabin-doors, crowded with beggars of the female sex, followed by three, four, or six children, all in rags, and importuning every passenger for an alms. These mothers, instead of being able to work for their honest livelihood, are forced to employ all their time in strolling to beg sustenance for their helpless infants; who, as they grow up, either turn thieves for want of work, or leave their dear native country to fight for the Pretender[2] in Spain, or sell themselves to the Barbadoes.[3]

I think it is agreed by all parties, that this prodigious number of children in the arms, or on the backs, or at the heels of their mothers, and frequently of their fathers, is, in the present deplorable state of the kingdom, a very great additional grievance; and, therefore, whoever could find out a fair, cheap, and easy method of making these children sound, useful members of the commonwealth, would deserve so well of the public, as to have his statue set up for a preserver of the nation.

But my intention is very far from being confined to provide only for the children of professed beggars; it is of a much greater extent, and shall take in the whole number of infants at a certain age, who are born of parents in effect as little able to support them, as those who demand our charity in the streets.

As to my own part, having turned my thoughts for many years upon this important subject, and maturely weighed the several schemes of our projectors, I have always found them grossly mistaken in their computation. It is true, a child, just dropped from its dam, may be supported by her milk for a solar year, with little other nourishment; at most, not above the value of two shillings, which the mother may certainly get, or the value in scraps, by her lawful occupation of begging; and it is exactly at one year old that I propose to provide for them in such a manner, as, instead of being a charge upon their parents, or the parish, or wanting food and raiment for

[1] Dublin. When Swift wrote this tract, Ireland had had three years of famine.]

[2] The Old Pretender, James Stuart, son of James II (who was deposed by the 'Glorious Revolution' of 1688) and claimant of the throne of Great Britain. He and his followers were constantly plotting to invade England.]

[3] As laborers on the West Indian plantations.]

the rest of their lives, they shall, on the contrary, contribute to the feeding and partly to the clothing,[4] of many thousands.

There is likewise another great advantage in my scheme, that it will prevent those voluntary abortions, and that horrid practice of women murdering their bastard children, alas, too frequent among us! sacrificing the poor innocent babes, I doubt[5] more to avoid the expense than the shame, which would move tears and pity in the most savage and inhuman breast.

The number of souls in this kingdom being usually reckoned one million and a half, of these I calculate there may be about two hundred thousand couple whose wives are breeders; from which number I subtract thirty thousand couple, who are able to maintain their own children, (although I apprehend there cannot be so many, under the present distresses of the kingdom;) but this being granted, there will remain a hundred and seventy thousand breeders. I again subtract fifty thousand, for those women who miscarry, or whose children die by accident or disease within the year. There only remain a hundred and twenty thousand children of poor parents annually born. The question therefore is, How this number shall be reared and provided for? which, as I have already said, under the present situation of affairs, is utterly impossible by all the methods hitherto proposed. For we can neither employ them in handicraft or agriculture; we neither build houses (I mean in the country,) nor cultivate land: they can very seldom pick up a livelihood by stealing, till they arrive at six years old, except where they are of towardly parts;[6] although I confess they learn the rudiments much earlier; during which time they can, however, be properly looked upon only as probationers; as I have been informed by a principal gentleman in the county of Cavan, who protested to me, that he never knew above one or two instances under the age of six, even in a part of the kingdom so renowned for the quickest proficiency in that art.

I am assured by our merchants, that a boy or a girl before twelve years old is no saleable commodity; and even when they come to this age they will not yield above three pounds, or three pounds and half-a-crown at most, on the exchange; which cannot turn to account either to the parents or kingdom, the charge of nutriment and rags having been at least four times that value.

I shall now, therefore, humbly propose my own thoughts, which I hope will not be liable to the least objection.

[4 When Gulliver lived among the Houyhnhnms, he repaired his shoes with 'the skins of Yahoos dried in the sun.']

[5 Suspect.]   [6 Bright. talented.]

I have been assured by a very knowing American [7] of my acquaintance in London, that a young healthy child, well nursed, is, at a year old, a most delicious, nourishing, and wholesome food, whether stewed, roasted, baked, or boiled; and I make no doubt that it will equally serve in a fricassee or a ragout.

I do therefore humbly offer it to public consideration, that of the hundred and twenty thousand children already computed, twenty thousand may be reserved for breed, whereof only one-fourth part to be males; which is more than we allow to sheep, black-cattle, or swine; and my reason is, that these children are seldom the fruits of marriage, a circumstance not much regarded by our savages, therefore one male will be sufficient to serve four females. That the remaining hundred thousand may, at a year old, be offered in sale to the persons of quality and fortune through the kingdom; always advising the mother to let them suck plentifully in the last month, so as to render them plump and fat for a good table. A child will make two dishes at an entertainment for friends; and when the family dines alone, the fore or hind quarter will make a reasonable dish, and, seasoned with a little pepper or salt, will be very good boiled on the fourth day, especially in winter.

I have reckoned, upon a medium, that a child just born will weigh twelve pounds, and in a solar year, if tolerably nursed, will increase to twenty-eight pounds.

I grant this food will be somewhat dear, and therefore very proper for landlords, who, as they have already devoured most of the parents, seem to have the best title to the children.

Infants' flesh will be in season throughout the year, but more plentifully in March, and a little before and after: for we are told by a grave author, an eminent French physician, that fish being a prolific diet, there are more children born in Roman Catholic countries about nine months after Lent, than at any other season; therefore, reckoning a year after Lent, the markets will be more glutted than usual, because the number of Popish infants is at least three to one in this kingdom; and therefore it will have one other collateral advantage, by lessening the number of Papists among us.

I have already computed the charge of nursing a beggar's child (in which list I reckon all cottagers, labourers, and four-fifths of the farmers) to be about two shillings per annum, rags included; and I believe no gentleman would repine to give ten shillings for the carcass of a good fat child, which,

[7 Some of the Indians were supposed by Europeans to be cannibals.]

as I have said, will make four dishes of excellent nutritive meat, when he has only some particular friend, or his own family, to dine with him. Thus the squire will learn to be a good landlord, and grow popular among his tenants; the mother will have eight shillings net profit, and be fit for work till she produces another child.

Those who are more thrifty (as I must confess the times require) may flay the carcass; the skin of which, artificially dressed, will make admirable gloves for ladies, and summer-boots for fine gentlemen.

As to our city of Dublin, shambles [8] may be appointed for this purpose in the most convenient parts of it, and butchers, we may be assured, will not be wanting; although I rather recommend buying the children alive, then dressing them hot from the knife, as we do roasting pigs.

A very worthy person, a true lover of his country, and whose virtues I highly esteem, was lately pleased, in discoursing on this matter, to offer a refinement upon my scheme. He said, that many gentlemen of this kingdom, having of late destroyed their deer, he conceived that the want of venison might be well supplied by the bodies of young lads and maidens, not exceeding fourteen years of age, nor under twelve; so great a number of both sexes in every country being now ready to starve for want of work and service; and these to be disposed of by their parents, if alive, or otherwise by their nearest relations. But, with due deference to so excellent a friend, and so deserving a patriot, I cannot be altogether in his sentiments; for as to the males, my American acquaintance assured me, from frequent experience, that their flesh was generally tough and lean, like that of our schoolboys, by continual exercise, and their taste disagreeable; and to fatten them would not answer the charge. Then as to the females, it would, I think, with humble submission, be a loss to the public, because they soon would become breeders themselves: and besides, it is not improbable that some scrupulous people might be apt to censure such a practice, (although indeed very unjustly,) as a little bordering upon cruelty; which, I confess, has always been with me the strongest objection against any project, how well soever intended.

But in order to justify my friend, he confessed that this expedient was put into his head by the famous Psalmanazar,[9] a native of the island Formosa, who came from thence to London above twenty years ago; and in conversation told my friend, that in his country, when any young person

[8 Slaughterhouses.]
[9 One George Psalmanazar posed as a native of Formosa and published a spurious *Description* of that island.]

happened to be put to death, the executioner sold the carcass to persons of quality as a prime dainty; and that in his time the body of a plump girl of fifteen, who was crucified for an attempt to poison the emperor, was sold to his imperial majesty's prime minister of state, and other great mandarins of the court, in joints from the gibbet, at four hundred crowns. Neither indeed can I deny, that, if the same use were made of several plump young girls in this town, who, without one single groat to their fortunes, cannot stir abroad without a chair, and appear at playhouse and assemblies in foreign fineries which they never will pay for, the kingdom would not be the worse.

Some persons of a desponding spirit are in great concern about that vast number of poor people, who are aged, diseased, or maimed; and I have been desired to employ my thoughts, what course may be taken to ease the nation of so grievous an encumbrance. But I am not in the least pain upon that matter, because it is very well known, that they are every day dying, and rotting, by cold and famine, and filth and vermin, as fast as can be reasonably expected. And as to the young labourers, they are now in almost as hopeful a condition: they cannot get work, and consequently pine away for want of nourishment, to a degree, that if at any time they are accidentally hired to common labour, they have not strength to perform it; and thus the country and themselves are happily delivered from the evils to come.

I have too long digressed, and therefore shall return to my subject. I think the advantages by the proposal which I have made are obvious and many, as well as of the highest importance.

For first, as I have already observed, it would greatly lessen the number of Papists, with whom we are yearly over-run, being the principal breeders of the nation, as well as our most dangerous enemies; and who stay at home on purpose to deliver the kingdom to the Pretender, hoping to take their advantage by the absence of so many good Protestants,[10] who have chosen rather to leave their country than stay at home and pay tithes against their conscience to an Episcopal curate.

Secondly, The poorer tenants will have something valuable of their own, which by law may be made liable to distress, and help to pay their landlord's rent; their corn and cattle being already seized, and money a thing unknown.

[10] This refers to Irish Dissenters, i.e. Protestants who did not belong to the Church of Ireland (the counterpart in that country of the Church of England, which, of course, was an established, official institution) but who were nevertheless taxed to support it.]

Thirdly, Whereas the maintenance of a hundred thousand children, from two years old and upward, cannot be computed at less than ten shillings a piece per annum, the nation's stock will be thereby increased fifty thousand pounds per annum, beside the profit of a new dish introduced to the tables of all gentlemen of fortune in the kingdom, who have any refinement in taste. And the money will circulate among ourselves,[11] the goods being entirely of our own growth and manufacture.

Fourthly, The constant breeders, beside the gain of eight shillings sterling per annum by the sale of their children, will be rid of the charge of maintaining them after the first year.

Fifthly, This food would likewise bring great custom [12] to taverns; where the vintners will certainly be so prudent as to procure the best receipts for dressing it to perfection, and, consequently, have their houses frequented by all the fine gentlemen, who justly value themselves upon their knowledge in good eating: and a skilful cook, who understands how to oblige his guests, will contrive to make it as expensive as they please.

Sixthly, This would be a great inducement to marriage, which all wise nations have either encouraged by rewards, or enforced by laws and penalties. It would increase the care and tenderness of mothers toward their children, when they were sure of a settlement for life to the poor babes, provided in some sort by the public, to their annual profit or expense. We should see an honest emulation among the married women, which of them could bring the fattest child to the market. Men would become as fond of their wives during the time of their pregnancy as they are now of their mares in foal, their cows in calf, their sows when they are ready to farrow; nor offer to beat or kick them (as is too frequent a practice) for fear of a miscarriage.

Many other advantages might be enumerated. For instance, the addition of some thousand carcasses in our exportation of barrelled beef; the propagation of swine's flesh, and improvement in the art of making good bacon, so much wanted among us by the great destruction of pigs, too frequent at our table; which are no way comparable in taste or magnificence to a well-grown, fat, yearling child, which, roasted whole, will make a considerable figure at a lord mayor's feast, or any other public entertainment. But this, and many others, I omit, being studious of brevity.

Supposing that one thousand families in this city would be constant customers for infants' flesh, beside others who might have it at merry-

[11 See introductory note.]
[12 Trade, patronage.]

meetings, particularly at weddings and christenings, I compute that Dublin would take off annually about twenty thousand carcasses; and the rest of the kingdom (where probably they will be sold somewhat cheaper) the remaining eighty thousand.

I can think of no one objection, that will possibly be raised against this proposal, unless it should be urged, that the number of people will be thereby much lessened in the kingdom. This I freely own, and it was indeed one principal design in offering it to the world. I desire the reader will observe, that I calculate my remedy for this one individual kingdom of Ireland, and for no other that ever was, is, or I think ever can be, upon earth. Therefore let no man talk to me of other expedients: of taxing our absentees at five shillings a pound: of using neither clothes, nor household furniture, except what is our own growth and manufacture: of utterly rejecting the materials and instruments that promote foreign luxury: of curing the expensiveness of pride, vanity, idleness, and gaming in our women: of introducing a vein of parsimony, prudence, and temperance: of learning to love our country, in the want of which we differ even from Laplanders, and the inhabitants of Topinamboo: [13] of quitting our animosities and factions, nor acting any longer like the Jews, who were murdering one another at the very moment their city was taken: of being a little cautious not to sell our country and conscience for nothing: of teaching landlords to have at least one degree of mercy toward their tenants: lastly, of putting a spirit of honesty, industry, and skill into our shopkeepers; who, if a resolution could now be taken to buy only our native goods, would immediately unite to cheat and exact upon us in the price, the measure, and the goodness, nor could ever yet be brought to make one fair proposal of just dealing, though often and earnestly invited to it.

Therefore I repeat, let no man talk to me of these and the like expedients, till he has at least some glimpse of hope, that there will be ever some hearty and sincere attempt to put them in practice.

But, as to myself, having been wearied out for many years with offering vain, idle, visionary thoughts, and at length utterly despairing of success, I fortunately fell upon this proposal; which, as it is wholly new, so it has something solid and real, of no expense and little trouble, full in our own power, and whereby we can incur no danger in disobliging England. For this kind of commodity will not bear exportation, the flesh being of too tender a consistence to admit a long continuance in salt, although per-

[13] In Brazil.]

haps I could name a country, which would be glad to eat up our whole nation without it.

After all, I am not so violently bent upon my own opinion as to reject any offer proposed by wise men, which shall be found equally innocent, cheap, easy and effectual. But before something of that kind shall be advanced in contradiction to my scheme, and offering a better, I desire the author, or authors, will be pleased maturely to consider two points. First, as things now stand, how they will be able to find food and raiment for a hundred thousand useless mouths and backs. And, secondly, there being a round million of creatures in human figure throughout this kingdom, whose whole subsistence put into a common stock would leave them in debt two millions of pounds sterling, adding those who are beggars by profession, to the bulk of farmers, cottagers, and labourers, with the wives and children who are beggars in effect; I desire those politicians who dislike my overture, and may perhaps be so bold as to attempt an answer, that they will first ask the parents of these mortals, whether they would not at this day think it a great happiness to have been sold for food at a year old, in the manner I prescribe, and thereby have avoided such a perpetual scene of misfortunes, as they have since gone through, by the oppression of landlords, the impossibility of paying rent without money or trade, the want of common sustenance, with neither house nor clothes to cover them from the inclemencies of the weather, and the most inevitable prospect of entailing the like, or greater miseries, upon their breed for ever.

I profess, in the sincerity of my heart, that I have not the least personal interest in endeavouring to promote this necessary work, having no other motive than the public good of my country, by advancing our trade, providing for infants, relieving the poor, and giving some pleasure to the rich. I have no children by which I can propose to get a single penny; the youngest being nine years old, and my wife past child-bearing.

Lord Chesterfield
LETTERS TO HIS SON

⟨ Chesterfield's reputation is lower than it deserves to be. Because his name became synonymous with correct and elegant taste, it has been vulgarized by attachment to cigarettes, overcoats, and other commodities, suggesting that he was a fop. Because he was the object of a celebrated letter by Dr. Johnson, it has been assumed by careless readers of Boswell that he was a prig. Because his tastes differed from Victorian ones, he has been considered completely immoral and hypocritical.

The reader of the letters will gain a somewhat different impression of Chesterfield. He was an efficient diplomat, a thoughtful friend—everybody knows his dying words, 'Give Dayrolles a chair' —an agreeable companion, and an uncomplaining victim of bad health. To understand him we should judge his letters by the standards not of Renaissance courtesy books, Victorian delineations of the gentleman, or the precepts of St. Paul, but of their own age. They express the aristocratic sentiment of that age, with its emphasis on polish, manners, form. Their ideal is Ciceronian decorum, restraint: 'Pray read frequently,' he writes to his son, 'nay, get by heart, if you can, that incomparable chapter in Cicero's Offices, upon the τὸ πρέπον, or the *Decorum*. It contains whatever is necessary for the dignity of manners.' 'Sacrifice to the Graces,' he is forever admonishing. Virtue is the companion of the Graces. 'Merit and good-breeding will make their way everywhere . . . politeness and good-breeding are absolutely necessary to adorn any, or all other good qualities or talents. Without them, no knowledge, no perfection whatever, is seen in its best light. The scholar, without good-breeding, is a pedant; the philosopher, a cynic; the soldier, a brute; and every man disagreeable.' Granted that these worldly, urbane standards are not the highest; but they are within their limits decent, in Chesterfield's sense of the word, and civilized.

FROM *Letters of Lord Chesterfield*, World's Classics Edition, Oxford University Press, 1929.

Dear Boy,

PLEASURE is the rock which most young people split upon:
they launch out with crowded sails in quest of it, but without a compass to direct their course, or reason sufficient to steer the vessel; for
want of which, pain and shame, instead of pleasure, are the returns of
their voyage. Do not think that I mean to snarl at pleasure, like a Stoic,[2]
or to preach against it, like a parson; no, I mean to point it out, and recommend it to you, like an Epicurean: I wish you a great deal; and my only
view is to hinder you from mistaking it.

The character which most young men first aim at is, that of a man
of pleasure; but they generally take it upon trust; and instead of consulting
their own taste and inclinations, they blindly adopt whatever those with
whom they chiefly converse, are pleased to call by the name of pleasure;
and a *man of pleasure*, in the vulgar acceptation of that phrase, means only
a beastly drunkard, an abandoned whore-master, and a profligate swearer
and curser. As it may be of use to you, I am not unwilling, though at the
same time ashamed, to own, that the vices of my youth proceeded much
more from my silly resolution of being what I heard called a man of pleasure, than from my own inclinations. I always naturally hated drinking; and
yet I have often drunk, with disgust at the time, attended by great sickness
the next day, only because I then considered drinking as a necessary qualification for a fine gentleman, and a man of pleasure.

The same as to gaming. I did not want [3] money, and consequently had
no occasion to play for it; but I thought play another necessary ingredient
in the composition of a man of pleasure, and accordingly I plunged into it
without desire, at first; sacrificed a thousand real pleasures to it; and made
myself solidly uneasy by it, for thirty the best years of my life.

[1] For 'Old Style,' that is, according to the Julian calendar. The Gregorian calendar,
which corrected an error in the Julian, was adopted in Great Britain in 1752; hence
many eighteenth-century writers added 'O.S.' or 'N.S.' to dates. Chesterfield himself
introduced in the House of Lords the bill for changing the calendar.]

[2] The ancient Stoic philosophers preached fortitude and austerity. The Epicureans
thought, or were popularly (and somewhat erroneously) accused of thinking, that pleasure is the chief good.]

[3] Lack, need.]

I was even absurd enough, for a little while, to swear, by way of adorning and completing the shining character which I affected; but this folly I soon laid aside, upon finding both the guilt and the indecency of it.

Thus seduced by fashion, and blindly adopting nominal pleasures, I lost real ones; and my fortune impaired, and my constitution shattered, are, I must confess, the just punishment of my errors.

Take warning then by them; choose your pleasures for yourself, and do not let them be imposed upon you. Follow nature and not fashion: weigh the present enjoyment of your pleasures against the necessary consequences of them, and then let your own common sense determine your choice.

Were I to begin the world again, with the experience which I now have of it, I would lead a life of real, not of imaginary pleasure. I would enjoy the pleasures of the table, and of wine; but stop short of the pains inseparably annexed to an excess in either. I would not, at twenty years, be a preaching missionary of abstemiousness and sobriety; and I should let other people do as they would, without formally and sententiously rebuking them for it: but I would be most firmly resolved not to destroy my own faculties and constitution; in complaisance to those who have no regard to their own. I would play to give me pleasure, but not to give me pain; that is, I would play for trifles, in mixed companies, to amuse myself, and conform to custom; but I would take care not to venture for sums which, if I won, I should not be the better for; but, if I lost, should be under a difficulty to pay; and when paid, would oblige me to retrench in several other articles. Not to mention the quarrels which deep play commonly occasions.

I would pass some of my time in reading, and the rest in the company of people of sense and learning, and chiefly those above me; and I would frequent the mixed companies of men and women of fashion, which, though often frivolous, yet they unbend and refresh the mind, not uselessly, because they certainly polish and soften the manners.

These would be my pleasures and amusements, if I were to live the last thirty years over again: they are rational ones; and moreover, I will tell you, they are really the fashionable ones: for the others are not, in truth, the pleasures of what I call people of fashion, but of those who only call themselves so. Does good company care to have a man reeling drunk among them? or to see another tearing his hair, and blaspheming, for having lost at play, more than he is able to pay? or a whore-master with half a nose, and crippled by coarse and infamous debauchery? No; those who practise, and much more those who brag of them, make no part of good company; and are most unwillingly, if ever, admitted into it. A real man of fashion and pleasures observes decency: at least neither borrows nor affects vices; and if he unfortunately has any, he gratifies them with choice, delicacy, and secrecy.

I have not mentioned the pleasures of the mind (which are the solid and permanent ones), because they do not come under the head of what people commonly call pleasures; which they seem to confine to the senses. The pleasure of virtue, of charity, and of learning, is true and lasting pleasure; with which I hope you will be well and long acquainted. Adieu!

LONDON, OCTOBER 9, O.S. 1747

DEAR BOY:

People of your age have, commonly, an unguarded frankness about them; which makes them the easy prey and bubbles of the artful and the experienced: they look upon every knave or fool, who tells them that he is their friend, to be really so; and pay that profession of simulated friendship with an indiscreet and unbounded confidence, always to their loss, often to their ruin. Beware, therefore, now that you are coming into the world, of these proffered friendships. Receive them with great civility, but with great incredulity too; and pay them with compliments, but not with confidence. Do not let your vanity and self-love make you suppose that people become your friends at first sight, or even upon a short acquaintance. Real friendship is a slow grower; and never thrives, unless ingrafted upon a stock of known and reciprocal merit. There is another kind of nominal friendship among young people, which is warm for the time, but, by good luck, of short duration. This friendship is hastily produced, by their being accidentally thrown together, and pursuing the same course of riot and debauchery. A fine friendship, truly; and well cemented by drunkenness and lewdness. It should rather be called a conspiracy against morals and good manners, and be punished as such by the civil magistrate. However, they have the impudence and folly to call this confederacy a friendship. They lend one another money, for bad purposes; they engage in quarrels, offensive and defensive, for their accomplices; they tell one another all they know, and often more too, when, of a sudden, some accident disperses them, and they think no more of each other, unless it be to betray and laugh at their imprudent confidence. Remember to make a great difference between companions and friends; for a very complaisant and agreeable companion may, and often does, prove a very improper and a very dangerous friend. People will, in a great degree, and not without reason, form their opinion of you, upon that which they have of your friends; and there is a Spanish proverb, which says very justly, *Tell me whom you live with, and I will tell you who you are.* One may fairly suppose, that a man, who makes a knave or a fool his friend, has something very bad to do or to conceal. But, at the same time that you carefully decline the friendship of knaves and fools, if it can be called friendship, there is no occasion to make either of them your enemies, wantonly, and unprovoked; for they are numerous bodies: and I would rather choose a secure neutrality, than alliance, or war, with either of them. You may be a declared enemy to their vices and follies, without being marked out by them as a personal one. Their enmity is the next dangerous thing to their friendship. Have a real reserve with almost everybody; and have a seeming reserve with almost nobody; for it is very disagreeable to seem reserved, and very dangerous not to be so. Few people find the true medium; many are ridiculously mysterious and reserved upon trifles; and many imprudently communicative of all they know.

The next thing to the choice of your friends, is the choice of your company. Endeavor, as much as you can, to keep company with people above you: there you rise, as much as you sink with people below you; for (as I have mentioned before) you are whatever the company you keep is. Do not mistake, when I say company above you, and think that I mean with regard to their birth: that is the least consideration; but I mean with regard to their merit, and the light in which the world considers them.

There are two sorts of good company; one, which is called the *beau monde,*[4] and consists of those people who have the lead in courts, and in the gay part of life; the other consists of those who are distinguished by some peculiar merit, or who excel in some particular and valuable art or science. For my own part, I used to think myself in company as much above me, when I was with Mr. Addison and Mr. Pope, as if I had been with all the Princes in Europe. What I mean by low company, which should by all means be avoided, is the company of those, who, absolutely insignificant and contemptible in themselves, think they are honoured by being in your company, and who flatter every vice and every folly you have, in order to engage you to converse with them. The pride of being the first of the company is but too common; but it is very silly, and very prejudicial. Nothing in the world lets down a character more than that wrong turn.

You may possibly ask me, whether a man has it always in his power to get into the best company? and how? I say, Yes, he has, by deserving it;

[4 Polite society.]

provided he is but in circumstances which enable him to appear upon the footing of a gentleman. Merit and good-breeding will make their way everywhere. Knowledge will introduce him, and good-breeding will endear him to the best companies; for, as I have often told you, politeness and good-breeding are absolutely necessary to adorn any, or all other good qualities or talents. Without them, no knowledge, no perfection whatever, is seen in its best light. The scholar, without good-breeding, is a pedant; the philosopher, a cynic; the soldier, a brute; and every man disagreeable.

I long to hear, from my several correspondents at Leipsig, of your arrival there, and what impression you make on them at first; for I have Arguses,[5] with an hundred eyes each, who will watch you narrowly, and relate to me faithfully. My accounts will certainly be true; it depends upon you, entirely, of what kind they shall be. Adieu.

LONDON, OCTOBER 16, O.S. 1747

DEAR BOY,

The art of pleasing is a very necessary one to possess; but a very difficult one to acquire. It can hardly be reduced to rules; and your own good sense and observation will teach you more of it than I can. Do as you would be done by, is the surest method that I know of pleasing. Observe carefully what pleases you in others, and probably the same things in you will please others. If you are pleased with the complaisance and attention of others to your humours, your tastes, or your weaknesses, depend upon it the same complaisance and attention, on your part to theirs, will equally please them. Take the tone of the company that you are in, and do not pretend to give it; be serious, gay, or even trifling, as you find the present humour of the company; this is an attention due from every individual to the majority. Do not tell stories in company; there is nothing more tedious and disagreeable; if by chance you know a very short story, and exceedingly applicable to the present subject of conversation, tell it in as few words as possible; and even then, throw out that you do not love to tell stories, but that the shortness of it tempted you. Of all things, banish the egotism out of your conversation, and never think of entertaining people with your own personal concerns or private affairs; though they are interesting to you they are tedious and impertinent to everybody else; besides that, one cannot keep one's own private affairs too secret. Whatever you think your own excellencies may be, do not affectedly display them in company; nor labour, as many people do, to give that turn to the conversation, which may supply you with an oppor-

[5 Argus was the hundred-eyed guardian of Io, whom Zeus had changed into a heifer.]

tunity of exhibiting them. If they are real, they will infallibly be discovered, without your pointing them out yourself, and with much more advantage. Never maintain an argument with heat and clamour, though you think or know yourself to be in the right; but give your opinion modestly and coolly, which is the only way to convince; and, if that does not do, try to change the conversation, by saying, with good-humour, 'We shall hardly convince one another; nor is it necessary that we should, so let us talk of something else.'

Remember that there is a local propriety to be observed in all companies; and that what is extremely proper in one company, may be, and often is, highly improper in another.

The jokes, the *bons mots*,[6] the little adventures, which may do very well in one company, will seem flat and tedious when related in another. The particular character, the habits, the cant of one company, may give credit to a word, or a gesture, which would have none at all if divested of those accidental circumstances. Here people very commonly err; and fond of something that has entertained them in one company, and in certain circumstances, repeat it with emphasis in another, where it is either insipid, or, it may be, offensive, by being ill-timed or misplaced. Nay, they often do it with this silly preamble: 'I will tell you an excellent thing'; or, 'the best thing in the world.' This raises expectations, which, when absolutely disappointed, make the relator of this excellent thing look, very deservedly, like a fool.

If you would particularly gain the affection and friendship of particular people, whether men or women, endeavour to find out their predominant excellency, if they have one, and their prevailing weakness, which everybody has; and do justice to the one, and something more than justice to the other. Men have various objects in which they may excel, or at least would be thought to excel; and, though they love to hear justice done to them, where they know that they excel, yet they are most and best flattered upon those points where they wish to excel, and yet are doubtful whether they do or not. As, for example: Cardinal Richelieu,[7] who was undoubtedly the ablest statesman of his time, or perhaps of any other, had the idle vanity of being thought the best poet too: he envied the great Corneille [8] his reputation, and ordered a criticism to be written upon the *Cid*. Those, therefore, who flattered skilfully, said little to him of his abili-

[6 Epigrams, witticisms.]
[7 He controlled the government of Louis XIII, 1624–42.]
[8 One of the greatest of French dramatists (1606–84).]

ties in state affairs, or at least but *en passant*,[9] and as it might naturally occur. But the incense which they gave him, the smoke of which they knew would turn his head in their favour, was as a *bel esprit* [10] and a poet. Why? Because he was sure of one excellency, and distrustful as to the other. You will easily discover every man's prevailing vanity, by observing his favourite topic of conversation; for every man talks most of what he has most a mind to be thought to excel in. Touch him but there, and you touch him to the quick. The late Sir Robert Walpole [11] (who was certainly an able man) was little open to flattery upon that head; for he was in no doubt himself about it; but his prevailing weakness was, to be thought to have a polite and happy turn to gallantry;—of which he had undoubtedly less than any man living: it was his favourite and frequent subject of conversation; which proved, to those who had any penetration, that it was his prevailing weakness. And they applied to it with success.

Women have, in general, but one object, which is their beauty; upon which, scarce any flattery is too gross for them to swallow. Nature has hardly formed a woman ugly enough to be insensible to flattery upon her person; if her face is so shocking, that she must in some degree be conscious of it, her figure and air, she trusts, make ample amends for it. If her figure is deformed, her face, she thinks, counterbalances it. If they are both bad, she comforts herself that she has graces; a certain manner; a *je ne sçais quoi*,[12] still more engaging than beauty. This truth is evident, from the studied and elaborate dress of the ugliest women in the world. An undoubted, uncontested, conscious beauty is, of all women, the least sensible of flattery upon that head; she knows that it is her due, and is therefore obliged to nobody for giving it her. She must be flattered upon her understanding; which, though she may possibly not doubt of herself, yet she suspects that men may distrust.

Do not mistake me, and think that I mean to recommend to you abject and criminal flattery: no; flatter nobody's vices or crimes: on the contrary, abhor and discourage them. But there is no living in the world without a complaisant indulgence for people's weaknesses, and innocent, though ridiculous vanities. If a man has a mind to be thought wiser, and a woman handsomer, than they really are, their error is a comfortable one to themselves, and an innocent one with regard to other people; and I would rather

[9] Incidentally.]
[10] Person of wit, grace, and intelligence.]
[11] Prime Minister, 1715–17, 1721–42.]
[12] I know not what.]

make them my friends, by indulging them in it, than my enemies, by endeavouring (and that to no purpose) to undeceive them.

There are little attentions likewise, which are infinitely engaging, and which sensibly affect that degree of pride and self-love, which is inseparable from human nature; as they are unquestionable proofs of the regard and consideration which we have for the persons to whom we pay them. As, for example, to observe the little habits, the likings, the antipathies, and the tastes of those whom we would gain; and then take care to provide them with the one, and to secure them from the other; giving them, genteelly, to understand, that you had observed they liked such a dish, or such a room; for which reason you had prepared it: or, on the contrary, that having observed they had an aversion to such a dish, a dislike to such a person, etc., you had taken care to avoid presenting them. Such attention to such trifles flatters self-love much more than greater things, as it makes people think themselves almost the only objects of your thoughts and care.

These are some of the *arcana* [13] necessary for your initiation in the great society of the world. I wish I had known them better at your age; I have paid the price of three and fifty years for them, and shall not grudge it, if you reap the advantage. Adieu.

BATH, FEBRUARY 22, O.S. 1748

DEAR BOY,

Every excellency, and every virtue, has its kindred vice or weakness; and if carried beyond certain bounds, sinks into the one or the other. Generosity often runs into profusion, œconomy into avarice, courage into rashness, caution into timidity, and so on;—insomuch that, I believe, there is more judgment required, for the proper conduct of our virtues, than for avoiding their opposite vices. Vice in its true light, is so deformed, that it shocks us at first sight, and would hardly ever seduce us, if it did not, at first, wear the mask of some virtue. But virtue is, in itself, so beautiful, that it charms us at first sight; engages us more and more upon farther acquaintance; and as with other beauties, we think excess impossible; it is here that judgment is necessary, to moderate and direct the effects of an excellent cause. I shall apply this reasoning, at present, not to any particular virtue, but to an excellency, which, for want of judgment, is often the cause of ridiculous and blameable effects; I mean, great learning; which, if not accompanied with sound judgment, frequently carries us into error, pride, and pedantry. As, I hope, you will possess that excellency in its utmost extent, and yet

[13 Secrets.]

without its too common failings, the hints, which my experience can suggest, may probably not be useless to you.

Some learned men, proud of their knowledge, only speak to decide, and give judgment without appeal; the consequence of which is, that mankind, provoked by the insult, and injured by the oppression, revolt; and in order to shake off the tyranny, even call the lawful authority in question. The more you know, the modester you should be: and (by-the-bye) that modesty is the surest way of gratifying your vanity. Even where you are sure, seem rather doubtful; represent, but do not pronounce, and if you would convince others, seem open to conviction yourself.

Others, to show their learning, or often from the prejudices of a school education, where they hear nothing else, are always talking of the ancients,[14] as something more than men, and of the moderns, as something less. They are never without a classic or two in their pockets; they stick to the old good sense; they read none of the modern trash; and will show you, plainly, that no improvement has been made, in any one art or science, these last seventeen hundred years. I would by no means have you disown your acquaintance with the ancients: but still less would I have you brag of an exclusive intimacy with them. Speak of the moderns without contempt, and of the ancients without idolatry; judge them all by their merits, but not by their ages; and if you happen to have an Elzevir classic [15] in your pocket, neither show it nor mention it.

Some great scholars, most absurdly, draw all their maxims, both for public and private life, from what they call parallel cases in the ancient authors; without considering that in the first place, there never were, since the creation of the world, two cases exactly parallel; and in the next place, that there never was a case stated, or even known, by any historian, with every one of its circumstances; which, however, ought to be known, in order to be reasoned from. Reason upon the case itself, and the several circumstances that attend it, and act accordingly; but not from the authority of ancient poets, or historians. Take into your consideration, if you please, cases seemingly analogous; but take them as helps only, not as guides. We are really so prejudiced by our education, that, as the ancients deified their heroes, we deify their mad-men; of which, with all due regard

[14 During the last part of the seventeenth and the first part of the eighteenth centuries there was a famous controversy in the literary world over the comparative merits of ancients and moderns. Swift's *Battle of the Books* was inspired by it.]

[15 A series of small, cheap editions of classics, somewhat like the modern Everyman's Library or Oxford World's Classics series.]

for antiquity, I take Leonidas and Curtius [16] to have been two distinguished ones. And yet a solid pedant would, in a speech in parliament, relative to a tax of twopence in the pound upon some commodity or other, quote those two heroes as examples of what we ought to do and suffer for our country. I have known these absurdities carried so far by people of injudicious learning, that I should not be surprised, if some of them were to propose, while we are at war with the Gauls, that a number of geese should be kept in the Tower, upon account of the infinite advantage which Rome received *in a parallel case*, from a certain number of geese in the Capitol.[17] This way of reasoning, and this way of speaking, will always form a poor politician, and a puerile declaimer.

There is another species of learned men who, though less dogmatical and supercilious, are not less impertinent. These are the communicative and shining pedants, who adorn their conversation, even with women, by happy quotations of Greek and Latin; and who have contracted such a familiarity with the Greek and Roman authors, that they call them by certain names or epithets denoting intimacy. As *old* Homer; that *sly rogue* Horace; *Maro*, instead of Virgil; and *Naso*, instead of Ovid. These are often imitated by coxcombs, who have no learning at all; but who have got some names and some scraps of ancient authors by heart, which they improperly and impertinently retail in all companies, in hopes of passing for scholars. If, therefore, you would avoid the accusation of pedantry on one hand, or the suspicion of ignorance on the other, abstain from learned ostentation. Speak the language of the company you are in; speak it purely, and unlarded with any other. Never seem wiser, nor more learned, than the people you are with. Wear your learning, like your watch, in a private pocket: and do not merely pull it out and strike it; merely to show that you have one. If you are asked what o'clock it is, tell it; but do not proclaim it hourly and unasked, like the watchman.

Upon the whole, remember that learning (I mean Greek and Roman learning) is a most useful and necessary ornament, which it is shameful not to be master of; but, at the same time, most carefully avoid those errors and abuses which I have mentioned, and which too often attend it. Re-

[16] Leonidas of Sparta defended Thermopylae against the Persian host in 480 B.C. A Roman legend told how, when the soothsayers proclaimed that a great crack in the Forum could be closed only by the sacrifice of Rome's greatest treasure, Curtius rode into the chasm. See Stevenson, p. 399.]

[17] The cackling of geese awakened Manlius Capitolinus when the Gauls began an attack on the Capitol (390 B.C.). He saved the Capitol, and ever afterward sacred geese were kept at public expense.]

member, too, that great modern knowledge is still more necessary than ancient; and that you had better know perfectly the present, than the old state of Europe; though I would have you well acquainted with both.

I have this moment received your letter of the 17th, N.S. Though, I confess, there is no great variety in your present manner of life, yet materials can never be wanting for a letter; you see, you hear, or you read something new every day; a short account of which, with your own reflections thereupon, will make out a letter very well. But since you desire a subject, pray send me an account of the Lutheran establishment in Germany; their religious tenets, their church government, the maintenance, authority, and titles of their clergy. . .

LONDON, SEPTEMBER 5, O.S. 1748

. . . As women are a considerable, or at least a pretty numerous part of company; and as their suffrages go a great way towards establishing a man's character in the fashionable part of the world (which is of great importance to the fortune and figure he proposes to make in it), it is necessary to please them. I will therefore, upon this subject, let you into certain *Arcana*, that will be very useful for you to know, but which you must, with the utmost care, conceal; and never seem to know. Women, then, are only children of a larger growth; they have an entertaining tattle, and sometimes wit; but for solid, reasoning good-sense, I never knew in my life one that had it, or who reasoned or acted consequentially for four and twenty hours together Some little passion or humour always break₃ in upon their best resolutions Their beauty neglected or controverted. their age increased, or their supposed understandings depreciated, instantly kindles their little passions, and overturns any system of consequential conduct, that in their most reasonable moments they might have been capable of forming. A man of sense only trifles with them, plays with them, humours and flatters them, as he does with a sprightly, forward child; but he neither consults them about, nor trusts them with serious matters; though he often makes them believe that he does both; which is the thing in the world that they are proud of; for they love mightily to be dabbling in business (which, by the way, they always spoil); and being justly distrustful, that men in general look upon them in a trifling light, they almost adore that man who talks more seriously to them, and who seems to consult and trust them; I say, who seems; for weak men really do, but wise ones only seem to do it. No flattery is either too high or too low for them. They will greedily swallow the highest, and gratefully accept of the lowest; and you may safely flatter any woman, from her understanding down to the exquisite taste of her fan. Women who are either indisputably beautiful, or indisputably ugly, are best flattered upon the score of their understandings; but those who are in a state of mediocrity, are best flattered upon their beauty, or at least their graces; for every woman, who is not absolutely ugly, thinks herself handsome; but not hearing often that she is so, is the more grateful, and the more obliged to the few who tell her so; whereas a decided and conscious beauty looks upon every tribute paid to her beauty only as her due; but wants to shine, and to be considered on the side of her understanding; and a woman who is ugly enough to know that she is so, knows that she has nothing left for it but her understanding, which is consequently (and probably in more senses than one) her weak side. But these are secrets, which you must keep inviolably, if you would not, like Orpheus,[18] be torn to pieces by the whole sex: on the contrary, a man who thinks of living in the great world, must be gallant, polite and attentive to please the women. They have, from the weakness of men, more or less influence in all courts; they absolutely stamp every man's character in the *beau monde*, and make it either current, or cry it down, and stop it in payments. It is, therefore, absolutely necessary to manage, please and flatter them: and never to discover the least mark of contempt, which is what they never forgive; but in this they are not singular, for it is the same with men; who will much sooner forgive an injustice than an insult. Every man is not ambitious, or covetous, or passionate; but every man has pride enough in his composition to feel and resent the least slight and contempt. Remember, therefore, most carefully to conceal your contempt, however just, wherever you would not make an implacable enemy. Men are much more unwilling to have their weaknesses and their imperfections known, than their crimes; and, if you hint to a man that you think him silly, ignorant, or even ill bred or awkward, he will hate you more and longer, than if you tell him plainly, that you think him a rogue. Never yield to that temptation, which to most young men is very strong, of exposing other people's weaknesses and infirmities, for the sake either of diverting the company, or showing your own superiority. You may get the laugh on your side by it for the present; but you will make enemies by it for ever; and even those who laugh with you then will, upon reflection fear, and consequently hate you: besides that it is ill natured, and a good heart desires rather to conceal than expose other people's weaknesses or misfortunes. If you have wit, use it to please, and

[18 He was torn to pieces by Thracian women.]

not to hurt: you may shine, like the sun in the temperate zones, without scorching. Here it is wished for: under the Line [19] it is dreaded.

These are some of the hints which my long experience in the great world enables me to give you; and which, if you attend to them, may prove useful to you, in your journey through it. I wish it may be a prosperous one; at least, I am sure that it must be your own fault if it is not.

Make my compliments to Mr. Harte,[20] who, I am very sorry to hear, is not well. I hope by this time he is recovered.

Adieu!

[19 The Equator.]
[20 His son's tutor and traveling companion.]

Virginia Woolf
LORD CHESTERFIELD'S LETTERS
TO HIS SON

❦ That subtle penetration into motive and character which is so remarkable in her fiction likewise distinguishes Virginia Woolf's biographical and critical essays. These are perhaps less widely known than *Mrs. Dalloway, To the Lighthouse, The Waves, Between the Acts,* and the other novels. Most of them are brief, some hardly more than miniatures; but they are all sharply focused and illuminating. And although miniatures, they frequently disclose the soul of the subject better than a full-length portrait could.

Mrs. Woolf's essays were collected in *The Common Reader* (1925), *The Second Common Reader* (1932), and three posthumous volumes, *The Death of the Moth* (1942), *The Moment* (1948), and *The Captain's Death Bed* (1950).

W̲HEN Lord Mahon edited the letters of Lord Chesterfield he thought it necessary to warn the intending reader that they are 'by no means fitted for early or indiscriminate perusal.' Only 'those people whose understandings are fixed and whose principles are matured' can, so his Lordship said, read them with impunity. But that was in 1845. And 1845 looks a little distant now. It seems to us now the age of enormous houses without any bathrooms. Men smoke in the kitchen after the cook has gone to bed. Albums lie upon drawing-room tables. The curtains are very thick and the women are very pure. But the eighteenth century also has undergone a change. To us in 1930 it looks less strange, less remote than those early Victorian years. Its civilisation seems more rational and more complete than the civilisation of Lord Mahon and his contempo-

FROM *The Second Common Reader,* by Virginia Woolf. Copyright 1932 by Harcourt, Brace, and Company, Inc. Reprinted by permission of Harcourt, Brace, and Company, Inc., and of The Hogarth Press, Ltd.

raries. Then at any rate a small group of highly educated people lived up
to their ideals. If the world was smaller it was also more compact; it knew
its own mind; it had its own standards. Its poetry is affected by the same
security. When we read the *Rape of the Lock* we seem to find ourselves in
an age so settled and so circumscribed that masterpieces were possible.
Then, we say to ourselves, a poet could address himself whole-heartedly to
his task and keep his mind upon it, so that the little boxes on a lady's
dressing-table are fixed among the solid possessions of our imaginations.
A game at cards or a summer's boating party upon the Thames has power
to suggest the same beauty and the same sense of things vanishing that we
receive from poems aimed directly at our deepest emotions. And just as the
poet could spend all his powers upon a pair of scissors and a lock of hair,
so too, secure in his world and its values, the aristocrat could lay down
precise laws for the education of his son. In that world also there was a
certainty, a security that we are now without. What with one thing and
another times have changed. We can now read Lord Chesterfield's letters
without blushing, or, if we do blush, we blush in the twentieth century at
passages that caused Lord Mahon no discomfort whatever.

When the letters begin, Philip Stanhope, Lord Chesterfield's natural
son by a Dutch governess, was a little boy of seven. And if we are to make
any complaint against the father's moral teaching, it is that the standard is
too high for such tender years. 'Let us return to oratory, or the art of speaking well; which should never be entirely out of our thoughts,' he writes to
the boy of seven. 'A man can make no figure without it in Parliament, or
the Church, or in the law,' he continues, as if the little boy were already
considering his career. It seems, indeed, that the father's fault, if fault it
be, is one common to distinguished men who have not themselves succeeded as they should have done and are determined to give their children
—and Philip was an only child—the chances that they have lacked. Indeed,
as the letters go on one may suppose that Lord Chesterfield wrote as much
to amuse himself by turning over the stores of his experience, his reading,
his knowledge of the world, as to instruct his son. The letters show an
eagerness, an animation which prove that to write to Philip was not a task,
but a delight. Tired, perhaps, with the duties of office and disillusioned
with its disappointments, he takes up his pen and, in the relief of free
communication at last, forgets that his correspondent is, after all, only a
schoolboy who cannot understand half the things that his father says to
him. But, even so, there is nothing to repel us in Lord Chesterfield's preliminary sketch of the unknown world. He is all on the side of moderation,

toleration, ratiocination. Never abuse whole bodies of people, he counsels; frequent all churches, laugh at none; inform yourself about all things. Devote your mornings to study, your evenings to good society. Dress as the best people dress, behave as they behave, never be eccentric, egotistical, or absent-minded. Observe the laws of proportion, and live every moment to the full.

So, step by step, he builds up the figure of the perfect man—the man that Philip may become, he is persuaded, if he will only—and here Lord Chesterfield lets fall the words which are to colour his teaching through and through—cultivate the Graces. These ladies are, at first, kept discreetly in the background. It is well that the boy should be indulged in fine sentiments about women and poets to begin with. Lord Chesterfield adjures him to respect them both. 'For my own part, I used to think myself in company as much above me when I was with Mr. Addison and Mr. Pope, as if I had been with all the Princes in Europe,' he writes. But as time goes on the Virtues are more and more taken for granted. They can be left to take care of themselves. But the Graces assume tremendous proportions. The Graces dominate the life of man in this world. Their service cannot for an instant be neglected. And the service is certainly exacting. For consider what it implies, this art of pleasing. To begin with, one must know how to come into a room and then how to go out again. As human arms and legs are notoriously perverse, this by itself is a matter needing considerable dexterity. Then one must be dressed so that one's clothes seem perfectly fashionable without being new or striking; one's teeth must be perfect; one's wig beyond reproach; one's finger-nails cut in the segment of a circle; one must be able to carve, able to dance, and, what is almost as great an art, able to sit gracefully in a chair. These things are the alphabet of the art of pleasing. We now come to speech. It is necessary to speak at least three languages to perfection. But before we open our lips we must take a further precaution—we must be on our guard never to laugh. Lord Chesterfield himself never laughed. He always smiled. When at length the young man is pronounced capable of speech he must avoid all proverbs and vulgar expressions; he must enunciate clearly and use perfect grammar; he must not argue; he must not tell stories; he must not talk about himself. Then, at last, the young man may begin to practise the finest of the arts of pleasing—the art of flattery. For every man and every woman has some prevailing vanity. Watch, wait, pry, seek out their weakness 'and you will then know what to bait your hook with to catch them.' For that is the secret of success in the world.

It is at this point, such is the idiosyncrasy of our age, that we begin to feel uneasy. Lord Chesterfield's views upon success are far more questionable than his views upon love. For what is to be the prize of this endless effort and self-abnegation? What do we gain when we have learnt to come into rooms and to go out again; to pry into people's secrets; to hold our tongues and to flatter, to forsake the society of low-born people which corrupts and the society of clever people which perverts? What is the prize which is to reward us? It is simply that we shall rise in the world. Press for a further definition, and it amounts perhaps to this: one will be popular with the best people. But if we are so exacting as to demand who the best people are we become involved in a labyrinth from which there is no returning. Nothing exists in itself. What is good society? It is the society that the best people believe to be good. What is wit? It is what the best people think to be witty. All value depends upon somebody else's opinion. For it is the essence of this philosophy that things have no independent existence, but live only in the eyes of other people. It is a looking-glass world, this, to which we climb so slowly; and its prizes are all reflections. That may account for our baffled feeling as we shuffle, and shuffle vainly, among these urbane pages for something hard to lay our hands upon. Hardness is the last thing we shall find. But, granted the deficiency, how much that is ignored by sterner moralists is here seized upon, and who shall deny, at least while Lord Chesterfield's enchantment is upon him, that these imponderable qualities have their value and these shining Graces have their radiance? Consider for a moment what the Graces have done for their devoted servant, the Earl.

Here is a disillusioned politician, who is prematurely aged, who has lost his office, who is losing his teeth, who, worst fate of all, is growing deafer day by day. Yet he never allows a groan to escape him. He is never dull; he is never boring; he is never slovenly. His mind is as well groomed as his body. Never for a second does he 'welter in an easy-chair.' Private though these letters are, and apparently spontaneous, they play with such ease in and about the single subject which absorbs them that it never becomes tedious or, what is still more remarkable, never becomes ridiculous. It may be that the art of pleasing has some connection with the art of writing. To be polite, considerate, controlled, to sink one's egotism, to conceal rather than to obtrude one's personality may profit the writer even as they profit the man of fashion.

Certainly there is much to be said in favour of the training, however we define it, which helped Lord Chesterfield to write his Characters. The little papers have the precision and formality of some old-fashioned minuet. Yet the symmetry is so natural to the artist that he can break it where he likes; it never becomes pinched and formal, as it would in the hands of an imitator. He can be sly; he can be witty; he can be sententious, but never for an instant does he lose his sense of time, and when the tune is over he calls a halt. 'Some succeeded, and others burst' he says of George the First's mistresses: the King liked them fat. Again, 'He was fixed in the house of lords, that hospital of incurables.' He smiles: he does not laugh. Here the eighteenth century, of course, came to his help. Lord Chesterfield, though he was polite to everything, even to the stars and Bishop Berkeley's [1] philosophy, firmly refused, as became a son of his age, to dally with infinity or to suppose that things are not quite as solid as they seem. The world was good enough and the world was big enough as it was. This prosaic temper, while it keeps him within the bounds of impeccable common sense, limits his outlook. No single phrase of his reverberates or penetrates as so many of La Bruyère's [2] do. But he would have been the first to deprecate any comparison with that great writer; besides, to write as La Bruyère wrote, one must perhaps believe in something, and then how difficult to observe the Graces! One might perhaps laugh; one might perhaps cry. Both are equally deplorable.

But while we amuse ourselves with this brilliant nobleman and his views on life we are aware, and the letters owe much of their fascination to this consciousness, of a dumb yet substantial figure on the farther side of the page. Philip Stanhope is always there. It is true that he says nothing, but we feel his presence in Dresden, in Berlin, in Paris, opening the letters and poring over them and looking dolefully at the thick packets which have been accumulating year after year since he was a child of seven. He had grown into a rather serious, rather stout, rather short young man. He had a taste for foreign politics. A little serious reading was rather to his liking. And by every post the letters came—urbane, polished, brilliant, imploring and commanding him to learn to dance, to learn to carve, to consider the management of his legs, and to seduce a lady of fashion. He did his best. He worked very hard in the school of the Graces, but their service was too exacting. He sat down half-way up the steep stairs which lead to the glittering hall with all the mirrors. He could not do it. He failed in the House of Commons; he subsided into some small post in Ratisbon; he died

[1] Irish philosopher (1685–1753). See the selection by Joad, pp. 505–11.]
[2] French author (1645–96) of *Caractères*, concise delineations of different human types.]

untimely. He left it to his widow to break the news which he had lacked the heart or the courage to tell his father—that he had been married all these years to a lady of low birth, who had borne him children.

The Earl took the blow like a gentleman. His letter to his daughter-in-law is a model of urbanity. He began the education of his grandsons. But he seems to have become a little indifferent to what happened to himself after that. He did not care greatly if he lived or died. But still to the very end he cared for the Graces. His last words were a tribute of respect to those goddesses. Some one [3] came into the room when he was dying; he roused himself: 'Give Dayrolles a chair,' he said, and said no more.

[3 Dayrolles was Chesterfield's godson, his secretary when Chesterfield was British Ambassador at The Hague, and his close friend.]

James Boswell

JOHNSON, CHESTERFIELD, AND
THE *DICTIONARY*

❬ Boswell's *Life of Johnson* has for a long time been adjudged the greatest biography in the English language. Boswell affirmed of his hero that 'he will be seen in this work more completely than any man who has ever yet lived.' Until a generation ago Johnson was, quite properly and quite naturally, the main subject of interest to students of Boswell's book. This is no longer true. Much of the interest and study has shifted to Boswell himself. Thanks to the astonishing number of Boswell's journals and papers discovered in recent years, we now know more about Boswell than about Johnson; in fact, more about Boswell than about any other writer in history. It is he, not Dr. Johnson, who, when these documents are published, will be seen 'more completely than any man who has ever yet lived.' As a man of letters Boswell has been frequently reappraised in recent years. These reappraisals are incomplete, but it seems agreed that his stature as biographer and literary artist will, in the future, be higher than ever.

L̲ORD CHESTERFIELD,[1] to whom Johnson had paid the high compliment of addressing to his Lordship the Plan of his Dictionary, had behaved to him in such a manner as to excite his contempt and indignation. The world has been for many years amused with a story confidently told, and as confidently repeated with additional circumstances, that a sudden disgust was taken by Johnson upon occasion of his having been one day kept long in waiting in his Lordship's antechamber, for which the reason assigned was, that he had company with him; and that at last, when the door opened, out walked Colley Cibber;[2] and that Johnson was so

[1 See pp. 338–57.]
[2 Playwright and poet (1671–1757); Poet Laureate from 1730. Pope ridiculed him in the *Dunciad*.]
F<small>ROM</small> Boswell's *Life of Johnson,* 1791.

violently provoked when he found for whom he had been so long excluded, that he went away in a passion, and never would return. I remember having mentioned this story to George Lord Lyttelton, who told me, he was very intimate with Lord Chesterfield; and holding it as a well-known truth, defended Lord Chesterfield by saying, that 'Cibber, who had been introduced familiarly by the backstairs, had probably not been there above ten minutes.' It may seem strange even to entertain a doubt concerning a story so long and so widely current, and thus implicitly adopted, if not sanctioned, by the authority which I have mentioned; but Johnson himself assured me, that there was not the least foundation for it. He told me, that there never was any particular incident which produced a quarrel between Lord Chesterfield and him; but that his Lordship's continued neglect was the reason why he resolved to have no connection with him. When the Dictionary was upon the eve of publication, Lord Chesterfield, who, it is said, had flattered himself with expectations that Johnson would dedicate the work to him, attempted, in a courtly manner, to soothe and insinuate himself with the Sage, conscious, as it should seem, of the cold indifference with which he had treated its learned authour; and further attempted to conciliate him, by writing two papers in 'The World,' in recommendation of the work; and it must be confessed, that they contain some studied compliments, so finely turned, that if there had been no previous offence, it is probable that Johnson would have been highly delighted. Praise, in general, was pleasing to him; but by praise from a man of rank and elegant accomplishments, he was peculiarly gratified.

His Lordship says, 'I think the publick in general, and the republick of letters in particular, are greatly obliged to Mr. Johnson, for having undertaken, and executed so great and desirable a work. Perfection is not to be expected from man; but if we are to judge by the various works of Johnson already published, we have good reason to believe, that he will bring this as near to perfection as any man could do. The Plan of it, which he published some years ago, seems to me to be a proof of it. Nothing can be more rationally imagined, or more accurately and elegantly expressed. I therefore recommend the previous perusal of it to all those who intend to buy the Dictionary, and who, I suppose, are all those who can afford it.'

'It must be owned, that our language is, at present, in a state of anarchy, and hitherto, perhaps, it may not have been the worse for it. During our free and open trade, many words and expressions have been imported, adopted, and naturalized from other languages, which have greatly enriched our own. Let it still preserve what real strength and beauty it may have borrowed from others; but let it not, like the Tarpeian maid,³ be overwhelmed and crushed by unnecessary ornaments. The time for discrimination seems to be now come. Toleration, adoption, and naturalization have run their lengths. Good order and authority are now necessary. But where shall we find them, and at the same time, the obedience due to them? We must have recourse to the old Roman expedient in times of confusion, and chuse a dictator. Upon this principle, I give my vote for Mr. Johnson to fill that great and arduous post. And I hereby declare, that I make a total surrender of all my rights and privileges in the English language, as a free-born British subject, to the said Mr. Johnson, during the term of his dictatorship. Nay more, I will not only obey him like an old Roman, as my dictator, but, like a modern Roman, I will implicitly believe in him as my Pope, and hold him to be infallible while in the chair, but no longer. More than this he cannot well require; for, I presume, that obedience can never be expected, where there is neither terrour to enforce, nor interest to invite it.'

'But a Grammar, a Dictionary, and a History of our Language, through its several stages, were still wanting at home, and importunately called for from abroad. Mr. Johnson's labours will now, I dare say, very fully supply that want, and greatly contribute to the farther spreading of our language in other countries. Learners were discouraged, by finding no standard to resort to; and, consequently, thought it incapable of any. They will now be undeceived and encouraged.'

This courtly device failed of its effect. Johnson, who thought that 'all was false and hollow,'⁴ despised the honeyed words, and was even indignant that Lord Chesterfield should, for a moment, imagine, that he could be the dupe of such an artifice. His expression to me concerning Lord Chesterfield, upon this occasion, was, 'Sir, after making great professions, he had, for many years, taken no notice of me; but when my Dictionary was coming out, he fell a scribbling in "The World" about it. Upon which, I wrote him a letter expressed in civil terms, but such as might shew him that I did not mind what he said or wrote, and that I had done with him.'

This is that celebrated letter of which so much has been said, and about

[³ Tarpeia treacherously opened the gates of Rome to the Sabines in return for their promise to give her what they had on their left arms, i.e. their bracelets. When the Sabine king entered the city, he threw his shield as well as his bracelet on her. His followers did the same, and she was killed by the weight of the shields.]

[⁴ Milton, *Paradise Lost*, II, 112.]

which curiosity has been so long excited, without being gratified. I for many years solicited Johnson to favour me with a copy of it, that so excellent a composition might not be lost to posterity. He delayed from time to time to give it me; * till at last in 1781, when we were on a visit at Mr. Dilly's, at Southill in Bedfordshire, he was pleased to dictate it to me from memory. He afterwards found among his papers a copy of it, which he had dictated to Mr. Baretti, with its title and corrections, in his own handwriting. This he gave to Mr. Langton; adding that if it were to come into print, he wished it to be from that copy. By Mr. Langton's kindness, I am enabled to enrich my work with a perfect transcript of what the world has so eagerly desired to see.

'TO THE RIGHT HONOURABLE THE EARL OF CHESTERFIELD.

'MY LORD,   FEBRUARY 7, 1755.

'I have been lately informed, by the proprietor of the World, that two papers, in which my Dictionary is recommended to the publick, were written by your Lordship. To be so distinguished, is an honour, which, being very little accustomed to favours from the great, I know not well how to receive, or in what terms to acknowledge.

'When, upon some slight encouragement, I first visited your Lordship, I was overpowered, like the rest of mankind, by the enchantment of your address, and could not forbear to wish that I might boast myself *Le vainqueur du vainqueur de la terre;*—⁵ that I might obtain that regard for which I saw the world contending; but I found my attendance so little encouraged, that neither pride nor modesty would suffer me to continue it. When I had once addressed your Lordship in publick, I had exhausted all the art of pleasing which a retired and uncourtly scholar can possess. I had done all that I could; and no man is well pleased to have his all neglected, be it ever so little.

'Seven years, my Lord, have now past, since I waited in your outward rooms, or was repulsed from your door; during which time I have been

---

* Dr. Johnson appeared to have had a remarkable delicacy with respect to the circulation of this letter; for Dr. Douglas, Bishop of Salisbury, informs me that having many years ago pressed him to be allowed to read it to the second Lord Hardwicke, who was very desirous to hear it (promising at the same time, that no copy of it should be taken), Johnson seemed much pleased that it had attracted the attention of a nobleman of such a respectable character; but after pausing some time, declined to comply with the request, saying, with a smile, 'No, Sir; I have hurt the dog too much already'; or words to that purpose.

[⁵ 'The conqueror of the conqueror of the earth.']

pushing on my work through difficulties, of which it is useless to complain, and have brought it, at last, to the verge of publication, without one act of assistance,* one word of encouragement, or one smile of favour. Such treatment I did not expect, for I never had a Patron before.

'The shepherd in Virgil⁶ grew at last acquainted with Love, and found him a native of the rocks.

'Is not a Patron, my Lord, one who looks with unconcern on a man struggling for life in the water, and, when he has reached ground, encumbers him with help? The notice which you have been pleased to take of my labours, had it been early, had been kind; but it has been delayed till I am indifferent, and cannot enjoy it; till I am solitary, and cannot impart it; * till I am known, and do not want it. I hope it is no very cynical asperity not to confess obligations where no benefit has been received, or to be unwilling that the Publick should consider me as owing that to a Patron, which Providence has enabled me to do for myself.

'Having carried on my work thus far with so little obligation to any favourer of learning, I shall not be disappointed though I should conclude it, if less be possible, with less; for I have been long wakened from that dream of hope, in which I once boasted myself with so much exultation,

'My Lord,

'Your Lordship's most humble

'Most obedient servant,

'SAM. JOHNSON.' †

* The following note is subjoined by Mr. Langton. 'Dr. Johnson, when he gave me this copy of his letter, desired that I would annex to it his information to me, that whereas it is said in the letter that "no assistance has been received," he did once receive from Lord Chesterfield the sum of ten pounds, but as that was so inconsiderable a sum, he thought the mention of it could not properly find a place in a letter of the kind that this was.'

[⁶ *Eclogues*, VIII, 43–5.]

* In this passage Dr. Johnson evidently alludes to the loss of his wife. We find the same tender recollection recurring to his mind upon innumerable occasions; and, perhaps no man ever more forcibly felt the truth of the sentiment so elegantly expressed by my friend Mr. Malone, in his Prologue to Mr. Jephson's tragedy of JULIA:

'Vain—wealth, and fame, and fortune's fostering care,
'If no fond breast the splendid blessings share;
'And, each day's bustling pageantry once past,
'There, only there, our bliss is found at last.'

† Upon comparing this copy with that which Dr. Johnson dictated to me from recollection, the variations are found to be so slight, that this must be added to the many other proofs which he gave of the wonderful extent and accuracy of his memory. To gratify the curious in composition, I have deposited both the copies in the British Museum.

There is a curious minute circumstance which struck me, in comparing the various editions of Johnson's Imitations of Juvenal. In the tenth Satire one of the couplets upon the vanity of wishes even for literary distinction stood thus:

> 'Yet think what ills the scholar's life assail,
> 'Toil, envy, want, the *garret*, and the jail.'

But after experiencing the uneasiness which Lord Chesterfield's fallacious patronage made him feel, he dismissed the word *garret* from the sad group, and in all the subsequent editions the line stands,

> 'Toil, envy, want, the *Patron*, and the jail.'

That Lord Chesterfield must have been mortified by the lofty contempt, and polite, yet keen, satire with which Johnson exhibited him to himself in this letter, it is impossible to doubt. He, however, with that glossy duplicity which was his constant study, affected to be quite unconcerned. Dr. Adams mentioned to Mr. Robert Dodsley [7] that he was sorry Johnson had written his letter to Lord Chesterfield. Dodsley, with the true feelings of trade, said 'he was very sorry too; for that he had a property in the Dictionary, to which his Lordship's patronage might have been of consequence.' He then told Dr. Adams, that Lord Chesterfield had shewn him the letter. 'I should have imagined (replied Dr. Adams) that Lord Chesterfield would have concealed it.' 'Poh! (said Dodsley) do you think a letter from Johnson could hurt Lord Chesterfield? Not at all, Sir. It lay upon his table, where any body might see it. He read it to me; said, "this man has great powers," pointed out the severest passages, and observed how well they were expressed.' This air of indifference, which imposed upon the worthy Dodsley, was certainly nothing but a specimen of that dissimulation which Lord Chesterfield inculcated as one of the most essential lessons for the conduct of life. His Lordship endeavoured to justify himself to Dodsley from the charges brought against him by Johnson; but we may judge of the flimsiness of his defence, from his having excused his neglect of Johnson, by saying, that 'he had heard he had changed his lodgings, and did not know where he lived'; as if there could have been the smallest difficulty to inform himself of that circumstance, by enquiring in the literary circle with which his Lordship was well acquainted, and was, indeed, himself, one of its ornaments.

Dr. Adams expostulated with Johnson, and suggested, that his not being

[7 A prominent bookseller.]

admitted when he called on him, was probably not to be imputed to Lord Chesterfield; for his Lordship had declared to Dodsley, that 'he would have turned off the best servant he ever had, if he had known that he denied him to a man who would have been always more than welcome'; and in confirmation of this, he insisted on Lord Chesterfield's general affability and easiness of access, especially to literary men. 'Sir, (said Johnson) that is not Lord Chesterfield; he is the proudest man this day existing.' 'No, (said Dr. Adams) there is one person, at least, as proud; I think, by your own account you are the prouder man of the two.' 'But mine (replied Johnson instantly) was *defensive* pride.' This, as Dr. Adams well observed, was one of those happy turns for which he was so remarkably ready.

Johnson having now explicitly avowed his opinion of Lord Chesterfield, did not refrain from expressing himself concerning that nobleman with pointed freedom: 'This man (said he) I thought had been a Lord among wits; but, I find, he is only a wit among Lords!' And when his Letters to his natural son were published, he observed, that 'they teach the morals of a whore, and the manners of a dancing-master.' *

The Dictionary, with a Grammar and History of the English Language, being now at length published, in two volumes folio, the world contemplated with wonder so stupendous a work achieved by one man, while other countries had thought such undertakings fit only for whole academies. Vast as his powers were, I cannot but think that his imagination deceived him, when he supposed that by constant application he might

* That collection of letters cannot be vindicated from the serious charge, of encouraging, in some passages, one of the vices most destructive to the good order and comfort of society, which his Lordship represents as mere fashionable gallantry; and, in others, of inculcating the base practice of dissimulation, and recommending, with disproportionate anxiety, a perpetual attention to external elegance of manners. But it must, at the same time, be allowed, that they contain many good precepts of conduct, and much genuine information upon life and manners, very happily expressed; and that there was considerable merit in paying so much attention to the improvement of one who was dependent upon his Lordship's protection; it has, probably, been exceeded in no instance by the most exemplary parent; and though I can by no means approve of confounding the distinction between lawful and illicit offspring, which is, in effect, insulting the civil establishment of our country, to look no higher; I cannot help thinking it laudable to be kindly attentive to those, of whose existence we have, in any way, been the cause. Mr. Stanhope's character has been unjustly represented as diametrically opposite to what Lord Chesterfield wished him to be. He has been called dull, gross, and aukward: but I knew him at Dresden, when he was Envoy to that court; and though he could not boast of the *graces,* he was, in truth, a sensible, civil, well-behaved man.

have performed the task in three years. Let the Preface be attentively perused, in which is given, in a clear, strong, and glowing style, a comprehensive, yet particular view of what he had done; and it will be evident, that the time he employed upon it was comparatively short. I am unwilling to swell my book with long quotations from what is in every body's hands, and I believe there are few prose compositions in the English language that are read with more delight, or are more impressed upon the memory, than that preliminary discourse. One of its excellencies has always struck me with peculiar admiration; I mean the perspicuity with which he has expressed abstract scientifick notions. As an instance of this, I shall quote the following sentence: 'When the radical idea branches out into parallel ramifications, how can a consecutive series be formed of senses in their own nature collateral?' We have here an example of what has been often said, and I believe with justice, that there is for every thought a certain nice adaptation of words which none other could equal, and which, when a man has been so fortunate as to hit, he has attained, in that particular case, the perfection of language.

The extensive reading which was absolutely necessary for the accumulation of authorities, and which alone may account for Johnson's retentive mind being enriched with a very large and various store of knowledge and imagery, must have occupied several years. The Preface furnishes an eminent instance of a double talent, of which Johnson was fully conscious. Sir Joshua Reynolds [8] heard him say, 'There are two things which I am confident I can do very well: one is an introduction to any literary work, stating what it is to contain, and how it should be executed in the most perfect manner: the other is a conclusion, shewing from various causes why the execution has not been equal to what the authour promised to himself and to the publick.'

How should puny scribblers be abashed and disappointed, when they find him displaying a perfect theory of lexicographical excellence, yet at the same time candidly and modestly allowing that he 'had not satisfied his own expectations.' Here was a fair occasion for the exercise of Johnson's modesty, when he was called upon to compare his own arduous performance, not with those of other individuals, (in which case his inflexible regard to truth would have been violated had he affected diffidence,) but with speculative perfection; as he, who can outstrip all his competitors in the race, may yet be sensible of his deficiency when he runs against time.

[8 The famous painter. He was a close friend of Dr. Johnson.]

Well might he say, that 'the English Dictionary was written with little assistance of the learned'; for he told me, that the only aid which he received was a paper containing twenty etymologies, sent to him by a person then unknown, who he was afterwards informed was Dr. Pearce, Bishop of Rochester. The etymologies, though they exhibit learning and judgement, are not, I think, entitled to the first praise amongst the various parts of this immense work. The definitions have always appeared to me such astonishing proofs of acuteness of intellect and precision of language, as indicate a genius of the highest rank. This it is which marks the superior excellence of Johnson's Dictionary over others equally or even more voluminous, and must have made it a work of much greater mental labour than mere Lexicons, or *Word-Books*, as the Dutch call them. They, who will make the experiment of trying how they can define a few words of whatever nature, will soon be satisfied of the unquestionable justice of this observation, which I can assure my readers is founded upon much study, and upon communication with more minds than my own.

A few of his definitions must be admitted to be erroneous. Thus, *Windward* and *Leeward*, though directly of opposite meaning, are defined identically the same way; as to which inconsiderable specks it is enough to observe, that his Preface announces that he was aware there might be many such in so immense a work; nor was he at all disconcerted when an instance was pointed out to him. A lady once asked him how he came to define *Pastern* the *knee* of a horse: instead of making an elaborate defence, as she expected, he at once answered, 'Ignorance, Madam, pure ignorance.' His definition of *Network* [9] has been often quoted with sportive malignity, as obscuring a thing in itself very plain. But to these frivolous censures no other answer is necessary than that with which we are furnished by his own Preface. 'To explain, requires the use of terms less abstruse than that which is to be explained, and such terms cannot always be found. For as nothing can be proved but by supposing something intuitively known, and evident without proof, so nothing can be defined but by the use of words too plain to admit of definition. Sometimes easier words are changed into harder; as *burial*, into *sepulture* or *interment*; *dry*, into *desiccative*; *dryness*, into *siccity*, or *aridity*; *fit*, into *paroxism*; for, the *easiest* word, whatever it be, can never be translated into one more easy.'

His introducing his own opinions, and even prejudices, under general definitions of words, while at the same time the original meaning of the

[9 'Network. Anything reticulated or decussated, at equal distances, with interstices between the intersections.']

words is not explained, as his *Tory*, *Whig*, *Pension*, *Oats*, *Excise*,* and a few more, cannot be fully defended, and must be placed to the account of capricious and humourous indulgence. Talking to me upon this subject when we were at Ashbourne in 1777, he mentioned a still stronger instance of the predominance of his private feelings in the composition of this work, than any now to be found in it. 'You know, Sir, Lord Gower forsook the old Jacobite interest. When I came to the *Renegado*, after telling that it meant "one who deserts to the enemy, a revolter," I added, *Sometimes we say a* GOWER. Thus it went to the press: but the printer had more wit than I, and struck it out.'

Let it, however, be remembered, that this indulgence does not display itself only in sarcasm towards others, but sometimes in playful allusion to the notions commonly entertained of his own laborious task. Thus: '*Grub-street*, the name of a street in London, much inhabited by writers of small histories, *dictionaries*, and temporary poems; whence any mean production is called *Grub-street*.'—'*Lexicographer*, a writer of dictionaries, a *harmless drudge*.'

At the time when he was concluding his very eloquent Preface, Johnson's mind appears to have been in such a state of depression, that we cannot contemplate without wonder the vigourous and splendid thoughts which so highly distinguish that performance. 'I (says he) may surely be contented without the praise of perfection, which if I could obtain in this gloom of solitude, what would it avail me? I have protracted my work till most of those whom I wished to please have sunk into the grave; and success and miscarriage are empty sounds. I therefore dismiss it with frigid tranquillity, having little to fear or hope from censure or from praise.' That

---

* He thus defines Excise: 'A hateful tax levied upon commodities, and adjudged not by the common judges of property, but wretches hired by those to whom Excise is paid.' The Commissioners of Excise being offended by this severe reflection, consulted Mr. Murray, then Attorney-General, to know whether redress could be legally obtained. I wished to have procured for my readers a copy of the opinion which he gave, and which may now be justly considered as history: but the mysterious secresy of office it seems would not permit it. I am, however, informed by very good authority, that its import was, that the passage might be considered as actionable; but that it would be more prudent in the board not to prosecute. Johnson never made the smallest alteration in this passage. We find he still retained his early prejudice against Excise; for in 'The Idler, No. 65,' there is the following very extraordinary paragraph: 'The authenticity of *Clarendon's* history, though printed with the sanction of one of the first Universities of the world, had not an unexpected manuscript been happily discovered, would, with the help of factious credulity, have been brought into question, by the two lowest of all human beings, a Scribbler for a party, and a Commissioner of Excise.' The persons to whom he alludes were Mr. John Oldmixon, and George Ducket, Esq.

this indifference was rather a temporary than an habitual feeling, appears, I think, from his letters to Mr. Warton; and however he may have been affected for the moment, certain it is that the honours which his great work procured him, both at home and abroad, were very grateful to him. His friend the Earl of Corke and Orrery, being at Florence, presented it to the *Academia della Crusca.* That Academy sent Johnson their *Vocabulario,* and the French Academy sent him their *Dictionnaire,* which Mr. Langton had the pleasure to convey to him.

It must undoubtedly seem strange, that the conclusion of his Preface should be expressed in terms so desponding, when it is considered that the authour was then only in his forty-sixth year. But we must ascribe its gloom to that miserable dejection of spirits to which he was constitutionally sub- ject, and which was aggravated by the death of his wife two years before. I have heard it ingeniously observed by a lady of rank and elegance, that 'his melancholy was then at its meridian.' It pleased God to grant him almost thirty years of life after this time; and once when he was in a placid frame of mind, he was obliged to own to me that he had enjoyed happier days, and had many more friends, since that gloomy hour, than before.

It is a sad saying, that 'most of those whom he wished to please had sunk into the grave'; and his case at forty-five was singularly unhappy, unless the circle of his friends was very narrow. I have often thought, that as longevity is generally desired, and I believe, generally expected, it would be wise to be continually adding to the number of our friends, that the loss of some may be supplied by others. Friendship, 'the wine of life,' should, like a well- stocked cellar, be thus continually renewed; and it is consolatory to think, that although we can seldom add what will equal the generous *first-growths* of our youth, yet friendship becomes insensibly old in much less time than is commonly imagined, and not many years are required to make it very mellow and pleasant. *Warmth* will, no doubt, make a considerable differ- ence. Men of affectionate temper and bright fancy will coalesce a great deal sooner than those who are cold and dull.

The proposition which I have now endeavoured to illustrate was, at a subsequent period of his life, the opinion of Johnson himself. He said to Sir Joshua Reynolds, 'If a man does not make new acquaintance as he advances through life, he will soon find himself left alone. A man, Sir, should keep his friendship *in constant repair.*'

The celebrated Mr. Wilkes, whose notions and habits of life were very opposite to his, but who was ever eminent for literature and vivacity, sallied forth with a little *Jeu d'Esprit* upon the following passage in his Grammar of the English Tongue, prefixed to the Dictionary: 'H seldom, perhaps never, begins any but the first syllable.' In an essay printed in 'the Public Advertiser,' this lively writer enumerated many instances in opposition to this remark; for example, 'The authour of this observation must be a man of a quick *appre-hension*, and of a most *compre-hensive* genius.' The position is undoubtedly expressed with too much latitude.

This light sally, we may suppose, made no great impression on our Lexicographer; for we find that he did not alter the passage till many years afterwards.*

He had the pleasure of being treated in a very different manner by his old pupil Mr. Garrick, in the following complimentary Epigram:

'On JOHNSON'S DICTIONARY.

'TALK of war with a Briton, he'll boldly advance,
'That one English soldier will beat ten of France;
'Would we alter the boast from the sword to the pen,
'Our odds are still greater, still greater our men;
'In the deep mines of science though Frenchmen may toil,
'Can their strength be compar'd to Locke, Newton, and Boyle?
'Let them rally their heroes, send forth all their pow'rs,
'Their verse-men and prose-men, then match them with ours!
'First Shakspeare and Milton, like Gods in the fight,
'Have put their whole drama and epick to flight;
'In satires, epistles, and odes, would they cope,
'Their numbers retreat before Dryden and Pope;
'And Johnson, well-arm'd like a hero of yore,
'Has beat forty French, † and will beat forty more!'

---

* In the third edition, published in 1773, he left out the words *perhaps never*, and added the following paragraph:

'It sometimes begins middle or final syllables in words compounded, as *block-head*, or derived from the Latin, as *comprehended*.'

† The number of the French Academy employed in settling their language.

David Hume

OF QUALITIES IMMEDIATELY AGREEABLE TO OTHERS *

❡ Hume is famous in the history of philosophy for the perplexing questions he asked in his *Treatise of Human Nature* (1739) and *Enquiry Concerning Human Understanding* (1748) about the nature of knowledge, and for his skeptical answers to those questions. He liked to think of himself as a man of letters rather than as a 'philosopher,' however, and he was as much concerned about the success of his *History of Great Britain* (1754–61) and his *Essays* as about the treatises on knowledge.

His *Enquiry Concerning the Principles of Morals* was, in his own judgment, 'of all my writings, historical, philosophical, or literary, incomparably the best.' He finds morality to be based on experience and utility; a custom is good because it is useful. And if it is useful, it receives our approbation. Hence 'Whatever is valuable in any kind so naturally classifies itself under the division of *useful* or *agreeable*, the *utile* or the *dulce*, that it is not easy to imagine why we should ever seek further, or consider the question as a matter of nice research or enquiry.' In the chapter on qualities agreeable to others, Hume's outlook is characteristic of much of the ethics and criticism of his age. Decorum is the ideal; in life, as in art, 'disproportions hurt the eye.' He himself was an example of agreeableness: 'a man,' as he says, 'of mild disposition, of command of temper, of an open, social, and cheerful humour, capable of attachment, but little susceptible of enmity, and of great moderation in all my passions.'

---

* It is the nature and, indeed, the definition of virtue, that it is *a quality of the mind agreeable to or approved of by every one who considers or contemplates it*. But some qualities produce pleasure, because they are useful to society, or useful or agreeable to the person himself; others produce it more immediately, which is the case with the class of virtues here considered.

FROM *An Enquiry Concerning the Principles of Morals*, 1751.

As the mutual shocks, in *society*, and the oppositions of interest and self-love have constrained mankind to establish the laws of *justice*, in order to preserve the advantages of mutual assistance and protection: in like manner, the eternal contrarieties, in *company*, of men's pride and self-conceit, have introduced the rules of Good Manners or Politeness, in order to facilitate the intercourse of minds, and an undisturbed commerce and conversation. Among well-bred people, a mutual deference is affected; contempt of others disguised; authority concealed; attention given to each in his turn; and an easy stream of conversation maintained, without vehemence, without interruption, without eagerness for victory, and without any airs of superiority. These attentions and regards are immediately *agreeable* to others, abstracted from any consideration of utility or beneficial tendencies: they conciliate affection, promote esteem, and extremely enhance the merit of the person who regulates his behaviour by them.

Many of the forms of breeding are arbitrary and casual; but the thing expressed by them is still the same. A Spaniard goes out of his own house before his guest, to signify that he leaves him master of all. In other countries, the landlord walks out last, as a common mark of deference and regard.

But, in order to render a man perfect *good company*, he must have Wit and Ingenuity as well as good manners. What wit is, it may not be easy to define; but it is easy surely to determine that it is a quality immediately *agreeable* to others, and communicating, on its first appearance, a lively joy and satisfaction to every one who has any comprehension of it. The most profound metaphysics, indeed, might be employed in explaining the various kinds and species of wit; and many classes of it, which are now received on the sole testimony of taste and sentiment, might, perhaps, be resolved into more general principles. But this is sufficient for our present purpose, that it does affect taste and sentiment, and bestowing an immediate enjoyment, is a sure source of approbation and affection.

In countries where men pass most of their time in conversation, and visits, and assemblies, these *companionable* qualities, so to speak, are of high estimation, and form a chief part of personal merit. In countries where men live a more domestic life, and either are employed in business, or amuse themselves in a narrower circle of acquaintance, the more solid qualities are chiefly regarded. Thus, I have often observed that among the French [1] the first questions with regard to a stranger are, *Is he polite? Has he wit?* In our own country, the chief praise bestowed is always that of a *good-natured, sensible fellow.*

In conversation, the lively spirit of dialogue is *agreeable,* even to those who desire not to have any share in the discourse: hence the teller of long stories, or the pompous declaimer, is very little approved of. But most men desire likewise their turn in the conversation, and regard, with a very evil eye, that *loquacity* which deprives them of a right they are naturally so jealous of.

There is a sort of harmless *liars,* frequently to be met with in company, who deal much in the marvellous. Their usual intention is to please and entertain; but as men are most delighted with what they conceive to be truth, these people mistake extremely the means of pleasing, and incur universal blame. Some indulgence, however, to lying or fiction is given in *humorous* stories; because it is there really agreeable and entertaining, and truth is not of any importance.

Eloquence, genius of all kinds, even good sense, and sound reasoning, when it rises to an eminent degree, and is employed upon subjects of any considerable dignity and nice discernment; all these endowments seem immediately agreeable, and have a merit distinct from their usefulness. Rarity, likewise, which so much enhances the price of every thing, must set an additional value on these noble talents of the human mind.

Modesty may be understood in different senses, even abstracted from chastity, which has been already treated of. It sometimes means that tenderness and nicety of honour, that apprehension of blame, that dread of intrusion or injury towards others, that Pudor, which is the proper guardian of every kind of virtue, and a sure preservative against vice and corruption. But its most usual meaning is when it is opposed to *impudence* and *arrogance,* and expresses a diffidence of our own judgement, and a due attention and regard for others. In young men chiefly, this quality is a sure sign of good sense; and is also the certain means of augmenting that endowment, by preserving their ears open to instruction, and making them still grasp after new attainments. But it has a further charm to every spectator; by flattering every man's vanity, and presenting the appearance of a docile pupil, who receives, with proper attention and respect, every word they utter.

[1 Hume lived in France from 1734 to 1737 and from 1763 to 1765.]

Men have, in general, a much greater propensity to overvalue than undervalue themselves; notwithstanding the opinion of Aristotle.* This makes us more jealous of the excess on the former side, and causes us to regard, with a peculiar indulgence, all tendency to modesty and self-diffidence; as esteeming the danger less of falling into any vicious extreme of that nature. It is thus in countries where men's bodies are apt to exceed in corpulency, personal beauty is placed in a much greater degree of slenderness, than in countries where that is the most usual defect. Being so often struck with instances of one species of deformity, men think they can never keep at too great a distance from it, and wish always to have a leaning to the opposite side. In like manner, were the door opened to self-praise, and were Montaigne's [3] maxim observed, that one should say as frankly, *I have sense, I have learning, I have courage, beauty, or wit*, as it is sure we often think so; were this the case, I say, every one is sensible that such a flood of impertinence would break in upon us, as would render society wholly intolerable. For this reason custom has established it as a rule, in common societies, that men should not indulge themselves in self-praise, or even speak much of themselves; and it is only among intimate friends or people of very manly behaviour, that one is allowed to do himself justice. Nobody finds fault with Maurice,[4] Prince of Orange, for his reply to one who asked him, whom he esteemed the first general of the age, *The Marquis of Spinola*, said he, *is the second*. Though it is observable, that the self-praise implied is here better implied, than if it had been directly expressed, without any cover or disguise.

He must be a very superficial thinker, who imagines that all instances of mutual deference are to be understood in earnest, and that a man would be more esteemable for being ignorant of his own merits and accomplishments. A small bias towards modesty, even in the internal sentiment, is favourably regarded, especially in young people; and a strong bias is required in the outward behaviour; but this excludes not a noble pride and spirit, which may openly display itself in its full extent, when one lies under calumny or oppression of any kind. The generous contumacy of Socrates, as Cicero calls it, has been highly celebrated in all ages; and when joined to the usual modesty of his behaviour, forms a shining character. Iphicrates, the Athenian, being accused of betraying the interests of his coun-

* Ethic. ad Nicomachum.[2]

[2 It is not clear which passage in the *Nicomachean Ethics* Hume alludes to. Compare IV, vii; IX, iv; IX, viii, 1–8.]

[3 Miguel de Montaigne (1533–92), famous for his *Essais*.]

[4 Maurice of Nassau (1567–1625).]

try, asked his accuser, *Would you*, says he, *have, on a like occasion, been guilty of that crime? By no means*, replied the other. *And can you then imagine*, cried the hero, *that* Iphicrates *would be guilty?* * In short, a generous spirit and self-value, well founded, decently disguised, and courageously supported under distress and calumny, is a great excellency, and seems to derive its merit from the noble elevation of its sentiment, or its immediate agreeableness to its possessor. In ordinary characters, we approve of a bias towards modesty, which is a quality immediately agreeable to others: the vicious excess of the former virtue, namely, insolence or haughtiness, is immediately disagreeable to others; the excess of the latter is so to the possessor. Thus are the boundaries of these duties adjusted.

A desire of fame, reputation, or a character with others, is so far from being blameable, that it seems inseparable from virtue, genius, capacity, and a generous or noble disposition. An attention even to trivial matters, in order to please, is also expected and demanded by society; and no one is surprised, if he find a man in company to observe a greater elegance of dress and more pleasant flow of conversation, than when he passes his time at home, and with his own family. Wherein, then, consists Vanity, which is so justly regarded as a fault or imperfection. It seems to consist chiefly in such an intemperate display of our advantages, honours, and accomplishments; in such an importunate and open demand of praise and admiration, as is offensive to others, and encroaches too far on *their* secret vanity and ambition. It is besides a sure symptom of the want of true dignity and elevation of mind, which is so great an ornament in any character. For why that impatient desire of applause; as if you were not justly entitled to it, and might not reasonably expect that it would for ever attend you? Why so anxious to inform us of the great company which you have kept; the obliging things which were said to you; the honours, the distinctions which you met with; as if these were not things of course, and what we could readily, of ourselves, have imagined, without being told of them?

Decency, or a proper regard to age, sex, character, and station in the world, may be ranked among the qualities which are immediately agreeable to others, and which, by that means, acquire praise and approbation. An effeminate behaviour in a man, a rough manner in a woman; these are ugly because unsuitable to each character, and different from the qualities which we expect in the sexes. It is as if a tragedy abounded in comic beauties, or

---

* Quinctil. lib. v. cap. 12.[5]

[5 Quintilian, whose *Institutio Oratoria* is the best exposition of the ideals and practice of Roman education.]

a comedy in tragic. The disproportions hurt the eye, and convey a disagreeable sentiment to the spectators, the source of blame and disapprobation. This is that *indecorum*, which is explained so much at large by Cicero in his Offices.[6]

Among the other virtues, we may also give Cleanliness a place; since it naturally renders us agreeable to others, and is no inconsiderable source of love and affection. No one will deny, that a negligence in this particular is a fault; and as faults are nothing but smaller vices, and this fault can have no other origin than the uneasy sensation which it excites in others; we may, in this instance, seemingly so trivial, clearly discover the origin of moral distinctions, about which the learned have involved themselves in such mazes of perplexity and error.

But besides all the *agreeable* qualities, the origin of whose beauty we can, in some degree, explain and account for, there still remains something mysterious and inexplicable, which conveys an immediate satisfaction to the spectator, but how, or why, or for what reason, he cannot pretend to determine. There is a manner, a grace, an ease, a genteelness, and I-know-not-what, which some men possess above others, which is very different from external beauty and comeliness, and which, however, catches our affection almost as suddenly and powerfully. And though this *manner* be chiefly talked of in the passion between the sexes, where the concealed magic is easily explained, yet surely much of it prevails in all our estimation of characters, and forms no inconsiderable part of personal merit. This class of accomplishments, therefore, must be trusted entirely to the blind, but sure testimony of taste and sentiment; and must be considered as a part of ethics, left by nature to baffle all the pride of philosophy, and make her sensible of her narrow boundaries and slender acquisitions.

We approve of another, because of his wit, politeness, modesty, decency, or any agreeable quality which he possesses; although he be not of our acquaintance, nor has ever given us any entertainment, by means of these accomplishments. The idea, which we form of their effect on his acquaintance, has an agreeable influence on our imagination, and gives us the sentiment of approbation. This principle enters into all the judgements which we form concerning manners and characters.

[6 Cicero's *De Officiis*, a treatise on moral duties, addressed to his son.]

Charles Lamb

THE SUPERANNUATED MAN

⟦ The *Essays of Elia* (Elia was the name of one of Lamb's fellow-clerks) were begun in 1820 and first appeared in *The London Magazine*. They were collected and republished in two series, 1823 and 1833.

Because of its informal and conversational style and its freedom from restrictions of subject, the familiar essay was a form perfectly suited to Lamb's temperament, to his insatiable curiosity about the oddities of human beings and customs and places: 'the cheerful cries of London, the music, and the ballad-singers—the buzz and stirring murmur of the streets.' Yet not all the essays deal with his beloved London. Like Montaigne, he treats of any topic that happens to interest him. His essays, like Montaigne's, delight us because the man himself delights us.

> Sera tamen respexit
> Libertas.   *Virgil.*[1]
> A Clerk I was in London gay.—*O'Keefe.*

I F PERADVENTURE, Reader, it has been thy lot to waste the golden years of thy life—thy shining youth—in the irksome confinement of an office; to have thy prison days prolonged through middle age down to decrepitude and silver hairs, without hope of release or respite; to have lived to forget that there are such things as holidays, or to remember them but as the prerogatives of childhood; then, and then only, will you be able to appreciate my deliverance.

It is now six-and-thirty years since I took my seat at the desk[2] in Mincing Lane. Melancholy was the transition at fourteen from the abundant play-

[1 'Yet freedom at length regarded (me).' *Eclogues*, I, 28.]
[2 Lamb was a clerk at the South Sea House from 1789 to 1792, and at the East India House from 1792 to 1825.]
FROM *Last Essays of Elia*, 1833.

time, and the frequently-intervening vacations of school days, to the eight, nine, and sometimes ten hours' a-day attendance at the counting-house. But time partially reconciles us to anything. I gradually became content— doggedly contented, as wild animals in cages.

It is true I had my Sundays to myself; but Sundays, admirable as the institution of them is for purposes of worship, are for that very reason the very worst adapted for days of unbending and recreation. In particular, there is a gloom for me attendant upon a city Sunday, a weight in the air. I miss the cheerful cries of London, the music, and the ballad-singers— the buzz and stirring murmur of the streets. Those eternal bells depress me. The closed shops repel me. Prints, pictures, all the glittering and end-less succession of knacks and gewgaws, and ostentatiously displayed wares of tradesmen, which make a weekday saunter through the less busy parts of the metropolis so delightful—are shut out. No bookstalls deliciously to idle over—no busy faces to recreate the idle man who contemplates them ever passing by—the very face of business a charm by contrast to his tem-porary relaxation from it. Nothing to be seen but unhappy countenances— or half-happy at best—of emancipated 'prentices and little tradesfolks, with here and there a servant-maid that has got leave to go out, who, slaving all the week, with the habit has lost almost the capacity of enjoying a free hour; and livelily expressing the hollowness of a day's pleasuring. The very strollers in the fields on that day look anything but comfortable.

But besides Sundays, I had a day at Easter, and a day at Christmas, with a full week in the summer to go and air myself in my native fields of Hert-fordshire. This last was a great indulgence; and the prospect of its recur-rence, I believe, alone kept me up through the year, and made my durance tolerable. But when the week came round, did the glittering phantom of the distance keep touch with me? or rather was it not a series of seven uneasy days, spent in restless pursuit of pleasure, and a wearisome anxiety to find out how to make the most of them? Where was the quiet, where the promised rest? Before I had a taste of it, it was vanished. I was at the desk again, counting upon the fifty-one tedious weeks that must intervene before such another snatch would come. Still the prospect of its coming threw something of an illumination upon the darker side of my captivity. Without it, as I have said, I could scarcely have sustained my thral-dom.

Independently of the rigours of attendance, I have ever been haunted with a sense (perhaps a mere caprice) of incapacity for business. This, dur-ing my latter years, had increased to such a degree, that it was visible in all the lines of my countenance. My health and my good spirits flagged. I had perpetually a dread of some crisis, to which I should be found unequal. Besides my daylight servitude, I served over again all night in my sleep, and would awake with terrors of imaginary false entries, errors in my accounts, and the like. I was fifty years of age, and no prospect of emancipation presented itself. I had grown to my desk, as it were; and the wood had entered into my soul.

My fellows in the office would sometimes rally me upon the trouble legible in my countenance; but I did not know that it had raised the suspicions of any of my employers, when, on the fifth of last month, a day ever to be remembered by me, L——, the junior partner in the firm, calling me on one side, directly taxed me with my bad looks, and frankly inquired the cause of them. So taxed, I honestly made confession of my infirmity, and added that I was afraid I should eventually be obliged to resign his service. He spoke some words of course to hearten me, and there the matter rested. A whole week I remained labouring under the impression that I had acted imprudently in my disclosure; that I had foolishly given a handle against myself, and had been anticipating my own dismissal. A week passed in this manner—the most anxious one, I verily believe, in my whole life— when on the evening of the 12th of April, just as I was about quitting my desk to go home (it might be about eight o'clock), I received an awful summons to attend the presence of the whole assembled firm in the formidable back parlour. I thought, now my time is surely come, I have done for myself, I am going to be told that they have no longer occasion for me. L——, I could see, smiled at the terror I was in, which was a little relief to me,—when to my utter astonishment B——, the eldest partner, began a formal harangue to me on the length of my services, my very meritorious conduct during the whole of the time (the deuce, thought I, how did he find out that? I protest I never had the confidence to think as much). He went on to descant on the expediency of retiring at a certain time of life, (how my heart panted!) and asking me a few questions as to the amount of my own property, of which I have a little, ended with a proposal, to which his three partners nodded a grave assent, that I should accept from the house, which I had served so well, a pension for life to the amount of two-thirds of my accustomed salary—a magnificent offer! I do not know what I answered between surprise and gratitude, but it was understood that I accepted their proposal, and I was told that I was free from that hour to leave their service. I stammered out a bow, and at just ten minutes after eight I went home—for ever. This noble benefit—gratitude forbids me to conceal their names—I owe to the kindness of the most munificent firm in the world—the house of Boldero, Merryweather, Bosanquet, and Lacy.

Esto perpetua! [3]

For the first day or two I felt stunned—overwhelmed. I could only apprehend my felicity; I was too confused to taste it sincerely. I wandered about, thinking I was happy, and knowing that I was not. I was in the condition of a prisoner in the old Bastile,[4] suddenly let loose after a forty years' confinement. I could scarce trust myself with myself. It was like passing out of Time into Eternity—for it is a sort of Eternity for a man to have all his Time to himself. It seemed to me that I had more time on my hands than I could ever manage. From a poor man, poor in Time, I was suddenly lifted up into a vast revenue; I could see no end of my possessions; I wanted some steward, or judicious bailiff, to manage my estates in Time for me. And here let me caution persons grown old in active business, not lightly nor without weighing their own resources, to forego their customary employment all at once, for there may be danger in it. I feel it by myself, but I know that my resources are sufficient; and now that those first giddy raptures have subsided, I have a quiet home-feeling of the blessedness of my condition. I am in no hurry. Having all holidays, I am as though I had none. If Time hung heavy upon me, I could walk it away; but I do *not* walk all day long, as I used to do in those old transient holidays, thirty miles a day, to make the most of them. If Time were troublesome, I could read it away; but I do *not* read in that violent measure, with which, having no Time my own but candlelight Time, I used to weary out my head and eyesight in bygone winters. I walk, read, or scribble (as now) just when the fit seizes me. I no longer hunt after pleasure; I let it come to me. I am like the man

> —that's born and has his years come to him,
> In some green desert.

'Years!' you will say; 'what is this superannuated simpleton calculating upon? He has already told us he is past fifty.'

I have indeed lived nominally fifty years, but deduct out of them the hours which I have lived to other people, and not to myself, and you will find me still a young fellow. For *that* is the only true Time, which a man

[3 'Be thou eternal!']
[4 A prison in Paris, destroyed by the mob on 14 July 1789, now the chief national anniversary in France.]

can properly call his own—that which he has all to himself; the rest, though in some sense he may be said to live it, is other people's Time, not his. The remnant of my poor days, long or short, is at least multiplied for me three-fold. My next ten years, if I stretch so far, will be as long as any preceding thirty. 'Tis a fair rule-of-three sum.

Among the strange fantasies which beset me at the commencement of my freedom, and of which all traces are not yet gone, one was, that a vast tract of time had intervened since I quitted the Counting House. I could not conceive of it as an affair of yesterday. The partners, and the clerks with whom I had for so many years, and for so many hours in each day of the year, been closely associated—being suddenly removed from them—they seemed as dead to me. There is a fine passage, which may serve to illustrate this fancy, in a Tragedy by Sir Robert Howard, speaking of a friend's death:—

> —'T was but just now he went away;
> I have not since had time to shed a tear;
> And yet the distance does the same appear
> As if he had been a thousand years from me.
> Time takes no measure in Eternity.

To dissipate this awkward feeling, I have been fain to go among them once or twice since; to visit my old desk-fellows—my co-brethren of the quill—that I had left below in the state militant. Not all the kindness with which they received me could quite restore to me that pleasant familiarity, which I had heretofore enjoyed among them. We cracked some of our old jokes, but methought they went off but faintly. My old desk; the peg where I hung my hat, were appropriated to another. I knew it must be, but I could not take it kindly. D——l take me, if I did not feel some remorse—beast, if I had not—at quitting my old compeers, the faithful partners of my toils for six-and-thirty years, that soothed for me with their jokes and conundrums the ruggedness of my professional road. Had it been so rugged then, after all? or was I a coward simply? Well, it is too late to repent; and I also know that these suggestions are a common fallacy of the mind on such occasions. But my heart smote me. I had violently broken the bands betwixt us. It was at least not courteous. I shall be some time before I get quite reconciled to the separation. Farewell, old cronies, yet not for long, for again and again I will come among ye, if I shall have your leave. Farewell, Ch——, dry, sarcastic, and friendly! Do——, mild, slow to move, and gentlemanly! Pl——, officious to do, and to volunteer, good services!—and thou, thou dreary pile, fit mansion for a Gresham or a Whittington [5] of old, stately house of Merchants; with thy labyrinthine passages, and light-excluding, pent-up offices, where candles for one-half the year supplied the place of the sun's light; unhealthy contributor to my weal, stern fosterer of my living, farewell! In thee remain, and not in the obscure collection of some wandering bookseller, my 'works!' There let them rest, as I do from my labours, piled on thy massy shelves, more MSS. in folio than ever Aquinas [6] left, and full as useful! My mantle I bequeath among ye.

A fortnight has passed since the date of my first communication. At that period I was approaching to tranquillity, but had not reached it. I boasted of a calm indeed, but it was comparative only. Something of the first flutter was left; an unsettling sense of novelty; the dazzle to weak eyes of unaccustomed light. I missed my old chains, forsooth, as if they had been some necessary part of my apparel. I was a poor Carthusian,[7] from strict cellular discipline suddenly by some revolution returned upon the world. I am now as if I had never been other than my own master. It is natural for me to go where I please, to do what I please. I find myself at 11 o'clock in the day in Bond Street, and it seems to me that I have been sauntering there at that very hour for years past. I digress into Soho, to explore a book-stall. Methinks I have been thirty years a collector. There is nothing strange nor new in it. I find myself before a fine picture in the morning. Was it ever otherwise? What is become of Fish Street Hill? Where is Fenchurch Street? Stones of old Mincing Lane, which I have worn with my daily pilgrimage for six-and-thirty years, to the footsteps of what toil-worn clerk are your everlasting flints now vocal? I indent the gayer flags of Pall Mall. It is 'Change time, and I am strangely among the Elgin marbles.[8] It was no hyperbole when I ventured to compare the change in my condition to passing into another world. Time stands still in a manner to me. I have lost all distinction of season. I do not know the day of the week or of the month. Each day used to be individually felt by me in its reference to the foreign post days; in its distance from, or propinquity to, the next Sunday. I had my Wednesday feelings, my Saturday nights' sensations. The genius of each day was upon me distinctly during the whole of it, affecting my

[5 Sir Thomas Gresham was an important financier in Elizabethan times. Sir Richard Whittington was Lord Mayor of London in 1397–8, 1406–7, and 1419–20.]

[6 St. Thomas Aquinas (1225–74), the greatest of medieval philosophers and theologians.]

[7 One of the stricter orders of monks.]

[8 Ancient sculptures from the Parthenon, collected by the Earl of Elgin and placed in the British Museum in 1816.]

appetite, spirits, etc. The phantom of the next day, with the dreary five to follow, sate as a load upon my poor Sabbath recreations. What charm has washed that Ethiop white? What is gone of Black Monday? All days are the same. Sunday itself—that unfortunate failure of a holiday, as it too often proved, what with my sense of its fugitiveness, and over-care to get the greatest quantity of pleasure out of it—is melted down into a week-day. I can spare to go to church now, without grudging the huge cantle [9] which it used to seem to cut out of the holiday. I have time for everything. I can visit a sick friend. I can interrupt the man of much occupation when he is busiest. I can insult over him with an invitation to take a day's pleasure with me to Windsor this fine May-morning. It is Lucretian pleasure [10] to behold the poor drudges, whom I have left behind in the world, carking and caring; like horses in a mill, drudging on in the same eternal round— and what is it all for? A man can never have too much Time to himself, nor too little to do. Had I a little son, I would christen him NOTHING-TO-DO; he should do nothing. Man, I verily believe, is out of his element as long as he is operative. I am altogether for the life contemplative. Will no kindly earthquake come and swallow up those accursed cotton-mills? Take me that lumber of a desk there, and bowl it down

As low as to the fiends.[11]

I am no longer * * * * * *, clerk to the Firm of, etc. I am Retired Leisure.[12] I am to be met with in trim gardens. I am already come to be known by my vacant face and careless gesture, perambulating at no fixed pace, nor with any settled purpose. I walk about; not to and from. They tell me, a certain *cum dignitate* [13] air, that has been buried so long with my other good parts, has begun to shoot forth in my person. I grow into gentility perceptibly. When I take up a newspaper, it is to read the state of the opera. *Opus operatum est.*[14] I have done all that I came into this world to do. I have worked task-work, and have the rest of the day to myself.

[9 Slice.]
[10 A celebrated passage at the opening of the second book of Lucretius' poem *De Rerum Natura* tells of the agreeable feeling one has when, safe himself, he watches the struggles of others. He pities them but rejoices that he is out of danger.]
[11 *Hamlet,* II, ii, 527.]
[12 See Milton, *Il Penseroso,* 49–50.]
[13 Dignified.]
[14 The task is performed.]

Henry David Thoreau

WHERE I LIVED, AND WHAT I LIVED FOR

⁅ Thoreau's narrative of his building a cabin by Walden Pond, near Concord, Massachusetts, and of his natural and spiritual life there is an indisputable classic, familiar today to many who never heard of his other writings and who perhaps never read even a page by his famous neighbor Emerson. *Walden* is unique; there is nothing to compare it with; it had no model, no predecessor. It is as genuine as Thoreau himself, as American as Concord.

Thoreau lived at Walden Pond for little more than two years, from July 1845 to September 1847. His was not a hermit's existence there by any means, nor was it intended to be one; he had callers now and then, and he frequently went to the village. When his 'experiment' satisfied him, he returned to Concord to live. 'I left the woods for as good a reason as I went there. Perhaps it seemed to me that I had several more lives to live, and could not spare any more time for that one.'

Most of *Walden* was written in 1846 or thereabouts, but parts of it were made not only from the journal Thoreau kept while he lived beside the pond but from his earlier journals as well. It was published in 1854.

See the essay by E. B. White, pp. 405–14.

A T A CERTAIN season of our life we are accustomed to consider every spot as the possible site of a house. I have thus surveyed the country on every side within a dozen miles of where I live. In imagination I have bought all the farms in succession, for all were to be bought, and I knew their price. I walked over each farmer's premises, tasted his wild apples, discoursed on husbandry with him, took his farm at his price, at any price, mortgaging it to him in my mind; even put a higher price on it,— took every thing but a deed of it,—took his word for his deed, for I dearly

FROM *Walden*, 1854.

love to talk,—cultivated it, and him too to some extent, I trust, and withdrew when I had enjoyed it long enough, leaving him to carry it on. This experience entitled me to be regarded as a sort of real-estate broker by my friends. Wherever I sat, there I might live, and the landscape radiated from me accordingly. What is a house but a *sedes*, a seat?—better if a country seat. I discovered many a site for a house not likely to be soon improved, which some might have thought too far from the village, but to my eyes the village was too far from it. Well, there I might live, I said; and there I did live, for an hour, a summer and a winter life; saw how I could let the years run off, buffet the winter through, and see the spring come in. The future inhabitants of this region, wherever they may place their houses, may be sure that they have been anticipated. An afternoon sufficed to lay out the land into orchard, woodlot, and pasture, and to decide what fine oaks or pines should be left to stand before the door, and whence each blasted tree could be seen to the best advantage; and then I let it lie, fallow perchance, for a man is rich in proportion to the number of things which he can afford to let alone.[1]

My imagination carried me so far that I even had the refusal of several farms,—the refusal was all I wanted,—but I never got my fingers burned by actual possession. The nearest that I came to actual possession was when I bought the Hollowell place, and had begun to sort my seeds, and collected materials with which to make a wheelbarrow to carry it on or off with; but before the owner gave me a deed of it, his wife—every man has such a wife —changed her mind and wished to keep it, and he offered me ten dollars to release him. Now, to speak the truth, I had but ten cents in the world, and it surpassed my arithmetic to tell, if I was that man who had ten cents, or who had a farm, or ten dollars, or all together. However, I let him keep the ten dollars and the farm too, for I had carried it far enough; or rather, to be generous, I sold him the farm for just what I gave for it, and, as he was not a rich man, made him a present of ten dollars, and still had my ten cents, and seeds, and materials for a wheelbarrow left. I found thus that I had been a rich man without any damage to my poverty. But I retained the landscape, and I have since annually carried off what it yielded without a wheelbarrow. With respect to landscapes,—

'I am monarch of all I *survey*,
My right there is none to dispute.' [2]

[1 Compare Luke, xii, 15.]
[2 Cowper, *Verses Supposed to be Written by Alexander Selkirk*.]

I have frequently seen a poet withdraw, having enjoyed the most valuable part of a farm, while the crusty farmer supposed that he had got a few wild apples only. Why, the owner does not know it for many years when a poet has put his farm in rhyme, the most admirable kind of invisible fence, has fairly impounded it, milked it, skimmed it, and got all the cream, and left the farmer only the skimmed milk.

The real attractions of the Hollowell farm, to me, were: its complete retirement, being about two miles from the village, half a mile from the nearest neighbor, and separated from the highway by a broad field; its bounding on the river, which the owner said protected it by its fogs from frosts in the spring, though that was nothing to me; the gray color and ruinous state of the house and barn, and the dilapidated fences, which put such an interval between me and the last occupant; the hollow and lichen-covered apple trees, gnawed by rabbits, showing what kind of neighbors I should have; but above all, the recollection I had of it from my earliest voyages up the river, when the house was concealed behind a dense grove of red maples, through which I heard the house-dog bark. I was in haste to buy it, before the proprietor finished getting out some rocks, cutting down the hollow apple trees, and grubbing up some young birches which had sprung up in the pasture, or, in short, had made any more of his improvements. To enjoy these advantages I was ready to carry it on; like Atlas, to take the world on my shoulders,—I never heard what compensation he received for that,—and do all those things which had no other motive or excuse but that I might pay for it and be unmolested in my possession of it; for I knew all the while that it would yield the most abundant crop of the kind I wanted if I could only afford to let it alone. But it turned out as I have said.

All that I could say, then, with respect to farming on a large scale (I have always cultivated a garden) was, that I had had my seeds ready. Many think that seeds improve with age. I have no doubt that time discriminates between the good and the bad; and when at last I shall plant, I shall be less likely to be disappointed. But I would say to my fellows, once for all, As long as possible live free and uncommitted. It makes but little difference whether you are committed to a farm or the county jail.

Old Cato,[3] whose 'De Re Rusticâ' is my 'Cultivator,' says, and the only translation I have seen makes sheer nonsense of the passage, 'When you think of getting a farm, turn it thus in your mind, not to buy greedily; nor spare your pains to look at it, and do not think it enough to go round it

[3 Cato the Elder, the Censor (234–149 B.C.); see Plutarch's life of him.]

once. The oftener you go there the more it will please you, if it is good.' I
think I shall not buy greedily, but go round and round it as long as I live,
and be buried in it first, that it may please me the more at last.

The present was my next experiment of this kind, which I purpose to
describe more at length, for convenience, putting the experience of two
years into one. As I have said, I do not propose to write an ode to dejection, but to brag as lustily as chanticleer in the morning, standing on his
roost, if only to wake my neighbors up.[4]

When first I took up my abode in the woods, that is, began to spend my
nights as well as days there, which, by accident, was on Independence day,
or the fourth of July, 1845, my house [5] was not finished for winter, but was
merely a defence against the rain, without plastering or chimney, the walls
being of rough weather-stained boards, with wide chinks, which made it
cool at night. The upright white hewn studs and freshly planed door and
window casings gave it a clean and airy look, especially in the morning,
when its timbers were saturated with dew, so that I fancied that by noon
some sweet gum would exude from them. To my imagination it retained
throughout the day more or less of this auroral character, reminding me of
a certain house on a mountain which I had visited the year before. This
was an airy and unplastered cabin, fit to entertain a travelling god, and
where a goddess might trail her garments. The winds which passed over
my dwelling were such as sweep over the ridges of mountains, bearing the
broken strains, or celestial parts only, of terrestrial music. The morning
wind forever blows, the poem of creation is uninterrupted; but few are the
ears that hear it. Olympus [6] is but the outside of the earth every where.

The only house I had been the owner of before, if I except a boat, was a
tent, which I used occasionally when making excursions in the summer,
and this is still rolled up in my garret; but the boat, after passing from hand
to hand, has gone down the stream of time. With this more substantial
shelter about me, I had made some progress toward settling in the world.
This frame, so slightly clad, was a sort of crystallization around me, and
reacted on the builder. It was suggestive somewhat as a picture in outlines.
I did not need to go out doors to take the air, for the atmosphere within
had lost none of its freshness. It was not so much within doors as behind
a door where I sat, even in the rainiest weather. The Harivansa [7] says, 'An

[4 This sentence appeared on the title page of the early editions of *Walden*.]
[5 See the first chapter of *Walden*, which describes the building of the house.]
[6 In classical mythology, the abode of the gods.]
[7 Supplement to the Hindu epic poem *Mahabharata*.]

abode without birds is like a meat without seasoning.' Such was not my abode, for I found myself suddenly neighbor to the birds; not by having imprisoned one, but having caged myself near them. I was not only nearer to some of those which commonly frequent the garden and the orchard, but to those wilder and more thrilling songsters of the forest which never, or rarely, serenade a villager,—the wood-thrush, the veery, the scarlet tanager, the field-sparrow, the whippoorwill, and many others.

I was seated [8] by the shore of a small pond, about a mile and a half south of the village of Concord and somewhat higher than it, in the midst of an extensive wood between that town and Lincoln, and about two miles south of that our only field known to fame, Concord Battle Ground; but I was so low in the woods that the opposite shore, half a mile off, like the rest, covered with wood, was my most distant horizon. For the first week, whenever I looked out on the pond it impressed me like a tarn high up on the side of a mountain, its bottom far above the surface of other lakes, and, as the sun arose, I saw it throwing off its nightly clothing of mist, and here and there, by degrees, its soft ripples or its smooth reflecting surface was revealed, while the mists, like ghosts, were stealthily withdrawing in every direction into the woods, as at the breaking up of some nocturnal conventicle. The very dew seemed to hang upon the trees later into the day than usual, as on the sides of mountains.

This small lake was of most value as a neighbor in the intervals of a gentle rain storm in August, when, both air and water being perfectly still, but the sky overcast, mid-afternoon had all the serenity of evening, and the wood-thrush sang around, and was heard from shore to shore. A lake like this is never smoother than at such a time; and the clear portion of the air above it being shallow and darkened by clouds, the water, full of light and reflections, becomes a lower heaven itself so much the more important. From a hill top near by, where the wood had been recently cut off, there was a pleasing vista southward across the pond, through a wide indentation in the hills which form the shore there, where their opposite sides sloping toward each other suggested a stream flowing out in that direction through a wooded valley, but stream there was none. That way I looked between and over the near green hills to some distant and higher ones in the horizon, tinged with blue. Indeed, by standing on tiptoe I could catch a glimpse of some of the peaks of the still bluer and more distant mountain ranges in the north-west, those true-blue coins from heaven's own mint, and also of some portion of the village. But in other directions, even from this point, I

[8 See p. 384.]

could not see over or beyond the woods which surrounded me. It is well to have some water in your neighborhood, to give buoyancy to and float the earth. One value even of the smallest well is, that when you look into it you see that earth is not continent but insular. This is as important as that it keeps butter cool. When I looked across the pond from this peak toward the Sudbury meadows, which in time of flood I distinguished elevated perhaps by a mirage in their seething valley, like a coin in a basin, all the earth beyond the pond appeared like a thin crust insulated and floated even by this small sheet of intervening water, and I was reminded that this on which I dwelt was but *dry land*.

Though the view from my door was still more contracted, I did not feel crowded or confined in the least. There was pasture enough for my imagination. The low shrub-oak plateau to which the opposite shore arose, stretched away toward the prairies of the West and the steppes of Tartary, affording ample room for all the roving families of men. 'There are none happy in the world but beings who enjoy freely a vast horizon,'—said Damodara,[9] when his herds required new and larger pastures.

Both place and time were changed, and I dwelt nearer to those parts of the universe and to those eras in history which had most attracted me. Where I lived was as far off as many a region viewed nightly by astronomers. We are wont to imagine rare and delectable places in some remote and more celestial corner of the system, behind the constellation of Cassiopeia's Chair, far from noise and disturbance. I discovered that my house actually had its site in such a withdrawn, but forever new and unprofaned, part of the universe. If it were worth the while to settle in those parts near to the Pleiades or the Hyades, to Aldebaran or Altair, then I was really there, or at an equal remoteness from the life which I had left behind, dwindled and twinkling with as fine a ray to my nearest neighbor, and to be seen only in moonless nights by him. Such was that part of creation where I had squatted;—

'There was a shepherd that did live,
    And held his thoughts as high
As were the mounts whereon his flocks
    Did hourly feed him by.'

What should we think of the shepherd's life if his flocks always wandered to higher pastures than his thoughts?

Every morning was a cheerful invitation to make my life of equal sim-

[9 Vishnu, the Preserver god in Hindu mythology.]

plicity, and I may say innocence, with Nature herself. I have been as sincere a worshipper of Aurora as the Greeks. I got up early and bathed in the pond; that was a religious exercise, and one of the best things which I did. They say that characters were engraven on the bathing tub of king Tching-thang to this effect: 'Renew thyself completely each day; do it again, and again, and forever again.' I can understand that. Morning brings back the heroic ages. I was as much affected by the faint hum of a mosquito making its invisible and unimaginable tour through my apartment at earliest dawn, when I was sitting with door and windows open, as I could be by any trumpet that ever sang of fame. It was Homer's requiem; itself an Iliad and Odyssey in the air, singing its own wrath and wanderings. There was something cosmical about it; a standing advertisement, till forbidden, of the everlasting vigor and fertility of the world. The morning, which is the most memorable season of the day, is the awakening hour. Then there is least somnolence in us; and for an hour, at least, some part of us awakes which slumbers all the rest of the day and night. Little is to be expected of that day, if it can be called a day, to which we are not awakened by our Genius, but by the mechanical nudgings of some servitor, are not awakened by our own newly-acquired force and aspirations from within, accompanied by the undulations of celestial music, instead of factory bells, and a fragrance filling the air—to a higher life than we fell asleep from; and thus the darkness bear its fruit, and prove itself to be good, no less than the light. That man who does not believe that each day contains an earlier, more sacred, and auroral hour than he has yet profaned, has despaired of life, and is pursuing a descending and darkening way. After a partial cessation of his sensuous life, the soul of man, or its organs rather, are reinvigorated each day, and his Genius tries again what noble life it can make. All memorable events, I should say, transpire in morning time and in a morning atmosphere. The Vedas [10] say, 'All intelligences awake with the morning.' Poetry and art, and the fairest and most memorable of the actions of men, date from such an hour. All poets and heroes, like Memnon,[11] are the children of Aurora, and emit their music at sunrise. To him whose elastic and vigorous thought keeps pace with the sun, the day is a perpetual morning. It matters not what the clocks say or the attitudes and labors of men. Morning is when I am awake and there is a dawn in me. Moral reform is the effort to throw off sleep. Why is it that men give so poor an account of

[10] Ancient Hindu scriptures.]
[11] A gigantic statue near Thebes, in Egypt, supposedly that of the hero Memnon, was said to utter musical sounds in the morning.]

their day if they have not been slumbering? They are not such poor calculators. If they had not been overcome with drowsiness they would have performed something. The millions are awake enough for physical labor; but only one in a million is awake enough for effective intellectual exertion, only one in a hundred millions to a poetic or divine life. To be awake is to be alive. I have never yet met a man who was quite awake. How could I have looked him in the face?

We must learn to reawaken and keep ourselves awake, not by mechanical aids, but by an infinite expectation of the dawn, which does not forsake us in our soundest sleep. I know of no more encouraging fact than the unquestionable ability of man to elevate his life by a conscious endeavor. It is something to be able to paint a particular picture, or to carve a statue, and so to make a few objects beautiful; but it is far more glorious to carve and paint the very atmosphere and medium through which we look, which morally we can do. To affect the quality of the day, that is the highest of arts. Every man is tasked to make his life, even in its details, worthy of the contemplation of his most elevated and critical hour. If we refused, or rather used up, such paltry information as we get, the oracles would distinctly inform us how this might be done.

I went to the woods because I wished to live deliberately, to front only the essential facts of life, and see if I could not learn what it had to teach, and not, when I came to die, discover that I had not lived. I did not wish to live what was not life, living is so dear; nor did I wish to practise resignation, unless it was quite necessary. I wanted to live deep and suck out all the marrow of life, to live so sturdily and Spartan-like as to put to rout all that was not life, to cut a broad swath and shave close, to drive life into a corner, and reduce it to its lowest terms, and, if it proved to be mean, why then to get the whole and genuine meanness of it, and publish its meanness to the world; or if it were sublime, to know it by experience, and be able to give a true account of it in my next excursion. For most men, it appears to me, are in a strange uncertainty about it, whether it is of the devil or of God, and have *somewhat hastily* concluded that it is the chief end of man here to 'glorify God and enjoy him forever.' [12]

Still we live meanly, like ants; though the fable tells us that we were long ago changed into men; like pygmies we fight with cranes; [13] it is error upon error, and clout upon clout, and our best virtue has for its occasion a superfluous and evitable wretchedness. Our life is frittered away by detail.

[12 From the Westminster (Presbyterian) Catechism.]
[13 According to an ancient fable the pygmies and cranes fought annually.]

An honest man has hardly need to count more than his ten fingers, or in extreme cases he may add his ten toes, and lump the rest. Simplicity, simplicity, simplicity! I say, let your affairs be as two or three, and not a hundred or a thousand; instead of a million count half a dozen, and keep your accounts on your thumb nail. In the midst of this chopping sea of civilized life, such are the clouds and storms and quicksands and thousand-and-one items to be allowed for, that a man has to live, if he would not founder and go to the bottom and not make his port at all, by dead reckoning, and he must be a great calculator indeed who succeeds. Simplify, simplify. Instead of three meals a day, if it be necessary eat but one; instead of a hundred dishes, five; and reduce other things in proportion. Our life is like a German Confederacy,[14] made up of petty states, with its boundary forever fluctuating, so that even a German cannot tell you how it is bounded at any moment. The nation itself, with all its so-called internal improvements, which, by the way, are all external and superficial, is just such an unwieldy and overgrown establishment, cluttered with furniture and tripped up by its own traps, ruined by luxury and heedless expense, by want of calculation and a worthy aim, as the million households in the land; and the only cure for it as for them is in a rigid economy, a stern and more than Spartan simplicity of life and elevation of purpose. It lives too fast. Men think that it is essential that the *Nation* have commerce, and export ice, and talk through a telegraph, and ride thirty miles an hour, without a doubt, whether *they* do or not; but whether we should live like baboons or like men, is a little uncertain. If we do not get out sleepers,[15] and forge rails, and devote days and nights to the work, but go to tinkering upon our *lives* to improve *them*, who will build railroads? And if railroads are not built, how shall we get to heaven in season? But if we stay at home and mind our business, who will want railroads? We do not ride on the railroad; it rides upon us. Did you ever think what those sleepers are that underlie the railroad? Each one is a man, an Irishman, or a Yankee man. The rails are laid on them, and they are covered with sand, and the cars run smoothly over them. They are sound sleepers, I assure you. And every few years a new lot is laid down and run over; so that, if some have the pleasure of riding on a rail, others have the misfortune to be ridden upon. And when they run over a man that is walking in his sleep, a supernumerary sleeper in the wrong position, and wake him up, they suddenly stop the cars, and

[14 When this was written, Germany was not yet a united nation but a collection of 'petty states.']

[15 Railroad ties.]

make a hue and cry about it, as if this were an exception. I am glad to know that it takes a gang of men for every five miles to keep the sleepers down and level in their beds as it is, for this is a sign that they may sometime get up again.

Why should we live with such hurry and waste of life? We are determined to be starved before we are hungry. Men say that a stitch in time saves nine, and so they take a thousand stitches to-day to save nine to-morrow. As for *work*, we haven't any of any consequence. We have the Saint Vitus' dance, and cannot possibly keep our heads still. If I should only give a few pulls at the parish bell-rope, as for a fire, that is, without setting the bell, there is hardly a man on his farm in the outskirts of Concord, notwithstanding that press of engagements which was his excuse so many times this morning, nor a boy, nor a woman, I might almost say, but would forsake all and follow that sound, not mainly to save property from the flames, but, if we will confess the truth, much more to see it burn, since burn it must, and we, be it known, did not set it on fire,—or to see it put out, and have a hand in it, if that is done as handsomely; yes, even if it were the parish church itself. Hardly a man takes a half hour's nap after dinner, but when he wakes he holds up his head and asks, 'What's the news?' as if the rest of mankind had stood his sentinels. Some give directions to be waked every half hour, doubtless for no other purpose; and then, to pay for it, they tell what they have dreamed. After a night's sleep the news is as indispensable as the breakfast. 'Pray tell me any thing new that has happened to a man any where on this globe,'—and he reads it over his coffee and rolls, that a man has had his eyes gouged out this morning on the Wachito River; never dreaming the while that he lives in the dark unfathomed mammoth cave of this world, and has but the rudiment of an eye himself.

For my part, I could easily do without the post-office. I think that there are very few important communications made through it. To speak critically, I never received more than one or two letters in my life—I wrote this some years ago—that were worth the postage. The penny-post is, commonly, an institution through which you seriously offer a man that penny for his thoughts which is so often safely offered in jest.[16] And I am sure that I never read any memorable news in a newspaper. If we read of one man robbed, or murdered, or killed by accident, or one house burned, or one vessel wrecked, or one steamboat blown up, or one cow run over on the

[16 At that time the postage might be paid by either the sender or the receiver of a letter.]

Western Railroad, or one mad dog killed, or one lot of grasshoppers in the winter,—we never need read of another. One is enough. If you are acquainted with the principle, what do you care for a myriad instances and applications? To a philosopher all *news*, as it is called, is gossip, and they who edit and read it are old women over their tea. Yet not a few are greedy after this gossip. There was such a rush, as I hear, the other day at one of the offices to learn the foreign news by the last arrival, that several large squares of plate glass belonging to the establishment were broken by the pressure,—news which I seriously think a ready wit might write a twelvemonth or twelve years beforehand with sufficient accuracy. As for Spain, for instance, if you know how to throw in Don Carlos and the Infanta, and Don Pedro and Seville and Granada, from time to time in the right proportions,—they may have changed the names a little since I saw the papers, —and serve up a bull-fight when other entertainments fail, it will be true to the letter, and give us as good an idea of the exact state or ruin of things in Spain as the most succinct and lucid reports under this head in the newspapers: and as for England, almost the last significant scrap of news from that quarter was the revolution of 1649; and if you have learned the history of her crops for an average year, you never need attend to that thing again, unless your speculations are of a merely pecuniary character. If one may judge who rarely looks into the newspapers, nothing new does ever happen in foreign parts, a French revolution not excepted.

What news! how much more important to know what that is which was never old! 'Kieou-he-yu (great dignitary of the state of Wei) sent a man to Khoung-tseu to know his news. Khoung-tseu caused the messenger to be seated near him, and questioned him in these terms: What is your master doing? The messenger answered with respect: My master desires to diminish the number of his faults, but he cannot come to the end of them. The messenger being gone, the philosopher remarked: What a worthy messenger! What a worthy messenger!' The preacher, instead of vexing the ears of drowsy farmers on their day of rest at the end of the week,—for Sunday is the fit conclusion of an ill-spent week, and not the fresh and brave beginning of a new one,—with this one other draggletail of a sermon, should shout with thundering voice,—'Pause! Avast! Why so seeming fast, but deadly slow?'

Shams and delusions are esteemed for soundest truths, while reality is fabulous. If men would steadily observe realities only, and not allow themselves to be deluded, life, to compare it with such things as we know, would be like a fairy tale and the Arabian Nights' Entertainments. If we respected only what is inevitable and has a right to be, music and poetry would resound along the streets. When we are unhurried and wise, we perceive that only great and worthy things have any permanent and absolute existence,—that petty fears and petty pleasures are but the shadow of the reality. This is always exhilarating and sublime. By closing the eyes and slumbering, and consenting to be deceived by shows, men establish and confirm their daily life of routine and habit every where, which still is built on purely illusory foundations. Children, who play life, discern its true law and relations more clearly than men, who fail to live it worthily, but who think that they are wiser by experience, that is, by failure. I have read in a Hindoo book, that 'there was a king's son, who, being expelled in infancy from his native city, was brought up by a forester, and, growing up to maturity in that state, imagined himself to belong to the barbarous race with which he lived. One of his father's ministers having discovered him, revealed to him what he was, and the misconception of his character was removed, and he knew himself to be a prince. So soul,' continues the Hindoo philosopher, 'from the circumstances in which it is placed, mistakes its own character, until the truth is revealed to it by some holy teacher, and then it knows itself to be *Brahme*.' [17] I perceive that we inhabitants of New England live this mean life that we do because our vision does not penetrate the surface of things. We think that that *is* which *appears* to be. If a man should walk through this town and see only the reality, where, think you, would the 'Mill-dam' go to? If he should give us an account of the realities he beheld there, we should not recognize the place in his description. Look at a meeting-house, or a court-house, or a jail, or a shop, or a dwelling-house, and say what that thing really is before a true gaze, and they would all go to pieces in your account of them. Men esteem truth remote, in the outskirts of the system, behind the farthest star, before Adam and after the last man. In eternity there is indeed something true and sublime. But all these times and places and occasions are now and here. God himself culminates in the present moment, and will never be more divine in the lapse of all the ages. And we are enabled to apprehend at all what is sublime and noble only by the perpetual instilling and drenching of the reality that surrounds us. The universe constantly and obediently answers to our conceptions; whether we travel fast or slow, the track is laid for us. Let us spend our lives in conceiving then. The poet or the artist never yet had so fair and noble a design but some of his posterity at least could accomplish it.

[17 Knows itself to be of the divine, eternal essence.]

Let us spend one day as deliberately as Nature, and not be thrown off the track by every nutshell and mosquito's wing that falls on the rails. Let us rise early and fast, or break fast, gently and without perturbation; let company come and let company go, let the bells ring and the children cry, —determined to make a day of it. Why should we knock under and go with the stream? Let us not be upset and overwhelmed in that terrible rapid and whirlpool called a dinner, situated in the meridian shallows. Weather this danger and you are safe, for the rest of the way is down hill. With unrelaxed nerves, with morning vigor, sail by it, looking another way, tied to the mast like Ulysses.[18] If the engine whistles, let it whistle till it is hoarse for its pains. If the bell rings, why should we run? We will consider what kind of music they are like. Let us settle ourselves, and work and wedge our feet downward through the mud and slush of opinion, and prejudice, and tradition, and delusion, and appearance, that alluvion which covers the globe, through Paris and London, through New York and Boston and Concord, through church and state, through poetry and philosophy and religion, till we come to a hard bottom and rocks in place, which we can call *reality*, and say, This is, and no mistake; and then begin, having a *point d'appui*,[19] below freshet and frost and fire, a place where you might found a wall or a state, or set a lamp-post safely, or perhaps a gauge, not a Nilometer,[20] but a Realometer, that future ages might know how deep a freshet of shams and appearances had gathered from time to time. If you stand right fronting and face to face to a fact, you will see the sun glimmer on both its surfaces, as if it were a cimeter, and feel its sweet edge dividing you through the heart and marrow, and so you will happily conclude your mortal career. Be it life or death, we crave only reality. If we are really dying, let us hear the rattle in our throats and feel cold in the extremities; if we are alive, let us go about our business.

Time is but the stream I go a-fishing in. I drink at it; but while I drink I see the sandy bottom and detect how shallow it is. Its thin current slides away, but eternity remains. I would drink deeper; fish in the sky, whose bottom is pebbly with stars. I cannot count one. I know not the first letter of the alphabet. I have always been regretting that I was not as wise as the day I was born. The intellect is a cleaver; it discerns and rifts its way into the secret of things. I do not wish to be any more busy with my hands than

[18 Ulysses had himself tied to the mast of his ship in order to resist the allurements of the Sirens.]

[19 Basis.]

[20 Instrument for measuring the height of the Nile.]

is necessary. My head is hands and feet. I feel all my best faculties concentrated in it. My instinct tells me that my head is an organ for burrowing, as some creatures use their snout and fore-paws, and with it I would mine and burrow my way through these hills. I think that the richest vein is somewhere hereabouts; so by the divining rod and thin rising vapors I judge; and here I will begin to mine.

Robert Louis Stevenson

ÆS TRIPLEX[1]

⟨ Robert Louis Stevenson's essays are less read now than they used to be, possibly because their style seems too polished, too finished, to please the taste of readers accustomed to other modes of writing. That his prose is sometimes overmannered is true, but by and large it is wonderfully clear, graceful, and easy. His ideas are as timely as ever. A reader coming to 'Aes Triplex' for the first time will be struck by many of Stevenson's observations; for example, 'This world itself, travelling blindly and swiftly in overcrowded space, among a million other worlds travelling blindly and swiftly in contrary directions, may very well come by a knock that would set it into explosion like a penny squib.' What better counsel for us nowadays than this: 'As courage and intelligence are the two qualities best worth a good man's cultivation, so it is the first part of intelligence to recognise our precarious estate in life, and the first part of courage to be not at all abashed before the fact'?

'Aes Triplex' first appeared in *The Cornhill Magazine* in 1878, and was included in the volume of essays entitled *Virginibus Puerisque* (1881).

T HE changes wrought by death are in themselves so sharp and final, and so terrible and melancholy in their consequences, that the thing stands alone in man's experience, and has no parallel upon earth. It outdoes all other accidents because it is the last of them. Sometimes it leaps suddenly upon its victims, like a Thug; sometimes it lays a regular siege and creeps upon their citadel during a score of years. And when the business is done, there is sore havoc made in other people's lives, and a pin knocked out by which many subsidiary friendships hung together.

[1 'Aes triplex' ('triple brass,' 'threefold armor') is synonymous with courage. The phrase is from Horace, *Odes*, I, iii, 9.]

FROM *The Cornhill Magazine*, 1878.

There are empty chairs, solitary walks and single beds at night. Again, in taking away our friends, death does not take them away utterly, but leaves behind a mocking, tragical, and soon intolerable residue, which must be hurriedly concealed. Hence a whole chapter of sights and customs striking to the mind, from the pyramids of Egypt to the gibbets and dule trees [2] of mediæval Europe. The poorest persons have a bit of pageant going towards the tomb; memorial stones are set up over the least memorable; and, in order to preserve some show of respect for what remains of our old loves and friendships, we must accompany it with much grimly ludicrous ceremonial, and the hired undertaker parades before the door. All this, and much more of the same sort, accompanied by the eloquence of poets, has gone a great way to put humanity in error; nay, in many philosophies the error has been embodied and laid down with every circumstance of logic; although in real life the bustle and swiftness, in leaving people little time to think, have not left them time enough to go dangerously wrong in practice.

As a matter of fact, although few things are spoken of with more fearful whisperings than this prospect of death, few have less influence on conduct under healthy circumstances. We have all heard of cities in South America built upon the side of fiery mountains, and how, even in this tremendous neighborhood, the inhabitants are not a jot more impressed by the solemnity of mortal conditions than if they were delving gardens in the greenest corner of England. There are serenades and suppers and much gallantry among the myrtles overhead; and meanwhile the foundation shudders underfoot, the bowels of the mountain growl, and at any moment living ruin may leap sky high into the moonlight, and tumble man and his merry-making in the dust. In the eyes of very young people, and very dull old ones, there is something indescribably reckless and desperate in such a picture. It seems not credible that respectable married people, with umbrellas, should find appetite for a bit of supper within quite a long distance of a fiery mountain; ordinary life begins to smell of high-handed debauch when it is carried on so close to a catastrophe; and even cheese and salad, it seems, could hardly be relished in such circumstances without something like a defiance of the Creator. It should be a place for nobody but hermits dwelling in prayer and maceration, or mere born-devils drowning care in a perpetual carouse. And yet, when one comes to think upon it calmly, the situation of these South American citizens forms only a very pale figure for the state of ordinary mankind. This world itself, travelling

[2 Mourning trees, i.e. hanging trees, gibbets.]

blindly and swiftly in overcrowded space, among a million other worlds
travelling blindly and swiftly in contrary directions, may very well come
by a knock that would set it into explosion like a penny squib. And what,
pathologically looked at, is the human body with all its organs, but a mere
bagful of petards? [3] The least of these is as dangerous to the whole economy as the ship's powder-magazine to the ship; and with every breath we
breathe, and every meal we eat, we are putting one or more of them in
peril. If we clung as devotedly as some philosophers pretend we do to the
abstract idea of life, or were half as frightened as they make out we are for
the subversive accident that ends it all, the trumpets might sound by the
hour and no one would follow them into battle—the blue-peter [4] might fly
at the truck,[5] but who would climb into a sea-going ship? Think (if these
philosophers were right) with what a preparation of spirit we should affront
the daily peril of the dinner-table: a deadlier spot than any battle-field in
history; where the far greater proportion of our ancestors have miserably
left their bones! What woman would ever be lured into marriage, so much
more dangerous than the wildest sea? And what would it be to grow old?
For, after a certain distance, every step we take in life we find the ice growing thinner below our feet, and all around us and behind us we see our
contemporaries going through. By the time a man gets well into the seven-
ties, his continued existence is a mere miracle; and when he lays his old
bones in bed for the night, there is an overwhelming probability that he
will never see the day. Do the old men mind it, as a matter of fact? Why,
no. They were never merrier; they have their grog at night, and tell the
raciest stories; they hear of the death of people about their own age, or
even younger, not as if it was a grisly warning, but with a simple childlike
pleasure at having outlived some one else; and when a draught might puff
them out like a guttering candle, or a bit of a stumble shatter them like so
much glass, their old hearts keep sound and unaffrighted, and they go on,
bubbling with laughter, through years of man's age compared to which the
valley at Balaklava [6] was as safe and peaceful as a village cricket-green on
Sunday. It may fairly be questioned (if we look to the peril only) whether
it was a much more daring feat for Curtius [7] to plunge into the gulf, than

[3 Firecrackers.]
[4 A blue and white signal flag used on ships.]
[5 Top of flagstaff or masthead.]
[6 Where, in the Crimean War, the 'six hundred' made their famous charge.]
[7 When a chasm suddenly opened in the Roman Forum, the soothsayers announced
that it would not close until Rome's chief strength was sacrificed. Curtius, armed and on
horseback, leaped into the chasm: Rome's strength was in her men and arms.]

for any old gentleman of ninety to doff his clothes and clamber into
bed.

Indeed, it is a memorable subject for consideration, with what unconcern and gaiety mankind pricks on along the Valley of the Shadow of
Death. The whole way is one wilderness of snares, and the end of it, for
those who fear the last pinch, is irrevocable ruin. And yet we go spinning
through it all, like a party for the Derby. Perhaps the reader remembers
one of the humourous devices of the deified Caligula: [8] how he encouraged
a vast concourse of holiday makers on to his bridge over Baiæ bay; and
when they were in the height of their enjoyment, turned loose the Præ-
torian guards among the company, and had them tossed into the sea. This
is no bad miniature of the dealings of nature with the transitory race of
man. Only, what a chequered picnic we have of it, even while it lasts! and
into what great waters, not to be crossed by any swimmer, God's pale Præ-
torian throws us over in the end! We live the time that a match flickers;
we pop the cork of a ginger-beer bottle, and the earthquake swallows us on
the instant. Is it not odd, is it not incongruous, is it not, in the highest sense
of human speech, incredible, that we should think so highly of the ginger-
beer, and trouble our heads so little about the devouring earthquake? The
love of Life and the fear of Death are two famous phrases that grow harder
to understand the more we think about them. It is a well-known fact that
an immense proportion of boat accidents would never happen if people
held the sheet in their hands instead of tying it; and yet, unless it be some
martinet of a professional mariner or some landsman with shattered nerves,
every one of God's creatures ties it. A strange instance of man's unconcern
and brazen boldness in the face of death!

We confound ourselves with metaphysical phrases, which we import
into daily talk with noble inappropriateness. We have no idea of what
death is, apart from its circumstances and some of its consequences to
others; and although we have some experience of living, there is not a man
on earth who has flown so high into abstraction as to have any practical
guess at the meaning of the word *life*. All literature, from Job and Omar
Khayyam to Thomas Carlyle or Walt Whitman, is but an attempt to look
upon the human state with such largeness of view as shall enable us to
rise from the consideration of living to the Definition of Life. And our
sages give us about the best satisfaction in their power when they say that
it is a vapour, or a show, or made out of the same stuff with dreams. Philosophy, in its more rigid sense, has been at the same work for ages; and

[8 Roman Emperor, A.D. 37–41.]

after a myriad bald heads have wagged over the problem, and piles of words have been heaped one upon another into dry and cloudy volumes without end, philosophy has the honour of laying before us, with modest pride, her contribution towards the subject: that life is a Permanent Possibility of Sensation. Truly a fine result! A man may very well love beef, or hunting, or a woman; but surely, surely, not a Permanent Possibility of Sensation! He may be afraid of a precipice, or a dentist, or a large enemy with a club, or even an undertaker's man; but not certainly of abstract death. We may trick with the word life in its dozen senses until we are weary of tricking; we may argue in terms of all the philosophies on earth, but one fact remains true throughout—that we do not love life, in the sense that we are greatly preoccupied about its conservation; that we do not, properly speaking, love life at all, but living. Into the views of the least careful there will enter some degree of providence; no man's eyes are fixed entirely on the passing hour; but although we have some anticipation of good health, good weather, wine, active employment, love, and self-approval, the sum of these anticipations does not amount to anything like a general view of life's possibilities and issues; nor are those who cherish them most vividly, at all the most scrupulous of their personal safety. To be deeply interested in the accidents of our existence, to enjoy keenly the mixed texture of human experience, rather leads a man to disregard precautions, and risk his neck against a straw. For surely the love of living is stronger in an Alpine climber roping over a peril, or a hunter riding merrily at a stiff fence, than in a creature who lives upon a diet and walks a measured distance in the interest of his constitution.

There is a great deal of very vile nonsense talked upon both sides of the matter: tearing divines reducing life to the dimensions of a mere funeral procession, so short as to be hardly decent; and melancholy unbelievers yearning for the tomb as if it were a world too far away. Both sides must feel a little ashamed of their performances now and again when they draw in their chairs to dinner. Indeed, a good meal and a bottle of wine is an answer to most standard works upon the question. When a man's heart warms to his viands, he forgets a great deal of sophistry, and soars into a rosy zone of contemplation. Death may be knocking at the door, like the Commander's statue; [9] we have something else in hand, thank God, and let him knock. Passing bells are ringing all the world over; all the world over, and every hour, some one is parting company with all his aches and ecstasies; for us also the trap is laid. But we are so fond of life that we have no

[9 In act II, scene iv of Mozart's opera, *Don Giovanni*.]

leisure to entertain the terror of death. 'Tis a honeymoon with us all through, and none of the longest. Small blame to us if we give our whole hearts to this glowing bride of ours, to the appetites, to honour, to the hungry curiosity of the mind, to the pleasure of the eyes in nature, and the pride of our own nimble bodies.

We all of us appreciate the sensations; but as for caring about the Permanence of the Possibility, a man's head is generally very bald, and his senses very dull, before he comes to that. Whether we regard life as a lane leading to a dead wall—a mere bag's end, as the French say—or whether we think of it as a vestibule or gymnasium, where we wait our turn and prepare our faculties for some more noble destiny; whether we thunder in a pulpit, or pule in little atheistic poetry-books, about its vanity and brevity; whether we look justly for years of health and vigour, or are about to mount into a bath-chair,[10] as a step towards the hearse; in each and all of these views and situations there is but one conclusion possible: that a man should stop his ears against paralysing terror, and run the race that is set before him [11] with a single mind. No one surely could have recoiled with more heartache and terror from the thought of death than our delightful lexicographer; [12] and yet we know how little it affected his conduct, how wisely and boldly he walked, and in what a fresh and lively vein he spoke of life. Already an old man, he ventured on his Highland tour; and his heart, bound with triple brass, did not recoil before twenty-seven individual cups of tea. As courage and intelligence are the two qualities best worth a good man's cultivation, so it is the first part of intelligence to recognise our precarious estate in life, and the first part of courage to be not at all abashed before the fact. A frank and somewhat headlong carriage, not looking too anxiously before, not dallying in maudlin regret over the past, stamps the man who is well armoured for this world.

And not only well armoured for himself, but a good friend and a good citizen to boot. We do not go to cowards for tender dealing; there is nothing so cruel as panic; the man who has least fear for his own carcase, has most time to consider others. That eminent chemist who took his walks abroad in tin shoes, and subsisted wholly upon tepid milk, had all his work cut out for him in considerate dealings with his own digestion. So soon as prudence has begun to grow up in the brain, like a dismal fungus, it finds its first expression in a paralysis of generous acts. The victim begins to

[10] Invalid's wheel chair.]
[11] Hebrews, xii, 1.]
[12] Dr. Johnson (see pp. 358–69).]

shrink spiritually; he develops a fancy for parlours with a regulated temperature, and takes his morality on the principle of tin shoes and tepid milk. The care of one important body or soul becomes so engrossing, that all the noises of the outer world begin to come thin and faint into the parlour with the regulated temperature; and the tin shoes go equably forward over blood and rain. To be overwise is to ossify; and the scruple-monger ends by standing stockstill. Now the man who has his heart on his sleeve,[13] and a good whirling weathercock of a brain, who reckons his life as a thing to be dashingly used and cheerfully hazarded, makes a very different acquaintance of the world, keeps all his pulses going true and fast, and gathers impetus as he runs, until, if he be running towards anything better than wildfire, he may shoot up and become a constellation in the end. Lord look after his health, Lord have a care of his soul, says he; and he has at the key of the position, and swashes through peril and incongruity towards his aim. Death is on all sides of him with pointed batteries, as he is on all sides of all of us; the nastiest chances pop out against him; mim-mouthed friends and relations hold up their hands in quite a little elegiacal synod about his path: and what cares he for all this? Being a true lover of living, a fellow with something pushing and spontaneous in his inside, he must, like any other soldier, in any other stirring, deadly warfare, push on at his best pace until he touch the goal. 'A peerage or Westminster Abbey!' cried Nelson[14] in his bright, boyish, heroic manner. These are great incentives; not for any of these, but for the plain satisfaction of living, of being about their business in some sort or other, do the brave, serviceable men of every nation tread down the nettle danger,[15] and pass flyingly over all the stumbling-blocks of prudence. Think of the heroism of Johnson, think of that superb indifference to mortal limitation that set him upon his dictionary, and carried him through triumphantly until the end! Who, if he were wisely considerate of things at large, would ever embark upon any work much more considerable than a halfpenny post card? Who would project a serial novel, after Thackeray and Dickens had each fallen in mid-course? Who would find heart enough to begin to live, if he dallied with the consideration of death?

And, after all, what sorry and pitiful quibbling all this is! To forego all the issues of living in a parlour with a regulated temperature—as if that

[13] *Othello*, I, i, 64.]

[14] He is said to have uttered some such words just before a naval battle. They are usually quoted as 'Westminster Abbey or victory!']

[15] *I Henry IV*, II, iii, 11–12.]

were not to die a hundred times over, and for ten years at a stretch! As if it were not to die in one's own lifetime, and without even the sad immunities of death! As if it were not to die, and yet be the patient spectators of our own pitiable change! The Permanent Possibility is preserved, but the sensations carefully held at arm's length, as if one kept a photographic plate in a dark chamber. It is better to lose health like a spendthrift than to waste it like a miser. It is better to live and be done with it, than to die daily in the sick-room. By all means begin your folio; even if the doctor does not give you a year, even if he hesitates about a month, make one brave push and see what can be accomplished in a week. It is not only in finished undertakings that we ought to honour useful labour. A spirit goes out of the man who means execution, which outlives the most untimely ending. All who have meant good work with their whole hearts, have done good work, although they may die before they have the time to sign it. Every heart that has beat strong and cheerfully has left a hopeful impulse behind it in the world, and bettered the tradition of mankind. And even if death catch people, like an open pitfall, and in mid-career, laying out vast projects, and planning monstrous foundations, flushed with hope, and their mouths full of boastful language, they should be at once tripped up and silenced: is there not something brave and spirited in such a termination? And does not life go down with a better grace, foaming in full body over a precipice, than miserably straggling to an end in sandy deltas? When the Greeks made their fine saying that those whom the gods love die young, I cannot help believing they had this sort of death also in their eye. For surely, at whatever age it overtake the man, this is to die young. Death has not been suffered to take so much as an illusion from his heart. In the hot-fit of life, a-tiptoe on the highest point of being, he passes at a bound on to the other side. The noise of the mallet and chisel is scarcely quenched, the trumpets are hardly done blowing, when, trailing with him clouds of glory,[16] this happy-starr'd, full-blooded spirit shoots into the spiritual land.

[16 Wordsworth, *Ode on Intimations of Immortality from Recollections of Early Childhood.*]

E. B. White

WALDEN

❴ Mr. White's publications include essays, sketches, editorials, and verse (*Quo Vadimus*, 1939; *One Man's Meat*, 1942; *The Second Tree from the Corner*, 1954), stories (*Stuart Little*, 1945; *Charlotte's Web*, 1952), and an anthology (A *Subtreasury of American Humor*, 1941). Many of his writings first appeared in *Harper's* and *The New Yorker*; he was one of the editors of *The New Yorker* for about a dozen years, and still contributes to it.

This essay on *Walden* was written for the hundredth anniversary of Thoreau's book. 'In our uneasy season, when all men unconsciously seek a retreat from a world that has got almost completely out of hand, his house in the Concord woods is a haven. In our culture of gadgetry and the multiplicity of convenience, his cry "Simplicity, simplicity, simplicity!" has the insistence of a fire alarm. In the brooding atmosphere of war and the gathering radioactive storm, the innocence and serenity of his summer afternoons are enough to burst the remembering heart, and one gazes back upon that pleasing interlude—its confidence, its purity, its deliberateness— with awe and wonder, as one would look upon the face of a child asleep.'

I n his journal for July 10–12, 1841, Thoreau wrote: 'A slight sound at evening lifts me up by the ears, and makes life seem inexpressibly serene and grand. It may be in Uranus, or it may be in the shutter.' The book into which he later managed to pack both Uranus and the shutter was published in 1854, and now, a hundred years having gone by, 'Walden,' its serenity and grandeur unimpaired, still lifts us up by the ears,

FROM *The Yale Review*, Autumn, 1954. Copyright by the Yale University Press. Reprinted by permission of the author and *The Yale Review*.

still translates for us that language we are in danger of forgetting, 'which all things and events speak without metaphor, which alone is copious and standard.'

'Walden' is an oddity in American letters. It may very well be the oddest of our distinguished oddities. For many it is a great deal too odd, and for many it is a particular bore. I have not found it to be a well-liked book among my acquaintances, although usually spoken of with respect, and one literary critic for whom I have the highest regard can find no reason why anyone gives 'Walden' a second thought. To admire the book is, in fact, something of an embarrassment, for the mass of men have an indistinct notion that its author was a sort of Nature Boy.

I think it is of some advantage to encounter the book at a period in one's life when the normal anxieties and enthusiasms and rebellions of youth closely resemble those of Thoreau in that spring of 1845 when he borrowed an axe, went out to the woods, and began to whack down some trees for timber. Received at such a juncture, the book is like an invitation to life's dance, assuring the troubled recipient that no matter what befalls him in the way of success or failure he will always be welcome at the party—that the music is played for him, too, if he will but listen and move his feet. In effect, that is what the book is—an invitation, unengraved; and it stirs one as a young girl is stirred by her first big party bid. Many think it a sermon; many set it down as an attempt to rearrange society; some think it an exercise in nature-loving; some find it a rather irritating collection of inspirational puffballs by an eccentric show-off. I think it none of these. It still seems to me the best youth's companion yet written by an American, for it carries a solemn warning against the loss of one's valuables, it advances a good argument for traveling light and trying new adventures, it rings with the power of positive adoration, it contains religious feeling without religious images, and it steadfastly refuses to record bad news. Even its pantheistic note is so pure as to be noncorrupting—pure as the flute-note blown across the pond on those faraway summer nights. If our colleges and universities were alert, they would present a cheap pocket edition of the book to every senior upon graduating, along with his sheepskin, or instead of it. Even if some senior were to take it literally and start felling trees, there could be worse mishaps: the axe is older than the Dictaphone and it is just as well for a young man to see what kind of chips he leaves before listening to the sound of his own voice. And even if some were to get no farther than the table of contents, they would learn how to name eighteen chapters by the use of only thirty-nine words and would see how sweet are the uses of brevity.

If Thoreau had merely left us an account of a man's life in the woods, or if he had simply retreated to the woods and there recorded his complaints about society, or even if he had contrived to include both records in one essay, 'Walden' would probably not have lived a hundred years. As things turned out, Thoreau, very likely without knowing quite what he was up to, took man's relation to nature and man's dilemma in society and man's capacity for elevating his spirit and he beat all these matters together, in a wild free interval of self-justification and delight, and produced an original omelette from which people can draw nourishment in a hungry day. 'Walden' is one of the first of the vitamin-enriched American dishes. If it were a little less good than it is, or even a little less queer, it would be an abominable book. Even as it is, it will continue to baffle and annoy the literal mind and all those who are unable to stomach its caprices and imbibe its theme. Certainly the plodding economist will continue to have rough going if he hopes to emerge from the book with a clear system of economic thought. Thoreau's assault on the Concord society of the mid-nineteenth century has the quality of a modern Western: he rides into the subject at top speed, shooting in all directions. Many of his shots ricochet and nick him on the rebound, and throughout the melee there is a horrendous cloud of inconsistencies and contradictions, and when the shooting dies down and the air clears, one is impressed chiefly by the courage of the rider and by how splendid it was that somebody should have ridden in there and raised all that ruckus.

When he went to the pond, Thoreau struck an attitude and did so deliberately, but his posturing was not to draw the attention of others to him but rather to draw his own attention more closely to himself. 'I learned this at least by my experiment: that if one advances confidently in the direction of his dreams, and endeavors to live the life which he has imagined, he will meet with a success unexpected in common hours.' The sentence has the power to resuscitate the youth drowning in his sea of doubt. I recall my exhilaration upon reading it, many years ago, in a time of hesitation and despair. It restored me to health. And now in 1954 when I salute Henry Thoreau on the hundredth birthday of his book, I am merely paying off an old score—or an installment on it.

In his journal for May 3-4, 1838—Boston to Portland—he wrote: 'Midnight—head over the boat's side—between sleeping and waking—with glimpses of one or more lights in the vicinity of Cape Ann. Bright moon-light—the effect heightened by seasickness.' The entry illuminates the man, as the moon the sea on that night in May. In Thoreau the natural scene was heightened, not depressed, by a disturbance of the stomach, and nausea met its match at last. There was a steadiness in at least one passenger if there was none in the boat. Such steadiness (which in some would be called intoxication) is at the heart of 'Walden'—confidence, faith, the discipline of looking always at what is to be seen, undeviating gratitude for the life-everlasting that he found growing in his front yard. 'There is nowhere recorded a simple and irrepressible satisfaction with the gift of life, any memorable praise of God.' He worked to correct that deficiency. 'Walden' is his acknowledgment of the gift of life. It is the testament of a man in a high state of indignation because (it seemed to him) so few ears heard the uninterrupted poem of creation, the morning wind that forever blows. If the man sometimes wrote as though all his readers were male, unmarried, and well-connected, it is because he gave his testimony during the callow years, and, for that matter, never really grew up. To reject the book because of the immaturity of the author and the bugs in the logic is to throw away a bottle of good wine because it contains bits of the cork.

Thoreau said he required of every writer, first and last, a simple and sincere account of his own life. Having delivered himself of this chesty dictum, he proceeded to ignore it. In his books and even in his enormous journal, he withheld or disguised most of the facts from which an under-standing of his life could be drawn. 'Walden,' subtitled 'Life in the Woods,' is not a simple and sincere account of a man's life, either in or out of the woods; it is an account of a man's journey into the mind, a toot on the trumpet to alert the neighbors. Thoreau was well aware that no one can alert his neighbors who is not wide awake himself, and he went to the woods (among other reasons) to make sure that he would stay awake during his broadcast. What actually took place during the years 1845–47 is largely unrecorded, and the reader is excluded from the private life of the author, who supplies almost no gossip about himself, a great deal about his neighbors and about the universe.

As for me, I cannot in this short ramble give a simple and sincere ac-count of my own life, but I think Thoreau might find it instructive to know that this memorial essay is being written in a house that, through no intent on my part, is the same size and shape as his own domicile on the pond—about ten by fifteen, tight, plainly finished, and at a little distance from my Concord. The house in which I sit this morning was built to accommodate a boat, not a man, but by long experience I have learned that in most respects it shelters me better than the larger dwelling where my bed is, and which, by design, is a manhouse not a boathouse. Here in the boathouse I am a wilder and, it would appear, a healthier man, by a safe margin. I have a chair, a bench, a table, and I can walk into the water if I tire of the land. My house fronts a cove. Two fishermen have just arrived to spot fish from the air—an osprey and a man in a small yellow plane who works for the fish company. The man, I have noticed, is less well equipped than the hawk, who can dive directly on his fish and carry it away, without telephoning. A mouse and a squirrel share the house with me. The building is, in fact, a multiple dwelling, a semidetached affair. It is because I am semidetached while here that I find it possible to transact this private business with the fewest obstacles.

There is also a woodchuck here, living forty feet away under the wharf. When the wind is right, he can smell my house; and when the wind is contrary, I can smell his. We both use the wharf for sunning, taking turns, each adjusting his schedule to the other's convenience. Thoreau once ate a woodchuck. I think he felt he owed it to his readers, and that it was little enough, considering the indignities they were suffering at his hands and the dressing-down they were taking. (Parts of 'Walden' are pure scold.) Or perhaps he ate the woodchuck because he believed every man should acquire strict business habits, and the woodchuck was destroying his market beans. I do not know. Thoreau had a strong experimental streak in him. It is probably no harder to eat a woodchuck than to construct a sentence that lasts a hundred years. At any rate, Thoreau is the only writer I know who prepared himself for his great ordeal by eating a woodchuck; also the only one who got a hangover from drinking too much water. (He was drunk the whole time, though he seldom touched wine or coffee or tea.)

Here in this compact house where I would spend one day as deliberately as Nature if I were not being pressed by THE YALE REVIEW, and with a woodchuck (as yet uneaten) for neighbor, I can feel the companionship of the occupant of the pondside cabin in Walden woods, a mile from the village, near the Fitchburg right of way. Even my immediate business is no barrier between us: Thoreau occasionally batted out a magazine piece, but was always suspicious of any sort of pur-

poseful work that cut into his time. A man, he said, should take care
not to be thrown off the track by every nutshell and mosquito's wing that
falls on the rails.[1]

There has been much guessing as to why he went to the pond. To
set it down to escapism is, of course, to misconstrue what happened.
Henry went forth to battle when he took to the woods, and 'Walden'
is the report of a man torn by two powerful and opposing drives—the
desire to enjoy the world (and not to be derailed by a mosquito wing)
and the urge to set the world straight. One cannot join these two successfully, but sometimes, in rare cases, something good or even great
results from the attempt of the tormented spirit to reconcile them. Henry
went forth to battle, and if he set the stage himself, if he fought on his
own terms and with his own weapons, it was because it was his nature
to do things differently from most men, and to act in a cocky fashion. If
the pond and the woods seemed a more plausible site for a house than
an in-town location, it was because a cowbell made for him a sweeter
sound than a churchbell. 'Walden,' the book, makes the sound of a
cowbell, more than a churchbell, and proves the point, although both
sounds are in it, and both remarkably clear and sweet. He simply preferred his churchbell at a little distance.

I think one reason he went to the woods was a perfectly simple and commonplace one—and apparently he thought so, too. 'At a certain season
of our life,' he wrote, 'we are accustomed to consider every spot as the possible site of a house.'[2] There spoke the young man, a few years out of
college, who had not yet broken away from home. He hadn't married,
and he had found no job that measured up to his rigid standards of
employment, and like any young man, or young animal, he felt uneasy and
on the defensive until he had fixed himself a den. Most young men, of
course, casting about for a site, are content merely to draw apart from
their kinfolks. Thoreau, convinced that the greater part of what his neighbors called good was bad, withdrew from a great deal more than family:
he pulled out of everything for a while, to serve everybody right for being
so stuffy, and to try his own prejudices on the dog.

The house-hunting sentence above, which starts the Chapter called
'Where I Lived, and What I Lived For,' is followed by another passage
that is worth quoting here because it so beautifully illustrates the offbeat

[1 See p. 395.]
[2 See p. 383.]

prose that Thoreau was master of, a prose at once strictly disciplined and wildly abandoned. 'I have surveyed the country on every side within a dozen miles of where I live,' continued this delirious young man. 'In imagination I have bought all the farms in succession, for all were to be bought, and I knew their price. I walked over each farmer's premises, tasted his wild apples, discoursed on husbandry with him, took his farm at his price, at any price, mortgaging it to him in my mind; even put a higher price on it—took everything but a deed of it—took his word for his deed, for I dearly love to talk—cultivated it, and him too to some extent, I trust, and withdrew when I had enjoyed it long enough, leaving him to carry it on.' A copydesk man would get a double hernia trying to clean up that sentence for the management, but the sentence needs no fixing, for it perfectly captures the meaning of the writer and the quality of the ramble.

'Wherever I sat, there I might live, and the landscape radiated from me accordingly.' [3] Thoreau, the home-seeker, sitting on his hummock with the entire State of Massachusetts radiating from him, is to me the most humorous of the New England figures, and 'Walden' the most humorous of the books, though its humor is almost continuously sub-surface and there is nothing funny anywhere, except a few weak jokes and bad puns that rise to the surface like the perch in the pond that rose to the sound of the maestro's flute. Thoreau tended to write in sentences, a feat not every writer is capable of, and 'Walden' is, rhetorically speaking, a collection of certified sentences, some of them, it would now appear, as indestructible as they are errant. The book is distilled from the vast journals, and this accounts for its intensity: he picked out bright particles that pleased his eye, whirled them in the kaleidoscope of his content, and produced the pattern that has endured—the color, the form, the light.

On this its hundredth birthday, Thoreau's 'Walden' is pertinent and timely. In our uneasy season, when all men unconsciously seek a retreat from a world that has got almost completely out of hand, his house in the Concord woods is a haven. In our culture of gadgetry and the multiplicity of convenience, his cry 'Simplicity, simplicity, simplicity!'[4] has the in-sistence of a fire alarm. In the brooding atmosphere of war and the gather-ing radioactive storm, the innocence and serenity of his summer after-

[3 See p. 384.]
[4 See p. 391.]

noons are enough to burst the remembering heart, and one gazes back upon that pleasing interlude—its confidence, its purity, its deliberateness— with awe and wonder, as one would look upon the face of a child asleep.

'This small lake was of most value as a neighbor in the intervals of a gentle rain-storm in August, when, both air and water being perfectly still, but the sky overcast, midafternoon had all the serenity of evening, and the wood-thrush sang around, and was heard from shore to shore.' [5] Now, in the perpetual overcast in which our days are spent, we hear with extra perception and deep gratitude that song, tying century to century.

I sometimes amuse myself by bringing Henry Thoreau back to life and showing him the sights. I escort him into a phone booth and let him dial Weather. 'This is a delicious evening,' the girl's voice says, 'when the whole body is one sense, and imbibes delight through every pore.' I show him the spot in the Pacific where an island used to be, before some magician made it vanish. 'We know not where we are,' I murmur. 'The light which puts out our eyes is darkness to us. Only that day dawns to which we are awake.' I thumb through the latest copy of 'Vogue' with him. 'Of two patterns which differ only by a few threads more or less of a particular color,' I read, 'the one will be sold readily, the other lie on the shelf, though it frequently happens that, after the lapse of a season, the latter becomes the most fashionable.' Together we go outboarding on the Assabet, looking for what we've lost—a hound, a bay horse, a turtledove. I show him a distracted farmer who is trying to repair a hay baler before the thunder shower breaks. 'This farmer,' I remark, 'is endeavoring to solve the problem of a livelihood by a formula more complicated than the problem itself. To get his shoe strings he speculates in herds of cattle.'

I take the celebrated author to Twenty-One for lunch, so the waiters may study his shoes. The proprietor welcomes us. 'The gross feeder,' remarks the proprietor, sweeping the room with his arm, 'is a man in the larva stage.' After lunch we visit a classroom in one of those schools con- ducted by big corporations to teach their superannuated executives how to retire from business without serious injury to their health. (The shock to men's systems these days when relieved of the exacting routine of amassing wealth is very great and must be cushioned.) 'It is not necessary,' says the teacher to his pupils, 'that a man should earn his living by the sweat

[5 See p. 387.]

of his brow, unless he sweats easier than I do. We are determined to be starved before we are hungry.'

I turn on the radio and let Thoreau hear Winchell beat the red hand around the clock. 'Time is but the stream I go a-fishing in,' shouts Mr. Winchell, rattling his telegraph key. 'Hardly a man takes a half hour's nap after dinner, but when he wakes he holds up his head and asks, "What's the news?" If we read of one man robbed, or murdered, or killed by accident, or one house burned, or one vessel wrecked, or one steamboat blown up, or one cow run over on the Western Railroad, or one mad dog killed, or one lot of grasshoppers in the winter—we need never read of another. One is enough.'

I doubt that Thoreau would be thrown off balance by the fantastic sights and sounds of the twentieth century. 'The Concord nights,' he once wrote, 'are stranger than the Arabian nights.' A four-engined air liner would merely serve to confirm his early views on travel. Everywhere he would observe, in new shapes and sizes, the old predicaments and follies of men—the desperation, the impedimenta, the meanness—along with the visible capacity for elevation of the mind and soul. 'This curious world which we inhabit is more wonderful than it is convenient; more beautiful than it is useful; it is more to be admired and enjoyed than used.' He would see that today ten thousand engineers are busy making sure that the world shall be convenient if they bust doing it, and others are determined to increase its usefulness even though its beauty is lost somewhere along the way.

At any rate, I'd like to stroll about the countryside in Thoreau's company for a day, observing the modern scene, inspecting today's snowstorm, pointing out the sights, and offering belated apologies for my sins. Thoreau is unique among writers in that those who admire him find him uncomfortable to live with—a regular hairshirt of a man. A little band of dedicated Thoreauvians would be a sorry sight indeed: fellows who hate compromise and have compromised, fellows who love wildness and have lived tamely, and at their side, censuring them and chiding them, the ghostly figure of this upright man, who long ago gave corroboration to impulses they perceived were right and issued warnings against the things they instinctively knew to be their enemies. I should hate to be called a Thoreauvian, yet I wince every time I walk into the barn I'm pushing before me, seventy-five feet by forty, and the author of 'Walden' has served as my conscience through the long stretches of my trivial days.

Hairshirt or no, he is a better companion than most, and I would not swap him for a soberer or more reasonable friend even if I could. I can reread his famous invitation with undiminished excitement. The sad thing is that not more acceptances have been received, that so many decline for one reason or another, pleading some previous engagement or ill health. But the invitation stands. It will beckon as long as this remarkable book stays in print—which will be as long as there are August afternoons in the intervals of a gentle rainstorm, as long as there are ears to catch the faint sounds of the orchestra. I find it agreeable to sit here this morning, in a house of correct proportions, and hear across a century of time his flute, his frogs, and his seductive summons to the wildest revels of them all.

Douglas Southall Freeman
THE PATTERN OF A LIFE

⟨ Freeman led a life of extreme regularity and industry, divided equally between journalism and biography. An early riser (2.30 a.m.), he would work until noon on *The Richmond News Leader*, of which he was editor from 1915 until 1949. Afternoons and Sundays he devoted to less ephemeral writing, his lives of great Southerners. He wrote other books on Southern subjects (*Calendar of Confederate Papers*, 1908; *The South to Posterity*, 1939), but will be remembered by his spacious studies of Washington, Lee, and Lee's generals. These were acknowledged at once to be unrivaled in their fields.

The earliest was *R. E. Lee* (1935), on which Freeman spent twenty years. To these four volumes were added three on *Lee's Lieutenants* (1942–4), regarded by the author as the best of all his books. Finally came the most elaborate work of all, the life of George Washington. Five of the seven volumes planned were published between 1948 and 1952, the sixth in 1954 after Freeman's death.

In a biographical preface to the sixth volume of *George Washington*, Freeman's friend and fellow historian, Professor Dumas Malone, writes of *R. E. Lee*: 'Lee may still seem almost too good to be true, but his memory inspires no jealousy—since his life was set on a background of dark tragedy, just as Lincoln's was. It seems safe to predict, therefore, that this classic portrait of him, done in the grand manner by patient and skillful hands, will be cherished as long as the ideals of the Republic shall endure. . . . The creators of noble books about noble men are public benefactors, and such a benefactor was Douglas Southall Freeman.'

THERE he lies, now that they have shrouded him, with his massive features so white against the lining of the casket that he seems already a marble statue for the veneration of the South. His cause died at Appomattox; now, in him, it is to have its apotheosis. Others survive who shared his battles and his vigils, but none who so completely embodies the glamour, the genius, and the graces with which the South has idealized a hideous war. His passing sets a period to the bloodiest chapter in the history of his country.

Yet even in the hour of his death there are omens that the future of the South is to be built not less on hope than on memory. The windows of the chamber do not look to the west but to the sunrise. He is not clad in the uniform of his army but in the wedding garment he bought when he went, all unwillingly, to the marriage feast in Petersburg and found the city of his last defense breathing with new life. Presently, the bells that are tolling his death will bring down from the highlands, like the clans at the sound of the pibroch, a host of those who had followed his standard. For the moment, the first mourners are the students of the college, younger brothers of his veterans, and the children of the schools of the town, abruptly dismissed from their classes when the first note from the church belfry announced his last battle ended.

Tomorrow a slow-footed procession will form to carry his body to the chapel of the college,[1] and the press of the country will be praising his feats as a soldier and his high intellect as a leader, or else, once more, will be branding him a traitor. We who have followed his career through many pages have already discussed these things. Let us speak of them no more, but, ere the silent undertaker screws down the lid of the coffin, let us look at him for the last time and read from his countenance the pattern of his life.

Because he was calm when others were frenzied, loving when they hated, and silent when they spoke with bitter tongue, they shook their heads and said he was a superman or a mysterious man. Beneath that untroubled exterior, they said, deep storms must rage; his dignity, his reserve, and his few words concealed sombre thoughts, repressed ambitions, livid resentments. They were mistaken. Robert Lee was one of the small company of great men in whom there is no inconsistency to be explained, no enigma

[1 Lee was president of Washington College (now Washington and Lee University) from 1865 until his death in 1870.]

to be solved. What he seemed, he was—a wholly human gentleman, the essential elements of whose positive character were two and only two, simplicity and spirituality.

When the nascent science of genetics is developed, Lee will be cited in the case-books along with those who appear in Galton's *Hereditary Genius*. For his most conspicuous qualities, it may be repeated, were derived in almost equal determinable proportions from his parents and from his grandparents. From his Grandfather Lee, came a sense of system, the power of critical analysis that kept him free of illusion, and, along with these, perhaps, his love of animals. His good looks were an endowment from his maternal grandmother, the 'Lowland Beauty' at the sight of whom the grave eyes of George Washington are said to have lighted up. To his Grandfather Carter, Robert E. Lee owed much of the religion of his nature, something of his kindness, his love of family life and his devotion to his kin. 'Light-Horse Harry' Lee [2] passed on to his youngest son his fine physique, his aptitude for military affairs, his great intelligence, his daring, his sense of public duty, and the charm of manner that made him so readily a captain. The characteristics of his mother that reppear were her religion, her thrift, her self-control, her social sense, and her patience in adversity. If it seem unscientific, at first glance, to speak with so much assurance of Lee's inherited characteristics, it may be said that the celebrity of his forebears and the diligence of the family genealogists make the facts more apparent than in most cases. Were as much known of other great American families as of the Lees, as much might be said of their descendants.

Fortunate in his ancestors, Lee was fortunate most of all in that he inherited nearly all their nobler qualities and none of their worse. Geneticists will say, perhaps, that this is the explanation of genius—a chance combination of genes. Beyond the frontier that these pioneers have yet crossed lies the fact that at least four generations of the ancestors of Lee, prior to that of his immediate grandparents, had all married well. Back to Richard the immigrant, whose wife's family name is unknown, there was not one instance in which a direct progenitor of Lee mated with a woman of blood and of station below his own. His line was not crossed in a century and a half with one that was degenerating. If blood means anything, he was entitled to be what he fundamentally was, a gentleman.

The first reference to Robert E. Lee in an extant letter is the significant statement of his father that 'Robert was always good and will be confirmed

[2 General Henry ('Light-Horse Harry') Lee was a daring cavalry officer in the Revolutionary army. After the war he was a member of Congress and Governor of Virginia.]

in his happy turn of mind by his everwatchful and affectionate mother. Does he strengthen his native tendency?' Penned when the boy was ten, this language registered the impression the absent father had formed when Robert was not more than seven years of age. The stamp of character must, then, have been upon him from childhood. When he emerges dimly as a personality, in the later days of his cadetship at West Point, many of his essential qualities are apparent. Thereafter, from the time he appears clearly at Cockspur Island and at Fort Monroe, he exhibits every characteristic that later distinguished him. Subsequent change in his character was negligible and is simply the development of the man by challenging circumstance. Of this there can be no question. So consistent is the description of the young lieutenant of engineers, in the early 1830's, alike by those who became his foes and by those who remained his friends, that one need not fear the picture is touched up with the later remembrance of qualities the grizzled General displayed when he had endured the hard ordeal of the War between the States.

This early development of character, like everything else that relates to Lee as an individual, is easily understood. Despite the ill-health of the mother and her unhappiness during her pregnancy, he had a strong and normal nervous system that was invigorated by a simple outdoor life. Although there is no evidence that Mrs. Ann Lee had any secret dread that her son would develop the recklessness of his father, there is abundant proof that, with tactful wisdom, she inculcated in him from childhood the principles of self-control. From earliest adolescence he had upon him the care of his mother. George Washington, the embodiment of character, was his hero, made real and personal in the environment of Alexandria. At West Point his ambition to excel in his class led Lee to subject himself willingly and with a whole heart to a discipline that confirmed every excellence he had acquired at home. Physically more developed than most of the cadets, he had from the outset a better appreciation of what the training of the academy was intended to accomplish. All his early assignments to engineering duty were of a sort to impose responsibility. These circumstances did not destroy his sunny exuberance of spirit, but they set his character so early and so definitely that it did not change with years or woes.

Whether it was at the Des Moines Rapids, or during his superintendency of West Point, or in the president's house at Washington College—wherever he was in full four decades when the burden of battle was not on him—an old acquaintance would have observed little difference in his daily outlook, his nature, or his manners. Only in four particulars was the man who went to that last vestry meeting at the Episcopal church in Lexington unlike the lieutenant who bantered the 'Beautiful Talcott' at Old Point in the moments he was not watching the contractors who might circumvent the government. His buoyant bearing had given place to a calmer cheerfulness, which might have been the case with any man who has bridged the chasm that divides the twenties of life from the sixties, even though no river of blood has flowed through the chasm. Again, the natural dignity of his person had settled into a more formal reserve, not because he had become less simple in heart or less approachable in manner, but because his conception of his duty to promote peace and national unity compelled him to put a wall between him and those who might have stirred unhappy memories and would certainly have kept open the old wounds of fratricidal war had he permitted them to talk of war. Even then it is quite likely that some of those who knew him after the war mistook their reverence for his reserve. He was changed, also, in that, after 1865, he put out of his heart the military career that long had fascinated him. All the misgivings he had felt before the war regarding the pursuit of arms were confirmed by five years at Lexington. He spoke his conviction, as always, when he told young Professor Humphreys that the great mistake of his life had been in pursuing the education of a soldier, and he was not jesting in his encomium to General Ewell on the delights of a civil life. It was not by chance that he failed to keep step with the superintendent of V. M. I. when the two walked together at the head of the column of cadets.

These things apart, any one who had worked with him on the wharf at Saint Louis would have felt at home in his office in Lexington and would have found him the same man in the habits of life, in the steady routine, and in the simplicity of spirit that were his very ego. He rose early and cheerfully and had his private devotions. If he was away from home, he would write his domestic letters before breakfast. At the meal hour he would appear promptly, with greetings to all and with gentle, bantering reproaches for his always tardy wife. Were his food the sumptuous fare of bountiful Arlington, he would enjoy and praise each dish, eating with heartiness; but when he sat down to the plain diet of the first hard days at Lexington he showed the same relish and made no complaint.

Family worship over, he would go to work immediately, neatly dressed and with the whitest of linens, but never ostentatiously apparelled. In his labor he was swift and diligent, prompt and accurate, always systematic and instinctively thrifty. His ambition was in his labor, whatever its nature. He did not covet praise. Blushing to receive it, he assumed that others would blush when he bestowed it, and he spared what he thought were their feelings, though no man was quicker to appreciate and, at the proper time, to acknowledge the achievement of others. Place and advancement never lured him, except as promotion held out the hope of larger opportunity and better provision for his family. Even then he was meticulous regarding the methods he would employ to further himself financially, and he would never capitalize his name or draw drafts on the good opinion of friends or public. Yet he had all his life the desire to excel at the task assigned him. That was the urge alike of conscience, of obligation, of his regard for detail, and of his devotion to thoroughness as the prime constituent of all labor. He never said so in plain words, but he desired everything that he did, whether it was to plan a battle or to greet a visitor, to be as nearly perfect as he could make it. No man was more critical of his own performance because none demanded more of himself. The engineer's impulse in him was most gratified if something was to be created or organized, but if it concerned another's happiness or had a place in the large design or worth-while things, he considered the smallest task proper to perform. Only the useless was irksome.

He endured interruption of his work without vexation. Rarely was he embarrassed in his dealings with men. He met every visitor, every fellow-worker, with a smile and a bow, no matter what the other's station in life. Always he seemed to keep others at a judicious distance and did not invite their confidences, but he sought as a gentleman to make every right-minded person comfortable in his presence. With a tact so delicate that others scarcely noticed it, when he was busy he kept conversation to the question at issue, and he sought to make his interviews brief; but even so, his consideration for the sensibilities of others cost him many a precious hour. Wrangles he avoided, and disagreeable persons he usually treated with a cold and freezing courtesy. Should his self-control be overborne by stupidity or ill-temper, his eyes would flash and his neck would redden. His rebuke would be swift and terse, and it might be two hours or more before he was completely master of himself. Whoever visited him meantime would perhaps find him irascible, though sure to make amends. Exacting of his subordinates, he still reconciled himself often to working with clumsy human tools. Resentments he never cherished. When he found men unworthy of his confidence, he made it his practice to see them as little as possible and to talk to them not at all. Silence was one of his strongest weapons. During the war he summarized his code when he wrote these words on a scrap of paper that nobody saw until after his death:

'The forbearing use of power does not only form a touchstone, but the manner in which an individual enjoys certain advantages over others is a test of a true gentleman.

'The power which the strong have over the weak, the employer over the employed, the educated over the unlettered, the experienced over the confiding, even the clever over the silly—the forbearing or inoffensive use of all this power or authority, or a total abstinence from it when the case admits it, will show the gentleman in a plain light. The gentleman does not needlessly and unnecessarily remind an offender of a wrong he may have committed against him. He can not only forgive, he can forget; and he strives for that nobleness of self and mildness of character which impart sufficient strength to let the past be but the past. A true man of honor feels humbled himself when he cannot help humbling others.'

Lee sought to conclude his work by early afternoon, even if that compelled him to set a late hour for the meal. When dinner was done he was glad of a brief period of relaxation and sometimes of a little sleep, usually upright in his chair. Then he sought his daily exercise in a ride on his horse. He delighted to have a companion, and if he had one, he talked of pleasant topics. Riding alone, which he often did, he would close his mind to the difficulties of the day and to the problems of the morrow and would soothe himself with the discovered beauties of the countryside. Nothing of a physical nature gave him the same thrill as a glowing sunset. Usually, on these rides, he paid his calls on the sick and on strangers, as diligently as if he had been the parson of the town. This he regarded as one of his social duties, and he discharged it not only with willingness but also with satisfaction. Whether his ride included social calls or simply carried him to a given objective, he was always on the alert for the children and he never passed them without a greeting, and, usually, a chat.

His return home, like all his other movements, was according to a precise schedule. Unless a sudden storm detained him, he would be at his door promptly at dusk, and would soon be ready for his light evening meal— 'tea' as the family called it. The hours then belonged to Mrs. Lee, to his children, and to his guests. He would read to them or converse cheerfully until bedtime, which was usually after 10 o'clock. When he retired to his own room he had his evening prayers and was soon asleep. His quarters at Lexington were always as neat as if he were still a cadet at West Point, but the only suggestion of the soldier was the army pistol that hung in its holster by the head of his bed. After Mrs. Lee's invalidism afflicted her, he rarely went out to social affairs. Before that time he sometimes attended her to parties or to dinners, where he preferred the company of women to that of men, and that of the daughters to the mothers'. Always his address was dignified, but to the young girls it was often bantering. Nothing delighted him more than gently to tease some blushing young beauty. He had neither high wit nor quick repartee, though occasionally he essayed a pun; but his smile, his manners, and his quick understanding made him socially irresistible. His conversation, however, never turned to forbidden topics, nor was there in it anything suggestive or of *double entente*. In all his letters, and there are several thousand of them, as in all his reported conversation, and there are countless anecdotes of him, no oath or vulgarism appears. He was clean-minded, though definitely and unfeignedly attracted to intelligent, handsome women.

Leaves and furloughs during his army services and vacations after the war found him ready to travel, not to distant lands but to the spas of Virginia or, better still, to the houses of congenial friends. Most of all did he relish a round of visits to his own kin, with whom he delighted to talk of the doings of their relatives. Chatter of this sort never bored him. Naturally sociable and devoted to his countless cousins, he sympathized with all their distresses and rejoiced in their little triumphs. Rarely was he too busy, when time allowed of his writing at all, to chronicle every wedding, every birth, every journey, every sickness, for the information of his family correspondents. At home, in his earlier periods of leisure, he shared in the sports of his sons, and to the end of his life he gave to each of his daughters a measure of courtly attention fitted to the temperament and age of each of them.

At intervals his habitual cheerfulness was marred by a sense of failure. This was most apt to overtake him when he was absent from home on long tours of military duty, for his simple nature made him dependent on his wife and children. Separated from them he often suffered loneliness and sometimes acute nostalgia. On occasion, and particularly during the difficult period when he was struggling to settle Mr. Custis's estate and to repair Arlington in 1857–59, this sense of frustration came upon him even at home. Then he would wonder why he did not advance more rapidly in the army and would puzzle himself to know how he could make adequate provision for his daughters, none of whom, in his heart of hearts, he wished to be married. These were the most unhappy times of his life, except perhaps those of his occasional illnesses. When sick, he would have few words even for his family, and was more than apt to lose his grip upon himself in dealing with others.

This was the pattern of his daily life. There is every reason to believe it was the mirror of his own soul. Those who look at him through the glamour of his victories or seek deep meaning in his silence will labor in vain to make him appear complicated. His language, his acts, and his personal life were simple for the unescapable reason that he was a simple gentleman.

Simple and spiritual—the two qualities which constitute the man cannot be separated. The strongest religious impulse in his life was that given him by his mother. After that, in youth, he probably came most under the indirect influence of Reverend William Meade, later bishop, the clergyman who did more than any one else to restore the Protestant Episcopal Church in Virginia from the ruin that had overtaken it during and after the American Revolution. Mr. Meade was rector in Alexandria for only eighteen months and then at a time when Robert was too young to heed his sermons; but he preached there often during Robert's youth and his spirit dominated the Episcopal Church in Virginia. He was a picturesque personality, one of the prophets of his generation. Holding to the beautiful forms of his faith, Mr. Meade breathed into its worship an evangelism as ardent as that of the younger American denominations. In his eyes, religion concerned itself equally with acts and with beliefs. No reformer was ever more uncompromising in his denunciation of cards or more unyielding in opposition to the old habit the barons of the Northern Neck had of staging races and of backing their horses with their dollars. None excoriated the stage with warnings more sulphurous than did Mr. Meade. Had he been sent to idolatrous Israel, he could not more solemnly have proclaimed the day of the vengeance of the Lord or have portrayed more darkly the fearsome punishment visited on the sinner for his hardness of heart. Yet he spoke 'comfortably to Jerusalem.' He gave the promise of forgiveness to the repentant, pictured glowingly to the faithful the bliss of a hard-won Heaven, and somehow planted in the hearts of the dominant class in that section of the Old Dominion a religion of simplicity, vigor, and sincerity.

It is a singular fact that young Robert Lee was not prompted by the exhortations of Mr. Meade or of like-minded clergymen to submit himself to confirmation. The reason cannot be surmised, unless it was that the theology of his youth had a vehemence and an emotionalism alien to his nature. He was content until he was past forty-five to hold to the code of a gentleman rather than to the formal creed of a church. The experiences of the Mexican War, the gentle piety of the Fitzhughs at Ravensworth, the example and death of Mrs. Custis, the simple faith of Mrs. Lee, and, more immediately, the purpose of his daughters to enter into the full fellowship of the church induced Lee in 1853 to renew his vows. After that time, first his sense of dependence on God for the uprearing of his boys during his long absences from home, and then the developing tragedy of the war, deepened every religious impulse of his soul.

And what did religion imply for him as he sent Pickett's men up Cemetery Ridge,[3] as he rode to the McLean house,[4] as he read of Military District No. 1,[5] and as he looked down from the chapel platform at the scarred faces and patched garments of his students?

To answer that question is to employ the terms of a theology that now seems to some outworn and perhaps archaic. It was, however, the *credo* of a man who met the supreme tests of life in that he accepted fame without vanity and defeat without repining. To understand the faith of Robert E. Lee is to fill out the picture of him as a gentleman of simple soul. For him as for his grandfather, Charles Carter, religion blended with the code of *noblesse oblige* to which he had been reared. Together, these two forces resolved every problem of his life into right and wrong. The clear light of conscience and of social obligation left no zone of gray in his heart: everything was black or white. There cannot be said to have been a 'secret' of his life, but this assuredly was the great, transparent truth, and this it was, primarily, that gave to his career its consistency and decision. Over his movements as a soldier he hesitated often, but over his acts as a man, never. There was but one question ever: What was his duty as a Christian and a gentleman? That he answered by the sure criterion of right and wrong, and, having answered, acted. Everywhere the two obligations went together; he never sought to expiate as a Christian for what he had failed to do as a gentleman, or to atone as a gentleman for what he had neglected as a Christian. He could not have conceived of a Christian who was not a gentleman.

Kindness was the first implication of religion in his mind—not the deliberate kindness of 'good works' to pacify exacting Deity but the instinctive kindness of a heart that had been schooled to regard others. His

[3 At Gettysburg.]

[4 Where the surrender papers were signed, at Appomattox.]

[5 The First Reconstruction Act of March 1867 divided the South into military districts. Virginia was in District No. 1.]

was not a nature to waste time in the perplexities of self-analysis; but if those about him at headquarters had understood him better they might often have asked themselves whether, when he brought a refreshing drink to a dusty lieutenant who called with dispatches, he was discharging the social duty of a host or was giving a 'cup of cold water' in his Master's name. His manner in either case would have been precisely the same.

Equally was his religion expressed in his unquestioning response to duty. In his clear creed, right was duty and must be discharged. 'There is,' he wrote down privately for his own guidance, 'a true glory and a true honor: the glory of duty done—the honor of the integrity of principle.' He probably never summed up this aspect of his religion more completely than in that self-revealing hour before he started to meet General Grant, when he answered all the appeals of his lieutenants with the simple statement: 'The question is, is it right to surrender this army? If it is right, then I will take all the responsibility.' It was a high creed—right at all times and at all costs—but daily self-discipline and a clear sense of justice made him able to adhere to it.

Humility was another major implication of his religion. So lofty was his conception of man's duty to his Maker and to his neighbors, so completely did his ambition extend, all unconsciously, into the realm of the spirit, that he was never satisfied with what he was. Those who stood with him on the red field of Appomattox thought that his composure was due to his belief that he had discharged his full duty, and in this they were partially correct; but he always felt, with a sincerity no man can challenge, that he had fallen immeasurably short of his ideal of a servant of God. 'So humble was he as a Christian,' wrote Mrs. Lee on the day of his death, 'that he said not long ago to me he wished he felt sure of his acceptance. I said all who love and trust in the Savior need not fear. He did not reply, but a more upright and conscientious Christian never lived.'

Born of this humility, this sense of unworthiness in the sight of God, was the submission to the Divine will that has so often been cited in these pages to explain his calmness in hours that would have wrecked the self-control of lesser men. There was nothing of blind fatalism in his faith. Resignation is scarcely the name for it. Believing that God was Infinite Wisdom and Eternal Love, he subjected himself to seeming ill-fortune in the confidence that God's will would work out for man's good. If it was a battle that had been won, to 'Almighty God' he gave the glory; if it was a death that had brought grief to the family, he reminded his wife that their 'Heavenly Father' knew better than they, and that there was eternal peace and sure reunion after life. Nothing of his serenity during the war or of his silent labor in defeat can be understood unless one realizes that he submitted himself in all things faithfully to the will of a Divinity which, in his simple faith, was directing wisely the fate of nations and the daily life of His children. This, and not the mere physical courage that defies danger, sustained him in battle; and this, at least equally with his sense of duty done, made him accept the results of the war without even a single gesture of complaint.

Of humility and submission was born a spirit of self-denial that prepared him for the hardships of the war and, still more, for the dark destitution that followed it. This self-denial was, in some sense, the spiritual counterpart of the social self-control his mother had inculcated in his boyhood days, and it grew in power throughout his life. He loved the luxury that wealth commanded. Had he been as rich as his Grandfather Carter, he would have lived in a style as hospitable. Fine horses and handsome clothes and lavish entertainments would have been his; Arlington would have been adorned, and his daughters would have enjoyed travel and the richest comfort. But Arlington was confiscated, its treasures were scattered, each stage of his sacrifice for the South brought him lower and lower in fortune until he was living in a borrowed tenant house and his wife was husbanding the scraps from a pair of trousers a farmer's wife had made for him. His own misfortunes typified the fate of the Confederacy and of its adherents. Through it all, his spirit of self-denial met every demand upon it, and even after he went to Washington College and had an income on which he could live easily, he continued to deny himself as an example to his people. Had his life been epitomized in one sentence of the Book he read so often, it would have been in the words, 'If any man will come after me, let him deny himself, and take up his cross daily, and follow me.' And if one, only one, of all the myriad incidents of his stirring life had to be selected to typify his message, as a man, to the young Americans who stood in hushed awe that rainy October morning as their parents wept at the passing of the Southern Arthur, who would hesitate in selecting that incident? It occurred in Northern Virginia, probably on his last visit there. A young mother brought her baby to him to be blessed. He took the infant in his arms and looked at it and then at her and slowly said, 'Teach him he must deny himself.'

That is all. There is no mystery in the coffin there in front of the windows that look to the sunrise.

Mark Twain (S. L. Clemens)
LIFE ON THE MISSISSIPPI

❪ As a narrative of youth and river life, Mark Twain's *Life on the Mississippi* is second to the immortal *Huckleberry Finn*, but it is a very good second. The first part of the book (chs. iv–xx), describing the author's years on the river as a steamboat pilot, was originally published in *The Atlantic Monthly*; the second part, which is a record of a revisit to the river many years after his career as a pilot had ended, was written seven years after the first. The book appeared in 1883. All of it is typical Mark Twain and therefore good, but the earlier chapters, with their vivid pictures of the cub pilot, of the superlative Mr. Bixby, and of the mighty river itself, are easily the favorite ones. They contain some of the best pages Mark Twain ever wrote.

THE BOYS' AMBITION

WHEN I was a boy, there was but one permanent ambition among my comrades in our village * on the west bank of the Mississippi River. That was, to be a steamboatman. We had transient ambitions of other sorts, but they were only transient. When a circus came and went, it left us all burning to become clowns; the first negro minstrel show that came to our section left us all suffering to try that kind of life; now and then we had a hope that if we lived and were good, God would permit us to be pirates. These ambitions faded out, each in its turn; but the ambition to be a steamboatman always remained.

Once a day a cheap, gaudy packet arrived upward from St. Louis, and another downward from Keokuk. Before these events had transpired, the day was glorious with expectancy; after they had transpired, the day was a dead and empty thing. Not only the boys, but the whole village, felt this.

* Hannibal, Missouri.
FROM *Life on the Mississippi*, 1875, 1883.

After all these years I can picture that old time to myself now, just as it was then: the white town drowsing in the sunshine of a summer's morning; the streets empty, or pretty nearly so; one or two clerks sitting in front of the Water Street stores, with their splint-bottomed chairs tilted back against the wall, chins on breasts, hats slouched over their faces, asleep— with shingle-shavings enough around to show what broke them down; a sow and a litter of pigs loafing along the sidewalk, doing a good business in water-melon rinds and seeds; two or three lonely little freight piles scattered about the 'levee'; a pile of 'skids' on the slope of the stone-paved wharf, and the fragrant town drunkard asleep in the shadow of them; two or three wood flats at the head of the wharf, but nobody to listen to the peaceful lapping of the wavelets against them; the great Mississippi, the majestic, the magnificent Mississippi, rolling its mile-wide tide along, shining in the sun; the dense forest away on the other side; the 'point' above the town, and the 'point' below, bounding the river-glimpse and turning it into a sort of sea, and withal a very still and brilliant and lonely one. Presently a film of dark smoke appears above one of those remote points; instantly a negro drayman, famous for his quick eye and prodigious voice, lifts up the cry, 'S-t-e-a-m-boat a-comin'!' and the scene changes! The town drunkard stirs, the clerks wake up, a furious clatter of drays follows, every house and store pours out a human contribution, and all in a twinkling the dead town is alive and moving. Drays, carts, men, boys, all go hurrying from many quarters to a common centre, the wharf. Assembled there, the people fasten their eyes upon the coming boat as upon a wonder they are seeing for the first time. And the boat *is* rather a handsome sight, too. She is long and sharp and trim and pretty; she has two tall, fancy-topped chimneys, with a gilded device of some kind swung between them; a fanciful pilot-house, all glass and 'gingerbread,' perched on top of the 'texas' deck [1] behind them; the paddle-boxes are gorgeous with a picture or with gilded rays above the boat's name; the boiler deck, the hurricane deck, and the texas deck are fenced and ornamented with clean white railings; there is a flag gallantly flying from the jack-staff; the furnace doors are open and the fires glaring bravely; the upper decks are black with passengers; the captain stands by the big bell, calm, imposing, the envy of all; great volumes of the blackest smoke are rolling and tumbling out of the chimneys—a husbanded grandeur created with a bit of pitch pine just before arriving at a town; the crew are grouped on the forecastle; the broad stage is run far out over the port

[1 Where both pilot house and officers' cabins were. The texas was on the hurricane, or upper, deck.]

bow, and an envied deck-hand stands picturesquely on the end of it with a coil of rope in his hand; the pent steam is screaming through the gauge-cocks; the captain lifts his hand, a bell rings, the wheels stop; then they turn back, churning the water to foam, and the steamer is at rest. Then such a scramble as there is to get aboard, and to get ashore, and to take in freight and to discharge freight, all at one and the same time; and such a yelling and cursing as the mates facilitate it all with! Ten minutes later the steamer is under way again, with no flag on the jack-staff and no black smoke issuing from the chimneys. After ten more minutes the town is dead again, and the town drunkard asleep by the skids once more.

My father was a justice of the peace, and I supposed he possessed the power of life and death over all men and could hang anybody that offended him. This was distinction enough for me as a general thing; but the desire to be a steamboatman kept intruding, nevertheless. I first wanted to be a cabin-boy, so that I could come out with a white apron on and shake a table-cloth over the side, where all my old comrades could see me; later I thought I would rather be the deck-hand who stood on the end of the stage-plank with the coil of rope in his hand, because he was particularly conspicuous. But these were only day-dreams—they were too heavenly to be contemplated as real possibilities. By and by one of our boys went away. He was not heard of for a long time. At last he turned up as apprentice engineer or 'striker' on a steamboat. This thing shook the bottom out of all my Sunday-school teachings. That boy had been notoriously worldly, and I just the reverse; yet he was exalted to this eminence, and I left in obscurity and misery. There was nothing generous about this fellow in his greatness. He would always manage to have a rusty bolt to scrub while his boat tarried at our town, and he would sit on the inside guard and scrub it, where we could all see him and envy him and loathe him. And whenever his boat was laid up he would come home and swell around the town in his blackest and greasiest clothes, so that nobody could help remembering that he was a steamboatman; and he used all sorts of steamboat technicalities in his talk, as if he were so used to them that he forgot common people could not understand them. He would speak of the 'labboard' side of a horse in an easy, natural way that would make one wish he was dead. And he was always talking about 'St. Looy' like an old citizen; he would refer casually to occasions when he 'was coming down Fourth Street,' or when he was 'passing by the Planter's House,' or when there was a fire and he took a turn on the brakes of 'the old Big Missouri,' and then he would go on and lie about how many towns the size of ours were burned down there that day. Two or three of the boys had long been persons of consideration among us because they had been to St. Louis once and had a vague general knowledge of its wonders, but the day of their glory was over now. They lapsed into a humble silence, and learned to disappear when the ruthless 'cub'-engineer approached. This fellow had money, too, and hair oil. Also an ignorant silver watch and a showy brass watch chain. He wore a leather belt and used no suspenders. If ever a youth was cordially admired and hated by his comrades, this one was. No girl could withstand his charms. He 'cut out' every boy in the village. When his boat blew up at last, it diffused a tranquil contentment among us such as we had not known for months. But when he came home the next week, alive, renowned, and appeared in church all battered up and bandaged, a shining hero, stared at and wondered over by everybody, it seemed to us that the partiality of Providence for an undeserving reptile had reached a point where it was open to criticism.

This creature's career could produce but one result, and it speedily followed. Boy after boy managed to get on the river. The minister's son became an engineer. The doctor's and the postmaster's sons became 'mud clerks'; the wholesale liquor dealer's son became a bar-keeper on a boat; four sons of the chief merchant, and two sons of the county judge, became pilots. Pilot was the grandest position of all. The pilot, even in those days of trivial wages, had a princely salary—from a hundred and fifty to two hundred and fifty dollars a month, and no board to pay. Two months of his wages would pay a preacher's salary for a year. Now some of us were left disconsolate. We could not get on the river—at least our parents would not let us.

So by and by I ran away. I said I never would come home again till I was a pilot and could come in glory. But somehow I could not manage it. I went meekly aboard a few of the boats that lay packed together like sardines at the long St. Louis wharf, and very humbly inquired for the pilots, but got only a cold shoulder and short words from mates and clerks. I had to make the best of this sort of treatment for the time being, but I had comforting day-dreams of a future when I should be a great and honored pilot, with plenty of money, and could kill some of these mates and clerks and pay for them.

A CUB-PILOT'S EXPERIENCE

WHAT with lying on the rocks four days at Louisville, and some other delays, the poor old Paul Jones fooled away about two weeks in making the voyage from Cincinnati to New Orleans. This gave me a chance to get acquainted with one of the pilots, and he taught me how to steer the boat, and thus made the fascination of river life more potent than ever for me.

It also gave me a chance to get acquainted with a youth who had taken deck passage—more's the pity; for he easily borrowed six dollars of me on a promise to return to the boat and pay it back to me the day after we should arrive. But he probably died or forgot, for he never came. It was doubtless the former, since he had said his parents were wealthy, and he only traveled deck passage because it was cooler.*

I soon discovered two things. One was that a vessel would not be likely to sail for the mouth of the Amazon ² under ten or twelve years; and the other was that the nine or ten dollars still left in my pocket would not suffice for so imposing an exploration as I had planned, even if I could afford to wait for a ship. Therefore it followed that I must contrive a new career. The Paul Jones was now bound for St. Louis. I planned a siege against my pilot, and at the end of three hard days he surrendered. He agreed to teach me the Mississippi River from New Orleans to St. Louis for five hundred dollars, payable out of the first wages I should receive after graduating. I entered upon the small enterprise of 'learning' twelve or thirteen hundred miles of the great Mississippi River with the easy confidence of my time of life. If I had really known what I was about to require of my faculties, I should not have had the courage to begin. I supposed that all a pilot had to do was to keep his boat in the river, and I did not consider that that could be much of a trick, since it was so wide.

The boat backed out from New Orleans at four in the afternoon, and it was 'our watch' until eight. Mr. Bixby, my chief, 'straightened her up,' plowed her along past the sterns of the other boats that lay at the Levee, and then said, 'Here, take her; shave those steamships as close as you'd peel an apple.' I took the wheel, and my heart went down into my boots; for it seemed to me that we were about to scrape the side off every ship in the line, we were so close. I held my breath and began to claw the boat away from the danger; and I had my own opinion of the pilot who had known no better than to get us into such peril, but I was too wise to express it. In half a minute I had a wide margin of safety intervening between the Paul Jones and the ships; and within ten seconds more I was set aside in disgrace, and Mr. Bixby was going into danger again and flaying me alive

* 'Deck' passage—i.e., steerage passage.

[² In an earlier chapter Mark Twain, then in Cincinnati, decided rather casually to explore the Amazon. and took passage to New Orleans on the *Paul Jones*.]

with abuse of my cowardice. I was stung, but I was obliged to admire the easy confidence with which my chief loafed from side to side of his wheel, and trimmed the ships so closely that disaster seemed ceaselessly imminent. When he had cooled a little he told me that the easy water was close ashore and the current outside, and therefore we must hug the bank, up-stream, to get the benefit of the former, and stay well out, down-stream, to take advantage of the latter. In my own mind I resolved to be a down-stream pilot and leave the up-streaming to people dead to prudence.

Now and then Mr. Bixby called my attention to certain things. Said he, 'This is Six-Mile Point.' I assented. It was pleasant enough information, but I could not see the bearing of it. I was not conscious that it was a matter of any interest to me. Another time he said, 'This is Nine-Mile Point.' Later he said, 'This is Twelve-Mile Point.' They were all about level with the water's edge; they all looked about alike to me; they were monotonously unpicturesque. I hoped Mr. Bixby would change the subject. But no; he would crowd up around a point, hugging the shore with affection, and then say: 'The slack water ends here, abreast this bunch of China-trees; now we cross over.' So he crossed over. He gave me the wheel once or twice, but I had no luck. I either came near chipping off the edge of a sugar plantation, or else I yawed too far from shore, and so I dropped back into disgrace again and got abused.

The watch was ended at last, and we took supper and went to bed. At midnight the glare of a lantern shone in my eyes, and the night watchman said:—

'Come! turn out!'

And then he left. I could not understand this extraordinary procedure; so I presently gave up trying to, and dozed off to sleep. Pretty soon the watchman was back again, and this time he was gruff. I was annoyed. I said:—

'What do you want to come bothering around here in the middle of the night for? Now as like as not I'll not get to sleep again to-night."

The watchman said:—

'Well, if this an't good, I'm blest.'

The 'off-watch' was just turning in, and I heard some brutal laughter from them, and such remarks as 'Hello, watchman! an't the new cub turned out yet? He's delicate, likely. Give him some sugar in a rag and send for the chambermaid to sing rock-a-by-baby to him.'

About this time Mr. Bixby appeared on the scene. Something like a minute later I was climbing the pilot-house steps with some of my clothes on and the rest in my arms. Mr. Bixby was close behind, commenting. Here was something fresh—this thing of getting up in the middle of the night to go to work. It was a detail in piloting that had never occurred to me at all. I knew that boats ran all night, but somehow I had never happened to reflect that somebody had to get up out of a warm bed to run them. I began to fear that piloting was not quite so romantic as I had imagined it was; there was something very real and work-like about this new phase of it.

It was a rather dingy night, although a fair number of stars were out. The big mate was at the wheel, and he had the old tub pointed at a star and was holding her straight up the middle of the river. The shores on either hand were not much more than a mile apart, but they seemed wonderfully far away and ever so vague and indistinct. The mate said:—

'We've got to land at Jones's plantation, sir.'

The vengeful spirit in me exulted. I said to myself, I wish you joy of your job, Mr. Bixby; you'll have a good time finding Mr. Jones's plantation such a night as this; and I hope you never *will* find it as long as you live.'

Mr. Bixby said to the mate:—

'Upper end of the plantation, or the lower?'

'Upper.'

'I can't do it. The stumps there are out of water at this stage. It's no great distance to the lower, and you'll have to get along with that.'

'All right, sir. If Jones don't like it he'll have to lump it, I reckon.'

And then the mate left. My exultation began to cool and my wonder to come up. Here was a man who not only proposed to find this plantation on such a night, but to find either end of it you preferred. I dreadfully wanted to ask a question, but I was carrying about as many short answers as my cargo-room would admit of, so I held my peace. All I desired to ask Mr. Bixby was the simple question whether he was ass enough to really imagine he was going to find that plantation on a night when all plantations were exactly alike and all the same color. But I held in. I used to have fine inspirations of prudence in those days.

Mr. Bixby made for the shore and soon was scraping it, just the same as if it had been daylight. And not only that, but singing—

'Father in heaven the day is declining,' etc.

It seemed to me that I had put my life in the keeping of a peculiarly reckless outcast. Presently he turned on me and said:—

'What's the name of the first point above New Orleans?'

I was gratified to be able to answer promptly, and I did. I said I didn't know.

'Don't *know?*'

This manner jolted me. I was down at the foot again, in a moment. But I had to say just what I had said before.

'Well, you're a smart one,' said Mr. Bixby. 'What's the name of the *next* point?'

Once more I didn't know.

'Well this beats anything. Tell me the name of *any* point or place I told you.'

I studied a while and decided that I couldn't.

'Look-a-here! What do you start out from, above Twelve-Mile Point, to cross over?'

'I—I—don't know.'

'You—you—don't know?' mimicking my drawling manner of speech. 'What *do* you know?'

'I—I—nothing, for certain.'

'By the great Cæsar's ghost I believe you! You're the stupidest dunderhead I ever saw or ever heard of, so help me Moses! The idea of *you* being a pilot—*you!* Why, you don't know enough to pilot a cow down a lane.'

Oh, but his wrath was up! He was a nervous man, and he shuffled from one side of his wheel to the other as if the floor was hot. He would boil a while to himself, and then overflow and scald me again.

'Look-a-here! What do you suppose I told you the names of those points for?'

I tremblingly considered a moment, and then the devil of temptation provoked me to say:—

'Well—to—to—be entertaining, I thought.'

This was a red rag to the bull. He raged and stormed so (he was crossing the river at the time) that I judge it made him blind, because he ran over the steering-oar of a trading-scow. Of course the traders sent up a volley of red-hot profanity. Never was a man so grateful as Mr. Bixby was: because he was brim full, and here were subjects who would *talk back*. He threw open a window, thrust his head out, and such an irruption followed as I never had heard before. The fainter and farther away the scowmen's curses drifted, the higher Mr. Bixby lifted his voice and the weightier his adjectives grew. When he closed the window he was empty. You could have drawn a seine through his system and not caught curses enough to disturb your mother with. Presently he said to me in the gentlest way:—

'My boy, you must get a little memorandum-book, and every time I tell you a thing, put it down right away. There's only one way to be a pilot, and that is to get this entire river by heart. You have to know it just like A B C.'

That was a dismal revelation to me; for my memory was never loaded with anything but blank cartridges. However, I did not feel discouraged long. I judged that it was best to make some allowances, for doubtless Mr. Bixby was 'stretching.' Presently he pulled a rope and struck a few strokes on the big bell. The stars were all gone, now, and the night was as black as ink. I could hear the wheels churn along the bank, but I was not entirely certain that I could see the shore. The voice of the invisible watchman called up from the hurricane deck:—

'What's this, sir?'

'Jones's plantation.'

I said to myself, I wish I might venture to offer a small bet that it isn't. But I did not chirp. I only waited to see. Mr. Bixby handled the engine bells, and in due time the boat's nose came to the land, a torch glowed from the forecastle, a man skipped ashore, a darky's voice on the bank said, 'Gimme de carpet-bag, Mars' Jones,' and the next moment we were standing up the river again, all serene. I reflected deeply a while and then said,—but not aloud,—Well, the finding of that plantation was the luckiest accident that ever happened; but it couldn't happen again in a hundred years. And I fully believed it *was* an accident, too.

By the time we had gone seven or eight hundred miles up the river, I had learned to be a tolerably plucky up-stream steersman, in daylight, and before we reached St. Louis I had made a trifle of progress in night-work, but only a trifle. I had a note-book that fairly bristled with the names of towns, 'points,' bars, islands, bends, reaches, etc.; but the information was to be found only in the note-book—none of it was in my head. It made my heart ache to think I had only got half of the river set down; for as our watch was four hours off and four hours on, day and night, there was a long four-hour gap in my book for every time I had slept since the voyage began.

My chief was presently hired to go on a big New Orleans boat, and I packed my satchel and went with him. She was a grand affair. When I stood in her pilot-house I was so far above the water that I seemed perched on a mountain; and her decks stretched so far away, fore and aft, below me, that I wondered how I could ever have considered the little Paul Jones a large craft. There were other differences, too. The Paul Jones's pilot-

house was a cheap, dingy, battered rattle-trap, cramped for room: but here
was a sumptuous glass temple; room enough to have a dance in; showy red
and gold window-curtains; an imposing sofa; leather cushions and a back to
the high bench where visiting pilots sit, to spin yarns and 'look at the river';
bright, fanciful 'cuspadores' instead of a broad wooden box filled with saw-
dust; nice new oil-cloth on the floor; a hospitable big stove for winter; a
wheel as high as my head, costly with inlaid work; a wire tiller-rope; bright
brass knobs for the bells; and a tidy, white-aproned, black 'texas-tender,'
to bring up tarts and ices and coffee during mid-watch, day and night. Now
this was 'something like'; and so I began to take heart once more to believe
that piloting was a romantic sort of occupation after all. The moment we
were under way I began to prowl about the great steamer and fill myself
with joy. She was as clean and as dainty as a drawing-room; when I looked
down her long, gilded saloon, it was like gazing through a splendid tunnel;
she had an oil-picture, by some gifted sign-painter, on every state-room
door; she glittered with no end of prism-fringed chandeliers; the clerk's
office was elegant, the bar was marvelous, and the bar-keeper had been
barbered and upholstered at incredible cost. The boiler deck (*i.e.*, the second
story of the boat, so to speak) was as spacious as a church, it seemed to
me; so with the forecastle; and there was no pitiful handful of deck-hands,
firemen, and roust-abouts down there, but a whole battalion of men. The
fires were fiercely glaring from a long row of furnaces, and over them were
eight huge boilers! This was unutterable pomp. The mighty engines—but
enough of this. I had never felt so fine before. And when I found that the
regiment of natty servants respectfully 'sir'd' me, my satisfaction was
complete.

A PILOT'S NEEDS

. . . FIRST of all, there is one faculty which a pilot must incessantly cultivate until he has brought it to absolute perfection. Nothing short of perfection will do. That faculty is memory. He cannot stop with merely thinking a thing is so and so; he must *know* it; for this is eminently one of the
'exact' sciences. With what scorn a pilot was looked upon, in the old
times, if he ever ventured to deal in that feeble phrase 'I think,' instead
of the vigorous one 'I know!' One cannot easily realize what a tremendous
thing it is to know every trivial detail of twelve hundred miles of river
and know it with absolute exactness. If you will take the longest street
in New York, and travel up and down it, conning its features patiently
until you know every house and window and door and lamp-post and big

and little sign by heart, and know them so accurately that you can instantly
name the one you are abreast of when you are set down at random in that
street in the middle of an inky black night, you will then have a tolerable
notion of the amount and the exactness of a pilot's knowledge who carries
the Mississippi River in his head. And then if you will go on until you
know every street crossing, the character, size, and position of the crossing-
stones, and the varying depth of mud in each of those numberless places,
you will have some idea of what the pilot must know in order to keep a
Mississippi steamer out of trouble. Next, if you will take half of the signs
in that long street, and *change their places* once a month, and still manage
to know their positions accurately on dark nights, and keep up with these
repeated changes without making any mistakes, you will understand what
is required of a pilot's peerless memory by the fickle Mississippi.

I think a pilot's memory is about the most wonderful thing in the
world. To know the Old and New Testaments by heart, and be able to
recite them glibly, forward or backward, or begin at random anywhere in
the book and recite both ways and never trip or make a mistake, is no
extravagant mass of knowledge, and no marvelous facility, compared to a
pilot's massed knowledge of the Mississippi and his marvelous facility in
the handling of it. I make this comparison deliberately, and I believe I am
not expanding the truth when I do it. Many will think my figure too
strong, but pilots will not.

And how easily and comfortably the pilot's memory does its work; how
placidly effortless is its way! how *unconsciously* it lays up its vast stores,
hour by hour, day by day, and never loses or mislays a single valuable
package of them all! Take an instance. Let a leadsman cry, 'Half twain!
half twain! half twain! half twain! half twain!' until it becomes as monotonous as the ticking of a clock; let conversation be going on all the time,
and the pilot be doing his share of the talking, and no longer listening to
the leadsman; and in the midst of this endless string of half twains let a
single 'quarter twain!' be interjected, without emphasis, and then the half
twain cry go on again, just as before: two or three weeks later that pilot
can describe with precision the boat's position in the river when that quarter
twain was uttered, and give you such a lot of head-marks, stern-marks,
and side-marks to guide you, that you ought to be able to take the boat
there and put her in that same spot again yourself! The cry of quarter twain
did not really take his mind from his talk, but his trained faculties instantly
photographed the bearings, noted the change of depth, and laid up the
important details for future reference without requiring any assistance from

him in the matter. If you were walking and talking with a friend, and another friend at your side kept up a monotonous repetition of the vowel sound A, for a couple of blocks, and then in the midst interjected an R, thus, A, A, A, A, A, R, A, A, A, etc., and gave the R no emphasis, you would not be able to state, two or three weeks afterward, that the R had been put in, nor be able to tell what objects you were passing at the moment it was done. But you could if your memory had been patiently and laboriously trained to do that sort of thing mechanically.

Give a man a tolerably fair memory to start with, and piloting will develop it into a very colossus of capability. But *only in the matters it is daily drilled in.* A time would come when the man's faculties could not help noticing landmarks and soundings, and his memory could not help holding on to them with the grip of a vice; but if you asked that same man at noon what he had had for breakfast, it would be ten chances to one that he could not tell you. Astonishing things can be done with the human memory if you will devote it faithfully to one particular line of business.

At the time that wages soared so high on the Missouri River, my chief, Mr. Bixby, went up there and learned more than a thousand miles of that stream with an ease and rapidity that were astonishing. When he had seen each division *once* in the daytime and *once* at night, his education was so nearly complete that he took out a 'daylight' license; a few trips later he took out a full license, and went to piloting day and night—and he ranked A 1, too.

Mr. Bixby placed me as steersman for a while under a pilot whose feats of memory were a constant marvel to me. However, his memory was born in him, I think, not built. For instance, somebody would mention a name. Instantly Mr. Brown would break in:—

'Oh, I knew *him*. Sallow-faced, red-headed fellow, with a little scar on the side of his throat like a splinter under the flesh. He was only in the Southern trade six months. That was thirteen years ago. I made a trip with him. There was five feet in the upper river then; the Henry Blake grounded at the foot of Tower Island, drawing four and a half; the George Elliott unshipped her rudder on the wreck of the Sunflower'—

'Why, the Sunflower didn't sink until'—

'I know when she sunk; it was three years before that, on the 2d of December; Asa Hardy was captain of her, and his brother John was first clerk; and it was his first trip in her, too; Tom Jones told me these things a week afterward in New Orleans; he was first mate of the Sunflower. Captain Hardy stuck a nail in his foot the 6th of July of the next year, and died of the lockjaw on the 15th. His brother John died two years after,—3d of March,—erysipelas. I never saw either of the Hardys,—they were Alleghany River men,—but people who knew them told me all these things. And they said Captain Hardy wore yarn socks winter and summer just the same, and his first wife's name was Jane Shook,—she was from New England,— and his second one died in a lunatic asylum. It was in the blood. She was from Lexington, Kentucky. Name was Horton before she was married.'

And so on, by the hour, the man's tongue would go. He could *not* forget anything. It was simply impossible. The most trivial details remained as distinct and luminous in his head, after they had lain there for years, as the most memorable events. His was not simply a pilot's memory; its grasp was universal. If he were talking about a trifling letter he had received seven years before, he was pretty sure to deliver you the entire screed from memory. And then, without observing that he was departing from the true line of his talk, he was more than likely to hurl in a long-drawn par- enthetical biography of the writer of that letter; and you were lucky indeed if he did not take up that writer's relatives, one by one, and give you their biographies, too.

Such a memory as that is a great misfortune. To it, all occurrences are of the same size. Its possessor cannot distinguish an interesting circum- stance from an uninteresting one. As a talker, he is bound to clog his narrative with tiresome details and make himself an insufferable bore. Moreover, he cannot stick to his subject. He picks up every little grain of memory he discerns in his way, and so is led aside. Mr. Brown would start out with the honest intention of telling you a vastly funny anecdote about a dog. He would be 'so full of laugh' that he could hardly begin; then his memory would start with the dog's breed and personal appearance; drift into a history of his owner; of his owner's family, with descriptions of weddings and burials that had occurred in it, together with recitals of congratulatory verses and obituary poetry provoked by the same; then this memory would recollect that one of these events occurred during the celebrated 'hard winter' of such and such a year, and a minute description of that winter would follow, along with the names of people who were frozen to death, and statistics showing the high figures which pork and hay went up to. Pork and hay would suggest corn and fodder; corn and fodder would suggest cows and horses; the latter would suggest the circus and certain celebrated bare-back riders; the transition from the circus to the menagerie was easy and natural; from the elephant to equatorial Africa was but a step; then of course the heathen savages would suggest religion; and at the end of three or four hours' tedious jaw, the watch would change and Brown would go out of the pilot-house muttering extracts from sermons he had heard years before about the efficacy of prayer as a means of grace. And the original first mention would be all you had learned about that dog, after all this waiting and hungering.

A pilot must have a memory; but there are two higher qualities which he must also have. He must have good and quick judgment and decision, and a cool, calm courage that no peril can shake. Give a man the merest trifle of pluck to start with, and by the time he has become a pilot he cannot be unmanned by any danger a steamboat can get into; but one cannot quite say the same for judgment. Judgment is a matter of brains, and a man must *start* with a good stock of that article or he will never succeed as a pilot.

The growth of courage in the pilot-house is steady all the time, but it does not reach a high and satisfactory condition until some time after the young pilot has been 'standing his own watch,' alone and under the staggering weight of all the responsibilities connected with the position. When an apprentice has become pretty thoroughly acquainted with the river, he goes clattering along so fearlessly with his steamboat, night or day, that he presently begins to imagine that it is *his* courage that animates him; but the first time the pilot steps out and leaves him to his own devices he finds out it was the other man's. He discovers that the article has been left out of his own cargo altogether. The whole river is bristling with exigencies in a moment; he is not prepared for them; he does not know how to meet them; all his knowledge forsakes him; and within fifteen minutes he is as white as a sheet and scared almost to death. Therefore pilots wisely train these cubs by various strategic tricks to look danger in the face a little more calmly. A favorite way of theirs is to play a friendly swindle upon the candidate.

Mr. Bixby served me in this fashion once, and for years afterward I used to blush even in my sleep when I thought of it. I had become a good steersman; so good, indeed, that I had all the work to do on our watch, night and day; Mr. Bixby seldom made a suggestion to me; all he ever did was to take the wheel on particularly bad nights or in particularly bad crossings, land the boat when she needed to be landed, play gentleman of leisure nine tenths of the watch, and collect the wages. The lower river was about bank-full, and if anybody had questioned my ability to run any crossing between Cairo and New Orleans without help or instruction, I should have felt irreparably hurt. The idea of being afraid of any crossing in the lot, in the *day-time*, was a thing too preposterous for contemplation. Well, one matchless summer's day I was bowling down the bend above island 66, brim full of self-conceit and carrying my nose as high as a giraffe's, when Mr. Bixby said,—

'I am going below a while. I suppose you know the next crossing?'

This was almost an affront. It was about the plainest and simplest crossing in the whole river. One couldn't come to any harm, whether he ran it right or not; and as for depth, there never had been any bottom there. I knew all this, perfectly well.

'Know how to *run* it? Why, I can run it with my eyes shut.'

'How much water is there in it?'

'Well, that is an odd question. I couldn't get bottom there with a church steeple.'

'You think so, do you?'

The very tone of the question shook my confidence. That was what Mr. Bixby was expecting. He left, without saying anything more. I began to imagine all sorts of things. Mr. Bixby, unknown to me, of course, sent somebody down to the forecastle with some mysterious instructions to the leadsman, another messenger was sent to whisper among the officers, and then Mr. Bixby went into hiding behind a smoke-stack where he could observe results. Presently the captain stepped out on the hurricane deck; next the chief mate appeared; then a clerk. Every moment or two a straggler was added to my audience; and before I got to the head of the island I had fifteen or twenty people assembled down there under my nose. I began to wonder what the trouble was. As I started across, the captain glanced aloft at me and said, with a sham uneasiness in his voice,—

'Where is Mr. Bixby?'

'Gone below, sir.'

But that did the business for me. My imagination began to construct dangers out of nothing, and they multiplied faster than I could keep the run of them. All at once I imagined I saw shoal water ahead! The wave of coward agony that surged through me then came near dislocating every joint in me. All my confidence in that crossing vanished. I seized the bell-rope; dropped it, ashamed; seized it again; dropped it once more; clutched it tremblingly once again, and pulled it so feebly that I could hardly hear the stroke myself. Captain and mate sang out instantly, and both together,—

'Starboard lead there! and quick about it!'

This was another shock. I began to climb the wheel like a squirrel; but I

would hardly get the boat started to port before I would see new dangers
on that side, and away I would spin to the other; only to find perils accumulating to starboard, and be crazy to get to port again. Then came the leadsman's sepulchral cry:—

'D-e-e-p four!'

Deep four in a bottomless crossing! The terror of it took my breath
away.

'M-a-r-k three! M-a-r-k three! Quarter less three! Half twain!'

This was frightful! I seized the bell-ropes and stopped the engines.

'Quarter twain! Quarter twain! *Mark* twain!'

I was helpless. I did not know what in the world to do. I was quaking
from head to foot, and I could have hung my hat on my eyes, they stuck
out so far.

'Quarter *less* twain! Nine and a *half!*'

We were *drawing* nine! My hands were in a nerveless flutter. I could
not ring a bell intelligibly with them. I flew to the speaking-tube and
shouted to the engineer,—

'Oh, Ben, if you love me, *back* her! Quick, Ben! Oh, back the immortal
soul out of her!'

I heard the door close gently. I looked around, and there stood Mr.
Bixby, smiling a bland, sweet smile. Then the audience on the hurricane
deck sent up a shout of humiliating laughter. I saw it all, now, and I felt
meaner than the meanest man in human history. I laid in the lead, set
the boat in her marks, came ahead on the engines, and said,—

'It was a fine trick to play on an orphan, *wasn't* it? I suppose I'll never
hear the last of how I was ass enough to heave the lead at the head of 66.'

'Well, no, you won't, maybe. In fact I hope you won't; for I want you
to learn something by that experience. Didn't you *know* there was no
bottom in that crossing?'

'Yes, sir, I did.'

'Very well, then. You shouldn't have allowed me or anybody else to
shake your confidence in that knowledge. Try to remember that. And
another thing: when you get into a dangerous place, don't turn coward.
That isn't going to help matters any.'

It was a good enough lesson, but pretty hardly learned. Yet about the
hardest part of it was that for months I so often had to hear a phrase which
I had conceived a particular distaste for. It was, 'Oh, Ben, if you love me,
back her!'

Stephen Vincent Benét

BY THE WATERS OF BABYLON

⟨ In a comparatively brief career, Benét (1898–1943) produced
many volumes of poetry and prose. He wrote several novels (*Spanish
Bayonet*, 1926, and *James Shore's Daughter*, 1934, were the more
successful ones), but his forte was verse and the short story. Like
Washington Irving, he had a special fondness and talent for making
legends and turning regional material into story. His best work in
this genre was 'The Devil and Daniel Webster' (1937), which
has been made into an opera and a moving picture. Most popular
of all his books was *John Brown's Body* (1928), a long narrative
poem about the Civil War. *John Brown's Body* and the later
Western Star (1943) won Pulitzer Prizes for verse.

'By the Waters of Babylon' is a good example of Benét's fiction.
The story attracted no particular attention when first printed; read
today, however, it has a relevance that is unmistakable. It 'speaks
to our condition.'

THE north and the west and the south are good hunting
ground, but it is forbidden to go east. It is forbidden to go to any of the
Dead Places except to search for metal and then he who touches the
metal must be a priest or the son of a priest. Afterwards, both the man and
the metal must be purified. These are the rules and the laws; they are well
made. It is forbidden to cross the great river and look upon the place that
was the Place of the Gods—this is most strictly forbidden. We do not even
say its name though we know its name. It is there that spirits live, and
demons—it is there that there are the ashes of the Great Burning. These
things are forbidden—they have been forbidden since the beginning of
time.

My father is a priest; I am the son of a priest. I have been in the Dead Places near us, with my father—at first, I was afraid. When my father went into the house to search for the metal, I stood by the door and my heart felt small and weak. It was a dead man's house, a spirit house. It did not have the smell of man, though there were old bones in a corner. But it is not fitting that a priest's son should show fear. I looked at the bones in the shadow and kept my voice still.

Then my father came out with the metal—a good, strong piece. He looked at me with both eyes but I had not run away. He gave me the metal to hold—I took it and did not die. So he knew that I was truly his son and would be a priest in my time. That was when I was very young— nevertheless, my brothers would not have done it, though they are good hunters. After that, they gave me the good piece of meat and the warm corner by the fire. My father watched over me—he was glad that I should be a priest. But when I boasted or wept without a reason, he punished me more strictly than my brothers. That was right.

After a time, I myself was allowed to go into the dead houses and search for metal. So I learned the ways of those houses—and if I saw bones, I was no longer afraid. The bones are light and old—sometimes they will fall into dust if you touch them. But that is a great sin.

I was taught the chants and the spells—I was taught how to stop the running of blood from a wound and many secrets. A priest must know many secrets—that was what my father said. If the hunters think we do all things by chants and spells, they may believe so—it does not hurt them. I was taught how to read in the old books and how to make the old writings —that was hard and took a long time. My knowledge made me happy—it was like a fire in my heart. Most of all, I liked to hear of the Old Days and the stories of the gods. I asked myself many questions that I could not answer, but it was good to ask them. At night, I would lie awake and listen to the wind—it seemed to me that it was the voice of the gods as they flew through the air.

We are not ignorant like the Forest People—our women spin wool on the wheel, our priests wear a white robe. We do not eat grubs from the tree, we have not forgotten the old writings, although they are hard to understand. Nevertheless, my knowledge and my lack of knowledge burned in me—I wished to know more. When I was a man at last, I came to my father and said, 'It is time for me to go on my journey. Give me your leave.'

He looked at me for a long time, stroking his beard, then he said at last, 'Yes. It is time.' That night, in the house of the priesthood, I asked for and received purification. My body hurt but my spirit was a cool stone. It was my father himself who questioned me about my dreams.

He bade me look into the smoke of the fire and see—I saw and told what I saw. It was what I have always seen—a river, and, beyond it, a great Dead Place and in it the gods walking. I have always thought about that. His eyes were stern when I told him—he was no longer my father but a priest. He said, 'This is a strong dream.'

'It is mine,' I said, while the smoke waved and my head felt light. They were singing the Star song in the outer chamber and it was like the buzzing of bees in my head.

He asked me how the gods were dressed and I told him how they were dressed. We know how they were dressed from the book, but I saw them as if they were before me. When I had finished, he threw the sticks three times and studied them as they fell.

'This is a very strong dream,' he said. 'It may eat you up.'

'I am not afraid,' I said and looked at him with both eyes. My voice sounded thin in my ears but that was because of the smoke.

He touched me on the breast and the forehead. He gave me the bow and the three arrows.

'Take them,' he said. 'It is forbidden to travel east. It is forbidden to cross the river. It is forbidden to go to the Place of the Gods. All these things are forbidden.'

'All these things are forbidden,' I said, but it was my voice that spoke and not my spirit. He looked at me again.

'My son,' he said. 'Once I had young dreams. If your dreams do not eat you up, you may be a great priest. If they eat you, you are still my son. Now go on your journey.'

I went fasting, as is the law. My body hurt but not my heart. When the dawn came, I was out of sight of the village. I prayed and purified myself, waiting for a sign. The sign was an eagle. It flew east.

Sometimes signs are sent by bad spirits. I waited again on the flat rock, fasting, taking no food. I was very still—I could feel the sky above me and the earth beneath. I waited till the sun was beginning to sink. Then three deer passed in the valley, going east—they did not wind me or see me. There was a white fawn with them—a very great sign.

I followed them, at a distance, waiting for what would happen. My heart was troubled about going east, yet I knew that I must go. My head hummed with my fasting—I did not even see the panther spring upon the white fawn. But, before I knew it, the bow was in my hand. I shouted and the panther lifted his head from the fawn. It is not easy to kill a panther with one arrow but the arrow went through his eye and into his brain. He died as he tried to spring—he rolled over, tearing at the ground. Then I knew I was meant to go east—I knew that was my journey. When the night came, I made my fire and roasted meat.

It is eight suns' journey to the east and a man passes by many Dead Places. The Forest People are afraid of them but I am not. Once I made my fire on the edge of a Dead Place at night and, next morning, in the dead house, I found a good knife, little rusted. That was small to what came afterward but it made my heart feel big. Always when I looked for game, it was in front of my arrow, and twice I passed hunting parties of the Forest People without their knowing. So I knew my magic was strong and my journey clean, in spite of the law.

Toward the setting of the eighth sun, I came to the banks of the great river. It was half-a-day's journey after I had left the god-road—we do not use the god-roads now for they are falling apart into great blocks of stone, and the forest is safer going. A long way off, I had seen the water through trees but the trees were thick. At last, I came out upon an open place at the top of a cliff. There was the great river below, like a giant in the sun. It is very long, very wide. It could eat all the streams we know and still be thirsty. Its name is Ou-dis-sun, the Sacred, the Long. No man of my tribe had seen it, not even my father, the priest. It was magic and I prayed.

Then I raised my eyes and looked south. It was there, the Place of the Gods.

How can I tell what it was like—you do not know. It was there, in the red light, and they were too big to be houses. It was there with the red light upon it, mighty and ruined. I knew that in another moment the gods would see me. I covered my eyes with my hands and crept back into the forest.

Surely, that was enough to do, and live. Surely it was enough to spend the night upon the cliff. The Forest People themselves do not come near. Yet, all through the night, I knew that I should have to cross the river and walk in the places of the gods, although the gods ate me up. My magic did not help me at all and yet there was a fire in my bowels, a fire in my mind. When the sun rose, I thought, 'My journey has been clean. Now I will go home from my journey.' But, even as I thought so, I knew I could not. If I went to the Place of the Gods, I would surely die, but, if I did not go, I could never be at peace with my spirit again. It is better to lose one's life than one's spirit, if one is a priest and the son of a priest.

Nevertheless, as I made the raft, the tears ran out of my eyes. The Forest People could have killed me without fight, if they had come upon me then, but they did not come. When the raft was made, I said the sayings for the dead and painted myself for death. My heart was cold as a frog and my knees like water, but the burning in my mind would not let me have peace. As I pushed the raft from the shore, I began my death song—I had the right. It was a fine song.

'I am John, son of John,' I sang. 'My people are the Hill People.
    They are the men.
I go into the Dead Places but I am not slain.
I take the metal from the Dead Places but I am not blasted.
I travel upon the god-roads and am not afraid. E-yah! I have killed the
    panther, I have killed the fawn!
E-yah! I have come to the great river. No man has come there before.
It is forbidden to go east, but I have gone, forbidden to go on the great
    river, but I am there.
Open your hearts, you spirits, and hear my song.
    Now I go to the Place of the Gods, I shall not return.
My body is painted for death and my limbs weak, but my heart is big as I
    go to the Place of the Gods!'

All the same, when I came to the Place of the Gods, I was afraid, afraid. The current of the great river is very strong—it gripped my raft with its hands. That was magic, for the river itself is wide and calm. I could feel evil spirits about me, in the bright morning; I could feel their breath on my neck as I was swept down the stream. Never have I been so much alone—I tried to think of my knowledge, but it was a squirrel's heap of winter nuts. There was no strength in my knowledge any more and I felt small and naked as a new-hatched bird—alone upon the great river, the servant of the gods.

Yet, after a while, my eyes were opened and I saw. I saw both banks of the river—I saw that once there had been god-roads across it, though now they were broken and fallen like broken vines. Very great they were, and wonderful and broken—broken in the time of the Great Burning when the fire fell out of the sky. And always the current took me nearer to the Place of the Gods, and the huge ruins rose before my eyes.

I do not know the customs of rivers—we are the People of the Hills. I tried to guide my raft with the pole but it spun around. I thought the river meant to take me past the Place of the Gods and out into the Bitter Water of the legends. I grew angry then—my heart felt strong. I said aloud, 'I am a priest and the son of a priest!' The gods heard me—they showed me how to paddle with the pole on one side of the raft. The current changed itself—I drew near to the Place of the Gods.

When I was very near, my raft struck and turned over. I can swim in our lakes—I swam to the shore. There was a great spike of rusted metal sticking out into the river—I hauled myself up upon it and sat there, panting. I had saved my bow and two arrows and the knife I found in the Dead Place but that was all. My raft went whirling downstream toward the Bitter Water. I looked after it, and thought if it had trod me under, at least I would be safely dead. Nevertheless, when I had dried my bow-string and re-strung it, I walked forward to the Place of the Gods.

It felt like ground underfoot; it did not burn me. It is not true what some of the tales say, that the ground there burns forever, for I have been there. Here and there were the marks and stains of the Great Burning, on the ruins, that is true. But they were old marks and old stains. It is not true either, what some of our priests say, that it is an island covered with fogs and enchantments. It is not. It is a great Dead Place—greater than any Dead Place we know. Everywhere in it there are god-roads, though most are cracked and broken. Everywhere there are the ruins of the high towers of the gods.

How shall I tell what I saw? I went carefully, my strung bow in my hand, my skin ready for danger. There should have been the wailings of spirits and the shrieks of demons, but there were not. It was very silent and sunny where I had landed—the wind and the rain and the birds that drop seeds had done their work—the grass grew in the cracks of the broken stone. It is a fair island—no wonder the gods built there. If I had come there, a god, I also would have built.

How shall I tell what I saw? The towers are not all broken—here and there one still stands, like a great tree in a forest, and the birds nest high. But the towers themselves look blind, for the gods are gone. I saw a fish-hawk, catching fish in the river. I saw a little dance of white butterflies over a great heap of broken stones and columns. I went there and looked about me—there was a carved stone with cut-letters, broken in half. I can read letters but I could not understand these. They said UBTREAS. There was also the shattered image of a man or a god. It had been made of white stone and he wore his hair tied back like a woman's. His name was ASHING, as I read on the cracked half of a stone. I thought it wise to pray to ASHING, though I do not know that god.

How shall I tell what I saw? There was no smell of man left, on stone or metal. Nor were there many trees in that wilderness of stone. There are many pigeons, nesting and dropping in the towers—the gods must have loved them, or, perhaps, they used them for sacrifices. There are wild cats that roam the god-roads, green-eyed, unafraid of man. At night they wail like demons but they are not demons. The wild dogs are more dangerous, for they hunt in a pack, but them I did not meet till later. Everywhere there are the carved stones, carved with magical numbers or words.

I went North—I did not try to hide myself. When a god or a demon saw me, then I would die, but meanwhile I was no longer afraid. My hunger for knowledge burned in me—there was so much that I could not understand. After awhile, I knew that my belly was hungry. I could have hunted for my meat, but I did not hunt. It is known that the gods did not hunt as we do—they got their food from enchanted boxes and jars. Sometimes these are still found in the Dead Places—once, when I was a child and foolish, I opened such a jar and tasted it and found the food sweet. But my father found out and punished me for it strictly, for, often, that food is death. Now, though, I had long gone past what was forbidden, and I entered the likeliest towers, looking for the food of the gods.

I found it at last in the ruins of a great temple in the mid-city. A mighty temple it must have been, for the roof was painted like the sky at night with its stars—that much I could see, though the colors were faint and dim. It went down into great caves and tunnels—perhaps they kept their slaves there. But when I started to climb down, I heard the squeaking of rats, so I did not go—rats are unclean, and there must have been many tribes of them, from the squeaking. But near there, I found food, in the heart of a ruin, behind a door that still opened. I ate only the fruits from the jars—they had a very sweet taste. There was drink, too, in bottles of glass—the drink of the gods was strong and made my head swim. After I had eaten and drunk, I slept on the top of a stone, my bow at my side.

When I woke, the sun was low. Looking down from where I lay, I saw a dog sitting on his haunches. His tongue was hanging out of his mouth; he looked as if he were laughing. He was a big dog, with a gray-brown coat, as big as a wolf. I sprang up and shouted at him but he did not move—he just sat there as if he were laughing. I did not like that. When I reached for a stone to throw, he moved swiftly out of the way of the stone.

He was not afraid of me; he looked at me as if I were meat. No doubt I could have killed him with an arrow, but I did not know if there were others. Moreover, night was falling.

I looked about me—not far away there was a great, broken god-road, leading North. The towers were high enough, but not so high, and while many of the dead-houses were wrecked, there were some that stood. I went toward this god-road, keeping to the heights of the ruins, while the dog followed. When I had reached the god-road, I saw that there were others behind him. If I had slept later, they would have come upon me asleep and torn out my throat. As it was, they were sure enough of me; they did not hurry. When I went into the dead-house, they kept watch at the entrance—doubtless they thought they would have a fine hunt. But a dog cannot open a door and I knew, from the books, that the gods did not like to live on the ground but on high.

I had just found a door I could open when the dogs decided to rush. Ha! They were surprised when I shut the door in their faces—it was a good door, of strong metal. I could hear their foolish baying beyond it but I did not stop to answer them. I was in darkness—I found stairs and climbed. There were many stairs, turning around till my head was dizzy. At the top was another door—I found the knob and opened it. I was in a long small chamber—on one side of it was a bronze door that could not be opened, for it had no handle. Perhaps there was a magic word to open it but I did not have the word. I turned to the door in the opposite side of the wall. The lock of it was broken and I opened it and went in.

Within, there was a place of great riches. The god who lived there must have been a powerful god. The first room was a small ante-room—I waited there for some time, telling the spirits of the place that I came in peace and not as a robber. When it seemed to me that they had had time to hear me, I went on. Ah, what riches! Few, even, of the windows had been broken—it was all as it had been. The great windows that looked over the city had not been broken at all though they were dusty and streaked with many years. There were coverings on the floors, the colors not greatly faded, and the chairs were soft and deep. There were pictures upon the walls, very strange, very wonderful—I remember one of a bunch of flowers in a jar —if you came close to it, you could see nothing but bits of color, but if you stood away from it, the flowers might have been picked yesterday. It made my heart feel strange to look at this picture—and to look at the figure of a bird, in some hard clay, on a table and see it so like our birds. Every-where there were books and writings, many in tongues that I could not read. The god who lived there must have been a wise god and full of knowledge. I felt I had right there, as I sought knowledge also.

Nevertheless, it was strange. There was a washing-place but no water—perhaps the gods washed in air. There was a cooking-place but no wood, and though there was a machine to cook food, there was no place to put fire in it. Nor were there candles or lamps—there were things that looked like lamps but they had neither oil nor wick. All these things were magic, but I touched them and lived—the magic had gone out of them. Let me tell one thing to show. In the washing-place, a thing said 'Hot' but it was not hot to the touch—another thing said 'Cold' but it was not cold. This must have been a strong magic but the magic was gone. I do not under-stand—they had ways—I wish that I knew.

It was close and dry and dusty in their house of the gods. I have said the magic was gone but that is not true—it had gone from the magic things but it had not gone from the place. I felt the spirits about me, weighing upon me. Nor had I ever slept in a Dead Place before—and yet, tonight, I must sleep there. When I thought of it, my tongue felt dry in my throat, in spite of my wish for knowledge. Almost I would have gone down again and faced the dogs, but I did not.

I had not gone through all the rooms when the darkness fell. When it fell, I went back to the big room looking over the city and made fire. There was a place to make fire and a box with wood in it, though I do not think they cooked there. I wrapped myself in a floor-covering and slept in front of the fire—I was very tired.

Now I tell what is very strong magic. I woke in the midst of the night. When I woke, the fire had gone out and I was cold. It seemed to me that all around me there were whisperings and voices. I closed my eyes to shut them out. Some will say that I slept again, but I do not think that I slept. I could feel the spirits drawing my spirit out of my body as a fish is drawn on a line.

Why should I lie about it? I am a priest and the son of a priest. If there are spirits, as they say, in the small Dead Places near us, what spirits must there not be in that great Place of the Gods? And would not they wish to speak? After such long years? I know that I felt myself drawn as a fish is drawn on a line. I had stepped out of my body—I could see my body asleep in front of the cold fire, but it was not I. I was drawn to look out upon the city of the gods.

It should have been dark, for it was night, but it was not dark. Every-where there were lights—lines of light—circles and blurs of light—ten

thousand torches would not have been the same. The sky itself was alight—
you could barely see the stars for the glow in the sky. I thought to myself
'This is strong magic' and trembled. There was a roaring in my ears like
the rushing of rivers. Then my eyes grew used to the light and my ears to
the sound. I knew that I was seeing the city as it had been when the gods
were alive.

That was a sight indeed—yes, that was a sight: I could not have seen it
in the body—my body would have died. Everywhere went the gods, on foot
and in chariots—there were gods beyond number and counting and their
chariots blocked the streets. They had turned night to day for their pleasure
—they did not sleep with the sun. The noise of their coming and going
was the noise of many waters. It was magic what they could do—it was
magic what they did.

I looked out of another window—the great vines of their bridges were
mended and the god-roads went East and West. Restless, restless, were the
gods and always in motion! They burrowed tunnels under rivers—they flew
in the air. With unbelievable tools they did giant works—no part of the
earth was safe from them, for, if they wished for a thing, they summoned
it from the other side of the world. And always, as they labored and rested,
as they feasted and made love, there was a drum in their ears—the pulse of
the giant city, beating and beating like a man's heart.

Were they happy? What is happiness to the gods? They were great, they
were mighty, they were wonderful and terrible. As I looked upon them and
their magic, I felt like a child—but a little more, it seemed to me, and
they would pull down the moon from the sky. I saw them with wisdom
beyond wisdom and knowledge beyond knowledge. And yet not all they
did was well done—even I could see that—and yet their wisdom could not
but grow until all was peace.

Then I saw their fate come upon them and that was terrible past speech.
It came upon them as they walked the streets of their city. I have been in
the fights with the Forest People—I have seen men die. But this was not
like that. When gods war with gods, they use weapons we do not know. It
was fire falling out of the sky and a mist that poisoned. It was the time of
the Great Burning and the Destruction. They ran about like ants in the
streets of their city—poor gods, poor gods! Then the towers began to fall.
A few escaped—yes, a few. The legends tell it. But, even after the city had
become a Dead Place, for many years the poison was still in the ground. I
saw it happen, I saw the last of them die. It was darkness over the broken
city and I wept.

All this, I saw. I saw it as I have told it, though not in the body. When I woke in the morning, I was hungry, but I did not think first of my hunger for my heart was perplexed and confused. I knew the reason for the Dead Places but I did not see why it had happened. It seemed to me it should not have happened, with all the magic they had. I went through the house looking for an answer. There was so much in the house I could not understand—and yet I am a priest and the son of a priest. It was like being on one side of the great river, at night, with no light to show the way.

Then I saw the dead god. He was sitting in his chair, by the window, in a room I had not entered before and, for the first moment, I thought that he was alive. Then I saw the skin on the back of his hand—it was like dry leather. The room was shut, hot and dry—no doubt that had kept him as he was. At first I was afraid to approach him—then the fear left me. He was sitting looking out over the city—he was dressed in the clothes of the gods. His age was neither young nor old—I could not tell his age. But there was wisdom in his face and great sadness. You could see that he would have not run away. He had sat at his window, watching his city die —then he himself had died. But it is better to lose one's life than one's spirit—and you could see from the face that his spirit had not been lost. I knew, that, if I touched him, he would fall into dust—and yet, there was something unconquered in the face.

That is all of my story, for then I knew he was a man—I knew then that they had been men, neither gods nor demons. It is a great knowledge, hard to tell and believe. They were men—they went a dark road, but they were men. I had no fear after that—I had no fear going home, though twice I fought off the dogs and once I was hunted for two days by the Forest People. When I saw my father again, I prayed and was purified. He touched my lips and my breast, he said, 'You went away a boy. You come back a man and a priest.' I said, 'Father, they were men! I have been in the Place of the Gods and seen it! Now slay me, if it is the law—but still I know they were men.'

He looked at me out of both eyes. He said, 'The law is not always the same shape—you have done what you have done. I could not have done it my time, but you come after me. Tell!'

I told and he listened. After that, I wished to tell all the people but he showed me otherwise. He said, 'Truth is a hard deer to hunt. If you eat too much truth at once, you may die of the truth. It was not idly that our fathers forbade the Dead Places.' He was right—it is better the truth should come little by little. I have learned that, being a priest. Perhaps, in the old days, they ate knowledge too fast.

Nevertheless, we make a beginning. It is not for the metal alone we go to the Dead Places now—there are the books and the writings. They are hard to learn. And the magic tools are broken—but we can look at them and wonder. At least, we make a beginning. And, when I am chief priest we shall go beyond the great river. We shall go to the Place of the Gods— the place newyork—not one man but a company. We shall look for the images of the gods and find the god ASHING and the others—the gods Licoln and Biltmore and Moses. But they were men who built the city, not gods or demons. They were men. I remember the dead man's face. They were men who were here before us. We must build again.

Samuel Butler

THE WAY OF ALL FLESH

❡ Butler's writings against Darwin, his translations of Homer, his contributions to the 'Homeric question,' and most of his other works are almost forgotten now, but his novels, *Erewhon, Erewhon Revisited,* and *The Way of All Flesh,* have become minor classics. Only the first two of these appeared in his lifetime. He began *The Way of All Flesh* in 1872, worked at it irregularly until 1884, and then laid it aside, not quite finished. It was published in 1903, after his death.

The irony, the pleasant perverseness, and the wit of *The Way of All Flesh* have delighted many readers who may never have heard how autobiographical it is—though they must have divined that before reading very far in it—and who did not realize that it was to some degree a serious effort on Butler's part to illustrate certain theories of heredity which he championed against Darwinism. Butler detested his parents, the Theobald and Christina of the novel. He shared the opinion of Swift's Lilliputians that parents are 'the last of all others to be trusted with the education of their own children.' He scorned all the Victorian shibboleths, smashed all the idols, and generally 'fought the good faith' in his books, while living a conventional Victorian gentleman's existence himself.

I

M R. PONTIFEX was not the man to trouble himself much about his motives. People were not so introspective then as we are now; they lived more according to a rule of thumb. Dr. Arnold [1] had not yet

[¹ English historian and divine (1795–1842), headmaster of Rugby School, 1828–42. His reforms in education were very influential and widely copied. He was the father of Matthew Arnold.]

FROM *The Way of All Flesh,* 1903, chs. vi, xx. Reprinted by permission of E. P. Dutton, Inc., New York; Jonathan Cape, Limited; and the Executors of Samuel Butler.

sown that crop of earnest thinkers which we are now harvesting, and men did not see why they should not have their own way if no evil consequences to themselves seemed likely to follow upon their doing so. Then as now, however, they sometimes let themselves in for more evil consequences than they had bargained for.

Like other rich men at the beginning of this century he ate and drank a good deal more than was enough to keep him in health. Even his excellent constitution was not proof against a prolonged course of overfeeding and what we should now consider overdrinking. His liver would not unfrequently get out of order, and he would come down to breakfast looking yellow about the eyes. Then the young people knew that they had better look out. It is not as a general rule the eating of sour grapes [2] that causes the children's teeth to be set on edge. Well-to-do parents seldom eat many sour grapes; the danger to the children lies in the parents eating too many sweet ones.

I grant that at first sight it seems very unjust, that the parents should have the fun and the children be punished for it, but young people should remember that for many years they were part and parcel of their parents and therefore had a good deal of the fun in the person of their parents. If they have forgotten the fun now, that is no more than people do who have a headache after having been tipsy overnight. The man with a headache does not pretend to be a different person from the man who got drunk, and claim that it is his self of the preceding night and not his self of this morning who should be punished; no more should offspring complain of the headache which it has earned when in the person of its parents, for the continuation of identity, though not so immediately apparent, is just as real in one case as in the other. What is really hard is when the parents have the fun after the children have been born, and the children are punished for this.

On these, his black days, he would take very gloomy views of things and say to himself that in spite of all his goodness to them his children did not love him. But who can love any man whose liver is out of order? How base, he would exclaim to himself, was such ingratitude! How especially hard upon himself, who had been such a model son, and always honoured and obeyed his parents though they had not spent one hundredth part of the money upon him which he had lavished upon his own children. 'It is always the same story,' he would say to himself, 'the more young people have the more they want, and the less thanks one gets; I have made a great mistake;

[2 See Jeremiah, xxxi, 29; Ezekiel, xviii, 2.]

I have been far too lenient with my children; never mind, I have done my duty by them, and more; if they fail in theirs to me it is a matter between God and them. I, at any rate, am guiltless. Why, I might have married again and become the father of a second and perhaps more affectionate family, etc., etc.' He pitied himself for the expensive education which he was giving his children; he did not see that the education cost the children far more than it cost him, inasmuch as it cost them the power of earning their living easily rather than helped them towards it, and ensured their being at the mercy of their father for years after they had come to an age when they should be independent. A public school [3] education cuts off a boy's retreat; he can no longer become a labourer or a mechanic, and these are the only people whose tenure of independence is not precarious—with the exception of course of those who are born inheritors of money or who are placed young in some safe and deep groove. Mr. Pontifex saw nothing of this; all he saw was that he was spending much more money upon his children than the law would have compelled him to do, and what more could you have? Might he not have apprenticed both his sons to green-grocers? Might he not even yet do so to-morrow morning if he were so minded? The possibility of this course being adopted was a favourite topic with him when he was out of temper; true, he never did apprentice either of his sons to greengrocers, but his boys comparing notes together had sometimes come to the conclusion that they wished he would.

At other times when not quite well he would have them in for the fun of shaking his will at them. He would in his imagination cut them all out one after another and leave his money to found almshouses, till at last he was obliged to put them back, so that he might have the pleasure of cutting them out again the next time he was in a passion.

Of course if young people allow their conduct to be in any way influenced by regard to the wills of living persons they are doing very wrong and must expect to be sufferers in the end, nevertheless the powers of will-dangling and will-shaking are so liable to abuse and are continually made so great an engine of torture that I would pass a law, if I could, to incapacitate any man from making a will for three months from the date of each offence in either of the above respects and let the bench of magistrates or judge, before whom he has been convicted, dispose of his property as they shall think right and reasonable if he dies during the time that his will-making power is suspended.

Mr. Pontifex would have the boys into the dining-room. 'My dear John,

[3 'Public school' here means what in the United States is called a 'private school.']

my dear Theobald,' he would say, 'look at me. I began life with nothing but the clothes with which my father and mother sent me up to London. My father gave me ten shillings and my mother five for pocket money and I thought them munificent. I never asked my father for a shilling in the whole course of my life, nor took aught from him beyond the small sum he used to allow me monthly till I was in receipt of a salary. I made my own way and I shall expect my sons to do the same. Pray don't take it into your heads that I am going to wear my life out making money that my sons may spend it for me. If you want money you must make it for yourselves as I did, for I give you my word I will not leave a penny to either of you unless you show that you deserve it. Young people seem nowadays to expect all kinds of luxuries and indulgences which were never heard of when I was a boy. Why, my father was a common carpenter, and here you are both of you at public schools, costing me ever so many hundreds a year, while I at your age was plodding away behind a desk in my Uncle Fairlie's counting house. What should I not have done if I had had one half of your advantages? You should become dukes or found new empires in undiscovered countries, and even then I doubt whether you would have done proportionately so much as I have done. No, no, I shall see you through school and college and then, if you please, you will make your own way in the world.'

In this manner he would work himself up into such a state of virtuous indignation that he would sometimes thrash the boys then and there upon some pretext invented at the moment.

And yet, as children went, the young Pontifexes were fortunate; there would be ten families of young people worse off for one better; they ate and drank good wholesome food, slept in comfortable beds, had the best doctors to attend them when they were ill and the best education that could be had for money. The want of fresh air does not seem much to affect the happiness of children in a London alley: the greater part of them sing and play as though they were on a moor in Scotland. So the absence of a genial mental atmosphere is not commonly recognized by children who have never known it. Young people have a marvellous faculty of either dying or adapting themselves to circumstances. Even if they are unhappy— very unhappy—it is astonishing how easily they can be prevented from finding it out, or at any rate from attributing it to any other cause than their own sinfulness.

To parents who wish to lead a quiet life I would say: Tell your children that they are very naughty—much naughtier than most children. Point to the young people of some acquaintances as models of perfection and impress your own children with a deep sense of their own inferiority. You carry so many more guns than they do that they cannot fight you. This is called moral influence, and it will enable you to bounce them as much as you please. They think you know and they will not have yet caught you lying often enough to suspect that you are not the unworldly and scrupulously truthful person which you represent yourself to be; nor yet will they know how great a coward you are, nor how soon you will run away, if they fight you with persistency and judgement. You keep the dice and throw them both for your children and yourself. Load them then, for you can easily manage to stop your children from examining them. Tell them how singularly indulgent you are; insist on the incalculable benefit you conferred upon them, firstly in bringing them into the world at all, but more particularly in bringing them into it as your own children rather than anyone else's. Say that you have their highest interests at stake whenever you are out of temper and wish to make yourself unpleasant by way of balm to your soul. Harp much upon these highest interests. Feed them spiritually upon such brimstone and treacle as the late Bishop of Winchester's Sunday stories. You hold all the trump cards, or if you do not you can filch them; if you play them with anything like judgement you will find yourselves heads of happy, united, God-fearing families, even as did my old friend Mr. Pontifex. True, your children will probably find out all about it some day, but not until too late to be of much service to them or inconvenience to yourself.

Some satirists have complained of life inasmuch as all the pleasures belong to the fore part of it and we must see them dwindle till we are left, it may be, with the miseries of a decrepit old age.

To me it seems that youth is like spring, an overpraised season—delightful if it happen to be a favoured one, but in practice very rarely favoured and more remarkable, as a general rule, for biting east winds than genial breezes. Autumn is the mellower season, and what we lose in flowers we more than gain in fruits. Fontenelle [4] at the age of ninety, being asked what was the happiest time of his life, said he did not know that he had ever been much happier than he then was, but that perhaps his best years had been those when he was between fifty-five and seventy-five, and Dr. Johnson placed the pleasures of old age far higher than those of youth. True, in old age we live under the shadow of Death, which, like a sword of Damocles, may descend at any moment, but we have so long found life to

[4 French writer (1657–1757).]

be an affair of being rather frightened than hurt that we have become like the people who live under Vesuvius,[5] and chance it without much misgiving.

II

The birth of his son opened Theobald's eyes to a good deal which he had but faintly realized hitherto. He had had no idea how great a nuisance a baby was. Babies come into the world so suddenly at the end, and upset everything so terribly when they do come: why cannot they steal in upon us with less of a shock to the domestic system? His wife, too, did not recover rapidly from her confinement; she remained an invalid for months; here was another nuisance and an expensive one, which interfered with the amount which Theobald liked to put by out of his income against, as he said, a rainy day, or to make provision for his family if he should have one. Now he was getting a family, so that it became all the more necessary to put money by, and here was the baby hindering him. Theorists may say what they like about a man's children being a continuation of his own identity, but it will generally be found that those who talk in this way have no children of their own. Practical family men know better.

About twelve months after the birth of Ernest there came a second, also a boy, who was christened Joseph, and in less than twelve months afterwards, a girl, to whom was given the name of Charlotte. A few months before this girl was born Christina paid a visit to the John Pontifexes in London, and, knowing her condition, passed a good deal of time at the Royal Academy exhibition looking at the types of female beauty portrayed by the Academicians, for she had made up her mind that the child this time was to be a girl. Alethea warned her not to do this, but she persisted, and certainly the child turned out plain, but whether the pictures caused this or no I cannot say.

Theobald had never liked children. He had always got away from them as soon as he could, and so had they from him; oh, why, he was inclined to ask himself, could not children be born into the world grown up? If Christina could have given birth to a few full-grown clergymen in priest's orders —of moderate views, but inclining rather to Evangelicalism, with comfortable livings and in all respects facsimiles of Theobald himself—why, there might have been more sense in it; or if people could buy ready-made children at a shop of whatever age and sex they liked, instead of always having

[5 See Stevenson, pp. 397–404.]

to make them at home and to begin at the beginning with them—that might do better, but as it was he did not like it. He felt as he had felt when he had been required to come and be married to Christina—that he had been going on for a long time quite nicely, and would much rather continue things on their present footing. In the matter of getting married he had been obliged to pretend he liked it; but times were changed, and if he did not like a thing now, he could find a hundred unexceptionable ways of making his dislike apparent.

It might have been better if Theobald in his younger days had kicked more against his father: the fact that he had not done so encouraged him to expect the most implicit obedience from his own children. He could trust himself, he said (and so did Christina), to be more lenient than perhaps his father had been to himself; his danger, he said (and so again did Christina), would be rather in the direction of being too indulgent; he must be on his guard against this, for no duty could be more important than that of teaching a child to obey its parents in all things.

He had read not long since of an Eastern traveller, who, while exploring somewhere in the more remote parts of Arabia and Asia Minor, had come upon a remarkably hardy, sober, industrious little Christian community— all of them in the best of health—who had turned out to be the actual living descendants of Jonadab,[6] the son of Rechab; and two men in European costume, indeed, but speaking English with a broken accent, and by their colour evidently Oriental, had come begging to Battersby soon afterwards, and represented themselves as belonging to this people; they had said they were collecting funds to promote the conversion of their fellow tribesmen to the English branch of the Christian religion. True, they turned out to be impostors, for when he gave them a pound and Christina five shillings from her private purse, they went and got drunk with it in the next village but one to Battersby; still, this did not invalidate the story of the Eastern traveller. Then there were the Romans—whose greatness was probably due to the wholesome authority exercised by the head of a family over all its members. Some Romans had even killed their children; this was going too far, but then the Romans were not Christians, and knew no better.

The practical outcome of the foregoing was a conviction in Theobald's mind, and if in his, then in Christina's, that it was their duty to begin training up their children in the way they should go, even from their earliest infancy. The first signs of self-will must be carefully looked for, and plucked

[6 See II Kings, x, 15; Jeremiah, xxxv, 6, 8, 14, 16, 19.]

undefinedSamuel Butler

462

up by the roots at once before they had time to grow. Theobald picked up this numb serpent of a metaphor and cherished it in his bosom.

Before Ernest could well crawl he was taught to kneel; before he could well speak he was taught to lisp the Lord's prayer, and the general confession. How was it possible that these things could be taught too early? If his attention flagged or his memory failed him, here was an ill weed which would grow apace, unless it were plucked out immediately, and the only way to pluck it out was to whip him, or shut him up in a cupboard, or dock him of some of the small pleasures of childhood. Before he was three years old he could read and, after a fashion, write. Before he was four he was learning Latin, and could do rule of three sums.

As for the child himself, he was naturally of an even temper; he doted upon his nurse, on kittens and puppies, and on all things that would do him the kindness of allowing him to be fond of them. He was fond of his mother, too, but as regards his father, he has told me in later life he could remember no feeling but fear and shrinking. Christina did not remonstrate with Theobald concerning the severity of the tasks imposed upon their boy, nor yet as to the continual whippings that were found necessary at lesson times. Indeed, when during any absence of Theobald's the lessons were entrusted to her, she found to her sorrow that it was the only thing to do, and she did it no less effectually than Theobald himself, nevertheless she was fond of her boy, which Theobald never was, and it was long before she could destroy all affection for herself in the mind of her first-born. But she persevered.

William James
TWO LETTERS ON DEATH

❨ William James as 'man thinking' is represented in this volume by an excerpt from one of his philosophical essays. Here it is James as son and brother who is revealed. He is the same James, unaffected, sympathetic, completely honest; only here we see him not in the lecture room but in the solitude of those moments in every life when out of the abundance of the heart the mouth speaketh. These two letters are in every sense characteristic: no rhetoric, no conventionalities, no sentimentalism, no 'O eloquent, just, and mighty Death!' but sincere, plainspoken affection: 'If you go, it will not be an inharmonious thing. . . Good-night, my sacred old Father.'

BOLTON ST., LONDON, DECEMBER 14, 1882

DARLING OLD FATHER,[1]—Two letters, one from my Alice [2] last night, and one from Aunt Kate to Harry [3] just now, have somewhat dispelled the mystery in which the telegrams left your condition; and although their

[1] James's father, Henry James, Sr., was the son of an Irish immigrant who made a fortune in business and became a prominent citizen of Albany, N.Y. Henry went to Union College and Princeton Theological Seminary, but after two years' study abandoned forever the Calvinistic divinity. He lived in New York City and, from time to time, in Europe.

He was a man of great independence of mind and decided opinion, religious by nature yet scornful of orthodox theologies (he turned to Swedenborg); full of kindness, sympathy, and curiosity—traits inherited by his more celebrated son William. He loved to argue with his five children, to sharpen their wits. An unusual man, he was repaid by unusual affection. His daughter's diary records that a week before his death she asked him whether he had thought what he should like to have done about his funeral. 'He was immediately very much interested, not having apparently thought of it before; he reflected for some time, and then said with the greatest solemnity and looking so majestic: "Tell him to say only this: 'Here lies a man, who has thought all his life that the ceremonies attending birth, marriage and death were all damned non-sense.' Don't let him say a word more!" ' (*Letters of William James*, I, 16).]

[2] His sister (1848–92). See the next letter.]

[3] Henry James (1843–1916), who became a famous novelist.]

FROM *The Letters of William James*, 1920, 1926. Reprinted by permission of the Executors of the Estate of Henry James.

news is several days earlier than the telegrams, I am free to suppose that the latter report only an aggravation of the symptoms the letters describe. It is far more agreeable to think of this than of some dreadful unknown and sudden malady.

We have been so long accustomed to the hypothesis of your being taken away from us, especially during the past ten months, that the thought that this may be your last illness conveys no very sudden shock. You are old enough, you've given your message to the world in many ways and will not be forgotten; you are here left alone, and on the other side, let us hope and pray, dear, dear old Mother is waiting for you to join her. If you go, it will not be an inharmonious thing. Only, if you are still in possession of your normal consciousness, I should like to see you once again before we part. I stayed here only in obedience to the last telegram, and am waiting now for Harry—who knows the exact state of my mind, and who will know yours—to telegraph again what I shall do. Meanwhile, my blessed old Father, I scribble this line (which may reach you though I should come too late), just to tell you how full of the tenderest memories and feelings about you my heart has for the last few days been filled. In that mysterious gulf of the past into which the present soon will fall and go back and back, yours is still for me the central figure. All my intellectual life I derive from you; and though we have often seemed at odds in the expression thereof, I'm sure there's a harmony somewhere, and that our strivings will combine. What my debt to you is goes beyond all my power of estimating,—so early, so penetrating and so constant has been the influence. You need be in no anxiety about your literary remains.[4] I will see them well taken care of, and that your words shall not suffer for being concealed. At Paris I heard that Milsand,[5] whose name you may remember in the 'Revue des Deux Mondes' and elsewhere, was an admirer of the 'Secret of Swedenborg,'[6] and Hodgson[7] told me your last book had deeply impressed him. So will it be; especially, I think, if a collection of *extracts* from your various writings were published, after the manner of the extracts from Carlyle, Ruskin, & Co. I have long thought such a volume would be the best monument to you.—As for us; we shall live on each in his way,—feeling somewhat unprotected, old as we are, for the absence of the parental bosoms as a refuge, but holding fast together in that common sacred memory. We will stand

[4 William James published them in 1885.]
[5 Joseph Milsand, a French writer.]
[6 A book by Henry James, Sr.]
[7 Shadworth Hodgson, English philosopher and friend of William James.]

by each other and by Alice, try to transmit the torch in our offspring as you did in us, and when the time comes for being gathered in, I pray we may, if not all, some at least, be as ripe as you. As for myself, I know what trouble I've given you at various times through my peculiarities; and as my own boys grow up, I shall learn more and more of the kind of trial you had to overcome in superintending the development of a creature different from yourself, for whom you felt responsible. I say this merely to show how my *sympathy* with you is likely to grow much livelier, rather than to fade—and not for the sake of regrets.—As for the other side, and Mother, and our all possibly meeting, I *can't* say anything. More than ever at this moment do I feel that if that *were* true, all would be solved and justified. And it comes strangely over me in bidding you good-bye how a life is but a day and expresses mainly but a single note. It is so much like the act of bidding an ordinary good-night. Good-night, my sacred old Father! If I don't see you again—Farewell! a blessed farewell! Your

WILLIAM

CHOCORUA, N.H., JULY 6, 1891.

DEAREST ALICE,—. . . Of course [this medical verdict on your case may mean] as all men know, a finite length of days; and then, good-bye to neurasthenia and neuralgia and headache, and weariness and palpitation and disgust all at one stroke—I should think you would be reconciled to the prospect with all its pluses and minuses! I know you've never cared for life, and to me, now at the age of nearly fifty, life and death seem singularly close together in all of us—and life a mere farce of frustration in all, so far as the realization of the innermost ideals go to which we are made respectively capable of feeling an affinity and responding. Your frustrations are only rather more flagrant than the rule; and you've been saved many forms of self-dissatisfaction and misery which appertain to such a multiplication of responsible relations to different people as I, for instance, have got into. Your fortitude, good spirits and unsentimentality have been simply unexampled in the midst of your physical woes; and when you're relieved from your post, just *that* bright note will remain behind, together with the inscrutable and mysterious character of the doom of nervous weakness which has chained you down for all these years. As for that, there's more in it than has ever been told to so-called science. These inhibitions, these split-up selves, all these new facts that are gradually coming to light about our organization, these enlargements of the self in trance, etc., are bringing me to turn for light in the direction of all sorts of despised spiritualistic and unscientific ideas. Father would find in me today a much more receptive listener—all *that* philosophy has got to be brought in. And what a queer contradiction comes to the ordinary scientific argument against immortality (based on body being mind's condition and mind going *out* when body is gone), when one must believe (as now, in these neurotic cases) that some infernality in the body *prevents* really existing parts of the mind from coming to their effective rights at all, suppresses them, and blots them out from participation in this world's experiences, although they are *there* all the time. When that which is *you* passes out of the body, I am sure that there will be an explosion of liberated force and life till then eclipsed and kept down. I can hardly imagine *your* transition without a great oscillation of both 'worlds' as they regain their new equilibrium after the change! Everyone will feel the shock, but you yourself will be more surprised than anybody else.

It may seem odd for me to talk to you in this cool way about your end; but, my dear little sister, if one has things present to one's mind, and I know they are present enough to *your* mind, why not speak them out? I am sure you appreciate that best. How many times I have thought, in the past year, when my days were so full of strong and varied impression and activities, of the long unchanging hours in bed which those days stood for with you, and wondered how you bore the slow-paced monotony at all, as you did! You can't tell how I've pitied you. But you *shall* come to your rights erelong. Meanwhile take things gently. Look for the little good in each day as if life were to last a hundred years. Above all things, save yourself from bodily pain, if it can be done. You've had too much of that. Take all the morphia (or other forms of opium if that disagrees) you want, and don't be afraid of becoming an opium-drunkard. What was opium created for except for such times as this? Beg the good Katharine (to whom *our* debt can never be extinguished) to write me a line every week, just to keep the currents flowing, and so farewell until I write again. Your ever loving,

W. J.

Joseph Conrad

IL CONDE

❨ On Conrad see pp. 63–7. 'Il Conde' was first published in *A Set of Six* (1908).

'*Vedi Napoli e poi mori.*'

T̃HE first time we got into conversation was in the National Museum in Naples, in the rooms on the ground floor containing the famous collection of bronzes from Herculaneum and Pompeii: that marvellous legacy of antique art whose delicate perfection has been preserved for us by the catastrophic fury of a volcano.

He addressed me first, over the celebrated Resting Hermes which we had been looking at side by side. He said the right things about the wholly admirable piece. Nothing profound. His taste was natural rather than cultivated. He had obviously seen many fine things in his life and appreciated them: but he had no jargon of a dilettante or the connoisseur. A hateful tribe. He spoke like a fairly intelligent man of the world, a perfectly unaffected gentleman.

We had known each other by sight for some few days past. Staying in the same hotel—good, but not extravagantly up to date—I had noticed him in the vestibule going in and out. I judged he was an old and valued client. The bow of the hotel-keeper was cordial in its deference, and he acknowledged it with familiar courtesy. For the servants he was *Il Conde*. There was some squabble over a man's parasol—yellow silk with white lining sort of thing—the waiters had discovered abandoned outside the dining-room door. Our gold-laced door-keeper recognized it and I heard him directing one of the lift boys to run after *Il Conde* with it. Perhaps he was the only Count staying in the hotel, or perhaps he had the distinction

Reprinted by permission of J. M. Dent & Sons, Ltd. Published in the United States by Doubleday and Company.

of being *the* Count *par excellence*, conferred upon him because of his tried fidelity to the house.

Having conversed at the Museo—(and by the by he had expressed his dislike of the busts and statues of Roman emperors in the gallery of marbles: their faces were too vigorous, too pronounced for him)—having conversed already in the morning, I did not think I was intruding when in the evening, finding the dining-room very full, I proposed to share his little table. Judging by the quiet urbanity of his consent he did not think so either. His smile was very attractive.

He dined in an evening waistcoat and a 'smoking' (he called it so) with a black tie. All this of very good cut, not new—just as these things should be. He was, morning or evening, very correct in his dress. I have no doubt that his whole existence had been correct, well ordered and conventional, undisturbed by startling events. His white hair brushed upward off a lofty forehead gave him the air of an idealist, of an imaginative man. His white moustache, heavy but carefully trimmed and arranged, was not unpleasantly tinted a golden yellow in the middle. The faint scent of some very good perfume, and of good cigars (that last odour quite remarkable to come upon in Italy) reached me across the table. It was in his eyes that his age showed most. They were a little weary with creased eyelids. He must have been sixty or a couple of years more. And he was communicative. I would not go so far as to call it garrulous—but distinctly communicative.

He had tried various climates, of Abbazia, of the Riviera, of other places, too, he told me, but the only one which suited him was the climate of the Gulf of Naples. The ancient Romans, who, he pointed out to me, were men expert in the art of living, knew very well what they were doing when they built their villas on these shores, in Baiæ, in Vico, in Capri. They came down to this seaside in search of health, bringing with them their trains of mimes and flute-players to amuse their leisure. He thought it extremely probable that the Romans of the higher classes were specially predisposed to painful rheumatic affections.

This was the only personal opinion I heard him express. It was based on no special erudition. He knew no more of the Romans than an average informed man of the world is expected to know. He argued from personal experience. He had suffered himself from a painful and dangerous rheumatic affection till he found relief in this particular spot of southern Europe.

This was three years ago, and ever since he had taken up his quarters on the shores of the gulf, either in one of the hotels in Sorrento or hiring a small villa in Capri. He had a piano, a few books: picked up transient acquaintances of a day, week, or month in the stream of travellers from all Europe. One can imagine him going out for his walks in the streets and lanes, becoming known to beggars, shopkeepers, children, country people; talking amiably over the walls to the contadini [1]—and coming back to his rooms or his villa to sit before the piano, with his white hair brushed up and his thick orderly moustache, 'to make a little music for myself.' And, of course, for a change there was Naples near by—life, movement, animation, opera. A little amusement, as he said, is necessary for health. Mimes and flute-players, in fact. Only, unlike the magnates of ancient Rome, he had no affairs of the city to call him away from these moderate delights. He had no affairs at all. Probably he had never had any grave affairs to attend to in his life. It was a kindly existence, with its joys and sorrows regulated by the course of Nature—marriages, births, deaths—ruled by the prescribed usages of good society and protected by the State.

He was a widower; but in the months of July and August he ventured to cross the Alps for six weeks on a visit to his married daughter. He told me her name. It was that of a very aristocratic family. She had a castle—in Bohemia, I think. This is as near as I ever came to ascertaining his nationality. His own name, strangely enough, he never mentioned. Perhaps he thought I had seen it on the published list. Truth to say, I never looked. At any rate, he was a good European—he spoke four languages to my certain knowledge—and a man of fortune. Not of great fortune, evidently and appropriately. I imagine that to be extremely rich would have appeared to him improper, outré [2]—too blatant altogether. And obviously, too, the fortune was not of his making. The making of a fortune cannot be achieved without some roughness. It is a matter of temperament. His nature was too kindly for strife. In the course of conversation he mentioned his estate quite by the way, in reference to that painful and alarming rheumatic affection. One year, staying incautiously beyond the Alps as late as the middle of September, he had been laid up for three months in that lonely country house with no one but his valet and the caretaking couple to attend to him. Because, as he expressed it, he 'kept no establishment there.' He had only gone for a couple of days to confer with his land agent. He promised himself never to be so imprudent in the future. The first weeks of September would find him on the shores of his beloved gulf.

Sometimes in travelling one comes upon such lonely men, whose only

[1 Peasants.]
[2 Extreme, excessive.]

business is to wait for the unavoidable. Deaths and marriages have made a solitude round them, and one really cannot blame their endeavours to make the waiting as easy as possible. As he remarked to me: 'At my time of life freedom from physical pain is a very important matter.'

It must not be imagined that he was a wearisome hypochondriac. He was really much too well-bred to be a nuisance. He had an eye for the small weaknesses of humanity. But it was a good-natured eye. He made a restful, easy, pleasant companion for the hours between dinner and bedtime. We spent three evenings together, and then I had to leave Naples in a hurry to look after a friend who had fallen seriously ill in Taormina. Having nothing to do, *Il Conde* came to see me off at the station. I was somewhat upset, and his idleness was always ready to take a kindly form. He was by no means an indolent man.

He went along the train peering into the carriages for a good seat for me, and then remained talking cheerily from below. He declared he would miss me that evening very much and announced his intention of going after dinner to listen to the band in the public garden, the Villa Nazionale. He would amuse himself by hearing excellent music and looking at the best society. There would be a lot of people, as usual.

I seem to see him yet—his raised face with a friendly smile under the thick moustaches, and his kind, fatigued eyes. As the train began to move, he addressed me in two languages: first in French, saying, *'Bon voyage'*; then, in his very good, somewhat emphatic English, encouragingly, because he could see my concern: 'All will—be—well—yet!'

My friend's illness having taken a decidedly favourable turn, I returned to Naples on the tenth day. I cannot say I had given much thought to *Il Conde* during my absence, but entering the dining-room I looked for him in his habitual place. I had an idea he might have gone back to Sorrento to his piano and his books and his fishing. He was great friends with all the boatmen, and fished a good deal with lines from a boat. But I made out his white head in a crowd of heads, and even from a distance noticed something unusual in his attitude. Instead of sitting erect, gazing all round with alert urbanity, he drooped over his plate. I stood opposite him for some time before he looked up, a little wildly, if such a strong word can be used in connection with his correct appearance.

'Ah, my dear sir! Is it you?' he greeted me. 'I hope all is well.'

He was very nice about my friend. Indeed, he was always nice, with the niceness of people whose hearts are genuinely humane. But this time it cost him an effort. His attempts at general conversation broke down into dulness. It occurred to me he might have been indisposed. But before I could frame the inquiry he muttered:

'You find me here very sad.'

'I am sorry for that,' I said. 'You haven't had bad news, I hope?'

It was very kind of me to take an interest. No. It was not that. No bad news, thank God. And he became very still, as if holding his breath. Then, leaning forward a little, and in an odd tone of awed embarrassment, he took me into his confidence.

'The truth is that I have had a very—a very—how shall I say?—abominable adventure happen to me.'

The energy of the epithet was sufficiently startling in that man of moderate feelings and toned-down vocabulary. The word unpleasant I should have thought would have fitted amply the worst experience likely to befall a man of his stamp. And an adventure, too. Incredible! But it is in human nature to believe the worst, and I confess I eyed him stealthily, wondering what he had been up to. In a moment, however, my unworthy suspicions vanished. There was a fundamental refinement of nature about the man which made me dismiss all idea of some more or less disreputable scrape.

'It is very serious. Very serious.' He went on nervously. 'I will tell you after dinner, if you will allow me.'

I expressed my perfect acquiescence by a little bow, nothing more. I wished him to understand that I was not likely to hold him to that offer, if he thought better of it later on. We talked of indifferent things, but with a sense of difficulty quite unlike our former easy, gossipy intercourse. The hand raising a piece of bread to his lips, I noticed, trembled slightly. This symptom, in regard of my reading of the man, was no less than startling.

In the smoking-room he did not hang back at all. Directly we had taken our usual seats he leaned sideways over the arm of his chair and looked straight into my eyes earnestly.

'You remember,' he began, 'that day you went away? I told you then I would go to the Villa Nazionale to hear some music in the evening.'

I remembered. His handsome old face, so fresh for his age, unmarked by any trying experience, appeared haggard for an instant. It was like the passing of a shadow. Returning his steadfast gaze, I took a sip of my black coffee. He was systematically minute in his narrative, simply in order, I think, not to let his excitement get the better of him.

After leaving the railway station, he had an ice, and read the paper in a café. Then he went back to the hotel, dressed for dinner, and dined with a good appetite. After dinner he lingered in the hall (there were chairs and

tables there) smoking his cigar; talked to the little girl of the Primo
Tenore of the San Carlo theatre, and exchanged a few words with that
'amiable lady,' the wife of the Primo Tenore. There was no performance
that evening, and these people were going to the Villa also. They went out
of the hotel. Very well.

At the moment of following their example—it was half-past nine already
—he remembered he had a rather large sum of money in his pocket-book.
He entered, therefore, the office and deposited the greater part of it with
the book-keeper of the hotel. This done, he took a carozella and drove to
the seashore. He got out of the cab and entered the Villa on foot from the
Largo di Vittoria end.

He stared at me very hard. And I understood then how really impres-
sionable he was. Every small fact and event of that evening stood out in
his memory as if endowed with mystic significance. If he did not mention
to me the colour of the pony which drew the carozella, and the aspect of
the man who drove, it was a mere oversight arising from his agitation,
which he repressed manfully.

He had then entered the Villa Nazionale from the Largo di Vittoria end.
The Villa Nazionale is a public pleasure-ground laid out in grass plots,
bushes, and flower-beds between the houses of the Riviera di Chiaja and
the waters of the bay. Alleys of trees, more or less parallel, stretch its whole
length—which is considerable. On the Riviera di Chiaja side the electric
tramcars run close to the railings. Between the garden and the sea is the
fashionable drive, a broad road bordered by a low wall, beyond which the
Mediterranean splashes with gentle murmurs when the weather is fine.

As life goes on late at night in Naples, the broad drive was all astir with
a brilliant swarm of carriage lamps moving in pairs, some creeping slowly,
others running rapidly under the thin, motionless line of electric lamps
defining the shore. And a brilliant swarm of stars hung above the land
humming with voices, piled up with houses, glittering with lights—and
over the silent flat shadows of the sea.

The gardens themselves are not very well lit. Our friend went forward in
the warm gloom, his eyes fixed upon a distant luminous region extending
nearly across the whole width of the Villa, as if the air had glowed there
with its own cold, bluish, and dazzling light. This magic spot, behind the
black trunks of trees and masses of inky foliage, breathed out sweet sounds
mingled with bursts of brassy roar, sudden clashes of metal, and grave,
vibrating thuds.

As he walked on, all these noises combined together into a piece of elaborate music whose harmonious phrases came persuasively through a great disorderly murmur of voices and shuffling of feet on the gravel of that open space. An enormous crowd immersed in the electric light, as if in a bath of some radiant and tenuous fluid shed upon their heads by luminous globes, drifted in its hundreds round the band. Hundreds more sat on chairs in more or less concentric circles, receiving unflinchingly the great waves of sonority that ebbed out into the darkness. The Count penetrated the throng, drifted with it in tranquil enjoyment, listening and looking at the faces. All people of good society: mothers with their daughters, parents and children, young men and young women all talking, smiling, nodding to each other. Very many pretty faces, and very many pretty toilettes. There was, of course, a quantity of diverse types: showy old fellows with white moustaches, fat men, thin men, officers in uniform; but what predominated, he told me, was the South Italian type of young man, with a colourless, clear complexion, red lips, jet-black little moustache and liquid black eyes so wonderfully effective in leering or scowling.

Withdrawing from the throng, the Count shared a little table in front of the café with a young man of just such a type. Our friend had some lemonade. The young man was sitting moodily before an empty glass. He looked up once, and then looked down again. He also tilted his hat forward. Like this——

The Count made a gesture of a man pulling his hat down over his brow, and went on:

'I think to myself: he is sad; something is wrong with him; young men have their troubles. I take no notice of him, of course. I pay for my lemonade, and go away.'

Strolling about in the neighbourhood of the band, the Count thinks he saw twice that young man wandering alone in the crowd. Once their eyes met. It must have been the same young man, but there were so many there of that type that he could not be certain. Moreover, he was not very much concerned except in so far that he had been struck by the marked, peevish discontent of that face.

Presently, tired of the feeling of confinement one experiences in a crowd, the Count edged away from the band. An alley, very sombre by contrast, presented itself invitingly with its promise of solitude and coolness. He entered it, walking slowly on till the sound of the orchestra became distinctly deadened. Then he walked back and turned about once more. He did this several times before he noticed that there was somebody occupying one of the benches.

The spot being midway between two lamp-posts the light was faint.

The man lolled back in the corner of his seat, his legs stretched out, his arms folded and his head drooping on his breast. He never stirred, as though he had fallen asleep there, but when the Count passed by next time he had changed his attitude. He sat leaning forward. His elbows were propped on his knees, and his hands were rolling a cigarette. He never looked up from that occupation.

The Count continued his stroll away from the band. He returned slowly, he said. I can imagine him enjoying to the full, but with his usual tranquillity, the balminess of this southern night and the sounds of music softened delightfully by the distance.

Presently, he approached for the third time the man on the garden seat, still leaning forward with his elbows on his knees. It was a dejected pose. In the semi-obscurity of the alley his high shirt collar and his cuffs made small patches of vivid whiteness. The Count said that he had noticed him getting up brusquely as if to walk away, but almost before he was aware of it the man stood before him asking in a low, gentle tone whether the signore would have the kindness to oblige him with a light.

The Count answered this request by a polite 'Certainly,' and dropped his hands with the intention of exploring both pockets of his trousers for the matches.

'I dropped my hands,' he said, 'but I never put them in my pockets. I felt a pressure there——'

He put the tip of his finger on a spot close under his breastbone, the very spot of the human body where a Japanese gentleman begins the operation of the harakiri, which is a form of suicide following upon dishonour, upon an intolerable outrage to the delicacy of one's feelings.

'I glance down,' the Count continued in an awe-struck voice, 'and what do I see? A knife! A long knife——'

'You don't mean to say,' I exclaimed amazed, 'that you have been held up like this in the Villa at half-past ten o'clock, within a stone's throw of a thousand people!'

He nodded several times, staring at me with all his might.

'The clarionet,' he declared solemnly, 'was finishing his solo, and I assure you I could hear every note. Then the band crashed *fortissimo*, and that creature rolled its eyes and gnashed its teeth, hissing at me with the greatest ferocity, "Be silent! No noise or——" '

I could not get over my astonishment.

'What sort of knife was it?' I asked stupidly.

'A long blade. A stiletto—perhaps a kitchen knife. A long narrow blade. It gleamed. And his eyes gleamed. His white teeth, too. I could see them. He was very ferocious. I thought to myself: "If I hit him he will kill me." How could I fight with him? He had the knife and I had nothing. I am nearly seventy, you know, and that was a young man. I seemed even to recognize him. The moody young man of the café. The young man I met in the crowd. But I could not tell. There are so many like him in this country.'

The distress of that moment was reflected in his face. I should think that physically he must have been paralyzed by surprise. His thoughts, however, remained extremely active. They ranged over every alarming possibility. The idea of setting up a vigorous shouting for help occurred to him, too. But he did nothing of the kind, and the reason why he refrained gave me a good opinion of his mental self-possession. He saw in a flash that nothing prevented the other from shouting, too.

'That young man might in an instant have thrown away his knife and pretended I was the aggressor. Why not? He might have said I attacked him. Why not? It was one incredible story against another! He might have said anything—bring some dishonouring charge against me—what do I know? By his dress he was no common robber. He seemed to belong to the better classes. What could I say? He was an Italian—I am a foreigner. Of course I have my passport, and there is our consul—but to be arrested, dragged at night to the police office like a criminal!'

He shuddered. It was in his character to shrink from scandal much more than from mere death. And certainly for many people this would have always remained—considering certain peculiarities of Neapolitan manners —a deucedly queer story. The Count was no fool. His belief in the respectable placidity of life having received this rude shock, he thought that now anything might happen. But also a notion came into his head that this young man was perhaps merely an infuriated lunatic.

This was for me the first hint of his attitude toward this adventure. In his exaggerated delicacy of sentiment he felt that nobody's self-esteem need be affected by what a madman may choose to do to one. It became apparent, that the Count was to be denied that consolation. He enlarged upon the abominably savage way in which that young man rolled his glistening eyes and gnashed his white teeth. The band was going now through a slow movement of solemn braying by all the trombones, with deliberately repeated bangs of the big drum.

'But what did you do?' I asked, greatly excited.

'Nothing,' answered the Count. 'I let my hands hang down very still. I told him quietly I did not intend making a noise. He snarled like a dog, then said in an ordinary voice:

' "*Vostro portofolio.*"

'So I naturally,' continued the Count—and from this point acted the whole thing in pantomime. Holding me with his eyes, he went through all the motions of reaching into his inside breast pocket, taking out a pocket-book, and handing it over. But that young man, still bearing steadily on the knife, refused to touch it.

He directed the Count to take the money out himself, received it into his left hand, motioned the pocket-book to be returned to the pocket, all this being done to the sweet thrilling of flutes and clarionets sustained by the emotional drone of the hautboys. And the 'young man,' as the Count called him, said: 'This seems very little.'

'It was, indeed, only 340 or 360 lire,' the Count pursued. 'I had left my money in the hotel, as you know. I told him this was all I had on me. He shook his head impatiently and said:

' "*Vostro orologio.*" '

The Count gave me the dumb show of pulling out his watch, detaching it. But, as it happened, the valuable gold half-chronometer he possessed had been left at a watch-maker's for cleaning. He wore that evening (on a leather guard) the Waterbury fifty-franc thing he used to take with him on his fishing expeditions. Perceiving the nature of this booty, the well-dressed robber made a contemptuous clicking sound with his tongue like this, 'Tse-Ah!' and waved it away hastily. Then, as the Count was returning the disdained object to his pocket, he demanded with a threateningly in-creased pressure of the knife on the epigastrum, by way of reminder:

'*Vostri anelli.*'

'One of the rings,' went on the Count, 'was given me many years ago by my wife; the other is the signet ring of my father. I said, "No. *That* you shall not have!" '

Here the Count reproduced the gesture corresponding to that declaration by clapping one hand upon the other, and pressing both thus against his chest. It was touching in its resignation. 'That you shall not have,' he repeated firmly and closed his eyes, fully expecting—I don't know whether I am right in recording that such an unpleasant word had passed his lips—fully expecting to feel himself being—I really hesitate to say—being dis-embowelled by the push of the long, sharp blade resting murderously against the pit of his stomach—the very seat, in all human beings, of anguishing sensations.

Great waves of harmony went on flowing from the band.

Suddenly the Count felt the nightmarish pressure removed from the sensitive spot. He opened his eyes. He was alone. He had heard nothing. It is probable that the 'young man' had departed, with light steps, some time before, but the sense of the horrid pressure had lingered even after the knife had gone. A feeling of weakness came over him. He had just time to stagger to the garden seat. He felt as though he had held his breath for a long time. He sat all in a heap, panting with the shock of the reaction.

The band was executing, with immense bravura, the complicated finale. It ended with a tremendous crash. He heard it unreal and remote, as if his ears had been stopped, and then the hard clapping of a thousand, more or less, pairs of hands, like a sudden hail-shower passing away. The profound silence which succeeded recalled him to himself.

A tramcar, resembling a long glass box wherein people sat with their heads strongly lighted, ran along swiftly within sixty yards of the spot where he had been robbed. Then another rustled by, and yet another going the other way. The audience about the band had broken up, and were entering the alley in small conversing groups. The Count sat up straight and tried to think calmly of what had happened to him. The vileness of it took his breath away again. As far as I can make it out he was disgusted with himself. I do not mean to say with his behaviour. Indeed, if his pantomimic rendering of it for my information was to be trusted, it was simply perfect. No, it was not that. He was not ashamed. He was shocked at being the selected victim, not of robbery so much as of contempt. His tranquillity had been wantonly desecrated. His lifelong, kindly nicety of outlook had been defaced.

Nevertheless, at that stage, before the iron had time to sink deep, he was able to argue himself into comparative equanimity. As his agitation calmed down somewhat, he became aware that he was frightfully hungry. Yes, hungry. The sheer emotion had made him simply ravenous. He left the seat and, after walking for some time, found himself outside the gardens and before an arrested tramcar, without knowing very well how he came there. He got in as if in a dream, by a sort of instinct. Fortunately he found in his trouser pocket a copper to satisfy the conductor. Then the car stopped, and as everybody was getting out he got out, too. He recognized the Piazza San Ferdinando, but apparently it did not occur to him to take a cab and drive to the hotel. He remained in distress on the Piazza like a lost dog, thinking vaguely of the best way of getting something to eat at once.

Suddenly he remembered his twenty-franc piece. He explained to me that he had that piece of French gold for something like three years. He used to carry it about with him as a sort of reserve in case of accident. Anybody is liable to have his pocket picked—a quite different thing from a brazen and insulting robbery.

The monumental arch of the Galleria Umberto faced him at the top of a noble flight of stairs. He climbed these without loss of time, and directed his steps toward the Café Umberto. All the tables outside were occupied by a lot of people who were drinking. But as he wanted something to eat, he went into the café, which is divided into aisles by square pillars set all round with long looking-glasses. The Count sat down on a red plush bench against one of these pillars, waiting for his risotto.[3] And his mind reverted to his abominable adventure.

He thought of the moody, well-dressed young man, with whom he had exchanged glances in the crowd around the bandstand, and who, he felt confident, was the robber. Would he recognize him again? Doubtless. But he did not want ever to see him again. The best thing was to forget this humiliating episode.

The Count looked round anxiously for the coming of his risotto, and, behold! to the left against the wall—there sat the young man. He was alone at a table, with a bottle of some sort of wine or syrup and a carafe of iced water before him. The smooth olive cheeks, the red lips, the little jet-black moustache turned up gallantly, the fine black eyes a little heavy and shaded by long eyelashes, that peculiar expression of cruel discontent to be seen only in the busts of some Roman emperors—it was he, no doubt at all. But that was a type. The Count looked away hastily. The young officer over there reading a paper was like that, too. Same type. Two young men farther away playing draughts also resembled——

The Count lowered his head with the fear in his heart of being everlastingly haunted by the vision of that young man. He began to eat his risotto. Presently he heard the young man on his left call the waiter in a bad-tempered tone.

At the call, not only his own waiter, but two other idle waiters belonging to a quite different row of tables, rushed toward him with obsequious alacrity, which is not the general characteristic of the waiters in the Café Umberto. The young man muttered something and one of the waiters walking rapidly to the nearest door called out into the Galleria: 'Pasquale! O! Pasquale!'

Everybody knows Pasquale, the shabby old fellow who, shuffling between

[3 A rice dish.]

the tables, offers for sale cigars, cigarettes, picture postcards, and matches to the clients of the café. He is in many respects an engaging scoundrel. The Count saw the gray-haired, unshaven ruffian enter the café, the glass case hanging from his neck by a leather strap, and, at a word from the waiter, make his shuffling way with a sudden spurt to the young man's table. The young man was in need of a cigar with which Pasquale served him fawningly. The old pedlar was going out, when the Count, on a sudden impulse, beckoned to him.

Pasquale approached, the smile of deferential recognition combining oddly with the cynical, searching expression of his eyes. Leaning his case on the table, he lifted the glass lid without a word. The Count took a box of cigarettes and urged by a fearful curiosity, asked as casually as he could——

'Tell me, Pasquale, who is that young signore sitting over there?'

The other bent over his box confidentially.

'That, *Signor Conde*,' he said, beginning to rearrange his wares busily and without looking up, 'that is a young *Cavaliere* of a very good family from Bari. He studies in the University here, and is the chief, *capo*, of an association of young men—of very nice young men.'

He paused, and then, with mingled discretion and pride of knowledge, murmured the explanatory word 'Camorra' [4] and shut down the lid. 'A very powerful Camorra,' he breathed out. 'The professors themselves respect it greatly . . . *una lira e cinquanti centesimi, Signor Conde*.'

Our friend paid with the gold piece. While Pasquale was making up the change, he observed that the young man, of whom he had heard so much in a few words, was watching the transaction covertly. After the old vagabond had withdrawn with a bow, the Count settled with the waiter and sat still. A numbness, he told me, had come over him.

The young man paid, too, got up and crossed over, apparently for the purpose of looking at himself in the mirror set in the pillar nearest to the Count's seat. He was dressed all in black with a dark green bow tie. The Count looked round, and was startled by meeting a vicious glance out of the corners of the other's eyes. The young *Cavaliere* from Bari (according to Pasquale; but Pasquale is, of course, an accomplished liar) went on arranging his tie, settling his hat before the glass, and meantime he spoke just loud enough to be heard by the Count. He spoke through his teeth with the most insulting venom of contempt and gazing straight into the mirror.

[⁴ Secret society.]

'Ah! So you have some gold on you—you old liar—you old *birba*—you *furfante!* [5] But you are not done with me yet.'

The fiendishness of his expression vanished like lightning, and he lounged out of the café with a moody, impassive face.

The poor Count, after telling me this last episode, fell back trembling in his chair. His forehead broke into perspiration. There was a wanton insolence in the spirit of this outrage which appalled even me. What it was to the Count's delicacy I won't attempt to guess. I am sure that if he had not been too refined to do such a blatantly vulgar thing as dying from apoplexy in a café, he would have had a fatal stroke there and then. All irony apart, my difficulty was to keep him from seeing the full extent of my commiseration. He shrank from every excessive sentiment, and my commiseration was practically unbounded. It did not surprise me to hear that he had been in bed a week. He had got up to make his arrangements for leaving southern Italy for good and all.

And the man was convinced that he could not live through a whole year in any other climate!

No argument of mine had any effect. It was not timidity, though he did say to me once: 'You do not know what a Camorra is, my dear sir. I am a marked man.' He was not afraid of what could be done to him. His delicate conception of his dignity was defiled by a degrading experience. He couldn't stand that. No Japanese gentleman, outraged in his exaggerated sense of honour, could have gone about his preparations for hara-kiri with greater resolution. To go home really amounted to suicide for the poor Count.

There is a saying of Neapolitan patriotism, intended for the information of foreigners, I presume: 'See Naples and then die.' *Vedi Napoli e poi mori.* It is a saying of excessive vanity, and everything excessive was abhorrent to the nice moderation of the poor Count. Yet, as I was seeing him off at the railway station, I thought he was behaving with singular fidelity to its conceited spirit. *Vedi Napoli!* . . . He had seen it! He had seen it with startling thoroughness—and now he was going to his grave. He was going to it by the *train de luxe* of the International Sleeping Car Company, *via* Trieste and Vienna. As the four long, sombre coaches pulled out of the station I raised my hat with the solemn feeling of paying the last tribute of respect to a funeral *cortège*. *Il Conde's* profile, much aged already, glided away from me in stony immobility, behind the lighted pane of glass —*Vedi Napoli e poi mori!*

[5 Good-for-nothing; rogue.]

James Thurber
UNIVERSITY DAYS

⟨ Mr. Thurber (1894—) grew up in Columbus, Ohio, and attended the Ohio State University he writes about in 'University
Days.' He records of his youth that 'There is no clearly traceable
figure or pattern in this phase of his life. If he knew where he was
going, it is not apparent from this distance. He fell down a great
deal during this period, because of a trick he had of walking into
himself. His gold-rimmed glasses forever needed straightening,
which gave him the appearance of a person who hears somebody
calling him but can't make out where the sound is coming from.'
After graduation, he worked for the State Department for two
years, was a reporter in Columbus and in Paris, and after 1926 a
member of the staff of *The New Yorker,* in which many of his
writings and drawings first appeared.

To anybody unfamiliar with Mr. Thurber's productions such an
outline tells little; besides, 'Thurber's life,' according to the first
authority, 'baffles and irritates the biographer because of its lack of
design. One has the disturbing feeling that the man contrived to be
some place without actually having gone there.' All that Mr. Thurber's admirers know, and all they need to know, about his life is
contained in his writings, especially *My Life and Hard Times,* from
which the selections here reprinted are taken.

Much of Mr. Thurber's best work is collected in *The Thurber
Carnival* (1945) and *The Thurber Album* (1952). 'University
Days' and 'Draft Board Nights' were first printed in *The New
Yorker.*

I PASSED all the other courses that I took at my University, but
I could never pass botany. This was because all botany students had to spend
several hours a week in a laboratory looking through a microscope at plant

cells, and I could never see through a microscope. I never once saw a cell through a microscope. This used to enrage my instructor. He would wander around the laboratory pleased with the progress all the students were making in drawing the involved and, so I am told, interesting structure of flower cells, until he came to me. I would just be standing there. 'I can't see anything,' I would say. He would begin patiently enough, explaining how anybody can see through a microscope, but he would always end up in a fury, claiming that I could *too* see through a microscope but just pretended that I couldn't. 'It takes away from the beauty of flowers anyway,' I used to tell him. 'We are not concerned with beauty in this course,' he would say. 'We are concerned solely with what I may call the *mechanics* of flars.' 'Well,' I'd say, 'I can't see anything.' 'Try it just once again,' he'd say, and I would put my eye to the microscope and see nothing at all, except now and again a nebulous milky substance—a phenomenon of maladjustment. We were supposed to see a vivid, restless clockwork of sharply defined plant cells. 'I see what looks like a lot of milk,' I would tell him. This, he claimed, was the result of my not having adjusted the microscope properly, so he would readjust it for me, or rather, for himself. And I would look again and see milk.

I finally took a deferred pass, as they called it, and waited a year and tried again. (You had to pass one of the biological sciences or you couldn't graduate.) The professor had come back from vacation brown as a berry, bright-eyed, and eager to explain cell-structure again to his classes. 'Well,' he said to me, cheerily, when we met in the first laboratory hour of the semester, 'we're going to see cells this time, aren't we?' 'Yes, sir,' I said. Students to right of me and to left of me and in front of me were seeing cells; what's more, they were quietly drawing pictures of them in their notebooks. Of course, I didn't see anything.

'We'll try it,' the professor said to me, grimly, 'with every adjustment of the microscope known to man. As God is my witness, I'll arrange this glass so that you see cells through it or I'll give up teaching. In twenty-two years of botany, I—' He cut off abruptly for he was beginning to quiver all over, like Lionel Barrymore, and he genuinely wished to hold onto his temper; his scenes with me had taken a great deal out of him.

So we tried it with every adjustment of the microscope known to man. With only one of them did I see anything but blackness or the familiar lacteal opacity, and that time I saw, to my pleasure and amazement, a variegated constellation of flecks, specks, and dots. These I hastily drew. The instructor, noting my activity, came back from an adjoining desk, a smile on his lips and his eyebrows high in hope. He looked at my cell drawing. 'What's that?' he demanded, with a hint of a squeal in his voice. 'That's what I saw,' I said. 'You didn't, you didn't, you *did*n't!' he screamed, losing control of his temper instantly, and he bent over and squinted into the microscope. His head snapped up. 'That's your eye!' he shouted. 'You've fixed the lens so that it reflects! You've drawn your eye!'

Another course that I didn't like, but somehow managed to pass, was economics. I went to that class straight from the botany class, which didn't help me any in understanding either subject. I used to get them mixed up. But not as mixed up as another student in my economics class who came there direct from a physics laboratory. He was a tackle on the football team, named Bolenciecwcz. At that time Ohio State University had one of the best football teams in the country, and Bolenciecwcz was one of its outstanding stars. In order to be eligible to play it was necessary for him to keep up in his studies, a very difficult matter, for while he was not dumber than an ox he was not any smarter. Most of his professors were lenient and helped him along. None gave him more hints, in answering questions, or asked him simpler ones than the economics professor, a thin, timid man named Bassum. One day when we were on the subject of transportation and distribution, it came Bolenciecwcz's turn to answer a question. 'Name one means of transportation,' the professor said to him. No light came into the big tackle's eyes. 'Just any means of transportation,' said the professor. Bolenciecwcz sat staring at him. 'That is,' pursued the professor, 'any medium, agency, or method of going from one place to another.' Bolenciecwcz had the look of a man who is being led into a trap. 'You may choose among steam, horse-drawn, or electrically propelled vehicles,' said the instructor. 'I might suggest the one which we commonly take in making long journeys across land.' There was a profound silence in which everybody stirred uneasily, including Bolenciecwcz and Mr. Bassum. Mr. Bassum abruptly broke this silence in an amazing manner. "Choo-choo-choo,' he said, in a low voice, and turned instantly scarlet. He glanced appealingly around the room. All of us, of course, shared Mr. Bassum's desire that Bolenciecwcz should stay abreast of the class in economics, for the Illinois game, one of the hardest and most important of the season, was only a week off. 'Toot, tooot, too-tooooooot!' some student with a deep voice moaned, and we all looked encouragingly at Bolenciecwcz. Somebody else gave a fine imitation of a locomotive letting off steam. Mr. Bassum himself rounded off the little show. 'Ding, dong, ding, dong,' he said hopefully. Bolenciecwcz was staring at the floor now, trying to think, his great brow furrowed, his huge hands rubbing together, his face red.

'How did you come to college this year, Mr. Bolenciecwcz?' asked the professor. '*Chuffa*, chuffa, *chuffa*, chuffa.'

'M'father sent me,' said the football player.

'What on?' asked Bassum.

'I git an 'lowance,' said the tackle, in a low, husky voice, obviously embarrassed.

'No, no,' said Bassum. 'Name a means of transportation. What did you *ride* here on?'

'Train,' said Bolenciecwcz.

'Quite right,' said the professor. 'Now, Mr. Nugent, will you tell us——'

If I went through anguish in botany and economics—for different reasons—gymnasium work was even worse. I don't even like to think about it. They wouldn't let you play games or join in the exercises with your glasses on and I couldn't see with mine off. I bumped into professors, horizontal bars, agricultural students, and swinging iron rings. Not being able to see, I could take it but I couldn't dish it out. Also, in order to pass gymnasium (and you had to pass it to graduate) you had to learn to swim if you didn't know how. I didn't like the swimming pool, I didn't like swimming, and I didn't like the swimming instructor, and after all these years I still don't. I never swam but I passed my gym work anyway, by having another student give my gymnasium number (978) and swim across the pool in my place. He was a quiet, amiable blonde youth, number 473, and he would have seen through a microscope for me if we could have got away with it, but we couldn't get away with it. Another thing I didn't like about gymnasium work was that they made you strip the day you registered. It is impossible for me to be happy when I am stripped and being asked a lot of questions. Still, I did better than a lanky agricultural student who was cross-examined just before I was. They asked each student what college he was in—that is, whether Arts, Engineering, Commerce or Agriculture. 'What college are you in?' the instructor snapped at the youth in front of me. 'Ohio State University,' he said promptly.

It wasn't that agricultural student but it was another a whole lot like him who decided to take up journalism, possibly on the ground that when farming went to hell he could fall back on newspaper work. He didn't realize, of course, that that would be very much like falling back full-length on a kit of carpenter's tools. Haskins didn't seem cut out for journalism, being too embarrassed to talk to anybody and unable to use a typewriter, but the editor of the college paper assigned him to the cow barns, the sheep house, the horse pavilion, and the animal husbandry department generally. This was a genuinely big 'beat,' for it took up five times as much ground and got ten times as great a legislative appropriation as the College of Liberal Arts. The agricultural student knew animals, but nevertheless his stories were dull and colorlessly written. He took all afternoon on each of them, on account of having to hunt for each letter on the typewriter. Once in a while he had to ask somebody to help him hunt. 'C' and 'L,' in particular, were hard letters for him to find. His editor finally got pretty much annoyed at the farmer-journalist because his pieces were so uninteresting. 'See here, Haskins,' he snapped at him one day, 'why is it we never have anything hot from you on the horse pavilion? Here we have two hundred head of horses on this campus—more than any other university in the Western Conference except Purdue—and yet you never get any real low down on them. Now shoot over to the horse barns and dig up something lively.' Haskins shambled out and came back in about an hour; he said he had something. 'Well, start it off snappily,' said the editor. 'Something people will read.' Haskins set to work and in a couple of hours brought a sheet of typewritten paper to the desk; it was a two-hundred word story about some disease that had broken out among the horses. Its opening sentence was simple but arresting. It read: 'Who has noticed the sores on the tops of the horses in the animal husbandry building?'

Ohio State was a land grant university and therefore two years of military drill was compulsory. We drilled with old Springfield rifles and studied the tactics of the Civil War even though the World War was going on at the time. At 11 o'clock each morning thousands of freshmen and sophomores used to deploy over the campus, moodily creeping up on the old chemistry building. It was good training for the kind of warfare that was waged at Shiloh [1] but it had no connection with what was going on in Europe. Some people used to think there was German money behind it, but they didn't dare say so or they would have been thrown in jail as German spies. It was a period of muddy thought and marked, I believe, the decline of higher education in the Middle West.

As a soldier I was never any good at all. Most of the cadets were glumly indifferent soldiers, but I was no good at all. Once General Littlefield, who was commandant of the cadet corps, popped up in front of me during regimental drill and snapped, 'You are the main trouble with this university!' I think he meant that my type was the main trouble with the univer-

[1 In Tennessee, 1862.]

sity but he may have meant me individually. I was mediocre at drill, certainly—that is, until my senior year. By that time I had drilled longer than anybody else in the Western Conference, having failed at military at the end of each preceding year so that I had to do it all over again. I was the only senior still in uniform. The uniform which, when new, had made me look like an interurban railway conductor, now that it had become faded and too tight made me look like Bert Williams in his bellboy act. This had a definitely bad effect on my morale. Even so, I had become by sheer practise little short of wonderful at squad manoeuvres.

One day General Littlefield picked our company out of the whole regiment and tried to get it mixed up by putting it through one movement after another as fast as we could execute them: squads right, squads left, squads on right into line, squads right about, squads left front into line etc. In about three minutes one hundred and nine men were marching in one direction and I was marching away from them at an angle of forty degrees, all alone. 'Company, halt!' shouted General Littlefield, 'That man is the only man who has it right!' I was made a corporal for my achievement.

The next day General Littlefield summoned me to his office. He was swatting flies when I went in. I was silent and he was silent too, for a long time. I don't think he remembered me or why he had sent for me, but he didn't want to admit it. He swatted some more flies, keeping his eyes on them narrowly before he let go with the swatter. 'Button up your coat!' he snapped. Looking back on it now I can see that he meant me although he was looking at a fly, but I just stood there. Another fly came to rest on a paper in front of the general and began rubbing its hind legs together. The general lifted the swatter cautiously. I moved restlessly and the fly flew away. 'You startled him!' barked General Littlefield, looking at me severely. I said I was sorry. 'That won't help the situation!' snapped the General, with cold military logic. I didn't see what I could do except offer to chase some more flies toward his desk, but I didn't say anything. He stared out the window at the faraway figures of co-eds crossing the campus toward the library. Finally, he told me I could go. So I went. He either didn't know which cadet I was or else he forgot what he wanted to see me about. It may have been that he wished to apologize for having called me the main trouble with the university; or maybe he had decided to compliment me on my brilliant drilling of the day before and then at the last minute decided not to. I don't know. I don't think about it much any more.

DRAFT BOARD NIGHTS

I LEFT the University in June, 1918, but I couldn't get into the army on account of my sight, just as grandfather couldn't get in on account of his age. He applied several times and each time he took off his coat and threatened to whip the men who said he was too old. The disappointment of not getting to Germany (he saw no sense in everybody going to France) and the strain of running around town seeing influential officials finally got him down in bed. He had wanted to lead a division and his chagrin at not even being able to enlist as a private was too much for him. His brother Jake, some fifteen years younger than he was, sat up at night with him after he took to bed, because we were afraid he might leave the house without even putting on his clothes. Grandfather was against the idea of Jake watching over him—he thought it was a lot of tomfoolery—but Jake hadn't been able to sleep at night for twenty-eight years, so he was the perfect person for such a vigil.

On the third night, grandfather was wakeful. He would open his eyes, look at Jake, and close them again, frowning. He never answered any question Jake asked him. About four o'clock that morning, he caught his brother sound asleep in the big leather chair beside the bed. When once Jake did fall asleep he slept deeply, so that grandfather was able to get up, dress himself, undress Jake, and put him in bed without waking him. When my Aunt Florence came into the room at seven o'clock, grandfather was sitting in the chair reading the *Memoirs of U. S. Grant* and Jake was sleeping in the bed. 'He watched while I slept,' said grandfather, 'so now I'm watchin' while he sleeps.' It seemed fair enough.

One reason we didn't want grandfather to roam around at night was that he had said something once or twice about going over to Lancaster, his old home town, and putting his problem up to 'Cump'—that is, General William Tecumseh Sherman, also an old Lancaster boy. We knew that his inability to find Sherman would be bad for him and we were afraid that he might try to get there in the little electric runabout that had been bought for my grandmother. She had become, surprisingly enough, quite skilful at getting around town in it. Grandfather was astonished and a little indignant when he saw her get into the contraption and drive off smoothly and easily. It was her first vehicular triumph over him in almost fifty years of married life and he determined to learn to drive the thing himself. A famous old horseman, he approached it as he might have approached a wild colt. His brow would darken and he would begin to curse. He always leaped into it quickly, as if it might pull out from under him if he didn't get into the seat fast enough. The first few times he tried to run the electric, he went swiftly around in a small circle, drove over the curb, across the sidewalk, and up onto the lawn. We all tried to persuade him to give up, but his spirit was aroused. 'Git that goddam buggy back in the road!' he would say, imperiously. So we would manoeuver it back into the street and he would try again. Pulling too savagely on the guiding-bar—to teach the electric a lesson—was what took him around in a circle, and it was difficult to make him understand that it was best to relax and not get mad. He had the notion that if you didn't hold her, she would throw you. And a man who (or so he often told us) had driven a four-horse McCormick reaper when he was five years old did not intend to be thrown by an electric runabout.

Since there was no way of getting him to give up learning to operate the electric, we would take him out to Franklin Park, where the roadways were wide and unfrequented, and spend an hour or so trying to explain the differences between driving a horse and carriage and driving an electric. He would keep muttering all the time; he never got it out of his head that when he took the driver's seat the machine flattened its ears on him, so to speak. After a few weeks, nevertheless, he got so he could run the electric for a hundred yards or so along a fairly straight line. But whenever he took a curve, he invariably pulled or pushed the bar too quickly and too hard and headed for a tree or a flower bed. Someone was always with him and we would never let him take the car out of the park.

One morning when grandmother was all ready to go to market, she called the garage and told them to send the electric around. They said that grandfather had already been there and taken it out. There was a tremendous to-do. We telephoned Uncle Will and he got out his Lozier and we started off to hunt for grandfather. It was not yet seven o'clock and there was fortunately little traffic. We headed for Franklin Park, figuring that he might have gone out there to try to break the car's spirit. One or two early pedestrians had seen a tall old gentleman with a white beard driving a little electric and cussing as he drove. We followed a tortuous trail and found them finally on Nelson Road, about four miles from the town of Shepard. Grandfather was standing in the road shouting, and the back wheels of the electric were deeply entangled in a barbed-wire fence. Two workmen and a farmhand were trying to get the thing loose. Grand-

father was in a state of high wrath about the electric. 'The —— —— ——
backed up on me!' he told us.

But to get back to the war. The Columbus draft board never called
grandfather for service, which was a lucky thing for them because they
would have had to take him. There were stories that several old men of
eighty or ninety had been summoned in the confusion, but somehow or
other grandfather was missed. He waited every day for the call, but it
never came. My own experience was quite different. I was called almost
every week, even though I had been exempted from service the first time
I went before the medical examiners. Either they were never convinced that
it was me or else there was some clerical error in the records which was
never cleared up. Anyway, there was usually a letter for me on Monday
ordering me to report for examination on the second floor of Memorial
Hall the following Wednesday at 9 P.M. The second time I went up I
tried to explain to one of the doctors that I had already been exempted.
'You're just a blur to me,' I said, taking off my glasses. 'You're absolutely
nothing to me,' he snapped, sharply.

I had to take off all my clothes each time and jog around the hall with
a lot of porters and bank presidents' sons and clerks and poets. Our hearts
and lungs would be examined, and then our feet; and finally our eyes. That
always came last. When the eye specialist got around to me, he would
always say, 'Why, you couldn't get into the service with sight like that!'
'I know,' I would say. Then a week or two later I would be summoned
again and go through the same rigmarole. The ninth or tenth time I was
called, I happened to pick up one of several stethoscopes that were lying
on a table and suddenly, instead of finding myself in the line of draft men,
I found myself in the line of examiners. 'Hello, doctor,' said one of them,
nodding. 'Hello,' I said. That, of course, was before I took my clothes off;
I might have managed it naked, but I doubt it. I was assigned, or rather
drifted, to the chest-and-lung section, where I began to examine every
other man, thus cutting old Dr. Ridgeway's work in two. 'I'm glad to have
you here, doctor,' he said.

I passed most of the men that came to me, but now and then I would
exempt one just to be on the safe side. I began by making each of them
hold his breath and then say 'mi, mi, mi, mi' until I noticed Ridgeway
looking at me curiously. He, I discovered, simply made them say 'ah,' and
sometimes he didn't make them say anything. Once I got hold of a man
who, it came out later, had swallowed a watch—to make the doctors believe
there was something wrong with him inside (it was common subterfuge:

men swallowed nails, hairpins, ink, etc., in an effort to be let out). Since I didn't know what you were supposed to hear through a stethoscope, the ticking of the watch at first didn't surprise me, but I decided to call Dr. Ridgeway into consultation, because nobody else had ticked. 'This man seems to tick,' I said to him. He looked at me in surprise but didn't say anything. Then he thumped the man, laid his ear to his chest, and finally tried the stethoscope. 'Sound as a dollar,' he said. 'Listen lower down,' I told him. The man indicated his stomach. Ridgeway gave him a haughty, indignant look. 'That is for the abdominal men to worry about,' he said, and moved off. A few minutes later, Dr. Blythe Ballomy got around to the man and listened, but he didn't blink an eye; his grim expression never changed. 'You have swallowed a watch, my man,' he said crisply. The draftee reddened in embarrassment and uncertainty. 'On *purpose?*' he asked. 'That I can't say,' the doctor told him, and went on.

I served with the draft board for about four months. Until the summonses ceased, I couldn't leave town and as long as I stayed and appeared promptly for examination, even though I did the examining, I felt that technically I could not be convicted of evasion. During the daytime, I worked as publicity agent for an amusement park, the manager of which was a tall, unexpected young man named Byron Landis. Some years before, he had dynamited the men's lounge in the statehouse annex for a prank; he enjoyed pouring buckets of water on sleeping persons, and once he had barely escaped arrest for jumping off the top of the old Columbus Transfer Company building with a homemade parachute.

He asked me one morning if I would like to take a ride in the new Scarlet Tornado, a steep and wavy roller-coaster. I didn't want to but I was afraid he would think I was afraid, so I went along. It was about ten o'clock and there was nobody at the park except workmen and attendants and concessionaires in their shirtsleeves. We climbed into one of the long gondolas of the roller-coaster and while I was looking around for the man who was going to run it, we began to move off. Landis, I discovered, was running it himself. But it was too late to get out; we had begun to climb, clickety-clockety, up the first steep incline, down the other side of which we careened at eighty miles an hour. 'I didn't know you could run this thing!' I bawled at my companion, as we catapulted up a sixty-degree arch and looped headlong into space. 'I didn't either!' he bawled back. The racket and the rush of air were terrific as we roared into the pitch-black Cave of Darkness and came out and down Monohan's Leap, so called because a workman named Monohan had been forced to jump from it when caught between two approaching experimental cars while it was being completed. That trip, although it ended safely, made a lasting impression on me. It is not too much to say that it has flavored my life. It is the reason I shout in my sleep, refuse to ride on the elevated, keep jerking the emergency brake in cars other people are driving, have the sensation of flying like a bird when I first lie down, and in certain months can't keep anything on my stomach.

During my last few trips to the draft board, I went again as a draft prospect, having grown tired of being an examiner. None of the doctors who had been my colleagues for so long recognized me, not even Dr. Ridgeway. When he examined my chest for the last time, I asked him if there hadn't been another doctor helping him. He said there had been. 'Did he look anything like me?' I asked. Dr. Ridgeway looked at me. 'I don't think so,' he said, 'he was taller.' (I had my shoes off while he was examining me.) 'A good pulmonary man,' added Ridgeway. 'Relative of yours?' I said yes. He sent me on to Dr. Quimby, the specialist who had examined my eyes twelve or fifteen times before. He gave me some simple reading tests. 'You could never get into the army with eyes like that,' he said. 'I know,' I told him.

Late one morning, shortly after my last examination, I was awakened by the sound of bells ringing and whistles blowing. It grew louder and more insistent and wilder. It was the Armistice.

Rachel L. Carson

THE BIRTH OF AN ISLAND

❨ The book from which this selection is taken, *The Sea Around Us*, is an admirably lucid, informative, and readable account of the ocean and its life history. Published in 1951 (a few chapters had appeared first in periodicals), it quickly became a 'best seller,' and brought its author many scientific and academic awards.

Miss Carson (1907——), after graduation from Pennsylvania College for Women, continued her studies at Johns Hopkins University and the Marine Biological Laboratory at Woods Hole, Massachusetts. She taught for a few years at Johns Hopkins and the University of Maryland; then, in 1936, joined the staff of the United States Bureau of Fisheries as an aquatic biologist. More recently she has been Editor-in-Chief of the United States Fish and Wildlife Service. In addition to *The Sea Around Us*, she has written *Under the Sea Wind* (1941), *The Edge of the Sea* (1955), and various articles on natural history.

> *Many a green isle needs must be*
> *In the deep, wide sea . . .*
>   SHELLEY

MILLIONS of years ago, a volcano built a mountain on the floor of the Atlantic. In eruption after eruption, it pushed up a great pile of volcanic rock, until it had accumulated a mass a hundred miles across at its base, reaching upward toward the surface of the sea. Finally its cone emerged as an island with an area of about 200 square miles. Thousands of years passed, and thousands of thousands. Eventually the waves of the Atlantic cut down the cone and reduced it to a shoal—all of it, that is, but a small fragment which remained above water. This fragment we know as Bermuda.

With variations, the life story of Bermuda has been repeated by almost every one of the islands that interrupt the watery expanses of the oceans far from land. For these isolated islands in the sea are fundamentally diffent from the continents. The major land masses and the ocean basins are today much as they have been throughout the greater part of geologic time. But islands are ephemeral, created today, destroyed tomorrow. With few exceptions, they are the result of the violent, explosive, earth-shaking eruptions of submarine volcanoes, working perhaps for millions of years to achieve their end. It is one of the paradoxes in the ways of earth and sea that a process seemingly so destructive, so catastrophic in nature, can result in an act of creation.

Islands have always fascinated the human mind. Perhaps it is the instinctive response of man, the land animal, welcoming a brief intrusion of earth in the vast, overwhelming expanse of sea. Here in a great ocean basin, a thousand miles from the nearest continent, with miles of water under our vessel, we come upon an island. Our imaginations can follow its slopes down through darkening waters to where it rests on the sea floor. We wonder why and how it arose here in the midst of the ocean.

The birth of a volcanic island is an event marked by prolonged and violent travail: the forces of the earth striving to create, and all the forces of the sea opposing. The sea floor, where an island begins, is probably nowhere more than about fifty miles thick—a thin covering over the vast bulk of the earth. In it are deep cracks and fissures, the results of unequal cooling and shrinkage in past ages. Along such lines of weakness the molten lava from the earth's interior presses up and finally bursts forth into the sea. But a submarine volcano is different from a terrestrial eruption, where the lava, molten rocks, gases, and other ejecta are hurled into the air through an open crater. Here on the bottom of the ocean the volcano has resisting it all the weight of the ocean water above it. Despite the immense pressure of, it may be, two or three miles of sea water, the new volcanic cone builds upward toward the surface, in flow after flow of lava. Once within reach of the waves, its soft ash and tuff are violently attacked, and for a long period the potential island may remain a shoal, unable to emerge. But, eventually, in new eruptions, the cone is pushed up into the air and a rampart against the attacks of the waves is built of hardened lava.

Navigators' charts are marked with numerous, recently discovered submarine mountains. Many of these are the submerged remnants of the islands of a geologic yesterday. The same charts show islands that emerged from the sea at least fifty million years ago, and others that arose within our own memory. Among the undersea mountains marked on the charts may be the islands of tomorrow, which at this moment are forming, unseen, on the floor of the ocean and are growing upward toward its surface.

For the sea is by no means done with submarine eruptions; they occur fairly commonly, sometimes detected only by instruments, sometimes obvious to the most casual observer. Ships in volcanic zones may suddenly find themselves in violently disturbed water. There are heavy discharges of steam. The sea appears to bubble or boil in a furious turbulence. Fountains spring from its surface. Floating up from the deep, hidden places of the actual eruption come the bodies of fishes and other deep-sea creatures, and quantities of volcanic ash and pumice.

One of the youngest of the large volcanic islands of the world is Ascension in the South Atlantic. During the Second World War the American airmen sang

> *If we don't find Ascension*
> *Our wives will get a pension*

this island being the only piece of dry land between the hump of Brazil and the bulge of Africa. It is a forbidding mass of cinders, in which the vents of no less than forty extinct volcanoes can be counted. It has not always been so barren, for its slopes have yielded the fossil remains of trees. What happened to the forests no one knows; the first men to explore the island, about the year 1500, found it treeless, and today it has no natural greenness except on its highest peak, known as Green Mountain.

In modern times we have never seen the birth of an island as large as Ascension. But now and then there is a report of a small island appearing where none was before. Perhaps a month, a year, five years later, the island has disappeared into the sea again. These are the little, stillborn islands, doomed to only a brief emergence above the sea.

About 1830 such an island suddenly appeared in the Mediterranean between Sicily and the coast of Africa, rising from 100-fathom depths after there had been signs of volanic activity in the area. It was little more than a black cinder pile, perhaps 200 feet high. Waves, wind, and rain attacked it. Its soft and porous materials were easily eroded; its substance was rapidly eaten away and it sank beneath the sea. Now it is a shoal, marked on the charts as Graham's Reef.

Falcon Island, the tip of a volcano projecting above the Pacific nearly two thousand miles east of Australia, suddenly disappeared in 1913. Thirteen years later, after violent eruptions in the vicinity, it as suddenly rose again above the surface and remained as a physical bit of the British Empire until 1949. Then it was reported by the Colonial Under Secretary to be missing again.

Almost from the moment of its creation, a volcanic island is fore-doomed to destruction. It has in itself the seeds of its own dissolution, for new explosions, or landslides of the soft soil, may violently accelerate its disintegration. Whether the destruction of an island comes quickly or only after long ages of geologic time may also depend on external forces: the rains that wear away the loftiest of land mountains, the sea, and even man himself.

South Trinidad, or in the Portuguese spelling, 'Ilha Trinidade,' is an example of an island that has been sculptured into bizarre forms through centuries of weathering—an island in which the signs of dissolution are clearly apparent. This group of volcanic peaks lies in the open Atlantic, about a thousand miles north-east of Rio de Janeiro. E. F. Knight wrote in 1907 that Trinidad 'is rotten throughout, its substance has been dis-integrated by volcanic fires and by the action of water, so that it is every-where tumbling to pieces.' During an interval of nine years between Knight's visits, a whole mountainside had collapsed in a great landslide of broken rocks and volcanic debris.

Sometimes the disintegration takes abrupt and violent form. The great-est explosion of historic time was the literal evisceration of the island of Krakatoa. In 1680 there had been a premonitory eruption on this small island in Sunda Strait, between Java and Sumatra in the Netherlands Indies. Two hundred years later there had been a series of earthquakes. In the spring of 1883, smoke and steam began to ascend from fissures in the volcanic cone. The ground became noticeably warm, and warning rum-blings and hissings came from the volcano. Then, on 27 August, Krakatoa literally exploded. In an appalling series of eruptions, that lasted two days, the whole northern half of the cone was carried away. The sudden inrush of ocean water added the fury of superheated steam to the cauldron. When the inferno of white-hot lava, molten rock, steam, and smoke had finally subsided, the island that had stood 1400 feet above the sea had become a cavity a thousand feet below sea level. Only along one edge of the former crater did a remnant of the island remain.

Krakatoa, in its destruction, became known to the entire world. The eruption gave rise to a hundred-foot wave that wiped out villages along the Strait and killed people by tens of thousands. The wave was felt on the shores of the Indian Ocean and at Cape Horn; rounding the Cape into the Atlantic, it sped northward and retained its identity even as far as the English Channel. The sound of the explosions was heard in the Philippine Islands, in Australia, and on the Island of Madagascar, nearly 3000 miles away. And clouds of volcanic dust, the pulverized rock that had been torn from the heart of Krakatoa, ascended into the stratosphere and were carried around the globe to give rise to a series of spectacular sunsets in every country of the world for nearly a year.

Although Krakatoa's dramatic passing was the most violent eruption that modern man has witnessed, Krakatoa itself seems to have been the product of an even greater one. There is evidence that an immense volcano once stood where the waters of Sunda Strait now lie. In some remote period a titanic explosion blew it away, leaving only its base represented by a broken ring of islands. The largest of these was Krakatoa, which, in its own demise, carried away what was left of the original crater ring. But in 1929 a new volcanic island arose in this place—Anak Krakatoa, Child of Krakatoa.

Subterranean fires and deep unrest disturb the whole area occupied by the Aleutians. The islands themselves are the peaks of a thousand-mile chain of undersea mountains, of which volcanic action was the chief architect. The geologic structure of the ridge is little known, but it rises abruptly from oceanic depths of about a mile on one side and two miles on the other. Apparently this narrow ridge indicates a deep fracture of the earth's crust. On many of the islands volcanoes are now active, or only temporarily quiescent. In the short history of modern navigation in this region, it has often happened that a new island has been reported but perhaps only the following year could not be found.

The small island of Bogoslof, since it was first discovered in 1796, has altered its shape and position several times and has even disappeared completely, only to emerge again. The original island was a mass of black rock, sculptured into fantastic, towering shapes. Explorers and sealers coming upon it in the fog were reminded of a castle and named it Castle Rock. At the present time there remain only one or two pinnacles of the castle, a long spit of black rocks where sea lions haul out, and a cluster of higher rocks resounding with the cries of thousands of sea birds. Each time the parent volcano erupts, as it has done at least half a dozen times since men have been observing it, new masses of steaming rocks emerge from the heated waters, some to reach heights of several hundred feet before they are destroyed in fresh explosions. Each new cone that appears is, as described by the volcanologist Jaggar, 'the live crest, equivalent to a crater, of a great submarine heap of lava six thousand feet high, piled above the floor of the Bering Sea where the Aleutian mountains fall off to the deep sea.'

One of the few exceptions to the almost universal rule that oceanic islands have a volcanic origin seems to be the remarkable and fascinating group of islets known as the Rocks of St. Paul. Lying in the open Atlantic between Brazil and Africa, St. Paul's Rocks are an obstruction thrust up from the floor of the ocean into the midst of the racing Equatorial Current, a mass against which the seas, which have rolled a thousand miles unhindered, break in sudden violence. The entire cluster of rocks covers not more than a quarter of a mile, running in a curved line like a horseshoe. The highest rock is not more than sixty feet above the sea; spray wets it to the summit. Abruptly the rocks dip under water and slope steeply down into great depths. Geologists since the time of Darwin have puzzled over the origin of these black, wave-washed islets. Most of them agree that they are composed of material like that of the sea floor itself. In some remote period, inconceivable stresses in the earth's crust must have pushed a solid rock mass upward more than two miles.

So bare and desolate that not even a lichen grows on them, St. Paul's Rocks would seem one of the most unpromising places in the world to look for a spider, spinning its web in arachnidan hope of snaring passing insects. Yet Darwin found spiders when he visited the Rocks in 1833, and forty years later the naturalists of H.M.S. *Challenger* also reported them, busy at their web-spinning. A few insects are there, too, some as parasites on the sea birds, three species of which nest on the Rocks. One of the insects is a small brown moth that lives on feathers. This very nearly completes the inventory of the inhabitants of St. Paul's Rocks, except for the grotesque crabs that swarm over the islets, living chiefly on the flying fish brought by the birds to their young.

St. Paul's Rocks are not alone in having an extraordinary assortment of inhabitants, for the faunas and floras of oceanic islands are amazingly different from those of the continents. The pattern of island life is peculiar and significant. Aside from forms recently introduced by man, islands remote from the continents are never inhabited by any land mammals, except sometimes the one mammal that has learned to fly—the bat. There are never any frogs, salamanders, or other amphibians. Of reptiles, there may be a few snakes, lizards, and turtles, but the more remote the island from a major land mass, the fewer reptiles there are, and the really isolated islands have none. There are usually a few species of land birds, some insects, and some spiders. So remote an island as Tristan da Cunha in the South Atlantic, 1500 miles from the nearest continent, has no land animals but these: three species of land birds, a few insects, and several small snails.

With so selective a list, it is hard to see how, as some biologists believe, the islands could have been colonized by migration across land bridges, even if there were good evidence for the existence of the bridges. The very animals missing from the islands are the ones that would have had to come dry-shod, over the hypothetical bridges. The plants and animals that we find on oceanic islands, on the other hand, are the ones that could have come by wind or water. As an alternative, then, we must suppose that the stocking of the islands has been accomplished by the strangest migration in earth's history—a migration that began long before man appeared on the earth and is still continuing, a migration that seems more like a series of cosmic accidents than an orderly process of nature.

We can only guess how long after its emergence from the sea an oceanic island may lie uninhabited. Certainly in its original state it is a land bare, harsh, and repelling beyond human experience. No living thing moves over the slopes of its volcanic hills; no plants cover its naked lava fields. But little by little, riding on the winds, drifting on the currents, or rafting in on logs, floating brush, or trees, the plants and animals that are to colonize it arrive from the distant continents.

So deliberate, so unhurried, so inexorable are the ways of nature that the stocking of an island may require thousands or millions of years. It may be that no more than half a dozen times in all these eons does a particular form, such as a tortoise, make a successful landing upon its shores. To wonder impatiently why man is not a constant witness of such arrivals is to fail to understand the majestic pace of the process.

Yet we have occasional glimpses of the method. Natural rafts of uprooted trees and matted vegetation have frequently been seen adrift at sea, more than a thousand miles off the mouths of such great tropical rivers as the Congo, the Ganges, the Amazon, and the Orinoco. Such rafts could easily carry an assortment of insect, reptile, or mollusk passengers. Some of the involuntary passengers might be able to withstand long weeks at sea; others would die during the first stages of the journey. Probably the ones best adapted for travel by raft are the wood-boring insects, which, of all the insect tribe, are most commonly found on oceanic islands. The poorest raft travelers must be the mammals. But even a mammal might cover short interisland distances. A few days after the explosion of Krakatoa, a small monkey was rescued from some drifting timber in Sunda Strait. She had been terribly burned, but survived the experience.

No less than the water, the winds and the air currents play their part in bringing inhabitants to the islands. The upper atmosphere, even during the ages before man entered it in his machines, was a place of congested traffic. Thousands of feet above the earth, the air is crowded with living creatures, drifting, flying, gliding, ballooning, or involuntarily swirling along on the high winds. Discovery of this rich aerial plankton had to wait until man himself had found means to make physical invasion of these regions. With special nets and traps, scientists have now collected from the upper atmosphere many of the forms that inhabit oceanic islands. Spiders, whose almost invariable presence on these islands is a fascinating problem, have been captured nearly three miles above the earth's surface. Airmen have passed through great numbers of the white, silken filaments of spiders' 'parachutes' at heights of two or three miles. At altitudes of 6,000 to 16,000 feet, and with wind velocities reaching 45 miles an hour, many living insects have been taken. At such heights and on such strong winds, they might well have been carried hundreds of miles. Seeds have been collected at altitudes up to 5,000 feet. Among those commonly taken are members of the Composite family, especially the so-called 'thistle-down' typical of oceanic islands.

An interesting point about transport of living plants and animals by wind is the fact that in the upper layers of the earth's atmosphere the winds do not necessarily blow in the same direction as at the earth's surface. The trade winds are notably shallow, so that a man standing on the cliffs of St. Helena, a thousand feet above the sea, is above the wind, which blows with great force below him. Once drawn into the upper air, insects, seeds, and the like can easily be carried in a direction contrary to that of the winds prevailing at island level.

The wide-ranging birds that visit islands of the ocean in migration may also have a good deal to do with the distribution of plants, and perhaps even of some insects and minute land shells. From a ball of mud taken from a bird's plumage, Charles Darwin raised 82 separate plants, belonging to 5 distinct species! Many plant seeds have hooks or prickles, ideal for attachment to feathers. Such birds as the Pacific golden plover, which annually flies from the mainland of Alaska to the Hawaiian Islands and even beyond, probably figure in many riddles of plant distribution.

The catastrophe of Krakatoa gave naturalists a perfect opportunity to observe the colonization of an island. With most of the island itself destroyed, and the remnant covered with a deep layer of lava and ash that remained hot for weeks, Krakatoa after the explosive eruptions of 1883 was, from a biological standpoint, a new volcanic island. As soon as it was possible to visit it, scientists searched for signs of life, although it was hard to imagine how any living thing could have survived. Not a single plant or animal could be found. It was not until nine months after the eruption that the naturalist Cotteau was able to report: 'I only discovered one microscopic spider—only one. This strange pioneer of the renovation was busy spinning its web.' Since there were no insects on the island, the web-spinning of the bold little spider was presumably in vain, and, except for a few blades of grass, practically nothing lived on Krakatoa for a quarter of a century. Then the colonists began to arrive—a few mammals in 1908; a number of birds, lizards, and snakes; various mollusks, insects, and earthworms. Ninety per cent of Krakatoa's new inhabitants, Dutch scientists found, were forms that could have arrived by air.

Isolated from the great mass of life on the continents, with no opportunity for the crossbreeding that tends to preserve the average and to eliminate the new and unusual, island life has developed in a remarkable manner. On these remote bits of earth, nature has excelled in the creation of strange and wonderful forms. As though to prove her incredible versatility, almost every island has developed species that are endemic—that is, they are peculiar to it alone and are duplicated nowhere else on earth.

It was from the pages of earth's history written on the lava fields of the Galapagos that young Charles Darwin got his first inkling of the great truths of the origin of species. Observing the strange plants and animals— giant tortoises, black, amazing lizards that hunted their food in the surf, sea lions, birds in extraordinary variety—Darwin was struck by their vague similarity to mainland species of South and Central America, yet was haunted by the differences, differences that distinguish them not only from the mainland species but from those on other islands of the archipelago. Years later he was to write in reminiscence: 'Both in space and time, we seem to be brought somewhat near to that great fact—that mystery of mysteries—the first appearance of new beings on earth.'

Of the 'new beings' evolved on islands, some of the most striking examples have been birds. In some remote age before there were men, a small, pigeonlike bird found its way to the island of Mauritius, in the Indian Ocean. By processes of change at which we can only guess, this bird lost the power of flight, developed short, stout legs, and grew larger until it reached the size of a modern turkey. Such was the origin of the fabulous dodo, which did not long survive the advent of man on Mauritius. New Zealand was the sole home of the moas. One species of these ostrich-like birds stood twelve feet high. Moas had roamed New Zealand from the early part of the Tertiary; those that remained when the Maoris arrived soon died out.

Other island forms besides the dodo and the moas have tended to become large. Perhaps the Galapagos tortoise became a giant after its arrival on the islands, although fossil remains on the continents cast doubt on this. The loss of wing use and even of the wings themselves (the moas had none) are common results of insular life. Insects on small, wind-swept islands tend to lose the power of flight—those that retain it are in danger of being blown out to sea. The Galapagos Islands have a flightless cormorant. There have been at least fourteen species of flightless rails on the islands of the Pacific alone.

One of the most interesting and engaging characteristics of island species is their extraordinary tameness—a lack of sophistication in dealings with the human race, which even the bitter teachings of experience do not quickly alter. When Robert Cushman Murphy visited the island of South Trinidad in 1913 with a party from the brig *Daisy*, terns alighted on the heads of the men in the whaleboat and peered inquiringly into their faces. Albatrosses on Laysan, whose habits include wonderful ceremonial dances, allowed naturalists to walk among their colonies and responded with a grave bow to similar polite greetings from the visitors. When the British ornithologist David Lack visited the Galapagos Islands, a century after Darwin, he found that the hawks allowed themselves to be touched, and the flycatchers tried to remove hair from the heads of the men for nesting material. 'It is a curious pleasure,' he wrote, 'to have the birds of the wilderness settling upon one's shoulders, and the pleasure could be much less rare were man less destructive.'

But man, unhappily, has written one of his blackest records as a destroyer on the oceanic islands. He has seldom set foot on an island that he has not brought about disastrous changes. He has destroyed environments by cutting, clearing, and burning; he has brought with him as a chance associate the nefarious rat; and almost invariably he has turned loose upon the islands a whole Noah's Ark of goats, hogs, cattle, dogs, cats, and other nonnative animals as well as plants. Upon species after species of island life, the black night of extinction has fallen.

In all the world of living things, it is doubtful whether there is a more delicately balanced relationship than that of island life to its environment. This environment is a remarkably uniform one. In the midst of a great ocean, ruled by currents and winds that rarely shift their course, climate changes little. There are few natural enemies, perhaps none at all. The harsh struggle for existence that is the normal lot of continental life is softened on the islands. When this gentle pattern of life is abruptly changed, the island creatures have little ability to make the adjustments necessary for survival.

Ernst Mayr tells of a steamer wrecked off Lord Howe Island east of Australia in 1918. Its rats swam ashore. In two years they had so nearly exterminated the native birds that an islander wrote, 'This paradise of birds has become a wilderness, and the quietness of death reigns where all was melody.'

On Tristan da Cunha almost all of the unique land birds that had evolved there in the course of the ages were exterminated by hogs and rats. The native fauna of the island of Tahiti is losing ground against the horde of alien species that man has introduced. The Hawaiian Islands, which have lost their native plants and animals faster than almost any other area in the world, are a classic example of the results of interfering with natural balances. Certain relations of animal to plant, and of plant to soil, had grown up through the centuries. When man came in and rudely disturbed the balance, he set off a whole series of chain reactions.

Vancouver brought cattle and goats to the Hawaiian Islands, and the resulting damage to forests and other vegetation was enormous. Many plant introductions were as bad. A plant known as the pamakani was brought in many years ago, according to report, by a Captain Makee for his beautiful gardens on the island of Maui. The pamakani, which has light, windborne seeds, quickly escaped from the captain's gardens, ruined the pasture lands on Maui, and proceeded to hop from island to island. The CCC boys [1] were at one time put to work to clear it out of the Honouliuli Forest Reserve, but as fast as they destroyed it, the seeds of new plants arrived on the wind. Lantana was another plant brought in as an ornamental species. Now it covers thousands of acres with a thorny,

[1 Members of the Civilian Conservation Corps, established in the 1930s by the Federal Government to give work to unemployed young men.]

scrambling growth—despite large sums of money spent to import parasitic insects to control it.

There was once a society in Hawaii for the special purpose of introducing exotic birds. Today when you go to the islands, you see, instead of the exquisite native birds that greeted Captain Cook, mynas from India, cardinals from the United States or Brazil, doves from Asia, weavers from Australia, skylarks from Europe, and titmice from Japan. Most of the original bird life has been wiped out, and to find its fugitive remnants you would have to search assiduously in the most remote hills.

Some of the island species have, at best, the most tenuous hold on life. The Laysan teal is found nowhere in the world but on the one small island of Laysan. Even on this island it occurs only on one end, where there is a seepage of fresh water. Probably the total population of this species does not exceed fifty individuals. Destruction of the small swampy bit of land that is its home, or the introduction of a hostile or competing species, could easily snap the slender thread of life.

Most of man's habitual tampering with nature's balance by introducing exotic species has been done in ignorance of the fatal chain of events that would follow. But in modern times, at least, we might profit by history. About the year 1513, the Portuguese introduced goats onto the recently discovered island of St. Helena, which had developed a magnificent forest of gumwood, ebony, and brazilwood. By 1560 or thereabouts, the goats had so multiplied that they wandered over the island by the thousand, in flocks a mile long. They trampled the young trees and ate the seedlings. By this time the colonists had begun to cut and burn the forests, so that it is hard to say whether men or goats were the more responsible for the destruction. But of the result there was no doubt. By the early 1800's the forests were gone, and the naturalist Alfred Wallace later described this once beautiful, forest-clad volcanic island as a 'rocky desert,' in which the remnants of the original flora persisted only in the most inaccessible peaks and crater ridges.

When the astronomer Halley visited the islands of the Atlantic about 1700, he put a few goats ashore on South Trinidad. This time, without the further aid of man, the work of deforestation proceeded so rapidly that it was nearly completed within the century. Today Trinidad's slopes are the place of a ghost forest, strewn with the fallen and decaying trunks of long-dead trees; its soft volcanic soils, no longer held by the interlacing roots, are sliding away into the sea.

One of the most interesting of the Pacific islands was Laysan, a tiny scrap of soil which is a far outrider of the Hawaiian chain. It once supported a forest of sandalwood and fanleaf palms and had five land birds, all peculiar to Laysan alone. One of them was the Laysan rail, a charming, gnomelike creature no more than six inches high, with wings that seemed too small (and were never used as wings), and feet that seemed too large, and a voice like distant, tinkling bells. About 1887, the captain of a visiting ship moved some of the rails to Midway, about 300 miles to the west, establishing a second colony. It seemed a fortunate move, for soon thereafter rabbits were introduced on Laysan. Within a quarter of a century, the rabbits had killed off the vegetation of the tiny island, reduced it to a sandy desert, and all but exterminated themselves. As for the rails, the devastation of their island was fatal, and the last rail died about 1924.

Perhaps the Laysan colony could later have been restored from the Midway group had not tragedy struck there also. During the war in the Pacific, rats went ashore to island after island from ships and landing craft. They invaded Midway in 1943. The adult rails were slaughtered. The eggs were eaten, and the young birds killed. The world's last Laysan rail was seen in 1944.

The tragedy of the oceanic islands lies in the uniqueness, the irreplaceability of the species they have developed by the slow processes of the ages. In a reasonable world men would have treated these islands as precious possessions, as natural museums filled with beautiful and curious works of creation, valuable beyond price because nowhere in the world are they duplicated. W. H. Hudson's [2] lament for the birds of the Argentine pampas might even more truly have been spoken of the islands: 'The beautiful has vanished and returns not.'

[² English writer and naturalist (1841–1922).]

C. E. M. Joad
WHAT DO WE KNOW OF
THE OUTSIDE WORLD?

❡ We reprint here the opening chapter of C. E. M. Joad's *Guide to Philosophy*, a remarkably readable introduction to metaphysics and the theory of knowledge, and probably the best known of his books.

After graduation from Oxford in 1914 Mr. Joad was in the Civil Service for sixteen years. In 1930 he became head of the Department of Philosophy and Psychology at Birkbeck College, University of London. Besides *Guide to Philosophy* and other works on philosophy (*The Meaning of Life; Matter, Life and Value; Philosophical Aspects of Modern Science; Guide to Modern Thought*) he wrote provocative books on politics, religion, war, and education. He died in 1953.

INTRODUCTORY. It is not easy to decide how to begin a book on philosophy. Philosophical problems are closely bound up with one another; so closely, that some philosophers think that a completely satisfactory solution of any one of them would entail the solution of them all. Whether this is so we cannot tell, since it is extremely unlikely that a completely satisfactory solution of any one of them will be reached by the human mind in the present state of its development. It is, however, true that most philosophical questions are found sooner or later to raise the same problems. In philosophy all roads lead if not to the same Rome, at least into the same maze, so that it is a matter of not very great moment which you choose at the outset of your journey.

But the fact that there is no very good reason for choosing one rather than another makes it very difficult to choose any, as the logical ass of the philosopher Buridan * (1300–1350), placed between two equally large and

* Actually the illustration of the ass does not appear anywhere in Buridan's writings. It is, however, always associated with him. A similar image appears in Dante's *Paradiso*, and the conceit seems to have been a popular one in the Middle Ages.

FROM *Guide to Philosophy*, 1936. Reprinted by permission of Random House, Inc., and of the author.

equally succulent bundles of hay, is said to have starved because of an inability to discover any reason why he should proceed in the direction of one rather than of the other.

On reflection I have decided to begin with the problem of sense perception; not because it is any easier or any nearer to solution than any other philosophical problem, but because it entails a consideration of issues which people can explore for themselves: can, and to some extent do, since, of all philosophical conclusions, the conclusion that the outside world is not really 'there' or is not really 'real' is most familiar to, and most frequently derided by, the non-philosophical. But whether people deride it, dismiss it, or embrace it for the controversial discomfiture of their friends, they are at least familiar with it.

COMMONSENSE VIEW OF EXTERNAL WORLD. The problem may be stated fairly simply in the form of a number of questions. What kind of information do our sense organs give us about the external world? Is it reliable information? If it is, what is the nature of the objects about which we receive it? Of what sort of things, in other words, is the external world composed? Common sense answers these questions without much hesitation on the following lines. (1) The external world, it declares, consists of substances which possess qualities; for example, of wood which is hard or soft, of metal which is yellow or silver. (2) These substances we perceive in the form of physical objects such as chairs and tables, gold rings and silver shillings —unless we happen to be scientists, when we perceive what are, presumably, more fundamental substances such as chemical compounds and molecules of which the ordinary substances are composed, and should perceive, if our instruments were delicate enough, which they are not, substances more fundamental still such as atoms and electrons. (3) Physical objects are 'out there' in the world and are revealed to us by our senses exactly as they are. In particular, they are not dependent for their existence upon our perception of them. When our sense organs, eyes, ears or noses, are brought into suitable spatial relations with them, then we are said to know them. But common sense would hold that that which actually *knows* is not itself a sense organ, but is the mind or consciousness. The sense organs, it would be said, are the channels by which knowledge of physical objects is conveyed to the mind.

Now each one of the above propositions is denied by many philosophers, and, although it is by no means clear what propositions ought to be substituted for them, it is reasonably certain that, in the form in which I have just stated them, none of them is true. The first proposition, that the world consists of substances possessing qualities, will be considered in Chapter VI. The consideration of the second and the third which are largely interdependent brings us to the problem of sense perception. In the present chapter we shall be mainly concerned with the third proposition, which asserts that the physical objects which we perceive are 'out there' in the world, and are in no sense dependent upon our perception of them for their existence. Most philosophers have held that they are not 'out there' in the world in any ordinary sense, and many have come to the conclusion that they are in some sense dependent for their existence upon the mind or minds which perceive them. Other philosophers, while maintaining that *something* exists in the world outside ourselves which is not dependent upon our minds for its existence, have, nevertheless, adduced good reasons for denying that this 'something' is in the least like the physical objects with which, if the commonsense account of the matter is to be believed, we are in contact. They have, that is to say, denied the second of the three propositions asserted above. With the reasons for this latter denial we shall be concerned in the second chapter.

WHAT DO OUR SENSES REVEAL?   Let us call the objects of which, common sense would say, our senses make us aware sensible objects. What do our senses tell us about them? At first sight it seems that they tell us a great deal; but on reflection we find that much of the information which our senses seem to give us relates not to what is going on outside ourselves, but to what is going on inside ourselves, not to sensible objects, but to our own experiences.

Let us suppose that I press my tongue against my teeth and ask the question: 'What is it that I experience or am aware of?' At first sight the answer would appear to be: 'I am aware of my teeth.' But is this answer really correct? Is not what I *really* experience a feeling in my tongue—a feeling caused perhaps by the contact between tongue and teeth, but a feeling nevertheless, and since it *is* a feeling, something that is mental? Suppose now, that I press my fingers against the table, is what I experience the table? Again, the obvious answer proves on examination to be doubtful. The *immediate* object of my experience, that of which I am directly aware, is, many would say, a sensation in my fingers, a sensation of smoothness, hardness, and coolness.

Let us take a further example. If I stand two feet away from the fire, I experience heat, and common sense tells me that this heat is a property of the fire. If, however, I move nearer to the fire, the heat increases in intensity, until it becomes pain. Now, the pain is clearly in me and not in the fire; since, then, the pain is only a more intense degree of the heat, the inference is that the heat also was a sensation of mine, and not a property of the fire. The leg of a cheese mite is so small that, except with the aid of a microscope, we cannot see it. Are we, then, to suppose that the cheese mite cannot see its own leg? This seems unlikely. We must infer, then, that the apparent size of the cheese mite's leg varies according to the nature of the mind perceiving it—that the leg, in fact, has one apparent size for the cheese mite and another for ourselves. But the leg cannot have two different sizes at the same time. Has it, then, any *real* size at all? May it not rather be the case that size is not an intrinsic quality of the object seen, a quality possessed by it in its own right, but is relative to and dependent upon the nature of the perceiver's mind.

THE CASE OF THE STEEPLE.   Let us consider the case of size in a little more detail. I am, we will suppose, looking at a church steeple. Its height appears to vary according to the distance from which I view it. It appears, for example, to have one height from a distance of half a mile, another from a distance of a hundred yards, and another from a distance of five yards, while, if I stand right underneath it, I am unable to estimate its height at all. There are thus a number of different heights which the steeple *appears* to have. How am I to tell which one of them is or represents its *real* height? The commonsense answer would probably be, by applying a measuring rod or tape-measure or whatever apparatus is normally used for measuring steeples, and noting the reading on the apparatus in question. Let us suppose that the reading on the piece of apparatus—we will call it a tape-measure—is 150 feet. Then we shall say that 150 feet is the *real* height of the steeple. But will this answer bear investigation? For practical purposes no doubt it will; but for philosophical ones it will not.

In the first place, we have admitted that the steeple *appears* to have different heights to different observers situated at different distances. What we want to know is, which one of these different appearances really *is* its height. Now, 150 feet is one of these heights, the height, namely, which it appears to have to a tape-measure extended to the whole of its very considerable length along the outside of the steeple. But why should the tape-measure be accorded the title of a privileged observer, and why should the position immediately contiguous to the outside wall be regarded as a privileged position, so that we are entitled to say that *to an observer occupying that position alone* is the *real* height revealed?

Secondly, what sort of information does a reading of 150 feet really give us? We want to know what is the real height of the steeple and we are informed that it is 150 feet. But what is 150 feet? It is a mathematical expression, a name that we give to certain sorts of height, for example to the height possessed by the steeple. Thus, when we want to know what is the real height of the steeple we are told that it is 150 feet, and when we want to know what 150 feet is, we find that it is the sort of height which the steeple, and whatever other things happen to be exactly as tall as the steeple are said to possess. Our information, in fact, is purely circular.

Thirdly, what account are we to give of the tape-measure itself? We have cited a number of illustrations above to suggest that the qualities apparently possessed by sensible objects do not belong to them in actual fact, but are either qualities of our own experience or, since our experience of them varies, are at any rate dependent upon and determined by our experience. But if this is so, we have no right to assume that a tape-measure is exempt from the conclusions suggested by the previous analysis, that it *really* owns in its own right the qualities that it appears to own, and that in particular it has a length which *really* is its length. If we may assume without question these facts about the tape-measure, there would be no need to raise questions about the height of the steeple. But whatever reasons there are for doubting whether the steeple *really* has a height are equally good reasons for doubting whether the tape-measure *really* has a length. We cannot in short establish the *real* height of the steeple by reference to the *real* length of the tape-measure, for it is precisely the meaning of the words 'real height' and 'real length' that is in doubt.

THE SHAPE OF THE PENNY. As with height so with shape. Let us consider as an example the shape of the penny. Common sense supposes the shape to be circular, but from almost any point of view from which the penny is looked at, the penny appears, as we quickly find out when we try to draw it, to be elliptical, the ellipses which we perceive varying in degrees of fatness and thinness according to the angle of vision from which we view the penny. From two positions only does the penny appear to be circular, and these, namely, the position vertically above and the position vertically below the penny, are rather peculiar positions which are comparatively rarely occupied by the human eye.

If the shape of the penny normally appears to be elliptical, why do we call it circular? It is not easy to say. In the first instance, perhaps, because of the prevalence of a general belief to the effect that it *is* circular, a belief so widespread and deep-seated that anyone who questioned it outside a philosophical discussion would be regarded as imperfectly sane. But how did this general belief arise? On what is it based? Probably it rests at bottom upon the fact that the penny conforms in respect of many of its attributes to the definition of a circle. There is, for example, a point on its surface such that all lines drawn from that point to the circumference are of equal length: its circumference again is equal to $2\pi r$, its area to πr^2. But, if we take our stand on this definition, similar difficulties arise to those which we considered in the case of the steeple. What we want to know is the nature of the shape to which these mathematical properties belong? If we answer that it is a *circular* shape the question arises, does a penny have it? Unfortunately the penny as usually seen does not. Nor does the penny as touched; to feel a penny is not to feel a circular shape but either a flat surface or, if a finger is crooked round its edge, a curving line of metal. Hence, to touch and to sight the penny does not normally *appear* to be circular. But to what, then, does it *appear* to be circular? Presumably to a pair of compasses. But why should its appearance to a pair of compasses, or if the expression be preferred, the reaction of a pair of compasses to it, be presumed to acquaint us with its *real* shape, in some sense in which its appearance to eyes and fingers does not acquaint us with its real shape? Why in fact are the compasses privileged 'observers'? Moreover, what are we to say of the properties of the pair of compasses? Can we, when the existence of physical objects possessing properties in their own right is in question, steal the answer to the question in the case of the compasses in order not to beg it in the case of the penny?

As it is with texture and temperature, as with size and shape, so it is with most, if not all, of the qualities which apparently belong to objects in the external world. In regard to most, if not to all, of these apparent qualities we can truly say that in the last resort they turn out to be relative to ourselves. We have only, for example, to raise the temperatures of our bodies a few degrees, and the world will look different. Still more obviously will it feel different. Yet there is no reason why that world alone should be privileged to be considered real which is perceived by a normal, Nordic adult possessing a body which is heated to a temperature of 98.4 degrees.

IMPLICATIONS OF MODERN SCIENCE. The force of these considerations, in so far as they purport to show the relativity to the perceiver of the qualities apparently existing in the external world, is considerably strengthened by the information which science in general and the sciences of physics and physiology in particular have obtained in regard to the machinery of perception. Before, however, we indicate the bearing of the conclusions of modern science upon the problems under consideration, it is necessary to guard ourselves against misinterpretation by the introduction of a word of warning.

In the first place, the whole question of the relation between science and philosophy is controversial, and many philosophers would maintain that no results reached by science do have or can have any bearing upon philosophical problems.

In the second place, the philosophers whose line of thought I have during the course of the foregoing illustrations been mainly following and with whose general conclusion, namely, that the objects revealed to us in perception are in some sense dependent upon the mind of the perceiver, we are in this chapter mainly concerned, did not introduce scientific considerations into their arguments, or did so only to a very small extent. The philosophers in question (who are sometimes known as subjective idealists) are Locke (1632–1704), Berkeley (1685–1753) and Hume (1711–1776) who lived in the seventeenth and eighteenth centuries when the sciences of physics and physiology were comparatively immature, and as a general rule they developed their arguments without reference to such results as these sciences had achieved.

In the third place, it is doubtful whether, even if they had been fully conversant with the conclusions of twentieth century scientists, these philosophers would have been able consistently to use them in support of their general position. At least we are entitled to hope that they would have been too clear headed to have made what would in effect have been a serious elementary blunder. . .

So much having been said by way of qualification and reservation, I propose to enumerate certain considerations afforded by the conclusions of modern science which tend to reinforce the view that the qualities of the objects which we know in sense experience do not belong to them in their own right, but depend in a large measure upon conditions prevailing in the perceiver. Hitherto it has been with the part played by the perceiver's mind that we have been chiefly concerned. We are now under the direction of science to emphasise rather the influence of the perceiver's body in determining what we perceive.

THE PHYSIOLOGIST'S ACCOUNT OF THE MACHINERY OF PERCEPTION. Let us suppose that I am looking at a star, Sirius say, on a dark night. If physics is to be believed, light waves which started to travel from Sirius many years ago reach (after a specified time which astronomers calculate) the earth, impinge upon my retinas and cause me to say that I am seeing Sirius. Now the Sirius about which they convey information to me is the Sirius which existed at the time when they started. This Sirius may, however, no longer exist; it may have disappeared in the interval. To say that one can see what no longer exists is absurd. It follows that, whatever it is that I am seeing, it is not Sirius. What, in fact, I do see is a yellow patch of a particular size, shape and intensity. I infer that this yellow patch had an origin (with which it is connected by a continuous chain of physical events) several years ago and many million miles away. But this inference may be mistaken; the origin of the yellow patch, which I call a star, may be a blow on the nose, or a lamp hanging on the mast of a ship.

Nor is this the only inference involved. It is true that I *think* I am seeing a yellow patch, but am I really justified in holding this belief? So far as physics and physiology are concerned, all that I am entitled to say is that my optic nerve is being stimulated in a certain way, as a result of which certain events are being caused in my brain. Am I really justified in saying any more than this?

In a celebrated example Bertrand Russell cites the case of a physiologist examining the brain of his patient. The physiologist undoubtedly believes himself to be looking at the brain of another person; yet, Russell points out, if physiology is correct in what it asserts, the *cause* of his seeing must be something which is happening in his own. Russell's account of the process is as follows: 'Light waves travel from the brain that is being observed to the eye of the physiologist, at which they only arrive after an interval of time, which is finite though short. The physiologist sees what he is observing only after the light waves have reached his eye; therefore the event which constitutes his seeing comes at the end of a series of events which travel from the observed brain into the brain of the physiologist. We cannot, without a preposterous kind of discontinuity, suppose that the physiologist's percept, which comes at the end of this series, is anywhere else but in the physiologist's head.' When we reflect that, during the period of time which is occupied by the occurrence of the series of events which precede the physiologist's seeing, the patient's brain may have gone out of existence, the difficulty of supposing that the physiologist is really looking at a brain outside his own becomes very great.

TOUCH AND SMELL. Perception by touch makes the matter even plainer. Let us consider in a little more detail the case of a person who presses his fingers against the table. I am doing it now, as I write. Ordinarily I should say that there was contact between two material substances, my fingers and the table. Modern physics, however, lends no countenance to this view. What happens according to the physicist is that electrical repulsion is developed between the atoms composing the finger and those composing the table. The harder I press the table, the stronger are the electrical forces which repel my finger. These electrical forces set up in the nerve cells at the end of my finger a current which reaches my brain, as the result of which I experience the sensation of touching the table. In fact, however, I am not in contact with any object outside my body and, if appropriate parts of my nervous system are suitably stimulated, I shall experience the same sensation of touching the table, although there is no table to touch. What is more, I can experience what appears to be a sensation of a pin prick in the non-existent finger of a hand which has been amputated, provided that the nerve terminals in my arm are suitably manipulated.

As with sight and touch, so with smell. I doubt very much whether even common sense assumes that the smell of a body is something which really belongs to it. Most people would probably agree that a thing's smell is at least not *in the same place* as that which is occupied by the thing. It is, they would say, something which the thing gives off—most people, I imagine, think of smell as a sort of gas composed of molecules—and it is only when the gas reaches the place where one's nostrils are and the molecules of which it is composed stimulate the sensitive tissues inside the nostrils, that certain nervous impulses are despatched to the brain, as a result of which we have the sensation of smelling.* But the connection of this 'something,' the smell which is smelt, with the object which is thought to have originated it remains vague. Similarly with sound! Waves travel through the atmosphere and impinge on the ear drums. Complex events take place in the outer, middle and inner ears. In the inner ear, for example, there is a shell-like bony receptacle, the cochlea, filled with fluid. When the vibrations of the bones and membranes in the middle ear reach the cochlea, the fluid is agitated. The agitation of the fluid imparts a swaying motion to certain long, hair-like threads, the cilia ranged along the inside of the cochlea. The swaying cilia send neural impulses to the brain, as a result

---

* In fact, odorous substances must be dissolved in the moisture which covers the nasal mucous membrane, before they can evoke the sensation of smell.

of which we hear a sound. But if we were to ask where or what is the sound that is heard, it is extremely difficult to answer.

EDDINGTON'S IDEALIST CONCLUSION. The teaching of physics and physiology with regard to the machinery of perception seems to point to the conclusion that what we actually know, when we have sensory experience, are not the movements of matter, but certain events in ourselves connected with or produced by these movements; not objects external to ourselves, but the effects of the impact of light rays, gases, atmospheric waves and other forms of energy proceeding from these objects upon our bodies.

The following quotation from Sir Arthur Eddington's book *Science and the Unseen World* clearly indicates how large a part of what we know of the external world is conceded by a modern physicist—and in this respect, at least, Eddington's views are in no sense unrepresentative—to be inferred by our minds, instead of being directly perceived by our senses.

'Consider,' says Sir Arthur Eddington, 'how our supposed acquaintance with a lump of matter is attained. Some influence emanating from it plays on the extremity of a nerve starting a series of physical and chemical changes which are propagated along the nerve to a brain cell; there a mystery happens, and an image or sensation arises in the mind which cannot purport to resemble the stimulus which excites it. Everything known about the material world must in one way or another have been inferred from these stimuli transmitted along the nerves. . . The mind as a central receiving station reads the dots and dashes of the incoming nerve-signals. By frequent repetition of their call-signals the various transmitting stations of the outside world become familiar. We begin to feel quite a homely acquaintance with 2LO and 5XX. But a broadcasting station is not *like* its call-signal; there is no commensurability in their natures. So, too, the chairs and tables around us which broadcast to us incessantly those signals which affect our sight and touch cannot in their nature be like unto the signals or to the sensations which the signals awake at the end of their journey. . . It is an astonishing feat of deciphering that we should have been able to infer an orderly scheme of natural knowledge from such indirect communication.'

From these considerations Sir Arthur Eddington proceeds to derive conclusions which, as the reader will see in the next chapter, are almost indistinguishable from those of idealist philosophers. Having stressed the round-about and inferential character of our knowledge of the external world, he proceeds to contrast it with the directness and immediacy of our knowledge of ourselves.

'Clearly,' he continues, 'there is one kind of knowledge which cannot pass through such channels, namely, knowledge of the intrinsic nature of that which lies at the far end of the lines of communication.'

This is not an inferred knowledge of outside things from the messages which they send us over the telephone lines of nervous communication; it is knowledge of something as it is in itself. And this something as it is in itself, the one thing we know directly as it really is, turns out to be mental; it is a mind. 'Mind,' Sir Arthur Eddington concludes, 'is the first and most direct thing in our experience; all else is remote inference.' We have, he adds, an acquaintance with the 'mental and spiritual nature of ourselves, known in our minds by an intimate contact transcending the methods of physics.'

SIGNIFICANCE OF CONCLUSIONS DERIVED FROM SCIENCE. I do not wish to suggest that the above conclusion is necessarily true. As we shall see below, any philosophy which asserts, as the subjective idealists did, that the objects which we know in perception are existent in or even dependent upon the mind of the perceiver is precluded from making use of any of the considerations upon which the scientist's conclusions are based. I have introduced the scientific account of perception at this stage because my present purpose is to accumulate considerations, from whatever source they may be derived, which militate against the commonsense view that the external world is composed of physical objects possessing qualities in their own right, which by a sort of divine revelation are presented to the mind exactly as they are. Whether we emphasise the part played by the mind in the process of perception or by the body and the sense organs, it seems almost impossible to resist the view that the qualities of the world we perceive depend very largely upon ourselves. For how otherwise, it may be asked, are we to explain the fact of differing perceptions of the same thing. If X sees a carnation blue, and Y, who is colour-blind, sees it green, it is very difficult to suppose that the carnation is both green and blue at the same time. On the other hand there seems no good ground for affirming that it *really* is blue because it is blue to normal vision, and that its appearance to the colour-blind man is not, therefore, its *real* appearance, merely because the colour-blind man is in a minority. The plain implication seems to be that the difference between the apparent colours is due to a difference in the physiological machineries of the two perceivers. Moreover, if we place santonin in our eyes, we see everything yellow. Since we cannot suppose that the alteration in our visual apparatus has produced a corresponding alteration in the world outside us, we can only conclude that the appearance of yellowness is the result of a peculiar condition of our visual organs. But, if this is true in regard to yellowness, there is no reason why it should not be true in regard to all the colours which we normally believe ourselves to perceive in the outside world.

Bertrand Russell

INDIVIDUAL AND SOCIAL KNOWLEDGE

⟨ Bertrand Russell (1872—), one of the foremost of living philosophers, has written some thirty books in the past half century. These range from manifestoes on manners and morals (*On Education,* 1926; *Marriage and Morals,* 1929; *The Conquest of Happiness,* 1930) and popular introductions to philosophy (*The Problems of Philosophy,* 1912; *History of Western Philosophy,* 1945), to treatises on logic, physics, and pure mathematics (*Introduction to Mathematical Philosophy,* 1919; *The Analysis of Matter,* 1927; *An Inquiry into Meaning and Truth,* 1940). In the world of learning the work for which he is best known is *Principia Mathematica* (1910), written in collaboration with A. N. Whitehead. He was awarded the Nobel prize for literature in 1950.

His recent book on *Human Knowledge* is an inquiry into the conditions, nature, and sources of our knowing. Like his other works it discusses difficult questions in plain and lucid language; for 'Philosophy,' as he writes in his preface, 'deals with matters of interest to the general educated public, and loses much of its value if only a few professionals can understand what is said.'

Scientific knowledge aims at being wholly impersonal, and tries to state what has been discovered by the collective intellect of mankind. In this chapter I shall consider how far it succeeds in this aim, and what elements of individual knowledge have to be sacrificed in order to achieve the measure of success that is possible.

The community knows both more and less than the individual: it knows, in its collective capacity, all the contents of the encyclopedia and all the contributions to the proceedings of learned bodies, but it does not know the warm and intimate things that make up the color and texture of an individual life. When a man says, 'I can never convey the horror I felt on seeing Buchenwald' or 'No words can express my joy at seeing the sea again after years in a prison camp,' he is saying something which is strictly and precisely true: he possesses, through his experience, knowledge not possessed by those whose experience has been different, and not completely capable of verbal expression. If he is a superb literary artist, he may create in sensitive readers a state of mind not wholly unlike his own, but if he tries scientific methods the stream of his experience will be lost and dissipated in a dusty desert.

Language, our sole means of communicating *scientific* knowledge, is essentially social in its origin and in its main functions. It is true that if a mathematician were wrecked on a desert island with a notebook and a pencil, he would, in all likelihood, seek to make his solitude endurable by calculations using the language of mathematics; it is true also that a man may keep a diary which he intends to conceal from all eyes but his own. On a more everyday plane, most of us use words in solitary thinking. Nevertheless, the chief purpose of language is communication, and to serve this purpose it must be public, not a private dialect invented by the speaker. It follows that what is most personal in each individual's experience tends to evaporate during the process of translation into language. What is more, the very publicity of language is in large part a delusion. A given form of words will usually be interpreted by competent hearers in such a way as to be true for all of them or false for all of them, but in spite of this it will not have the same meaning for all of them. Differences which do not affect the truth or falsehood of a statement are usually of little practical importance and are therefore ignored, with the result that we all believe our private world to be much more like the public world than it really is.

This is easily proved by considering the process of learning to understand language. There are two ways of getting to know what a word means: one is by a definition in terms of other words, which is called *verbal* definition; the other is by frequently hearing the word when the object which it denotes is present, which is called *ostensive* definition. It is obvious that ostensive definition is alone possible in the beginning, since verbal definition presupposes a knowledge of the words used in the *definiens*.[1] You can learn by a verbal definition that a pentagon is a plane figure with five sides, but a child does not learn in this way the meaning of everyday words such as 'rain,' 'sun,' 'dinner,' or 'bed.' These are taught by using the appropriate

[1 Defining part.]

word emphatically while the child is noticing the object concerned. Consequently the meaning that the child comes to attach to the word is a product of his personal experience, and varies according to his circumstances and his sensorium. A child who frequently experiences a mild drizzle will attach a different idea to the word 'rain' from that formed by a child who has only experienced tropical torrents. A short-sighted and a long-sighted child will connect different images with the word 'bed.'

It is true that education tries to depersonalize language, and with a certain measure of success. 'Rain' is no longer the familiar phenomenon, but 'drops of water falling from clouds toward the earth,' and 'water' is no longer what makes you wet, but H_2O. As for hydrogen and oxygen, they have verbal definitions which have to be learned by heart; whether you understand them does not matter. And so, as your instruction proceeds, the world of words becomes more and more separated from the world of the senses; you acquire the art of using words correctly, as you might acquire the art of playing the fiddle; in the end you become such a virtuoso in the manipulation of phrases that you need hardly ever remember that words have meanings. You have then become completely a public character, and even your inmost thoughts are suitable for the encyclopedia. But you can no longer hope to be a poet, and if you try to be a lover you will find your depersonalized language not very successful in generating the desired emotions. You have sacrificed expression to communication, and what you can communicate turns out to be abstract and dry.

It is an important fact that the nearer we come to the complete abstractness of logic, the less is the unavoidable difference between different people in the meaning attached to a word. I see no reason why there should be any difference at all between two suitably educated persons in the idea conveyed to them by the word '3481.' The words 'or' and 'not' are capable of having exactly the same meaning for two different logicians. Pure mathematics, throughout, works with concepts which are capable of being completely public and impersonal. The reason is that they derive nothing from the senses, and that the senses are the source of privacy. The body is a sensitive recording instrument, constantly transmitting messages from the outside world; the messages reaching one body are never quite the same as those reaching another, though practical and social exigencies have taught us ways of disregarding the differences between the percepts of neighboring persons. In constructing physics we have emphasized the spatio-temporal aspect of our perceptions, which is the aspect that is most abstract and most nearly akin to logic and mathematics. This we have done in the pursuit of publicity, in order to communicate what is communicable and to cover up the rest in a dark mantle of oblivion.

Space and time, however, as human beings know them, are not in reality so impersonal as science pretends. Theologians conceive God as viewing both space and time from without, impartially, and with a uniform awareness of the whole; science tries to imitate this impartiality with some apparent success, but the success is in part illusory. Human beings differ from the theologians' God in the fact that their space and time have a *here* and *now*. What is here and now is vivid; what is remote has a gradually increasing dimness. All our knowledge of events radiates from a space-time center, which is the little region that we are occupying at the moment. 'Here' is a vague term: in astronomical cosmology the Milky Way may count as 'here'; in the study of the Milky Way 'here' is the solar system; in the study of the solar system 'here' is the earth; in geography it is the town or district in which we live; in physiological studies of sensation it is the brain as opposed to the rest of the body. Larger 'heres' always contain smaller ones as parts; all 'heres' contain the brain of the speaker, or part of it. Similar considerations apply to 'now.'

Science professes to eliminate 'here' and 'now.' When some event occurs on the earth's surface, we give its position in the space-time manifold by assigning latitude, longitude, and date. We have developed a technique which insures that all accurate observers with accurate instruments will arrive at the same estimate of latitude, longitude, and date. Consequently there is no longer anything personal in these estimates, in so far as we are content with numerical statements of which the meaning is not too closely investigated. Having arbitrarily decided that the longitude of Greenwich and the latitude of the equator are to be zero, other latitudes and longitudes follow. But what is 'Greenwich'? This is hardly the sort of term that ought to occur in an impartial survey of the universe, and its definition is not mathematical. The best way to define 'Greenwich' is to take a man to it and say, 'Here is Greenwich.' If someone else has already determined the latitude and longitude of the place where you are, 'Greenwich' can be defined by its latitude and longitude relative to that place; it is, for example, so many degrees east and so many degrees north of New York. But this does not get rid of 'here,' which is now New York instead of Greenwich.

Moreover it is absurd to *define* either Greenwich or New York by its latitude and longitude. Greenwich is an actual place, inhabited by actual people, and containing buildings which antedate its longitudinal pre-eminence. You can, of course, describe Greenwich, but there always might be another town with the same characteristics. If you want to be *sure* that your description applies to no other place, the only way is to mention its relation to some other place—for instance, by saying that it is so many miles down the Thames from London Bridge. But then you will have to define 'London Bridge.' Sooner or later you are faced with the necessity of defining some place as 'here,' and this is an egocentric definition, since the place in question is not 'here' for everybody. There may be a way of escape from this conclusion; at a later stage, we will resume the question. But there is no obvious or easy way of escape, and until one is found all determinations of latitude and longitude are infected with the subjectivity of 'here.' This means that although different people assign the same latitude and longitude to a place, they do not, in ultimate analysis, attach the same meaning to the figures at which they arrive.

The common world in which we believe ourselves to live is a construction, partly scientific, partly pre-scientific. We perceive tables as circular or rectangular, in spite of the fact that a painter, to reproduce their appearance, has to paint ellipses or non-rectangular quadrilaterals. We see a person as of about the same size whether he is two feet from us or twelve. Until our attention is drawn to the facts, we are quite unconscious of the corrections that experience has led us to make in interpreting sensible appearances. There is a long journey from the child who draws two eyes in a profile to the physicist who talks of electrons and protons, but throughout this journey there is one constant purpose: to eliminate the subjectivity of sensation and substitute a kind of knowledge which can be the same for all percipients. Gradually the difference between what is sensed and what is believed to be objective grows greater; the child's profile with two eyes is still very like what is seen, but the electrons and protons have only a remote resemblance of logical structure. The electrons and protons, however, have the merit that they *may* be what actually exists where there are no sense organs, whereas our immediate visual data, owing to their subjectivity, are almost certainly not what takes place in the physical objects that we are said to see.

The electrons and protons—assuming it scientifically correct to believe in them—do not depend for their existence upon being perceived; on the contrary, there is every reason to believe that they existed for countless ages before there were any percipients in the universe. But although perception is not needed for their existence, it is needed to give us a reason for believing in their existence. Hundreds of thousands of years ago, a vast and remote region emitted incredible numbers of photons, which wandered through the universe in all directions. At last a very few of them hit a photographic plate, in which they caused chemical changes which made parts of the plate look black instead of white when examined by an astronomer. This tiny effect upon a minute but highly educated organism is our only reason for believing in the existence of a nebula comparable in size with the Milky Way. The order for knowledge is the inverse of the causal order. In the order for knowledge, what comes first is the brief subjective experience of the astronomer looking at a pattern of black and white, and what comes last is the nebula, vast, remote, and belonging to the distant past.

In considering the reasons for believing in any empirical statement, we cannot escape from perception with all its personal limitations. How far the information which we obtain from this tainted source can be purified in the filter of scientific method, and emerge resplendently godlike in its impartiality, is a difficult question, with which we shall be much concerned. But there is one thing that is obvious from the start: Only in so far as the initial perceptual datum [2] is trustworthy can there be any reason for accepting the vast cosmic edifice of inference which is based upon it.

I am not suggesting that the initial perceptual datum must be accepted as indubitable; that is by no means the case. There are well-known methods of strengthening or weakening the force of individual testimony; certain methods are used in the law courts, somewhat different ones are used in science. But all depend upon the principle that *some* weight is to be attached to every piece of testimony, for it is only in virtue of this principle that a number of concordant testimonies are held to give a high probability. Individual percepts are the basis of all our knowledge, and no method exists by which we can begin with data which are public to many observers.

[2 What is 'given,' assumed.]

William James

PRAGMATISM'S CONCEPTION OF TRUTH

❡ William James (1842–1910) credited his friend C. S. Peirce with the invention of the term 'pragmatism,' but it was James himself who did most to expound it, popularize it, and make it a party slogan in philosophical disputes. The word may not be so challenging nowadays as it used to be, but the questions that gave rise to it, and that it sought to answer, are as debatable as ever, even though the old wine of pragmatism may be in new bottles labeled 'instrumentalism.' James's best explanations of his views are found in his volume of lectures, *Pragmatism. A New Name for Some Old Ways of Thinking* (1907). He permitted himself to say in a letter to his brother that 'I shouldn't be surprised if ten years hence it should be rated as "epoch-making," for of the definitive triumph of that general way of thinking I can entertain no doubt whatever—I believe it to be something quite like the protestant reformation.' Whether the book was indeed so epoch-making may be decided by the historians of philosophy; but there is no doubt that it is an excellent and representative statement of a way of thinking extremely characteristic and influential in the twentieth century.

Only the first half of the chapter on 'Pragmatism's Conception of Truth' is reprinted here, and the opening paragraph is omitted.

. . . I FULLY expect to see the pragmatist [1] view of truth run through the classic stages of a theory's career. First, you know, a new theory is attacked as absurd; then it is admitted to be true, but obvious and insignificant; finally it is seen to be so important that its adversaries claim that they themselves discovered it. Our doctrine of truth is at present in the first of these three stages, with symptoms of the second stage having begun in certain quarters. I wish that this lecture might help it beyond the first stage in the eyes of many of you.

[1 The word comes from Greek 'pragma,' an act or deed.]

FROM *Pragmatism*, 1907. Reprinted by permission of Paul R. Reynolds & Son, New York.

Truth, as any dictionary will tell you, is a property of certain of our ideas. It means their 'agreement,' as falsity means their disagreement, with 'reality.' Pragmatists and intellectualists both accept this definition as a matter of course. They begin to quarrel only after the question is raised as to what may precisely be meant by the term 'agreement,' and what by the term 'reality,' when reality is taken as something for our ideas to agree with.

In answering these questions the pragmatists are more analytic and painstaking, the intellectualists more offhand and irreflective. The popular notion is that a true idea must copy its reality. Like other popular views, this one follows the analogy of the most usual experience. Our true ideas of sensible things do indeed copy them. Shut your eyes and think of yonder clock on the wall, and you get just such a true picture or copy of its dial. But your idea of its 'works' (unless you are a clock-maker) is much less of a copy, yet it passes muster, for it in no way clashes with the reality. Even though it should shrink to the mere word 'works,' that word still serves you truly; and when you speak of the 'time-keeping function' of the clock, or of its spring's 'elasticity,' it is hard to see exactly what your ideas can copy.

You perceive that there is a problem here. Where our ideas cannot copy definitely their object, what does agreement with that object mean? Some idealists seem to say that they are true whenever they are what God means that we ought to think about that object. Others hold the copy-view all through, and speak as if our ideas possessed truth just in proportion as they approach to being copies of the Absolute's eternal way of thinking.

These views, you see, invite pragmatistic discussion. But the great assumption of the intellectualists is that truth means essentially an inert static relation. When you've got your true idea of anything, there's an end of the matter. You're in possession; you *know*; you have fulfilled your thinking destiny. You are where you ought to be mentally; you have obeyed your categorical imperative; [2] and nothing more need follow on that climax of your rational destiny. Epistemologically you are in stable equilibrium.

Pragmatism, on the other hand, asks its usual question. 'Grant an idea or belief to be true,' it says, 'what concrete difference will its being true make in any one's actual life? How will the truth be realized? What experiences will be different from those which would obtain if the belief were false? What, in short, is the truth's cash-value in experiential terms?'

The moment pragmatism asks this question, it sees the answer: *True ideas are those that we can assimilate, validate, corroborate and verify.*

[2 A famous phrase in Kant's ethical writings. The imperative is 'Act as if the maxim of thy action were to become by thy will a universal law of nature.']

False ideas are those that we can not. That is the practical difference it makes to us to have true ideas; that, therefore, is the meaning of truth, for it is all that truth is known-as.

This thesis is what I have to defend. The truth of an idea is not a stagnant property inherent in it. Truth *happens* to an idea. It *becomes* true, is *made* true by events. Its verity *is* in fact an event, a process: the process namely of its verifying itself, its veri-*fication*. Its validity is the process of its valid-*ation*.

But what do the words verification and validation themselves pragmatically mean? They again signify certain practical consequences of the verified and validated idea. It is hard to find any one phrase that characterizes these consequences better than the ordinary agreement-formula—just such consequences being what we have in mind whenever we say that our ideas 'agree' with reality. They lead us, namely, through the acts and other ideas which they instigate, into or up to, or towards, other parts of experience with which we feel all the while—such feeling being among our potentialities—that the original ideas remain in agreement. The connexions and transitions come to us from point to point as being progressive, harmonious, satisfactory. This function of agreeable leading is what we mean by an idea's verification. Such an account is vague and it sounds at first quite trivial, but it has results which it will take the rest of my hour to explain.

Let me begin by reminding you of the fact that the possession of true thoughts means everywhere the possession of invaluable instruments of action; and that our duty to gain truth, so far from being a blank command from out of the blue, or a 'stunt' self-imposed by our intellect, can account for itself by excellent practical reasons.

The importance to human life of having true beliefs about matters of fact is a thing too notorious. We live in a world of realities that can be infinitely useful or infinitely harmful. Ideas that tell us which of them to expect count as the true ideas in all this primary sphere of verification, and the pursuit of such ideas is a primary human duty. The possession of truth, so far from being here an end in itself, is only a preliminary means towards other vital satisfactions. If I am lost in the woods and starved, and find what looks like a cow-path, it is of the utmost importance that I should think of a human habitation at the end of it, for if I do so and follow it, I save myself. The true thought is useful here because the house which is its object is useful. The practical value of true ideas is thus primarily derived from the practical importance of their objects to us. Their objects are, indeed, not important at all times. I may on another occasion have no use for the house; and then my idea of it, however verifiable, will be practically irrelevant, and had better remain latent. Yet since almost any object may some day become temporarily important, the advantage of having a general stock of *extra* truths, of ideas that shall be true of merely possible situations, is obvious. We store such extra truths away in our memories, and with the overflow we fill our books of reference. Whenever such an extra truth becomes practically relevant to one of our emergencies, it passes from cold-storage to do work in the world and our belief in it grows active. You can say of it then either that 'it is useful because it is true' or that 'it is true because it is useful.' Both these phrases mean exactly the same thing, namely that here is an idea that gets fulfilled and can be verified. True is the name for whatever idea starts the verification-process, useful is the name for its completed function in experience. True ideas would never have been singled out as such, would never have acquired a class-name, least of all a name suggesting value, unless they had been useful from the outset in this way.

From this simple cue pragmatism gets her general notion of truth as something essentially bound up with the way in which one moment in our experience may lead us towards other moments which it will be worth while to have been led to. Primarily, and on the common-sense level, the truth of a state of mind means this function of *a leading that is worth while*. When a moment in our experience, of any kind whatever, inspires us with a thought that is true, that means that sooner or later we dip by that thought's guidance into the particulars of experience again and make advantageous connexion with them. This is a vague enough statement, but I beg you to retain it, for it is essential.

Our experience meanwhile is all shot through with regularities. One bit of it can warn us to get ready for another bit, can 'intend' or be 'significant of' that remoter object. The object's advent is the significance's verification. Truth, in these cases, meaning nothing but eventual verification, is manifestly incompatible with waywardness on our part. Woe to him whose beliefs play fast and loose with the order which realities follow in his experience; they will lead him nowhere or else make false connexions.

By 'realities' or 'objects' here, we mean either things of common sense, sensibly present, or else common-sense relations, such as dates, places, distances, kinds, activities. Following our mental image of a house along the cow-path, we actually come to see the house; we get the image's full verification. *Such simply and fully verified leadings are certainly the originals and prototypes of the truth-process.* Experience offers indeed other forms of truth-process, but they are all conceivable as being primary verifications arrested, multiplied or substituted one for another.

Take, for instance, yonder object on the wall. You and I consider it to be a 'clock,' altho no one of us has seen the hidden works that make it one. We let our notion pass for true without attempting to verify. If truths mean verification-process essentially, ought we then to call such unverified truths as this abortive? No, for they form the overwhelmingly large number of the truths we live by. Indirect as well as direct verifications pass muster. Where circumstantial evidence is sufficient, we can go without eye-witnessing. Just as we here assume Japan to exist without ever having been there, because it *works* to do so, everything we know conspiring with the belief, and nothing interfering, so we assume that thing to be a clock. We *use* it as a clock, regulating the length of our lecture by it. The verification of the assumption here means its leading to no frustration or contradiction. Verifi*ability* of wheels and weights and pendulum is as good as verification. For one truth-process completed there are a million in our lives that function in this state of nascency. They turn us *towards* direct verification; lead us into the *surroundings* of the objects they envisage; and then, if everything runs on harmoniously, we are so sure that verification is possible that we omit it, and are usually justified by all that happens.

Truth lives, in fact, for the most part on a credit system. Our thoughts and beliefs 'pass,' so long as nothing challenges them, just as bank-notes pass so long as nobody refuses them. But this all points to direct face-to-face verifications somewhere, without which the fabric of truth collapses like a financial system with no cash-basis whatever. You accept my verification of one thing, I yours of another. We trade on each other's truth. But beliefs verified concretely by *somebody* are the posts of the whole superstructure.

'Another great reason—beside economy of time—for waiving complete verification in the usual business of life is that all things exist in kinds and not singly. Our world is found once for all to have that peculiarity. So that when we have once directly verified our ideas about one specimen of a kind, we consider ourselves free to apply them to other specimens without verification. A mind that habitually discerns the kind of thing before it, and acts by the law of the kind immediately, without pausing to verify, will be a 'true' mind in ninety-nine out of a hundred emergencies, proved so by its conduct fitting everything it meets, and getting no refutation.

Indirectly or only potentially verifying processes may thus be true as well as full verification-processes. They work as true processes would work, give us the same advantages, and claim our recognition for the same reasons. All this on the common-sense level of matters of fact, which we are alone considering.

But matters of fact are not our only stock in trade. *Relations among purely mental ideas* form another sphere where true and false beliefs obtain, and here the beliefs are absolute, or unconditional. When they are true they bear the name either of definitions or of principles. It is either a principle or a definition that 1 and 1 make 2, that 2 and 1 make 3, and so on; that white differs less from gray than it does from black; that when the cause begins to act the effect also commences. Such propositions hold of all possible 'ones,' of all conceivable 'whites' and 'grays' and 'causes.' The objects here are mental objects. Their relations are perceptually obvious at a glance, and no sense-verification is necessary. Moreover, once true, always true, of those same mental objects. Truth here has an 'eternal' character. If you can find a concrete thing anywhere that is 'one' or 'white' or 'gray' or an 'effect,' then your principles will everlastingly apply to it. It is but a case of ascertaining the kind, and then applying the law of its kind to the particular object. You are sure to get truth if you can but name the kind rightly, for your mental relations hold good of everything of that kind without exception. If you then, nevertheless, failed to get truth concretely, you would say that you had classed your real objects wrongly.

In this realm of mental relations, truth again is an affair of leading. We relate one abstract idea with another, framing in the end great systems of logical and mathematical truth, under the respective terms of which the sensible facts of experience eventually arrange themselves, so that our eternal truths hold good of realities also. This marriage of fact and theory is endlessly fertile. What we say is here already true in advance of special verification, *if we have subsumed our objects rightly.* Our ready-made ideal framework for all sorts of possible objects follows from the very structure of our thinking. We can no more play fast and loose with these abstract relations than we can do so with our sense-experiences. They coerce us; we must treat them consistently, whether or not we like the results. The rules of addition apply to our debts as rigorously as to our assets. The hundredth decimal of π, the ratio of the circumference to its diameter, is predetermined ideally now, tho no one may have computed it. If we should ever need the figure in our dealings with an actual circle we should need to have it given rightly, calculated by the usual rules; for it is the same kind of truth that those rules elsewhere calculate.

Between the coercions of the sensible order and those of the ideal order, our mind is thus wedged tightly. Our ideas must agree with realities, be such realities concrete or abstract, be they facts or be they principles, under penalty of endless inconsistency and frustration.

So far, intellectualists can raise no protest. They can only say that we have barely touched the skin of the matter.

Realities mean, then, either concrete facts, or abstract kinds of thing and relations perceived intuitively between them. They furthermore and thirdly mean, as things that new ideas of ours must no less take account of, the whole body of other truths already in our possession. But what now does 'agreement' with such threefold realities mean?—to use again the definition that is current.

Here it is that pragmatism and intellectualism begin to part company. Primarily, no doubt, to agree means to copy, but we saw that the mere word 'clock' would do instead of a mental picture of its works, and that of many realities our ideas can only be symbols and not copies. 'Past time,' 'power,' 'spontaneity,'—how can our mind copy such realities?

To 'agree' in the widest sense with a reality *can only mean to be guided either straight up to it or into its surroundings, or to be put into such working touch with it as to handle either it or something connected with it better than if we disagreed.* Better either intellectually or practically! And often agreement will only mean the negative fact that nothing contradictory from the quarter of that reality comes to interfere with the way in which our ideas guide us elsewhere. To copy a reality is, indeed, one very important way of agreeing with it, but it is far from being essential. The essential thing is the process of being guided. Any idea that helps us to *deal*, whether practically or intellectually, with either the reality or its belongings, that doesn't entangle our progress in frustrations, that *fits*, in fact, and adapts our life to the reality's whole setting, will agree sufficiently to meet the requirement. It will hold true of that reality.

Thus, *names* are just as 'true' or 'false' as definite mental pictures are. They set up similar verification-processes, and lead to fully equivalent practical results.

All human thinking gets discursified; we exchange ideas; we lend and borrow verifications, get them from one another by means of social intercourse. All truth thus gets verbally built out, stored up, and made available for every one. Hence, we must *talk* consistently just as we must *think* consistently: for both in talk and thought we deal with kinds. Names are arbitrary, but once understood they must be kept to. We mustn't now call Abel 'Cain' or Cain 'Abel.' If we do, we ungear ourselves from the whole book of Genesis, and from all its connexions with the universe of speech and fact down to the present time. We throw ourselves out of whatever truth that entire system of speech and fact may embody.

The overwhelming majority of our true ideas admit of no direct or face-to-face verification—those of past history, for example, as of Cain and Abel. The stream of time can be remounted only verbally, or verified indirectly by the present prolongations or effects of what the past harbored. Yet if they agree with these verbalities and effects, we can know that our ideas of the past are true. As *true as past time itself was*, so true was Julius Cæsar, so true were antediluvian monsters, all in their proper dates and settings. That past time itself was, is guaranteed by its coherence with everything that's present. True as the present *is*, the past *was* also.

Agreement thus turns out to be essentially an affair of leading—leading that is useful because it is into quarters that contain objects that are important. True ideas lead us into useful verbal and conceptual quarters as well as directly up to useful sensible termini. They lead to consistency, stability and flowing human intercourse. They lead away from excentricity and isolation, from foiled and barren thinking. The untrammelled flowing of the leading-process, its general freedom from clash and contradiction, passes for its indirect verification; but all roads lead to Rome, and in the end and eventually, all true processes must lead to the face of directly verifying sensible experiences *somewhere*, which somebody's ideas have copied.

Such is the large loose way in which the pragmatist interprets the word agreement. He treats it altogether practically. He lets it cover any process of conduction from a present idea to a future terminus, provided only it run prosperously. It is only thus that 'scientific' ideas, flying as they do beyond common sense, can be said to agree with their realities. It is, as I have already said, *as if* reality were made of ether, atoms or electrons, but we mustn't think so literally. The term 'energy' doesn't even pretend to stand for anything 'objective.' It is only a way of measuring the surface of phenomena so as to string their changes on a simple formula.

Yet in the choice of these man-made formulas we can not be capricious with impunity any more than we can be capricious on the common-sense practical level. We must find a theory that will *work*; and that means something extremely difficult; for our theory must mediate between all previous truths and certain new experiences. It must derange common sense and previous belief as little as possible, and it must lead to some sensible terminus or other that can be verified exactly. To 'work' means both these things; and the squeeze is so tight that there is little loose play for any hypothesis. Our theories are wedged and controlled as nothing else is. Yet sometimes alternative theoretic formulas are equally compatible with all the truths we know, and then we choose between them for subjective reasons. We choose the kind of theory to which we are already partial; we follow 'elegance' or 'economy.' Clerk-Maxwell [3] somewhere says it would be 'poor scientific taste' to choose the more complicated of two equally well-evidenced conceptions; and you will all agree with him. Truth in science is what gives us the maximum possible sum of satisfactions, taste included, but consistency both with previous truth and with novel fact is always the most imperious claimant. . .

[3] Experimental physicist at Cambridge, celebrated for his work on the kinetic theory of gases, on electricity, and on magnetism. One of the foremost scientists of the nineteenth century.]

George *Santayana*

WILLIAM JAMES

❲ 'Only an American—and I am not one except by long association—can speak for the heart of America. I try to understand it, as a family friend may who has a different temperament.' So Mr. Santayana writes in the preface to *Character and Opinion in the United States*. The 'United States' of his title consists of the environs of Boston, to be sure, but this limitation in no way diminishes the excellence of the essays. They are not intended as a guidebook to the country or a set of tourist's impressions, like Henry James's *The American Scene*. They are mostly meditations on the persons, customs, and opinions that Mr. Santayana knew long and intimately in America: Harvard, William James, Josiah Royce, and their milieu. When he does generalize about the American character, however, his observations are wise and just.

Readers interested in Mr. Santayana's further reminiscences of the United States, and especially of the Boston and Harvard of his day, should not fail to read the second volume of his autobiography, *The Middle Span* (1945).

WILLIAM JAMES enjoyed in his youth what are called advantages: he lived among cultivated people, travelled, had teachers of various nationalities. His father [1] was one of those somewhat obscure sages whom early America produced: mystics of independent mind, hermits in the desert of business, and heretics in the churches. They were intense individualists, full of veneration for the free souls of their children, and convinced that every one should paddle his own canoe, especially on the high seas. William James accordingly enjoyed a stimulating if slightly irregular

[¹ See pp. 463–6.]

FROM *Character and Opinion in the United States*, 1920. Reprinted by permission of Charles Scribner's Sons.

education: he never acquired that reposeful mastery of particular authors and those safe ways of feeling and judging which are fostered in great schools and universities. In consequence he showed an almost physical horror of club sentiment and of the stifling atmosphere of all officialdom. He had a knack for drawing, and rather the temperament of the artist; but the unlovely secrets of nature and the troubles of man preoccupied him, and he chose medicine for his profession. Instead of practising, however, he turned to teaching physiology, and from that passed gradually to psychology and philosophy.

In his earlier years he retained some traces of polyglot student days at Paris, Bonn, Vienna, or Geneva; he slipped sometimes into foreign phrases, uttered in their full vernacular; and there was an occasional afterglow of Bohemia about him, in the bright stripe of a shirt or the exuberance of a tie. On points of art or medicine he retained a professional touch and an unconscious ease which he hardly acquired in metaphysics. I suspect he had heartily admired some of his masters in those other subjects, but had never seen a philosopher whom he would have cared to resemble. Of course there was nothing of the artist in William James, as the artist is sometimes conceived in England, nothing of the æsthete, nothing affected or limp. In person he was short rather than tall, erect, brisk, bearded, intensely masculine. While he shone in expression and would have wished his style to be noble if it could also be strong, he preferred in the end to be spontaneous, and to leave it at that; he tolerated slang in himself rather than primness. The rough, homely, picturesque phrase, whatever was graphic and racy, recommended itself to him; and his conversation outdid his writing in this respect. He believed in improvisation, even in thought; his lectures were not minutely prepared. Know your subject thoroughly, he used to say, and trust to luck for the rest. There was a deep sense of insecurity in him, a mixture of humility with romanticism: we were likely to be more or less wrong anyhow, but we might be wholly sincere. One moment should respect the insight of another, without trying to establish too regimental a uniformity. If you corrected yourself tartly, how could you know that the correction was not the worse mistake? All our opinions were born free and equal, all children of the Lord, and if they were not consistent that was the Lord's business, not theirs. In reality, James was consistent enough, as even Emerson (more extreme in this sort of irresponsibility) was too. Inspiration has its limits, sometimes very narrow ones. But James was not consecutive, not insistent; he turned to a subject afresh, without egotism or pedantry; he dropped his old points, sometimes very good ones; and he modestly looked for light from others, who had less light than himself.

His excursions into philosophy were accordingly in the nature of raids, and it is easy for those who are attracted by one part of his work to ignore other parts, in themselves perhaps more valuable. I think that in fact his popularity does not rest on his best achievements. His popularity rests on three somewhat incidental books, *The Will to Believe, Pragmatism,* and *The Varieties of Religious Experience,* whereas, as it seems to me, his best achievement is his *Principles of Psychology.* In this book he surveys, in a way which for him is very systematic, a subject made to his hand. In its ostensible outlook it is a treatise like any other, but what distinguishes it is the author's gift for evoking vividly the very life of the mind. This is a work of imagination; and the subject as he conceived it, which is the flux of immediate experience in men in general, requires imagination to read it at all. It is a literary subject, like autobiography or psychological fiction, and can be treated only poetically; and in this sense Shakespeare is a better psychologist than Locke or Kant. Yet this gift of imagination is not merely literary; it is not useless in divining the truths of science, and it is invaluable in throwing off prejudice and scientific shams. The fresh imagination and vitality of William James led him to break through many a false convention. He saw that experience, as we endure it, is not a mosaic of distinct sensations, nor the expression of separate hostile faculties, such as reason and the passions, or sense and the categories; it is rather a flow of mental discourse, like a dream, in which all divisions and units are vague and shifting, and the whole is continually merging together and drifting apart. It fades gradually in the rear, like the wake of a ship, and bites into the future, like the bow cutting the water. For the candid psychologist, carried bodily on this voyage of discovery, the past is but a questionable report, and the future wholly indeterminate; everything is simply what it is experienced as being.

At the same time, psychology is supposed to be a science, a claim which would tend to confine it to the natural history of man, or the study of behaviour, as is actually proposed by Auguste Comte and by some of James's own disciples, more jejune if more clear-headed than he. As matters now stand, however, psychology as a whole is not a science, but a branch of philosophy; it brings together the literary description of mental discourse and the scientific description of material life, in order to consider the relation between them, which is the nexus of human nature.

What was James's position on this crucial question? It is impossible to reply unequivocally. He approached philosophy as mankind originally approached it, without having a philosophy, and he lent himself to various hypotheses in various directions. He professed to begin his study on the assumptions of common sense, that there is a material world which the animals that live in it are able to perceive and to think about. He gave a congruous extension to this view in his theory that emotion is purely bodily sensation, and also in his habit of conceiving the mind as a total shifting sensibility. To pursue this path, however, would have led him to admit that nature was automatic and mind simply cognitive, conclusions from which every instinct in him recoiled. He preferred to believe that mind and matter had independent energies and could lend one another a hand, matter operating by motion and mind by intention. This dramatic, amphibious way of picturing causation is natural to common sense, and might be defended if it were clearly defined; but James was insensibly carried away from it by a subtle implication of his method. This implication was that experience or mental discourse not only constituted a set of substantive facts, but the *only* substantive facts; all else, even that material world which his psychology had postulated, could be nothing but a verbal or fantastic symbol for sensations in their experienced order. So that while nominally the door was kept open to any hypothesis regarding the conditions of the psychological flux, in truth the question was prejudged. The hypotheses, which were parts of this psychological flux, could have no object save other parts of it. That flux itself, therefore, which he could picture so vividly, was the fundamental existence. The *sense* of bounding over the waves, the *sense* of being on an adventurous voyage, was the living fact; the rest was dead reckoning. Where one's gift is, there will one's faith be also; and to this poet appearance was the only reality.

This sentiment, which always lay at the back of his mind, reached something like formal expression in his latest writings, where he sketched what he called radical empiricism. The word experience is like a shrapnel shell, and bursts into a thousand meanings. Here we must no longer think of its setting, its discoveries, or its march; to treat it radically we must abstract its immediate objects and reduce it to pure data. It is obvious (and the sequel has already proved) that experience so understood would lose its romantic signification, as a personal adventure or a response to the shocks of fortune. 'Experience' would turn into a cosmic dance of absolute entities created and destroyed *in vacuo* [2] according to universal laws, or perhaps by chance. No minds would gather this experience, and no material agencies would impose it; but the immediate objects present to any one would

[² In empty space.]

simply be parts of the universal fireworks, continuous with the rest, and all
the parts, even if not present to anybody, would have the same status.
Experience would then not at all resemble what Shakespeare reports or
what James himself had described in his psychology. If it could be experienced as it flows in its entirety (which is fortunately impracticable), it
would be a perpetual mathematical nightmare. Every whirling atom, every
changing relation, and every incidental perspective would be a part of it.
I am far from wishing to deny for a moment the scientific value of such a
cosmic system, if it can be worked out; physics and mathematics seem to
me to plunge far deeper than literary psychology into the groundwork of
this world; but human experience is the stuff of literary psychology; we
cannot reach the stuff of physics and mathematics except by arresting or
even hypostatising [3] some elements of appearance, and expanding them on
an abstracted and hypothetical plane of their own. Experience, as memory
and literature rehearse it, remains nearer to us than that: it is something
dreamful, passionate, dramatic, and significative.

Certainly this personal human experience, expressible in literature and
in talk, and no cosmic system however profound, was what James knew
best and trusted most. Had he seen the developments of his radical empiricism, I cannot help thinking he would have marvelled that such logical
mechanisms should have been hatched out of that egg. The principal problems and aspirations that haunted him all his life long would lose their
meaning in that cosmic atmosphere. The pragmatic nature of truth, for
instance, would never suggest itself in the presence of pure data; but a
romantic mind soaked in agnosticism, conscious of its own habits and
assuming an environment the exact structure of which can never be observed, may well convince itself that, for experience, truth is nothing but
a happy use of signs—which is indeed the truth of literature. But if we
once accept *any* system of the universe as literally true, the value of convenient signs to prepare us for such experience as is yet absent cannot be called
truth: it is plainly nothing but a necessary inaccuracy. So, too, with the
question of the survival of the human individual after death. For radical
empiricism a human individual is simply a certain cycle or complex of
terms, like any other natural fact; that some echoes of his mind should
recur after the regular chimes have ceased, would have nothing paradoxical
about it. A mathematical world is a good deal like music, with its repetitions and transpositions, and a little trill, which you might call a person,
might well peep up here and there all over a vast composition. Something

[3 Assuming to be substantial realities.]

of that sort may be the truth of spiritualism; but it is not what the spiritualists imagine. Their whole interest lies not in the experiences they have, but in the interpretation they give to them, assigning them to troubled spirits in another world; but both another world and a spirit are notions repugnant to a radical empiricism.

I think it is important to remember, if we are not to misunderstand William James, that his radical empiricism and pragmatism were in his own mind only methods; his doctrine, if he may be said to have had one, was agnosticism. And just because he was an agnostic (feeling instinctively that beliefs and opinions, if they had any objective beyond themselves, could never be sure they had attained it), he seemed in one sense so favourable to credulity. He was not credulous himself, far from it; he was well aware that the trust he put in people or ideas might betray him. For that very reason he was respectful and pitiful to the trustfulness of others. Doubtless they were wrong, but who were we to say so? In his own person he was ready enough to face the mystery of things, and whatever the womb of time might bring forth; but until the curtain was rung down on the last act of the drama (and it might have no last act!) he wished the intellectual cripples and the moral hunchbacks not to be jeered at; perhaps they might turn out to be the heroes of the play. Who could tell what heavenly influences might not pierce to these sensitive half-flayed creatures, which are lost on the thick-skinned, the sane, and the duly goggled? We must not suppose, however, that James meant these contrite and romantic suggestions dogmatically. The agnostic, as well as the physician and neurologist in him, was never quite eclipsed. The hope that some new revelation might come from the lowly and weak could never mean to him what it meant to the early Christians. For him it was only a right conceded to them to experiment with their special faiths; he did not expect such faiths to be discoveries of absolute fact, which everybody else might be constrained to recognise. If any one had made such a claim, and had seemed to have some chance of imposing it universally, James would have been the first to turn against him; not, of course, on the ground that it was *impossible* that such an orthodoxy should be true, but with a profound conviction that it was to be feared and distrusted. No: the degree of authority and honour to be accorded to various human faiths was a moral question, not a theoretical one. All faiths were what they were experienced as being, in their capacity of faiths; these faiths, not their objects, were the hard facts we must respect. We cannot pass, except under the illusion of the moment, to anything firmer or on a deeper level. There was accordingly no sense of security, no joy, in James's apology for personal religion. He did not really believe; he merely believed in the right of believing that you might be right if you believed.

It is this underlying agnosticism that explains an incoherence which we might find in his popular works, where the story and the moral do not seem to hang together. Professedly they are works of psychological observation; but the tendency and suasion in them seems to run to disintegrating the idea of truth, recommending belief without reason, and encouraging superstition. A psychologist who was not an agnostic would have indicated, as far as possible, whether the beliefs and experiences he was describing were instances of delusion or of rare and fine perception, or in what measure they were a mixture of both. But James—and this is what gives such romantic warmth to these writings of his—disclaims all antecedent or superior knowledge, listens to the testimony of each witness in turn, and only by accident allows us to feel that he is swayed by the eloquence and vehemence of some of them rather than of others. This method is modest, generous, and impartial; but if James intended, as I think he did, to picture the *drama* of human belief, with its risks and triumphs, the method was inadequate. Dramatists never hesitate to assume, and to let the audience perceive, who is good and who bad, who wise and who foolish, in their pieces; otherwise their work would be as impotent dramatically as scientifically. The tragedy and comedy of life lie precisely in the contrast between the illusions or passions of the characters and their true condition and fate, hidden from them at first, but evident to the author and the public. If in our diffidence and scrupulous fairness we refuse to take this judicial attitude, we shall be led to strange conclusions. The navigator, for instance, trusting his 'experience' (which here, as in the case of religious people, means his imagination and his art), insists on believing that the earth is spherical; he has sailed round it. That is to say, he has seemed to himself to steer westward and westward, and has seemed to get home again. But how should he know that home is now where it was before, or that his past and present impressions of it come from the same, or from any, material object? How should he know that space is as trim and tri-dimensional as the discredited Euclidians used to say it was? If, on the contrary, my worthy aunt, trusting to her longer and less ambiguous experience of her garden, insists that the earth is flat, and observes that the theory that it is round, which is only a theory, is much less often tested and found useful than her own perception of its flatness, and that moreover that theory is pedantic, intellectualistic, and a product of academies, and a rash dogma to impose on mankind for ever and ever, it might seem that on James's principle we ought to agree with her. But no; on James's real principles we need not agree with her, nor with the navigator either. Radical empiricism, which is radical agnosticism, delivers us from so benighted a choice. For the quarrel becomes unmeaning when we remember that the earth is *both* flat and round, if it is experienced as being both. The substantive fact is not a single object on which both the perception and the theory are expected to converge; the substantive facts are the theory and the perception themselves. And we may note in passing that empiricism, when it ceases to value experience as a means of discovering external things, can give up its ancient prejudice in favour of sense as against imagination, for imagination and thought are immediate experiences as much as sensation is; they are therefore, for absolute empiricism, no less actual ingredients of reality.

In *The Varieties of Religious Experience* we find the same apologetic intention running through a vivid account of what seems for the most part (as James acknowledged) religious disease. Normal religious experience is hardly described in it. Religious experience, for the great mass of mankind, consists in simple faith in the truth and benefit of their religious traditions. But to James something so conventional and rationalistic seemed hardly experience and hardly religious; he was thinking only of irruptive visions and feelings as interpreted by the mystics who had them. These interpretations he ostensibly presents, with more or less wistful sympathy for what they were worth; but emotionally he wished to champion them. The religions that had sprung up in America spontaneously—communistic, hysterical, spiritistic, or medicinal—were despised by select and superior people. You might inquire into them, as you might go slumming, but they remained suspect and distasteful. This picking up of genteel skirts on the part of his acquaintance prompted William James to roll up his sleeves— not for a knock-out blow, but for a thorough clinical demonstration. He would tenderly vivisect the experiences in question, to show how living they were, though of course he could not guarantee, more than other surgeons do, that the patient would survive the operation. An operation that eventually kills may be technically successful, and the man may die cured; and so a description of religion that showed it to be madness might first show how real and how warm it was, so that if it perished, at least it would perish understood.

I never observed in William James any personal anxiety or enthusiasm for any of these dubious tenets. His conception even of such a thing as free-will, which he always ardently defended, remained vague; he avoided defining even what he conceived to be desirable in such matters. But he wished to protect the weak against the strong, and what he hated beyond everything was the *non possumus* [4] of any constituted authority. Philosophy for him had a Polish constitution; so long as a single vote was cast against the majority, nothing could pass. The suspense of judgement which he had imposed on himself as a duty, became almost a necessity. I think it would have depressed him if he had had to confess that any important question was finally settled. He would still have hoped that something might turn up on the other side, and that just as the scientific hangman was about to despatch the poor convicted prisoner, an unexpected witness would ride up in hot haste, and prove him innocent. Experience seems to most of us to lead to conclusions, but empiricism has sworn never to draw them.

In the discourse on 'The Energies of Men,' certain physiological marvels are recorded, as if to suggest that the resources of our minds and bodies are infinite, or can be infinitely enlarged by divine grace. Yet James would not, I am sure, have accepted that inference. He would, under pressure, have drawn in his mystical horns under his scientific shell; but he was not naturalist enough to feel instinctively that the wonderful and the natural are all of a piece, and that only our degree of habituation distinguishes them. A nucleus, which we may poetically call the soul, certainly lies within us, by which our bodies and minds are generated and controlled, like an army by a government. In this nucleus, since nature in a small compass has room for anything, vast quantities of energy may well be stored up, which may be tapped on occasion, or which may serve like an electric spark to let loose energy previously existing in the grosser parts. But the absolute autocracy of this central power, or its success in imposing extraordinary trials on its subjects, is not an obvious good. Perhaps, like a democratic government, the soul is at its best when it merely collects and coordinates the impulses coming from the senses. The inner man is at times a tyrant, parasitical, wasteful, and voluptuous. At other times he is fanatical and mad. When he asks for and obtains violent exertions from the body, the question often is, as with the exploits of conquerors and conjurers, whether the impulse to do such prodigious things was not gratuitous, and the things nugatory. Who would wish to be a mystic? James himself, who by nature was a spirited rather than a spiritual man, had no liking for sanctimonious transcendentalists, visionaries, or ascetics; he hated minds that run thin. But he hastened to correct this manly impulse, lest it should be unjust, and forced himself to overcome his repugnance. This was

[4 'We cannot.']

made easier when the unearthly phenomenon had a healing or saving function in the everyday material world; miracle then re-established its ancient identity with medicine, and both of them were humanised. Even when this union was not attained, James was reconciled to the miracle-workers partly by his great charity, and partly by his hunter's instinct to follow a scent, for he believed discoveries to be imminent. Besides, a philosopher who is a teacher of youth is more concerned to give people a right start than a right conclusion. James fell in with the hortatory tradition of college sages; he turned his psychology, whenever he could do so honestly, to purposes of edification; and his little sermons on habit, on will, on faith, and this on the latent capacities of men, were fine and stirring, and just the sermons to preach to the young Christian soldier. He was much less sceptical in morals than in science. He seems to have felt sure that certain thoughts and hopes —those familiar to a liberal Protestantism—were every man's true friends in life. This assumption would have been hard to defend if he or those he habitually addressed had ever questioned it; yet his whole argument for voluntarily cultivating these beliefs rests on this assumption, that they are beneficent. Since, whether we will or no, we cannot escape the risk of error, and must succumb to some human or pathological bias, at least we might do so gracefully and in the form that would profit us most, by clinging to those prejudices which help us to lead what we all feel is a good life. But what is a good life? Had William James, had the people about him, had modern philosophers anywhere, any notion of that? I cannot think so. They had much experience of personal goodness, and love of it; they had standards of character and right conduct; but as to what might render human existence good, excellent, beautiful, happy, and worth having as a whole, their notions were utterly thin and barbarous. They had forgotten the Greeks, or never known them.

This argument accordingly suffers from the same weakness as the similar argument of Pascal in favour of Catholic orthodoxy. You should force yourself to believe in it, he said, because if you do so and are right you win heaven, while if you are wrong you lose nothing. What would Protestants, Mohammedans, and Hindus say to that? Those alternatives of Pascal's are not the sole nor the true alternatives; such a wager—betting on the improbable because you are offered big odds—is an unworthy parody of the real choice between wisdom and folly. There is no heaven to be won in such a spirit, and if there was, a philosopher would despise it. So William James would have us bet on immortality, or bet on our power to succeed, because if we win the wager we can live to congratulate ourselves on our true instinct, while we lose nothing if we have made a mistake; for unless you have the satisfaction of finding that you have been right, the dignity of having been right is apparently nothing. Or if the argument is rather that these beliefs, whether true or false, make life better in this world, the thing is simply false. To be boosted by an illusion is not to live better than to live in harmony with the truth; it is not nearly so safe, not nearly so sweet, and not nearly so fruitful. These refusals to part with a decayed illusion are really an infection to the mind. Believe, certainly; we cannot help believing; but believe rationally, holding what seems certain for certain, what seems probable for probable, what seems desirable for desirable, and what seems false for false.

In this matter, as usual, James had a true psychological fact and a generous instinct behind his confused moral suggestions. It is a psychological fact that men are influenced in their beliefs by their will and desires; indeed, I think we can go further and say that in its essence belief is an expression of impulse, of readiness to act. It is only peripherally, as our action is gradually adjusted to things, and our impulses to our possible or necessary action, that our ideas begin to hug the facts, and to acquire a true, if still a symbolic, significance. We do not need a will to believe; we only need a will to study the object in which we are inevitably believing. But James was thinking less of belief in what we find than of belief in what we hope for: a belief which is not at all clear and not at all necessary in the life of mortals. Like most Americans, however, only more lyrically, James felt the call of the future and the assurance that it could be made far better, totally other, than the past. The pictures that religion had painted of heaven or the millennium were not what he prized, although his Swedenborgian connection [5] might have made him tender to them, as perhaps it did to familiar spirits. It was the moral succour offered by religion, its open spaces, the possibility of miracles *in extremis*,[6] that must be retained. If we recoiled at the thought of being dupes (which is perhaps what nature intended us to be), were we less likely to be dupes in disbelieving these sustaining truths than in believing them? Faith was needed to bring about the reform of faith itself, as well as all other reforms.

In some cases faith in success could nerve us to bring success about, and so justify itself by its own operation. This is a thought typical of James at his worst—a worst in which there is always a good side. Here again psychological observation is used with the best intentions to hearten oneself and

[5] James's father was much influenced by Swedenborgian doctrines. See p. 464.]
[6] At the last.]

other people; but the fact observed is not at all understood, and a moral twist is given to it which (besides being morally questionable) almost amounts to falsifying the fact itself. Why does belief that you can jump a ditch help you to jump it? Because it is a symptom of the fact that you *could* jump it, that your legs were fit and that the ditch was two yards wide and not twenty. A rapid and just appreciation of these facts has given you your confidence, or at least has made it reasonable, manly, and prophetic; otherwise you would have been a fool and got a ducking for it. Assurance is contemptible and fatal unless it is self-knowledge. If you had been rattled you might have failed, because that would have been a symptom of the fact that you were out of gear; you would have been afraid because you trembled, as James at his best proclaimed. You would never have quailed if your system had been reacting smoothly to its opportunities, any more than you would totter and see double if you were not intoxicated. Fear is a sensation of actual nervousness and disarray, and confidence a sensation of actual readiness; they are not disembodied feelings, existing for no reason, the devil Funk and the angel Courage, one or the other of whom may come down arbitrarily into your body, and revolutionise it. That is childish mythology, which survives innocently enough as a figure of speech, until a philosopher is found to take that figure of speech seriously. Nor is the moral suggestion here less unsound. What is good is not the presumption of power, but the possession of it: a clear head, aware of its resources, not a fuddled optimism, calling up spirits from the vasty deep.[7] Courage is not a virtue, said Socrates, unless it is also wisdom. Could anything be truer both of courage in doing and of courage in believing? But it takes tenacity, it takes *reasonable* courage, to stick to scientific insights such as this of Socrates or that of James about the emotions; it is easier to lapse into the traditional manner, to search natural philosophy for miracles and moral lessons, and in morals proper, in the reasoned expression of preference, to splash about without a philosophy.

William James shared the passions of liberalism. He belonged to the left, which, as they say in Spain, is the side of the heart, as the right is that of the liver; at any rate there was much blood and no gall in his philosophy. He was one of those elder Americans still disquieted by the ghost of tyranny, social and ecclesiastical. Even the beauties of the past troubled him; he had a puritan feeling that they were tainted. They had been cruel and frivolous, and must have suppressed far better things. But what, we may ask, might these better things be? It may do for a revolutionary politician

[7 See *I Henry IV*, iii, i, 53.]

to say: 'I may not know what I want—except office—but I know what I don't want'; it will never do for a philosopher. Aversions and fears imply principles of preference, goods acknowledged; and it is the philosopher's business to make these goods explicit. Liberty is not an art, liberty must be used to bring some natural art to fruition. Shall it be simply eating and drinking and wondering what will happen next? If there is some deep and settled need in the heart of man, to give direction to his efforts, what else should a philosopher do but discover and announce what that need is?

There is a sense in which James was not a philosopher at all. He once said to me: 'What a curse philosophy would be if we couldn't forget all about it!' In other words, philosophy was not to him what it has been to so many, a consolation and sanctuary in a life which would have been unsatisfying without it. It would be incongruous, therefore, to expect of him that he should build a philosophy like an edifice to go and live in for good. Philosophy to him was rather like a maze in which he happened to find himself wandering, and what he was looking for was the way out. In the presence of theories of any sort he was attentive, puzzled, suspicious, with a certain inner prompting to disregard them. He lived all his life among them, as a child lives among grown-up people; what a relief to turn from those stolid giants, with their prohibitions and exactions and tiresome talk, to another real child or a nice animal! Of course grown-up people are useful, and so James considered that theories might be; but in themselves, to live with, they were rather in the way, and at bottom our natural enemies. It was well to challenge one or another of them when you got a chance; perhaps that challenge might break some spell, transform the strange landscape, and simplify life. A theory while you were creating or using it was like a story you were telling yourself or a game you were playing; it was a warm, self-justifying thing then; but when the glow of creation or expectation was over, a theory was a phantom, like a ghost, or like the minds of other people. To all other people, even to ghosts, William James was the soul of courtesy; and he was civil to most theories as well, as to more or less interesting strangers that invaded him. Nobody ever recognised more heartily the chance that others had of being right, and the right they had to be different. Yet when it came to understanding what they meant, whether they were theories or persons, his intuition outran his patience; he made some brilliant impressionistic sketch in his fancy and called it by their name. This sketch was as often flattered as distorted, and he was at times the dupe of his desire to be appreciative and give the devil his due; he was too impulsive for exact sympathy; too subjective, too romantic, to be just.

Love is very penetrating, but it penetrates to possibilities rather than to facts. The logic of opinions, as well as the exact opinions themselves, were not things James saw easily, or traced with pleasure. He liked to take things one by one, rather than to put two and two together. He was a mystic, a mystic in love with life. He was comparable to Rousseau and to Walt Whitman; he expressed a generous and tender sensibility, rebelling against sophistication, and preferring daily sights and sounds, and a vague but indomitable faith in fortune, to any settled intellectual tradition calling itself science or philosophy.

A prophet is not without honour save in his own country; [8] and until the return wave of James's reputation reached America from Europe, his pupils and friends were hardly aware that he was such a distinguished man. Everybody liked him, and delighted in him for his generous, gullible nature and brilliant sallies. He was a sort of Irishman among the Brahmins, and seemed hardly imposing enough for a great man. They laughed at his erratic views and his undisguised limitations. Of course a conscientious professor ought to know everything he professes to know, but then, they thought, a dignified professor ought to seem to know everything. The precise theologians and panoplied idealists, who exist even in America, shook their heads. What sound philosophy, said they to themselves, could be expected from an irresponsible doctor, who was not even a college graduate, a crude empiricist, and vivisector of frogs? On the other hand, the solid men of business were not entirely reassured concerning a teacher of youth who seemed to have no system in particular—the ignorant rather demand that the learned should have a system in store, to be applied at a pinch; and they could not quite swallow a private gentleman who dabbled in hypnotism, frequented mediums, didn't talk like a book, and didn't write like a book, except like one of his own. Even his pupils, attached as they invariably were to his person, felt some doubts about the profundity of one who was so very natural, and who after some interruption during a lecture—and he said life was a series of interruptions—would slap his forehead and ask the man in the front row 'What *was* I talking about?' Perhaps in the first years of his teaching he felt a little in the professor's chair as a military man might feel when obliged to read the prayers at a funeral. He probably conceived what he said more deeply than a more scholastic mind might have conceived it; yet he would have been more comfortable if some one else had said it for him. He liked to open the window, and look out for a moment. I think he was glad when the bell rang, and he could be himself

[8 Matthew, xiii, 57.]

again until the next day. But in the midst of this routine of the class-room the spirit would sometimes come upon him, and, leaning his head on his hand, he would let fall golden words, picturesque, fresh from the heart, full of the knowledge of good and evil. Incidentally there would crop up some humorous characterisation, some candid confession of doubt or of instinctive preference, some pungent scrap of learning; radicalisms plunging sometimes into the sub-soil of all human philosophies; and, on occasion, thoughts of simple wisdom and wistful piety, the most unfeigned and manly that anybody ever had.

Thomas Babington Macaulay
PLATO AND BACON

❰ Macaulay has not fared too well in the twentieth century. His Whiggism, his Protestantism, his enthusiasm about the social progress of Victorian England, his confidence in *laissez-faire* arrangements in society have given him a reputation, no doubt an exaggerated one, for complacency. Everybody knows the remark of a contemporary that he wished he were as sure of anything as Macaulay was of everything. This Olympian assurance is particularly distasteful to readers who have turned to other dogmas, other social systems, and other views of history than Macaulay's, including some that he thought wholly pernicious and others that he considered dead and buried.

Whatever may be thought of some of his ideas, there is no denying his power as a writer. He may oversimplify issues and overcolor scenes—what historian does not?—but he makes the issues live ones and the scenes brilliant and memorable. His long essay on Bacon (1837), from which this contrast between Plato and Bacon is taken, is a good example both of his magisterial manner and of the ideas he cherished.

. . . THE difference between the philosophy of Bacon and that of his predecessors cannot, we think, be better illustrated than by comparing his views on some important subjects with those of Plato. We select Plato, because we conceive that he did more than any other person towards giving to the minds of speculative men that bent which they retained till they received from Bacon a new impulse in a diametrically opposite direction.

It is curious to observe how differently these great men estimated the value of every kind of knowledge. Take Arithmetic for example. Plato, after speaking slightly of the convenience of being able to reckon and compute

FROM *The Edinburgh Review,* July 1837.

in the ordinary transactions of life, passes to what he considers as a far more important advantage. The study of the properties of numbers, he tells us, habituates the mind to the contemplation of pure truth, and raises it above the material universe. He would have his disciples apply themselves to this study,—not that they may be able to buy or sell,—not that they may qualify themselves to be shopkeepers or travelling merchants,—but that they may learn to withdraw their minds from the ever-shifting spectacle of this visible and tangible world, and to fix them on the immutable essence of things.*

Bacon on the other hand, valued this branch of knowledge only on account of its uses with reference to that visible and tangible world which Plato so much despised. He speaks with scorn of the mystical arithmetic of the later Platonists; and laments the propensity of mankind to employ, on mere matters of curiosity, powers, the whole exertion of which is required for purposes of solid advantage. He advises arithmeticians to leave these trifles, and to employ themselves in framing convenient expressions, which may be of use in physical researches.†

The same reasons which led Plato to recommend the study of arithmetic, led him to recommend also the study of mathematics. The vulgar crowd of geometricians, he says, will not understand him. They have practice always in view. They do not know that the real use of the science is to lead man to the knowledge of abstract, essential, eternal truth.‡ Indeed, if we are to believe Plutarch, Plato carried this feeling so far, that he considered geometry as degraded by being applied to any purpose of vulgar utility. Archytas,[1] it seems, had framed machines of extraordinary power, on mathematical principles.§ Plato remonstrated with his friend; and declared that this was to degrade a noble intellectual exercise into a low craft, fit only for carpenters and wheelwrights. The office of geometry, he said, was to discipline the mind, not to minister to the base wants of the body. His interference was successful; and from that time, according to Plutarch, the science of mechanics was considered as unworthy of the attention of a philosopher.

Archimedes in a later age imitated and surpassed Archytas. But even Archimedes was not free from the prevailing notion that geometry was degraded by being employed to produce any thing useful. It was with diffi-

* Plato's *Republic*, Book 7.
† *De Augmentis*, Lib. 3, Cap. 6.
‡ Plato's *Republic*, Book 7.
[1 He was credited with having invented the screw and the pulley.]
§ Plutarch, *Sympos.*, viii, and *Life of Marcellus*. The machines of Archytas are also mentioned by Aulus Gellius and Diogenes Laertius.

culty that he was induced to stoop from speculation to practice. He was half ashamed of those inventions [2] which were the wonder of hostile nations; and always spoke of them slightingly as mere amusements—as trifles in which a mathematician might be suffered to relax his mind after intense application to the higher parts of his science.

The opinion of Bacon on this subject was diametrically opposed to that of the ancient philosophers. He valued geometry chiefly, if not solely, on account of those uses which to Plato appeared so base. And it is remarkable that the longer he lived the stronger this feeling became. When, in 1605, he wrote the two books on the 'Advancement of Learning,' he dwelt on the advantages which mankind derived from mixed mathematics; but he at the same time admitted, that the beneficial effect produced by mathematical study on the intellect, though a collateral advantage, was 'no less worthy than that which was principal and intended.' But it is evident that his views underwent a change. When, nearly twenty years later, he published the *De Augmentis*, which is the treatise on the 'Advancement of Learning,' greatly expanded and carefully corrected, he made important alterations in the part which related to mathematics. He condemned with severity the high pretensions of the mathematicians,—'delicias et fastum mathematicorum.' Assuming the well-being of the human race to be the end of knowledge,[*] he pronounced that mathematical science could claim no higher rank than that of an appendage, or an auxiliary to other sciences. Mathematical science, he says, is the handmaid of natural philosophy—she ought to demean herself as such—and he declares that he cannot conceive by what ill chance it has happened that she presumes to claim precedence over her mistress. He predicts,—a prediction which would have made Plato shudder,—that as more and more discoveries are made in physics, there will be more and more branches of mixed mathematics. Of that collateral advantage, the value of which, twenty years before, he rated so highly, he says not one word. This omission cannot have been the effect of mere inadvertence. His own treatise was before him. From that treatise he deliberately expunged whatever was favorable to the study of pure mathematics, and inserted several keen reflections on the ardent votaries of that study. This fact in our opinion, admits of only one explanation. Bacon's love of those pursuits which directly tend to improve the condition of mankind, and his

[2 Among them the water-screw, military machines, and a planetarium. He founded the science of hydrostatics.]

* Usui et commodis hominum consulimus.[3]

[3 'We have considered the profit and interests of men.']

jealousy of all pursuits merely curious, had grown upon him, and had, it may be, become immoderate. He was afraid of using any expression which might have the effect of inducing any man of talents to employ in speculations, useful only to the mind of the speculator, a single hour which might be employed in extending the empire of man over matter.* If Bacon erred here, we must acknowledge that we greatly prefer his error to the opposite error of Plato.—We have no patience with a philosophy which, like those Roman matrons who swallowed abortives in order to preserve their shapes, takes pains to be barren for fear of being homely.

Let us pass to astronomy. This was one of the sciences which Plato exhorted his disciples to learn, but for reasons far removed from common habits of thinking. 'Shall we set down astronomy,' says Socrates, 'among the subjects of study?' † 'I think so,' answers his young friend Glaucon: 'to know something about the seasons, about the months and the years is of use for military purposes, as well as for agriculture and navigation.' 'It amuses me,' says Socrates, 'to see how afraid you are lest the common herd of people should accuse you of recommending useless studies.' He then proceeds in that pure and magnificent diction, which, as Cicero said Jupiter would use if Jupiter spoke Greek, to explain, that the use of astronomy is not to add to the vulgar comforts of life, but to assist in raising the mind to the contemplation of things which are to be perceived by the pure intellect alone. The knowledge of the actual motions of the heavenly bodies he considers as of little value. The appearances which make the sky beautiful at night are, he tells us, like the figures which a geometrician draws on the sand, mere examples, mere helps to feeble minds. We must get beyond them; we must neglect them; we must attain to an astronomy which is as independent of the actual stars as geometrical truth is independent of the lines of an ill-drawn diagram. This is, we imagine, very nearly, if not exactly, the astronomy which Bacon compared to the ox of Prometheus ‡—a sleek, well shaped hide, stuffed with rubbish, goodly to look at, but containing nothing to eat. He complained that astronomy had, to its great injury, been separated from natural philosophy, of which it was one of the noblest provinces, and annexed to the domain of mathematics. The world stood in need, he said, of a very different astronomy—of a *living astronomy,* § of an

---

* Compare the passage relating to mathematics in the Second Book of the Advancement of Learning with the *De Augmentis*, Lib. 3, Cap. 6.

† Plato's *Republic*, Book 7.

‡ *De Augmentis*, Lib. 3, Cap. 4.

§ Astronomia viva.

astronomy which should set * forth the nature, the motion, and the influences of the heavenly bodies, as they really are.

On the greatest and most useful of all inventions,—the invention of
alphabetical writing,—Plato did not look with much complacency. He
seems to have thought that the use of letters had operated on the human
mind as the use of the go-cart in learning to walk, or of corks in learning to
swim, is said to operate on the human body. It was a support which soon
became indispensable to those who used it,—which made vigorous exertion
first unnecessary, and then impossible. The powers of the intellect would,
he conceived, have been more fully developed without this delusive aid.
Men would have been compelled to exercise the understanding and the
memory; and, by deep and assiduous meditation, to make truth thoroughly
their own. Now, on the contrary, much knowledge is traced on paper, but
little is engraved in the soul. A man is certain that he can find information
at a moment's notice when he wants it. He therefore suffers it to fade from
his mind. Such a man cannot in strictness be said to know any thing. He
has the show without the reality of wisdom. These opinions Plato has put
into the mouth of an ancient King of Egypt.† But it is evident from the
context that they were his own; and so they were understood to be by
Quinctilian.‡ Indeed they are in perfect accordance with the whole Platonic
system.

Bacon's views, as may easily be supposed, were widely different.§ The
powers of the memory, he observes, without the help of writing, can do
little towards the advancement of any useful science. He acknowledges that
the memory may be disciplined to such a point as to be able to perform
very extraordinary feats. But on such feats he sets little value. The habits of
his mind, he tells us, are such that he is not disposed to rate highly any
accomplishment, however rare, which is of no practical use to mankind. As
to these prodigious achievements of the memory, he ranks them with the
exhibitions of rope-dancers and tumblers. 'The two performances,' he says,
'are of much the same sort. The one is an abuse of the powers of the body;
the other is an abuse of the powers of the mind. Both may perhaps excite
our wonder; but neither is entitled to our respect.'

To Plato, the science of medicine appeared one of very disputable advan-

* 'Quæ substantiam et motum et influxum cœlestium, prout re vera sunt proponat.'
Compare this language with Plato's, ' τὰ δ'ἐν τῷ οὐρανῷ ἐάσομεν.' [4]
[4 'Things in the heavens we shall leave out of consideration.']
† Plato's *Phædrus.*
‡ Quinctilian, xi.
§ *De Augmentis,* Lib. 5, Cap. 5.

tage.* He did not indeed object to quick cures for acute disorders, or for injuries produced by accidents. But the art which resists the slow sap of a chronic disease—which repairs frames enervated by lust, swollen by gluttony, or inflamed by wine—which encourages sensuality, by mitigating the natural punishment of the sensualist, and prolongs existence when the intellect has ceased to retain its entire energy—had no share of his esteem. A life protracted by medical skill he pronounced to be a long death. The exercise of the art of medicine ought, he said, to be tolerated so far as that art may serve to cure the occasional distempers of men whose constitutions are good. As to those who have bad constitutions, let them die;—and the sooner the better. Such men are unfit for war, for magistracy, for the management of their domestic affairs. That however is comparatively of little consequence. But they are incapable of study and speculation. If they engage in any severe mental exercise, they are troubled with giddiness and fulness of the head; all which they lay to the account of philosophy. The best thing that can happen to such wretches is to have done with life at once. He quotes mythical authority in support of this doctrine; and reminds his disciples that the practice of the sons of Æsculapius,[5] as described by Homer, extended only to the cure of external injuries.

Far different was the philosophy of Bacon. Of all the sciences, that which he seems to have regarded with the greatest interest was the science which, in Plato's opinion, would not be tolerated in a well regulated community. To make men perfect was no part of Bacon's plan. His humble aim was to make imperfect men comfortable. The beneficence of his philosophy resembled the beneficence of the common Father, whose sun rises on the evil and the good—whose rain descends for the just and the unjust. In Plato's opinion man was made for philosophy; in Bacon's opinion philosophy was made for man; it was a means to an end;—and that end was to increase the pleasures, and to mitigate the pains of millions who are not and cannot be philosophers. That a valetudinarian who took great pleasure in being wheeled along his terrace, who relished his boiled chicken and his weak wine and water, and who enjoyed a hearty laugh over the Queen of Navarre's tales,[6] should be treated as a *caput lupinum* [7] because he could not read the Timæus [8] without a headache, was a notion which the humane

---

* Plato's *Republic*, Book 3.

[5 God of medicine.]

[6 The *Heptameron*, love stories by Queen Margaret of Navarre (1492–1549).]

[7 Wolf's head. 'Let him be treated like a wolf's head' meant treated like an outlaw, killed on sight.]

[8 One of Plato's major works.]

spirit of the English school of wisdom altogether rejected. Bacon would not have thought it beneath the dignity of a philosopher to contrive an improved garden chair for such a valetudinarian,—to devise some way of rendering his medicines more palatable,—to invent repasts which he might enjoy, and pillows on which he might sleep soundly; and this though there might not be the smallest hope that the mind of the poor invalid would ever rise to the contemplation of the ideal beautiful and the ideal good. As Plato had cited the religious legends of Greece to justify his contempt for the more recondite parts of the art of healing, Bacon vindicated the dignity of that art by appealing to the example of Christ; and reminded his readers that the great physician of the soul did not disdain to be also the physician of the body.*

When we pass from the science of medicine to that of legislation, we find the same difference between the systems of these two great men. Plato, at the commencement of the fine Dialogue on Laws, lays it down as a fundamental principle, that the end of legislation is to make men virtuous. It is unnecessary to point out the extravagant conclusions to which such a proposition leads. Bacon well knew to how great an extent the happiness of every society must depend on the virtue of its members; and he also knew what legislators can, and what they cannot do for the purpose of promoting virtue. The view which he has given of the end of legislation and of the principal means for the attainment of that end, has always seemed to us eminently happy; even among the many happy passages of the same kind with which his works abound. 'Finis et scopus quem leges intueri atque ad quem jussiones et sanctiones suas dirigere debent, non alius est quam ut cives feliciter degant. Id fiet si pietate et religione recte instituti, moribus honesti, armis adversus hostes externos tuti, legum auxilio adversus seditiones et privatas injurias muniti, imperio et magistratibus obsequentes, copiis et opibus locupletes et florentes fuerint.' † The end is the well-being of the people. The means are the imparting of moral and religious education; the providing of every thing necessary for defence against foreign enemies; the maintaining of internal order; the establishing of a judicial, financial, and commercial system, under which wealth may be rapidly accumulated and securely enjoyed.

Even with respect to the form in which laws ought to be drawn, there is a remarkable difference of opinion between the Greek and the Englishman. Plato thought a preamble essential; Bacon thought it mischievous. Each

* *De Augmentis*, Lib. 4, Cap. 2.
† *De Augmentis*, Lib. 8, Cap. 3, Alph. 5 [translated by the rest of the paragraph].

was consistent with himself. Plato, considering the moral improvement of the people as the end of legislation, justly inferred that a law which commanded and threatened, but which neither convinced the reason nor touched the heart, must be a most imperfect law. He was not content with deterring from theft a man who still continued to be a thief at heart,—with restraining a son who hated his mother from beating his mother. The only obedience on which he set so much value, was the obedience which an enlightened understanding yields to reason, and which a virtuous disposition yields to precepts of virtue. He really seems to have believed that, by prefixing to every law an eloquent and pathetic exhortation, he should, to a great extent, render penal enactments superfluous. Bacon entertained no such romantic hopes; and he well knew the practical inconveniences of the course which Plato recommended. 'Neque nobis,' says he, 'prologi legum qui inepti olim habiti sunt et leges introducunt disputantes non jubentes utique placerent si priscos mores ferre possemus. . . Quantum fieri potest prologi evitentur et lex incipiat a jussione.' * 9

Had Plato lived to finish the 'Critias,' a comparison between that noble fiction and the 'New Atlantis,' would probably have furnished us with still more striking instances. It is amusing to think with what horror he would have seen such an institution as 'Solomon's House' 10 rising in his republic; with what vehemence he would have ordered the brewhouses, the perfume-houses, and the dispensatories to be pulled down; and with what inexorable rigor he would have driven beyond the frontier all the Fellows of the College, Merchants of light and Depredators, Lamps and Pioneers.

To sum up the whole: we should say that the aim of the Platonic philosophy was to exalt man into a god. The aim of the Baconian philosophy was to provide man with what he requires while he continues to be man. The aim of the Platonic philosophy was to raise us far above vulgar wants. The aim of the Baconian philosophy was to supply our vulgar wants. The former aim was noble; but the latter was attainable. Plato drew a good bow; but, like Acestes in Virgil,11 he aimed at the stars; and therefore, though there was no want of strength or skill, the shot was thrown away. His arrow was indeed followed by a track of dazzling radiance, but it struck nothing.

* *De Augmentis*, Lib. 8, Cap. 3, Alph. 69.

[9 'If we could hold to ancient customs, preambles of laws, anciently considered foolish and introducing laws by disputing and not by commanding, would certainly displease us. . . So far as possible, let preambles be avoided, and let the law begin by commanding.']

[10 A research institute in Bacon's *New Atlantis*.]

[11 *Aeneid*, v, 519–29.]

'Volens liquidis in nubibus arsit arundo
Signavitque viam flammis, tenuisque recessit
Consumpta in ventos.' [12]

Bacon fixed his eye on a mark which was placed on the earth and within bow-shot, and hit it in the white. The philosophy of Plato began in words and ended in words,—noble words indeed,—words such as were to be expected from the finest of human intellects exercising boundless dominion over the finest of human languages. The philosophy of Bacon began in observations and ended in arts.

The boast of the ancient philosophers was, that their doctrine formed the minds of men to a high degree of wisdom and virtue. This was indeed the only practical good which the most celebrated of those teachers even pretended to effect; and undoubtedly if they had effected this, they would have deserved the greatest praise. But the truth is, that in those very matters in which alone they professed to do any good to mankind, in those very matters for the sake of which they neglected all the vulgar interests of mankind, they did nothing, or worse than nothing. They promised what was impracticable; they despised what was practicable; they filled the world with long words and long beards; and they left it as wicked and as ignorant as they found it. . .

[12   Chafed by the speed, it fired; and, as it flew,
A train of following flames, ascending, drew:
Kindling they mount, and mark the shiny way,
Across the skies as falling meteors play,
And vanish into wind, or in a blaze decay (Dryden).]

Hans Zinsser

RATS AND MEN

❲ Hans Zinsser (1878–1940) was a bacteriologist who taught at Stanford, Columbia, and Harvard universities, wrote several text books on his specialty, and won many honors in the scientific world. To the public, however, he was known as the author of *Rats, Lice and History*, an uncommonly readable book, learned but unpedantic, about typhus and its effects on civilization. Written 'at odd moments as a relaxation from studies of typhus fever in the laboratory and in the field,' it is intended not only to tell the story of typhus but to be a 'protest against the American attitude which tends to insist that a specialist should have no interests beyond his chosen field.' Zinsser believed that 'one type of intelligent occupation should, in all but exceptional cases, increase the capacity for comprehension in general . . . that art and sciences have much in common and both may profit by mutual appraisal.' His book shows that he himself had both the scientific and the artistic temperament.

Iᴛ ɪs quite impossible to make a case for the presence of true rats in Europe proper during classical times, much as this would clarify the epidemiological situation. It is conceivable that the manner of transmission of plague and typhus may have undergone modification since the Peloponnesian Wars [1] by changed adaptations to hosts, both insect and rodent. But it would seem much more likely that the zoölogical differentiations between rodents so similar and closely related as mice and rats were inaccurate in ancient records, and that rats may have existed—though undomesticated. This would give us a wider latitude for speculation regarding the nature of epidemics, which, to be sure, were rarely, under the circumstances of ancient life, as widespread or deadly as they became with the

[1 Between Athens and Sparta, 431–404 B.C.]

later concentrations of population and of urban habits. At any rate, if rats had been present in those times in anything like the numbers in which they are found to-day, we should probably have reliable records. It may well be that the frugality of well-run households, like that of Penelope,[2] gave little encouragement to house rats to become parasitic on man to the extent to which they have since.

All this is conjecture. According to the wisest students of the subject, there is no certain knowledge of rats in Europe, within historic periods, until shortly after the Crusades. In prehistoric days they certainly existed there—but later disappeared. Fossil remains of rats have been found in the Pliocene period of Lombardy (the Mastodon period of Europe) and in the later Pleistocene of Crete. They were present during the glacial period with the lake dwellers, whom they pestered in Mecklenburg and Western Germany. From that time on, there were either few or no rats until thousands of years later.

In regard to the reappearance of rats in Europe, our industrious colleagues, the zoölogists, have gathered an immense amount of information, much of which has been interestingly summarized by Barrett-Hamilton and Hinton in their *History of British Mammals,* and by Donaldson in his *Memoir on the Rat.* Before we proceed to this subject, however, it will be profitable to consider the striking analogy between rats and men. More than any other species of animal, the rat and mouse have become dependent on man, and in so doing they have developed characteristics which are amazingly human.

In the first place, like man, the rat has become practically omnivorous. It eats anything that lets it and—like man—devours its own kind, under stress. It breeds at all seasons and—again like man—it is most amorous in the springtime.* It hybridizes easily and, judging by the strained relation-

[2 In Homer's *Odyssey.*]

* On first sight, the fertility of rats would seem far to outstrip that of man; for rats reach adolescence when a little more than half grown, and produce one or two litters a year, averaging from five to ten in number. The difference from man, however, is not so striking if one remembers Donaldson's calculation that one rat year equals thirty years for man, and makes the comparison with human society of former years—in savage communities, or before the humane and sane practice of birth control had begun to weaken the inhibitions of religion in such matters. Many examples not too unlike conditions among rats could be cited—such as, for instance, the story of Samuel Wesley, father of John, which we take from a review by J. C. Minot of Laver's biography of Wesley. Samuel had fourteen children with his good Sukey before 1701, when he left her because she refused to pray for William III as the lawful King of England. On the accession of Queen Anne, he was reconciled and bestowed five more children upon the fortunate woman. The oldest of these pledges of reconciliation was the immortal John Wesley.

ship between the black and the brown rat, develops social or racial prejudices against this practice. The sex proportions are like those among us. Inbreeding takes place readily. The males are larger, the females fatter. It adapts itself to all kinds of climates. It makes ferocious war upon its own kind, but has not, as yet, become nationalized. So far, it has still stuck to tribal wars—like man before nations were invented. If it continues to ape man as heretofore, we may, in a few centuries, have French rats eating German ones, or Nazi rats attacking Communist or Jewish rats; however, such a degree of civilization is probably not within the capacities of any mere animal. Also—like man—the rat is individualistic until it needs help. That is, it fights bravely alone against weaker rivals, for food or for love; but it knows how to organize armies and fight in hordes when necessary.

Donaldson, basing his calculations mainly on stages in the development of the nervous system, reckons three years of a rat life as ninety years for man. By this scale, the rat reaches puberty at about sixteen, and arrives at the menopause at the equivalent of forty-five. In following man about all over the earth, the rat has—more than any other living creature except man—been able to adapt itself to any conditions of seasonal changes or climate.

The first rat to arrive in Europe was *Mus rattus*—the black rat, house rat, or ship rat. It may have wandered in between 400 and 1100 A.D., with the hordes that swept into Europe from the East in that period of great unrest—the *Völkerwanderung*.[3] It may not have arrived until somewhat later, when the first Crusaders returned. It is not mentioned in the Epinal Glossary of 700 A.D., but may have been meant by the word 'raet' in the English Archbishop Ælfric's Vocabulary of 1000 A.D. But the authorities from whom we cite this call attention to the fact that the word 'rata' was the Provençal for the domestic mouse of that time, and the word may have been introduced into England.* Hamilton and Hinton say that the first clear differentiation between rats and mice is found in the writings of

[3 Migration of peoples.]

* Rats and mice belong to the same genus, and the closeness of the relationship is attested by the experiment of Ivanoff, who artificially inseminated a white mouse with the sperm of a white rat, and obtained two hybrids after a pregnancy of twenty-seven days. Mice may have developed out of rats under circumstances which made it less desirable to be large and ferocious than to be able to get into a smaller hole—the advantages of which may be appreciated by those of us who have lived in the world during the post-war years.

Giraldus Cambrensis (1147–1223). After that date, it is referred to frequently.

As to the Eastern origin of the black rat, there seems to be no difference of opinion among authorities, though there is much uncertainty about the exact part of the Orient from which it came. De L'Isle believes that the *Mus alexandrinus* represents the source stock of the European *Mus rattus*. This—the Alexandrine rat—did not, according to him, become parasitic on human society until the seventh century—living before this time a wild existence, possibly in the Arabian deserts, a fact which would account for its failure to migrate into classical Europe with trade, and, in the early Middle Ages, with Saracen invasions. By the time of the Crusaders, it had begun to domesticate and consequently to follow human travel. Being a climber and therefore a ship rat, it spread rapidly to Mediterranean ports, where, according to Hamilton and Hinton, its arrival by sea is witnessed to by the name πόντικος [4] applied to it by the modern Greeks; 'pantagena' by the Venetians. The Genoese mistook it for a mole, calling it 'Salpa,' another point of evidence that it may have been new to them.

From the time of its arrival, the rat spread across Europe with a speed superior even to that of the white man in the Americas. Before the end of the thirteenth century, it had become a pest. The legend of the *Rattenfänger von Hameln*,[5] who piped the children into the hollow Koppenberg because the town refused his pay for piping the rats into the Weser, is placed at or about 1284. By this time, the rat had penetrated into England. It had reached Ireland some time before this, where it was the 'foreign' or 'French' mouse, 'ean francach.' Our authorities tell us that in Ireland, even until very recent times, everything foreign was called 'francach,' or French. A little later, the rat was in Denmark, Norway, and the adjacent islands. By Shakespeare's time, the black rat was so formidable a nuisance that days of prayer for protection against its ravages were set aside, and rat catchers (see *Romeo and Juliet*, Act III) were important officials, probably calling themselves, as they would to-day, scientists or artists (or 'rattors' —*cf.* 'realtors' and 'morticians').

For twice as long as the Vandals had their day in North Africa, or the Saracens in Spain, or the Normans in Italy, the black rats had their own way in Europe. Their reign covered the periods of the devastating epidemics of plague that swept through the battle areas of the Thirty Years' War and the later ones of the seventeenth century. And during the centuries of its

[4 Of the sea.]
[5 The Pied Piper of Hamelin.]

supremacy there occurred the most destructive typhus epidemics, accompanying wars and famines, that have occurred up to our own time. Whether the black rats of mediæval Europe played a rôle in these remains uncertain. That they played the leading part in the plague epidemics of this time seems beyond question.

But just as the established civilizations of Northern Europe were swept aside by the mass invasions of barbarians from the East, so the established hegemony of the black rat was eventually wiped out with the incursion of the hordes of the brown rat, or *Mus decumanus*—the ferocious, short-nosed, and short-tailed Asiatic that swept across the Continent in the early eighteenth century; until at the present time, the slender-nosed, long-tailed, climbing *Mus rattus* has been all but exterminated in its former strongholds, and continues to thrive only in relatively small groups along the littoral, in seaports, on islands, or in countries like South American and other tropical regions where it is not confined to parasitic life in competition with its larger and more barbaric rival, or where the brown *conquistadores* have not yet arrived. It maintains its former superiority only on ships, where, because of its greater ability in climbing, it can still hold its own.*

The brown rat, too, came from the East. It is now known as the 'common' rat and, because of a mistaken notion of its origin, as *Mus norvegicus*. Its true origin, according to Hamilton and Hinton, is probably Chinese Mongolia or the region east of Lake Baikal, in both of which places forms resembling it have been found indigenous. The same writers quote Blasius, who believes that the ancients about the Caspian Sea may have known this rat. Claudius Ælianus, a Roman rhetorician of the second century, in his *De Animalium Natura*, speaks of 'little less than Ichneumons, making periodical raids in infinite numbers' in the countries along the Caspian, 'swimming over rivers holding each other's tails.' This may or may not be so; but it seems certain that this rat was not known in Western Europe until the eighteenth century.

Pallas (1831), in his *Zoögraphica Rosso-Asiatica*, records that in 1727 —a mouse year—great masses of these rats swam across the Volga after an earthquake. They invaded Astrakhan, and thence rapidly spread westward. They reached England, probably by ship, in 1728, and were unjustly called the 'Hanoverian rat' because of the unpopularity of the House of Hanover, though probably they had not arrived in Germany at that time. They were seen in Prussia in 1750, and were common by 1780. This rat

* In a recent rat survey of Boston, black rats were found in only a single small and circumscribed area, close to the docks.

was unknown to Buffon in 1753 and to Linnæus in 1758—but both of these gentlemen were already 'famous' scientists at this time, and most likely occupied in attending committee meetings. The brown rat arrived in Norway in 1762, a little later in Spain, and in Scotland about 1770. By 1775 it had come to America from England. It appears to have had a hard time only in countries where the population is what is spoken as of 'thrifty.' In Scotland, it took from 1776 to 1834 to get from Selkirk to Morayshire; it did not dare enter Switzerland until 1869, and has never done very well among the Switzers. It spread slowly across our continent, owing to deserts, rivers, and long distances between 'hand-outs.' Consequently, it did not arrive in California until shortly after 1851. Now that it is there, it thrives in that wonderful climate as hardly elsewhere. At the present time the rat has spread across the North American Continent from Panama to Alaska, has penetrated to all the less tropical parts of South America, to the South Sea Islands, to New Zealand, and to Australia. In fact, it has conquered the world. Only the extreme cold of Greenland does not seem to attract it. Unlike the Eskimo, it has had the good sense, whenever introduced to the arctic regions, to wander southward at the first opportunity.

Wherever it has gone, it has driven out the black rat and all rival rodents that compete with it. From the point of view of all other living creatures, the rat is an unmitigated nuisance and pest. There is nothing that can be said in its favor.* It can live anywhere and eat anything. It burrows for itself when it has to, but, when it can, it takes over the habitations of other animals, such as rabbits, and kills them and their young. It climbs and it swims.

It carries diseases of man and animals—plague, typhus, trichinella spiralis, rat-bite fever, infectious jaundice, possibly Trench fever, probably foot-and-mouth disease and a form of equine 'influenza.' Its destructiveness is

---

* Of course, rats might form a cheap source of food. They have been eaten without harm under stress—at the siege of Paris in 1871, and before that by the French garrison at Malta in 1798, where, according to Lantz, food was so scarce that a rat carcass brought a high price. The same writer states that Dr. Kane of the arctic ship *Advance* ate rats through the winter, and avoided scurvy—from which his more fastidious companions all suffered. For the following story we cannot vouch. It is related to us that a learned specialist on rodents was lecturing, some years ago, in one of the more distinguished university centres in the United States. After the lecture, he was taken to a restaurant famous for its terrapin. He enjoyed his meal and praised the quality of the *pièce de résistance*, but recognized the bones on his plate as those of rats. He is said later to have visited the albino rattery where the 'terrapin' was bred. The matter might be looked into as a commercial possibility. Robert Southey once suggested that the first requisite to successful rat eradication was to make them a table delicacy.

almost unlimited. Lantz, of the United States Department of Agriculture, has made some approximate estimates of this, as follows (we abbreviate) :—

Rats destroy cultivated grain as seeds, sprouts, or after ripening.

They eat Indian corn, both during growth and in the cribs, and have been known to get away with half of the crop. A single rat can eat from forty to fifty pounds a year.

They destroy merchandise, both stored and in transit, books, leather, harness, gloves, cloth, fruit, vegetables, peanuts, and so forth.

The rat is the greatest enemy of poultry, killing chicks, young turkeys, ducks, pigeons; also eating enormous numbers of eggs.

Rats destroy wild birds, ducks, woodcocks, and song birds.

They attack bulbs, seeds, and young plants or flowers.

They cause enormous damage to buildings, by gnawing wood, pipes, walls, and foundations.

Hagenbeck had to kill three elephants because the rats had gnawed their feet. Rats have killed young lambs and gnawed holes in the bellies of fat swine.

They have gnawed holes in dams and started floods; they have started fires by gnawing matches; they have bitten holes in mail sacks and eaten the mail; they have actually caused famines in India by wholesale crop destruction in scant years.

They have nibbled at the ears and noses of infants in their cribs; starving rats once devoured a man who entered a disused coal mine.

A rat census is obviously impossible. It is quite certain, however, that they breed more rapidly than they are destroyed in many places in the world. We can appraise the rat population only by the numbers that are killed in organized rat campaigns and by the amount of destruction they cause. In about 1860, Shipley tells us, there was a slaughterhouse for horses on Montfaucon, which it was planned to remove farther away from Paris. The carcasses of horses amounted to sometimes thirty-five a day, and were regularly cleaned up completely by rats in the following night. Dusaussois had the idea of trying to find out how many rats were engaged in this gruesome traffic. He set horse-meat bait in enclosures from which the exit of rats could be prevented, and in the course of the first night killed 2650. By the end of a month, he had killed over 16,000. Shipley estimates that there are about forty million rats in England at one time. In 1881 there was a rat plague in certain districts of India. The crops of the preceding two years were below average and a large part of them had been destroyed by rats. Rewards offered for rat destruction led to a killing of over 12,000,000 rats. Shipley estimates that a single rat does about 7s. 6d. worth of damage in a year, which makes a charge of £15,000,000 upon Great Britain and Ireland. It costs about sixty cents to two dollars a year to feed a rat on grain. Every rat on a farm costs about fifty cents a year. Lantz adds to this that hotel managers estimate five dollars a year as a low estimate of the loss inflicted by a rat. He thinks that in the thickly populated parts of the country an estimate of one rat per acre is not excessive, and that in most of our cities there are as many rats as people. He investigated, in 1909, the approximate total damage by rats in the cities of Washington and Baltimore. From the data he obtained, he calculated the annual damage in the two cities as amounting to $400,000 and $700,000 respectively—which, considering the populations, amounted to an average loss of $1.27 a year per person. On the same basis, the urban population of the United States, at that time 28,000,000 people, sustained an annual direct injury of $35,-000,000 a year. In Denmark, the estimated rat cost is about $1.20 a person; in Germany, eighty-five cents a person; in France, a little over a dollar. Add to this the inestimable depreciation of property and the costs of protection.

All this has nothing to do with our main subject, but we were started on rats, and it is just as well to give thought to the problem of what rat extermination for sanitary purposes is likely to mean in other respects.

The tremendous speed with which rats swarmed over the continents of the world can be readily understood if one reads the observations of actual rat migrations made in modern times. The seasonal migration of rats from buildings to the open fields takes place with the coming of the warm weather and the growth of vegetation; and a return to shelter follows with the cold weather. Dr. Lantz tells us that in 1903 hordes of rats migrated over several counties in Western Illinois, suddenly appearing when for several years no abnormal numbers had been seen. An eyewitness stated to Lantz that, as he was returning to his home on a moonlight night, he heard a rustling in a near-by field, and saw a great army of rats cross the road in front of him. The army of rats stretched away as far as he could see in the moonlight. This, to be sure, was before the Eighteenth Amendment,[6] but there must have been some fact behind it, since heavy damage was caused by rats in the entire surrounding country of farms and villages in the ensuing winter and summer. On one farm, in the month of April, about 3500 rats were caught in traps. Lantz himself saw a similar migration in the valley of the Kansas River, in 1904; and Lantz, being at that time an

[6 Prohibiting the manufacture and sale of alcoholic liquors.]

officer and gentleman of the United States Agricultural Service, cannot be under the suspicion that is aroused by accounts of armies of rats seen by moonshine. In England a general movement of rats inland from the coast occurs every October, and this migration is connected with the closing of the herring season. During the herring catch, rats swarm all over the coast, attracted by the food supply of herring cleaning; when it is over, they go back to their regular haunts. In South America, Lantz advises us, rat plagues are periodic in Paraná, in Brazil, and occur at intervals of about thirty years. In Chile, the same thing has been observed, at intervals of fifteen to twenty-five years. Studies of these migrations have shown that the rat plagues are associated with the ripening and decay of a dominant species of bamboo in each country. For a year or two, the ripening seed in the forests supplies a favorite food for the rats. They multiply enormously, and eventually, this food supply failing, they go back to the cultivated areas. A famine was caused in 1878 in the state of Paraná by the wholesale destruction of the corn, rice, and mandioca crops by rats. The invasion of Bermuda by rats in 1615, and their sudden disappearance, are as dramatic as the rise and fall of some of the short-lived Indian empires of Central and South America. Black rats appeared in that year, and within the two following ones increased with alarming rapidity. They devoured fruits, plants, and trees to such an extent that a famine resulted, and a law required every man in the islands to keep twelve traps set. Nothing, however, was of any use, until finally the rats disappeared with a suddenness that makes it almost necessary to assume that they died of a pestilence.

As we have indicated in a preceding paragraph, the natural history of the rat is tragically similar to that of man. Offspring of widely divergent evolutionary directions, men and rats reached present stages of physical development within a few hundred thousand years of each other—since remnants of both are found in the fossils of the glacial period.

Some of the more obvious qualities in which rats resemble men—ferocity, omnivorousness, and adaptability to all climates—have been mentioned above. We have also alluded to the irresponsible fecundity with which both species breed at all seasons of the year with a heedlessness of consequences which subjects them to wholesale disaster on the inevitable, occasional failure of the food supply. In this regard, it is only fair to state—in justice to man—that, as far as we can tell, the rat does this of its own free and stupid gluttony, while man has tradition, piety, and the duty of furnishing cannon fodder to contend with, in addition to his lower instincts. But these are, after all, phenomena of human biology, and man cannot be absolved of responsibility for his stupidities because they are the results of wrong-headedness rather than the consequences of pure instinct—certainly not if they result in identical disasters.

Neither rat nor man has achieved social, commercial, or economic stability. This has been, either perfectly or to some extent, achieved by ants and by bees, by some birds, and by some of the fishes in the sea. Man and the rat are merely, so far, the most successful animals of prey. They are utterly destructive of other forms of life. Neither of them is of the slightest earthly use to any other species of living things. Bacteria nourish plants; plants nourish man and beast. Insects, in their well-organized societies, are destructive of one form of living creature, but helpful to another. Most other animals are content to lead peaceful and adjusted lives, rejoicing in vigor, grateful for this gift of living, and doing the minimum of injury to obtain the things they require. Man and the rat are utterly destructive. All that nature offers is taken for their own purposes, plant or beast.

Gradually these two have spread across the earth, keeping pace with each other and unable to destroy each other, though continually hostile. They have wandered from East to West, driven by their physical needs, and—unlike any other species of living things—have made war upon their own kind. The gradual, relentless, progressive extermination of the black rat by the brown has no parallel in nature so close as that of the similar extermination of one race of man by another. Did the Danes conquer England; or the Normans the Saxon-Danes; or the Normans the Sicilian-Mohammedans; or the Moors the Latin-Iberians; or the Franks the Moors; or the Spanish the Aztecs and the Incas; or the Europeans in general the simple aborigines of the world by qualities other than those by which *Mus decumanus* has driven out *Mus rattus?* In both species, the battle has been pitilessly to the strong. And the strong have been pitiless. The physically weak have been driven before the strong—annihilated, or constrained to the slavery of doing without the bounties which were provided for all equally. Isolated colonies of black rats survive, as weaker nations survive until the stronger ones desire the little they still possess.

The rat has an excuse. As far as we know, it does not appear to have developed a soul, or that intangible quality of justice, mercy, and reason that psychic evolution has bestowed upon man. We must not expect too much. It takes a hundred thousand years to alter the protuberances on a bone, the direction of a muscle; much longer than this to develop a lung from a gill, or to atrophy a tail. It is only about twenty-five hundred years since Plato, Buddha, and Confucius; only two thousand years since Christ.

In the meantime, we have had Homer and Saint Francis, Copernicus and Galileo; Shakespeare, Pascal, Newton, Goethe, Bach, and Beethoven, and a great number of lesser men and women of genius who have demonstrated the evolutionary possibilities of the human spirit. If such minds have been rare, and spread thinly over three thousand years, after all, they still represent the sports that indicate the high possibilities of fortunate genetic combinations. And these must inevitably increase if the environment remains at all favorable. If no upward progress in spirit or intelligence seems apparent, let us say, between the best modern minds and that of Aristotle, we must remember that, in terms of evolutionary change, three thousand years are negligible. If, as in the last war and its subsequent imbecilities, mankind returns completely to the rat stage of civilization, this surely shows how very rudimentary an emergence from the Neanderthal our present civilization represents—how easily the thin, spiritual veneer is cracked under any strain that awakens the neolithic beast within. Nevertheless, for perhaps three or five thousand years, the beast has begun to ponder and grope. Isolated achievements have demonstrated of what the mind and spirit are capable when a happy combination of genes occurs under circumstances that permit the favored individual to mature. And the most incomprehensible but hopeful aspect of the matter is the fact that successive generations have always bred an adequate number of individuals sufficiently superior to the brutal mass to keep alive a reverence for these supreme achievements and make them a cumulative heritage. It is more than likely —biologically considered—that by reason of this progressive accumulation of the best that superior specimens of our species have produced, the evolution toward higher things may gain velocity with time, and that in another hundred thousand years the comparison of the race of men with that of rats may be less humiliatingly obvious.

Man and the rat will always be pitted against each other as implacable enemies. And the rat's most potent weapons against mankind have been its perpetual maintenance of the infectious agents of plague and of typhus fever.

Julian Huxley

THE UNIQUENESS OF MAN

❰ Julian Huxley (1887—), like his famous grandfather Thomas Henry Huxley, is both a professional biologist and a humanist, and like his grandfather, he has written on social as well as scientific problems. He taught biology at Oxford, the Rice Institute in Texas, and the University of London, and from 1935 to 1942 was Secretary of the Zoological Society of London. In 1947-8 he served as Director General of UNESCO.

His reflections on life and the condition of man are represented by *Essays of a Biologist* (1923) and *The Stream of Life* (1926), to mention only two of his earlier writings, and by half a dozen books published in the 1940's: *Man Stands Alone* (1941), *Evolution, the Modern Synthesis* (1942), *On Living in a Revolution* (1944), *TVA: Adventure in Planning* (1943), *Man in the Modern World* (1947), *Evolution and Ethics* (1947). 'The most vital task of the present age,' he believes, 'is to formulate a social basis for civilization, to dethrone economic ideals and replace them by human ones.' To this task biology can contribute by providing what Mr. Huxley considers the proper background of a new world-picture. 'Man as an organism, but a unique and very strange organism, human evolution as an integral part of life's evolution, but operating through novel and peculiar mechanisms—without this background our world-picture will be falsified, and our attempts at transforming our civilization will wholly or partly fail.'

Man's opinion of his own position in relation to the rest of the animals has swung pendulum-wise between too great or too little a conceit of himself, fixing now too large a gap between himself and the animals, now too small. The gap, of course, can be diminished or increased at either the animal or the human end. One can, like Descartes,[1] make animals too mechanical, or, like most unsophisticated people, humanize them too much. Or one can work at the human end of the gap, and then either de-humanize one's own kind into an animal species like any other, or super-humanize it into beings a little lower than the angels.[2]

Primitive and savage man, the world over, not only accepts his obvious kinship with the animals but also projects into them many of his own attributes. So far as we can judge, he has very little pride in his own humanity. With the advent of settled civilization, economic stratification, and the development of an elaborate religion as the ideological mortar of a now class-ridden society, the pendulum began slowly to swing into the other direction. Animal divinities and various physiological functions such as fertility gradually lost their sacred importance. Gods became anthropo-morphic and human psychological qualities pre-eminent. Man saw him-self as a being set apart, with the rest of the animal kingdom created to serve his needs and pleasure, with no share in salvation, no position in eter-nity. In Western civilization this swing of the pendulum reached its limit in developed Christian theology and in the philosophy of Descartes: both alike inserted a qualitative and unbridgeable barrier between all men and any animals.

With Darwin, the reverse swing was started. Man was once again re-garded as an animal, but now in the light of science rather than of un-sophisticated sensibility. At the outset, the consequences of the changed outlook were not fully explored. The unconscious prejudices and attitudes of an earlier age survived, disguising many of the moral and philosophical implications of the new outlook. But gradually the pendulum reached the furthest point of its swing. What seemed the logical consequences of the Darwinian postulates were faced: man is an animal like any other; accord-ingly, his views as to the special meaning of human life and human ideals need merit no more consideration in the light of eternity (or of evolution) than those of a bacillus or a tapeworm. Survival is the only criterion of evolutionary success: therefore, all existing organisms are of equal value. The idea of progress is a mere anthropomorphism. Man happens to be the dominant type at the moment, but he might be replaced by the ant or the rat. And so on.

The gap between man and animal was here reduced not by exaggerating

[1 French philosopher and mathematician (1596–1650). He considered animals mere automata.]

[2 Psalm viii, 5.]

the human qualities of animals, but by minimizing the human qualities of men. Of late years, however, a new tendency has become apparent. It may be that this is due mainly to the mere increase of knowledge and the extension of scientific analysis. It may be that it has been determined by social and psychological causes. Disillusionment with *laisser faire* [3] in the human economic sphere may well have spread to the planetary system of *laisser faire* that we call natural selection. With the crash of old religious, ethical, and political systems, man's desperate need for some scheme of values and ideals may have prompted a more critical re-examination of his biological position. Whether this be so is a point that I must leave to the social historians. The fact remains that the pendulum is again on the swing, the man-animal gap again broadening. After Darwin, man could no longer avoid considering himself as an animal; but he is beginning to see himself as a very peculiar and in many ways a unique animal. The analysis of man's biological uniqueness is as yet incomplete. This essay is an attempt to review its present position.

The first and most obviously unique characteristic of man is his capacity for conceptual thought; if you prefer objective terms, you will say his employment of true speech, but that is only another way of saying the same thing. True speech involves the use of verbal signs for objects, not merely for feelings. Plenty of animals can express the fact that they are hungry; but none except man can ask for an egg or a banana. And to have words for objects at once implies conceptual thought, since an object is always one of a class. No doubt, children and savages are as unaware of using conceptual thought as Monsieur Jourdain [4] was unaware of speaking in prose; but they cannot avoid it. Words are tools which automatically carve concepts out of experience. The faculty of recognizing objects as members of a class provides the potential basis for the concept: the use of words at once actualizes the potentiality.

This basic human property has had many consequences. The most important was the development of a cumulative tradition. The beginnings of tradition, by which experience is transmitted from one generation to the next, are to be seen in many higher animals. But in no case is the tradition cumulative. Offspring learn from parents, but they learn the same kind and quantity of lessons as they, in turn, impart: the transmission of experience never bridges more than one generation. In man, however, tradition is an independent and potentially permanent activity, capable of indefinite im-

[3 In economics, 'free enterprise,' i.e. freedom from governmental regulation.]
[4 In Molière's comedy, *Le Bourgeois Gentilhomme*.]

provement in quality and increase in quantity. It constitutes a new acces-
sory process of heredity in evolution, running side by side with the biological process, a heredity of experience to supplement the universal heredity
of living substance.

The existence of a cumulative tradition has as its chief consequence—
or if you prefer, its chief objective manifestation—the progressive improvement of human tools and machinery. Many animals employ tools; but they
are always crude tools employed in a crude way. Elaborate tools and skilled
technique can develop only with the aid of speech and tradition.

In the perspective of evolution, tradition and tools are the characters
which have given man his dominant position among organisms. This biological dominance is, at present, another of man's unique properties. In
each geological epoch of which we have knowledge, there have been types
which must be styled biologically dominant: they multiply, they extin-
guish or reduce competing types, they extend their range, they radiate into
new modes of life. Usually at any one time there is one such type—the
placental mammals, for instance, in the Cenozoic Epoch; but sometimes
there is more than one. The Mesozoic is usually called the Age of Reptiles,
but in reality the reptiles were then competing for dominance with the
insects: in earlier periods we should be hard put to it to decide whether
trilobites, nautiloids, or early fish were *the* dominant type. To-day, however, there is general agreement that man is the sole type meriting the title.
Since the early Pleistocene, widespread extinction has diminished the previously dominant group of placental mammals, and man has not merely
multiplied, but has evolved, extended his range, and increased the variety
of his modes of life.

Biology thus reinstates man in a position analogous to that conferred on
him as Lord of Creation by theology. There are, however, differences, and
differences of some importance for our general outlook. In the biological
view, the other animals have not been created to serve man's needs, but
man has evolved in such a way that he has been able to eliminate some
competing types, to enslave others by domestication, and to modify physical and biological conditions over the larger part of the earth's land area.
The theological view was not true in detail or in many of its implications;
but it had a solid biological basis.

Speech, tradition, and tools have led to many other unique properties of
man. These are, for the most part, obvious and well known, and I propose
to leave them aside until I have dealt with some less familiar human characteristics. For the human species, considered as a species, is unique in cer-

tain purely biological attributes; and these have not received the attention they deserve, either from the zoological or the sociological standpoint.

In the first place, man is by far the most variable wild species known. Domesticated species like dog, horse, or fowl may rival or exceed him in this particular, but their variability has obvious reasons, and is irrelevant to our inquiry.

In correlation with his wide variability, man has a far wider range than any other animal species, with the possible exception of some of his parasites. Man is also unique as a dominant type. All other dominant types have evolved into many hundreds or thousands of separate species, grouped in numerous genera, families, and larger classificatory groups. The human type has maintained its dominance without splitting: man's variety has been achieved within the limits of a single species.

Finally, man is unique among higher animals in the method of his evolution. Whereas, in general, animal evolution is divergent, human evolution is reticulate. By this is meant that in animals, evolution occurs by the isolation of groups which then become progressively more different in their genetic characteristics, so that the course of evolution can be represented as a divergent radiation of separate lines, some of which become extinct, others continue unbranched, and still others divergently branch again. Whereas in man, after incipient divergence, the branches have come together again, and have generated new diversity from their Mendelian recombinations,[5] this process being repeated until the course of human descent is like a network.

All these biological peculiarities are interconnected. They depend on man's migratory propensities, which themselves arise from his fundamental peculiarities, of speech, social life, and relative independence of environment. They depend again on his capacity, when choosing mates, for neglecting large differences of colour and appearance which would almost certainly be more than enough to deter more instinctive and less plastic animals. Thus divergence, though it appears to have gone quite a long way in early human evolution, generating the very distinct white, black, and yellow subspecies and perhaps others, was never permitted to attain its normal culmination. Mutually infertile groups were never produced; man remained a single species. Furthermore, crossing between distinct types, which is a rare and extraordinary phenomenon in other animals, in him

[5 Refers to laws of heredity formulated by the Austrian botanist G. J. Mendel (1822–84).]

became normal and of major importance. According to Mendelian laws, such crosses generate much excess variability by producing new recombinations. Man is thus more variable than other species for two reasons. First, because migration has recaptured for the single interbreeding group divergences of a magnitude that in animals would escape into the isolation of separate species; and secondly, because the resultant crossing has generated recombinations which both quantitatively and qualitatively are on a far bigger scale than is supplied by the internal variability of even the numerically most abundant animal species.

We may contrast this with the state of affairs among ants, the dominant insect group. The ant type is more varied than the human type; but it has achieved this variability by intense divergent evolution. Several thousand species of ants are known, and the number is being added to each year with the increase of biological exploration. Ways of life among ants are divided among different subtypes, each rigidly confined to its own methods. Thus even if ants were capable of accumulating experience, there could exist no single world-wide ant tradition. The fact that the human type comprises but one biological species is a consequence of his capacity for tradition, and also permits his exploitation of that unique capacity to the utmost.

Let us remind ourselves that superposed upon this purely biological or genetic variability is the even greater amount of variability due to differences of upbringing, profession, and personal tastes. The final result is a degree of variation that would be staggering if it were not so familiar. It would be fair to say that, in respect to mind and outlook, individual human beings are separated by differences as profound as those which distinguish the major groups of the animal kingdom. The difference between a somewhat subnormal member of a savage tribe and a Beethoven or a Newton is assuredly comparable in extent with that between a sponge and a higher mammal. Leaving aside such vertical differences, the lateral difference between the mind of, say, a distinguished general or engineer of extrovert type and of an introvert genius in mathematics or religious mysticism is no less than that between an insect and a vertebrate. This enormous range of individual variation in human minds often leads to misunderstanding and even mutual incomprehensibility; but it also provides the necessary basis for fruitful division of labour in human society.

Another biological peculiarity of man is the uniqueness of his evolutionary history. Writers have indulged their speculative fancy by imagining other organisms endowed with speech and conceptual thought—talking rats, rational ants, philosophic dogs, and the like. But closer analysis shows that these fantasies are impossible. A brain capable of conceptual thought could not have been developed elsewhere than in a human body.

The course followed by evolution appears to have been broadly as follows. From a generalized early type, various lines radiate out, exploiting the environment in various ways. Some of these comparatively soon reach a limit to their evolution, at least as regards major alteration. Thereafter they are limited to minor changes such as the formation of new genera and species. Others, on the other hand, are so constructed that they can continue their career, generating new types which are successful in the struggle for existence because of their greater control over the environment and their greater independence of it. Such changes are legitimately called 'progressive.' The new type repeats the process. It radiates out into a number of lines, each specializing in a particular direction. The great majority of these come up against dead ends and can advance no further: specialization is one-sided progress, and after a longer or shorter time, reaches a biomechanical limit. The horse stock cannot reduce its digits below one; the elephants are near the limits of size for terrestrial animals; feathered flight cannot become aerodynamically more efficient than in existing birds, and so on.

Sometimes all the branches of a given stock have come up against their limit, and then either have become extinct or have persisted without major change. This happened, for instance, to the echinoderms, which with their sea-urchins, starfish, brittle-stars, sea-lilies, sea-cucumbers, and other types now extinct had pushed the life that was in them into a series of blind alleys: they have not advanced for perhaps a hundred million years, nor have they given rise to other major types.

In other cases, all but one or two of the lines suffer this fate, while the rest repeat the process. All reptilian lines were blind alleys save two—one which was transformed into the birds, and another which became the mammals. Of the bird stock, all lines came to a dead end; of the mammals, all but one—the one which became man.

Evolution is thus seen as an enormous number of blind alleys, with a very occasional path of progress. It is like a maze in which almost all turnings are wrong turnings. The goal of the evolutionary maze, however, is not a central chamber, but a road which will lead indefinitely onwards.

If now we look back upon the past history of life, we shall see that the avenues of progress have been steadily reduced in number, until by the Pleistocene period, or even earlier, only one was left. Let us remember that we can and must judge early progress in the light of its latest steps. The most recent step has been the acquisition of conceptual thought, which has enabled man to dethrone the non-human mammals from their previous position of dominance. It is biologically obvious that conceptual thought could never have arisen save in an animal, so that all plants, both green and otherwise, are at once eliminated. As regards animals, I need not detail all the early steps in their progressive evolution. Since some degree of bulk helps to confer independence of the forces of nature, it is obvious that the combination of many cells to form a large individual was one necessary step, thus eliminating all single-celled forms from such progress. Similarly, progress is barred to specialized animals with no blood-system, like planarian worms; to internal parasites, like tapeworms; to animals with radial symmetry and consequently no head, like echinoderms.

Of the three highest animal groups—the molluscs, the arthropods, and the vertebrates—the molluscs advanced least far. One condition for the later steps in biological progress was land life. The demands made upon the organism by exposure to air and gravity called forth biological mechanisms, such as limbs, sense-organs, protective skin, and sheltered development, which were necessary foundations for later advance. And the molluscs have never been able to produce efficient terrestrial forms: their culmination is in marine types like squid and octopus.

The arthropods, on the other hand, have scored their greatest successes on land, with the spiders and especially the insects. Yet the fossil record reveals a lack of all advance, even in the most successful types such as ants, for a long time back—certainly during the last thirty million years, probably during the whole of the Tertiary epoch. Even during the shorter of these periods, the mammals were still evolving rapidly, and man's rise is contained in a fraction of this time.

What was it that cut the insects off from progress? The answer appears to lie in their breathing mechanism. The land arthropods have adopted the method of air-tubes or tracheae, branching to microscopic size and conveying gases directly to and from the tissues, instead of using the dual mechanism of lungs and bloodstream. The laws of gaseous diffusion are such that respiration by tracheae is extremely efficient for very small animals, but becomes rapidly less efficient with increase of size, until it ceases to be of use at a bulk below that of a house mouse. It is for this reason that no insect has ever become, by vertebrate standards, even moderately large.

It is for the same reason that no insect has ever become even moderately intelligent. The fixed pathways of instinct, however elaborate, require far fewer nerve-cells than the multiple switchboards that underlie intelligence. It appears to be impossible to build a brain mechanism for flexible behaviour with less than a quite large minimum of neurones; and no insect has reached a size to provide this minimum.

Thus only the land vertebrates are left. The reptiles shared biological dominance with the insects in the Mesozoic. But while the insects had reached the end of their blind alley, the reptiles showed themselves capable of further advance. Temperature regulation is a necessary basis for final progress, since without it the rate of bodily function could never be stabilized, and without such stabilization, higher mental processes could never become accurate and dependable.

Two reptilian lines achieved this next step, in the guise of the birds and the mammals. The birds soon, however, came to a dead end, chiefly because their forelimbs were entirely taken up in the specialization for flight. The subhuman mammals made another fundamental advance, in the shape of internal development, permitting the young animal to arrive at a much more advanced stage before it was called upon to face the world. They also (like the birds) developed true family life.

Most mammalian lines, however, cut themselves off from indefinite progress by one-sided evolution, turning their limbs and jaws into specialized and therefore limited instruments. And, for the most part, they relied mainly on the crude sense of smell, which cannot present as differentiated a pattern of detailed knowledge as can sight. Finally, the majority continued to produce their young several at a time, in litters. As J. B. S. Haldane has pointed out, this gives rise to an acute struggle for existence in the prenatal period, a considerable percentage of embryos being aborted or resorbed. Such intra-uterine selection will put a premium upon rapidity of growth and differentiation, since the devil takes the hindmost; and this rapidity of development will tend automatically to be carried on into postnatal growth.

As everyone knows, man is characterized by a rate of development which is abnormally slow as compared with that of any other mammal. The period from birth to the first onset of sexual maturity comprises nearly a quarter of the normal span of his life, instead of an eighth, a tenth or twelfth, as in some other animals. This again is in one sense a unique characteristic of man, although from the evolutionary point of view it represents merely the exaggeration of a tendency which is operative in other Primates. In any case, it is a necessary condition for the evolution and proper utilization of rational thought. If men and women were, like mice, confronted with the problems of adult life and parenthood after a few weeks, or even, like whales, after a couple of years, they could never acquire the skills of body and mind that they now absorb from and contribute to the social heritage of the species.

This slowing (or 'foetalization,' as Bolk has called it, since it prolongs the foetal characteristics of earlier ancestral forms into postnatal development and even into adult life) has had other important by-products for man. Here I will mention but one—his nakedness. The distribution of hair on man is extremely similar to that on a late foetus of a chimpanzee, and there can be little doubt that it represents an extension of this temporary anthropoid phase into permanence. Hairlessness of body is not a unique biological characteristic of man; but it is unique among terrestrial mammals, save for a few desert creatures, and some others which have compensated for loss of hair by developing a pachydermatous skin. In any case, it has important biological consequences, since it must have encouraged the comparatively defenceless human creatures in their efforts to protect themselves against animal enemies and the elements, and so has been a spur to the improvement of intelligence.

Now, foetalization could never have occurred in a mammal producing many young at a time, since intra-uterine competition would have encouraged the opposing tendency. Thus we may conclude that conceptual thought could develop only in a mammalian stock which normally brings forth but one young at a birth. Such a stock is provided in the Primates—lemurs, monkeys, and apes.

The Primates also have another characteristic which was necessary for the ancestor of a rational animal—they are arboreal. It may seem curious that living in trees is a pre-requisite of conceptual thought. But Elliot Smith's analysis has abundantly shown that only in an arboreal mammal could the forelimb become a true hand, and sight become dominant over smell. Hands obtain an elaborate tactile pattern of what they handle, eyes an elaborate visual pattern of what they see. The combination of the two kinds of pattern, with the aid of binocular vision, in the higher centres of the brain allowed the Primate to acquire a wholly new richness of knowledge about objects, a wholly new possibility of manipulating them. Tree life laid the foundation both for the fuller definition of objects by conceptual thought and for the fuller control of them by tools and machines.

Higher Primates have yet another pre-requisite of human intelligence—they are all gregarious. Speech, it is obvious, could never have been evolved in a solitary type. And speech is as much the physical basis of conceptual thought as is protoplasm the physical basis of life.

For the passage, however, of the critical point between subhuman and human, between the biological subordination and the biological primacy of intelligence, between a limited and a potentially unlimited tradition— for this it was necessary for the arboreal animal to descend to the ground again. Only in a terrestrial creature could fully erect posture be acquired; and this was essential for the final conversion of the arms from locomotor limbs into manipulative hands. Furthermore, just as land life, ages previously, had demanded and developed a greater variety of response than had been required in the water, so now it did the same in relation to what had been required in the trees. An arboreal animal could never have evolved the skill of the hunting savage, nor ever have proceeded to the domestication of other animals or to agriculture.

We are now in a position to define the uniqueness of human evolution. The essential character of man as a dominant organism is conceptual thought. And conceptual thought could have arisen only in a multicellular animal, an animal with bilateral symmetry, head and blood system, a vertebrate as against a mollusc or an arthropod, a land vertebrate among vertebrates, a mammal among land vertebrates. Finally, it could have arisen only in a mammalian line which was gregarious, which produced one young at a birth instead of several, and which had recently become terrestrial after a long period of arboreal life.

There is only one group of animals which fulfils these conditions—a terrestrial offshoot of the higher Primates. Thus not merely has conceptual thought been evolved only in man: it could not have been evolved except in man. There is but one path of unlimited progress through the evolutionary maze. The course of human evolution is as unique as its result. It is unique not in the trivial sense of being a different course from that of any other organism, but in the profounder sense of being the only path that could have achieved the essential characters of man. Conceptual thought on this planet is inevitably associated with a particular type of Primate body and Primate brain.

A further property of man in which he is unique among higher animals concerns his sexual life. Man is prepared to mate at any time: animals are not. To start with, most animals have a definite breeding season; only during this period are their reproductive organs fully developed and functional. In addition to this, higher animals have one or more sexual cycles within their breeding seasons, and only at one phase of the cycle are they prepared to mate. In general, either a sexual season or a sexual cycle, or both, operates to restrict mating.

In man, however, neither of these factors is at work. There appear to be indications of a breeding season in some primitive peoples like the Eskimo, but even there they are but relics. Similarly, while there still exist physiological differences in sexual desire at different phases of the female sexual cycle, these are purely quantitative, and may readily be overridden by psychological factors. Man, to put it briefly, is continuously sexed: animals are discontinuously sexed. If we try to imagine what a human society would be like in which the sexes were interested in each other only during the summer, as in songbirds, or, as in female dogs, experienced sexual desire only once every few months, or even only once in a lifetime, as in ants, we can realize what this peculiarity has meant. In this, as in his slow growth and prolonged period of dependence, man is not abruptly marked off from all other animals, but represents the culmination of a process that can be clearly traced among other Primates. What the biological meaning of this evolutionary trend may be is difficult to understand. One suggestion is that it may be associated with the rise of mind to dominance. The bodily functions, in lower mammals rigidly determined by physiological mechanisms, come gradually under the more plastic control of the brain. But this, for what it is worth, is a mere speculation.

Another of the purely biological characters in which man is unique is his reproductive variability. In a given species of animals, the maximum litter-size may, on occasions, reach perhaps double the minimum, according to circumstances of food and temperature, or even perhaps threefold. But during a period of years, these variations will be largely equalized within a range of perhaps fifty percent either way from the average, and the percentage of wholly infertile adults is very low. In man, on the other hand, the range of positive fertility is enormous—from one to over a dozen, and in exceptional cases to over twenty; and the number of wholly infertile adults is considerable. This fact, in addition to providing a great diversity of patterns of family life, has important bearings on evolution. It means that in the human species differential fertility is more important as a basis for selection than is differential mortality; and it provides the possibility of much more rapid selective change than that found in wild animal species. Such rapidity of evolution would, of course, be effectively realized only if the stocks with large families possessed a markedly different hereditary constitution from those with few children; but the high differential fertility of unskilled workers as against the professional classes in England, or of the French Canadians against the rest of the inhabitants of Canada, demonstrates how rapidly populations may change by this means.

Still another point in which man is biologically unique is the length and relative importance of his period of what we may call 'post-maturity.' If we consider the female sex, in which the transition from reproductive maturity to non-reproductive post-maturity is more sharply defined than in the male, we find, in the first place, that in animals a comparatively small percentage of the population survives beyond the period of reproduction; in the second place, that such individuals rarely survive long, and so far as known never for a period equal to or greater than the period during which reproduction was possible; and thirdly, that such individuals are rarely of importance in the life of the species. The same is true of the male sex, provided we do not take the incapacity to produce fertile gametes as the criterion of post-maturity, but rather the appearance of signs of age, such as the beginnings of loss of vigour and weight, decreased sexual activity, or greying hair.

It is true that in some social mammals, notably among ruminants and Primates, an old male or old female is frequently found as leader of the herd. Such cases, however, provide the only examples of the special biological utility of post-mature individuals among animals; they are confined to a very small proportion of the population, and it is uncertain to what extent such individuals are post-mature in the sense we have defined. In any event, it is improbable that the period of post-maturity is anywhere near so long as that of maturity. But in civilized man the average expectation of life now includes over ten post-mature years, and about a sixth of the population enjoys a longer post-maturity than maturity. What is more, in all advanced human societies a large proportion of the leaders of the community are always post-mature. All the members of the British War Cabinet are post-mature.

This is truly a remarkable phenomenon. Through the new social mechanisms made possible by speech and tradition, man has been able to utilize for the benefit of the species a period of life which in almost all other creatures is a mere superfluity. We know that the dominance of the old can be over-emphasized; but it is equally obvious that society cannot do without the post-mature. To act on the slogan 'Too old at forty'—or even at forty-five—would be to rob man of one of his unique characteristics, whereby he utilizes tradition to the best advantage.

We have now dealt in a broad way with the unique properties of man both from the comparative and the evolutionary point of view. Now we can return to the present and the particular and discuss these properties and their consequences a little more in detail. First, let us remind ourselves that the gap between human and animal thought is much greater than is usually supposed. The tendency to project familiar human qualities into animals is very strong, and colours the ideas of nearly all people who have not special familiarity both with animal behaviour and scientific method.

Let us recall a few cases illustrating the unhuman characteristics of animal behaviour. Everyone is familiar with the rigidity of instinct in insects. Worker ants emerge from their pupal case equipped not with the instincts to care for ant grubs in general, but solely with those suitable to ant grubs of their own species. They will attempt to care for the grubs of other species, but appear incapable of learning new methods if their instincts kill their foster children. Or again, a worker wasp, without food for a hungry grub, has been known to bite off its charge's tail and present it to its head. But even in the fine flowers of vertebrate evolution, the birds and mammals, behaviour, though it may be more plastic than in the insects, is as essentially irrational. Birds, for instance, seem incapable of analysing unfamiliar situations. For them some element in the situation may act as its dominant symbol, the only stimulus to which they can react. At other times, it is the organization of the situation as a whole which is the stimulus: if the whole is interfered with, analysis fails to dissect out the essential element. A hen meadow-pipit feeds her young when it gapes and squeaks in the nest. But if it has been ejected by a young cuckoo, gaping and squeaking has no effect, and the rightful offsping is neglected and allowed to die, while the usurper in the nest is fed. The pipit normally cares for its own young, but not because it recognizes them as such.

Mammals are no better. A cow deprived of its calf will be quieted by the provision of a crudely stuffed calfskin. Even the Primates are no exception. Female baboons whose offspring have died will continue carrying the corpses until they have not merely putrefied but mummified. This appears to be due not to any profundity of grief, but to a contact stimulus: the mother will react similarly to any moderately small and furry object.

Birds and especially mammals are, of course, capable of a certain degree of analysis, but this is effected, in the main, by means of trial and error through concrete experience. A brain capable of conceptual thought appears to be the necessary basis for speedy and habitual analysis. Without it, the practice of splitting up situations into their components and assigning real degrees of significance to the various elements remains rudimentary and rare, whereas with man, even when habit and trial and error are prevalent, conceptual thought is of major biological importance. The behaviour of animals is essentially arbitrary, in that it is fixed within narrow limits. In man it has become relatively free—free at the incoming and the outgoing ends alike. His capacity for acquiring knowledge has been largely released from arbitrary symbolism, his capacity for action, from arbitrary canalizations of instinct. He can thus rearrange the patterns of experience and action in a far greater variety, and can escape from the particular into the general.

Thus man is more intelligent than the animals because his brain mechanism is more plastic. This fact also gives him, of course, the opportunity of being more nonsensical and perverse: but its primary effects have been more analytical knowledge and more varied control. The essential fact, from my present standpoint, is that the change has been profound and in an evolutionary sense rapid. Although it has been brought about by the gradual quantitative enlargement of the association areas of the brain, the result has been almost as abrupt as the change (also brought about quantitatively) from solid ice to liquid water. We should remember that the machinery of the change has been an increase in plasticity and potential variety: it is by a natural selection of ideas and actions that the result has been greater rationality instead of greater irrationality.

This increase of flexibility has also had other psychological consequences which rational philosophers are apt to forget: and in some of these, too, man is unique. It has led, for instance, to the fact that man is the only organism normally and inevitably subject to psychological conflict. You can give a dog neurosis, as Pavlov did, by a complicated laboratory experiment: you can find cases of brief emotional conflict in the lives of wild birds and animals. But, for the most part, psychological conflict is shirked by the simple expedient of arranging that now one and now another instinct should dominate the animal's behaviour. I remember in Spitsbergen finding the nest of a Red-throated Diver on the shore of an inland pool. The sitting bird was remarkably bold. After leaving the nest for the water, she stayed very close. She did not, however, remain in a state of conflict between fear of intruders and desire to return to her brooding. She would gradually approach as if to land, but eventually fear became dominant, and when a few feet from the shore she suddenly dived, and emerged a good way farther out—only to repeat the process. Here the external circumstances were such as to encourage conflict, but even so what are the most serious features of human conflict were minimized by the outlet of alternate action.

Those who take up bird-watching as a hobby tend at first to be surprised at the way in which a bird will turn, apparently without transition or hesitation, from one activity to another—from fighting to peaceable feeding, from courtship to uninterested preening, from panic flight to unconcern.

However, all experienced naturalists or those habitually concerned with animals recognize such behaviour as characteristic of the subhuman level. It represents another aspect of the type of behaviour I have just been describing for the Red-throated Diver. In this case, the internal state of the bird changes, presumably owing to some form of physiological fatigue or to a diminution of intensity of a stimulus with time or distance; the type of behaviour which had been dominant ceases to have command over the machinery of action, and is replaced by another which just before had been subordinate and latent.

As a matter of fact, the prevention of conflict between opposed modes of action is a very general phenomenon, of obvious biological utility, and it is only the peculiarities of the human mind which have forced its partial abandonment on man. It begins on the purely mechanical level with the nervous machinery controlling our muscles. The main muscles of a limb, for instance, are arranged in two antagonistic sets, the flexors bending and the extensors straightening it. It would obviously be futile to throw both sets into action at the same time, and economical when one set is in action to reduce to the minimum any resistance offered by the other. This has actually been provided for. The nervous connections in the spinal cord are so arranged that when a given muscle receives an impulse to contract, its antagonist receives an impulse causing it to lose some of its tone and thus, by relaxing below its normal level, to offer the least possible resistance to the action of the active muscle.

Sherrington discovered that the same type of mechanism was operative in regard to the groups of muscles involved in whole reflexes. A dog, for instance, cannot very well walk and scratch itself at the same time. To avoid the waste involved in conflict between the walking and the scratching reflex, the spinal cord is constructed in such a way that throwing one reflex into action automatically inhibits the other. In both these cases, the machinery for preventing conflicts of activity resides in the spinal cord. Although the matter has not yet been analysed physiologically, it would appear that the normal lack of conflict between instincts which we have just been discussing is due to some similar type of nervous mechanism in the brain.

When we reach the human level, there are new complications; for, as we have seen, one of the peculiarities of man is the abandonment of any rigidity of instinct, and the provision of association-mechanisms by which any activity of the mind, whether in the spheres of knowing, feeling, or willing, can be brought into relation with any other. It is through this that man has acquired the possibility of a unified mental life. But, by the same token, the door is opened to the forces of disruption, which may destroy any such unity and even prevent him from enjoying the efficiency of behaviour attained by animals. For, as Sherrington has emphasized, the nervous system is like a funnel, with a much larger space for intake than for outflow. The intake cone of the funnel is represented by the receptor nerves, conveying impulses inward to the central nervous system from the sense-organs: the outflow tube is, then, through the effector nerves, conveying impulses outwards to the muscles, and there are many more of the former than of the latter. If we like to look at the matter from a rather different standpoint, we may say that, since action can be effected only by muscles (strictly speaking, also by the glands, which are disregarded here for simplicity's sake), and since there are a limited number of muscles in the body, the only way for useful activity to be carried out is for the nervous system to impose a particular pattern of action on them, and for all other competing or opposing patterns to be cut out. Each pattern, when it has seized control of the machinery of action, *should* be in supreme command, like the captain of a ship. Animals are, in many ways, like ships which are commanded by a number of captains in turn, each specializing in one kind of action, and popping up and down between the authority of the bridge and the obscurity of their private cabins according to the business on hand. Man is on the way to achieving permanent unity of command, but the captain has a disconcerting way of dissolving into a wrangling committee.

Even on the new basis, however, mechanisms exist for minimizing conflict. They are what are known by psychologists as suppression and repression. From our point of view, repression is the more interesting. It implies the forcible imprisonment of one of two conflicting impulses in the dungeons of the unconscious mind. The metaphor is, however, imperfect. For the prisoner in the mental dungeon can continue to influence the tyrant above in the daylight of consciousness. In addition to a general neurosis, compulsive thoughts and acts may be thrust upon the personality. Repression may thus be harmful; but it can also be regarded as a biological necessity for dealing with inevitable conflict in the early years of life, before rational judgment and control are possible. Better to have the capacity for more or less unimpeded action, even at the expense of possible neurosis, than an organism constantly inactivated like the ass between the two bundles of hay, balanced in irresolution.[6]

In repression, not only is the defeated impulse banished to the uncon-

[6 See pp. 281, 505–6.]

scious, but the very process of banishment is itself unconscious. The inhibitory mechanisms concerned in it must have been evolved to counteract the more obvious possibilities of conflict, especially in early life, which arose as by-products of the human type of mind.

In suppression, the banishment is conscious, so that neurosis is not likely to appear. Finally, in rational judgment, neither of the conflicting impulses is relegated to the unconscious, but they are balanced in the light of reason and experience, and control of action is consciously exercised.

I need not pursue the subject further. Here I am only concerned to show that the great biological advantages conferred on man by the unification of mind have inevitably brought with them certain counterbalancing defects. The freedom of association between all aspects and processes of the mind has provided the basis for conceptual thought and tradition; but it has also provided potential antagonists, which in lower organisms were carefully kept apart, with the opportunity of meeting face to face, and has thus made some degree of conflict unavoidable.

In rather similar fashion, man's upright posture has brought with it certain consequential disadvantages in regard to the functioning of his internal organs and his proneness to rupture. Thus man's unique characteristics are by no means wholly beneficial.

In close correlation with our subjection to conflict is our proneness to laughter. So characteristic of our species is laughter that man has been defined as the laughing animal. It is true that, like so much else of man's uniqueness, it has its roots among the animals, where it reveals itself as an expression of a certain kind of general pleasure—and thus in truth perhaps more of a smile than a laugh. And in a few animals—ravens, for example,— there are traces of a malicious sense of humour. Laughter in man, however, is much more than this. There are many theories of laughter, many of them containing a partial truth. But biologically the important feature of human laughter seems to lie in its providing a release for conflict, a resolution of troublesome situations.

This and other functions of laughter can be exaggerated so that it becomes as the crackling of thorns under the pot, and prevents men from taking anything seriously; but in due proportion its value is very great as a lubricant against troublesome friction and a lightener of the inevitable gravity and horror of life, which would otherwise become portentous and overshadowing. True laughter, like true speech, is a unique possession of man.

Those of man's unique characteristics which may better be called psychological and social than narrowly biological spring from one or other of three characteristics. The first is his capacity for abstract and general thought: the second is the relative unification of his mental processes, as against the much more rigid compartmentalization of animal mind and behaviour: the third is the existence of social units, such as tribe, nation, party, and church, with a continuity of their own, based on organized tradition and culture.

There are various by-products of the change from pre-human to the human type of mind which are, of course, also unique biologically. Let us enumerate a few: pure mathematics; musical gifts; artistic appreciation and creation; religion; romantic love.

Mathematical ability appears, almost inevitably, as something mysterious. Yet the attainment of speech, abstraction, and logical thought, bring it into potential being. It may remain in a very rudimentary state of development; but even the simplest arithmetical calculations are a manifestation of its existence. Like any other human activity, it requires proper tools and machinery. Arabic numerals, algebraic conventions, logarithms, the differential calculus, are such tools: each one unlocks new possibilities of mathematical achievement. But just as there is no essential difference between man's conscious use of a chipped flint as an implement and his design of the most elaborate machine, so there is none between such simple operations as numeration or addition and the comprehensive flights of higher mathematics. Again, some people are by nature more gifted than others in this field; yet no normal human being is unable to perform some mathematical operations. Thus the capacity for mathematics is, as I have said, a by-product of the human type of mind.

We have seen, however, that the human type of mind is distinguished by two somewhat opposed attributes. One is the capacity for abstraction, the other for synthesis. Mathematics is one of the extreme by-products of our capacity for abstraction. Arithmetic abstracts objects of all qualities save their enumerability; the symbol π abstracts in a single Greek letter a complicated relation between the parts of all circles. Art, on the other hand, is an extreme by-product of our capacity for synthesis. In one unique production, the painter can bring together form, colour, arrangement, associations of memory, emotion, and idea. Dim adumbrations of art are to be found in a few creatures such as bower-birds; but nothing is found to which the word can rightly be applied until man's mind gave the possibility of freely mingling observations, emotions, memories, and ideas, and subjecting the mixture to deliberate control.

But it is not enough here to enumerate a few special activities. In point of fact, the great majority of man's activities and characteristics are by-products of his primary distinctive characteristics, and therefore, like them, biologically unique.

On the one hand, conversation, organized games, education, sport, paid work, gardening, the theatre; on the other, conscience, duty, sin, humiliation, vice, penitence—these are all such unique by-products. The trouble, indeed, is to find any human activities which are not unique. Even the fundamental biological attributes such as eating, sleeping, and mating have been tricked out by man with all kinds of unique frills and peculiarities.

There may be other by-products of man's basic uniqueness which have not yet been exploited. For let us remember that such by-products may remain almost wholly latent until demand stimulates invention and invention facilitates development. It is asserted that there exist human tribes who cannot count above two; certainly some savages stop at ten. Here the mathematical faculty is restricted to numeration, and stops short at a very rudimentary stage of this rudimentary process. Similarly, there are human societies in which art has never been developed beyond the stage of personal decoration. It is probable that during the first half of the Pleistocene period, none of the human race had developed either their mathematical or their artistic potentialities beyond such a rudimentary stage.

It is perfectly possible that to-day man's so-called super-normal or extra-sensory faculties are in the same case as were his mathematical faculties during the first or second glaciations of the Ice Age—barely more than a potentiality, with no technique for eliciting and developing them, no tradition behind them to give them continuity and intellectual respectability. Even such simple performances as multiplying two three-figure numbers would have appeared entirely magical to early Stone Age men.

Experiments such as those of Rhine and Tyrrell on extra-sensory guessing, experiences like those of Gilbert Murray on thought transference, and the numerous sporadic records of telepathy and clairvoyance suggest that some people at least possess possibilities of knowledge which are not confined within the ordinary channels of sense-perception. Tyrrell's work is particularly interesting in this connection. As a result of an enormous number of trials with apparatus ingeniously designed to exclude all alternative explanation, he finds that those best endowed with this extra-sensory gift can guess right about once in four times when once in five would be expected on chance alone. The results are definite, and significant in the statistical sense, yet the faculty is rudimentary: it does not permit its possessor to guess right all the time or even most of the time—merely to achieve a small rise in the percentage of right guessing. If, however, we could discover in what this faculty really consists, on what mechanism it depends, and by what conditions and agencies it can be influenced, it should be capable of development like any other human faculty. Man may thus be unique in more ways than he now suspects.

So far we have been considering the fact of human uniqueness. It remains to consider man's attitude to these unique qualities of his. Professor Everett, of the University of California, in an interesting paper bearing the same title as this essay, but dealing with the topic from the standpoint of the philosopher and the humanist rather than that of the biologist, has stressed man's fear of his own uniqueness. Man has often not been able to tolerate the feeling that he inhabits an alien world, whose laws do not make sense in the light of his intelligence, and in which the writ of his human values does not run. Faced with the prospect of such intellectual and moral loneliness, he has projected personality into the cosmic scheme. Here he has found a will, there a purpose; here a creative intelligence, and there a divine compassion. At one time, he has deified animals, or personified natural forces. At others, he has created a superhuman pantheon, a single tyrannical world ruler, a subtle and satisfying Trinity in Unity. Philosophers have postulated an Absolute of the same nature as mind.

It is only exceptionally that men have dared to uphold their uniqueness and to be proud of their human superiority to the impersonality and irrationality of the rest of the universe. It is time now, in the light of our knowledge, to be brave and face the fact and the consequences of our uniqueness. That is Dr. Everett's view, as it was also that of T. H. Huxley in his famous Romanes lecture. I agree with them; but I would suggest that the antinomy between man and the universe is not quite so sharp as they have made out. Man represents the culmination of that process of organic evolution which has been proceeding on this planet for over a thousand million years. That process, however wasteful and cruel it may be, and into however many blind alleys it may have been diverted, is also in one aspect progressive. Man has now become the sole representative of life in that progressive aspect and its sole trustee for any progress in the future.

Meanwhile it is true that the appearance of the human type of mind, the latest step in evolutionary progress, has introduced both new methods and new standards. By means of his conscious reason and its chief offspring, science, man has the power of substituting less dilatory, less wasteful, and less cruel methods of effective progressive change than those of natural selection, which alone are available to lower organisms. And by means of his conscious purpose and his set of values, he has the power of substituting new and higher standards for change than those of mere survival and adaptation to immediate circumstances, which alone are inherent in pre-human evolution. To put the matter in another way, progress has hitherto been a rare and fitful by-product of evolution. Man has the possibility of making it the main feature of his own future evolution, and of guiding its course in relation to a deliberate aim.

But he must not be afraid of his uniqueness. There may be other beings in this vast universe endowed with reason, purpose, and aspiration: but we know nothing of them. So far as our knowledge goes, human mind and personality are unique and constitute the highest product yet achieved by the cosmos. Let us not put off our responsibilities onto the shoulders of mythical gods or philosophical absolutes, but shoulder them in the hopefulness of tempered pride. In the perspective of biology, our business in the world is seen to be the imposition of the best and most enduring of our human standards upon ourselves and our planet. The enjoyment of beauty and interest, the achievement of goodness and efficiency, the enhancement of life and its variety—these are the harvest which our human uniqueness should be called upon to yield.

Questions

Noah Webster

THE FUTURE OF ENGLISH IN AMERICA

1. What geographical and social conditions in America would, in Webster's opinion, make American English increasingly divergent from British English?
2. Why does he reject British usage as the standard for Americans?
3. Which of his predictions about American English were correct, and which were wrong? (Consult H. L. Mencken's *The American Language*, G. P. Krapp's *The English Language in America*, A. C. Baugh's *History of the English Language*, ch. xi.)
4. What political consequences does Webster expect from a uniform standard of English in America?
5. To what extent, in your judgment, does his nationalism affect his views on language? What part does it play in his predictions?
6. Why does he expect pronunciation in America to be more nearly uniform than in Great Britain?
7. What are his standards or tests for correctness in speech? Do they seem applicable today?
8. Which adjectives fit Webster's arguments best: 'arbitrary,' 'empirical,' 'authoritarian,' 'analytical,' 'democratic'?
9. What is his 'principle of analogy'?
10. Does his assertion that 'principles of propriety are founded in the very nature of things' (p. 6) seem consistent with his other arguments?
11. Compare Orwell, 'Politics and the English Language,' pp. 252–64.

C. E. Montague

THE BLESSING OF ADAM

1. Find the sentence that best expresses the author's thesis.
2. What, in your opinion, is the author's purpose? Is he serious? Convincing?
3. What can you say about the tone of this essay? What does the tone contribute to meaning and effect?

4. How does Montague make it plausible that artists have a 'congenital disinclination to striking'? What sort of artist has he in mind?

5. What effect does he think machinery and mass-production have on 'the natural delightfulness of work'? Does 'delightfulness' seem the right word here? What force or emphasis has it that 'pleasure' would not have?

6. Does the sentence in the final paragraph, 'Art is only work utterly unspoilt, and drudgery is only art gone utterly wrong,' seem a logical conclusion from the arguments and examples in the essay? Use the sentence just quoted as the opening one of an essay on some success or failure of your own.

7. Explain the connotations and appropriateness of: 'darling' (p. 10), 'a fine set of abstract nouns' (p. 10), 'gladiatorial' (p. 13), 'featly' (p. 15).

8. Do the author's opinions on art and artists agree with those of Forster (pp. 37–43), Maugham (pp. 54–62), and Conrad (pp. 63–7)?

Jacques Barzun

HOW TO WRITE AND BE READ

1. What does Mr. Barzun mean by telling us that writing 'comes before' reading?

2. 'Writing can only be taught by the united efforts of the entire teaching staff.' Is that the way it is taught in your school or college?

3. 'This conscious brutality' (p. 18): why call it that?

4. What is the author's opinion of French methods of teaching writing? What is yours? If you want to learn more about writing in French schools, look up *How the French Boy Learns to Write*, by Rollo W. Brown.

5. Why does Mr. Barzun emphasize preciseness so much? Is his own writing precise?

6. 'As regards writing' (p. 23): but isn't 'as regards' as trite as the 'however's' and the 'Thus we see's' Mr. Barzun objects to?

7. Translate into your English: 'the school does not work in a vacuum but rather in a vortex of destructive forces.' What does he mean?

8. Why is the sentence about Mr. McCaffrey (p. 26) called poetry?

9. Do you think Mr. Barzun understands students and their writing problems? Does this chapter succeed in treating the subject more amiably or more sensibly than other discussions of it that you have been assigned to read?

10. Compare these ideas on writing with those of Maugham and Highet (pp. 54–62 and 167–176). On jargon or cant phrases you should read an essay by Sir Arthur Quiller-Couch in his *The Art of Writing*.

11. If you liked this chapter, you will probably like the one on reading that is referred to in the final sentence. See pp. 61–80 of *Teacher in America*.

Henry David Thoreau

READING

1. Why 'essentially' students and observers (p. 28)?

2. What is shallow about books of travel (see p. 29)?

3. Find examples of paradox, exaggeration, and epigram in these pages.
4. 'Books must be read as deliberately and reservedly as they were written' (p. 29). Why must they? (Make sure you know exactly what 'deliberately' means.)
5. 'It is worth the expense . . . suggestions and provocations' (p. 29). Do you think Thoreau would approve of 'Classics in Translation' courses or other substitutes for the classics?
6. What does he mean by 'What is called eloquence in the forum is commonly found to be rhetoric in the study'? Do you know of any examples?
7. Why does he say the woodchopper was 'above' an interest in the news (p. 33)? Is there anything wrong with being interested in news? What does Thoreau say about it in 'Where I Lived, and What I Lived For'?
8. Why does Thoreau think it 'adventurous' to study classics (p. 29)? Do you find it so?
9. Compare Thoreau's chapter with the essay by E. M. Forster (pp. 44–53).
10. You ought now to read Emerson's 'The American Scholar' and to compare his ideas of men and books with Thoreau's.

E. M. Forster

ART FOR ART'S SAKE

1. What is the main thesis of this lecture?
2. What exactly does the author mean by 'art for art's sake'? What fundamental distinction does he make between 'art for art's sake' and the 'silly idea' that 'only art matters'?
3. What does he mean by the statement that a work of art is 'a self-contained entity'?
4. What kinds of order, according to the lecture, are attainable?
5. What makes a work of art unique?
6. What, in the author's view, is the true relation of artist to society?
7. 'Artists always seek a new technique': why?
8. Put into your own language the paragraph beginning 'If our present society should disintegrate . . .'
9. 'His power to impose form': why is this, according to Mr. Forster's argument, proof of an artist's importance?
10. Explain: 'pointillism' (p. 38), 'mateyness' (p. 41), 'démodé' (p. 42).
11. Compare Mr. Forster's ideas on art and the artist with those of Conrad (pp. 63–7). Also, read Mr. Forster's 'Anonymity: an Enquiry' (pp. 44–53).

E. M. Forster

ANONYMITY: AN ENQUIRY

1. What implications has the word 'Enquiry'? Does it seem appropriate? What can you say of the tone of this composition?

2. 'Lyric poetry is absolutely no use' (p. 46). What does 'use' mean here? What 'use' has drama or fiction?

3. In a theme, apply the distinction between 'information' and 'atmosphere' to some of the selections in this book.

4. What produces the 'atmosphere' of words?

5. 'Information is relative. A poem is absolute.' What does this mean, and how does the author support it?

6. Read carefully the criticism of Lamb and Stevenson (p. 50). Then read the essays on pp. 376–82, 397–404 of this book, and see whether you agree with Mr. Forster's judgments. Do Lamb and Stevenson 'always write with their surface-personalities'? Can you find examples in Stevenson of mannerisms, sentimentality, quaintness?

7. 'Literature tries to be unsigned' (p. 50). What does 'tries' mean in this sentence?

8. 'Study is only a serious form of gossip.' Why so?

9. Do you find that you are more impressed by an unsigned than a signed article in a newspaper (see p. 52)?

10. See Mr. Forster's 'Art for Art's Sake,' pp. 37–43 and the selection from Conrad, pp. 63–7. Other essays by Mr. Forster that may interest you are 'The Duty of Society to the Artist' and 'The *Raison d'Etre* of Criticism in the Arts,' in *Two Cheers for Democracy.*

W. Somerset Maugham

WRITER AND READER

1. What qualities in prose does Mr. Maugham admire most? Judging by this specimen only, do you think his own writing exemplifies those qualities?

2. 'For to write good prose is an affair of good manners' (p. 58). What does he mean? '. . . good prose should be like the clothes of a well-dressed man, appropriate but unobtrusive' (p. 59). Chesterfield suggests a well-dressed man. Does his prose (pp. 339–51) meet the requirement? Are there, in this volume, any examples of prose that does not seem 'like the clothes of a well-dressed man'?

3. Is what Mr. Maugham says of Hume (p. 54) true of the passage from Hume on pp. 371–5? (That passage is not the philosophical kind Mr. Maugham means, probably, but it does illustrate Hume's style.)

4. Read twenty pages of Ruskin and see whether your impression of his style is like Mr. Maugham's (p. 56).

5. Why does the author regret the influence of the Bible on English prose style? (See the modern translation on pp. 78–109.)

6. What examples of 'elegance' and 'sobriety' (p. 57) can you find in Arnold's 'Literature and Science' (pp. 120–37)?

7. Find out what 'baroque' and 'rococo' mean. Why is poetry called baroque and prose rococo (p. 58)?

8. Swift, Newman, and Arnold, whose prose styles Mr. Maugham thinks among the best, are represented by selections in this book. Study those selections; try to

describe the styles; and compare your opinions with Mr. Maugham's, to see if you agree with his description of the writers' characteristics.

9. 'No reading is worth while unless you enjoy it.' Is that true in your experience? Write a short essay defending or refuting this dictum.

Joseph Conrad

Preface to THE NIGGER OF THE 'NARCISSUS'

1. Restate Conrad's definition of art in your own words. What does he mean, in his definition, by rendering 'justice' to the visible universe?
2. What does the artist have in common with the philosopher and the scientist, and how does he differ fundamentally from them? (See also E. M. Forster, pp. 37–43.)
3. Summarize the two sentences 'But the artist . . . to the unborn' (p. 64). Which 'part of our being' is it, precisely, that the artist appeals to?
4. Which art does Conrad consider the highest?
5. With the sentence about 'an unremitting never-discouraged care for the shape and ring of sentences' (p. 65) compare the final pages of Orwell's essay (pp. 262–4).
6. 'The light of magic suggestiveness' (p. 65). Can you find examples in Conrad's novels, in 'Il Conde' (pp. 467–80) or in any other selections in this book?
7. 'All art, therefore, appeals primarily to the senses.' How can this be as true of literature as of painting or music?
8. What is Conrad's conception of the use of fiction?
9. 'To snatch in a moment of courage . . . beginning of the task' (p. 65): and note the phrase 'and without fear' in the following sentence. Why is courage needed?
10. Look up in an unabridged dictionary definitions of realism, romanticism, naturalism, and sentimentalism (see p. 66). Why does Conrad call these 'temporary' formulas?

Robert E. Sherwood

HOW F. D. R.'S SPEECHES WERE WRITTEN

1. Why did President Roosevelt take speeches so seriously?
2. Why did he need a 'sounding board for discussions of the best means of attaining the goals that the President set for himself'?
3. Why did the speeches intended for radio delivery have to be treated differently from others? Why did their punctuation matter so much?
4. Look up Mr. Sherwood's dramatic reconstructions of Lincoln's and Douglas's speeches in his play *Abe Lincoln in Illinois*. What factors (besides radio) have most affected political speeches since Lincoln's day?
5. What is the use of the reference to 'some anonymous citizen in Council Bluffs' (p. 74) and of the phrase 'with the deliberation of an alchemist' (p. 71).

6. Why do you think the writer adds the digression on the President's eating and drinking habits? What impression do you get from these pages of the President's character? Of the White House routine?

7. What evidence is there in this selection that 'Roosevelt knew that he was the voice of America to the rest of the world'?

8. What evidence does the writer provide to support his observation that Roosevelt was 'normally the most untemperamental genius I have ever encountered'?

THE STORY OF JOSEPH

1. If you were previously acquainted with the King James but not the American translation, what do you think of the latter after reading it for the first time? If you were not well acquainted with either one, which do you like better, and why? Which is the more intelligible?

2. Consider the story of Joseph as a narrative. What can you say about its construction and characterization? It is often praised as one of the greatest stories ever written. Do you think it deserves such praise? Test it by the standards that you think a supremely good story must meet.

3. 'But my opinion of the merits of the story is bound to be affected by whether I can accept the religious parts of it.' How sensible and how important does this criticism seem to you?

4. Is the emotion in the story mostly explicit or implicit?

5. If there is a moral or religious idea dominating the story, what is it?

6. Does the frequency of sentences beginning with 'and' in the King James translation diminish your satisfaction in reading it? Why do you suppose the translators used 'and' so often?

7. One of the early sixteenth-century translators of the Bible rendered one sentence: 'And the Lord was with Joseph, and he was a lucky fellow.' Would 'lucky fellow' be an acceptable translation today, even though accurate enough?

8. The literary merits and influence of the King James Bible have been highly praised for generations, but see Maugham's criticism on p. 57 of this book. Does it sound plausible? (Naturally your opinion on such matters will not be worth much unless you are familiar with the different prose styles he mentions, but his comments on the King James Bible are nevertheless worth thinking about.)

9. Compare the American translation with the aims as stated in the quotation at the end of the introductory note, p. 77. Do you think the translators succeeded in their effort to produce a translation in idiomatic, clear language? They wanted to steer a middle course between the elevated and the mean in language (do you agree that this is what the quotation says?). Do they use any words or phrases that you dislike?

John Henry Newman

LIBERAL KNOWLEDGE

1. What does Newman mean by the word 'liberal' when he uses it in the phrase 'liberal knowledge'?

2. Which sentence best expresses Newman's conception of liberal education? What, according to him, is the fundamental purpose of liberal education?

3. What does Newman think of the supposed connection between liberal education and religious training? What dignities and what failures of philosophy does he describe?

4. 'To detect what is sophistical, and to discard what is irrelevant': does your education enable you to do this? How do you know?

5. What distinctions does Newman make between true humility, ordinary condescension, modesty, and self-respect? What is the importance of the distinctions in his argument?

6. Why is the 'gentleman' the product of civilization rather than of Christianity? Cannot a Christian be a gentleman or a gentleman a Christian?

7. Compare Newman's description of the gentleman with the passages from Hume (pp. 371–5) and Chesterfield (pp. 338–51). Which of the three passages do you like the best? Which tells you the most?

8. Do not fail to observe that the gentleman whom Newman delineates (on pp. 117–19) is a *mere* gentleman, not a Christian; therefore, despite his virtures, he is deficient. Would this have made as much difference to Hume and Chesterfield as it does to Newman? Why?

Matthew Arnold

LITERATURE AND SCIENCE

1. What is the principal issue in the essay? What is Arnold's thesis concerning it?

2. What is his conception of culture? What does he mean by the humanities? Find his definition. What does he mean by 'literature'? Why does he hold science to be one of the humanities?

3. How does the contrast between Plato's outlook and the one Plato satirizes (pp. 120–21) serve to introduce Arnold's theme?

4. 'The English House of Lords or for the pork trade in Chicago' (p. 122). Is this ironical?

5. 'Man is the cynosure of things terrestrial' (p. 125). What does 'cynosure' mean? Find out its source.

6. Why does Arnold believe it is more important for most people to know 'the great results of the scientific investigation of nature' than 'the processes by which those results are reached'? Do you agree?

7. Why does he leave specialists out of consideration when he talks about the best education?

8. What is his chief criticism of those who wish to give physical science the largest place in the curriculum? What do you think of the criticism?

9. How does literature satisfy 'the sense for conduct' and 'the sense for beauty'? Why does he think physical science does not satisfy them so well?

10. Just why is it more important for a student to be able to paraphrase *Macbeth* correctly than to know the diameter of the moon (see pp. 134–5)? What is the point of this illustration?

11. What makes Arnold so certain (p. 136) that the instinct for beauty is served best by Greek literature and art? (How many students in your college or university study Greek?)

12. Try to reconstruct Huxley's argument in 'Science and Culture' from your reading of Arnold's essay. Then read Huxley's lecture. Does Arnold quote it accurately? Is he fair toward it? Are the two men talking about the same things? Which argument is more convincing to you?

13. What would you say are the main characteristics of Arnold's style? Why does he repeat some phrases so often? Why does he use a conversational tone?

14. See Whitehead's essay, pp. 138–51.

A. N. *Whitehead*

TECHNICAL EDUCATION AND ITS RELATION TO SCIENCE AND LITERATURE

1. Compare Whitehead's conclusions about literary education with those of Arnold (pp. 120–37). Which seem more persuasive to you? More relevant to your times and your education? Why?

2. Both Arnold and Whitehead refer to Platonic culture. How do their views of it differ?

3. What is Whitehead's conception of the nature and use of 'liberal' education? Is it like Newman's (pp. 110–14)?

4. Do you agree with Whitehead's remark (see headnote, p. 138) that the general principles of this essay apply to America as much as to England?

5. Do you agree that liberal education is 'an aristocratic education implying leisure'? Is this the way you commonly hear it described or advocated?

6. 'No man of science wants merely to know.' Why not? What else does he want?

7. Why does Whitehead maintain that 'the antithesis between a technical and a liberal education is fallacious'?

8. What distinction does he make between scientific and technical education? What connections between the two does he stress? What are their characteristic merits?

9. 'Education should turn out the pupil with something he knows well and something he can do well.' Is yours likely to do this?

10. Do Whitehead's remarks (see pp. 146–8) about the teaching of mathematics and science fit your courses in those subjects?

C. H. *Haskins*

THE EARLIEST UNIVERSITIES

1. What essentially is a university?

2. Sum up the main similarities and differences between mediaeval universities and the ones you know best.

3. What distinction is made between the mediaeval university and the mediaeval college?

4. To what extent does the author appear to admire or approve of the aims of mediaeval universities? Of their methods? After you have read about mediaeval curricula, see Whitehead's remarks on modern studies, pp. 141–51.

5. Were the objects of the mediaeval universities those that Newman says (see pp. 110–12) the universities of his time had? Those that today's have?

6. Do you agree with the final sentence of the essay? What evidence is there that the American world has 'given too little attention' to this tradition?

7. How does the lecturer make his remarks interesting—assuming that you find them so? If you do not, what is your criticism of them?

8. Write a Socratic dialogue or essay on the theme suggested in the opening paragraph of the lecture.

9. If you are interested in mediaeval universities, look up *University Records and Life in the Middle Ages* (1944), ed. Lynn Thorndike, which contains translations of documents illustrating all the topics Haskins discusses.

Gilbert Highet

THE AMERICAN STUDENT AS I SEE HIM

1. Why is the distinction between 'student' and 'scholar' needed in writing and reading this essay?

2. If Mr. Highet had published his impressions this year instead of in 1941, which ones do you think might have been different, and why?

3. What are the most serious defects he finds in American schools (not colleges)? What are the reasons for them?

4. Explain: 'crofter' (p. 168), 'labyrinthine' (p. 169), 'mandarinate' (p. 171), 'myriad' (p. 171), 'bombinating' (p. 172), 'dichotomy' (p. 172), 'anomalous' (p. 175).

5. What does the writer think are the three main characteristics of American students as contrasted with the European students he knew?

6. 'When you and I make jokes . . . margin' (p. 169). Do you believe this?

7. '. . . a few eccentric universities' (p. 171). Do you know which ones?

8. '. . . read and understand *Hamlet*' (p. 172). Is there any connection here between 'understand' and 'reproduce the various explanations' a few lines later? Is reproducing somebody else's explanations a sign of understanding? Or is this an unfair interpretation of Mr. Highet's meaning? If it is, what does he mean?

9. Does he share Mr. Hutton's opinion (see p. 183) that American schools hold back the abler students?

10. '. . . other reasons . . . too controversial' (p. 174). What, for instance?

11. What does the phrase 'democracy in education' mean to you? This essay seems to imply that in the United States it is commonly, and unfortunately, confused with political democracy. In what way? And why unfortunately?

12. 'The task of the university . . . the inessential' (p. 176). The sentence is a metaphorical description of the nature of a university's function, but does it define the function? What does the entire essay assume to be the primary function of a university? Do you think the author would endorse the dictum of President Wilson

that 'The object of a university is intellect; as a university its only object is intellect'?

Graham Hutton

THE CULT OF THE AVERAGE

1. If you live in the Midwest, do you think Mr. Hutton knows what he is talking about? Is this a fair and accurate picture of education, so far as you know it, in that region? If you do not live in the Midwest, what can you say about the likeness or difference between the education described here and that prevalent in your own section of the country?

2. Can you tell from the text alone that the writer is a foreigner? For what readers does he seem to be writing?

3. Why is the phrase 'leading forth from' (p. 179) within quotation marks?

4. What are said to be the aims of education in the Midwest? (Are they different in the east, north, or south?)

5. Do you accept his statement that 'The midwesterner always distrusted intellectually outstanding people'? How would he, or how would you, prove it? Does it imply, conversely, that northerners, easterners, and southerners always trusted intellectually outstanding people?

6. What significance does the author attach to the fact that many private colleges in the Midwest were founded by easterners but the state universities by the midwesterners themselves?

7. 'Work their way through' (p. 180). This feature of American collegiate life never fails to astound Europeans. Compare Highet, pp. 167–8.

8. 'Strange reverence for books' (p. 181). Do you believe this?

9. Consider Mr. Hutton's criticism that the schools and colleges indoctrinate rather than educate. Is he right? How do you know? What has your own experience been? What seems to be his criterion of a good education?

10. In his discussion of the religion of patriotism on p. 184, is his sentence 'The Midwest has proved that' ironic?

11. Apropros of the typical midwestern query 'Will it work?' see the selection on pragmatism (pp. 523–31 in this volume) by William James.

12. 'Treats them as men in almost all respects, but agrees in the main not to teach them anything on controversial issues' (p. 188). Is this a correct description?

13. 'Can read, but cannot understand, the great speeches of Calhoun, Webster, Clay, and Douglas' (p. 184). Can you read them and understand them?

14. Compare Mr. Hutton's impressions with Mr. Highet's, pp. 167–76 (but remember that Mr. Highet writes from New York, not from Chicago).

George Santayana

CLASSIC LIBERTY

1. What definition of liberty is implicit in the essay?

2. How can liberty be 'vindicated' by martyrdom, as Santayana says it was at Thermopylae?

3. Explain the meaning of these phrases: 'public experimental study' (p. 191), 'loquacious, festive little ant-hills' (p. 191), 'impassibility' (p. 191), 'the unanswerable scepticism of silence' (p. 191).

4. 'The conservatives . . . so intelligent were they' (p. 191). Why is it intelligent for conservatives to be radical?

5. 'A prescription to a diseased old man' (p. 191). Who is the old man?

6. What analogy does the author draw between the liberty of Greek cities and the liberty of Greek philosophers?

7. In what ways did the early Christian Church adopt and practice the classic conception of liberty? For what reasons?

8. 'Our modern liberty to drift in the dark' (p. 193). What does he mean?

9. What are the main effects of modern 'liberty,' according to this essay? What kind of liberty do you think the author esteems most highly? Is he an uncritical admirer of Greek liberty? Find passages to support your answer.

10. The essay was written during the First World War. Are any of its ideas 'dated'? Are there any that you think particularly relevant today?

Jefferson and Adams

NATURAL ARISTOCRACY

1. What is the problem treated by Jefferson and Adams? Does it still exist? In the same form?

2. Tell in your own words exactly what Jefferson and Adams mean by 'aristocracy.'

3. Is Jefferson's division of aristocracies into 'natural' and 'artificial' as convincing to you after you have read Adams's reply? Does Adams's letter cause you to think the subject less simple than Jefferson's exposition seemed to make it?

4. What does Jefferson mean by 'mutually indulging its [reason's] errors' (p. 195)?

5. Does Adams agree with Jefferson that enough of the wealthy 'will find their way into every branch of the legislature to protect themselves'? For the same reasons? Do you think the writers are correct about this?

6. Was Jefferson's confidence that voters 'in general . . . will elect the really good and wise' (p. 195) justifiable? Do you think him too optimistic in this? Or Adams too skeptical? How would you establish the correctness of your answer? For other opinions on the promises and perils of popular government, see selections by Madison, Burke, Paine, Emerson, and Becker.

7. What are the advantages of the 'little republics' Jefferson has in mind? Are there any disadvantages?

8. How 'democratic' is Jefferson's scheme of education? Note that he would not allow all graduates of district high schools to attend the university, or even most of them, but only the best ones. Note also that the words 'democracy' and 'democratic' do not appear in his letter. In Jefferson's time 'democracy' was a word of rather disreputable associations—for example, with 'the mobs of the cities' (p. 198); Jefferson himself habitually described his principles as 'republican.' 'Jefferson was not in any social sense a democrat, and only in a political sense by contrast with

his contemporaries' (S. E. Morison and H. S. Commager, *The Growth of the American Republic*, 1950, 1, 382).

Which parts of Jefferson's plan for a system of public education seem closest to our present system? Read Hutton's 'The Cult of the Average' (pp. 177–89). Are these school systems he describes, and the ideals of education they express, Jeffersonian?

James Madison

THE FEDERALIST. NO. X

1. Madison states a problem, defines his terms, presents arguments, and finds a solution. Make an outline of his arguments.
2. Is the language like Jefferson's? Does it inspire confidence in the reasonableness of his arguments? What sort of audience is he addressing? Is he appealing to their minds or their emotions? How persuasive does his essay seem to you as propaganda?
3. What does 'specious' (p. 202) mean?
4. Why does Madison make such a careful contrast between a 'pure democracy' and a republic, and why does he insist that the United States can succeed only as a republic? What does Madison hold to be the most important differences between a democracy and a republic? Why does he think a republic has more advantages? And why has a large republic more advantages than a small one? Can you support or question his opinion by examples from modern history?

For another example of Madison's views on republics look up his *Federalist* No. XXXIX, from which the following definition is taken:

If we resort for a criterion to the different principles on which different forms of government are established, we may define a republic to be, or at least bestow that name on, a government which derives all its powers directly or indirectly from the great body of the people, and is administered by persons holding their offices during pleasure, for a limited period, or during good behavior. It is *essential* to such a government that it be derived from the great body of the society, not from an inconsiderable proportion, or a favored class of it; otherwise a handful of tyrannical nobles, exercising their oppressions by a delegation of their powers, might aspire to the rank of republicans, and claim for their government the honorable title of republic.

5. Why does Madison put so much emphasis on the conflicts between economic interests in his treatment of political groups? How does he think different economic interests can get along harmoniously enough to form and preserve a stable government?
6. How closely do Madison's views of the rights of man and of governments resemble Jefferson's, as Jefferson's are suggested by his letter to Adams?
7. 'Enlightened statesmen will not always be at the helm' (p. 205). Does this prophecy reflect the same attitude as Jefferson's toward the wisdom of the electorate? Does it agree with Emerson's ('Politics')? Before answering reread pp. 207–8.

8. 'The influence of factious leaders . . . the other States' (p. 208). Can you show whether this is still true?

Ralph Waldo Emerson

POLITICS

1. What is Emerson's principal thesis in this essay? Find a good statement of it.
2. Which passages remind you most of Thoreau's 'Where I Lived, and What I Lived For'?
3. 'The State must follow, and not lead the character and progress of the citizen' (p. 211). Why is the opposite view so prevalent today (assuming you allow that it is prevalent)? Would Mill (see pp. 222–34) agree with the sentence?
4. 'The law is only a memorandum.' 'Good men must not obey the laws too well.' What do these sentences mean? Do you accept them? Can you be law-abiding without obeying the laws 'too well'?
5. 'In this country . . . only fitter for us' (p. 214). Do you agree that our political institutions are no better inherently but 'only fitter for us'? Do you think most Americans would agree? Why should they, or why should they not?
6. Do Emerson's opinions on property oppose Madison's (see pp. 202–9)?
7. 'A party is perpetually corrupted by personality.' Translate that into your own terms. Is it true? Does a politician corrupt a party, or a party a politician?
8. What would you say to this comment: 'Emerson's fine talk about individualism and the conquest of the state by character is all very well, but he didn't live in the twentieth century; if he had, he wouldn't have been so sure of this'? Is Emerson excessively optimistic about moral progress? What solid reasons can you give for your answer?
9. Read Becker, 'The Reality.' Is he any more or less observant or realistic about the nature of political institutions than Emerson is? Can you prove it?
10. What relevance to these matters does Paul (p. 211) have? What did he know, or say, about politics and liberty?
11. Is Emerson's contrast of the characters of the liberal and conservative parties of his day (pp. 214–16) valid for our liberal and conservative parties now?
12. 'Hence, the less government we have, the better' (p. 218). Has he demonstrated this to your satisfaction? Is it a logical conclusion from his premises?

John Stuart Mill

ON LIBERTY

1. Some students complain that Mill is hard to read. Do you find him so? He often writes long sentences, but his thought may require them. Provided it is clear, a long sentence shows the writer's control of a complicated subject. He is putting things in order, subordinating certain facts or ideas to others. If a subject is in-

volved or profound, any oversimplifying of it—for example, by using short sentences —may misrepresent its real nature.

Style is a 'thinking out into language'; it comes from the writer's character and his habit of mind, not merely from his practice in writing. What qualities of mind does Mill's style suggest?

2. What is the purpose of the essay?
3. What kind of liberty does he discuss?
4. 'The vital question of the future.' Can you show whether or not it has been a vital one, or the vital one, since Mill wrote his essay? How vital is it today?
5. 'The tyranny of the majority': tyranny in what? by what means?
6. 'Another grand determining principle' (p. 227). What does 'grand' mean here?
7. 'The majority have not yet learnt . . . public opinion' (p. 229). Has this prophecy come true? Can you prove it?
8. For what part of your conduct does Mill think you should be 'amenable' to society?
9. What is his principle in deciding ethical questions?
10. Find out what utilitarianism is. How does Mill's argument illustrate utilitarianism?
11. 'The only freedom which deserves the name, is that of pursuing our own good in our own way.' Do you believe this? Can you defend it or refute it?
12. Compare Madison (pp. 202-9), Emerson (pp. 210-21), and Becker (pp. 235-51).

Carl Becker

THE REALITY

1. Outline the essay.
2. Which paragraph states the writer's main thesis?
3. What does he mean by 'exploiting' (p. 238), 'bourgeoisie' (p. 238), 'rococo' (p. 239), 'proletarian peasants and workers' (p. 240)?
4. What are some of the most important impediments to democracy? What caused them? Why did not Jefferson and Madison recognize them?
5. How do Becker, Madison, and Mill differ in their treatment of liberty?
6. Which liberties were most emphasized by the doctrinaires of the eighteenth century? Which ones were least emphasized? Why? Which does Becker think most urgent in the twentieth century?
7. Which segment of society did the bourgeoisie exclude from 'the political country'? Why did it exclude them?
8. How did the technological revolution exert 'a decisive influence in modifying all the habitual patterns of thought and conduct'? How did it change political ideas?
9. Why is self-government called an 'expensive luxury'?
10. 'In any society there is bound to be a close connection between economic and political power.' What other writings (in this book) have discussed or stressed this fact?
11. What criticism does Becker make of the 'traditional concept of individual liberty'?
12. Does Becker have any remedies to propose for the ills of modern democracy? If so, what remedies? Does he think modern democracy will survive?

George Orwell

POLITICS AND THE ENGLISH LANGUAGE

1. What assumptions or convictions about the nature of language underlie the opinions expressed in this essay?
2. 'It is clear that the decline of a language must ultimately have political and economic causes.' Why must it? What does Webster have to say (see pp. 1–9) about connections between language and politics?
3. Why is it more important to be careful about words than about phrases?
4. Can you refute the contention that 'Orthodoxy, of whatever color, seems to demand a lifeless, imitative style'?
5. Compare what Orwell says about political writing with Mr. Sherwood's account (pp. 68–76) of President Roosevelt's speeches. Test those speeches, or excerpts from them, by Orwell's assertion that 'In our time it is broadly true that political writing is bad writing. Where it is not true, it will generally be found that the writer is some kind of rebel, expressing his private opinions and not a "party line." '
6. Make a list of ambiguous and euphemistic words and phrases used in American political propaganda and 'Government prose.'
7. Can you find in Orwell's own writing any of the faults his essay condemns? For example, is his use of 'régime' (p. 257) consistent with what he says about foreign words and phrases on p. 256?
8. What do you suppose Orwell would think of the assertion by Maugham (p. 58) that 'To write good prose is an affair of good manners'?
9. Using Orwell's 'To think clearly is a necessary first step towards political regeneration' as the topic sentence of your opening paragraph, write an essay illustrating some of the relations between current American language and current American politics.
10. Do not fail to read the appendix to 1984 on "The Principles of Newspeak.'

Edmund Burke

REFLECTIONS ON THE REVOLUTION IN FRANCE

1. Which passages seem most persuasive to you? Least persuasive? Why?
2. What are Burke's main reasons for denying the 'right to choose our own *governors*'?
3. What does he think are the '*real* rights of men'?
4. What is his definition of government?
5. Is his principle that 'Whatever each man can separately do, without trespassing upon others, he has a right to do for himself' the same as Mill's (see pp. 222–34)?
6. 'Government is not made in virtue of natural rights.' What would Paine's answer be (see pp. 275–81)?
7. 'The restraints on men, as well as their liberties, are to be reckoned among their rights' (pp. 269–70). What does he mean?

8. 'Men have no right to what is not reasonable, and to what is not for their benefit' (p. 271). Could you refute this? What would Mill's answer be?

9. In the famous passage on chivalry (pp. 272–3), what is Burke's chief regret? Why is 'chivalry' so important? Why does he think the loss of it has important political consequences? Do you find the passage convincing? Sincere?

10. 'Society is indeed a contract.' What sort of contract? How binding, in Burke's opinion, is this contract?

11. How would you describe Burke's style?

12. Compare Burke's ideas on government with Madison's (pp. 202–9). Study Paine's reply to Burke (pp. 275–81).

Thomas Paine

THE RIGHTS OF MAN

1. What is his main idea? What are the best statements of it?

2. Does he represent Burke's arguments fairly?

3. Compare Paine's opinions on the rights of man with those of Madison (pp. 202–9) and Jefferson (pp. 194–9). See also Mill (pp. 222–34) and Becker (pp. 235–51). Do Paine's principles agree with those of the Declaration of Independence?

4. 'The right of the people is almost always sophistically confounded with their power' (p. 271), according to Burke. Does Paine seem to you guilty of such confusion?

5. Does Paine's scorn of Burke's praise of chivalry seem justified? Do you think Paine makes his point?

6. What different assumptions do Burke and Paine make about human nature?

7. What do you think Paine would have said of Emerson's dictum (see p. 214) that 'Good men must not obey the laws too well'?

8. 'Man has no property in man.' What does he mean? What place does this idea have in Paine's argument?

9. What differences are there between Burke's and Paine's styles?

Arnold J. Toynbee

CIVILIZATION ON TRIAL

1. What are the theses maintained?

2. In what sense is civilization 'on trial'? Why is it on trial now any more than it ever was?

3. Why does Mr. Toynbee think our 'pre-nationalist mediaeval ancestors' had a better historical vision than we have?

4. Throughout this essay there is a contrast between 'historical horizon' and 'historical vision.' What does the writer mean by these terms, and why are they contrasted? What is the 'unified vision' he urges, and what difference is it to make?

5. 'And even if they were mistaken . . . Hengist and Horsa' (p. 284): why is it better?

6. What are 'higher' religions?

7. Why does he select mostly founders of religions as 'the greatest benefactors' of the living generation of mankind (p. 287)? If he does not tell you explicitly, can you infer the reason?

8. What has been the consequence, in his opinion, of the simultaneous development in modern society of humanitarianism and nationalism?

9. How does Christendom differ from Christianity? What connections does he suggest between Christianity and civilization? Why does he emphasize them? (If this subject interests you, see Mr. Toynbee's 'Christianity and Civilization,' printed in *Civilization on Trial.*)

10. Why does he call North and South America 'a couple of large islands' (p. 285) instead of 'the two continents'? What is the effect of 'batch' in 'this batch of world wars' (p. 290)? of the 'more unpleasant' alternative (p. 290)?

11. This brief essay touches on some topics that Mr. Toynbee treats at length in his *A Study of History.* If you want to explore his ideas further, look up the one-volume condensation of *A Study of History* by D. C. Somervell.

12. This essay appeared in its original form in 1947. Do you think the author would change anything in it if he were writing it today?

Benjamin Franklin

REMARKS

CONCERNING THE SAVAGES OF NORTH AMERICA

1. What difference does it make that Franklin uses the word 'savages' instead of 'Indians' in his title?

2. What are the main objects of Franklin's satire?

3. How much sympathy do you suppose Franklin had with the missionaries' efforts to convert the Indians?

4. What similarities and what differences are there between the irony of these 'Remarks' and that of Swift's *A Modest Proposal* (pp. 329–37)?

5. If you know Swift's *Gulliver's Travels,* what resemblances do you find between Swift's methods of satire and Franklin's?

6. Do Franklin's 'savages' measure up to Hume's standards of polite behavior (see pp. 370–75)?

7. What do you think of the Indians' customs, for example, 'not to answer a public Proposition the same day that it is made,' and observing 'a profound Silence' for five or six minutes after a man has made a speech? What does Franklin intend us to think of them?

8. Why does Franklin add the word 'historical' in 'the principal historical Facts' (p. 296)? Why does he have the Indian orator refer to 'these Things which you have heard from your Mothers' and not 'fathers'?

9. Why does he add the note at the end of his 'Remarks'?

Samuel Eliot Morison
and Henry Steele Commager

THE UNITED STATES IN 1790

1. Which facts about the United States in 1790 do you find most surprising?
2. Why is it said that 'The United States of 1790 was not a nation'?
3. What is meant by 'the cruder phases of democracy' (p. 308)?
4. What were the three political experiments America was attempting, and why was their success so doubtful?
5. What different European opinions of the future of the United States are mentioned? Which of them seems to you the best grounded or the most prophetic?
6. What is implied by the statement that 'no one found much to admire in America in the works of man' (p. 305)?
7. What political habits of Americans today are discernible in this report of America in 1790?
8. Is this description supported by sufficient illustrations or anecdotes to make it convincing as well as vivid?
9. Why are the observations of so many foreigners quoted?
10. Why was Pennsylvania a 'microcosm of the America to be'? Why the social contrasts in Virginia? Why so many slaves in New York State?
11. What seeds of future sectional conflicts can you find in the America of 1790?
12. Which of the physical conditions of America in 1790 most affected the social and political character of the society?
13. What characteristics of the America of 1790, as described by Professors Morison and Commager, do you perceive in the sketches of modern America or Americans by Brogan and Hutton (pp. 322–8, 177–89)?
14. In an essay, examine and elaborate some of Turgot's assertions in his letter to Dr. Price (p. 319).
15. How would you illustrate the statements of this chapter by passages from Jefferson, Adams, and Madison (pp. 194–201, 202–9)?

D. W. Brogan

AMERICAN CLIMATE

1. By what means does the author, without resorting to statistics, manage to give the reader enough facts to prove his thesis? What is his thesis?
2. How much knowledge of American climate does he take for granted in the readers? Who are the readers he seems to be writing for? Why is he writing this account?
3. How well do you think he knows the United States? Does he make you realize better the effect of the climate on American civilization?
4. Why is 'capricious,' near the beginning of the first paragraph, an apt word in this context? Which phrase in the same paragraph explains it?

5. Point out some examples of irony of statement and irony of fact.

6. What is the tone of this selection? What is the author's 'approach'? Is it one of amusement, superiority, wonder?

7. If you judge by Mr. Brogan's account, which section of the country has the most deplorable climate?

8. To what 'highly paradoxical destiny' of Los Angeles does he refer (p. 324)?

9. What does he mean by 'had later toughened the New Englanders' (p. 325)? Why does he express it in this way?

10. What is 'the more exigent type of American tourist' (p. 326)?

11. What effect has the American climate had on fashions?

12. You may be interested in comparing parts of Mr. Brogan's book with another recent British examination of the United States, Graham Hutton's *Midwest at Noon*, a chapter from which is reprinted on pp. 177–89 of this book. Do these two writers have similar opinions about America?

    Morison and Commager's 'The United States in 1790' (pp. 300–321) should be read with Mr. Brogan's pages.

Jonathan Swift
A MODEST PROPOSAL

1. This selection can serve to test your comprehension of the nature of satire and irony. First, find out what the words 'satire' and 'irony' mean; find out what they are supposed to do; then reread the selection until you see *how* they do it. Does satire differ from sarcasm? If so, how? Does it differ from the sardonic? Do satire and irony require the same sort of perceptiveness on the reader's part? What various meanings does the adjective 'ironical' have? Is Swift's irony like that of Arnold, Butler, or Thoreau (all of whom are represented in this volume)? Is understatement an essential part of irony? Such questions as these, if you try seriously to answer them, should sharpen your understanding of the ways of language as well as the ways of thought.

2. 'A child, just dropped from its dam.' What is gained by putting it in this way instead of 'a child just born'? Note how often Swift uses of human beings terms usually employed of animals, especially those raised for food. Why does he do this?

3. How far did you read before you realized what the 'modest proposal' was? Note that Swift does not give it in so many words until p. 331, where it suddenly confronts us in the phrase 'contribute to the feeding.'

4. On p. 333, what is the effect of 'A very worthy person, a true lover of his country' and 'so deserving a patriot'?

5. What other writings on social or political problems have you read that make successful use of irony and satire? Have irony and satire any disadvantages in the treatment of such subjects?

6. What objections to his public-spirited scheme does Swift anticipate, and how does he meet the objections?

7. The last sentence on the last page deserves special study. What is its purpose, and what would the pamphlet lose if it were omitted?

8. Does writing about human beings in such fashion show Swift to be callous?

Lord Chesterfield

LETTERS TO HIS SON

1. Is it good advice? Do you think Chesterfield understood human nature and society? Which precepts does he emphasize most? Why is he so insistent on reserve and decorum?
2. 'Take the tone of the company that you are in' (p. 343). Why should you?
3. What sort of company does he consider the best? He gives reasons; are they good ones?
4. The passage beginning 'Vice in its true light' and ending 'effects of an excellent cause' (p. 346) is important as a statement typical of eighteenth-century ethical literature. (Compare what Newman says of Shaftesbury, pp. 114–15.) Restate it in your own words. How true do you think it is?
5. Chesterfield calls Leonidas and Curtius madmen (pp. 347–8). Why?
6. Do his admonitions amount to anything more than tips on 'how to win friends and influence people'? What is their object, and how worthy is it, in your opinion?
7. Burke, referring to pre-Revolutionary France, declared that 'vice itself lost half its evil by losing half its grossness.' Would Chesterfield endorse the implied proposition that grossness and viciousness are so closely related? Are they?
8. Do your impressions of Chesterfield's character and intelligence conform to those you get after reading Virginia Woolf's essay (pp. 352–7)? Is the one selection of much help in understanding the other?
9. See Newman's description of a gentleman (pp. 117–19), written a century after Chesterfield's letters. Is his gentleman a Chesterfieldian one?
10. Read Hume (pp. 370–75). Do he and Chesterfield have the same point of view? Which selection do you like better, and why?
11. How would you describe Chesterfield's estimate of women? Is it cynical, naïve, patronizing, sensible, fantastic?
12. See pp. 358–69 on Chesterfield and Dr. Johnson.

Virginia Woolf

LORD CHESTERFIELD'S LETTERS TO HIS SON

1. 'The little papers [Chesterfield's letters] have the precision and formality of some old-fashioned minuet.' Explain and criticize this description.
2. 'The curtains are very thick and the women are very pure' (p. 352). What is the effect of joining the two statements in this fashion? What judgments of Victorian society do they imply?
3. The *Rape of the Lock* (p. 353). Read or reread the poem; and note Chesterfield's remark about Pope on p. 342.
4. What does 'even to the stars' (p. 356) mean?
5. 'One must perhaps believe in something, and then how difficult to observe the Graces!' (p. 356). Why difficult?

6. What faults in Chesterfield are suggested?
7. 'He sat down . . . all the mirrors' (p. 356). Explain the figure. Is it appropriate?
8. 'Lord Chesterfield himself never laughed. He always smiled.' How much does this tell you about him?
9. Why did Chesterfield's letters fail to have the desired effect?
10. How do Chesterfield's dying words, 'Give Dayrolles a chair,' sum up the doctrine of the letters?
11. How would you describe Mrs. Woolf's attitude toward Chesterfield? Does she admire him? Is she ironical about him?

James Boswell

JOHNSON, CHESTERFIELD, AND THE *DICTIONARY*

1. On p. 360 what difference would 'wrote' make if substituted for 'fell a scribbling'?
2. What does Chesterfield's treatment of Johnson's letter (p. 363) tell you about Chesterfield? Does it confirm the impression you get from Chesterfield's letters?
3. Does Chesterfield's letter about the *Dictionary* seem cordial enough?
4. How appropriate is Johnson's letter to Chesterfield? Why is the language so restrained and polite?
5. How much does his account of the Johnson-Chesterfield episode tell you about Boswell's attitude toward Johnson?
6. Look up the Preface to the *Dictionary*, and compare your impressions of it with Boswell's praise. Also look up Johnson's definition of 'Tory,' 'Whig,' 'pension,' and 'oats' in the *Dictionary*.
7. What does Boswell consider the most remarkable feature of the *Dictionary*?
8. What aspects of Johnson's character and temperament are brought out most strongly in these passages?
9. Why does Boswell quote examples of the *Dictionary*'s capricious and inaccurate definitions?
10. What evidence is there that Boswell made efforts to verify stories he heard about Johnson?

David Hume

OF QUALITIES IMMEDIATELY AGREEABLE TO OTHERS

1. What does Hume consider the main social virtues?
2. How does he explain the origin of manners? What, according to him, is the relation between morals and manners?
3. 'What wit is, it may not be easy to define.' Aristotle calls it 'well-bred insolence.' Is this a good definition?

4. Does 'politeness,' as Hume uses the word, mean exactly what it means in common usage today?

5. What kind of self-praise is allowed, and in what circumstances?

6. 'Decency' and 'modesty' are key words in this chapter. What does Hume mean by them? Why are they so important?

7. What name would you give to the 'something mysterious and inexplicable' described in the next to last paragraph?

8. 'The passion between the sexes' (p. 375): can you think of any reason for his use of this phrase instead of the word 'love'?

9. What inferences can you make from this chapter about the author's character and tastes?

10. With Hume's description of qualities agreeable to others, compare a famous nineteenth-century delineation of the gentleman, reprinted from Newman on pp. 117–19. Do Hume and Newman stress the same qualities? Which passage is more precise, and which is more to your liking?

Also to be read with this selection are the pages from Chesterfield's letters (pp. 338–51). How closely do he and Hume agree?

Charles Lamb

THE SUPERANNUATED MAN

1. What does 'superannuated' mean? What term is more common now?

2. Why does Lamb begin in mock-formal style, with 'thy' and 'Reader' and a long periodic sentence? (Can you define a periodic sentence?) What advantages has the conversational manner in which the rest of the essay is composed?

3. How much does the addition of 'as wild animals in cages' add to the meaning of 'doggedly contented' (p. 377)?

4. Sum up in a sentence the idea of the essay.

5. Are Lamb's feelings on retirement like those of other persons you know or have read about? If they are, how does he manage to say anything about them that is worth reading?

6. How much do you learn from the essay about Lamb's tastes and habits?

7. How can Lamb compare his 'works' with those of Aquinas (p. 381)?

8. Would you call the essay regretful, melancholy, or pensive?

9. What is its purpose—to convey a mood, to paint a picture, to give advice?

10. In the final paragraph why is 'perambulating' a better word than 'walking' would be?

11. See Forster's criticism of Lamb. p. 50.

Henry David Thoreau

WHERE I LIVED, AND WHAT I LIVED FOR

1. After reading the selection explain what a critic meant by saying that Thoreau's 'profession was living.' What states of life and what moral standards does Thoreau

value most? What reasons does he give for valuing them most? State in your own language what Thoreau's 'philosophy' is.

2. What, specifically, does Thoreau think is wrong with the lives most people live? How would he have them live instead?

3. Find examples of irony in this chapter. What is the purpose of Thoreau's irony? How does irony differ from satire? Which does Thoreau use more often?

4. Is Thoreau didactic, critical, sententious, hortatory? Which of these terms fits him best?

5. Explain: 'I had had my seeds ready' (p. 385); 'I have never yet met a man who was quite awake. How could I have looked him in the face?' (p. 390).

6. 'A religious exercise' (p. 389): 'religious' in what sense?

7. Thoreau wrote in his *Journal* (12 November 1851): 'Those sentences are good and well discharged which are like so many little resiliences from the spring floor of our life. . . Sentences uttered with your back to the wall. . . Sentences in which there is no strain.' What does he mean? Can you find in 'Where I Lived, and What I Lived For' any sentences that seem to be 'uttered with your back to the wall'? Why do you choose those sentences as examples instead of others?

8. Paraphrase or summarize the final paragraph, in order to show whether you know what it says.

9. Is Thoreau anti-social?

10. Which sentence in the chapter gives the clearest statement of why Thoreau went to live by Walden Pond?

11. Read the essay by E. B. White (pp. 405–14). Does it add anything to your understanding or appreciation of Thoreau?

Robert Louis Stevenson

ÆS TRIPLEX

1. Has the Latin title any advantages that an English one might not have? What English title would you give to the selection?

2. Which sentence first states the main idea of the essay?

3. Why does Stevenson think funerals 'ludicrous' (p. 398)?

4. What practical advice does he give against the fear of death? How practical does it seem to you?

5. Why is the 'accident that ends it all' called subversive (p. 399)? Why are the dry volumes 'cloudy' (p. 401)?

6. Explain these phrases: 'pule in little atheistic poetry-books' (p. 402); 'mim-mouthed friends and relations' (p. 403); 'to be overwise is to ossify' (p. 403).

7. 'We do not, properly speaking, love life at all, but living.' What is the distinction? Is he consistent about it? Compare, for instance, the sentence on pp. 401–2: 'But we are so fond of life that we have no leisure to entertain the terror of death.'

8. What is the purpose of referring to death by such commonplace terms as 'the thing' and 'the business' (p. 397, find other examples)?

9. Does his mood seem to you one of forced cheerfulness or of sincere, temperamental zest for life?

10. Stevenson admired Thoreau's writings. Do you find in this essay any thoughts, any points of view, that Thoreau would have shared?

11. Is Stevenson morally consistent? Why should one take his advice on these questions? What does the essay suggest concerning his religious views?

12. Read some of Stevenson's other essays to find out whether 'Aes Triplex' is characteristic of his outlook. 'El Dorado,' 'An Apology for Idlers,' and 'Virginibus Puerisque' are good ones to start with.

13. See E. M. Forster's criticism of Stevenson (p. 50). Do you agree with it?

E. B. White

WALDEN

1. What means does the writer use to convince the reader that *Walden* is 'pertinent and timely'? Are you convinced?

2. Does the essay tell you anything about *Walden* that you did not find out from 'Where I Lived, and What I Lived For' (pp. 383–96)?

3. What, according to the essay, are *Walden*'s main virtues? Why is it 'the best youth's companion yet written by an American'?

4. *Walden* is said to have 'a horrendous cloud of inconsistencies and contradictions.' Can you find any in the selections from *Walden* reprinted in this book (pp. 28–36, 383–96)?

5. 'Parts of "Walden" are pure scold' (p. 409). Do you find any examples on pp. 28–36, 383–96?

6. Why can *Walden* be called a humorous but not a funny book (see p. 411)?

7. How would you describe the language of this essay? Is it appropriate to the theme? What effect or what advantage have such words as 'whack' (p. 406), 'first big party bid' (p. 406), 'original omelette' (p. 407), 'all that ruckus' (p. 407), 'the bugs in the logic' (p. 408), 'batted out' (p. 409), 'if they bust doing it' (p. 413)?

8. Explain 'it contains religious feeling without religious images' (p. 406); 'It is probably no harder to eat a woodchuck than to construct a sentence that lasts a hundred years' (p. 409); 'the multiplicity of convenience' (p. 411); 'a regular hairshirt of a man' (p. 413); 'a house of correct proportions' (p. 414).

9. What ills and paradoxes of our society are brought out in the last half a dozen paragraphs? How do they compare with the ones Thoreau criticizes?

10. What's wrong with being called a Thoreauvian (see p. 413)?

Douglas Southall Freeman

THE PATTERN OF A LIFE

1. What were the 'essential elements' of Lee's character, and how are they emphasized in this selection?

2. 'If blood means anything, he was entitled to be what he fundamentally was, a gentleman.' Does the author seem to think 'blood' tells? Read Newman's descrip-

tion of a gentleman (pp. 114–9). Does it fit Lee? Does Newman place any emphasis on blood? What is meant by a 'simple' gentleman (p. 423)?

3. 'He could not have conceived of a Christian who was not a gentleman.' Could Newman?

4. 'Everything was black or white.' How much does this tell you about Lee? How is it illustrated in this chapter?

5. Compare Lee's qualities, as set forth by Freeman, with those described or implied in Jefferson's letter on natural aristocracy (pp. 194–9) and Hume's 'Of Qualities Immediately Agreeable to Others' (pp. 370–75).

6. Explain: 'have its apotheosis' (p. 416), 'the graces with which the South has idealized a hideous war' (p. 416), 'the clear light of conscience and of social obligation' (p. 424), 'the Southern Arthur' (p. 426).

7. What surmises about the author do you make from this chapter? His veneration of Lee is obvious enough, but consider how he expresses his admiration. Do you infer that he shares Lee's religious faith? That he too believes in the supreme importance of 'simplicity and spirituality'?

8. Consider also that this is the final chapter of a four-volume work. Read as much in those volumes as you can—at the very least, vol. IV, chs. ix, xi, xxvii—and then compare your impressions of Lee with those you get from 'The Pattern of a Life.'

9. Why is Lee's failure to keep in step (p. 419) worth mention?

Mark Twain (S. L. Clemens)

LIFE ON THE MISSISSIPPI

1. What different devices does the author use to prove that piloting is an 'exact science'?

2. Did piloting turn out to be as romantic an occupation as the boy had expected?

3. How well acquainted with Mr. Bixby do you feel after reading these chapters? What made him so masterly a pilot? How is he made to seem of heroic stature?

4. How many different 'levels' or kinds of language are used in these chapters?

5. Note and study the phrases that make the narrative picturesque. Substitute others of your own; what is the difference? For example, what would be the difference in the first paragraph on p. 426 if Mark Twain had written 'if we lived and were good we could become pirates' instead of 'if we lived and were good, God would permit us to be pirates'; in the second paragraph, 'what made them sleepy' instead of 'what broke them down'; 'eating water-melon rinds and seeds' instead of 'doing a good business in water-melon rinds and seeds'? Try to rewrite the first two pages in your own language, omitting none of the persons or things mentioned. Exercises of this kind, if you take them seriously enough, can sharpen your appreciation of preciseness and vividness in writing.

6. What are the most important and most obvious qualities of Mark Twain's humor? Is it satirical? Does he depend on 'tall tales'? On vivid description of ordinary happenings? On local color?

7. What scenes or situations in these chapters depend for their success on the fact that they are presented from a boy's point of view?
8. 'This fellow had money, too, and hair oil' (p. 429). What does the addition of 'and hair oil' contribute to the description?
9. Who is the chief character in these chapters—Mark Twain, Mr. Bixby, or the river?
10. Read *Huckleberry Finn*, if you have never done so.

Stephen Vincent Benét

BY THE WATERS OF BABYLON

1. What is the theme or idea of this story? How is the main character made to 'fit' this theme? Has the story a moral?
2. What does the title signify (see Psalm cxxxvii)?
3. How much of the story did you read before you guessed what was coming?
4. What kind of story is it—allegory? fable? apologue? fantasy? How would you describe it?
5. Where is the climax?
6. What effect has the refrain-like 'I am a priest and the son of a priest'?
7. How successful is the story, in your judgment, as a study of fear and courage?
8. The story seems to have an unusual number of short, simple sentences. Why? What is their effect?
9. 'Were they happy? What is happiness to the gods? They were great, they were mighty, they were wonderful and terrible'; 'I saw them with wisdom beyond wisdom and knowledge beyond knowledge'; 'poor gods, poor gods!' How do these passages suggest or illustrate the meaning of the story?
10. Do you think mention of the Dead Place's name (final paragraph) is a mistake; that it would have been better to let the reader guess it? Would there have been any difficulty in guessing it?

Samuel Butler

THE WAY OF ALL FLESH

1. Study the irony. Is it malicious? amusing? bitter? Is Butler sarcastic or sardonic? How would you describe his mood in these chapters?
2. Does Butler imply that relations between parents and children are usually as he describes them, or that such relations were peculiar to Victorian families, or to his own experience? Does he intend his generalizations on these subjects to be taken seriously? How do you know?
3. What does he mean by 'moral influence'?
4. Do you agree, or do you suppose you will agree, that 'youth is like spring, an overpraised season'?
5. What are Theobald's most obvious (to you, not to himself) characteristics?

6. What does 'this numb serpent of a metaphor' (p. 462) mean?
7. What does 'the education cost the children far more than it cost him' mean? Is Butler suggesting that this is what usually happens?
8. How much do the parenthetical statements '(and so did Christina)' on p. 461, and the last sentence on p. 462, 'But she persevered,' tell you about Christina?
9. 'No duty could be more important than that of teaching a child to obey its parents in all things.' 'Some Romans had even killed their children; this was going too far. . .' How do these sentences illustrate Theobald's views on 'moral influence'?
10. 'Young people . . . circumstances' (p. 458). Use this as the first sentence in an essay on some experience of your own childhood.

William James

TWO LETTERS ON DEATH

1. What, in your judgment, is most noteworthy in these two letters?
2. What do they suggest about the writer? Do they strike you as honest? candid? too candid? more emotional or less emotional than the occasion might require?
3. How much can you infer from the letters about the father and sister? Whose character emerges most clearly?
4. What does James mean by 'If you go, it will not be an inharmonious thing'?
5. What does the phrase 'believing agnostic' suggest when applied to William James? Is there any 'believing agnosticism' in these letters?
6. Assuming the letters were read by the persons to whom they were addressed, do you suppose they gave comfort and reassurance?
7. Read the final sentence of George Santayana's 'William James' (p. 546 in this book). Is it supported by these letters?
8. Read James's 'Pragmatism's Conception of Truth.' Does it have anything in common with the letters?

Joseph Conrad

IL CONDE

1. State in your own words the theme of the story. What is its point? Find the sentence or sentences that seem to express this best.
2. Read the preface to Conrad's *Nigger of the 'Narcissus'* (pp. 63–7), and try to judge 'Il Conde' by its artistic and critical standards. Does this story seem to you to 'carry its justification in every line,' to bring truth to light (see p. 63)? Truth about what?
3. Conrad says that 'Fiction—if it at all aspires to be art—appeals to temperament. And in truth it must be, like painting, like music, like all art, the appeal of one temperament to all the other innumerable temperaments whose subtle and resistless power endows passing events with their true meaning, and creates the moral,

the emotional atmosphere of the place and time' (pp. 64–5). What type of temperament would 'Il Conde' appeal to, and why? How much can you infer about the narrator's temperament? Study, for example, the sentence on p. 480: 'There was a wanton insolence in the spirit of this outrage which appalled even me.' How understanding and sympathetic is the narrator?

4. What part does irony play in the story?

5. What, in your opinion, is the climax of the story?

6. How much do these phrases contribute to our understanding of Il Conde's character: 'unaffected gentleman' (p. 467), 'quiet urbanity' (p. 468), 'no affairs at all' (p. 469), 'wait for the unavoidable' (p. 470), 'such a blatantly vulgar thing as dying from apoplexy in a café' (p. 480), 'singular fidelity' (p. 480)?

7. Is it possible to call Il Conde either cowardly or heroic?

8. What significance has the utterance, 'That you shall not have!' (p. 476)?

9. Write several paragraphs on 'Il Conde' as a study of aristocracy, or of sensibility, or of 'atmosphere.'

James Thurber

UNIVERSITY DAYS and DRAFT BOARD NIGHTS

Although sober analysis often spoils humor, it may be worth while asking yourself just why these pieces are amusing. (If you are not amused by them, it will be worth while analyzing yourself.)

1. What can you infer from the fact that 'University Days' has often been reprinted in anthologies made by teachers?

2. What difference does it make in the first paragraph that *too* and *mechanics* are italicized, and that the botany teacher says 'flars' instead of 'flowers'?

3. The writer of these questions once read 'University Days' with a class that included the son of one of the country's best-known football coaches. The boy was indignant about the satire of Mr. Bolenciecwcz; he thought it lowered the dignity of the sport. 'Anybody as dumb as that couldn't play modern football,' he said. What do you think of his criticism?

4. 'Professors, horizontal bars, agricultural students, and swinging iron rings' (p. 484). Is there any reason for listing them in this order?

5. How much does the word 'moodily' add in 'moodily creeping up on the old chemistry building' (p. 485), and 'unexpected' in 'a tall, unexpected young man' (p. 490)?

6. What is wrong with the opening sentence of Haskins's article (p. 485)?

7. Do the university types described by Mr. Thurber have anything in common with those of Highet's essay (pp. 167–76)?

8. Which of the two sketches by Mr. Thurber do you like better, and why?

9. Try your hand at describing some teachers or college experiences you have had.

Rachel L. Carson

THE BIRTH OF AN ISLAND

1. Study the means used to make the subject interesting. What are the merits of the

essay as exposition and description? Does the writer use scientific terms? Those only? What kinds of readers does she seem to be writing for?

2. How does the introductory paragraph set the tone of the essay? What good is the epigraph from Shelley?

3. What sources of evidence does the writer seem to rely upon the most?

4. How do the adjectives in the following phrases affect meaning and emphasis: 'islands are ephemeral' (p. 493), 'forbidding mass' (p. 494), 'literal evisceration' (p. 495), 'appalling series' (p. 495), 'dramatic passing' (p. 496), 'fascinating group' (p. 497), 'majestic pace' (p. 498), 'engaging characteristics' (p. 501), 'black night of extinction' (p. 502), 'gentle pattern' (p. 502)?

5. What relevance has the criticism of men in this essay (note 'one of his blackest records as a destroyer,' p. 501; 'man's habitual tampering,' p. 503; 'without the further aid of man,' p. 503; 'in a reasonable world,' p. 504)? Do you find anything comparable in Zinsser's 'Rats and Men' (pp. 556–66)?

6. What importance in this essay has Krakatoa?

7. If there is a key sentence in the essay, what is it?

8. Does the essay have a thesis? What is it? Which paragraph or paragraphs state it best?

9. Why is the loss of certain species on oceanic islands called a 'tragedy' (p. 504)? Would 'misfortune,' 'calamity,' 'bad luck' do as well?

C. E. M. Joad

WHAT DO WE KNOW OF THE OUTSIDE WORLD?

Even a person unacquainted with philosophical writings should find 'What Do We Know of the Outside World?' an intelligible and interesting introduction to one of the basic subjects of philosophical inquiry—the nature of human knowledge. He should not need explanatory notes in reading this selection, though one or two questions might be useful to him.

The chapter is, obviously, an essay in exposition. How well do you think the writer succeeds in summarizing quite familiar, apparently simple, but (as it turns out) really complex experiences? Does he convince you that 'common-sense' views of what constitutes knowledge are inadequate? Does he have enough illustrations to make his points? Are you dissatisfied with any of the illustrations? Does he define his terms and use them consistently? After you have finished reading, can you say, if not what knowledge is, what it is not?

The author knows when he begins that his subject is difficult, and evidently he is anxious to present it in clear, nontechnical terms. The reader—certainly this is true of some readers at any rate—thinks when *he* begins that the problem is no great one, but he soon begins to realize that it is far from simple after all. The writer has succeeded only if the reader is in fact made to see that there are real issues here, is enabled to see clearly what they are, and is forced to re-examine his own previous assumptions about them. To appreciate better the skill needed in handling a difficult topic in exposition, try writing a plain explanation of something common but complex: for example, motion, existence, beauty, truth.

Russell's 'Individual and Social Knowledge' (pp. 517-22) should be read with this selection. Do the authors use similar methods in trying to make their ideas clear? Do you think one writer has been more successful than the other?

Bertrand Russell

INDIVIDUAL AND SOCIAL KNOWLEDGE

1. Does the author think that science succeeds in being 'wholly impersonal'? Does it eliminate 'here' and 'now'?
2. Why is it that 'the very publicity of language is in large part a delusion'?
3. What connections between language and science are emphasized?
4. What is the distinction between verbal and ostensive definition?
5. How does language become depersonalized? What are some examples of depersonalized words?
6. He speaks of 'the common world in which we believe ourselves to live' (p. 521). Do we not know whether we live in it? Why does he call this common world a 'construction'?
7. Does the chapter make you skeptical of common-sense assumptions about knowledge? Is it intended to? (Compare Joad, pp. 505-16.)
8. Explain this sentence: 'The order for knowledge is the inverse of the causal order.'
9. Do you think this chapter is, for you, a successful exposition? Does it pose a problem clearly and make you see what is involved? Does it define terms? Does it assume agreement about the meanings of terms?
10. What is his conclusion?
11. See the selections by Joad (pp. 505-16), James (pp. 523-31), and Santayana (pp. 532-46).

William James

PRAGMATISM'S CONCEPTION OF TRUTH

You should read the selection several times before attempting the questions. Outlining James's argument will be helpful.

1. What is the problem? Summarize James's solution of it in your own language.
2. How much light do the selections by Joad (pp. 505-16) and Russell (pp. 517-22) throw on the problem?
3. Why is pragmatism called a philosophy of 'instrumentalism'?
4. Is truth, as defined by pragmatism, a matter of expediency? of mere expediency?
5. Consider the statements, 'It is useful because it is true' and 'It is true because it is useful.' Do they mean the same thing?
6. Pragmatism's critics accuse it of holding that truth is 'man-made.' Is the accusation justified?

7. What arguments can you bring against the dictum that 'truth is what works'?

8. What is 'the practical difference it makes to us to have true ideas'? What does James mean by 'realizing' a truth?

9. What difference does or might the pragmatist view of truth make to moral behavior?

10. Read Santayana's portrait of James (pp. 532–46). What criticisms of pragmatism does he make? If you suppose Santayana's picture of James is accurate (a supposition that some critics might not accept), what can you infer about the connection between a man's temperament and the kind of philosophy he adopts?

11. Write an argument for or against these assertions by James: 'Truth *happens* to an idea. It *becomes* true, is *made* true by events' (p. 525). Begin by searching for an adequate definition—your own, not a dictionary's—of 'truth,' and then consider whether James's sentences satisfy you.

12. Criticize the lecture as an exposition of ideas. Does it present the issues clearly, with enough illustrations? Is the lecture dogmatic, modest, confident, persuasive? Why does he try to expound complex ideas in informal or colloquial language? How well does he succeed?

George Santayana

WILLIAM JAMES

1. Read with this essay the two letters by James and the excerpt from one of his philosophical essays (pp. 463–6, 523–31). Do they seem to you to confirm the observations of Santayana?

 The paragraphs on James's philosophical ideas on pp. 534–43 may puzzle you, but if you reread them several times you should be able to make something of them. (It is questionable whether James would have accepted them as an accurate representation of his views.) The portrait of James the man ought to be clear enough.

2. Is Santayana critical, patronizing, ironic? How would you sum up his opinions of James?

3. How does the addition of the phrase 'especially on the high seas' clarify and expand the meaning of 'every one should paddle his own canoe' (p. 532)?

4. What is the effect of the word 'exuberance' in 'the exuberance of a tie' (p. 533)? of 'raids' (p. 534)? of 'lyrically' (p. 542)?

5. 'His doctrine . . . was agnosticism' (p. 537). Is this supported by the letters on pp. 463–6?

6. What does the writer mean when he calls James 'a spirited rather than a spiritual man'?

7. What does he mean by 'the hortatory tradition of college sages' (p. 541)? Have you encountered this tradition? Is the phrase 'little sermons' ironic or depreciatory? What of the phrase about 'the young Christian soldier' on p. 541?

8. How much, if anything, can you infer about Santayana's own beliefs?

9. Which passages make James most real or most attractive to you? What is your

final impression of him? Was your impression influenced by the final sentence of
the essay?

Thomas Babington Macaulay

PLATO AND BACON

1. What, according to Macaulay, are the most important defects of Plato's philosophy
    and the most important merits of Bacon's?
2. Which sentence or sentences best sum up the essential differences (in Macaulay's
    opinion) between the Platonic and Baconian philosophies?
3. What methods does Macaulay use to prove Bacon's superiority? Does he prove
    it or argue it or assume it?
4. This selection is an excellent example of the use of balance, antithesis, and contrast.
    Find examples of these in whole paragraphs and in sentences. Is each paragraph
    on Plato balanced by one on Bacon? How effective, in your judgment, is this use
    of balance and antithesis?
5. No reader could possibly miss Macaulay's preference for the Baconian philosophy,
    but study his method of making this sympathy plain. Does he do it mostly by
    statement, by implication, or by phrases?
6. What assumption about progress underlies this passage?
7. What do you infer regarding Macaulay's conception of the purposes of legislation?
8. If Macaulay is so convinced of the superiority of Bacon's ideas, is he inconsistent
    in calling Plato the 'finest of human intellects' (p. 555)? And if Plato was indeed
    the finest of human intellects, why was he so blind to truths that Bacon and
    Macaulay saw so clearly?
9. 'He really . . . superfluous' (p. 554). Why does Macaulay add the 'really'? What
    does 'pathetic' mean? In the next sentence why does Macaulay call Plato's hopes
    'romantic'?
10. Does he define terms sufficiently—for instance 'mere matters of curiosity' (p. 548),
    'useful' (p. 548), 'well-being' (p. 549)?
11. 'The beneficence of his [Bacon's] philosophy resembled the beneficence of the
    common Father' (p. 552). Is there anything objectionable in this sentence? Is it
    logically sound? Is it fair?

Hans Zinsser

RATS AND MEN

1. How does the writer make his unpleasant subject readable?
2. Which sentence on p. 557 gives the main theme or idea of the chapter?
3. Does Zinsser make the analogy between rats and men convincing? Why does he
    insist upon it at such length? How important does it seem to you?
4. Is this, in your opinion, a successful piece of writing? Does it interest you? (Do not
    answer this too glibly. Reread the text, and balance the author's evident purposes
    against his accomplishment before you answer.)

5. 'We may, in a few centuries . . . any mere animal' (p. 558): why does he say 'civilization'?

6. What is the point about 'realtors' and 'morticians' (p. 559)? What is wrong with those terms?

7. Does he make rats seem more human than we are wont to think them, or men more rat-like?

8. What social and ethical standards does he seem to prize most?

9. In comparing small things with great, or mean with splendid ones (as Zinsser does, for example, on p. 564, comparing the invasion of Bermuda by rats and their sudden disappearance with the rise and fall of Indian empires), a writer may be trying either to amuse us or to impress us with satiric or ironic meanings we do not ordinarily think of. Which is Zinsser trying to do? How well does he succeed? Does he ever fail?

10. Why does he add, or what is the effect of his adding, 'the duty of furnishing cannon fodder' (p. 564); 'the rat has an excuse' (p. 565); 'less humiliatingly obvious' (p. 566)?

11. What is his tone? Is it one of irony, of sarcasm, of moralism? Is this scientist writing as a scientist, as a historian, as a journalist, or as a preacher?

Julian Huxley

THE UNIQUENESS OF MAN

1. What are the biological, psychological, and social characteristics Huxley finds to be unique in man? Does he account for their uniqueness?

2. '. . . dehumanize one's own kind' (p. 568). In what different ways is this done in the selections by Swift and Zinsser (pp. 329–37, 556–66)?

3. What evidence does Huxley give that evolution is 'an enormous number of blind alleys, with a very occasional path of progress'?

4. Why could a brain capable of conceptual thought develop only in man?

5. How much scientific jargon does the writer use? What kind or kinds of readers does he appear to be writing for?

6. 'The fixed pathways of instinct . . . intelligence' (p. 574). How useful, and how justifiable, in 'scientific' writing is a figure of speech like 'multiple switchboards'? Find other metaphors in this selection and try to determine how much they contribute to clarity and emphasis.

7. What are the main differences, in style and manner, between this essay and the one by Zinsser (pp. 556–66)? Which interests you more? Why?

8. Huxley emphasizes man's unique capacity for intellectual and social achievement as much as Zinsser does man's capacity for destructiveness and selfish cruelty. Which writer paints the truer picture? Does each paint the one that seems to him more important or serves his argument best? How does Huxley's purpose differ from Zinsser's?

9. Why is it important to this argument to show the lack of affection in animals?

10. Note the phrase 'the perspective of biology' (p. 588). Why define our business in the world by the perspective of biology rather than by other perspectives?

11. '. . . tempered pride' (p. 588). Why should it be tempered?

12. Look up *Hamlet*, II, ii, 313–29. How does that judgment of man's nature compare with Zinsser's and Huxley's?

13. Why does the author think it takes courage to face the 'consequences of our uniqueness'?